CRITICAL SURVEY
OF
DRAMA

CRITICAL SURVEY
OF
DRAMA

English Language Series

Authors
Hal-Mas

3

Edited by
FRANK N. MAGILL

SALEM PRESS
Englewood Cliffs, N. J.

LIBRARY OF CONGRESS CATALOG CARD NUMBER: 85-50962
Complete Set: ISBN 0-89356-375-7
Volume 3:   ISBN 0-89356-378-1

PRINTED IN THE UNITED STATES OF AMERICA

LIST OF AUTHORS IN VOLUME 3

	page
Hall, Willis	865
Hansberry, Lorraine	874
Hardy, Thomas	885
Hart, Lorenz	895
Hart, Moss	906
Hellman, Lillian	914
Henshaw, James Ene	925
Heyward, DuBose	934
Heywood, John	940
Heywood, Thomas	948
Horovitz, Israel	957
Howard, Bronson	965
Howard, Sidney	973
Inge, William	979
James, Henry	989
Jones, Henry Arthur	999
Jones, Preston	1007
Jonson, Ben	1014
Kaufman, George S.	1026
Kingsley, Sidney	1035
Kirkland, Jack	1045
Knowles, James Sheridan	1055
Kopit, Arthur	1064
Kops, Bernard	1077
Kyd, Thomas	1086
Laurents, Arthur	1098
Lawler, Ray	1109
Lee, Nathaniel	1118
Lewis, Matthew Gregory	1124
Lillo, George	1141
Livings, Henry	1151
Lodge, Thomas	1158
Lonsdale, Frederick	1165
Lyly, John	1178

CRITICAL SURVEY OF DRAMA

                                                                    page
McCullers, Carson 1190
MacDonagh, Donagh 1201
MacLeish, Archibald 1213
McNally, Terrence 1226
Mamet, David 1234
Marlowe, Christopher 1246
Marston, John 1265
Martyn, Edward 1275
Masefield, John 1283
Massinger, Philip 1292

CRITICAL SURVEY
OF
DRAMA

WILLIS HALL

Born: Leeds, England; April 6, 1929

Principal drama

The Long and the Short and the Tall, pr. 1958, pb. 1959; *A Glimpse of the Sea and Last Day in Dreamland*, pr. 1959, pb. 1961; *Billy Liar*, pr., pb. 1960 (with Keith Waterhouse; adaptation of Waterhouse's novel); *Chin-Chin*, pr. 1960 (adaptation of François Billetdoux's play); *A Glimpse of the Sea: Three Short Plays*, pb. 1961 (includes *Last Day in Dreamland* and the teleplay *Return to the Sea*); *Celebration*, pr., pb. 1961 (with Waterhouse); *England, Our England*, pr. 1962, pb. 1964 (musical, with Waterhouse; music by Dudley Moore); *The Sponge Room*, pr. 1962, pb. 1963 (one act, with Waterhouse); *Squat Betty*, pr. 1962, pb. 1963 (one act, with Waterhouse); *Yer What?*, pr. 1962 (revue, with others; music by Lance Mulcahy); *Come Laughing Home*, pr. 1964 (with Waterhouse; originally as *They Called the Bastard Stephen*, pb. 1965); *Say Who You Are*, pr. 1965, pb. 1966 (with Waterhouse); *Joey, Joey*, pr. 1966 (musical, with Waterhouse; music by Ron Moody); *Whoops-a-Daisy*, pr. 1968, pb. 1978 (with Waterhouse); *Who's Who*, pr. 1971, pb. 1974 (with Waterhouse); *Saturday, Sunday, Monday*, pr. 1973, pb. 1974 (with Waterhouse; adaptation of Eduardo de Filippo's play); *The Card*, pr. 1973 (musical, with Waterhouse; music and lyrics by Tony Hatch and Jackie Trent; adaptation of Arnold Bennett's novel); *Walk On, Walk On*, pr. 1975, pb. 1976; *Filumena*, pr. 1977, pb. 1978 (with Waterhouse; adaptation of de Filippo's play); *The Wind in the Willows*, pr. 1984 (musical); *Treasure Island*, pr. 1984 (musical).

Other literary forms

Willis Hall has become familiar to English audiences through a variety of media and genres. He and Keith Waterhouse, with whom he regularly collaborates, are highly regarded for their screenplays; some of their more notable efforts are *Whistle Down the Wind* (1961) and *Billy Liar* (1963). With Wolf Mankowitz, Hall has adapted for the screen *The Long and the Short and the Tall* (1961). Hall has also worked extensively in television, writing for programs such as *The Fuzz* and *Secret Army*, coauthoring half a dozen other series with Waterhouse, and writing a number of television plays, often for children. Hall has written musicals—*England, Our England*, with music by Dudley Moore, was reviewed with great praise—books on sports, the text for a documentary, pantomimes, novels, award-winning adaptations of foreign drama, and scripts for television series. The sheer bulk of Hall's work and its rich variety testify to his artistic strength and durability.

Achievements

It is difficult to find any single descriptive category or term under which Hall's achievements as a dramatist will fit with accuracy. *The Long and the Short and the Tall* (commissioned by the Oxford Theatre Group for the Edinburgh Festival of 1958, and winner of the *Evening Standard* Drama Award for Best Play in 1959), associated him with the new drama appearing in the wake of John Osborne's *Look Back in Anger* (pr. 1956), and comparisons have often been made between Hall's Private Bamforth and Osborne's Jimmy Porter. At the same time, Hall's early collaborations with Keith Waterhouse have been considered in terms of regional realism, as authentic representations of life in the North of England. Plays such as *Billy Liar* and *Celebration* reflect their authors' feel for the idiosyncrasies of regional language, serving as reminders that Hall and Waterhouse often draw with success upon their shared Yorkshire background. These descriptions are somewhat helpful; yet with plays such as *The Sponge Room* or *Squat Betty* they plainly break down, since these are expressly nonrealistic plays. Such descriptions also do not apply well to later plays, such as *Say Who You Are* and *Who's Who*, which move away from realistic Northern themes and introduce elements of farce.

If Hall's work resists any single-phrase summary, this in itself is perhaps an indication of his achievement as a writer. He has directed his efforts toward a wide variety of literary ventures in a variety of genres, each demanding its own kind of discipline, and he has performed with some success in all of them. Further, his writings with Waterhouse represent the foremost dramatic collaboration in England today, and both are admired for their professional competence and consistency. In addition to their own work, they have been successful adapters of two plays by Eduardo de Filippo, *Saturday, Sunday, Monday*, which starred Sir Laurence Olivier and Joan Plowright, and *Filumena*, which enjoyed a two-year run in England. On his own, Hall has written and staged a successful adaptation of François Billetdoux's *Chin-Chin*. Hall, then, has written on his own and in collaboration, for children and adults, for the stage and for the radio and screen.

While praising Hall's versatility and the range of his work, reviewers and critics have at times questioned its depth, and indeed it is difficult to avoid feeling that some of the plays are too light or are perhaps dominated by an adept dramatic technique that masks other and more profound limitations. One might say simply that the aims of the plays are sometimes modest but that they achieve those aims with delightful flair and insight and offer genuine rewards for their readers.

Biography

Willis Hall was born on April 6, 1929, in Leeds, England, the son of

Walter and Gladys Hall, and was educated in Leeds at the Cockburn High School. As a youth, he became friends with Keith Waterhouse, with whom he worked on a youth-club magazine and collaborated on a wide variety of projects for the stage, television, film, and radio. That friendship was interrupted in 1947 by Hall's five-year stint in the British Regular Army, during which time he served in the Far East as a radio playwright for Forces Radio. The military provided the background for Hall's first major stage success after his return to England, *The Long and the Short and the Tall*, which included Peter O'Toole and Robert Shaw in the cast. Hall resumed his friendship with Waterhouse, and together they adapted Waterhouse's novel *Billy Liar* for the stage in 1960, a highly successful production that established Albert Finney and Tom Courtenay, each of whom had a turn at the title role, as exceptionally gifted actors. From that time on, Hall has occupied himself with a remarkably prolific and consistent literary life.

Analysis

Many of Willis Hall's plays (including those he coauthored with Keith Waterhouse) concern the discrepancy between the real world and the world that people invent for themselves. Again and again one comes upon figures who have created their own drama about the world and their own part in it, only to find that reality is an entirely different drama which proceeds indifferent to its characters. This theme lends itself to a variety of treatments: In a play such as *Billy Liar*, it can create a pathetic character whose imagination defends him from the world and masks his lack of courage, and who, when he sees beyond the veil of his own private fictions, knows that he is alone and insignificant; it can also produce the lighthearted farce of a play such as *Who's Who*, in which the distortions of reality create a complex series of mix-ups and mistaken identities culminating in comic disclosures, admissions, embarrassments, and reconciliations. In many of the plays, the imagination is a kind of obstacle to a character's growth, for it substitutes the satisfying (and effortless) vision of distant success and security for any real development.

The Long and the Short and the Tall, Hall's first major success, is a realistic war drama about a small unit of British soldiers in the Malayan jungle, set during the Japanese advance on Singapore in 1942. It seems at first to have little to do with the themes or subjects of Hall's subsequent work, but much of the play's conflict grows out of the soldiers' storybook ideas about war, their visions of themselves as heroic and moral men defending the side of good—visions that are denied by the reality of the war as it quickly closes in on them. This theme is suggested in an early scene. As the men rest in a deserted store-hut where nearly all of the action takes place, Private Evans sits reading the serial story in an issue of *Ladies Companion and Home* (his mother sends it to him each week), a romantic tale about a second lieutenant who must leave his girl behind when he is posted overseas. The story takes its hero through a variety of exciting and fantastic adventures, the last installment having left him in the hands of some Bedouins who have bound and suspended him above a roaring fire. Evans is puzzled, though, because the current issue finds the hero inexplicably escaped from the Bedouins and enjoying a honeymoon in Brighton with the girl he had left behind, who has waited faithfully for him. The events of the play contradict everything about this kind of story. The petulant Private Bamforth quickly questions the fidelity of Evans' own girl, taunting him with the suggestion that by now she has probably found a variety of substitutes for him. Bamforth also rejects the heroic ideal of the magazine story by describing his plans for a fast exit in the event of a Japanese invasion. Often, Bamforth's remarks have a disturbing edge of reality to them that deflates the *Ladies Companion and Home* image of war, and this is one reason that he is often at odds with his comrades, who still cling to that image. At the play's conclusion, that image is finally destroyed. Far from effecting any miraculous escape, the men are surrounded by the Japanese and killed, except for Corporal Johnstone, who is wounded and surrenders.

The romantic view of the war is attacked in the second act of the play by Sergeant Mitchem, in his speech on women. The context of that speech is important. The unit has captured a Japanese soldier, separated from his patrol, who has wandered into the hut, and in the initial struggle several of the men find that they are unable to kill the soldier when called upon to do so, largely because they realize for the first time that war involves killing men very much like themselves. "He's human at least," Private Macleish later explains to Mitchem after the captured soldier has shown them a picture of his family; for Mitchem, however, the point is obvious: "What do you want for your money? Dracula?" He is annoyed by the naïve assumptions about war that the men have brought with them to battle, and he lays the blame on "bints," on women, who give a man a heroic image of himself in uniform as he heads gallantly off to war. "Few weeks after that," Mitchem concludes, "he's on his back with his feet in the air and a hole as big as your fist in his belly. And he's nothing." This remark might just as easily have come from Bamforth's mouth, for he shares with Mitchem an unflinching sense of the truth that lies covered by the men's self-deceiving fictions.

The Long and the Short and the Tall examines the nature of war, the ways in which it changes the moral relations between men, the almost unbearable demands that it makes upon the human conscience. Hall demonstrated, in this play, his skill with dialogue and pace; he also demonstrated a subtlety in his handling of theme that often goes overlooked. At its heart, the play is a study of the fundamental human tendency to believe and act according to the stories we tell ourselves about life and the problems that arise when these stories are contradicted by the sometimes harsh facts of the world.

In Billy Fisher, the main character of *Billy Liar*, this storytelling tendency is taken to an extreme. Billy is a conscious fabricator who deceives his family, his friends, his employers, and perhaps most of all himself, for reasons so obscure that one is tempted to agree with his friend Arthur in saying that Billy's condition is pathological.

Billy Liar is set in the industrial North of England, and the play's action describes the affairs of the Fishers, a lower-middle-class household whose father, Geoffrey Fisher, has recently lifted his family above his own working-class background through his success as a garage owner. The father is plainly expecting something of the same initiative from Billy, his nineteen-year-old son, but as one meets him in the opening moments of the play, he seems an unlikely successor to his father. He has risen late from bed, and comes downstairs in his pajamas and an old raincoat. Billy is also pressured by his mother, Alice, and by her mother, Florence Boothroyd, who is living in the Fisher household and who habitually directs her remarks to the sideboard. The house is decorated in poor taste, and this contributes to the tense and oppressive atmosphere, in which Billy is almost constantly derided by his father for being lazy and also for mismanaging his affairs. In some sense, it is understandable that Billy retreats into the worlds created by his imagination.

Billy is in a bad position from the very start of the play. His job with Shadrack and Duxbury, Funeral Furnishers, is in jeopardy because he has been absent on days when he was supposed to have been at work (including the day on which the play takes place); he has also apparently been taking money from the firm, and he has failed to mail the company's Christmas calendars as he has been asked to do. The calendars are crammed into a cupboard that Billy uses for his "private" things, but which he opens for Arthur when Arthur asks him about the calendars. In the cupboard, also, is a letter from Alice Fisher to the host of a radio show called "Housewives' Choice," asking him to play an old favorite for her. She concludes the letter with a postscript saying that her son also writes songs but that he probably will amount to little in that line because he lacks the training. She ends with a remark about the family being just "ordinary folk," and upon reading this Billy abruptly tosses the letter back into the cupboard, denying the limitations his mother seems to be putting on his abilities. One senses in this scene that Billy's stories and fantasies are part of an effort to escape from the mediocrity of his life, an attempt to be something more than ordinary. One soon discovers, however, that he lacks the courage to make any significant break with his environment and that his only escape is to change his world by inventing it anew in his own mind. When Billy threatens to make some practical effort to change his life by quitting his job, Arthur recognizes the characteristic bravado that masks a deeper fear of change and he scoffs at Billy's threat by saying that he has heard it before.

At first, Billy's fictions strike us as wonderfully absurd, as flashes of life in a generally dull existence. He has apparently told his parents and others that his friend Arthur's mother is pregnant—a lie—and this story has gotten back to her. When Arthur's mother threatens to come and see Mr. Fisher about it, Billy complains to Arthur that she cannot do that, because Billy has since told his parents that she has had a miscarriage to prevent his own mother from delivering a present for the baby. This is good fun, but it suggests other more serious problems that will confront Billy later. Often his stories have significant effects on people around him, and his insensitivity to the problems he may be causing for others reveals a certain self-centeredness.

Billy also seems unaware of the problems he may be causing for himself when the real world breaks through his artifice; his stories have a way of turning on him, as, for example, in his relationships with women. He is expecting a visit in the afternoon from Barbara, a girl to whom he is supposedly engaged and whom he plans to try to seduce by dropping some "passion pills" in her drink. He also needs to convince her to return her engagement ring to him for a time, since he needs it to give to another girl—Rita—to whom he is also engaged. The plan backfires when the passion pills prove worthless and Barbara refuses to give up the ring, and when Rita suddenly appears at the Fishers' door demanding her engagement ring there is an angry and embarrassing exchange among the saucy Rita, Barbara, and the astonished Mrs. Fisher. In this scene, Billy has lost control over events that his lies set in motion; he is clearly to blame for the situation, and any comic element in it is overshadowed by his apparent indifference to the feelings of others and his inability to foresee the consequences of his actions.

Billy nevertheless wins a measure of sympathy in the play's conclusion, where we see him as a frustrated dreamer whose imagination is marvelously agile but who is unable to get beyond that agility to the more profound courage required by genuine growth and maturity. In the third act, he meets an old girlfriend, Liz, a much more levelheaded and insightful girl than are the others, and with her Billy at least approaches self-recognition. By this time, his deceptions have landed him in a complicated mess that even involves a physical threat from Rita's brother, and Billy for the first time seems to sense that he has only himself to blame. His fantasies become visions of self-extinction, and he imagines going to London with Liz to lose himself, to become "invisible." Liz plainly shares his feelings, and they arrange to meet at the train station at midnight to run off to London. The vision, however, succumbs to reality, and the play closes with Billy's silent return to the house after his parents are in bed. Just why he cannot bring himself to go is left to the reader's judgment. Billy may realize that a life of invisibility is as much a lie as is the life that he is living now, or it may be that he is lured back by the prospect of manipulating the world, in the hope that someday it may match his own desires. In any case, the fertility of his imagination is inextricably tied to his frustrations and his lack of growth, and the play's ending leaves little hope for any immediate change in his life. The last line of the play, appropriately, is Rita's, shouting from outside the Fisher house that she will be back in the morning for her ring, her angry voice an emblem of the world outside Billy's imagination, demanding satisfaction.

Last Day in Dreamland is a shorter and less ambitious play than *Billy Liar*, but it illustrates how deftly Hall can establish atmosphere and mood and how, even in a short play, his attention to language can give solidity to half a dozen different characters. The play is related to *Billy Liar* in dealing with characters who seem trapped in an unsatisfying way of life, powerless to take the actions that might create some real change.

Like *Billy Liar*, too, *Last Day in Dreamland* is set in the North, but in a seaside town. It centers on the owner and operators of an amusement arcade during what turns out to be the last day of the season, though none of them knows this at the start. Still, they know that the end of the season is very near and that they will soon be out of work again until the next season comes around, and it is this atmosphere of melancholy anticipation that hangs over the action throughout, ironically heightened by the backdrop of festivity.

The play begins with a strong sense of pattern and repetition, a strong sense that each of these characters has been at his job for countless years, for they move about with a clear understanding of both their own responsibilities on the job and their relationships to the other workers. In his production notes to the play, Hall emphasizes its "group construction" and the importance of each actor's studying the parts of the others, because the mood of the action depends on a complete familiarity among the characters and on their displaying the sense that they have done all of this hundreds of times before. Tich Curtis' question about whether today is their last day is met with affectionate scorn by the manager and mechanic, Coppin, who has heard the same question for fourteen years from Curtis when the season comes to an end. Though he is young, George Fentrill is already noted by the others for claiming that each year at the arcade is his last, and each year Sailor Beeson seems to come closer to losing his job because of his tardiness. The repetition, the sameness, helps to give these figures identity, yet it is an identity that each of them might willingly forsake for a different life.

Coppin's history is representative of the others'. One of the younger members of the crew, Harry Lomax, announces that he plans to leave and try his hand at lorry driving after this season, and Coppin responds by recalling his own youthful dreams. He had, he says, planned to open his own shop, repairing wirelesses, but like the others, Coppin's dream simply slipped away. "So what happened?" Lomax asks, and Coppin's response gives us some insight into his sympathies with the men who work under him: "Nothing. That's all—nothing. For years I talked about having that shop—the summers I've spent in here dreaming about that joint don't bear thinking about. So one day, before you know where you are, you're fifty-two and all you've got is a screwdriver, a fistful of loose change and six months' work a year." In some ways, the speech recalls Sergeant Mitchem's in *The Long and the Short and the Tall*, because it breaks through the haze of dreams and fantasies to a level of reality that few of the characters are willing to face. In the end, Coppin's description of his own life proves to be true for the others; both Lomax and Fentrill hedge their plans to get away at the end of the season, and the audience is left with a strong sense—as in *Billy Liar*—that despite the dreams of the characters, a new season at the arcade will find all of them there, lacking the will to escape.

In other plays, Hall has allowed his form to echo these themes, so that while their characters avoid reality by arranging their own worlds of fantasy, the works become less realistic. This is true of plays such as *The Sponge Room* and *Squat Betty*, which, as Hall and Waterhouse observe in their production notes, depend on a "mood of suspended disbelief in which the audience will be ready to go along with the incongruities of the plot while at the same time appreciating the basic truths about loneliness, fear and fantasy." *The Sponge Room* in particular puts the audience in a situation somewhat analogous to that of the characters: The young "lovers" are also suspending their disbelief by pretending to plan an intimate rendezvous, though neither really wants to carry it out. "The play is about three dreamers," say the authors, "who will never have the courage to carry out their dreams—for the dreams themselves are a substitute for courage." The later farce, *Who's Who*, is another example of this nonrealistic treatment. The play's two acts are divided by a discussion between the two actors playing Bernard White and Timothy Black in which they agree to reenact the events of the first act with some important changes in the scenario. In some ways, the play represents a comic flip side to *Billy Liar* in that Black, like Billy, runs his life on deception, but without the kind of consequences suffered by Billy. It is a highly stylized, artificial play, but, as in *The Sponge Room*, the technique seems curiously appropriate here, applied as it is to a work about that fundamental human drive to orchestrate the events of one's life and re-create a world according to one's desires.

The Sponge Room and *Who's Who* demonstrate the diversity of Hall's talents, and his longevity and consistency as a writer must in some degree be attributed to his skill for finding new and varied methods of handling his subjects. Though they depart from the earlier, more conventional techniques, they share with Hall's other plays the insight and feeling that make his art worth experiencing. It is an art full of sympathy for its characters, perhaps because Hall sees in the human urge to dream, to fantasize, to imagine a world and to believe in it, an impulse very much like the dramatist's.

Other major works

NOVEL: *The Fuzz*, 1977 (novelization of television series).

NONFICTION: *The A to Z of Soccer*, 1970 (with Michael Parkinson); *The A to Z of Television*, 1971 (with Bob Monkhouse).

SCREENPLAYS: *The Long and the Short and the Tall*, 1961 (with Wolf Mankowitz); *Whistle Down the Wind*, 1961 (with Keith Waterhouse); *The Valiant*, 1962 (with Waterhouse); *A Kind of Loving*, 1963 (with Waterhouse); *Billy Liar*, 1963 (with Waterhouse); *West Eleven*, 1963 (with Waterhouse); *Man in the Middle*, 1963 (with Waterhouse); *Pretty Polly (A Matter of Innocence)*, 1967 (with Waterhouse); *Lock Up Your Daughters*, 1969 (with Waterhouse).

TELEPLAYS: *Air Mail from Cyprus*, 1958; *Return to the Sea*, 1960; *On the Night of the Murder*, 1962; *Happy Moorings*, 1963 (with Waterhouse); *How Many Angels*, 1964 (with Waterhouse); *The Ticket*, 1969; *The Railwayman's New Clothes*, 1971; *The Villa Maroc*, 1972; *They Don't All Open Men's Boutiques*, 1972; *Song at Twilight*, 1973; *Friendly Encounter*, 1974; *The Piano-Smashers of the Golden Sun*, 1974; *Illegal Approach*, 1974; *Midgley*, 1975; *Match-Fit*, 1976 (from Brian Glanville's story); *A Flash of Inspiration*, 1976; *Danedyke Mystery*, 1979 (from a work by Stephen Chance); *National Pelmet*, 1980; *Christmas Spirits*, 1981.

CHILDREN'S LITERATURE: *The Play of the Royal Astrologers*, 1958 (play); *The Gentle Knight*, 1964 (radio play); *Kidnapped at Christmas*, 1975 (play); *Christmas Crackers*, 1976 (play); *A Right Christmas Caper*, 1977 (play); *Worzel Gummidge*, 1980 (play, with Waterhouse); *The Inflatable Shop*, 1984 (novel); *Dragon Days*, 1984 (novel).

Bibliography

Armstrong, William A., ed. *Experimental Drama*, 1963.
Taylor, John Russell. *The Angry Theatre: New British Drama*, 1969.

Steven Reese

LORRAINE HANSBERRY

Born: Chicago, Illinois; May 19, 1930
Died: New York, New York; January 12, 1965

Principal drama

A Raisin in the Sun, pr., pb. 1959; *The Sign in Sidney Brustein's Window*, pr. 1964, pb. 1965; *To Be Young, Gifted, and Black*, pr. 1969; *Les Blancs*, pr. 1970, pb. 1972 (edited by Robert Nemiroff); *The Drinking Gourd*, pb. 1972 (edited by Nemiroff); *What Use Are Flowers?*, pb. 1972 (edited by Nemiroff); *Les Blancs: The Collected Last Plays of Lorraine Hansberry*, pb. 1972 (includes *Les Blancs*, *The Drinking Gourd*, and *What Use Are Flowers?*).

Other literary forms

As a result of her involvement in the civil rights movement, Lorraine Hansberry wrote the narrative for *The Movement: Documentary of a Struggle for Equality* (1964), a book of photographs, for the Student Nonviolent Coordinating Committee (SNCC). Because she died at such a young age, Hansberry left much of her work unpublished, but her husband, Robert Nemiroff, the literary executor of her estate, edited and submitted some of it for publication and, in the case of *Les Blancs*, production. In addition, he arranged excerpts from Hansberry's various writings into a seven-and-a-half-hour radio program entitled *To Be Young, Gifted, and Black*, which was broadcast on radio station WBAI in 1967. This program was later adapted for the stage, opening at the Cherry Lane Theatre in New York on January 2, 1969, and becoming the longest running production of the 1968-1969 season. Many readers know Hansberry through the anthology of her writings edited by Nemiroff, *To Be Young, Gifted, and Black: A Portrait of Lorraine Hansberry in Her Own Words* (1969), a book which has enjoyed very wide circulation.

Achievements

Hansberry's career was very brief, only two of her plays being produced in her lifetime, yet she recorded some very impressive theatrical achievements. She was only twenty-nine when *A Raisin in the Sun* appeared on Broadway, and its great success earned for her recognition that continues to this day. When *A Raisin in the Sun* was voted best play of the year by the New York Drama Critics Circle, she became the first black person as well as the youngest person to win the award. In 1973, a musical adapted from *A Raisin in the Sun*, entitled *Raisin* (with libretto by Nemiroff), won a Tony Award as best musical of the year (1974). She was respected and befriended by such figures as Paul Robeson and James Baldwin, and she helped in an active way to further the work of the civil rights movement. Though her later work has received far less recognition than her first play, *A Raisin in the Sun* continues to enjoy a broad popularity.

Biography

Lorraine Vivian Hansberry was born on May 19, 1930, in the South Side of Chicago, the black section of that segregated city. Her parents, Carl and Mamie Hansberry, were well-off; he was a United States deputy marshal for a time and then opened a successful real estate business in Chicago. Despite their affluence, they were forced by local covenants to live in the poor South Side. When Hansberry was eight years old, her father decided to test the legality of those covenants by buying a home in a white section of the city. Hansberry later recalled one incident which occurred shortly after the family's move to a white neighborhood: A mob gathered outside their home, and a brick, thrown through a window, barely missed her before embedding itself in a wall.

In order to stay in the house, to which he was not given clear title, Carl Hansberry instituted a civil rights suit against such restrictive covenants. When he lost in Illinois courts, he and the N.A.A.C.P. carried an appeal to the United States Supreme Court, which, on November 12, 1940, reversed the ruling of the Illinois Supreme Court and declared the local covenants illegal. Thus, Lorraine had a consciousness of the need to struggle for civil rights from a very young age. Her father, despite his legal victory, grew increasingly pessimistic about the prospects for change in the racial situation, and he finally decided to leave the country and retire in Mexico City. He had a stroke on a visit to Mexico, however, and died in 1945.

Hansberry's uncle, William Leo Hansberry, was also an important influence on her. A scholar of African history who taught at Howard University, his pupils included Nnamdi Azikewe, the first president of Nigeria, and Kwame Nkrumah of Ghana. Indeed, William Leo Hansberry was such a significant figure in African studies that in 1963, the University of Nigeria named its College of African Studies at Nsakka after him. While Lorraine was growing up, she was frequently exposed to the perspectives of young African students who were invited to family dinners, and this exposure helped to shape many of the attitudes later found in her plays.

Lorraine, the youngest of four children, was encouraged to excel and was expected to succeed. After attending Englewood High School, she enrolled in the University of Wisconsin as a journalism student. She did not fare very well at the university, however, and felt restricted by the many requirements of the school. After two years, she left Wisconsin and enrolled in the New School for Social Research in New York, where she was permitted greater leeway in choosing courses.

Once in New York, Hansberry began writing for several periodicals, including *Freedom*, Paul Robeson's monthly magazine. She quickly became a reporter and then an associate editor of the magazine. In New York, she met Robert Nemiroff, then a student at New York University, and they were married in June of 1953. By this time, Hansberry had decided to be a writer, and while the bulk of her energies went into writing, she did hold a variety of jobs during the next few years. When Nemiroff acquired a good position with music publisher Phil Rose, she quit working and began writing full-time.

Hansberry's first completed work was *A Raisin in the Sun*, which, after an initial struggle for financial backing, opened on Broadway at the Ethel Barrymore Theatre on March 11, 1959. The play, starring Sidney Poitier, Ruby Dee, Louis Gossett, Jr., and Claudia McNeil, was an enormous success, running for 530 performances, and in May, winning the New York Drama Critics Circle Award.

Soon thereafter, Hansberry and Nemiroff moved from their apartment in Greenwich Village to a home in Croton, New York, in order for Hansberry to have more privacy for her work. At the same time, her success made her a public figure, and she used her newfound fame to champion the causes of civil rights and African independence. She made important speeches in a variety of places and once confronted then Attorney General Robert Kennedy on the issue of civil rights.

It was not until 1964 that Hansberry produced another play, *The Sign in Sidney Brustein's Window*, and by that time she was seriously ill. The play opened at the Longacre Theatre on October 15, 1964, to generally good but unenthusiastic reviews, and Nemiroff had to struggle to keep it open, a number of times placing advertisements in newspapers asking for support, accepting financial support from friends and associates, and once accepting the proceeds from a spontaneous collection taken up by the audience when it was announced that without additional funds, the play would have to close. On this uncertain financial basis, production of the play continued from week to week.

Hansberry's life continued in much the same way. While the play struggled, she was in a hospital bed dying of cancer. She once lapsed into a coma and was not expected to recover, but for a brief time she did rally, recovering all of her faculties. Her strength gave out, however, and on January 12, 1965, she died. That night, the Longacre Theatre closed its doors in mourning, and *The Sign in Sidney Brustein's Window* closed after 101 performances.

Analysis

Lorraine Hansberry claimed Sean O'Casey as one of the earliest and strongest influences on her work and cited his realistic portrayal of character as the source of strength in his plays. In *To Be Young, Gifted, and*

Black, she praised O'Casey for describing

> the human personality in its totality. O'Casey never fools you about the Irish . . . the
> Irish drunkard, the Irish braggart, the Irish liar . . . and the genuine heroism which
> must naturally emerge when you tell the truth about people. This . . . is the height of
> artistic perception . . . because when you believe people so completely . . . then you
> also believe them in their moments of heroic assertion: you don't doubt them.

In her three most significant plays, *A Raisin in the Sun*, *The Sign in Sidney
Brustein's Window*, and *Les Blancs*, one can see Hansberry's devotion to
the principles that she valued in O'Casey. First, she espoused realistic
drama; second, she believed that the ordinary individual has a capacity for
heroism; finally, she believed that drama should reveal to the audience its
own humanity and its own capacity for heroism.

Hansberry claimed that her work was realistic rather than naturalistic,
explaining that "naturalism tends to take the world as it is and say: this is
what it is . . . it is 'true' because we see it every day in life . . . you simply
photograph the garbage can. But in realism . . . the artist . . . imposes . . .
not only what *is* but what is *possible* . . . because that is part of reality too."
For Hansberry, then, realism involved more than a photographic faithfulness to the real world. She sought to deliver a universal message but realized that "in order to create the universal you must pay very great attention to the specific. Universality . . . emerges from truthful identity of what
is." This concern for realism was present from the very beginning of
Hansberry's career and persists in her work, though she did occasionally
depart from it in small ways, such as in the symbolic rather than literal
presence of "The Woman" in *Les Blancs*, that character symbolizing the
spirit of liberty and freedom which lives inside man.

Essential to Hansberry's vision of reality was the belief that the average
person has within him the capacity for heroism. Hansberry believed that
each human being is not only "dramatically interesting" but also a "creature of stature," and this is one of the most compelling features of her
drama. Like O'Casey, Hansberry paints a full picture of each character,
complete with flaws and weaknesses, yet she does not permit these flaws to
hide the characters' "stature." Perhaps she expressed this idea best in *A
Raisin in the Sun*, when Lena Younger berates her daughter Beneatha for
condemning her brother, Walter Lee. Lena says, "When you start measur-
ing somebody, measure him right, child, measure him right. Make sure you
done taken into account what hills and valleys he come through before he
got to wherever he is." For Hansberry, each character's life is marked by
suffering, struggle, and weakness, yet in each case, the final word has not
been written. Just as Beneatha's brother can rise from his degradation, just
as Sidney (in *The Sign in Sidney Brustein's Window*) can overcome his en-
nui, so each of her characters possesses not only a story already written but

also possibilities for growth, accomplishment, heroism. Hansberry permits no stereotypes in her drama, opting instead for characters that present a mixture of positive and negative forces.

Hansberry's realistic style and her stress on the possibilities for heroism within each of her characters have everything to do with the purpose that she saw in drama. As James Baldwin observed, Hansberry made no bones about asserting that art has a purpose, that it contained "the energy that could change things." In *A Raisin in the Sun*, Hansberry describes a poor black family living in Chicago's South Side, her own childhood home, and through her realistic portrayal of their financial, emotional, and racial struggles, as well as in her depiction of their ability to prevail, she offers her audience a model of hope and perseverance, and shows the commonality of human aspirations, regardless of color. In *The Sign in Sidney Brustein's Window*, she takes as her subject the disillusioned liberal Sidney Brustein, who has lost faith in the possibility of creating a better world. After all of his disillusionment, he realizes that despair is not an answer, that the only answer is hope despite all odds and logic, that change depends upon his commitment to it. So too, in *Les Blancs*, Hansberry gives her audience a character, Tshembe Matoseh, who has a comfortable, pleasant, secure life and who seeks to avoid commitment to the cause of African independence, though he believes in the justness of that cause. He learns that change comes about only through commitment, and that such commitment often means the abandonment of personal comfort on behalf of something larger.

Hansberry's earliest play, *A Raisin in the Sun*, is also her finest and most successful work. The play is set in the South Side of Chicago, Hansberry's childhood home, and focuses on the events that transpire during a few days in the life of the Younger family, a family headed by Lena Younger, the mother; the other family members are her daughter, Beneatha, her son, Walter Lee, and his wife, Ruth, and son, Travis. The play focuses on the problem of what the family should do with ten thousand dollars that Lena receives as an insurance payment after the death of her husband, Walter Lee, Sr. The money seems a blessing at first, but the family is torn, disagreeing on how the money should be spent.

The play's title is taken from Langston Hughes's poem "Harlem" and calls attention to the dreams of the various characters, and the effects of having those dreams deferred. The set itself, fully realistic, emphasizes this theme from the first moment of the play. The furniture, once chosen with care, has been well cared for, yet it is drab, undistinguished, worn out from long years of service. The late Walter Lee, Sr., was a man of dreams, but he could never catch up with them, and he died, exhausted and wasted, worn out like the furniture, at an early age. His family is threatened with the same fate, but his insurance money holds out hope for the fulfillment of dreams. Lena and Walter Lee, however, disagree about what to do with the money. Walter Lee hates his job as a chauffeur and plans to become his own man by opening a liquor store with some friends, but Lena instead makes a down payment on a house with one-third of the money, and plans to use another third to finance Beneatha's medical studies. After the two argue, Lena realizes that she has not permitted her son to be a man and has stifled him, just as the rest of the world has. In order to make up for the past, she entrusts him with the remaining two-thirds of the money, directing him to take Beneatha's portion and put it into a savings account for her, using the final third as he sees fit. Walter Lee, however, invests all of the money in a foolhardy scheme and discovers shortly thereafter that one of his partners has bilked him of the money.

The house that Lena has purchased is in a white neighborhood, and a Mr. Lindner has approached the Youngers, offering to buy back the house—at a profit to the Youngers—because the members of the community do not want blacks living there. Walter Lee at first scornfully refuses Lindner's offer, but once he has lost all the money he is desperate to recoup his losses and calls Lindner, willing to sell the house. The family is horrified at how low Walter has sunk, but when Beneatha rejects him, claiming there is "nothing left to love" in him, Lena reminds her that "There is always something to love. And if you ain't learned that, you ain't learned nothing." Lena asks Beneatha, "You give him up for me? You wrote his epitaph too—like the rest of the world? Well, who give you the privilege?" The epitaph is indeed premature, for when Lindner arrives and Walter is forced to speak in his son's presence, Walter gains heroic stature by rejecting the offer, telling Lindner in simple, direct terms that they will move into their house because his father "earned it." It is a moment during which Walter comes into manhood, and if it has taken him a long while to do so, the moment is all the richer in heroism.

The theme of heroism found in an unlikely place is perhaps best conveyed through the symbol of Lena's plant. Throughout the play, Lena has tended a small, sickly plant that clings tenaciously to life despite the lack of sunlight in the apartment. Its environment is harsh, unfavorable, yet it clings to life anyway—somewhat like Walter, whose life should long ago have extinguished any trace of heroism in him. Hansberry gives her audience a message of hope.

Hansberry also reminds her audience of the common needs and aspirations of all humanity, and she does so without oversimplification. None of the characters in the play is a simple type, not even Lindner, who might easily have been presented as an incarnation of evil. Instead, Lindner is conveyed as a human being. When asked why she portrayed Lindner in this manner, Hansberry replied "I have treated Mr. Lindner as a human being merely because he is one; that does not make the meaning of his call less malignant, less sick." Here is where Hansberry calls her audience to action. She reminds the audience of what it is to be human and enjoins them to respect the dignity of all their fellows.

An interesting subtheme in the play, one that would be developed far more fully later in *Les Blancs*, is introduced by Joseph Asagai, an African student with a romantic interest in Beneatha. Some of the most moving speeches in the play belong to Asagai, and when Beneatha temporarily loses hope after Walter has lost all the money, Asagai reminds her of her ideals and the need to keep working toward improvement in the future. When Beneatha asks where it will all end, Asagai rejects the question, asking, "End? Who even spoke of an end? To life? To living?" Beneatha does not fully understand Asagai's argument at the time, but its meaning must be clear enough to the audience, who will see at the end of the play that Walter's victory is not an end, but rather one small, glorious advance. There will be other trials, other problems to overcome, but, as Asagai says, any other problem "will be the problem of another time."

Hansberry's second play, *The Sign in Sidney Brustein's Window*, never matched the success of her first, but it, too, uses a realistic format and was drawn from her own life. Instead of South Side Chicago, it is set in Greenwich Village, Hansberry's home during the early years of her marriage with Robert Nemiroff, and the central character is one who must have resembled many of Hansberry's friends. He is Sidney Brustein, a lapsed liberal, an intellectual, a former insurgent who has lost faith in his ability to bring about constructive change. As the play opens, Sidney moves from one project, a nightclub that failed, to another, the publication of a local newspaper, which Sidney insists will be apolitical. His motto at the opening of the play is "Presume no commitment, disavow all engagement, mock all great expectations. And above all else, avoid the impulse to correct." Sidney's past efforts have failed, and his lost faith is much the same as Beneatha's in *A Raisin in the Sun*.

The surrounding environment goes a long way toward explaining Sidney's cynicism. His wife, Iris, has been in psychoanalysis for two years, and her troubled soul threatens their marriage. Iris' older sister, Mavis, is anti-Semitic, and her other sister, Gloria, is a high-class call girl who masquerades as a model. Sidney's upstairs neighbor, David Ragin, is a homosexual playwright whose plays invariably assert "the isolation of the soul of man, the alienation of the human spirit, the desolation of all love, all possible communication." Organized crime controls politics in the neighborhood, and drug addiction is rampant; one of Sidney's employees at the defunct nightclub, Sal Peretti, died of addiction at the age of seventeen, despite Sidney's efforts to help him. Faced with these grim realities, Sidney longs to live in a high, wooded land, far from civilization, in a simpler, easier world.

The resultant atmosphere is one of disillusionment as characters lash out in anger while trying to protect themselves from pain. One of the targets of the intellectual barbs of the group is Mavis, an average, settled housewife who fusses over Iris and pretends to no intellectual stature. When the wit gets too pointed, though, Mavis cuts through the verbiage with a telling remark: "I was taught to believe that creativity and great intelligence ought to make one expansive and understanding. That if ordinary people . . . could not expect understanding from artists . . . then where indeed might we look for it at all." Only Sidney is moved by this remark; he is unable to maintain the pretense of cynicism, admitting, "I *care*. I care about it all. It takes too much energy *not* to care." Thus, Sidney lets himself be drawn into another cause, the election of Wally O'Hara to public office as an independent, someone who will oppose the drug culture and gangster rule of the neighborhood.

As Sidney throws himself into this new cause, he uses his newspaper to further the campaign, and even puts a sign, "Vote for Wally O'Hara," in his window. Idealism seems to have won out, and indeed Wally wins the election, but Sidney is put to a severe test as Iris seems about to leave him, and it is discovered that Wally is on the payroll of the gangsters. Added to all of this is Gloria's suicide in Sidney's bathroom. Her death brings Sidney to a moment of crisis, and when Wally O'Hara comes into the room to offer condolences and to warn against any hasty actions, Sidney achieves a clarity of vision that reveals his heroism. Sidney says, *"This world*—this swirling, seething madness—which you ask us to accept, to maintain—has done this . . . maimed my friends . . . emptied these rooms and my very bed. And now it has taken my sister. *This* world. Therefore, to live, to breathe—I shall *have* to fight it." When Wally accuses him of being a fool, he agrees: "A fool who believes that death is waste and love is sweet and that the earth turns and that men change every day . . . and that people wanna be better than they are . . . and that I hurt terribly today, and that hurt is desperation and desperation is energy and energy can *move* things." In this moment, Sidney learns true commitment and his responsibility to make the world what it ought to be. The play closes with Iris and Sidney holding each other on the couch, Iris crying in pain, with Sidney enjoining her: "Yes . . . weep now, darling, weep. Let us both weep. That is the first thing: to let ourselves feel again . . . then, tomorrow, we shall make something strong of this sorrow."

As the curtain closes, the audience can scarcely fail to apply these closing words to themselves. Only if they permit themselves to feel the pain, Hansberry claims, will it be possible to do anything to ease that pain in the future. James Baldwin, referring to the play, said, "it is about nothing less than our responsibility to ourselves and to others," a consistent theme in Hansberry's drama. Again and again, she reminds the audience of their responsibility to act in behalf of a better future, and the basis for this message is her affirmative vision. Robert Nemiroff says that she found reason to hope "in the most unlikely place of all: the lives most of us lead today. Precisely, in short, where *we* cannot find it. It was the mark of her respect for us all."

Hansberry's last play of significance, *Les Blancs*, was not in finished form when she died and did not open on stage until November 15, 1970, at the Longacre Theatre, years after her death. Nemiroff completed and edited the text, though it is to a very large degree Hansberry's play. It was her least successful play, running for only forty-seven performances, but it did spark considerable controversy, garnering both extravagant praise and passionate denunciation. Some attacked the play as advocating racial warfare, while others claimed it was the best play of the year, incisive and compassionate. The play is set not in a locale drawn from Hansberry's own experience but in a place that long held her interest: Africa.

Les Blancs is Hansberry's most complex and difficult play. It takes as its subject white colonialism and various possible responses to it. At the center of the play are the members of the Matoseh family: Abioseh Senior, the father, who is not actually part of the play, having died before it opens, but who is important in that his whole life defined the various responses possible (acceptance, attempts at lawful change, rebellion); in addition, there are his sons, Abioseh, Eric, and, most important, Tshembe. Hansberry attempts to shed some light on the movement for African independence by showing the relationships of the Matosehs to the whites living in Africa. The whites of importance are Major Rice, the military commander of the colony; Charlie Morris, a reporter; Madame Neilsen, and her husband, Dr. Neilsen, a character never appearing on stage but one responsible for the presence of all the others.

Dr. Neilsen has for many years run a makeshift hospital in the jungle; he is cut in the mold of Albert Schweitzer, for he has dedicated his life to tending the medical ills of the natives. It is because of him that all of the other doctors are there and because of him too that Charlie Morris is in Africa, for Charlie has come to write a story about the famous doctor.

Whereas Charlie comes to Africa for the first time, Tshembe and Abioseh are called back to Africa by the death of their father. Abioseh comes back a Catholic priest, having renounced his African heritage and embraced the culture and beliefs of the colonialists. Tshembe too has taken much from the colonial culture, including his education and a European bride. He has not, however, rejected his heritage, and he is sensitive to the injustice of the colonial system. Though he sees colonialism as evil, he does not want to commit himself to opposing it. He wants to return to his wife and child and lead a comfortable, secure life.

For both Charlie and Tshembe, the visit to Africa brings the unexpected, for they return in the midst of an uprising, called "terror" by the whites and "resistance" by the blacks. Charlie gradually learns the true nature of colonialism, and Tshembe, after great struggle, learns that he cannot avoid his obligation to oppose colonialism actively.

While Charlie waits for Dr. Neilsen to return from another village, he learns from Madame Neilsen that the doctor's efforts seem to be less and less appreciated. When Tshembe comes on the scene, Charlie is immediately interested in him and repeatedly tries to engage the former student of Madame Neilsen and the doctor in conversation, but they fail to understand each other. Tshembe will accept none of the assumptions that Charlie has brought with him to Africa: He rejects the efforts of Dr. Neilsen, however well-intentioned, as representing the guilty conscience of colonialism while perpetrating the system; he rejects Charlie's confident assumption that the facilities are so backward because of the superstitions of the natives. Charlie, on the other hand, cannot understand how Tshembe can speak so bitterly against colonialism yet not do anything to oppose it. Tshembe explains that he is one of those "who see too much to take sides," but his position becomes increasingly untenable. He is approached by members of the resistance and is asked to lead them, at which point he learns that it was his father who conceived the movement when it became clear that the colonialists, including Dr. Neilsen, saw themselves in the position of father rather than brother to the natives and would never give them freedom.

Still, Tshembe resists the commitment, but Charlie, as he leaves the scene, convinced now that the resistance is necessary, asks Tshembe, "Where are you running, man? Back to Europe? To watch the action on your telly?" Charlie reminds Tshembe that "we do what we can." Madame Neilsen herself makes Tshembe face the needs of his people. Tshembe by this time knows what his choice must be, but is unable to make it. In his despair, he turns to Madame Neilsen, imploring her help. She tells him, "You have forgotten your geometry if you are despairing, Tshembe. I once taught you that a line goes into infinity unless it is bisected. Our country needs *warriors*, Tshembe Matoseh."

In the final scene of the play, Tshembe takes up arms against the colonialists, and Hansberry makes his decision all the more dramatic by having him kill his brother Abioseh, who has taken the colonial side. Yet, lest anyone misunderstand the agony of his choice, Hansberry ends the play with Tshembe on his knees before the bodies of those he has loved, committed but in agony, deeply engulfed by grief that such commitment is necessary.

Les Blancs is less an answer to the problem of colonialism than it is another expression of Hansberry's deep and abiding belief in the need for individual commitment, and in the ability of the individual, once committed, to bring about positive change for the future, even if that requires suffering in the present. Surely her commitment to her writing will guarantee her work an audience far into the future.

Other major works

NONFICTION: *The Movement: Documentary of a Struggle for Equality*, 1964 (includes photographs); *To Be Young, Gifted, and Black: A Portrait of Lorraine Hansberry in Her Own Words*, 1969 (Robert Nemiroff, editor).

Bibliography

Abramson, Doris E. *Negro Playwrights in the American Theatre, 1925-1959*, 1969.

Bisgby, C. W. E. *Confrontation and Commitment: A Study of Contemporary American Drama 1959-1966*, 1968.

Cruse, Harold. *The Crises of the Negro Intellectual*, 1967.

Farrison, W. E. "Lorraine Hansberry's Last Dramas," in *College Language Association Journal*. December, 1972, pp. 188-197.

Lewis, Theopilus. "Social Protest in *A Raisin in the Sun*, " in *Catholic World*. CXC (October, 1959), pp. 31-35.

Hugh Short

THOMAS HARDY

Born: Higher Bockhampton, England; June 2, 1840
Died: Dorchester, England; January 11, 1928

Principal drama

The Dynasts: A Drama of the Napoleonic Wars, pb. 1903, 1906, 1908, 1910 (verse drama), pr. 1914 (abridged by Harley Granville-Barker); *The Famous Tragedy of the Queen of Cornwall*, pr., pb. 1923 (one act).

Other literary forms

Thomas Hardy is best known for his fiction. He was the author of fourteen novels, four collections of short stories containing more than forty tales, and several volumes of poetry comprising some nine hundred poems, as well as a large assortment of nonfiction prose, prefaces, and essays. His letters, diaries, notebooks, and private papers have survived, despite Hardy's intention that this material be destroyed. Several volumes of his correspondence have been published. In addition, there are two books of autobiography, *The Early Life of Hardy* (1928) and *The Later Years of Thomas Hardy* (1930), which Hardy dictated to his wife.

Achievements

While Hardy's achievements as a novelist and poet are widely recognized, his achievements as a playwright are less well-known. Hardy's training as an architect has been taken to explain his intricately plotted novels, and it might also be seen as the reason Hardy liked the conventions of dramatic structure. Hardy had a lifelong interest in drama and the theater, and it was his original literary ambition to be a playwright, although he did not produce any plays until near the end of his career and then wrote only two. Although he was sometimes tempted by London theatrical agents and friends to turn his talents to the stage, he largely resisted the lure of stagelights, being unwilling to compromise with the demands of actors and directors in the commercial theater, a position he explains in an essay, "Why I Don't Write Plays" (1892). Alternately fearful of the limitations and fascinated by the possibilities of drama, Hardy finally wrote his first "play," *The Dynasts*, which is something of a composite literary form. Intended for a mental rather than a real stage, it is epic in size and scope. This immense verse play, about which one might remark, as Samuel Johnson did of John Milton's *Paradise Lost* (1667, 1674), "none would wish it longer," has attracted some critical attention, but it has never drawn many readers from the general public. As a closet drama, it is a major artistic accomplishment, and it rivals Leo Tolstoy's *War and Peace* (1865, 1869) as a work that most vividly chronicles the defeat of Napoleon's dynastic ambitions. Hardy's hope of reviving interest in the verse drama, however, was not fulfilled with *The Dynasts* or with his second verse play, *The Famous Tragedy of the Queen of Cornwall*, which was conceived for actual stage production. The one-act *The Famous Tragedy of the Queen of Cornwall* was a coda to Hardy's brief career as a playwright; an extremely different type of poetic drama from *The Dynasts*, it shows what Hardy might have been able to do with stage conventions had he kept to his early ambition "to write a few fine plays."

Biography

Thomas Hardy was born on June 2, 1840, in a thatched-roof cottage at Higher Bockhampton, a village near the small city of Dorchester in the southern shire of Dorset—an area that was known as Wessex in ancient times and that has many historical associations with the Druids, the Celts, and the Romans. Hardy's father, a music-loving building contractor, was ambitious for young Thomas; thus, after he completed his education through grammar school, Hardy was apprenticed at age sixteen to an architect. Whatever of his education did not pertain to his vocation he had to pick up on his own, and it was in this fashion that he continued to study Latin and Greek. He also began writing poetry during his late teens, imitating the style and substance of the dialect verses of the Reverend William Barnes, a local curate and poetaster.

Hardy's apprenticeship under the ecclesiastical architect John Hicks lasted until 1862, after which he went up to London at the age of twenty-one to study architecture further. Under the tutelage of John Blomfield, Hardy became proficient enough in his professional life to win a prize given by the Royal Institute of British Architects for an essay on the use of ancient building materials in modern architecture. Hardy's expository talent was further demonstrated in a sketch, "How I Built Myself a House," in *Chamber's Journal*. During this period, Hardy's life was somewhat inchoate. He began at this time, however, to become more deeply interested in literature, writing stories as well as poetry and availing himself of the cultural opportunities London provided. He used his free time to visit the British Museum and the art galleries and spent his evenings at Kings College, studying French. The routine of work and study and the rigors of urban life placed a strain on Hardy's health, which had been delicate since his childhood, and after five years, he sought rustication, returning to Bockhampton to recover. While he was at home and employed only part-time with church restorations, he began to write his first novel, "The Poor Man and the Lady." He sent the manuscript to a publisher, but it was rejected because the story lacked plot and suspense. Despite this disappointment, Hardy was encouraged by the editor's praise, and he attempted a second novel, *Desperate Remedies*, which satisfied the requirement for plot ingenuity and was published anonymously in 1871. This book was quickly followed by *Under the Greenwood Tree* (1872) and *A Pair of Blue Eyes* (1873); neither novel was a popular success, but both received positive notice from the reviewers.

At the time, Hardy was encouraged by the editor of *Cornhill Magazine* to write a serial novel. The result was Hardy's first popular and financial success, the pastoral novel *Far from the Madding Crowd* (1874). Success with this book enabled Hardy to marry Emma Lavinia Gifford in the same year. He also gave up his practice as an architect, for he was assured of an income from his writing. After a honeymoon trip to France, Hardy settled down at Max Gate, his home near Dorchester, where he spent the next twenty-five years writing stories and novels. Although he wrote continuously and preferred a retired life, Hardy was by no means a recluse. He made many friends in literary circles and was active on the London social scene as his reputation as a major writer grew. During these decades, when Hardy's creative productivity was at its peak, he published the five major novels that he came to call stories of "Character and Environment": *The Return of the Native* (1878), *The Mayor of Casterbridge* (1886), *Tess of the D'Urbervilles* (1891), and *Jude the Obscure* (1895).

Although Hardy's career as a writer was flourishing throughout the 1870's, the 1880's, and the 1890's, his marriage to Emma was not. The couple was childless, which put a strain on their relationship, and the evidence points to sexual difficulties between Hardy and his wife. Although Emma was a conventional helpmate as a wife, tending to Hardy's business affairs and making fair copies of his manuscripts, she was not a mate to him in the full sense. As the years passed, each was embittered against the other, and the difficulties of their marriage increased. Emma Hardy's death in 1912 was an occasion of mixed relief and bereavement for Hardy, but after two years of mourning he married, at age seventy-four, for a second time. His new wife was Florence Emily Dugdale, who was a longtime friend of the Hardys and had served as his secretary following Mrs. Hardy's death.

During the later years of his writing career, after the hostile reception of *Jude the Obscure* in 1895, Hardy turned again to poetry and worked primarily in this medium for the rest of his life, producing two experiments in drama—the epic drama in verse, *The Dynasts*, and a second verse play, *The Famous Tragedy of the Queen of Cornwall*.

Honors and recognition came to Hardy in abundance in his later years. He was awarded the Order of Merit by King Edward; his home of Max Gate was a shrine visited with veneration by the literati of the English-speaking world. Although Hardy had wished to be buried in his native Dorset, at his death in 1928, he was honored by the nation with a burial in the Poets' Corner of Westminster Abbey. His heart, however, was taken home, where it was interred in the village graveyard of his native heath.

Analysis
Thomas Hardy's *The Dynasts* is, along with John Milton's *Samson Agonistes* (1671) and Percy Bysshe Shelley's *Prometheus Unbound* (1820), one of the longest closet dramas in English literature. This vast epic drama, consisting of nineteen acts and 130 scenes, traces the Napoleonic Wars from 1805 to 1815. Upon its publication, *The Dynasts* was hailed as a major achievement, but subsequent generations have found the massive work more problematic. Indeed, while Hardy's novels continue to be read and are available in numerous editions in any bookstore, only Victorian scholars are likely to plough their way through the 10,553 lines of *The Dynasts*. As Hardy's importance as a novelist increases, his importance as a dramatic poet seems to be fading, despite pleading by some critics to justify *The Dynasts* categorically either as an epic or as a drama.

The Dynasts, which was published in three separate parts in 1903, 1906, and 1908, was initially untitled and was referred to simply as "A Drama of Kings." When all three parts of the completed work were published together in 1910, Hardy labeled it an epic drama and gave it the title by which it is now known. Hardy's title comes from a line on the last page of the final act: " . . . who hurlest Dynasts from their thrones?" As to his choice of this title, Hardy wrote, "it was the best and shortest inclusive one I could think of to express the rulers of Europe in their desperate struggle to maintain their dynasties rather than to benefit their people."

It is not really surprising that Hardy should have turned his talents to the production of dramatic poetry. There are many indications of an early and lifelong interest in the drama—both folk and professional. Hardy enjoyed plays both in the study and on the stage, and he read widely among the classical Greek, Elizabethan, modern Continental, and modern English playwrights. He was a frequent playgoer in London and knew many theatrical people, among them Harley Granville-Barker, Sir James Barrie, George Bernard Shaw, and John Galsworthy. In fact, at one point in his life Hardy had thought of becoming a playwright himself, and as early as 1867, he was considering writing plays in blank verse but postponed this project after being discouraged by the realities of a stage production.

Hardy's interest in playwriting lay dormant for many years, but, having abandoned the writing of fiction, disgusted by the adverse critical reaction to his later novels, he turned to poetry and drama—his interest in the latter whetted by stage adaptations of *Far from the Madding Crowd* and *Tess of the D'Urbervilles*. Thus, near the end of the 1890's, Hardy plunged into the writing of a verse drama; "nothing could interfere with it," as he said, for it was intended for a "mental performance."

The Dynasts required all of Hardy's skills as a writer. Written in a variety of verse forms, the drama tells an epic story with a cast of thousands. Hardy's forte as a novelist was his ability to tell a story with interest and suspense, and his talent with plot did not desert him here. *The Dynasts* relates a well-known story—the rise and fall of Napoleon—with vivid and fresh appeal. There are scenes of battle, of political intrigue, and of the ordinary life of the people that provide spectacle on the scale of the films of the late Cecil B. De Mille. Unlike previous closet dramas, such as Lord Byron's *Manfred* (pb. 1817), Shelley's *The Cenci* (pb. 1819), or Alfred, Lord Tennyson's *Harold* (pb. 1876), Hardy selected a recent historical event as his subject, as he did in his novels, in which the setting is generally only a few decades removed from the telling; in *The Dynasts*, the time of the action is 1805-1815. Whereas in his fiction Hardy was concerned with the fate of common people in the grips of an indifferent destiny, in the epic drama his concern was to show how princes and powerful men, who often seem to control the fate of the masses, are in turn moved and influenced by the same blind forces that govern the humblest of men.

Hardy's epic drama was the result of his lifelong interest in Napoleon's character and career, a subject that had attracted many other writers of his own and earlier generations. It was his intention to do more than dramatize the turbulent period of the Napoleonic Wars; Hardy's purpose was to show how the events that led up to the period of conflict had been shaped by blind causes rather than human will; the major premise underlying *The Dynasts* is that all human thought and action are predestined—an expression of the anthropomorphic force that Hardy called the "Immanent Will," rather than of Divine Providence. While this was an advanced idea for 1904, it seems to make the drama passé to modern readers, who are not as concerned with questions of ultimate causation as were the post-Victorians.

The cast of characters in Hardy's drama, epic in proportions, is arranged on three levels: first, the celestial abstractions—the Will, the Ironies, the Spirit Sinister, the Shade of the Earth, and the Earth of the Years; next, the great historical figures—Napoleon, the Duke of Wellington, Lord Nelson, George III, William Pitt, the Younger, and the various kings, princes, and generals of Prussia, Austria, Spain, and Russia (these are the dynasts of Europe, all of whom are concerned only to maintain their rule); and finally, the ordinary people, the suffering masses who are puppets caught in the grip of political and historical forces beyond their control. Hardy makes these lower-class characters his collective protagonists, the heroes of the play. On the other hand, the conquerors and kings, the so-called dynasts, are cast as the antagonists, indifferent to the plight of the people and concerned only with expanding their borders; they side with Napoleon when he is up and combine against him when he is down. In the struggles on the human level among the dynasts and their nations, only England stands above the sordid schemes of the Continental kings as the British defy Napoleon's design for world conquest. Among the British generals, Wellington emerges as a worthy rival, whose tenacity will prove to be a match for

Napoleon's brilliant strategies.

Of all the characters in the drama, Napoleon is by far the most interesting. He is a complex and evolving personality, whose career as depicted by Hardy is a working out of the Immanent Will in the history of the world. At first, Napoleon functions as an agent of order as he imposes his dream of a unified Europe upon the chaos unleashed by the French Revolution. When he crowns himself emperor, however, his decline into egotistical megalomania begins. His march of conquest across Russia is undertaken only for selfish reasons, and from this point on he is pursued by a Nemesis-like retribution for his overwhelming hubris. The human actions in *The Dynasts* culminate in Napoleon's defeat at Waterloo, the battle scenes being presented from a panoramic perspective to which only a motion picture could do justice in visual terms. Hardy's careful historical research, which included interviews with surviving veterans of the battle of Waterloo, is particularly evident here as every battalion and regiment are cataloged in the best epic tradition. Hardy lavishes admiring detail on the exploits of the Scots Greys, the Black Watch, and the British Grenadiers as they hold the thin red line against the furious but futile charge of the French Imperial Guard.

As the numerous acts of the historical drama are played out, scenes are interspersed in which the spirits play their part, acting as symbols of abstract powers that are personified as actual characters. The Immanent Will influences events through its attendant spirits—the personified Pities, the Years, and Ironies—but the Will itself, because it stands for the all-inclusive mind or ultimate reality of the universe, is never depicted. Its operation is keenly felt at numerous points in the drama when its human puppets, including Napoleon himself, act on impulses or instincts that they cannot resist.

The Pities, Years, and Ironies are indicative of human traits, attitudes, and perspectives. The Spirit of Pities symbolizes sympathy and altruism. The Spirit of Years stands for rejective reason as time places distance between emotions and events. His outlook on human affairs is rationalistic and unsentimental. The Spirit of Pities, with all its compassion, is the obvious foil of the Spirit of Years, who has no feeling.

The debate between the spirits creates the effect of a Greek chorus and lends a traditional dramatic ingredient to the otherwise unique drama. Other allegorical characters, such as the Spirit Sinister, the Spirit of Rumor, and the Shade of Earth, enter the scene and attempt to interpret the meaning of the unfolding historical events. Their debate, however, is inconclusive, and though their final chorus ends with a weak note of optimism, on the hope that the current "rages of the ages shall be cancelled," to be followed by a future period when human reason will overcome selfish aggression and destructive impulses, it is clear that it will take ages of evolution to turn human instincts of passion into compassion. This evolutionary process, which Hardy termed "meliorism," was his faint but larger hope for mankind.

The foregoing summary can only suggest the total scope of Hardy's *The Dynasts*, which in volume exceeds all the other poetry that he wrote during his career. The work is no less than a poetic representation in dramatic terms of Hardy's personal philosophy and understanding of history. The magnitude of Hardy's poem, however, makes it difficult to come to terms with critically and even artistically. Though Hardy issued the caveat that *The Dynasts* was written for a "mental" staging, he agreed in 1914 to an abridged version that was adapted for a theater production by Granville-Barker, who cut the original to a tenth of its size. The operation was necessary to bring *The Dynasts* within the practical range of time for a theatrical performance, since it is estimated that it would have required two entire days and nights of consecutive stage time to dramatize the whole text. As it was, Granville-Barker's abridgment was a strain on audiences and actors, and it caused some reviewers to conclude that *The Dynasts* was an "unplayable play." Its excessive length was not the only fault found with the stage version: The chopped-up plot lacked any sense of progression, and the play had no climax; even more debilitating was the replacement of Hardy's philosophical concerns with an overlay of patriotic sentiment that was devised by Granville-Barker to fit the nationalistic mood fostered in England by the outbreak of World War I.

Hardy's final attempt at a dramatic work was a one-act play entitled *The Famous Tragedy of the Queen of Cornwall*, which was published in 1923. In this play, Hardy's aim was exactly opposite from the purpose of *The Dynasts*: Here, he aimed at concentration rather than expansiveness in his choice of plot, characters, and setting, as he consciously tried to observe the unities. His subject for this play is the tragic love story of Tristram and Iseult, whose story attracted a number of nineteenth century authors, most notably Tennyson, Matthew Arnold, and Algernon Charles Swinburne, who had all written versions of the ill-starred romance.

Hardy dedicated his one-act verse drama to the memory of Emma Gifford, his first wife, and the play has associations with the courtship that took place in the spring of 1870 when he and Emma visited King Arthur's castle, Tintagel, in Lyonnesse—a place he called "the region of dream and mystery." The legends associated with this area lingered in his mind for fifty years and led to the composition of *The Famous Tragedy of the Queen of Cornwall*, which he began in 1916 but did not finish until 1923.

Hardy develops the Tristram story in a unique way, though his basic conception of the romance depends upon Sir Thomas Malory's *Le Morte d'Arthur* (1485). The use of the dramatic format forced Hardy to compress a good many details in his version. For example, to maintain unity of place, he has all the action take place at Tintagel. Furthermore, Hardy begins his drama immediately before the catastrophe, the events of his play taking place during the last hours of the lovers' lives. Moreover, Hardy adds several original details to the story of the doomed couple who are victims of the irresistible and fatal force of love. He employs a chorus (termed "chanters") and Merlin, the wizard, to provide necessary exposition at the start of the play. We learn that while King Mark has been away on a hunt, Queen Iseult has been called to come to Brittany by Tristram, her lover, who, she believes, is dying. She is prevented from seeing him by Iseult of the White Hands, Tristram's wife, who informs her falsely that he is dead. Queen Iseult returns to Lyonnesse thinking that her suspicious husband is none the wiser about her flight to Tristram's bedside; informants, however, have told Mark of her actions. In a subsequent scene, Tristram recovers and comes to Cornwall, traveling incognito, to see Iseult, who is gratified to learn that he is not dead. He lays bare his heart to her, saying that he has been forced into a miserable marriage with Iseult of the White Hands. Shortly thereafter, a strange ship arrives bringing Tristram's wife, who has followed him upon discovering that he has returned to his former love.

In a poignant scene that was added by Hardy, the deserted wife and passionate mistress meet. It is clearly shown by this episode that the theme of the play is the tragedy of mismatched mates. Queen Iseult cannot love Mark, who is cruel by nature; she is compelled by a love potion to love Tristram. Tristram is loved by both women, but he is too weak to do what is right, his fate also having been sealed by the same love potion. Meanwhile, Mark discovers Tristram's presence at the castle and, catching him in an embrace with Iseult, stabs him in the back with a dagger. The queen plucks the knife from the body of her dying lover and kills her husband with it. Then she leaps over the ledge of the castle and plunges to her death in the sea below, providing to the legendary story an ending that was entirely Hardy's own.

Whatever the intentions of this play, Hardy's revision of the legend created a great deal more sympathy for Iseult of the White Hands than had previous versions. Hardy was able to renew, in this, his last work, the old formula of tragedy that ruled so many of his own doomed pairs of lovers, from Eustacia Vye and Clem Yeobright in *The Return of the Native* to Jude Fawley and Sue Bridehead in *Jude the Obscure*—lovers whose destinies were shaped, like Tristram and Iseult's, by the dual compulsion of character and fate.

The Famous Tragedy of the Queen of Cornwall was Hardy's only work written expressly for the stage. It was first produced by the Hardy Players in Dorchester on November 21, 1923. There was also an operatic version produced in 1924, which Rutland Boughton scored. In writing *The Famous Tragedy of the Queen of Cornwall*, Hardy was perhaps trying to meet the objections of those critics who had indicted him for an inability to write a concentrated play in *The Dynasts*. In the case of this short poetic drama, Hardy proved that he could indeed create plays for the commercial theater. It is ironic in the best Hardyesque fashion that he succeeded at last with a genre that had been his first aspiration as a literary artist—the poetic drama.

Other major works

NOVELS: *Desperate Remedies*, 1871; *Under the Greenwood Tree*, 1872; *A Pair of Blue Eyes*, 1873; *Far from the Madding Crowd*, 1874; *The Hand of Ethelberta*, 1876; *The Return of the Native*, 1878; *The Trumpet-Major*, 1880; *A Laodicean*, 1881; *Two on a Tower*, 1882; *The Mayor of Casterbridge*, 1886; *The Woodlanders*, 1887; *Tess of the D'Urbervilles*, 1891; *Jude the Obscure*, 1895; *The Well-Beloved*, 1897.

SHORT FICTION: *Wessex Tales*, 1888; *A Group of Noble Dames*, 1891; *Life's Little Ironies*, 1894; *A Changed Man, The Waiting Supper and Other Tales*, 1913.

POETRY: *Wessex Poems and Other Verses*, 1898; *Poems of the Past and Present*, 1901; *Time's Laughingstocks and Other Verses*, 1909; *Satires of Circumstance*, 1914; *Moments of Vision and Miscellaneous Verses*, 1917; *Late Lyrics and Earlier*, 1922; *Human Shows, Far Phantasies: Songs and Trifles*, 1925; *Winter Words*, 1928; *Collected Poems*, 1931.

NONFICTION: *Life and Art*, 1925; *The Early Life of Hardy*, 1928; *The Later Years of Thomas Hardy*, 1930; *Hardy's Personal Writings*, 1966 (Harold Orel, editor); *The Collected Letters of Thomas Hardy*, 1978, 1980 (2 volumes; Richard Little Purdy and Michael Millgate, editors).

Bibliography

Bailey, J. O. *Thomas Hardy and the Cosmic Mind: A New Reading of "The Dynasts,"* 1956.
Carpenter, Richard C. *Thomas Hardy*, 1964.
Church, Richard. "Thomas Hardy as Revealed in *The Dynasts*," in *Essays by Divers Hands: Being the Transactions of the Royal Society of Literature, Volume XXIX*, 1958. Edited by E. V. Rieu.
Dean, Susan. *Hardy's Poetic Vision in "The Dynasts,"* 1977.
DuHin, Henry C. *Thomas Hardy: A Study of the Novels, Poems, and "The Dynasts,"* 1937.
Garrison, Chester A. *The Vast Venture: Hardy's Epic-Drama "The Dynasts,"* 1973.
Guerrard, Albert J. *Thomas Hardy*, 1964.
Howe, Irving. *Thomas Hardy*, 1967.
Hynes, Samuel. *The Pattern of Hardy's Poetry*, 1961.
Lawrence, D. H. "A Study of Thomas Hardy," in *D. H. Lawrence: Se-*

lected Literary Criticism, 1955. Edited by Anthony Beal.
Roberts, Marguerite. *Hardy's Poetic Drama and the Theatre: "The Dynasts"
and "The Famous Tragedy of the Queen of Cornwall,"* 1965.
Wright, Walter F. *The Shaping of "The Dynasts,"* 1967.

Hallman B. Bryant

LORENZ HART

Born: New York, New York; May 2, 1895
Died: New York, New York; November 22, 1943

Principal drama

Fly with Me, pr. 1920 (lyrics; libretto by Milton Kroopf and Philip Leavitt; music by Richard Rodgers); *The Melody Man*, pr. 1924 (libretto, with Rodgers and Herbert Fields); *The Garrick Gaieties*, pr. 1925, pb. 1951 (lyrics; sketches by Sir Arthur Sullivan, Morrie Ryskind, and others; music by Rodgers); *Dearest Enemy*, pr. 1925 (lyrics; libretto by Fields; music by Rodgers; based on Jean Gilbert's operetta *Die Frau im Hermelin*); *The Girl Friend*, pr. 1926 (lyrics; libretto by Fields; music by Rodgers); *Peggy-Ann*, pr. 1926 (lyrics; libretto by Fields; music by Rodgers); *A Connecticut Yankee*, pr. 1927 (lyrics; libretto by Fields; music by Rodgers); *Chee-Chee*, pr. 1928 (lyrics; libretto by Fields; music by Rodgers); *Present Arms*, pr. 1928 (lyrics; libretto by Fields; music by Rodgers); *Jumbo*, pr. 1935 (lyrics; libretto by Ben Hecht and Charles MacArthur; music by Rodgers); *On Your Toes*, pr. 1936 (lyrics; libretto, with Rodgers and George Abbott; music by Rodgers); *Babes in Arms*, pr. 1937, pb. 1951 (libretto, with Rodgers; music by Rodgers); *I'd Rather Be Right*, pr., pb. 1937 (lyrics; libretto by George S. Kaufman and Moss Hart; music by Rodgers); *I Married an Angel*, pr. 1938 (libretto, with Rodgers; music by Rodgers; adaptation of James Vasarzy's play); *The Boys from Syracuse*, pr. 1938 (lyrics; libretto by Abbott; music by Rodgers); *Pal Joey*, pr. 1940, pb. 1952 (lyrics; libretto by John O'Hara; music by Rodgers); *By Jupiter*, pr. 1942, pb. 1951 (lyrics; libretto, with Rodgers; music by Rodgers; adaptation of Julian Thompson's play *The Warrior's Husband*).

Other literary forms

Lorenz Hart is known primarily as a lyricist. Although he collaborated on several librettos for stage comedies, he wrote more than a thousand song lyrics for those and twenty-four other stage comedies and revues and for ten motion-picture musicals, of which *Love Me Tonight* (1932) is representative. Hart also translated plays, operettas (such as Jean Gilbert's *Die Frau im Hermelin*), and lyrics (such as those to the 1934 motion picture *The Merry Widow*, often without receiving credit).

Achievements

Lorenz Hart played a major role in advancing the musical theater from the level of vaudeville, revue, and spectacle to that of musical drama. He was not the first to take this step, nor did he take it alone, but he was one of the pioneers in an era that included such other musical-theater giants as

George and Ira Gershwin, Herbert and Dorothy Fields, George M. Cohan, Irving Berlin, Arthur Schwartz and Howard Dietz, Oscar Hammerstein II, Cole Porter, and Hart's partner Richard Rodgers. In the early 1900's, W. S. Gilbert and Sir Arthur Sullivan were writing their satiric light operas in England; Sigmund Romberg, Vincent Youmans, Victor Herbert, and Rudolf Friml were writing operettas in the romantic Viennese tradition; and the team of Jerome Kern, Guy Bolton, and P. G. Wodehouse had just begun to adapt these European forms to an American form influenced by music-hall traditions. The satiric lyrics of Gilbert and Wodehouse strongly influenced the young Hart, and the stories that held these musicals together inspired him to want musical comedies in which the songs were closely integrated with the plots and characters.

When Hart and Richard Rodgers met, they found that they shared this vision of the musical theater, and their partnership thrived on their commitment to it. Their attempt to integrate song and drama began in the early shows, as with "Old Enough to Love," a song for mature lovers in *Dearest Enemy*. It continued improving throughout their partnership to the Amazon's defiant "Nobody's Heart" in *By Jupiter*. In their early shows, the integration was not entirely successful, but the partners learned quite a lot about musical integration from their motion-picture experiences in the 1930's. When they returned to Broadway from Hollywood, they began writing their own librettos in which the songs could be inherent parts of the action and dialogue. The epitome of Hart's achievement in integrating lyrics into drama is considered to be *Pal Joey*, with its character pieces, Joey's hypocritical "I Could Write a Book" and Vera's cynical "Bewitched, Bothered, and Bewildered."

In addition to their importance in integrating the music into the drama, Rodgers and Hart also pioneered the use of subjects and stories that had previously been disregarded for the musical theater. For example, *Dearest Enemy* was based on a historical incident of the Revolutionary War; *Peggy-Ann* was the first musical to use Freudian dream theories; *A Connecticut Yankee* used Mark Twain's satire on Yankeeism; *I'd Rather Be Right* was the first musical satire of in-office government officials; *The Boys from Syracuse* set a Shakespearean comedy (*The Comedy of Errors*) to music; and *Pal Joey* dealt with sleazy, small-time nightclub entertainers and criminals. Rodgers and Hart were determined to turn musical comedy away from the stock plots and characters of the early stage. *Pal Joey*, which was not well received at its introduction, is now considered to be the masterpiece that brought Broadway musicals to maturity. Its 1952 revival won the New York Drama Critics Circle Award for Best Musical and eleven out of sixteen Donaldson Awards.

Hart was equally concerned with breaking the "June, moon, soon" mold of the Tin Pan Alley rhyme. An avid reader, he had an understanding of rhyme theory and poetic rhythm that allowed him to write witty, subtle, complex lyrics that impressed nearly everyone who heard them. One has only to compare his "Manhattan" lyrics ("Manhattan" rhymed with "Staten," "Coney" with "baloney") with those of another song, "East Side, West Side" ("town," "down," "O'Rourke," "York") to see the difference. He had an excellent understanding of dialect and could range from the slangy in "The Girl Friend" to the archaic in "Thou Swell" through the romantic in "Isn't It Romantic" and the tender in "My Funny Valentine," from the ironic in "I Wish I Were in Love Again" to the satiric in "Dear Old Syracuse" and the impudent in "Girls, Girls, Girls." Hart may have been the first truly literate American lyricist; certainly he was the first to achieve equal credit with the composer for the songwriting and to have his name, along with those of the author and composer, in lights on the theater marquee.

Biography

Lorenz Milton Hart was born in New York City on May 2, 1895, to Max Hart and Frieda Isenberg Hart. He had one brother, Theodore Van Wyck Hart, who also gained theatrical fame, as comic actor Teddy Hart. Lorenz Hart was educated at Columbia Grammar School, DeWitt Clinton, Weingart Institute, and Columbia University. In school, he belonged to literary societies and wrote for and edited the school papers.

Hart grew up in a highly literary environment. His mother, Frieda, had wanted to be an actress, and from the age of six, he was taken to the theater. He began to write poetry when he was six, and he wrote and performed skits and satires of plays he had seen both on and off Broadway. He loved the Gilbert and Sullivan and Kern-Bolton-Wodehouse musicals, but he never liked Herbert's "schmaltzy" music. At the Weingart Institute summer school, he belonged to the Weingart Literary Society and wrote articles for the literary magazine, often satires and humorous essays. In 1909, he became the editor of *The Weingart Review*. Also at Weingart, he acted in school dramas, farces, and minstrel shows. At fifteen, he began to attend Paradox Lake Camp, where he was active in weekly shows. He was nicknamed "Shakespeare" because he brought to camp a trunkload of books, including a fifteen-volume set of William Shakespeare's works, and performed Hamlet's soliloquy in one of the camp shows.

In 1917, Hart became the dramatic counselor at Brant Lake Camp; there he wrote comedy acts for small-time vaudeville shows. While he was there, Arthur Schwartz (who later composed "That's Entertainment" and "Dancing in the Dark") heard some of Hart's lyrics and took a job at Brant Lake Camp in order to meet Hart and work with him on camp productions. While working at Brant Lake in the summers, Hart also worked for United Plays, a reading and translating company associated with the Shubert theaters. Between 1920 and 1925, he translated and adapted French and German plays and Viennese operettas. Notably, he translated *Die Frau im Hermelin* by Jean Gilbert as "The Lady in Ermine," which was never published or produced but from which he adapted material to use in *Dearest Enemy*. He also is recognized to have done part of what is now the standard translation of Ferenc Molnár's *Liliom*, although he did not receive credit. Schwartz claims that Hart also wrote lyrics for three songs by Billy Rose for which he did not receive credit or royalties. Hart was working in both instances for salary, and his material became the property of the employer.

In 1919, he was introduced to Richard Rodgers by a friend who knew that Rodgers was looking for a lyricist. Hart was twenty-three, Rodgers sixteen. The two collaborated on a number of amateur shows. One of their early songs, "Any Old Place with You," was purchased by Lew Fields for *A Lonely Romeo* (pr. 1919); this was their first song performed on Broadway. While Hart (and later Rodgers, too) was at Columbia University, he and Rodgers collaborated on musicals produced in New York hotel ballrooms. These amateur university productions were often clever enough to attract theatergoers and critics; they provided excellent training for potential theatrical talent.

Rodgers and Hart created more than twenty-five preprofessional musicals. The partners were unable to sell any of their work to Broadway producers for about four years. Hart was continuing to translate, and Rodgers was considering changing his career goal, when Rodgers was offered the chance to write songs for *The Garrick Gaieties*, and he insisted on having Hart as lyricist. They were not paid for this work, but the show was on Broadway, produced by the Theatre Guild, and attended by professional critics. The show, intended for two performances, was so original and witty that it received rave notices and was extended for a six-month run. The hit of the show was the Rodgers and Hart song "Manhattan," which established their reputations on Broadway. Their first big success, however, was "My Heart Stood Still," which was written for the British show *One Dam Thing After Another* (pr. 1927). Its popularity preceded their return to the United States, and the song was then introduced to Broadway in *A Connecticut Yankee*. After that hit production, with few exceptions, Rodgers and Hart's musicals enjoyed one success after another.

After the Crash of 1929 depressed Broadway production, the songwriting team worked in Hollywood periodically in the early 1930's. Their film experiences, particularly when working with Rouben Mamoulian, taught them much about enhancing their story with music and making songs a part of the dialogue. These were ideas which they had already used in such musical dramas as *A Connecticut Yankee*. Innovations in the use of song in the motion picture *Love Me Tonight* prompted improvements in the music of the great Rodgers and Hart Broadway shows of the late 1930's and early 1940's. Motion-picture production techniques, however, were frustrating to them, being so different from their ingrained Broadway techniques. They were unhappy with the long periods of inactivity enforced by studio contracts, with the arbitrary and unexpected rejection or substitution of songs, and with the cancellation of entire film projects deemed noncommercial. They missed their customary participation with their Broadway colleagues in other aspects of stage production: interpreting, staging, choreographing, revising, and directing. When they read "Whatever happened to Rodgers and Hart?" in the Los Angeles *Examiner*, they were convinced that they should return to Broadway.

Drinking had already become a problem for Hart. Indeed, when Hart began his collaboration with Rodgers at age twenty-three, Rodgers' mother had predicted that Hart would not live to be twenty-five. Hart grew up in a fun-loving family. His father had plenty of money most of the time, and the family lived in large New York apartments and had two maids, a chauffeur, and a footman. Max Hart enjoyed living well and indulging his sons. Although Frieda Hart was a good housekeeper, she never minded disruptions caused by her sons and their numerous friends, who made the home a center for games, parties, poetry readings, and dramatic and musical performances. From childhood, Hart developed a taste for high living, conviviality, and incessant activity. He inherited a small size: He was only five feet tall, and his brother was only two inches taller. Furthermore, his head was slightly large for his body, so that he had a somewhat dwarfish look. Although people said they did not notice his size and proportions because his personality was so charming, he remained sensitive about his appearance all of his life. Still, Rodgers recalled that Hart was actually handsome, with animated features and warm brown eyes. When he was young, his father unstintingly gave him money for dates and treating his friends, and it is possible that his father's largess taught him an unintended lesson—that he could gain love and friendship only by paying for them. Certainly he delighted throughout his life in picking up the check for whatever group he was with or even for everyone in the room.

Hart's friend Mel Shauer, however, believed that Hart's drinking was an attempt to quiet the incessant, restless activity of his brain. As boys, Hart and his friends joked that his vertical growth was held down by the size of his brain. He read voraciously, was fluent in three languages, loved conversation and entertaining, and kept constantly on the move, motoring, attending the theater, the opera, the ballet. George Balanchine, commenting about Hart's quick mind, said that whatever was needed on a show Hart would do in a moment, and then he would be off doing something else; he had a certain intuition about what techniques and what talents would work. He was described as "impish" and "puckish"; he might disappear in the middle of a conversation; he loved to tease; he laughed easily and readily. His vocabulary was immense and expressive; as far as anyone knew, he never used a rhyming dictionary. He was a perfectionist about lyrics and shows.

Whatever the reason, Hart's drinking increased during the 1930's, although it did not yet interfere with his work. After he and Rodgers returned from Hollywood, they wrote the songs for eight of their greatest musicals. For four of these, they also coauthored the librettos. These were the years of *On Your Toes*, *Babes in Arms*, *I Married an Angel*, *The Boys from Syracuse*, and what is now considered Rodgers and Hart's masterpiece, *Pal Joey*. Hart, however, became increasingly undependable; he would disappear and be inaccessible for lengthening periods of time. Rodgers sometimes had to track him down and stay with him to get a lyric written. Hart would not discipline himself to write until a rehearsal simply could not proceed until he did. Still, he would turn out brilliant lyrics under these adverse conditions.

By the onset of the 1940's, Hart's alcoholism was becoming a serious detriment to his work. After *By Jupiter*, Hart no longer wished to work with Rodgers, and he went to Mexico to avoid the pressure of doing *Oklahoma!* (pr. 1943) because he did not like the original play. When he returned, although in ill health, he was enthusiastic about working with Rodgers again on an adaptation of Henry Fielding's *Tom Jones* (1749), but he was unable to carry it out. Rodgers had already begun working with Oscar Hammerstein II. The former partners did collaborate on a 1943 revival of *A Connecticut Yankee*, and Hart's last song was "To Keep My Love Alive," a new one for that production. Its quality and critical acclaim proved that his lyric ability was still unimpaired. He developed pneumonia after attending the opening of the revival on November 17, and died at Doctors Hospital on November 22, 1943.

Analysis

"Amusing, breezy, contagious, energetic, fresh, gay, impudent, joyful, sophisticated, unhackneyed, versatile, witty, youthful, zestful"—such are the critical reactions to the works of Rodgers and Hart. Perhaps Lorenz Hart's failure to grow up physically and emotionally, a failure that destroyed him personally, was also what gave his lyrics and plots those fun-loving qualities which contributed to his success professionally. Youthful vitality and wit are the first characteristics common to all the shows of Rodgers and Hart. Hart evidenced a satiric turn of mind from his earliest attempts at writing, and he kept it until his death; Rodgers commented that Hart "really didn't know how not to be clever." All of their plots, those they wrote and those they set to music, were witty satires, in which Hart's irreverent lyrics could play their role.

Another characteristic of Rodgers and Hart's shows is their variety. Both partners believed in avoiding formulas, other people's or their own, and in never doing the same thing twice in a row—or twice at all, if possible. Subject matter for their shows includes anything from grand opera, the Depression, and long-distance bicycle racing to Freudian dreams, Chinese eunuchs, and Amazons. In the six librettos that they wrote themselves, there is a somewhat more consistent use of show business themes. Nevertheless, they made a deliberate policy of turning to a story quite different from whatever they had just completed, no matter how successful. For example, the political satire *I'd Rather Be Right* was followed by the fantasy *I Married an Angel*, which was followed in turn by the Shakespearean farce *The Boys from Syracuse*.

A third important characteristic of Rodgers and Hart's artistry was their effort to make the musical comedy a more completely integrated musical drama, in which the songs advanced the plot and portrayed character. As youngsters, both were impressed with the Kern-Bolton-Wodehouse musicals, in which the plots were not episodic or situational but were motivated by the characters, and the songs were not interludes but were part of the drama. Both writers wished to emulate and indeed surpass what they had admired. Their first Broadway comedy, *Dearest Enemy*, was such a drama, and the history of their songs and librettos is the history of improvements in song as drama.

Dearest Enemy was based on an incident in American history: Some ladies of New York entertained the officers of British General William Howe's staff with cakes and ale, enabling American forces to make a strategic retreat. The show was turned down by several producers who could not imagine the commercial success of a musical based on American history. Rodgers and Hart, however, could see the possibilities of an element of sexual enticement in the delay of the British, and the situation allowed them to counterplay a genuine love affair between a young American girl and a British officer against a strategic flirtation by an older woman. Two contrasting love songs were used to emphasize the differences between these relationships: "Here in My Arms" and "Old Enough to Love." Tired of the traditional love ballad, typically a stock love song with little appropriateness to the singer, the composers were looking for new ways to sing about love. "Old Enough to Love" allowed two variations on the theme; first, it was a love song between mature adults rather than ingenues, and second, it ironically used a tender lyric as a medium for a harsher emotion. (The latter was a technique which Rodgers and Hart used again in many later shows.) Furthermore, Hart suited the dialect of each song to the character singing it. In translating "The Lady in Ermine" a few years earlier, he had researched the eighteenth century, and in writing *Dearest Enemy* he was able to draw on this research in creating dialogue and lyrics that suggested the period. *Dearest Enemy* was one of the first musical comedies to achieve such authenticity; in general, comedy had simply placed a modern story in period costumes and settings. Besides the period dialect, Hart also used simple, ingenuous language for the girl's song and more complex, sophisticated language for the woman's. Thus he began his adaptation of lyric to the portrayal of dramatic character. *Dearest Enemy* also introduced the type of spunky, resourceful females that typically populate Rodgers and Hart musicals.

Although *The Girl Friend* was one of Rodgers and Hart's most popular and profitable productions, it did not add a great deal to their growth as artists. *Peggy-Ann* was the next significant step in their career. Based on a popular play, *Tillie's Nightmare*, in which the heroine had a series of comic dreams, the Rodgers-Hart-Fields team reinterpreted the dreams as Freudian fantasies. It was one of the first musical comedies to use Freudian theory. It also made use of a non-Broadway, balletic style of dancing, which along with the music was an integral part of the dream action. The dream, in turn, constituted the main plot, for the frame story was simply a young girl's coming to terms through her fantasies with the unromantic realities of her everyday life. In accordance with the Freudian background, the songs featured sexual innuendo to a degree unusual for the time, as in "A Little Birdie Told Me So" and "A Tree in the Park."

Chee-Chee, Rodgers and Hart's worst flop, was nevertheless one of their most daring experiments. It was based on a story about a young Chinese man who is trying to avoid inheriting his father's office as Grand Eunuch; the subject of castration was even more daring than the Freudian content of *Peggy-Ann*. The comedy did not appeal widely to critics or audiences; indeed, the satiric treatment of the subject impressed critics as tasteless and sophomoric, at best. This reception was vastly different from the raves Hart usually received for his witty words. Nevertheless, *Chee-Chee* integrated music and drama more completely than did any other Rodgers and Hart musical. So completely did the music become a part of the dialogue that only six songs had titles, compared with between ten and fifteen songs in most musicals. Most of the music consisted of snatches of songs and brief bits of musical dialogue interwoven in the progress of the plot. If the story of *Chee-Chee* had been more palatable to the public, it might have become one of Rodgers and Hart's most highly admired works, but even its failure taught the partners several important lessons: first, that music alone cannot make an unpopular subject acceptable; second, that having at least one and preferably more popular favorites among the songs is almost essential to the success of a musical comedy; third, that it is possible to achieve a nearly complete integration of music and drama; but, fourth, that they had not yet mastered that art. As a result of *Chee-Chee*'s failure, the next five Rodgers and Hart shows were far less venturesome. On the other hand, without the failure, the partners might not have been so receptive to some of the lessons which they learned from motion-picture techniques.

The Depression took Rodgers and Hart to Hollywood, which was less affected by hard times than Broadway had been. They did not enjoy working on films, but they were impressed by the technique by which a song was made to seem a natural extension of the dialogue; they were to use this technique in many of their subsequent stage shows. In *Love Me Tonight*, they also adapted the musically accompanied preliminary dialogue into a form they called "rhythmic dialogue" or "musical dialogue," a form of nonmelodic singing which they used again, as did many other musical comedy writers. For example, the technique was very useful in *My Fair Lady* (pr. 1956) and *Camelot* (pr. 1960) for Rex Harrison and Richard Burton, neither of whom had singing voices. A camera that moved about as a song was playing very likely gave Hart the idea for using the reprise to show character development. In *Love Me Tonight*, the camera moved across seven characters whistling or singing "Isn't It Romantic?" Three different sets of lyrics presented three different attitudes toward love. Hart had the reprise of "There's a Small Hotel" in *On Your Toes* serve a similar purpose. Later, he extended the technique to emphasize plot and character change. In *Pal Joey*, for example, Vera's reprise shows she is no longer "Bewitched, Bothered, and Bewildered." Another lesson came from Mamoulian, director of *Love Me Tonight*, who insisted that Rodgers write not only the songs but also all the background music, in order to achieve musical coherence throughout the film. What was true of musical coherence might also be true of literary coherence, and it was after this experience with Mamoulian that Rodgers and Hart began to write their own books. The ones they wrote themselves—the products of their fully matured talents—are accounted the best of their collaborations.

On Your Toes, the first of their books, did not have a very original plot, but it did bring together all that Rodgers and Hart had learned from their twenty-three years of collaboration. It was a fairly standard show-within-a-show plot, but it made ballet as well as song an essential part of the plot and characterization. The story concerns a former vaudeville dancer with classical yearnings, who becomes involved with a ballet company, fumbles traditional ballet in a comic travesty of classical dance forms, but finally introduces a jazz ballet in which his style succeeds very well. The ballet serves as the climax to the story, and not merely in the traditional "would-be star makes good" sense: In a confusion of identity, two gangsters are trying to shoot the hero, and at the conclusion of the jazz ballet performance, he signals the orchestra to continue playing so that he can keep on dancing and avoid being a stationary target for their guns. Meanwhile, his girlfriend calls the police, who arrive at the moment he becomes too exhausted to continue dancing. Thus, the satiric ballet, the jazz ballet, and the songs advance the plot and show the hero realizing his abilities.

Babes in Arms was a return to the type of joyous revue that had succeeded so well in the 1920's. There is not much to be said about the book, which Rodgers and Hart wrote this time without a collaborator. It is, however, notable that not one or two but five of their greatest songs came from this one show: "Where or When," "My Funny Valentine," "The Lady Is a Tramp," "Johnny One-Note," and "I Wish I Were in Love Again." Their songwriting skills had obviously reached an apex at this time, along with their dramatic skills.

I Married an Angel was a triumphantly witty account of an angel trying to adapt to the ways of this faulty world. In this show and in *By Jupiter*, all of their dramatic and lyric skills came together in what are still among the most memorable productions of musical comedy entertainment.

It was *Pal Joey*, however, that made the greatest impact on the Broadway musical tradition. The idea of doing this cynical, gritty show instead of the usual lighthearted comedy was suggested to them by John O'Hara, who wrote the book, and Rodgers and Hart were quick to see its possibilities. *Pal Joey* concerns a small-time nightclub entertainer who aspires to greater success. He is a handsome but unscrupulous opportunist who lies and seduces his way nearly to the top. Through a liaison with Vera, a wealthy older woman who is willing to pay for sexual excitement, he acquires his own nightclub. Upon a threat of blackmail, however, she quickly becomes disenchanted and drops him. There are no likable characters in this story, with the exception of a girl whom Joey attracts at the beginning of the play but drops in favor of Vera's money. The satire in *Pal Joey* is bitter and disillusioned instead of gay and youthful, and the wit is found in the slangy dialogue and sharp repartee. The show songs are designed to be trite and shoddy, as one might expect in a low-class nightclub, and even the love songs are hypocritical mockeries of genuine love songs. Critical reception of *Pal Joey* was mixed. Some critics found it distasteful; others recognized it as excellent drama and a trailblazing departure from the Broadway traditions. The latter critical opinion was supported by the show's success. It had a long initial run and an even longer run on its revival in 1952, when it also won the New York Drama Critics Circle Award for Best Musical. As Rodgers observed, "The show . . . forced the musical comedy theatre to wear long pants for the first time."

Indeed, this witty observation perhaps best sums up Rodgers and Hart's contribution to the musical theater. Along with Ira Gershwin and Cole Porter, Hart set a new standard in musical comedy for poetic excellence, semantic and phonetic appropriateness, and perfect rhythmic phrasing of lines to his partner's music. Together, Rodgers and Hart, with their collaborators, dared to break the mold of musical theater tradition and open the way to the great musical dramas of the 1950's and 1960's.

Bibliography

Craig, Warren. *Sweet and Lowdown*, 1978.
Ewen, David. *Men of Popular Music*, 1944.
——————. *New Complete Book of the American Musical Theater*, 1970.
Geisinger, Marion. *Plays, Players, and Playwrights*, 1971.
Green, Stanley. *The World of Musical Comedy*, 1960.
Hart, Dorothy. *Thou Swell, Thou Witty*, 1976.

Carol Croxton

MOSS HART

Born: New York, New York; October 24, 1904
Died: Palm Springs, California; December 20, 1961

Principal drama

The Hold-up Man, pr. 1923; *Jonica*, pr. 1930 (with Dorothy Heyward); *Once in a Lifetime*, pr., pb. 1930 (with George S. Kaufman); *Face the Music*, pr. 1932 (libretto; music by Irving Berlin); *As Thousands Cheer*, pr. 1933 (revue; music by Berlin); *The Great Waltz*, pr. 1934; *Merrily We Roll Along*, pr., pb. 1934 (with Kaufman); *Jubilee*, pr. 1935 (music by Cole Porter); *You Can't Take It with You*, pr. 1936, pb. 1937 (with Kaufman); *I'd Rather Be Right*, pr., pb. 1937 (with Kaufman; score by Richard Rodgers and Lorenz Hart); *The Fabulous Invalid*, pr., pb. 1938 (with Kaufman); *The American Way*, pr., pb. 1939 (with Kaufman); *The Man Who Came to Dinner*, pr., pb. 1939 (with Kaufman); *George Washington Slept Here*, pr., pb. 1940 (with Kaufman); *Lady in the Dark*, pr., pb. 1941 (music by Kurt Weill); *Winged Victory*, pr., pb. 1943; *Christopher Blake*, pr., pb. 1946; *Light Up the Sky*, pr. 1948, pb. 1949; *The Climate of Eden*, pr. 1952, pb. 1953 (adaptation of Edgar Mittelholzer's *Shadows Among Them*).

Other literary forms

Moss Hart is known primarily for his plays. He also achieved success as a screenwriter; among his best-known screenplays are those for *Gentleman's Agreement* (1947) and *A Star Is Born* (1954). In 1959, Hart published his autobiography, *Act One*, which was made into a film in 1963, as were many of his plays. Finally, Hart published a handful of miscellaneous articles on theater subjects.

Achievements

Moss Hart was one of the great comic playwrights of American drama. In works such as *Once in a Lifetime*, *You Can't Take It with You*, and *The Man Who Came to Dinner*, he gave the theater some of its most amusing moments. He was awarded the Roi Cooper Megrue Award in 1930 for *Once in a Lifetime* and in 1937, with George S. Kaufman, the Pulitzer Prize for *You Can't Take It with You*.

Since Hart's best works are his collaborations with Kaufman, his critical stature will always be obscured by that of the older, more famous dramatist. It would be a mistake, however, to think of Hart as simply Kaufman's collaborator. Kaufman worked with several partners in his career, including such talents as Ring Lardner, Alexander Woollcott, and Edna Ferber, but none of them produced such fine results with Kaufman as Hart did, nor were any of the Kaufman and Hart plays the work of one man more than the other. Theirs was a true collaboration, with each man contributing equally to the final product. Moreover, Hart's solo works, such as *Lady in the Dark*, with its innovative staging and probing of psychological conflicts, show that he could create significant drama on his own.

In addition to playwriting and screenwriting, Hart directed such plays as Alan Jay Lerner and Frederick Loewe's *Camelot* (pr. 1960) and *My Fair Lady* (pr. 1956); the latter won for Hart a Tony Award.

Biography

Moss Hart was born in the Bronx section of New York, the son of Barnett Hart, a cigar maker who was left without a trade when a cigar-making machine was developed. The family survived as best they could, but Hart's early life was dominated by a sense of poverty. The two most important influences in his childhood were his grandfather and his Aunt Kate. These impractical, domineering people, though a great drain on the family finances, were the only sources of color and vitality for the young Hart. Aunt Kate, an avid theatergoer, introduced Hart to the world of drama, which formed in his mind a desire to escape from his squalid surroundings via the glittering stage.

At the age of seventeen, Hart got his first theatrical job as office boy to Augustus Pitou, a touring-show producer known as "the King of the One-Night Stands." While reading plays that were submitted to Pitou, Hart began writing a play of his own, replete with the sentimental and hackneyed elements of those he had read. He presented the play to Pitou, who was enthusiastic about it and agreed to produce it. Entitled *The Hold-up Man*, it opened in Rochester in 1923 and flopped.

The failure of his first play also cost Hart his job. He worked as a director for little theater companies and as an actor, once playing the role of Smithers in Eugene O'Neill's *The Emperor Jones* (pr. 1920) to glowing reviews. He spent his summers as a social director in various resort camps. During this time, he still nursed a desire to write plays in the manner of O'Neill and George Bernard Shaw, but he learned that his talent lay not with serious drama but with light comedy. In the late 1920's, Hart began writing a comedy in the manner of his idol, the comedic writer George S. Kaufman, dealing with the advent of sound in motion pictures. Producer Sam Harris agreed to do the play only if Hart collaborated on it with Kaufman himself. The play, *Once in a Lifetime*, after dubious early showings and several major rewrites, was a smash hit and marked the beginning of one of the greatest writing teams in American drama. It also marked Hart's escape from the poverty of his early years. After reading the enthusiastic reviews of *Once in a Lifetime*, Hart moved his family from their Bronx apartment to rooms in the fashionable Edison Hotel.

In the following years, Hart wrote some of his best plays. These

included musicals with Irving Berlin and Cole Porter and further collaborations with Kaufman, including their greatest works, *You Can't Take It with
You* and *The Man Who Came to Dinner*. With the money from these plays,
Hart was able to buy a large country estate in the Poconos, yet he found
that success did not bring the solution to all of his problems. In 1934, he
began seeing a psychiatrist and came to believe that he was too dependent
on Kaufman. Finally, Hart, acting on the advice of his psychiatrist, broke
off his collaboration with Kaufman, although the two remained friends.

Hart's first play after the break, *Lady in the Dark*, proved that he could
write without Kaufman's support. He went on to write other successful
plays but never with the popularity of his work with Kaufman. In 1945, he
married actress Kitty Carlisle; they had two children. After World War II,
Hart wrote some of his finest screenplays, including *Gentleman's Agreement* and *A Star Is Born*. Hart served as president of the Dramatists Guild
from 1947 to 1955 and of the Authors League from 1955 to 1961. Hart also
returned to directing, winning a Tony Award in 1957 for *My Fair Lady*. In
1961, he died of a heart attack.

Analysis

Those who approach the plays of Moss Hart as literary products to be
analyzed and placed in some dramatic category will be disappointed. Hart
wrote his plays to give pleasure to large crowds. He learned early in his
career that his talent lay in witty light comedy rather than serious drama.
Though his plays satirized every institution of the time, from the New Deal
to the motion picture industry, their prevailing tone is one of wild spoofing,
not serious criticism. This is not to dismiss Hart as merely a pleasant hack.
With Kaufman, he created some of America's funniest plays. Hart stayed
within the limits of the popular theater, though he did try to extend those
limits. As a result, he created superior entertainment that continues to
delight audiences even today.

A good example of the Kaufman and Hart comedy is their first
collaboration, *Once in a Lifetime*. It concerns three down-and-out vaudeville actors: the likable-but-dumb straight man George Lewis; the tough,
clever May Daniels; and the enterprising Jerry Hylands. They sell their act
and travel to Hollywood in the first days of sound pictures to open an
elocution school for movie actors, who must now be heard as well as seen.
The school, operating in Glogauer Studios, is a failure, but when George
repeats some unflattering comments on motion pictures in general and
Glogauer in particular (comments that he has picked up from Lawrence
Vail, a disgruntled playwright hired by Glogauer to turn out film scripts),
he is taken by the producer to be an outspoken genius and is made studio
supervisor. With Jerry and May as his assistants, George oversees the production of *Gingham and Orchids*, a movie that has the script of another

film, a set only half-lit, and the noise of George incessantly cracking Indian nuts throughout the sound track. To everyone's surprise, the film becomes a financial and critical success, and George is the hero of the hour. Jerry and May, realizing that George does not need their guidance in order to get along in pictures, return to New York to get married.

There is scarcely any facet of Hollywood in the early 1930's that *Once in a Lifetime* does not ridicule, whether it is the "early De Mille" architecture, vapid movie columnists, temperamental German directors, or stars who cannot act. Many of the authors' opinions are put into the mouth of Lawrence Vail, a representative figure among the successful Broadway dramatists who went to Hollywood to write for the studios and then were given nothing to do. (Vail's part was played in the original run of *Once in a Lifetime* by Kaufman himself.) According to Vail, the film industry is "the most God-awful thing I have ever run into."

Given the topsy-turvy nature of movies, the success of George Lewis is perfectly logical. George takes everything at face value and therefore is perfect in a business that runs on hype. He is incompetent and thus is able to excel in a business that cannot tell the difference between a good film and a bad one. Ironically, Jerry and May decide to leave Hollywood, even though it was Jerry who suggested that they go there and May who came up with the elocution idea. Hart and Kaufman imply that intelligence has no value in pictures.

The major targets of the play's satire are stupidity and vanity, rather than the darker flaws revealed in such a work as Nathanael West's *The Day of the Locust* (1939). The only hint of such depths in *Once in a Lifetime* comes when Jerry denies any involvement with the making of *Gingham and Orchids* because the movie looks initially like a flop, but Jerry's duplicity is soon atoned for when he nobly tells off Glogauer and gets himself fired. Even Glogauer, though he is as inaccessible and arbitrary as an Eastern potentate, is not genuinely corrupt; he is simply a silly, vulgar little man puffed up with money. The play does not try to expose Hollywood as much as it tries to have fun at its expense. The film industry was not particularly offended by the play and even made it into a movie.

Another example of Kaufman and Hart's good-natured humor is *The Man Who Came to Dinner*. The main character, Sheridan Whiteside, was largely based on the authors' friend Alexander Woollcott, radio commentator, wit, and man of letters. Whiteside slips on a piece of ice on the doorstep of the Stanleys, a prominent family in Mesalia, Ohio, and fractures his hip. Convalescing for several weeks in the Stanleys' home, he turns their lives inside out. He does his radio broadcasts from the library, sends and receives messages from all over the world, and populates the house with murderers, penguins, and other exotic creatures. Worse, he encourages the Stanleys' son and daughter to direct their lives independently of their parents' wishes and blackmails Mr. Stanley into submitting. Whiteside also tries to break up and then restore the romance between his secretary, Maggie Cutler, and Burt Jefferson, a Mesalia reporter. Just as the play ends and Whiteside is leaving, he slips on the ice again and announces that he is suing Mr. Stanley for $350,000.

The comedy in *The Man Who Came to Dinner* is based on the fantastic characters that populate it, the greatest of whom is Whiteside. In fact, the personality of Whiteside, his eccentricities, his talent for insults and witty repartee, his scheming mind, and his carefully concealed streak of compassion dominate the play and win the audience to him in spite of his boorishness and his impositions on the Stanleys. Whiteside is supported in his comic antics by such figures as the nymphomaniac actress Lorraine Sheldon, the playwright Beverly Carlton (based on Noël Coward), and the movie clown Banjo (based on Harpo Marx). These figures are part of the great world in which Whiteside lives, the world of such figures as Mahatma Gandhi, Walt Disney, and H. G. Wells, all of whom provide some of the play's fun.

Hart and Kaufman's finest play is probably *You Can't Take It with You*, which to some extent resembles *The Man Who Came to Dinner*. Both plays portray the collision of a group of wild eccentrics with a respectable family. The eccentrics in *You Can't Take It with You* are Martin Vanderhof and his family. Martin, called Grandpa in the play, was once a businessman who felt that he was missing the fun of life. For thirty-five years, he has dedicated his life to enjoying himself, and his family has done likewise. While Grandpa collects snakes and attends commencements, his daughter Penny Sycamore writes plays; her husband, Paul, makes fireworks; their older daughter, Essie Carmichael, studies ballet with an expatriate Russian tutor; and Essie's husband, Ed, plays the xylophone and operates a small printing press. The only "normal" member of the group is Penny's younger daughter, Alice, a secretary for a Wall Street firm who has fallen in love with Tony Kirby, Jr., her boss's son. Even though she loves the members of her family, and even though Tony himself is charmed by them, Alice fears that their somewhat anarchistic life-style will clash with the values of the ultra-respectable Kirbys.

Alice's fears are justified when the Kirbys arrive for dinner on the night before they are expected. A drunken actress flirts with Mr. Kirby, Penny tells Mrs. Kirby that the Spiritualism in which she devoutly believes is a fake, and Kolenkhov, the Russian dance instructor, wrestles with Mr. Kirby. At the evening's climax, federal agents, suspecting Ed of subversive activities, arrest everyone just as Paul's fireworks go off. Alice and Tony's wedding seems doomed until Grandpa explains his way of life to Mr. Kirby. According to Grandpa, the quest for material success and social acceptance should never be pursued at the cost of personal happiness. When Tony reminds his father that he once dreamed of being a trapeze artist and later a saxophone player, the elder Kirby becomes reconciled to the Vanderhofs' unusual ways and his son's refusal to follow in his footsteps, and he joins his future in-laws for dinner.

You Can't Take It with You contrasts two families who have in different ways achieved the American Dream. The Kirbys, through hard work, sobriety, and duty, have attained wealth and respectability. The cost of their success has been the sacrifice of their personal happiness. Mr. Kirby suffers from indigestion and regrets that he has lost his youthful ideals. Mrs. Kirby takes solace in the fashionable humbug of Spiritualism and, in a game of word-association, responds to "sex" with "Wall Street." Tony feels that his parents do not understand him and plans to leave his father's firm to become a bricklayer. Even Mr. Kirby's hobby of growing orchids has been taken up as a refuge from business cares and not for its own sake. His remarks concerning the orchids center on the time it takes to grow one, as the Kirbys' lives are, in general, centered on time and schedules.

The Vanderhofs are another side of the American Dream, the individualistic side of the Dream represented by Walden Pond. They do exactly as they like and live off the money from Grandpa's land. They have no desire to make money or to win other people's respect, only to be happy and to make others happy. Their hobbies are taken up spontaneously; Penny became a dramatist only because a typewriter was accidentally delivered to the house. Their meals are largely impromptu affairs. The house is shared by various people, including Donald, the boyfriend of their housekeeper Rheba, and Mr. De Pinna, who used to be their iceman. While the Kirby's live by the clock, time is not quite real to the Vanderhofs; when Alice asks the time, her family's replies are confused.

Like many radical individualists in American history, the Vanderhofs are at odds with the government. Not only is Ed thought to be a subversive, but also Grandpa is harassed for not paying his income tax. Mr. Kirby calls their way of life Communism, but it is really closer to the American ideals of life, liberty, and the pursuit of happiness than is his own way of life. The play does not really answer the arguments against living exactly as one pleases, nor is it meant to do so. What attracts the audience to the Vanderhofs is not the cogency of their arguments but the delight in seeing people do things that others would like to do and the charm with which the Vanderhofs succeed. In this sense, the play is an American pastoral presenting an idyllic world to relieve the frustrated Kirbys in the audience. Interestingly, *You Can't Take It with You* was not originally as successful in England as in America; perhaps its celebration of individualism was too extreme for English tastes.

No survey of Moss Hart's work would be complete without notice of his solo plays, of which the best is *Lady in the Dark*. Lacking the slapstick situations and witty dialogue of his best work with Kaufman, the play examines the psychological state of Liza Elliot, editor of *Allure*, the most popular women's magazine in the country. Liza has reached the top of her profession yet is going through a psychological crisis. She undergoes analysis to find the cause of her problems, and her psychological states are dramatized in a series of fantasy sequences. In one sequence, Liza is a glamour girl adored by every man, even though in real life, she tries to appear totally unglamorous. The fantasy ends when a man resembling Charley Johnson, the advertising manager, paints a portrait of Liza as she really appears.

As Liza's analysis continues, she realizes that her problems relate to a sense of inferiority as a woman, derived from an unconscious belief that she can never be as beautiful as her celebrated mother, who died when Liza was young. Thus, Liza tries to make other women beautiful while remaining plain herself. Her lover, Kendall Nesbitt, is a married man for whom Liza does not have to compete; when Kendall gets a divorce, Liza does not wish to marry him. Similarly, she has a brief romance with Randy Curtis, an insecure movie star who looks to Liza as a mother figure rather than as a lover. Only when Liza understands her neurosis can she love the man who really loves her, Charley Johnson, who appears in her fantasies as her nemesis. Charley sees behind Liza's unfeminine pose and infuriates Liza until she realizes that he is the only man who can fulfill her needs as a woman.

Lady in the Dark, with its concern for psychological complexity, its innovative dramatic techniques, and serious theme, was a marked departure from Hart's previous work, although similarities to the earlier plays exist. Like *Once in a Lifetime* and *You Can't Take It with You*, this play explores the somewhat dubious value of success. Hart comments in his autobiography, *Act One*, that, as sweet as success is, it does not bring personal happiness and indeed often makes unhappiness more noticeable and difficult to bear. Just as success has given no joy to Mr. Kirby, so it has given none to Liza, since it is largely a flight from her unconscious fears. Only when Liza faces these fears can she achieve happiness.

Hart's technique of alternating fantasy and reality in the play through the use of four revolving stages is a brilliant and innovative method for dramatizing what occurs in Liza's mind. Especially effective is the device of using people from the real world as characters in Liza's dreams. Thus, Charley Johnson exposes Liza's self-imposed plainness in her glamour fantasy, exactly as he destroys her unglamorous competent-executive image in reality. The technique's effectiveness is weakened, however, by having Dr. Brooks explain what the fantasies mean rather than having the audience interpret them on its own.

Lady in the Dark demonstrated that Hart could work alone as well as in collaboration and in serious drama as well as in comedy, yet it also proves that his real talent lay in comedy, for although the play received popular and critical praise, it does not have the bite or sparkle of *The Man Who Came to Dinner* or *You Can't Take It with You*. It is good serious drama but not superlative entertainment, and it is for his superlative work that any artist should be remembered.

Other major works

NONFICTION: *Act One*, 1959.

SCREENPLAYS: *Flesh*, 1932; *The Masquerader*, 1933; *Broadway Melody of 1936*, 1935; *Frankie and Johnny*, 1936; *Winged Victory*, 1944; *Gentleman's Agreement*, 1947; *Hans Christian Andersen*, 1952; *Prince of Players*, 1954; *A Star Is Born*, 1954.

Bibliography

Ashley, Leonard R. N. "Moss Hart," in *Great Writers of the English Language: Dramatists*, 1979. Edited by James Vinson.

Ferber, Edna. "A Rolling Stone Gathers Considerable Heart," in *Stage*. XIV (December, 1936), pp. 41-43.

Harriman, H. C. "Hi-Yo Platinum!" in *The New Yorker*. XIX (September 11, 1943), pp. 29-34.

Meredith, Scott. *George S. Kaufman and His Friends*, 1974.

Ross, Walter R. "Moss Hart," in *The Dictionary of National Biography, Volume VII: Twentieth Century American Dramatists, Part I*, 1981. Edited by John MacNicholas.

Anthony Bernardo

LILLIAN HELLMAN

Born: New Orleans, Louisiana; June 20, 1905
Died: Martha's Vineyard, Massachusetts; June 30, 1984

Principal drama

The Children's Hour, pr., pb. 1934; *Days to Come*, pr., pb. 1936; *The Little Foxes*, pr., pb. 1939; *Watch on the Rhine*, pr., pb. 1941; *The Searching Wind*, pr., pb. 1944; *Another Part of the Forest*, pr. 1946, pb. 1947; *Montserrat*, pr. 1949, pb. 1950 (adaptation of Emmanuel Robles' play); *The Autumn Garden*, pr., pb. 1951; *The Lark*, pr. 1955, pb. 1956 (adaptation of Jean Anouilh's play *L'Alouette*); *Candide*, pr. 1956, pb. 1957 (libretto; music by Leonard Bernstein, lyrics by Richard Wilbur, John Latouche, and Dorothy Parker; adaptation of Voltaire's novel); *Toys in the Attic*, pr., pb. 1960; *My Mother, My Father and Me*, pr., pb. 1963 (adaptation of Burt Blechman's novel *How Much?*).

Other literary forms

In addition to her original stageplays, Lillian Hellman published original screenplays, a collection of the letters of Anton Chekhov, her adaptations of two French plays (*Montserrat*, *L'Alouette*) and of an American novel (*How Much?*), an operetta adapted from Voltaire's *Candide*, many uncollected articles, and several volumes of memoirs, the first two of which have received as much acclaim as her best plays.

Achievements

Hellman was the most important American follower of Henrik Ibsen after Arthur Miller. Like Ibsen in his middle period, she wrote strong, well-made plays involving significant social issues. Like Ibsen, she created memorable female characters, some strong, some weak; and her most important female character, Regina Giddens of *The Little Foxes* and *Another Part of the Forest*, seems at least partially modeled on Ibsen's Hedda Gabler. Both Hellman and Ibsen were exceptional in depicting believable, memorable children. Like him, though more frequently, she used blackmail as a dramatic ploy. Her plays, like Ibsen's, can be strongly and tightly dramatic, and, like his, some, notably *The Little Foxes*, have a question ending: one, that is, in which the eventual outcome for the major characters is left ironically uncertain.

Her last two original plays, however, recall Chekhov more than Ibsen in their depiction of feckless characters and, in one of the two, an apparent, though only apparent, plotlessness. She has been blamed for her employment of melodramatic plot elements, but her use of them is often valid and essential and does not interfere with accurate character analysis, convincing dramatic dialogue, and adroit handling of social issues. Hellman was, after Tennessee Williams, the most important dramatist writing primarily about the American South. Two of her plays, *Watch on the Rhine* and *Toys in the Attic*, won the New York Drama Critics Circle Award. Hellman received many other awards, including the Brandeis University Creative Arts Medal and the National Institute of Arts and Letters Gold Medal.

Biography

Lillian Florence Hellman was born in New Orleans of Jewish parents. Her father was also born in New Orleans, and her mother in Alabama, of a family long established there. Part of her mother's family moved to New York, and when Hellman was five years old, her parents moved there and commenced a routine of spending six months of each year in New York and six in New Orleans with her father's two unmarried sisters. As her memoirs make clear, Hellman's plays are strongly influenced by her Southern, urban background; her mother's family was a source for the Hubbards in *The Little Foxes* and *Another Part of the Forest*; her paternal aunts, for the sisters in *Toys in the Attic*. All of her original plays except the first two (*The Children's Hour* and *Days to Come*) are set in the South: in the Washington area, in Alabama towns, or in New Orleans. Hellman was graduated from high school in New York in 1922, attended New York University from 1922 to 1924, and briefly attended Columbia University in 1924, without completing a degree at either school. She worked for a time thereafter in New York and Hollywood in the areas of publishing, book reviewing, and reading manuscripts of plays and movie scenarios. In 1925, she married Arthur Kober; they were divorced in 1932. Two years later, her first play, *The Children's Hour*, was a tremendous hit, achieving a longer original run (691 performances) than any of her later plays. From that success until her last play in 1963, she was primarily a playwright and occasionally a scriptwriter, though she was never really happy in the theater.

Over the years, Hellman made various visits to Russia, to Civil War Spain, and elsewhere in Europe, including a very dangerous visit to Nazi Germany to take money to the underground at the request of a friend. For many years, she was the companion of the novelist Dashiell Hammett, though they lived together only sporadically. Congressional investigations of Communism in the United States in the early 1950's caused serious trouble for both her and Hammett, though she denied having sufficiently consistent or deep political convictions to belong to any party. As a result of the investigations, Hellman and Hammett were both blacklisted in Hollywood; she also lost the home she owned and shared with Hammett in upstate New York, as well as various friends. Hammett was imprisoned; soon after his release, he became ill, and Hellman took care of him until his death in 1961. In her later years, Hellman devoted herself to her four books of memoirs and taught at Harvard, the Massachusetts Institute of Technology, and the University of California at Berkeley. She died of cardiac arrest on June 30, 1984, on Martha's Vineyard.

Analysis

The Children's Hour, Lillian Hellman's first play, was based on an actual lawsuit, the Great Drumsheugh Case. The play displays almost all the dramatic characteristics for which Hellman is noted: crisp, forceful, realistic dialogue; clear character construction and analysis; a clear-cut plot line in the tradition of the well-made play, with fast movement and adroitly handled suspense which kept (and can still keep) audiences enthralled. Some of Hellman's later plays display these characteristics with greater skill, but they are all there in her first. *The Children's Hour* and most of the others can also be called melodramatic, because of the suspense, because of the use of violence and of blackmail, and because of obvious authorial manipulation to achieve a neat conclusion. The plays are never, however, pure melodrama, since pure melodrama would not include valid, well-drawn characters or significant themes. *The Children's Hour*, like many of Hellman's plays, concerns the destructive power of evil, its ability to erode human relationships and destroy lives. In this play, evil is manifested by a child's malicious lie and its repercussions in the lives of two women.

The Children's Hour opens on a class in progress at a girls' boarding school in Massachusetts. The teacher, Lily Mortar, is the aunt of Martha Dobie, one of the two young women who own and operate the school. Presently, Mary Tilford enters, very late for class, carrying a bunch of flowers with which she appeases the teacher. Then the other owner, Karen Wright, enters. Karen has lost her bracelet and asks one of the girls, Helen, if she has found it, an important issue in the play. Karen asks Mary where she got the flowers. Mary repeats her claim that she picked them. Karen, apparently recognizing them, says Mary got them out of the garbage pail and has been lying. Mary's response is, and continues to be, that the teachers are against her, that they never believe her, and that she is telling the truth. Karen grounds her for two weeks. Mary says her heart hurts and pretends to fall into a faint. She is carried to her room.

Martha enters, and she and Karen discuss Mary as a troublemaker, send for Karen's fiancé (Joe Cardin, who is a doctor and also Mary's cousin), discuss getting rid of Mrs. Mortar, and discuss Karen's plans to marry Joe as soon as school is out. Martha is clearly upset at the imminent marriage, although she likes Joe. She hates interference with a friendship that has gone on since college and hates the possibility that Karen might leave the school. Joe arrives and goes off to examine Mary.

At this point in the play, the audience cannot be sure of the meaning of Martha's jealousy, of whether Mary's feelings are in any sense justified, of whether the events thus far are more taut with emotion than what might be expected on a day-by-day basis in a girls' boarding school. Mrs. Mortar, deeply insulted at Martha's desire to get her away from the school and at her offer to send her to London and support her there, indirectly accuses her niece of homosexual feelings toward Karen. Mary's two roommates are caught eavesdropping. Joe has a friendly confrontation with Martha, who apologizes and falls into his arms, weeping. It is reasonably clear that she does not recognize her feelings for Karen as homosexual, if they are. Mary comes in, and it is clear that Joe considers her a troublemaker, as do the women. Then, as the adults leave and the audience sees Mary for the first time alone with other girls, her character becomes only too clear.

Indeed, one becomes more and more convinced that Mary's lies, her manipulation, her dictatorial attitude toward her schoolmates, and presently her outright blackmail of one of them and her cruelty to another represent more than mere naughtiness or adolescent confusion. Mary is psychotic, and dangerously so. Feeling no affection for anyone, she lives for manipulation and power. As soon as the teachers leave the room, she throws a cushion at the door and kicks a table. Apparently, her one genuine feeling other than hatred is the belief that the teachers hate her as much as she hates them. She tells her roommates that if she cannot go to the boat races (since she has been grounded), she will see to it that they do not go either. She forces a girl named Rosalie to do some work for her by hinting of knowledge that Rosalie stole the bracelet that Karen asked about earlier. She forces her roommates to report the conversation that they overheard, and while Mary certainly does not completely understand its import, she nevertheless recognizes it as a weapon she can use. She immediately announces that she is going to walk out and go home, and by physical force, she makes one of the girls give her the money to get there. On this moment of tension, typical of a well-made play, act 1 closes.

The Children's Hour is unusual among Hellman's plays in that it does not all take place in one setting. Act 2 takes place in the living room of the home of Mary's grandmother in Boston. As scene 1 of the act opens, Mary arrives and is admitted by the maid, Agatha, who clearly does not trust her for an instant. Left alone while Agatha goes to fetch Mrs. Tilford, Mary tries with the aid of a mirror to make herself look sick. Mrs. Tilford enters, and Mary dashes into her arms, in tears. It soon becomes clear that Mrs. Tilford is an intelligent woman but that, unlike Agatha, she can be taken in by her granddaughter. It is an irony of the play, however, that she cannot be taken in easily. Had Mary been able to deceive her by simple lies, there would have been no play. Her usual tricks—tears, stories of being mistreated—do not work. Mrs. Tilford has supported Martha and Karen in their establishment of the school, has encouraged her friends to send their daughters there, and certainly trusts the schoolmistresses. Mary, therefore, begins to use the story she has heard secondhand, mentioning it at first vaguely and uncertainly, but then, as she sees that it is having an effect, more positively and specifically. Mrs. Tilford is deeply disturbed and obviously finds it difficult to believe that such a story could be invented. She starts to phone Karen but decides against it. She calls Joe and urgently asks him to come over; she calls a friend, perhaps one with a daughter or granddaughter at the school, asking her to come over as well. Scene 2 opens with Agatha telling Mary that Rosalie is coming to spend the night; a few moments later, Rosalie arrives. The audience learns, partly now and fully later, that Mrs. Tilford has communicated with the parents of all the girls and told them Mary's story, with the result that all the girls have been called home. Rosalie is spending the night with Mary because her mother is in New York.

These circumstances represent significant flaws in the structure of *The Children's Hour*, though they are not as noticeable in performance: First, it is difficult to believe that a woman of Mrs. Tilford's maturity and intelligence would take such drastic action on the basis of her granddaughter's word alone; second, it has to be Rosalie, among all the students, whose mother is out of town, or the play would simply grind to a halt. About the first, one might say in Hellman's defense that it would be emotionally and even intellectually difficult for Mrs. Tilford to believe that her granddaughter would have either the desire or the knowledge to invent such a lie; that to seek external verification of the story would be, even if it were true, almost surely fruitless; and that, given the time and place, it would have been irresponsible of her not to inform the other parents. Problems remain, even so. Surely Mrs. Tilford could have spoken with Joe first. True, Hellman arranges that Joe arrives late, on the plausible ground that he had to stop at a hospital, but would one more night have mattered so much? Doubtless, Mrs. Tilford's urgency is partly emotional, on the ground that most, if not all, of the girls have been at the school on her recommendation. This does not explain, however, her calm assurance later in the play that the story is true. She takes the logical attitude that Martha's, Karen's, and Joe's denials are meaningless, since they are to be expected regardless of whether the story is accurate. She is also a woman who, given her class, her money, and her intelligence, is not prone to being wrong. Perhaps one should regard her attitude as a typical Hellman irony: It is her very sense of responsibility that has made her act irresponsibly. Less defense can be offered for the presence of Rosalie. All one can say is that her presence is essential to the play, and that in a well-made play this represents perhaps the minimum of manipulation.

The scene develops very dramatically. Mary blackmails Rosalie into being prepared to support her lies if necessary. Joe arrives, and very soon he and his aunt are battling. Karen and Martha arrive, and the battle enlarges, with strong emotions on one side and calm assurance on the other. Mrs. Tilford is not even moved by the threat of a libel suit. Finally, Joe insists that Mary be questioned and, against Mrs. Tilford's wishes, brings Mary in. Mary, genuinely nervous, tells her story, making it more and more circumstantial, until finally the circumstances catch her in a lie. She has said that she has seen things through Karen's keyhole, and Karen announces that her door has no keyhole. Mary is therefore forced to say that it was Martha's room, not Karen's; Martha announces that she lives on a different floor, at the other end of the house, and, moreover, shares her room with Mrs. Mortar. Mrs. Tilford is severely shaken. Backed into a corner, Mary says that it was not she but Rosalie who saw them, and that she saw them because Karen's door was halfway open. Rosalie is summoned and at first denies the story, but when Mary makes it plain that she will, if necessary, expose Rosalie as a thief, Rosalie agrees that the story is true and collapses in tears. The curtain falls.

After so tense a moment, act 3 is almost anticlimactic. It opens on the same scene as act 1. Karen and Martha are alone in the house. They have lost their case; the townspeople are against them; they feel so persecuted that they refuse even to answer the phone; and they have not even dared to leave the house. In a rather surprising anticipation of Samuel Beckett and the Absurdists, Martha says that they are "waiting," with the implication that that is all they—or at any rate, she—will ever do. Martha hopes that Karen will escape through marrying Joe, but Karen seems doubtful. Mrs. Mortar, who had left when told to by Martha, unexpectedly enters, and the audience learns that she would have been the key witness at the trial, that she refused to return, and thus the case was lost. Her failure to return was owing to her reluctance to become involved in such a scandal. She returns now because she has run out of money, but Martha has no more to give her. She leaves the room, and Joe enters. He is planning for the marriage and for all three of them to leave together permanently, even though he would thus be giving up a promising career. Martha leaves, and in his words and attitude toward Karen it becomes clear that Joe is uncertain of the truth. Karen quietly denies any homosexual relationship, and he apparently accepts the denial, but it is uncertain whether his doubts have been laid to rest. Karen asks him to think things over for a day or two and make a decision. He reluctantly agrees and leaves, insisting that he will come back, though Karen is sure that he will not. Martha returns and, in a scene of high emotion, tells Karen that, though she had not previously been aware of it, the story that had been told about them was, at least so far as her feelings went, true. She loves Karen "that way." She leaves the room, and presently, a muffled shot is heard. Karen opens the door and sees that Martha has killed herself. Mrs. Mortar rushes in, sees what has happened, and expresses her remorse. The doorbell rings, and she answers it. It is

Agatha. Mrs. Tilford is waiting in her car. Mrs. Mortar tries to keep her
from coming in, but Karen allows her to enter, and Mrs. Mortar rushes out
sobbing.

The final dialogue is between Karen and Mrs. Tilford. Mrs. Tilford has
learned the truth. The bracelet was found among Rosalie's things, and
Rosalie confessed. Apparently, Mary has confessed, too. The judge at the
trial will arrange a public apology and explanation, and Mrs. Tilford will
pay the amount of the damages and as much more as they will take. Karen
announces Martha's death and expresses her bitter feelings toward Mrs.
Tilford and her attempts to relieve her conscience through money. Gradually, however, Karen recognizes Mrs. Tilford's sincerity and sees that the
old woman will be the greater sufferer, since she has refused to commit
Mary to an institution and will hence have to live permanently in her company, and since Martha's suicide will inevitably burden her memory. Karen
agrees to accept Mrs. Tilford's money. She disagrees with Mrs. Tilford's
hope that she and Joe will marry. The two separate amicably, and Karen is
left alone at the play's end.

Hellman expressed the feeling later that the final scene was unnecessary,
that it was simply evidence of her personal compulsion to spell things out.
Certainly none of her important later plays spells things out so thoroughly,
but in *The Children's Hour*, the final scene provides desirable satisfaction
for the audience. The only valid objection to the scene is that it raises a
new possibility: Mrs. Tilford appears soon after Martha's suicide, rather
than earlier, perhaps in time to prevent it. Once Martha's feelings are clear,
however, it seems doubtful, given the time and circumstances, that anything
could have kept her alive, and Hellman properly leaves Karen with an uncertain future. Karen's belief in Joe's permanent defection may be wrong;
it may not. The possibility of a happy outcome for her is a valid comfort to
an audience after so much bitter emotion, but the certainty of a happy
ending would be difficult to accept.

The play was in part a *succès de scandale* on Broadway, since open treatment of homosexuality was very unusual at the time. Hellman wrote the
scenario for the first film version, *These Three* (1936), in which the homosexuality was changed to a traditional triangle. A later version restored
both title and content.

The Little Foxes is, and almost surely will remain, Hellman's standard
play. It represents significant advances in technique over *The Children's
Hour* and is in various ways more typical of Hellman's overall production.
First, it is set in the Deep South (small-town Alabama), as are three of
Hellman's four most significant later plays. Second, the characters are more
sharply distinguished and more deeply realized, and the dialogue is more
individualized. Third, Hellman displays three significant qualities which are
not fully realized in *The Children's Hour*: compassion, humor, and irony.

Fourth, *The Little Foxes* displays more clearly a sociopolitical theme than does the earlier play: These are "the little foxes who spoil the vines" (a quotation from the Song of Solomon), whom Hellman sees as twentieth century capitalists in embryo.

The Little Foxes concentrates on a rapacious small-town Alabama family, the Hubbards, and on some of their victims. The year is 1900. As the play opens, Regina Giddens is giving a dinner party for a businessman from Chicago, William Marshall, with whom her brothers are negotiating to join them in opening one of the first cotton mills in the South. All the characters in the play are present except Regina's husband, Horace, the town banker, long confined at The Johns Hopkins Hospital with a bad heart. The remaining characters are Regina's brothers, Ben and Oscar Hubbard; Oscar's wife, Birdie, the last member of an aristocratic family impoverished by the Civil War; Oscar and Birdie's son, Leo; Horace and Regina's daughter, Alexandra; and the servants, Addie and Cal. Unlike the Hubbards, Birdie has cultural interests; she is a frightened woman, bullied by her husband. Ben is a jovial hypocrite whose hypocrisy has become so practiced that he is sometimes almost unaware of it. He and Regina are the dominant Hubbards. Oscar is relatively weak, obtuse, and blustery, while Leo is a lesser version of Oscar. Alexandra shares Birdie's cultural interests and seems not at all Hubbard-like. Regina herself is a handsome woman, a smooth and clever conniver, who takes in Marshall to a degree that Ben, for all of his hypocrisy, cannot.

When the deal for the cotton mill has been struck, the young couple drive Marshall to the station to return to Chicago. The Hubbards are triumphant, looking forward to being rich. One problem remains: The three siblings are supposed to contribute equal sums to the mill project, enough to make them together the majority shareholders, but while Ben and Oscar are ready to put up their share, Regina must get hers from Horace, who has ignored all letters on the subject. In a piece of typical Hubbard trickery, Regina declares that Horace is holding out because he wants a larger share, and Ben finally agrees that he should have a larger share and that the difference will come out of Oscar's. Oscar is furious, but he is mollified by Regina's quite specious assurance that she will consider something that Oscar very much wants: a marriage between Leo and Alexandra. A plan is then made to send Alexandra, who is devoted to Horace, to bring him home.

Many modern plays, including several of Henrik Ibsen's, involve the return of someone long gone, but the return is almost always early in the play. In *The Little Foxes*, the audience must wait, with anticipation, for what Horace's return in the second act will bring. Before Horace's arrival, Oscar and Leo conceive a plan to steal eighty thousand dollars' worth of bonds from Horace's safety deposit box, to finance their venture. (If they can do this, they will not need Regina as a partner.) Horace then arrives, stiff and ill, accompanied by Alexandra, who has his heart medicine. During the course of the act, it becomes clear that Horace and Regina are, and have been, at odds during most of their marriage, that Horace will not agree to finance the proposed project, and that he will not consent to a marriage between Alexandra and Leo. It is also clear that Regina will not be thwarted and that Horace is too physically frail to withstand her will.

In act 3, Horace, who has discovered the crime, informs Regina about the theft and tells her that he will pretend that the theft was a loan. Moreover, he will change his will, leaving Regina the bonds and all of his other property to Alexandra. Regina will thus lose the opportunity to invest in the business venture (since the partners will no longer need her money), and she will lose her inheritance from Horace. Furiously, she tells him that she married him only for money. He becomes distraught, reaches for his medicine, spills it, and asks her to get his new bottle. She simply stands there as he collapses and dies. Regina is now in a position to blackmail her brothers into assigning her a seventy-five-percent interest in the mill, lest she prosecute them. Regina is triumphant; nevertheless, she now faces a life of loneliness because Alexandra has discovered her mother's treachery and will leave her.

The play ends with a question and is the better for it, since, if the ending represented a total and final triumph, it would emphasize the play's kinship to pure melodrama, and since, given the characters, an ending that had finality would be unlikely. Ben is too clear-sighted, too ironically aware, too psychologically healthy to give up. Alexandra's potential for fighting is probably small, but one cannot be sure. Moreover, the Hubbard siblings are more complex than a recital of the plot might make them seem. Ben retains an incompetent servant because she has always been in the family. Ben and Oscar both seem genuinely moved by Horace's death. Ben and Regina are both capable of viewing their own, and others', behavior ironically, and there is humor in some of their dialogue. Regina is frightened at what she has done, or rather not done. Wicked as the two may be, and much as they might remind one of nineteenth century melodramatic villains, they are human beings, complex enough to be believable.

The play, moreover, has other ironies which remove it from total melodrama. It is ironic that Leo should be Birdie's son and Alexandra Regina's daughter, because Leo is an extreme version of Oscar, and Alexandra has the outlook of Horace. For most of his life, however, Horace has been weak, yielding to his wife, as Birdie has to her husband. Birdie, for whom one is made to feel compassion, gains enough strength to tell Alexandra the truth, and Horace gains enough strength to stand up to Regina. These are highly individualized human beings, and the play is skillfully constructed, absorbing, and genuinely insightful.

Like *The Little Foxes*, *Watch on the Rhine* contains murder and black-mail, but it is a very different kind of play, peopled with a very different set of characters. It takes place entirely in the living room of Fanny Farrelly, in her country mansion near Washington, D.C. Fanny is a wealthy, eccentric matriarch in her sixties, a character typical of comedy of manners: basically good-hearted, sparklingly alert, and accustomed to having her own way. The time of the play is the spring of 1940. Germany is Nazi-ruled, and there is war in Europe in which the United States has not yet become involved.

The pattern of the first two acts of the play consists of alternating conversation of three kinds: humorous and witty, at times gossipy, as is appropriate to comedy of manners; affectionate; and tense, either because of personally threatening political maneuvers or because of the triangle that is a subplot in the play. The shifts from one type to another can be sudden, but they are always appropriate. Tension can lapse into humor, or an unexpected remark can turn humor into tension.

The characters include, besides Fanny, the other permanent residents of the mansion: Fanny's son, David, a lawyer in his deceased father's firm in Washington, in his late thirties; Fanny's longtime companion Anise, a Frenchwoman; and one of the servants, Joseph. There are also two house-guests who have long overstayed their welcome, Marthe de Brancovis, the daughter of an old friend of Fanny, and her husband, Teck, a Romanian count. Fanny's daughter Sara, her husband Kurt Müller, a member of the anti-Nazi underground and a German in exile, and their children arrive. The audience learns that Kurt has collected twenty-three thousand dollars to aid the resistance in Germany. In brief, Teck discovers the money and threatens to expose Kurt to the German embassy officials unless he is paid ten thousand dollars. Kurt is forced to kill Teck and flee the country, aided by Fanny, who during the course of the play has come to realize the Nazi threat and to be lifted above her own private concerns. The killing is presented, strangely, as an absence of the need to fight evil on all fronts, whether on a conventional battlefield or in one's own environment.

Watch on the Rhine is probably the best American play concerning World War II. It demonstrates that war is not limited to battlefronts and that the world is too small for anyone, anywhere, to be unaffected by large-scale violence. It demonstrates that such violence affects the cultured and the humane, whether they are poor, like Kurt, or wealthy, like Sara's family. The play is highly unusual in being a comedy of manners in which the central subject is war. In spite of the attempted blackmail and actual murder which figure prominently in its plot, it is among the least melodramatic of any of Hellman's plays, and to call the murder melodramatic has its own irony, since this particular murder constitutes an act of war.

The characters in *Watch on the Rhine* are developed with clarity and depth. Fanny is a far more individualized portrait of a wealthy, dominant older woman than is Mrs. Tilford in *The Children's Hour*. Unlike Mary Tilford or Ben and Regina, Teck is a flaccid, unwilling villain. Unlike Birdie, Horace, and Alexandra, the good people are strong, and for the only time in all of her plays, Hellman presents, in Kurt, an admirable hero and a marriage based on strong and permanent love. A believable presentation of either of these is indeed a rarity in modern drama. The children in *Watch on the Rhine* are more fully portrayed than those in *The Children's Hour*. The theme has universal validity; oppression is indeed a major issue throughout Hellman's plays. In *The Children's Hour*, it is oppression by the established rich, by a psychotic child, by established standards of behavior. In *The Little Foxes*, it is anticipated oppression on a broad scale by a rising class of capitalists, and actual oppression on a narrower scale by moneyed Southerners against blacks, poor whites, fallen aristocrats, and one another. *Watch on the Rhine* widens the range in dealing with oppression by Fascists and would-be Fascists. Blackmail itself, in all three plays, is a form of oppression. Later in Hellman's work, in *The Autumn Garden* and *Toys in the Attic*, she showed that even generosity and love can be forms of blackmail; those plays, like *Watch on the Rhine*, give the theme a universality which Hellman's first two successes lack. *The Little Foxes* will probably remain the most popular Hellman play in dramatic repertory, but *Watch on the Rhine* is certainly among her most effective.

Other major works

NONFICTION: *The Selected Letters of Anton Chekhov*, 1955 (editor); *An Unfinished Woman: A Memoir*, 1969; *Pentimento*, 1973; *Scoundrel Time*, 1976; *Maybe*, 1980; *Eating Together: Recipes and Recollections*, 1984 (with Peter Feibleman).

SCREENPLAYS: *The Dark Angel*, 1935 (with Mordaunt Shairp); *These Three*, 1936; *Dead End*, 1937 (adaptation of Sidney Kingsley's play); *The Little Foxes*, 1941 (with Dorothy Parker, Arthur Kober, Alan Campbell); *Watch on the Rhine*, 1943 (with Dashiell Hammett); *The North Star: A Motion Picture About Some Russian People*, 1943; *The Searching Wind*, 1946; *The Chase*, 1966.

ANTHOLOGY: *The Big Knockover: Selected Stories and Short Novels of Dashiell Hammett*, 1966 (editor, with introduction).

Bibliography

Adler, Jacob H. *Lillian Hellman*, 1969.
Falk, Doris V. *Lillian Hellman*, 1978.
Lederer, Katherine. *Lillian Hellman*, 1979.
Moody, Richard. *Lillian Hellman, Playwright*, 1972.

Jacob H. Adler

JAMES ENE HENSHAW

Born: Calabar, Nigeria; August 29, 1924

Principal drama

This Is Our Chance, pr. 1948, pb. 1956; *The Jewels of the Shrine*, pr. 1952, pb. 1956 (one act); *A Man of Character*, pb. 1956; *This Is Our Chance: Plays from West Africa*, pb. 1956 (includes *The Jewels of the Shrine* and *A Man of Character*; also as *The Jewels of the Shrine*, pb. 1956); *Children of the Goddess and Other Plays*, pb. 1964 (includes *Companion for a Chief* and *Magic in the Blood*); *Medicine for Love: A Comedy in Three Acts*, pb. 1964; *Dinner for Promotion: A Comedy in Three Acts*, pb. 1967; *Enough Is Enough: A Play of the Nigerian Civil War*, pr. 1975, pb. 1976.

Other literary forms

James Ene Henshaw is known only for his drama.

Achievements

As one of the pioneering dramatists in Nigeria, Henshaw was also one of the first to be published outside West Africa. *This Is Our Chance*, which has undergone many reprintings, has been extremely popular in West Africa since its first production by the Association of Students of African Descent in Dublin in 1948. It has been staged by professional companies as well as school and amateur groups.

In 1952, Henshaw's dramatic talents were acknowledged when his play *The Jewels of the Shrine* won the Henry Carr Memorial Cup as the best one-act play in the All-Nigeria Festival of the Arts. Henshaw's reputation was enhanced when *A Man of Character* was mentioned in *Nigeria 10*, the tenth-anniversary commemorative publication in honor of Nigerian independence compiled by the Federal Military Government.

Henshaw's influence, impact, and success as a dramatist in Nigeria stem from the fact that he is a very direct, matter-of-fact dramatic artist. Compared to such contemporary Nigerian writers as Wole Soyinka and John Pepper Clark, Henshaw's work is less intellectually oriented. His plays are straightforward, not bookishly philosophical, and are written in simple language. Most of the works are aimed both at the adult reader and at school-children. The beguiling simplicity of plot and style facilitates the staging of his plays, making him one of the most frequently produced playwrights in West Africa. He is also adept at stagecraft (although some critics have complained of implausibility in this regard), giving precise, detailed directions and analysis as to how his work is to be produced at every stage, whether for a school production or for adults.

Henshaw's dramatic philosophy contributes greatly to his popularity. His subject matter, which deals directly with African culture and traditions, focuses on major issues familiar to both his African and his Western audience. For this reason, Henshaw prefaces most of his plays, in the manner of George Bernard Shaw, with elaborate introductions which discuss thematic concerns and other ancillary matters connected with the work. Thus, both the foreign and African producer/reader are helped to see the proper perspective from which the work is to be approached, studied, analyzed, and evaluated. Henshaw himself views the function of his drama, in part, as providing a positive impact upon his society. Joseph Bruchac believes that Henshaw's cardinal aim in writing is to forge, through the dramatic medium, a unity and understanding among Africans, who share closely related traditions and heritage, rather than "explaining the African to the non-African."

Biography

James Ene Ewa Henshaw was born in 1924 in Calabar, South Eastern Nigeria, West Africa, into a large family, the youngest of nine sons. His father was of royal ancestry, descended from the Efik lineage in Calabar, where in the days before independence his importance gave him a position within the colonial Nigerian Legislative Council, an august lawmaking body.

Having been brought up by his eldest brother, Dr. Lawrence Eken Richard Henshaw, following the death of their father, James Henshaw was encouraged to continue his schooling at the Sacred Heart Primary School in Calabar. He then went on to Christ the King College, a secondary school in Onitsha, a well-known commercial center in what was then the Eastern region (now known as Cross River State) of Nigeria.

Upon graduation from Christ the King College, Henshaw traveled abroad to Ireland and in 1943 enrolled as a medical student at the National University of Ireland in Dublin. He took bachelor of science and bachelor of medicine degrees and in 1949 qualified as a physician. In 1954, Henshaw had the opportunity to pursue a course for specialized training in cardiovascular diseases and was awarded the T.D.D. degree by the University of Wales.

Henshaw's professional practice as a physician began in earnest upon his return to Nigeria in 1955, where he first served as a senior consultant in tuberculosis treatment for the government of Eastern Nigeria, in Port Harcourt, until 1978. From 1968 to 1972, he served as the First Controller of Medical Services in Cross River State. Thereafter he became medical consultant in thoracic medicine to the Ministry of Health at the chest clinic in his hometown, Calabar.

In 1973, Henshaw was appointed senior consultant on tuberculosis control at Rivers State, a post he held until 1978. He has since been interested in participating in national programs connected with the medical profession in Nigeria and has held membership in the National Council of Health (1968-1972) and the Nigerian Medical Council (1970-1972). In spite of his demanding professional commitments, James Henshaw is a family man. He married Caroline Nchelem Amada in 1958; they have eight children.

Analysis

Most of James Ene Henshaw's early, short plays share two thematic threads: tradition and its conflict with modern life, and the worldwide problems of corruption, crime, and materialism. *This Is Our Chance*, one of Henshaw's most popular plays, revolves around Kudaro, the Crown Princess; her father, Chief Damba; her mother, Ansa; her suitor, Prince Ndamu; her tutor, Bambulu; and other village folk whose offices bring them into the story. Set in the royal household and village-kingdom of Koloro and in the rival village of Udura, the play addresses the typically Henshawian preoccupation with the conflict between tradition and modernity and the need to assimilate the best of both African and Western cultures.

From the outset of the play, Chief Damba's obsession with tradition is clear: Tradition compels him to keep the fortune-teller at court, to forbid extravillage marriages, to opt for age-old customs instead of experimenting with new ideas. In Damba's opinion, Koloro's strict adherence to tradition is the key to the village's superiority. He will declare war on any village that threatens traditional values. Yet when the conflict of interest compels him to take his daughter's life—in eloping with Ndamu, the prince of the rival village, Udura, she has broken one of the most important tenets of Koloro tradition—Damba bends tradition to fit the circumstances, thereby opening new avenues for progress in his village.

Ajugo, Damba's prime minister, is a diehard protector of tradition, convinced that the old ways must never succumb to new ideas, no matter what the cost. Ajugo states categorically that matrimonial links outside the village of Koloro are punishable, in the case of the commoner, by banishment, and, in the case of royalty, by death. Damba, faced with the options of war, his daughter's death, or his own loss of life, must choose. Ajugo, ever faithful to tradition, prepares the hemlock for Damba's punishment. Damba's life is spared, however, by the sudden arrival of Princess Kudaro. Even though tradition now dictates Ajugo's death, the prime minister is spared and a new prime minister, Enusi, appointed. Ajugo remains the uncompromising custodian of the indigenous culture.

There is a dichotomy between those characters who favor modernity (Enusi, Bambulu, Princess Kudaro, Ansa, Ayi the maid, Udura's ambassador, and Prince Ndamu) and those who stand for tradition (Damba, Ajugo, and Chief Mboli of Udura). Princess Kudaro, having lived in the city, where she attended school, is at once sophisticated and down-to-earth. Although she is the Crown Princess, she frequently states how much she detests village life. Her elopement with Prince Ndamu is one of the greatest of village taboos. As a character, she represents progress. Princess Kudaro's elopement and the subsequent events, especially her use of Bambulu's antivenom serum, help to bring about peace between the perennially feuding villages.

The bombastic Bambulu, although a foreigner, wields great influence in the village. An accomplished scientist, educated in the Western tradition, and a good teacher, Bambulu the radical is always dressed in Western style. He refers to himself as the catalyst in the village. Under the cloak of teaching about vitamins, he succeeds in sowing the seeds of revolution which undermine the traditional values of Koloro. He is opposed to the blind adherence to tradition that breeds ignorance, hatred, war, disease, bigotry, poverty, and backwardness. As an apostle of progress, good-neighborliness, and reconciliation, Bambulu is mainly responsible for introducing Western ideas and civilization to the village. With Chief Damba's support, he opens more schools and is given full autonomy to teach basic scientific skills, reading, and writing, as well as agriculture.

Chief Damba thus rises out of adversity and seizes the chance to bring peace, progress, and prosperity to his village. Enusi's metaphoric description of their tradition being a sword of Damocles ties in neatly with the problems raised by tradition in the village of Koloro.

A Man of Character foreshadows in its thematic concerns many of the issues addressed in contemporary African writing. One of the most urgent of these is the problem of corruption. In the play, an honest, sincere, dedicated man—a man of character—who refuses to be corrupted in a corrupt society must suffer the consequences of his decision.

As in most Henshaw plays, with the exception of *Magic in the Blood*, when the protagonist runs into an intricate problem, he manages both to extricate and to vindicate himself. In this play, the serene, happy family life of Kobina and his wife, Ayodele, is disrupted by the negative influence of Ayodele's mercenary, domineering sister, Serinya, and her venal husband, Anosse. Kobina, a God-fearing man, refuses to be influenced by Anosse's offer of a bribe. His moral position is that West African society needs people of conscience and that appointments and promotions should be based on merit, not on nepotism or bribery. His refusal to enter into this system of institutionalized corruption breaks apart the family, since Serinya's values have influenced the once content Ayodele. Ayodele now desires a house of her own, new clothes, money for trips abroad, and security for their child, Ibitam. Kobina obviously cannot afford all of these luxuries, since his modest income is being used to educate his daughter. After a quarrel, Ayodele and Ibitam leave Kobina, whose misfortunes are compounded by the suspicious loss of five hundred pounds from his office safe. He becomes the prime suspect, and the onus of proof of innocence rests upon him. In fact, Seboh, Kobina's servant, together with Seboh's crooked, vicious-looking brother, has engineered the entire plot. Seboh, who is referred to as the "stranger" in the play, attempts to blackmail Kobina and his associates (the lawyer Diyego, the magistrate Kopechi, and Sergeant Mbedu), but the judge's quick thinking neutralizes the stranger's malevolent plan. Seboh, the servant, filled with remorse, is apprehended by the police as he attempts to return the money. The two Seboh brothers are hauled off to prison, with the stranger's strong avowal to turn over a new leaf.

The series of coincidences in the play dilutes the plausibility of the plot somewhat, since it is unlikely that all of Kobina's important associates would suddenly and simultaneously converge, uninvited, upon his home. The moral preoccupations of the protagonist render him rather too saintly, even somewhat self-righteous, although his depression and subsequent drinking do indicate that he is indeed human and vulnerable.

As many critics have remarked, the language in the play is inflated and bookish; the characters hardly speak as typical Nigerians do. The ending, as in Henshaw's *Companion for a Chief, Children of the Goddess, Dinner for Promotion*, and *This Is Our Chance*, takes the form of a happy reconciliation. Equilibrium is restored. The moral lesson that *A Man of Character* teaches is the age-old adage that crime does not pay. The upright are vindicated, truth stands, and honesty is shown to be the best policy. The characters become wiser and more determined to continue living in an upright way.

Medicine for Love, subtitled *A Comedy in Three Acts*, is a humorous examination of politics, politicians, and political practices in modern West Africa. It also explores the concept of the African marriage system, examining the issue of traditional wives and arranged marriages—an ancient custom being forced upon a modern city-dweller, Ewia Ekunyah. Henshaw, in his introduction to the piece, succinctly sums up these motifs: monogamy, polygamy, medicine men, tradition, and the African.

Ewia Ekunyah, the hero of the play and would-be politician, finds his life complicated by the unexpected arrival in the city of no less than three traditional wives, Bekin Wari, Ibiere Sua, and Nene Katsina, married to him through the agency of various relatives. According to tradition, these wives cannot be returned. Naturally, rivalry and suspicion are rampant among the three women and their assorted relatives, who resort to medicine for love in order to win Ewia Ekunyah's favor. The machinations begin when Ibiere Sua and Bekin Wari team up against Nene Katsina, the youngest, best educated, and most beautiful of the three. Apart from Nene

Katsina, who displays the characteristics of good humor, romance, and seriousness, the women are eminently unsuitable as wives of a prospective politician. Auntie Dupeh, a dowager-duchess type, is too domineering and aggressive in trying to push Ewia's interests. Auntie Dupeh's imposition as chairperson of Ewia's political planning committee and her recommendation of Agatarata the medicine man as spiritual adviser destroy Ewia's political career.

The array of Ewia's dishonest advisers clearly indicates that the political policymakers active in urban affairs are no better than the candidates themselves. Mr. Joss, Ewia's political agent, using his Machiavellian expertise, spends eighty-one hundred pounds and manages to swindle the poor Ewia into selling his last house to finance the campaign; the Reverend Sanctus Kyei cannot, in times of trouble, give Ewia any sensible advice regarding Ewia's concrete, everyday problems; Agatarata's ignorance of the chemical composition of the ink that becomes invisible on Ewia's application form leads to Ewia's downfall. Henshaw touches here on the very delicate interconnection between Christianity, tradition, and politics. That a modern educated African politician such as Ewia Ekunyah thinks he can win an election or solve his marital entanglements through a juju priest or a Christian minister is preposterous and ironic; these services, in fact, cost Ewia the election.

Henshaw has given a comic look at the operation of politics in contemporary Africa. The fundamental concept of democracy does not seem to be fully understood by the politicians, who tend to think that the survival of the fittest, by any means, foul or fair, is a more appropriate tenet. Instead of honest people of integrity and dignity, there is a multiplicity of crooked, politically self-serving, corrupt candidates and political advisers. The unqualified Ewia resorts to bribery to edge out honest, sincere, and dedicated rivals such as Mr. Sonrillo.

There is no poetic justice in *Medicine for Love*. At the end, all characters, good or bad, gain: Ewia and Nene Katsina gain marital bliss; Auntie Dupeh marries a VIP, Kiudu Bonga; Bekin Wari marries Ewia Ekunya's secretary, Olu Ita, who finds a new job; Ibiere Sua marries Dr. Sigismond Marsey. Finally, Papa Garuka marries Mama Ebunde, Ibiere Sua's mother. The matrimonial ceremony of the entire cast is presided over by the Reverend Kyei.

Dinner for Promotion, as the title implies, centers on the plans of Tikku and Seyil, two young and ambitious employees of Sipo Amalgamated, to get to the top. In the play, promotion depends upon a sumptuous dinner for the Sipo family and upon marrying the boss's daughter rather than upon merit. *Dinner for Promotion* thus touches upon the relationships between employer and employee, between friends, between parents and children, and between in-laws, and deals with the life of the young, educated urban group. Through *Dinner for Promotion*, Henshaw portrays the callous disregard for decency or ethical behavior or even loyalty among friends when personal interests are at stake.

Each character seems to have an ulterior motive. Tikku has his eye on Sharia, the boss's daughter, but his interest is purely selfish; he sees her only as a means for promotion. Seyil, not knowing Sharia's family connections, courts Sharia and takes the advice of Tikku to speak ill of Mr. Sipo, their employer. Naturally, Sharia takes offense as Seyil heaps insults upon her father's head, then promptly walks into Tikku's waiting arms. Through a series of deceptive moves, Seyil plots Tikku's downfall both as suitor to Sharia and as prospective executive in Sipo Amalgamated by sabotaging Tikku's "dinner for promotion," but his plans backfire. In spite of all this confusion and hostility, the ending of the play is typically amicable: The two sisters-in-law, Madam Pamphilia Sipo and Madam Una, are reconciled; Tikku and Sharia, blessed by their parents, are about to be married; Tikku does get his promotion and material gain; and even Seyil gains by being offered a much better job elsewhere. A form of equity reigns.

Enough Is Enough is a contemporary drama set in a detention camp during the last weeks of the Nigerian Civil War. The play documents the incarceration and plight, both psychological and physical, of six detainees and their guards. Henshaw's introduction to the work concentrates upon the personal attitudes and feelings of the detainees, the reactions of Nigerians to the war, and the complex human emotions which permeated the detainees' existence.

Set against the prison backdrop, *Enough Is Enough* centers upon the notion of reconciliation, the woes and gloom of the war, and the role of charitable and relief organizations at that time. The outcry "genocide and pogrom," which became the Biafran slogan during the course of the war, is alluded to throughout the work.

Apart from Ufanko, Bisong, and the disembodied voice of Nwakego, the major characters enacting the drama are Peter Emeribe, a very important member of Parliament; the lawyer Linus Nosikeh; Dr. Dagogo, a politician and medical practitioner; and the arrogant Professor Ezuba, who apparently masterminded the rebellion against the revolution. The remaining characters—the Superintendent, the warder, Mother Cecilia, Sister Lucinda, Major Maxy, and others—serve to highlight the suffering and anguish of the main characters. Referred to as detainees, saboteurs, and criminals, the incarcerated men seem to have rebelled against those advocating war and secession. This rebellion is regarded as treason and is the cause of their detention.

Divided into four acts, each with a distinct thematic concern, *Enough Is Enough* gives a concrete insight into the ravages of war, which claims the lives of healthy, innocent, able-bodied people (sometimes civilians). While all wars are destructive, this war is especially so: It is a civil war, with brother killing brother, creating a generation of orphans and cripples.

Henshaw is here concerned with the brutal treatment of the detainees, the resultant psychological problems of both the long-term detainees and their guards, the economic difficulties, and ecological destruction. There is a general lack of trust, a lack of freedom to speak or even to remain silent, and a very real lack of decent food and water. The detainees are denied such amenities as radios and the right to receive visitors or uncensored mail. Everyone in the camp is vulnerable to the constant attacks from bombing and disease. Survival becomes a critical issue; the detainees, in spite of their former privileged positions, have had to resort to sordid, subservient practices to survive. Part of the irony of Peter Emeribe's case is that the warder is his former houseboy.

The psychological problems range from insanity to alcoholism. The Superintendent, for example, a brilliant zoologist in civilian life, unsure of his competence in his present position, ends up a nervous, alcoholic wreck. Dr. Dagogo becomes moody, embittered, and mentally unstable after four years of detention at Umudali camp. Ufanko has turned into a cynic, while Peter Emeribe burns with a strong sense of injustice. The lack of privacy, and the constant harassment to which they are subject, cause the prisoners, understandably, to lash out at one another. As for Professor Ezuba, his arrogance leads to the eventual destruction of most of the group. Treating the warders as a pack of ignorant, unqualified upstarts, he insults his captors without considering the consequences for his fellow prisoners, always reminding the world of his former importance. On the other side, the presence of Major Maxy—a mere child trying to behave as an adult soldier, a boy who, at the age of fourteen, functions as an undercover agent—points out the absurdity and unprepared nature of the revolutionaries. Ironically, Maxy, in contrast with his dead brothers, displays filial devotion by trying to protect his father.

One important motif present in this drama is that of peace and reconciliation. The war, having taken its impartial toll of destruction, ends with the signing of the Lagos peace treaty. Umudali Camp is disbanded, and some of the detainees are released. As a consequence of the personal vengeance of the Superintendent, however, the most vocal of the detainees are killed, although, unbeknown to them, the war has already been over for four days.

The play's title, *Enough Is Enough*, fittingly expresses a yearning for peace, unity, reconciliation, and a return to normal life; as the first voice in act 3 cries, "Let's waste no further time. Let's spill no further blood. Let's rebuild the nation anew." Dagogo poignantly replies that the fighting should cease because there has been enough of brother killing brother, of suffering, of dying from bullets, of hunger and disease—enough of everything connected with the war and the prisoners' detention. The emotional demands of such a painful, historical moment give this later play an uncharacteristic slant in the Henshaw canon. The language itself strikes a note of pathos and patriotism, while the imagery constantly reverts to horror and bestiality (references to vampires, lizards, boa constrictors, hawks) to underscore the reality of human suffering.

Bibliography
Axworthy, G. J. "Criticism on the Works of James Henshaw," in *West African Journal of Education*. IX, no. 2 (June, 1965), p. 103.
——————. *"This is Our Chance: Three Plays from West Africa*, by James Ene Henshaw," in *Ibadan*. October, 1957, pp. 27-28.
Banham, Martin. "A Piece That We May Fairly Call Our Own," in *Ibadan*. June, 1961, pp. 15-18.
Dathorne, O. R. "Recent Staged Drama: Social Reality and the Inner Life," in *African Literature in the Twentieth Century*, 1975.
Kennard, Peter. "Recent African Drama," in *Bulletin of the Association for African Literature in English*. No. 1 (1964), pp. 11-18.
Ogunba, Oyin. "Modern Drama in West Africa," in *Perspectives on African Literature*, 1971. Edited by Christopher Heywood.
Taiwo, Oladele. "Nigerian Drama," in *An Introduction to West African Literature*, 1967.

Kwaku Amoabeng
Carrol Lasker

DuBOSE HEYWARD

Born: Charleston, South Carolina; August 31, 1885
Died: Tryon, North Carolina; June 16, 1940

Principal drama

Porgy, pr., pb. 1927 (with Dorothy Heyward; adaptation of his novel); *Brass Ankle*, pr., pb. 1931; *Porgy and Bess*, pr., pb. 1935 (libretto; music by George Gershwin; adaptation of *Porgy*); *Mamba's Daughters*, pr., pb. 1939 (with Dorothy Heyward; adaptation of his novel).

Other literary forms

In addition to three plays and the libretto for *Porgy and Bess*, DuBose Heyward was the author of poetry, short stories, and novels. In his own time, he probably achieved more recognition as a novelist than as a playwright. In fact, his plays *Porgy* and *Mamba's Daughters* are dramatizations of his novels of the same titles, set in black communities in and around Charleston, South Carolina. Heyward's final novel, *Star Spangled Virgin* (1939), also has black characters, but it is set on St. Croix in the Virgin Islands. Heyward also wrote three novels featuring white characters; *Angel* (1926) is about the mountaineers of North Carolina's Blue Ridge Mountains; *Lost Morning* (1936), set in the Piedmont, deals with an artist trying to regain his artistic integrity; and *Peter Ashley* (1932) is a historical novel set in Charleston at the beginning of the Civil War. *The Half Pint Flask* (1929), Heyward's best short story, was published separately as a book. Heyward also published poetry: *Carolina Chansons* (1922), *Skylines and Horizons* (1924), and *Jasbo Brown and Selected Poems* (1931).

Achievements

Heyward, a famous writer in his own time, is a comparatively obscure figure today. His characters, however, have become part of the American folklore. People who have not heard of DuBose Heyward nevertheless do know Porgy, thanks primarily to the success of what has come to be thought of as George Gershwin's *Porgy and Bess*. It must be remembered, though, that Heyward wrote the libretto as well as many of the lyrics of *Porgy and Bess*. According to virtually all sources, he also helped shape all other aspects of the production of what was undeniably America's first folk opera. Through *Porgy and Bess*, *Mamba's Daughters*, and *Brass Ankle*, Heyward made at least two other contributions to American theater: Arguably, he was the first American playwright to treat blacks as human beings in their own right, not as mere accessories to whites, and to portray them in this way in their own communities; Langston Hughes describes Heyward as one who saw "with his white eyes, wonderful poetic, human qualities in the inhabitants of Catfish Row. . . ." Heyward's plays with black characters also hastened the acceptance of blacks as serious actors. Ethel Waters in *Mamba's Daughters*, for example, was the first black actress ever to be starred on Broadway in a dramatic play.

Biography

Edwin DuBose Heyward was born in Charleston, South Carolina, into an old Charleston family. When he was two years old, his father was killed in an accident, and his mother began a struggle to support DuBose and his younger sister. Both of these events were to shape his work.

Heyward's writing, both his fiction and his plays, often portrays life in Charleston, most notably life in the black quarter. His contact with the black community probably came principally from his employment as a checker on a steamship company wharf, where he developed understanding and appreciation of the lives of the black stevedores with whom he worked. Afterward, he became successful in the real estate and insurance businesses. He was to pursue this career until his decision to commit himself to full-time writing.

Three people, in particular, influenced Heyward's decision to commit himself to writing as a career. He developed friendships with John Bennett, a critic and author of children's books, and Hervey Allen, who was later to write *Anthony Adverse* (1933). From these friendships grew the founding of the Poetry Society of South Carolina and Heyward's serious involvement with writing. Heyward's marriage to Dorothy Hartzell Kuhns also influenced his commitment to a writing career. He met her at the McDowell Colony, a retreat founded by the composer Edward McDowell for the purpose of encouraging artistic achievement. A graduate of the Harvard School of Drama, Kuhns had a play produced in the fall of 1923, the year in which she and Heyward were married. For the rest of his life, she gave her husband encouragement and the benefit of her own expertise as a dramatist, and collaborated with him on two successful Broadway dramas, *Porgy* and *Mamba's Daughters*, although she consistently claimed that his contribution was greater than hers.

Ira and George Gershwin were collaborators with Heyward for *Porgy and Bess*, first produced in 1935. Ironically, though the libretto and part of the lyrics are Heyward's, *Porgy and Bess* has come to be associated almost totally with the Gershwin name, as the opera has gone through numerous revivals over the years.

Heyward and Gershwin discussed yet another collaboration, a dramatization of Heyward's novel *Star Spangled Virgin*, but Heyward's death at the age of fifty-four ended those plans. Heyward died in Tryon, North Carolina, on June 16, 1940, and was buried in Saint Phillips Churchyard in Charleston.

Analysis

DuBose Heyward's contributions to American drama are minor but nevertheless important. He was one of the first American dramatists to portray blacks seriously and sympathetically. The use of black music in his plays, as well as in the folk opera *Porgy and Bess*, helped create acceptance of black folk expression as an art form. His influence helped black writers realize the value of their own culture and experience.

Heyward's plays also provided access to the stage for black performers. In fact, when *Porgy* was being cast, vaudeville performers had to be recruited and trained for their roles in a dramatic play, since at that time there were no black performers with experience in serious drama. The blues singer, Ethel Waters, who played Hagar in *Mamba's Daughters*, was the first black woman to be starred on Broadway in a dramatic play.

Despite the pioneering significance of Heyward's work, he had severe limitations as a dramatist. Virtually all of his critics point to his tendency to rely too heavily on melodrama and to a lack of character development. Many also feel that his critique of white society lacks depth. Nevertheless, Heyward provided the American theater with a positive treatment of a black community and its inner spirit—a spirit which Heyward referred to as "rhythm." "Rhythm," for him, was the spirit of a people close to their God and the earth and bound together in their community by suffering, hope, and joy.

Porgy was Heyward's first play. Although Dorothy Heyward wrote a first draft of the play, she asserts that her role was minor, that the play versions of both *Porgy* and *Mamba's Daughters* were nine-tenths DuBose's.

The basic plot of *Porgy*, well-known because of *Porgy and Bess*, concerns a summer in Catfish Row, the black quarter in Charleston. The time is the 1920's (a change from the turn-of-the-century setting of the novel). Porgy, the central character, a crippled beggar, is drawn about the streets on a cart made from a soapbox and pulled by a goat.

The play centers on Porgy's brief time of happiness and love with Bess. Bess seeks protection and shelter from Porgy after her brutal lover, Crown, murders Robbins at the beginning of the play. Ostracized by the other women of Catfish Row, Bess slowly finds acceptance and a new life with Porgy. From the beginning, though, the couple's happiness is threatened by Sportin Life, a Harlem drug dealer, and by the possibility of Crown's return.

Their summer of love comes to an end when Crown, who is hiding on Kittiwah Island, brutally forces Bess to resume her relationship with him (she has come to the island on a holiday picnic with others from Catfish Row). Shortly afterward, during a great storm, Crown returns to the Row. Although people at first believe that he has died in the storm, he actually returns to the Row later that night, determined to murder Porgy and take

Bess back. Instead, he is killed by Porgy. The storm also orphans a baby whom Bess claims as her own, after the mother leaves it with her and then goes out into the storm.

Although Porgy is not charged with Crown's murder, he is taken to jail to identify the dead man. Terrified by having to identify the man he has murdered, Porgy tries to escape, urged on by Sportin Life. After the police have caught Porgy and taken him into custody, Sportin Life convinces the people of the Row and Bess that Porgy will be in jail for a year. In fact, Porgy is in jail for only a week, and comes back happy, bringing money and presents for Bess and the baby and other friends. Joyfully, he searches for Bess and the baby, only to find that Sportin Life has lured her away with lies and a drug called "happy dust." As the play ends, Porgy drives his goat through the gate out of the Row on the way to New York to look for Bess.

The great achievement of *Porgy* (and the novel on which it was based) lies in Heyward's treatment of his black hero and the black community of which he was a part. The play succeeds as theater, primarily through its use of music and group expression—through spirituals, chants, shouts, parading—and the crowd movements associated with all of these. Its saucer burial scene and hurricane scene are, in particular, made powerful through the use of spirituals to express emotion that could not be conveyed by words.

While the play is powerful on the emotional level, it is marred by an excess of melodrama and, more seriously, a failure to provide the characters with adequate motivation. The audience is not prepared for Bess's crucial decision to leave Porgy and go with Sportin Life, whose character is never developed sufficiently to explain his actions. Even Porgy, the protagonist, is essentially a static character. In addition, in adapting his novel for the stage, Heyward minimized the element of racial conflict and added some incidents and characters which give to certain scenes in the play a condescending, minstrel-show quality. Yet the play does succeed, as an expression of "rhythm" and as a depiction of the significance and humanity of its black characters.

Porgy and Bess, the folk opera that made the Gershwins more famous than its librettist, succeeds in the same ways as the play on which it is based, and in some other ways as well. In comparison to that of *Porgy*, the plot of *Porgy and Bess* is simplified—some of the extraneous minstrel-show scenes are cut—but the songs and chants and "rhythm" of the play are retained and heightened, allowing the folk opera to profit "both by its escape from the play's clutter and the opportunity its songs provided for the characters to express their personal feelings," according to William H. Slavick (*DuBose Heyward*, 1981). Indeed, there are critics who were disappointed with the oversimplification of the opera in comparison with the play from which it was taken, yet, as Slavick notes, *Porgy and Bess* was unique in realizing "the rhythms, color, music, movement, and passion" that bestow upon it "more merit than vaudeville."

Mamba's Daughters, like Porgy and Porgy and Bess, derives much of its success from the use of music and songs. In fact, one of the characters, a black singer named Lissa, transforms the expression of her people into art. The play's central character, however, is not Lissa, but her mother, Hagar. The play focuses on Hagar's loneliness and separation from the daughter whom she has her own mother, Mamba, rear while she is in prison. Men are Hagar's adversaries—the sailors who refuse to pay her for delivering wash, the white men who administer a mockery of justice, but above all Gilly Bluton, whose life she saves at the expense of her freedom, when she takes him to the hospital in Charleston after being forbidden to return to the city from the plantation to which she was sent. In return for this sacrifice, Bluton rapes Lissa and then blackmails her after she achieves some success. The play ends with Hagar protecting Lissa's name by murdering Bluton and then committing suicide.

Aside from the music in the play—Lissa's music and the song with which Hagar consoles herself—Mamba's Daughters derives its power from its focus on the suffering figure of Hagar, who is separated from the daughter whom she loves and for whom she sacrifices everything—even her life. The theme of love as a weapon against injustice, and the song through which Hagar (and Lissa) express their love and suffering, give the play its power. Its weakness lies in its overly melodramatic plot.

Unlike Porgy, Porgy and Bess, and Mamba's Daughters, Brass Ankle was unsuccessful on Broadway. Also unlike the previous works, Brass Ankle was a play from the start, and Heyward had no collaborator. The play is about interracial marriage and passing. The white protagonist, Larry Leamer, must confront the knowledge of his wife Ruth's black ancestry when she bears him a dark-skinned son after previously bearing a blonde daughter, June. The play fails primarily because Heyward resolves the conflict through Ruth protecting her husband from the truth by claiming, falsely, that she has taken a lover. Leamer then kills her and their son—and is thus not forced to come to terms with his knowledge of her race.

Judged by the standards of a later generation, Heyward's dramatic portraits of the black community are deeply flawed; the notion of "rhythm" as the defining characteristic of the black spirit is a notorious stereotype, all too representative of Heyward's baggage of cultural assumptions. Judged by the standards of their own time, however, Heyward's works were courageous, pioneering efforts, and they played a significant role in bringing the black experience to the American stage.

Other major works

NOVELS: Porgy, 1925; Angel, 1926; Mamba's Daughters, 1929; Peter Ashley, 1932; Lost Morning, 1936; Star Spangled Virgin, 1939.

SHORT FICTION: *The Half Pint Flask*, 1929.
POETRY: *Carolina Chansons*, 1922; *Skylines and Horizons*, 1924; *Jasbo Brown and Selected Poems*, 1931.

Bibliography

Davidson, Donald. *Southern Writers in the Modern World*, 1958.
Durham, Frank. *DuBose Heyward: The Man Who Wrote Porgy*, 1954.
_____ . "The Reputed Demises of Uncle Tom: On the Treatment of the Negro in Fiction by White Authors in the 1920's," in *Southern Literary Journal*. II (Spring, 1970), pp. 26-50.
Slavick, William H. *DuBose Heyward*, 1981.

Doris Walters

JOHN HEYWOOD

Born: London(?), England; c. 1497
Died: Louvain(?), Spanish Netherlands; October, 1578

Principal drama

The Play of Love, pr. c. 1528-1529, pb. 1533; *The Pardoner and the Friar*, pb. 1533 (possibly based on *Farce nouvelle d'un pardonneur, d'un triacleur, et d'une tavernière*); *Johan Johan the Husband, Tyb His Wife, and Sir Johan the Priest*, pb. 1533 (commonly known as *Johan Johan*; adaptation of *Farce nouvelle et fort joyeuse du pasté*); *The Play of the Weather*, pb. 1533; *The Playe of the Foure P.P.: A Newe and a Very Mery Enterlude of a Palmer, a Pardoner, a Potycary, a Pedler*, pb. 1541-1547 (commonly known as *The Four P.P.*; possibly based on *Farce nouvelle d'un pardonneur, d'un triacleur, et d'une tavernière*); *Witty and Witless*, pb. 1846 (abridged), 1909; *The Dramatic Writings of John Heywood*, pb. 1905 (John S. Farmer, editor).

Other literary forms

In his own time, John Heywood was best known for his published collections of epigrams, not for his plays, even though the dramas were printed earlier. His first published poetic work was *A Dialogue of Proverbs* (1546), a versified discussion of marriage incorporating more than twelve hundred proverbs. Heywood's reputation was made by his several collections of original versified epigrams, six hundred in all, published beginning 1550 and collected in his *Works* in 1562; these quips and anecdotes, ranging from two to scores of lines apiece, are sometimes turgid, but they often shine with the wit for which Heywood was famous. He also wrote short occasional poems, songs and ballads, and a lengthy and obscure verse allegory, *The Spider and the Fly* (1556).

Achievements

John Heywood was one of the first writers of secular English drama who portrayed not abstractions but individual persons as characters. Most early Tudor plays represented Bible stories or saints' legends, or dramatized the conflict of such allegorical characters as Wisdom and Treason. Heywood's interludes portray husbands, pardoners, scholars, and fools; while most are unnamed types, each is individualized deftly and many have more than one dimension of character. Although Heywood's three disputation plays are heavy with choplogic, his three farces retain their vigor and interest. In plotting, character-drawing, and versifying, Heywood was far more skilled, at his best, than were other Tudor playwrights. It must be said, however, that Heywood's direct influence on later dramatists seems to have been

small; the flowering of Elizabethan comedy, some fifty years after his interludes were published, developed without evident influence from his plays.

Biography

The two hallmarks of John Heywood's life were his ready wit and his
loyal Catholicism. Through a long life and drastic swings in religious opinion at the English court, he kept in royal favor by his wit until finally, as an
old man, he was driven into exile for his faith. His birth, parentage, and
early life are obscure. He was born about 1497, possibly in London; he
may have been the son of a lawyer, William Heywood, sometime of Coventry. He may have spent some time at Oxford; the early historian of Oxford, Anthony Wood, claimed that Heywood had been a short time at
Broadgates Hall but that "the crabbedness of logic not suiting with his airy
genie, he retired to his native place, and became noted to all witty men,
especially to Sir Thomas More (with whom he was very familiar)."

Heywood certainly became an intimate of the Humanist circle centered
on More, and it is probably no coincidence that Heywood first appears as a
salaried appointee at the court of King Henry VIII in the summer of 1519,
at about the time that More resigned as under sheriff to concentrate on his
duties as privy councillor. Heywood's position at court, at first, was as
"singer" and "player on the virginals" (an early keyboard instrument); his
skills were appreciated by King Henry, himself an accomplished musician,
and were rewarded with grants of money and leases on land in addition to
his quarterly stipend. The exact time when Heywood became involved with
dramatic activities at court is unknown, but it seems likely that his six
extant plays were written in the 1520's. He was later renowned for his varied skills as an entertainer. John Bale, for example, wrote in 1557 that
Heywood "was accomplished in the arts of music and poesy in his own
tongue, and ingenious without great learning; he spent much time in
conducting merry dances after banquets and in presenting pageants, plays,
masques, and other 'disports.'" In 1528, he received a life annuity of ten
pounds and may have left the court; on January 20, 1530, he was admitted
to the London company of mercers and appointed to the office of mea-
surer of linen cloths.

Sometime during the period 1523-1529, Heywood married Eliza Rastell,
daughter of the Humanist author and printer John Rastell. Eliza's mother
was a sister of Sir Thomas More, and thus Heywood by his marriage cemented his relationship to the More circle at the time More was approach-
ing his zenith at court as chancellor. In 1533, Eliza's brother, William
Rastell, publisher four of Heywood's plays. These interludes and the poet's
epigrams reflect at many points the Humanists' social ideas, critical temper,
and harsh clerical satire. The circle was soon to be split, however, divided
by the rise of Protestantism in England.

In 1532, More resigned the chancellorship, and in 1535, he was executed for his Catholicism. The Rastell family was torn by the controversy; Heywood's father-in-law converted to Protestantism, while the son, William Rastell, remained loyal to the old faith. Heywood likewise retained his Catholic sympathies, and near the end of Henry's reign the dramatist became involved in a Catholic plot against Archbishop Cranmer that nearly cost him his life. The plot was discovered and several participants were executed. Heywood himself was condemned and his property ordered forfeit, but he "escaped hanging with his mirth," according to the 1596 report of John Harington, since King Henry was "truly persuaded that a man that wrote so pleasant and harmless verses, could not have any harmful conceit against his proceedings." Heywood read a public recantation in London on July 6, 1544.

Not only were Heywood's properties restored to him after his public humbling, but also he was reinstated at court. At the request of none other than Archbishop Thomas Cranmer, he wrote an interlude, "The Parts of Man," of which only fourteen lines survive, recorded in the manuscript autobiography of Thomas Whythorne, the dramatist's secretary from 1545 to 1548. When the Catholic Queen Mary Tudor came to the throne in 1553, Heywood's prospects brightened, for he had been faithful to her through her years of eclipse after her mother's divorce from Henry VIII. In 1534, he had written her a flattering poem, and in 1538, "with his Children" he presented a play before her; later, he delivered an oration at her coronation and penned a fulsome poem about her marriage. She rewarded him with a higher annuity and more gifts of land. Soon, however, it became obvious that the Protestant Elizabeth would succeed Mary, who was in ill health, and only five days before Mary's death, Heywood resigned his annuity and Mary granted him a forty-year lease on the substantial Bolmer manor in Yorkshire. Mary apparently wanted to protect Heywood from possible loss of income under her successor.

Under the new queen, Heywood managed for some time to remain active at court. In 1559, he aided in presenting a play for Elizabeth at Nonesuch during her summer "progress" or tour. Matters became increasingly difficult for Catholics in England, however, and on July 20, 1564, Heywood and his son Ellis fled to the Low Countries. Heywood lived for some time in Malines, then was granted a place at the Jesuit college of his son Ellis at Antwerp. When in 1578 the college was overrun by a Protestant mob, he barely escaped along with the Jesuits to Louvain. It was probably there that, late in 1578, more than eighty years of age, he died. Even on his deathbed, Heywood retained his wit; when his confessor kept intoning "The flesh is frail," the master epigrammatist twitted him: "You seem to be blaming God for not making me a fish." Heywood's career spanned the Tudor age: Linked to Erasmus by wit and to More by marriage, he survived at four Tudor monarchs' courts by his gifts as poet and dramatist; his son Jasper translated three tragedies of Seneca, and his daughter was the mother of the poet John Donne.

Analysis

The six plays of John Heywood's canon fall naturally into two groups: three debate plays, rhetorical disputations on set topics, and three farces, which include considerable argumentation but also feature rudimentary plots and lively onstage action. Of the former three, the simplest is *Witty and Witless*, with only three characters. John and James debate the latter's paradoxical proposition that it is "better to be a fool, than a wise man." James triumphs by showing that the Witless and the Witty equally suffer bodily pain, that Witless suffers lesser mental pain, and that Witless, being innocent, is sure of the supreme pleasure—salvation. At this point, a third interlocutor, Jerome, intervenes; he upbraids John for yielding and proceeds to overturn all three conclusions. He ends in a terse sermon showing that good deeds affect heavenly rewards proportionally—an anti-Lutheran view which at the time would have pleased Henry VIII, who in 1521 was named Defender of the Faith for his anti-Lutheran writing. Heywood's debate is in the ironic Humanist tradition of Erasmus' *Encomium moriae* (1509; *The Praise of Folly*); it also is indebted to a French farce, *Dyalogue du fol et du sage*, but goes beyond this source, which ends with the victory of the fool, to make a pious nonironic ending.

A considerable step up from this play in rhetorical complexity is *The Play of Love*, a disputation in which two pairs of debaters consider the pains and pleasures of love. This play may have been produced about 1528-1529 for a Christmas revel before an Inns of Court audience who would have followed the legalistic arguments with interest. The four characters comprise the possible permutations of love pairings. Lover Not Loved begins by asserting that of all pains, his is the worst. Beloved Not Loving, a woman, challenges him with a claim that her pain from incessant and unwelcome wooing is worse. After fruitless argument, they go off to find an arbitrator. Meanwhile the joyful Lover Loved enters with a song and declares that "The highest pleasure man can obtain,/ Is to be a lover beloved again." He in turn is challenged by the cocky, taunting Vice named Neither Lover Nor Loved, who avers that a lover is always torn by some passion but that he, being passionless, lives in quiet. When Lover Loved goes to find an indifferent judge of their dispute, the Vice relates to the audience his own love experience, in which he and a sweet damsel deceived each other; this story provides plausible motivation (unusual for a Vice character) for his mocking attitude toward all love. Each pair of disputants chooses the other as judges, with the result that both disputes end, anti-climactically, in a tie: Lover Not Loved and Beloved Not Loving are judged to suffer equal pains, while Lover Loved and Neither Lover Nor Loved enjoy equivalent pleasures. While the arguments are tedious, the play has its moment of excitement: At one point, the Vice runs in "among the audience with a high copper tank on his head full of squibs fired crying . . . fire! fire!" His prank has a purpose: He tells Lover Loved that his mistress has been burned, and the Lover's misery amply proves the Vice's contention that lovers are anxiety-ridden.

The third of the debate plays, *The Play of the Weather*, has the largest cast among Heywood's dramas, with ten characters. Heywood makes an entertaining play from the most trifling of subjects: complaints about the weather. When the great god Jupiter resolves to hear and redress grievances about the weather, eight characters representing a cross section of social types come in turn to make their conflicting pleas; in the end, Jupiter decides the issue in the only possible way: He will continue the weather "even as it was." Heywood enlivens this unpromising material in two ways: He arranges for lively antitheses between pairs of petitioners, and he selects as Jupiter's "cryer" (and the play's chief character) a Vice named Merry Report, whose quips and mocks enliven each episode. The successive pairs of petitioners make directly opposed requests; the Gentleman, for example, wants fair weather for hunting, while the Ranger desires terrific storms to level trees for his prerogative of windfall. Some pairs are set off by simultaneous appearance; the preening, fashion-conscious Gentlewoman is disdained for her vanity by the coarse, robustious Launder. The final complainant, a masterpiece of economical characterization, is the boy, "the least that can play," who comically mistakes the jaunty Merry Report for "master God" and then petitions for frost and snow, for all of his "pleasure is in catching of birds,/ And making of snow-balls and throwing the same." The boy's artless egotism highlights the selfishness of all the petitioners.

Though the ostensible topic is commonplace, the real subject of *The Play of the Weather* is social strife among competing interests and the need for a strong ruler to keep the peace. Particularly under the threat of religious innovation, Heywood is suggesting, England needs a powerful monarch to maintain the harmony of the ancient commonwealth.

Quite different from the *débat* plays are Heywood's three farces. These represent Heywood's most distinctive dramatic contribution, yet they are mostly derivative of French originals, two in part and the third substantially. Like any farce, these three feature fast-moving verbal and physical strife, single-line plots, and an absence of theme or idea; they are designed to dissolve all tensions in laughter. All three plays sharply satirize one or more clerics, or, as Francis Kirkman put it in his 1671 playlist, Heywood "makes notable work with the then Clergy."

The simplest and probably earliest of the three, *The Pardoner and the*

Friar, is little more than an extended quarrel between two itinerant preachers. The supposed setting is a parish church, with the dramatic audience as congregation, where the two title characters have come to raise money for their respective brotherhood or almshouse. The Friar begins first; while he prays before his sermon, the Pardoner displays his papal bulls and holy relics. Like Geoffrey Chaucer's pardoner in *The Canterbury Tales* (1387-1400), this pardoner carries a collection of ludicrous relics that includes such treasures as Saint Michael's brain-pan, the arm of Saint Sunday, and "the great toe of the Holy Trinity." When the Friar begins preaching, the Pardoner refuses to yield the floor, so the two harangue in tandem, in rapid line-by-line alternation, pausing occasionally to rail at one another. Finally they fall to hair-pulling, scratching, and biting just as the parish priest, scandalized, rushes in to part them, calling on Neighbor Pratt the constable for assistance. The two charlatans, facing a night in the stocks, thrash their captors and make their escape. The basic situation of the flyting between two itinerants may derive from the short French play, *Farce nouvelle d'un pardonneur, d'un triacleur, et d'une tavernière* (a new farce of a pardoner, an apothecary, and a tavern-girl); the similarities are, however, slight and perhaps coincidental.

The Four P.P. exhibits a lively lying contest among a Pardoner, a Palmer, and a Potyecary, with a Pedler as judge. (This play may also be indebted to the French farce mentioned above.) After considerable quarreling, the Pardoner tells a coarse tall tale of a remarkable cure, topping it with an exotic story of a woman rescued from Hell. Both stories make sport of women; when the Potyecary in reaction swears he never knew "any one woman out of patience," the three others involuntarily exclaim at his monstrous lie and the Pedler immediately awards him the prize. Lest we take the satire of corrupt churchmen too much to heart, the play ends, somewhat incongruously, with the Pedler's advice that we should "judge the best" of clerics and receive them "as the church doth judge or take them." The Palmer follows, speaking for the author, with an apology and disavowal of "all that hath scaped us here by negligence." The apology seems needless; the play's satire is light and harmless enough.

Heywood's most entertaining play is a vigorous domestic farce, *Johan Johan the Husband, Tyb His Wife, and Sir Johan the Priest*; this play has by far the most complicated plot, the most developed characterization, and the liveliest dialogue in the Heywood canon. Most of the credit, however, is not Heywood's, for his play is a fairly close translation of a French original, *Farce nouvelle et fort joyeuse du pasté* (a new and merry farce of a pie). At many points the translation is phrase-for-phrase; in other sections, Heywood shows originality and often improves on the French version. The story is simple enough: A husband vows to beat his wayward wife, but she easily outfaces him, sends him to fetch her lover the Priest, and dallies with the lover, eating a meat pie while poor Johan Johan is kept busy at the fire warming wax to fix a leaky bucket. Tyb the Wife snickers to Sir Johan about her cuckolded mate, who "chafeth the wax" and "for his life, dareth not look hitherward"; she gloats over her "pretty jape" of making "her husband her ape." Poor Johan Johan complains that "the smoke putteth out my eyes two: I burn my face . . . / And yet I dare not say one word" as his wife and her paramour eat his pie and taunt him. Finally his rage spills out and he beats the two of them soundly and drives them out of the house. From this simple situation, Heywood's version develops considerable human interest; the husband's vacillation between boastful manliness and sniveling servility is the mainspring of the action. He is caught in repeated ironies: He goes at his wife's bidding to fetch her lover to dine because he hopes the Priest will quell their strife; he has to beg the apparently reluctant Sir Johan to accept his invitation; he watches, famished, while the guest eats up his share of a pie; he drives wife and lover from the house at the end, only to run after them in fear of what the pair may be up to at the Priest's house. Apart from its picture of a corrupt cleric, the play makes no statement and has no moral; it is simply good fun.

Heywood's reputation as a dramatist rests on these six plays, though he is known to have written others, along with masques at court, and he has sometimes been credited with the authorship of the two-part interlude *Gentleness and Nobility* (pb. 1535), by John Rastell. Heywood's accomplishment was that he detached the interlude from its dependency on allegorical figures and introduced flesh-and-blood people into his simple plots; in his farces, Heywood created vivid characters whose interests and passions the audience shares even while it laughs at them. His plays benefit from his wide metrical range and considerable skills as a versifier; he makes good use, too, of his extensive proverb lore and of his famous facility with the quick quip. Despite the long passages of tedious dispute in some of the plays, at its best Heywood's dramatic dialogue sparkles with vivid homely diction, lively rhythms, and clever rhymes.

Other major works

POETRY: *A Dialogue of Proverbs*, 1546, 1963 (Rudolph E. Habenicht, editor); *The Spider and the Fly*, 1556.

MISCELLANEOUS: *Works*, 1562 (epigrams and poems); *Works and Miscellaneous Short Poems*, 1956 (Burton A. Milligan, editor).

Bibliography

Bevington, David M. *Tudor Drama and Politics*, 1968.
Bolwell, Robert W. *The Life and Works of John Heywood*, 1966.
Cameron, Kenneth. *John Heywood's "Play of the Wether,"* 1941.
Craik, T. W. "The True Source of John Heywood's *Johan Johan*," in *Mod-*

ern Language Review. XLV (1950), pp. 289-295.

_____ . *The Tudor Interlude*, 1958.

De La Bere, Rupert. *John Heywood: Entertainer*, 1937.

Maxwell, Ian. *French Farce and John Heywood*, 1946.

Phy, Wesley. "Chronology of John Heywood's Plays," in *Englische Studien*. LXXIV (1940), pp. 27-41.

Reed, A. W. *Early Tudor Drama*, 1926.

William M. Baillie

THOMAS HEYWOOD

Born: Lincolnshire, England; c. 1573
Died: London, England; August, 1641

Principal drama

The Four Prentices of London, pr. c. 1594, pb. 1615; *Edward IV, Parts I and II*, pr. 1599, pb. 1600; *The Royal King and the Loyal Subject*, pr. c. 1602, pb. 1637; *A Woman Killed with Kindness*, pr. 1603, pb. 1607; *The Wise Woman of Hogsdon*, pr. c. 1604, pb. 1638; *If You Know Not Me, You Know Nobody: Or, The Troubles of Queen Elizabeth, Part I*, pr., pb. 1605, *Part II*, pr. 1605, pb. 1606; *Fortune by Land and Sea*, pr. c. 1607, pb. 1655; *The Rape of Lucrece*, pb. 1608, pr. before 1611; *The Fair Maid of the West: Or, A Girl Worth Gold, Part I*, pr. before 1610, pb. 1631, *Part II*, pr. c. 1630, pb. 1631; *The Golden Age: Or, The Lives of Jupiter and Saturn*, pr. before 1611, pb. 1611; *The Silver Age*, pr. 1612, pb. 1613; *The Brazen Age*, pr., pb. 1613; *The Iron Age, Parts I and II*, pr. c. 1613, pb. 1632; *The Captives: Or, The Lost Recovered*, pr. 1624, pb. 1885; *A Maidenhead Well Lost*, pr. c. 1625-1634, pb. 1634; *The English Traveler*, pr. c. 1627, pb. 1633; *London's Jus Honorarium*, pr., pb. 1631 (masque); *Londini Artium et Scientiarum Scaturigo*, pr., pb. 1632 (masque); *Londini Emporia: Or, London's Mercatura*, pr., pb. 1633 (masque); *The Late Lancashire Witches*, pr., pb. 1634 (with Richard Brome); *A Challenge for Beauty*, pr. c. 1634, pb. 1636; *Love's Mistress*, pr. 1634, pb. 1636 (masque); *Londini Sinus Salutis: Or, London's Harbour of Health and Happiness*, pr., pb. 1635 (masque); *Londini Speculum: Or, London's Mirror*, pr., pb. 1637 (masque); *Porta Pietatis*, pr., pb. 1638 (masque); *Londini Status Pacatus: Or, London's Peaceable Estate*, pr., pb. 1639; *The Dramatic Works of Thomas Heywood*, 1964.

Other literary forms

Thomas Heywood was as prolific in other forms of writing as he was in the drama. Very little of his other work, however, has any particular literary merit. The long poem *Troia Britannica* (1609) was based on material that Heywood had earlier put into dramatic form, but the poetry is generally considered to be poor, Heywood having never shown a particular flair for verse. *An Apology for Actors* (1612), on the other hand, is an excellent critical work that defends the Jacobean stage on didactic grounds. Because Heywood so often used women as the protagonists of his plays, his *Gunaikeion: Or, Nine Books of Various History Concerning Women, Inscribed by the Nine Muses* (1624) is of interest to the modern reader because it suggests even further the degree to which Heywood was interested in the nature of women and their sufferings. None of these works, however, can lay claim to the merit of Heywood's best plays, and they have received little critical attention.

Achievements

In 1633, Heywood claimed to have written either all or most of some 220 plays, in addition to his volumes of poetry and prose. Yet only *A Woman Killed with Kindness* is well-known or anthologized with any regularity. To measure Heywood's significance in such terms would be to ignore the impact he had on the theater of his day and particularly on the development of the theater since the Restoration, both in England and in Europe. Heywood was the first English playwright to demonstrate consistently the potential of the sentimental drama, particularly the domestic tragedy, to produce effective theater. Restoration writers such as Nicholas Rowe and Thomas Otway followed in their "she-tragedies" Heywood's use of the female protagonist, and George Lillo in *The London Merchant: Or, The History of George Barnwell* (pr. 1731) employed the middle-class ethic of *A Woman Killed with Kindness* and *The English Traveler* to effect a similar pathos. Gotthold Ephraim Lessing, Friedrich Schiller, and Denis Diderot also saw the potential of the sentimental drama as Heywood had used it, although they were more directly influenced by the Restoration dramatists. In Heywood, one can find the beginning of a type of drama that has had a profound impact on Western dramatic literature. Although he did not have the dramatic and artistic talents of those who developed his forms, his plays solidly established the notion that pathos built on a foundation of basically bourgeois morality has both popular appeal and literary merit.

Biography

The facts of Thomas Heywood's early life are scarce. Heywood was apparently born sometime in 1573 to the Reverend Robert Heywood and his wife, Elizabeth. Probably a Cambridge graduate, Robert Heywood migrated prior to Thomas' birth from Cheshire to Lincolnshire, where he served as rector first at Rothwell and then at Ashby-cum-Fenley. Thomas was one of eleven children; there is, however, no record of any dealings between him and his siblings after he arrived in London.

The Heywoods were, it would seem, a family of gentility, evidenced by the application of Heywood's Uncle Edmund for a grant of arms. At sixteen or seventeen, Heywood entered Emmanuel College, Cambridge, a stronghold of Puritanism, which may explain the moral thrust in much of his writing, particularly in the pamphlets of his later career. His college work ended early, however, when his father died in 1593. At this point, Heywood, like so many young men with talent and a bit of learning but no degree, accepted the challenges of the London stage and began his career as an actor.

In 1593, Heywood was hired by Philip Henslowe as an actor for the Admiral's Men. Heywood, however, turned his hand very quickly to writing, sharing in the revision of works being done by the company; among these may have been, in 1599, *The Siege of London*.

Around 1600, Heywood began writing for Derby's Men, although the specifics of his relationship with this company are relatively obscure. *Edward IV* was produced by Derby's Men before Heywood broke the connection in 1601, when he became an actor-sharer with Worcester's Men and entered the service of Queen Anne, under the auspices of Henslowe. This new association connected Heywood with Henry Chettle, Thomas Dekker, Wentworth Smith, and John Webster, with whom he wrote *Lady Jane* (pr. 1602). By this time, as A. M. Clark notes, Heywood was financially well off as a result of his hasty writing, which, according to Clark, was "fatal to [the] literary quality" of his scripts but which "did not greatly diminish their price." Whatever effect Heywood's mercenary spirit may generally have had on his work, he did in 1603 write *A Woman Killed with Kindness*, the play on which his reputation rests.

A successful actor-sharer and playwright in 1603, Heywood married Ann Butler on June 13, with whom he had six children. Although no record of Ann Heywood's death has been found, Heywood apparently married Jane Span in 1632.

In 1608, after fifteen years of increasing success as a dramatist, Heywood turned his energies to other forms of literary achievement. His decision was probably spurred by the financial problems the theater experienced because of a new outbreak of the plague in London. More to the point, however, Heywood had always envisioned himself as a literary figure whose talent had been absorbed by his efforts to earn a living rather than achieve recognition as a poet. In 1609, he published *Troia Britannica*, certainly his best effort at poetry. Yet, whatever its merits, *Troia Britannica* is not as accomplished a piece as his series known as *The Ages* (*The Golden Age, The Silver Age, The Brazen Age,* and *The Iron Age*), his dramatizations of basically the same material. In 1612, Heywood published his major piece of criticism, *An Apology for Actors*, which defended on didactic grounds the London theater. This work remains a major piece of criticism, its value being enhanced by the fact that it was written by a major figure of the Jacobean theater.

For approximately the next ten years, Heywood had his finger in a number of activities but produced very little himself. In 1619, he joined the Lady Elizabeth's Men when the Queen's Company split. His new troupe produced *The Captives* just before he moved in 1625 to Queen Henrietta's Company, for which he wrote *The Fair Maid of the West, Part II*, which enjoyed a successful Christmas performance at court. Again, Heywood's interests began to turn from the stage, although he did write *The English*

Traveler, *The Late Lancashire Witches*, and his last play, either *A Challenge for Beauty* or *Love's Mistress* (the dates are somewhat uncertain), all of which were performed by the Lady Elizabeth's Men.

In 1631, Heywood began a series of city pageants which displayed his limited abilities with the masque. At the same time, he published a number of didactic journalistic pieces, such as the pamphlet *Philocothonista: Or, The Drunkard, Open, Dissected, and Anatomized* (1635), a treatise against the abuses of drinking. His *A Curtain Lecture* (1636) celebrates the value of marriage and further glorifies the domestic virtues which Heywood championed throughout his career. All of these works, however, have little to recommend them other than their support of our understanding of the changes in thought that Heywood experienced as he grew older.

When Heywood was buried at the Church of St. James, Clerkenwell, on August 16, 1641, he had had his hand in the writing of more than two hundred plays that had appeared between the years 1592 and 1641.

Analysis

In an age that produced William Shakespeare, Ben Jonson, and Christopher Marlowe, Thomas Heywood achieved a popular success on the stage that very likely dimmed even that of the masters; he was extremely popular in the pit with an audience that sought entertainment more than enlightenment. A. M. Clark has said that Heywood "was the journeyman-playwright *par excellence*, with a facility, not unlike the knack of a skilled artisan, with a dramatic insight which never altogether failed him, and without the vagaries and transcendences of a conscious literature." Heywood's plays presented characters and plots with which his audience could identify. That Heywood was able to present such middle-class characters, speaking naturally and responding to their conflicts with a morality consistent with their station in life, is not surprising, nor is it necessarily commendable. That he was able to do it and still produce within such strict boundaries effective scripts, always with dramatic and sometimes with literary quality, is more than commendable; as a result, Heywood became, in a genuine sense, the founder of the middle-class drama.

Heywood's plots were often borrowed from the chapbook literature that was popular during the early seventeenth century, and those that were not were framed as if they had been. Thus, his settings and actions were familiar to theatergoers. *The Wise Woman of Hogsdon*, for example, follows from the interest of his contemporaries in witches—an interest on which Heywood later capitalized in *The Late Lancashire Witches*—and the play effectively uses the comic potential in the fraud of such persons as the Wise Woman proves to be. Such con artists were familiar to Heywood's audience; thus, the Wise Woman's various intrigues were of considerable interest. *The Fair Maid of the West*, although spiced with a certain amount of romance, also demonstrates this sense of immediacy; the audience would have found themselves quite at home during the tavern scenes or laughing with recognition at the clown Clem, who, with typical English decorum, takes himself a bit too seriously for his own good. The central plots of *A Woman Killed with Kindness* and *The English Traveler*, however, best demonstrate this point. Such accounts of infidelity and lovers' intrigues were common in the popular literature of the day, materials that certainly would have been familiar to Heywood's audience. They are, moreover, stories of characters from the middle class.

It is in fact the characters more than the plots in Heywood's plays that do the most to break down barriers between the playwright and his audience. In *A Woman Killed with Kindness*, Frankford, though a member of the landed gentry, is not a member of the nobility; his grief is not that brought on by the peculiar circumstances of lofty birth but, rather, the kind of sorrow that anyone in the audience might experience. Anne's sin, moreover, is not one she commits because of some gruesome sense of fate. Hers is the weakness of human nature—again, a weakness shared with the audience. Bess, the heroine of *The Fair Maid of the West*, despite her excessive virtues, would have greatly pleased the audience, as she was a tavern mistress, a member of their own plebeian class. These few examples well illustrate the generalization that the characters of Heywood's plays, at least the better works, held up a mirror to early seventeenth century life.

To depict the experiences of such middle-class characters confronting what were generally the conflicts of the middle class, Heywood used what could well be regarded as pedestrian language. Poetry was the appropriate language for Shakespeare's noble characters, just as Heywood's prose and simple diction are completely in line with the thematic structure of his plays. His characters are lower in stature than are Shakespeare's; his themes are domestic. For his characters to speak in lofty tones would be out of place, and Heywood was enough of a dramatist to realize that his characters should use language and express sentiments appropriate to their station in life and the conflicts they faced.

Clark has labeled *The Fair Maid of the West* the "quintessence of popular literature," referring primarily to its excellent fusion of romantic elements with those of the domestic comedy. Heywood's success in combining these seemingly disparate elements also makes this his best comedy, containing characters from the domestic mode and plot from the romantic. Both work well to illustrate a theme basic to the Heywood canon: that fidelity, chastity, and married love are virtues that ennoble men and women of the middle class.

Bess Bridges, the heroine of *The Fair Maid of the West*, is reputed to be unmatched in virtue as well as in beauty, making the tavern where she works a popular gathering place for a lively crowd of suitors, including the gallant Spencer, who in her defense kills the overbearing Carroll and is forced to flee to Fayal to avoid being arrested. There he is wounded and, thinking that he will die, sends Goodlack to entrust his entire estate to Bess if she has remained faithful to him. She has, and after hearing that her love is dead, she sets out to Fayal to see his grave. While on the sea, she purges it of Spanish pirates until she is reunited with and married to Spencer at the court of Mullisheg.

This summary illustrates the romantic aspects of the play. It includes voyages on the high seas, suggestive of the many chronicles of travel that were popular at the time. Bess takes on heroic if improbable stature as she captures ships that have been terrorizing the English merchant fleet; thus, the play rings with patriotism such as would have been applauded by an audience who had within recent memory seen the defeat of the Spanish Armada. The settings shift from the tavern at Fay, in the domestic comedy tradition, to the court of Mullisheg, in the realm of romance. Yet throughout, the basic theme of the play is that the fundamental chastity of simple characters such as Bess and the faithfulness to love characteristic of Spencer are ennobling—that it is virtue, not birth, which confers true nobility.

In one sense, all of Heywood's plays, including the comedies, are concerned with the nobility of virtue, particularly the virtue of fidelity. In Heywood's terms, this virtue alone could ennoble even the most lowly characters on the social scale. *The Fair Maid of the West* treats this theme in various ways. First, there is the chastity that distinguishes Bess from the beginning. There is, moreover, the faithful love that she and Spencer share and that finally overcomes all the problems they face. There is, as well, the conversion of the two schemers Roughman and Goodlack, effected by Bess's virtue. Under her influence, these two become her true friends and loyal companions in her search for Spencer. Mullisheg, the pagan, serves as the final yardstick by which these characters, particularly Bess, can be measured. Despite his non-Christian frame of reference, he is so overcome with Bess's morality and her nobility of spirit that he ensures her marriage to Spencer and, despite his own loss, rewards all the characters in her entourage.

In *The Fair Maid of the West*, Heywood masks his seriousness of purpose, one that dominates all of his plays, with comedy and occasionally with sheer farce. He was well aware that audiences came to the theater more for entertainment than for enlightenment, but he demonstrates that they could well appreciate homily and entertainment together if the playwright suitably fused the two.

The Wise Woman of Hogsdon is perhaps Heywood's best example of what can legitimately be called domestic comedy. Lacking the ornamentation of romance elements that spice the action of *The Fair Maid of the West*, the play points up Heywood's place as a link in the chain that connects Renaissance and Restoration comedy. His role in linking the domestic tragedy of the two periods is well-known, but too often his role in connecting the comedy of the two periods goes unacknowledged.

The action of *The Wise Woman of Hogsdon* revolves around the antics of the rake Young Chartley, who has deserted Luce from the city, has contracted to marry Luce from the country, and has left his marriage bed to pursue the lovely Gratiana, the daughter of Sir Harry. These intrigues are complicated even further when the country Luce contracts the Wise Woman, whom Young Chartley has insulted, to handle the wedding arrangements; in order to avenge herself on Young Chartley, the Wise Woman mixes wedding partners. All is finally resolved when Young Chartley, who does in fact end up married to Luce from the city, repents, and all the others are satisfied with the mates they have been left holding.

The Wise Woman of Hogsdon is an acknowledgment of the virtues of chastity, fidelity, and married love. Here Heywood's recurring theme is treated within a completely comic framework. Here, moreover, the content is purely middle-class, suggesting strongly the notion that these virtues glorify even the common folk. Two other aspects from the play demonstrate further the fact that Heywood was directing his homily chiefly at a middle-class audience. First, the Wise Woman herself is a character drawn from contemporary life; she is a fraud and a charlatan akin to the witches, alchemists, and other con artists who were constantly being exposed both in the courts and in the popular literature of the day. Her antics are precisely what Heywood's audience would have expected from her; her duping of Young Chartley and the others would have been much to their appreciation. One scene in particular demonstrates Heywood's awareness of his audience. In the combat between Sir Boniface and Sencer, disguised as Sir Timothy, in which the Latin of the farcical schoolmaster is used by Sencer as a weapon against him, Heywood is clearly painting a comic picture of the pedants, the pretenders to learning, who in their own way were seen by the middle-class audience as even more absurd than con artists such as the Wise Woman. This is low comedy perhaps, but the scene works well to illustrate the folly not only of Sir Boniface but of the pretentious Sir Harry as well.

The gulling of Sir Boniface is reminiscent of the slapstick humor that Jonson fell into in plays such as *The Alchemist* (pr. 1610), as when Face and Subtle dupe the Puritans. The overall style of the play, however, is much more in line with the works of Sir George Etherege and William Wycherley; its action is not unlike that of Etheredge's *The Man of Mode* (pr. 1676) or Wycherley's *The Country Wife* (pr. 1675). Young Chartley, too, reminds one a great deal of Horner and Dorimant, whose quests for women trap them in a web of comic intrigue. For Heywood, however, there is a stronger moral bent at the denouement, not the essentially immoral conclusion typical of Wycherley or the amorality typical of Etherege. Young Chartley is penitent, and all the lovers are satisfied that they have ended up with the partners they should have. No character is totally humiliated. Even the con artists of the play have used their talents to ensure a proper resolution to the basic conflict. Thus, whatever this play may have in common with Restoration comedy, its morality sharply distinguishes it from the masterpieces of that licentious period.

A Woman Killed with Kindness is generally regarded as Heywood's masterpiece, and it has ensured him of a lasting place in the history of English literature. It is a sentimental or domestic tragedy constructed, like his other works, to appeal to a popular audience. The play has, moreover, a subplot which causes many of the same distractions caused by the secondary action in works such as *The English Traveler*. There is, however, one significant difference between this play and Heywood's lesser-known works. In *A Woman Killed with Kindness*, the poet in Heywood shines; his language, although appropriate to his domestic framework and therefore still somewhat pedestrian, is used so well to express meaning consistent with the theme and the characters of the work that there is a harmony between language and sentiment which is characteristic only of great literature

The central plot of *A Woman Killed with Kindness* begins with the marriage of Frankford and Anne, a marriage viewed by their friends as the perfect union. Frankford, however, takes Wendoll into his home, only to have his friend tempt Anne to infidelity. Upon discovering her adultery, Frankford banishes Anne to a secluded cottage on their estate. Anne refuses to eat and soon lies on her deathbed. Frankford, however, comes to her and forgives her, reinstating her to her position as wife and mother.

A Woman Killed with Kindness is Heywood's best statement of his constant theme: the ennobling grace of married love and fidelity. In this work, however, the statement is enhanced by an explicitly Christian sentiment. Frankford overcomes his initial rage and his desire to kill Anne and Wendoll, determined that he will not destroy two souls that Christ died to save. In this way, the revenge tragedy motif so characteristic of Renaissance theater is shattered by Christian sentiment. His punishment of Anne, suggested by the title of the work, is also characteristic of his goodness, as is his final forgiveness of her. Such is Frankford's virtue that scholars generally refer to him as the ultimate Christian hero.

While the goodness of Frankford accounts in part for the overwhelming sentimentality of the play, the genuine repentance of Anne and Wendoll adds significantly to the final pathos. They accept the tortures of their guilt and do not at any point try to justify their actions. Anne dies—Heywood's morality would not have allowed otherwise—but there is beauty in her death, the beauty of justice matched by forgiveness.

What makes *A Woman Killed with Kindness* a superior work, recognized as such even by those critics who do not accept the possibility of domestic tragedy and do not call Heywood's work a tragedy, is the language. The play's powerful fusion of language and sentiment is particularly clear in the scene in which Frankford confronts Anne about her infidelity. With a series of short questions, pointedly delivered, he asks her what failings as a husband he had demonstrated that would make her turn from him. She denies there being any, until at last Frankford explodes with a declaration of innocence from such failings that demonstrates well the grief he feels. This whole scene is built upon the assumption that the marital vows are sacred and that Frankford's faithfulness as a husband should preclude such treachery by his wife.

Of all of Heywood's plays, *A Woman Killed with Kindness* has had the most lasting interest to scholars; more important, the play has had an enormous impact on dramatic literature. Writers interested in the possibilities of sentimental tragedy have taken it as their model; Diderot referred explicitly to the success of *A Woman Killed with Kindness* as justifying the writing of domestic tragedy. Though the bulk of his work has been forgotten, Heywood has achieved a permanent place in the history of drama.

Other major works

POETRY: *Troia Britannica*, 1609; *The Hierarchy of the Blessed Angels*, 1635.

NONFICTION: *Philocothonista: Or, The Drunkard, Open, Dissected, Anatomized*, 1635; *A Curtain Lecture*, 1636.

MISCELLANEOUS: *An Apology for Actors*, 1612; *Gunaikeion: Or, Nine Books of Various History Concerning Women, Inscribed by the Nine Muses*, 1624; *England's Elizabeth, Her Life and Troubles During Her Minority from the Cradle to the Crown*, 1632; *Exemplary Lives and Memorable Acts of Nine of the Most Worthy Women of the World: Three Jews, Three Gentiles, Three Christians*, 1640.

Bibliography

Adams, Henry H. *English Domestic or Homiletic Tragedy, 1575-1642*, 1943.

Boas, Frederick. *Thomas Heywood*, 1950.

Brown, Arthur. "Thomas Heywood's Dramatic Art," in *Essays on Shakespeare and Elizabethan Drama*, 1962. Edited by Richard Hosley.

Clark, A. M. *Thomas Heywood*, 1931.

Eliot, T. S. *Elizabethan Essays*, 1934.

Velte, H. Mowbray. *The Bourgeois Elements in the Dramas of Thomas Heywood*, 1924.

Gerald W. Morton

ISRAEL HOROVITZ

Born: Wakefield, Massachusetts; March 31, 1939

Principal drama

The Comeback, pr. 1958; *Line*, pr. 1967, pb. 1968 (one act); *It's Called the Sugar Plum*, pr. 1967, pb. 1968 (one act); *The Indian Wants the Bronx*, pr., pb. 1968 (one act); *Rats*, pr., pb. 1968 (one act); *Acrobats*, pr. 1968, pb. 1971; *Morning*, pr. 1968 (as *Chiaroscuro*), pb. 1969 (one act); *The Honest-to-God Schnozzola*, pr. 1968, pb. 1971; *Leader*, pr. 1969, pb. 1970; *Clair-Obscur*, pr. 1970, pb. 1972; *Dr. Hero*, pr. 1971 (as *Hero*), pr. 1972 (revision of *Dr. Hero*), pb. 1973; *Shooting Gallery*, pr. 1971, pb. 1973; *Alfred the Great*, pr. 1972, pb. 1974; *Our Father's Failing*, pr. 1973, pb. 1979; *Spared*, pr. 1974, pb. 1975 (one act); *Hopscotch*, pr. 1974, pb. 1977; *Uncle Snake: An Independence Day Pageant*, pr. 1975, pb. 1976; *The Primary English Class*, pr. 1975, pb. 1976; *Stage Directions*, pr. 1976, pb. 1977; *The Reason We Eat*, pr. 1976; *Alfred Dies*, pr. 1976, pb. 1979; *The Former One-on-One Basketball Champion*, pr. 1977, pb. 1982; *The 75th*, pr., pb. 1977; *Man with Bags*, pr., pb. 1977 (adaptation of a translation of Eugène Ionesco's play); *Mackerel*, pr. 1978, pb. 1979; *A Christmas Carol: Scrooge and Marley*, pr. 1978, pb. 1979 (adaptation of Charles Dickens' story); *The Widow's Blind Date*, pr. 1978, pb. 1982; *The Wakefield Plays*, pb. 1979 (includes the Alfred Trilogy—*Alfred the Great, Our Father's Failing, Alfred Dies*—and the Quannapowitt Quartet—*Hopscotch, The 75th, Stage Directions, Spared*); *Park Your Car in the Harvard Yard*, pr. 1980; *The Good Parts*, pr. 1982, pb. 1983.

Other literary forms

The relish with which Israel Horovitz approaches language has found its way into two novels, *Cappella* (1973) and *Nobody Loves Me* (1975), and a book of poetry, *Spider Poems and Other Writings* (1973). None of these works, however, has approached the effectiveness of his drama. *Cappella* does show a dramatist's flair for vivid monologue, but the Beckett-like stream of consciousness that pervades much of the novel is rather irritating and often impenetrable. Not surprisingly, it is Horovitz's work in film that comes closest to the level of his stage works. His first produced film script, *The Strawberry Statement* (1970), based on the book by James Simon Kunen, conveyed the atmosphere of the Columbia University student riots in the late 1960's with shrewd social and psychological observations. His next major screenplay was the frankly autobiographical *Author! Author!* (1982), one of his most humane and least ironic works. It depicts the problems of a playwright whose second wife leaves him for another man and who must then deal with five children as well as the preparation for his first Broadway play, entitled *The Reason We Eat* (one of Horovitz's own, lesser-known plays). Ivan Travalian's life and work mirror Horovitz's quite closely, but Horovitz can view his own experience with much humor, giving some satiric insights into theater production. The screenplay is filled as well with a great deal of warmth and love between Ivan and the five children (four of whom are not even biologically his). Horovitz has also written a number of plays for television, sometimes with a social message (*VD Blues*, concerning venereal disease, in 1972; *Play for Trees*, on the importance of saving trees, in 1969). His television adaptation of Herman Melville's *Bartleby the Scrivener* (1977) effectively captured the gloom and poignancy of the original. In 1978, Horovitz wrote a cycle of plays for television called *Growing Up Jewish in Sault Ste. Marie*, adaptations of Morley Torgov's novel *A Nice Place to Come From*. Finally, Horovitz has contributed to a number of periodicals, most notably as a lively, refreshing, and personal art critic for *Crafts Horizons* from 1968 to 1970.

Achievements

Horovitz early staked out his claim to a share in the Beckett-Ionesco tradition of modern absurdity. He dramatizes the alienation of characters trapped in their own realities, often at cross-purposes, unable to communicate. Horovitz examines the violent roots of much human interaction; in his plays, submerged fears and hostilities rise to the surface and take concrete shape in often senseless acts of aggression.

Horovitz is a master of modern metropolitan malaise, yet he has also exposed the decay at work in small-town New England, setting most of his later plays either in Wakefield or Gloucester, Massachusetts. A native of Wakefield, Horovitz has returned to it in a series of plays, linked by related characters, similar themes and moods, and even repeated lines. Through these Wakefield plays, he portrays the constriction, pettiness, and desperation of life in a small town, where people are trapped for generations and where those who have escaped return only to be caught up in the same power struggles.

Horovitz's stark view of contemporary human relationships assures him a significant position in the history of Off-Broadway, a theater tradition given to intense engagement of the audience in ways diverging from the more familiar and comfortable realistic tradition of Broadway (and London's West End). Although, as a consequence, most of his plays have gone unreviewed by the national press, his work has been translated into more than twenty languages, and theaters across the United States and around the world are continually performing his plays. His keen vision earned for him Obie Awards for both *The Indian Wants the Bronx* and *The Honest-to-God Schnozzola*, both of which have also been otherwise honored, while awards have also gone to *Line*, *Rats*, and *It's Called the Sugar Plum*. As one of the creators of sketches for the television special *VD Blues*, he received an Emmy Award, and his script for *The Strawberry Statement* won for him the Cannes Film Festival Prix du Jury.

Biography

Israel Horovitz was born in Wakefield, Massachusetts, a town of more than twenty thousand people not far from Boston. Its impact upon him is clear in much of his later work—notably *The Wakefield Plays* and *The Widow's Blind Date*, with their evocation of a stifling small-town atmosphere. Although one source, *Contemporary Authors* (1978), says that his father, Julius Charles Horovitz, was a lawyer, a 1982 interview in *New York* indicates that his father was a truck driver. Bright but lower-middle-class, Horovitz did not attend college. When asked in 1972 to teach playwriting at City College of New York, he listed on his employment form, "Harvard, B.A." for his college education. When this falsification was discovered, Horovitz lost the job. Comparison of various biographical sketches in his published works and other sources reveals a number of discrepancies.

Horovitz's first play, *The Comeback*, was written when Horovitz was seventeen and was produced in Boston in 1958, when he was nineteen. He continued to write and to have plays produced throughout the early 1960's. During this period, he was a fellow in playwriting at the Royal Academy of Dramatic Art and was honored as the first American to be selected as playwright-in-residence with the Royal Shakespeare Company's Aldwych Theatre, in 1965. It was not until *Line*, in 1967, however, that his work was produced in New York, by Ellen Stewart's Café La Mama, an important force in the theater scene of the 1960's. For the next two or three years, Horovitz's work was much produced and much discussed, but a hiatus came in his New York work in the early 1970's, and thereafter his work enjoyed only rare major productions there; instead, he offered world premieres of his work to major regional theaters in Chicago, Los Angeles, and other cities, especially those in New England.

Although Horovitz early supported himself by working in an advertising agency (an experience he was able to use in *Dr. Hero*), he soon began making a satisfactory income from his writing, not only because of his early plays' striking successes but also because of his prolific output. He has written more than thirty-five plays, many of them unpublished.

Horovitz is very much a man of the theater. During the early and mid-1960's, he stage-managed in and around New York; he has directed a number of his plays; he has even acted in several of them, sometimes replacing an actor at the last moment. He is active in groups that develop new plays and playwrights, and he has taught playwriting at New York University as well as at other locations.

Horovitz's family life was revealed to audiences across the country in the 1982 film *Author! Author!*, and while certain details were changed, the spirit of the script is accurate. The film's title character has been once divorced and has custody of a son from that marriage; as the film begins, he is in the middle of a separation from his second wife, who has brought into their marriage four children from three previous marriages. Horovitz, on the other hand, was first married in 1959—to Elaine Abber—and divorced in 1960; he was married to Doris Keefe in 1960 and had three children with her, divorcing in 1972; and he then married Gillian Adams, an Englishwoman sharing his love of running.

Analysis

In *Waiting for Godot* (pb. 1952), Samuel Beckett created an indelible image of modern humanity: two bums cut off from any reality other than their immediate present and each other. The image of two men bound together in a mutually dependent but uncomfortable relationship was central also in Beckett's next play, *Endgame* (pr. 1957). The tradition continues in the work of Israel Horovitz. In his plays, the most characteristic relationship is not that of man and woman, as in Tennessee Williams and Edward Albee, nor that of parent and child, as in Eugene O'Neill and Arthur Miller. Rather, it is the relationship of two men, generally equals in age, intelligence, and social class but bound by mutual insecurity, the unrelenting need each has for reinforcement of his masculinity and his own sense of identity. Though considered friends, the two men share a deep undercurrent of hostility based on an insecurity related to both work and sex.

Such relationships in Horovitz's work, however, are not homosexual in any sense. In fact, in contrast to Lanford Wilson—who, in a 1984 issue of *The Advocate*, said, "Since ten percent of the population is gay, then every tenth character is going to be also"—Horovitz portrays virtually no homosexuality in his work beyond the transvestite in *The Honest-to-God Schnozzola*, with whom two American executives engage in sex under the impression that the transvestite is really a woman. The disgust and shame that they feel, like the feeling of Murph in *The Indian Wants the Bronx* when he makes his friend Joey take back a joking suggestion that Murph likes men, are evidence of a fear of homosexuality underlying this kind of relationship.

Because of this fear, the men in Horovitz's plays find any expression of affection difficult. A moment of tenderness may occur—even in that most tension-fraught of Horovitz's plays, *The Indian Wants the Bronx*—but it is only a moment, and the "true" masculine stance, hard and aggressive, is bound to return with greater force. When Joey is left by himself at the bus stop with the non-English-speaking man from India, he begins to make friends, instead of merely taunting him, as he and Murph had been doing before. He begins confiding in the Indian, though the Indian can understand only the emotions Joey's face and voice reveal. Joey's anxiety leads the Indian to comfort him with a hug, which Joey accepts as fatherly affection. Yet Joey's propensity for violence, along with the language barrier, betrays this moment: He takes out his knife to show as a cherished possession, but the Indian interprets this act as a threat, and when the Indian begins to move surreptitiously away, Joey believes that he is going to Murph to reveal what Joey had told him in confidence. Thus, the Indian's attempted escape provokes Joey to hit him and triggers the increasing hostility that culminates in Murph's wounding the Indian's hand.

The play, Horovitz's best known and certainly one of his most powerful, is filled with ironies. Like most of Horovitz's work, it explores failed connections: Joey and Murph are friends, yet their friendship is marred by taunts and insults, signs of a constant quest to make the other seem inferior; the Indian is trying to reach his son, and here are two men in their early twenties whom he could reach (one of whom he does reach, for a moment), yet they finally offer him only hostility and bloodshed. The mutual misinterpretation from which Joey and the Indian suffer results in the exact opposite of what each of them actually wants. Most important, the knife that instigates the misunderstanding and resulting violence is actually being shown by Joey in mockery—it and another like it were given to Joey and Murph as Christmas presents by a girlfriend, even though Murph had been arrested for stabbing someone. Joey is not a truly violent person— much less so than Murph is—but his need to prove himself the equal of Murph, to assert his manhood, outweighs his decent instincts. Murph, too, is acting out imagined male behavior rather than his real emotional responses. Both young men, living basically aimless lives with no real hope for escape, are essentially dispossessed and seek a bogus manhood in tough behavior and aggressive action.

Compassion, in this postmodern world, simply does not pay. Jebbie, one of the title figures in the one-act *Rats*, has been enjoying a blissful coexistence with a human baby, whom he protects rather than attacks, when his territory is invaded by a younger rat, Bobby. Bobby has idolized Jebbie, and he feels betrayed when he sees that the older rat, a hero to numerous rats before him, is keeping company with the enemy. When Bobby tries to get a piece of the action (a piece of baby's flesh), Jebbie stops him—in fact strangling him in order to do so. All should therefore be well—but the baby becomes upset and yells to its parents that there are rats, thus ensuring Jebbie's death. Jebbie's compassion for the human infant is largely a matter of self-protection, a kind of middle-aged complacence and gratitude for being free from worry, struggle, and "the rat race." This desire for peace and comfort, like Joey's deprecation of violence and desire for sympathetic human contact, results ironically in a return to violence and, in Jebbie's case, to his own defeat. An ironic god is looking down and laughing at the intentions that never quite work out, and Horovitz is right there with him, finding as a touchstone these words of Beckett, which he has quoted in his film script *Author! Author!*: "The highest laugh is the laugh which laughs at that which is unhappy."

There is certainly plenty of unhappiness in Horovitz's plays—especially the insecurity reflected in constant one-upmanship, whether involving rats, street punks, the working class (in *The Widow's Blind Date*), the professional class (*The Good Parts*), old men in a rest home (*Our Father's Failing*), or the corporate world (*The Honest-to-God Schnozzola, Dr. Hero*). Some of Horovitz's funniest dialogue comes from the banter between male friends as each tries to come out on top by putting the other down. Sam and Pa, two centenarians sharing their declining years in a home for the aged (or the insane) in *Our Father's Failing*, provide the most memorable scenes in Horovitz's Alfred Trilogy, part of his longer series entitled *The Wakefield Plays*. Constantly mocking each other, cutting in on each other's jokes (far too familiar to them), and mishearing or misinterpreting each other, they provide a hilarious image of old age and the undying competition between two men whose lives have overlapped for decades. Their competition is not without its sardonic side, for it is based on secret upon secret, what they are keeping from others as well as what one is keeping from the other. The long-concealed violence is bound to erupt at last, and it does, with serious repercussions. Such grim consequences—the dissolution of a lifelong friendship, disillusionment regarding other people, and the destruction of several lives—seem inevitable when competition, rather than cooperation, is the prime motivator.

Competition does produce interesting drama, and at his best, Horovitz exploits this potential to the full, dramatizing conflict through superbly observed dialogue that is often inarticulate, ungrammatical, and fragmentary, but also sharp and believable. Characters interrupt one another, stumble and hesitate, repeat themselves, very rarely engaging in typical stage rhetoric. Horovitz has clearly listened to people and their often inconsequential talk and has re-created such talk for his very ordinary characters. Through their talk, their numerous conflicts emerge.

Since much of his work deals with men's relationships to one another, and heterosexual men specifically, a major instigator of conflict and competition is the opposite sex: Friends become rivals for a woman's attentions. *The Good Parts*, for example, presents this rivalry comically, while *The Widow's Blind Date* treats the same theme with great seriousness. Here the motivating sexual rivalry is complex, rooted in the past, about twelve years before the time of the play, when George and Archie, the principal male characters, and several high school friends gang-raped Margie, now a widow, who, as the play begins, has returned to Wakefield, Massachusetts, from a sophisticated intellectual life in New York.

Margie, who has tried to forget the whole rape experience, has returned to be with her dying brother, a friend of George and Archie, and she asks Archie over for dinner, though they have not seen each other for years. George resents the attention that Archie receives from her, and Archie, recalling the distant past, resents the terrible experience of his first (and only) sexual intercourse with the girl whom he had secretly loved, when he went second in the gang-rape after George had coolly taken Margie's virginity. That the past endures is made explicit when Archie kills George by pushing him against a sharp object which, years before, had almost killed another man with whom Archie had fought. Before Margie leaves, she tells Archie that her revenge is still not finished. In return for her gang-rape, she has destroyed not only a friendship but two men's lives.

It is generally difficult in a Horovitz play to label one character the villain, since most of his characters have unappealing traits and are often to be viewed as victims, but in *The Widow's Blind Date*, it is difficult at the end to see Margie as anything but a villain. The increasing tension and violence in the two acts of the play suddenly appear as part of a revenge plot, and it is this widow—like a black widow spider—who is responsible for one man's death and the other's inevitable arrest.

Such characterizations of women are frequent in Horovitz's work. His women exist solely in relation to men; they are often motivated by a desire to get back at a man (or several men) for some sexual injustice in the past. In turn, the men in Horovitz's plays are often motivated by resentment against women, though without this same need to get back at them; they are apparently content merely to feel oppressed by women.

The resentment, conflict, and hostility pervading Horovitz's work find their inevitable result in some act of violence, or several, most frequently as the conclusion to the play—George's death in *The Widow's Blind Date*, the stabbing of the Indian's hand in *The Indian Wants the Bronx*, the shootings ending two of the Alfred plays, a hideous self-brutalization in *Stage Directions*. Horovitz's purpose is to provoke a strong reaction from his audience rather than allow them to sit back and let the play wash over them.

This provocative approach, largely a result of the influence of Edward Albee's *The Zoo Story* (pr. 1959), was effective in the 1960's, when Horovitz began his career, as Albee did, Off-Broadway. A quarter-century after *The Zoo Story*, however, and nearly two decades after *The Indian Wants the Bronx*—not to mention films such as *Bonnie and Clyde* (1967), or the work of Sam Peckinpah and Francis Ford Coppola—such violence, in and of itself, is not sufficient to make a play powerful. David Rabe and Sam Shepard, in plays such as *Streamers* (pr. 1976), *In the Boom Boom*

Room (pr. 1974), *Curse of the Starving Class* (pb. 1976), and *True West* (pr. 1983), can revivify the use of violence by giving it mythic or sociological resonance, but the violence in *The Wakefield Plays*, for example, is both predictable and inadequately prepared for by emotional involvement with the characters. Horovitz's work is more potent when presenting instead the psychic violence people inflict on one another.

Horovitz is too much a realist—Absurdist though he may be—to show his audiences a world where destructive competition does not prevail, yet he is capable of evoking real warmth and love, most notably in his screenplay *Author! Author!*, which depicts father-child relationships in a manner both touching and credible. Thus, his sardonic vision of the world is leavened with compassion.

Other major works

NOVELS: *Cappella*, 1973; *Nobody Loves Me*, 1975.

POETRY: *Spider Poems and Other Writings*, 1973.

SCREENPLAYS: *The Strawberry Statement*, 1970 (adaptation of James Simon Kunen's book); *Alfredo*, 1970; *Believe in Me*, 1970; *Machine Gun McCain*, 1970; *Acrobats*, 1972 (adaptation of his play); *Author! Author!*, 1982.

TELEPLAYS: *Play for Trees*, 1969; *VD Blues*, 1972 (as *Play for Germs*, pb. 1973); *The Making and Breaking of Splinters Braun*, 1975; *Start to Finish*, 1975; *Bartleby the Scrivener*, 1977 (adaptation of Herman Melville's story); *Growing Up Jewish in Sault Ste. Marie*, 1978 (adaptations of Morley Torgov's novel *A Nice Place to Come From*).

Bibliography

French, Philip. "Campus and Ghetto," in *The New Statesman*. September 6, 1968, pp. 296-297.

Gottfried, Martin. *Opening Nights*, 1970.

Gussow, Mel. "The New Playwrights," in *Newsweek*. LXXI (May 20, 1968), pp. 114-115.

Kalem, T. E. "Cosmic Jokers," in *Time*. XCVII (March 1, 1971), p. 67.

Kerr, Walter. *Thirty Days Hath November*, 1969.

Little, Stuart W., and Arthur Cantor. *The Playmakers*, 1970.

Oliver, Edith. "*Acrobats* and *Line*," in *The New Yorker*. XLVII (February 27, 1971), pp. 82-84.

Wetzsteon, Ross. "Author! Author!—It's Horovitz," in *New York*. XV (August 2, 1982), pp. 28-35.

Witham, Barry B. "Images of America: Wilson, Weller and Horovitz," in *Theater Journal*. XXXIV (May, 1982), pp. 223-232.

Scott Giantvalley

BRONSON HOWARD

Born: Detroit, Michigan; October 7, 1842
Died: Avon-by-the-Sea, New Jersey; August 4, 1908

Principal drama

Saratoga: Or, Pistols for Seven, pr. 1870, pb. c. 1870 (also known as *Brighton*); *Diamonds*, pr. 1872; *Hurricanes*, wr. 1873, pr. 1878, pb. 1941; *Moorcroft: Or, The Double Wedding*, pr. 1874; *Old Love Letters*, pr. 1878, pb. 1897; *The Banker's Daughter*, pr., pb. 1878 (revised; originally as *Lillian's Last Love*, pr. 1873); *Wives*, pr. 1879 (adaptation of Molière's plays *The School for Husbands* and *The School for Wives*); *Knave and Queen*, wr. 1882(?), pb. 1940 (with Sir Charles L. Young); *Young Mrs. Winthrop*, pr. 1882, pb. c. 1899; *One of Our Girls*, pr. 1885, pb. 1897; *Baron Rudolph*, pr. 1887, pb. 1941 (with David Belasco); *The Henrietta*, pr. 1887, pb. 1901 (revised by Winchell Smith and Victor Mapes as *The New Henrietta*, pr. 1913); *Met by Chance*, pr. 1887; *Shenandoah*, pr. 1888, pb. 1897; *Aristocracy*, pr. 1892, pb. 1898; *Peter Stuyvesant*, pr. 1899 (with Brander Matthews); *The Banker's Daughter and Other Plays*, pb. 1941.

Other literary forms

Bronson Howard is remembered primarily as a dramatist. Given his place as the first American to make a profession of writing plays, his comments on playwriting and the theater in America are important for the student of American dramatic literature. In 1906, for example, he surveyed, in New York's *Sunday Magazine*, the accomplishments of American playwrights and their critics after 1890 in an essay entitled "The American Drama." He commented on the art of acting in "Our Schools for the Stage," which appeared in *Century Magazine* in 1900. In one of the most revealing contemporary articles on late nineteenth century American dramatists—"American Playwrights on the American Drama," appearing in *Harper's Weekly* on February 2, 1889—Howard described his own approach to drama. Howard was a man of very definite opinions, and his most significant explanation of his theory of the "laws of dramatic composition" was first given as a lecture before the Shakespeare Club at Harvard College in March, 1886. This speech, in which he discussed at some length the origin and development of his play *The Banker's Daughter*, was repeated for the Nineteenth Century Club in New York in December, 1889, and was printed by the American Dramatists Club in New York and published as *The Autobiography of a Play* in 1914. This volume also included "Trash on the Stage and the Lost Dramatists of America," in which Howard outlined his approach to the theater and expressed his optimism regarding the future of American drama.

Achievements

Bronson Howard's most significant achievement was his ability to earn a living by writing plays. Prior to his time, many Americans had written plays; some were better plays than Howard wrote—plays by William Dunlap, John Howard Payne, Robert Montgomery Bird, Nathaniel Bannister, Cornelius Mathews, George H. Boker, or Epes Sargent and Nathaniel Parker Willis, for example. Although professional in the sense that they made money by writing plays, these writers were unable to sustain themselves with the income from their plays alone.

There is neither an extensive nor an impressive body of dramatic theory from pre-twentieth century American dramatists. Prior to Howard's lecture "The Laws of Dramatic Composition," commentary on dramatic theory was often scattered, slight, and haphazard. Basing his observations on one of his own plays, *The Banker's Daughter*, Howard outlined certain laws of dramatic construction that are significant in the history of dramatic theory in the United States, in particular illuminating those practices that made the melodramas of late nineteenth century America among the best that have been written. For Howard, the laws of dramatic composition were derived from an understanding of the sympathies of the audience as well as from the expected actions and motives of characters; to follow these laws, he believed, the dramatist had only to use common sense—to remain in touch with human nature. An audience will accept as "satisfactory" an occurrence that is, in a sense, deserved. For example, while an audience will accept the death of a good person in a tragedy, this acceptance will not be forthcoming in an ordinary play. Here, the death must be deserved or the audience will not be satisfied. Further, if a character is evil, the audience will not be satisfied unless that character is punished.

Howard's understanding of the importance of American business during the late nineteenth century and his ability to portray this characteristic of society effectively in his plays is both evidence of his insight and an achievement which distinguishes his work. His first work to explore the world of business, and, in fact, the first in its genre, was *Young Mrs. Winthrop*, a play in which business affairs consume the time and energies of the title character's husband, whose neglect of his society-minded wife threatens their life together. *The Henrietta*, considered by some critics to be his most successful play, reflects the stressful life of Wall Street financiers.

A creator of popular social melodramas on both the American stage and the English stage, Howard also left his mark upon the future of professional American dramatists as the founder, in 1891, of the American Dramatists Club, later the Society of American Dramatists and Composers, the forerunner of the Dramatists Guild. Concerned with promoting a sense of community among dramatists, Howard used his prestige as the first president of the club to bring into existence an amendment to copyright laws which threatened severe punishment for any individual who attempted to steal the work of a playwright.

Biography

Bronson Howard was the son of Charles Howard, a merchant in Detroit, Michigan, whose grandfather, Seabury Howard, fought for the English in the French and Indian War and against them in the American Revolution. After a public school education in Detroit, Howard attended an eastern preparatory school, intending to go on to Yale University. Instead, after suffering from eye problems, he returned to Detroit, where he began his writing career with a series of humorous sketches for the *Detroit Free Press*. In 1864, the *Detroit Free Press* published his first play, *Fantine*, a dramatization of a portion of Victor Hugo's *Les Misérables*.

Howard's interest in writing plays made him aware of the need to know and to understand the commercial theater, and he moved to New York in 1865. Although he continued to write plays, his innocence of the demands of his chosen profession rendered his early efforts fit only for the fireplace. He persisted, however, until he learned the accepted theater conventions of his day, eventually evolving his own principles of dramaturgy. As he studied his craft, he attended theatrical performances, observed the society around him in New York, and made his living by writing for the New York *Tribune* and *Evening Post*.

One of the major problems facing American dramatists of this period was the dual demand placed upon them: to satisfy the immediate theater audience while also providing dialogue that could be enjoyed by a literate public. Before Howard, American literary dramatists had generally eschewed the theatrical techniques that brought people into the theaters, while the actor-playwrights gave little thought to anything but the action upon the stage. As a consequence of this split, there were few fully satisfactory American plays. Although Howard started as a journalist writing plays, he soon learned that plays were to be seen and must present interesting spectacles to the eye. At the same time, he was aware of the importance of the written word, particularly of dialogue that would reflect the interests of society.

Like all successful dramatists, Howard realized that his work would have to be judged not wholly as literature but according to the laws of the theater. Indeed, he objected to the publication of his plays and felt a slight contempt for literary people such as William Dean Howells, resenting their assumption that a true American drama might be realized only through their efforts. Late in his life, he went so far as to argue that drama should be absolutely divorced from literature, and he insisted on being called a "dramatist" rather than a "literary man."

Howard's first success in the theater came with the production in 1870 of a farce entitled *Saratoga*, which ran for 101 nights in Augustin Daly's Fifth Avenue Theatre. Two years later, Daly opened another Howard play, *Diamonds*, a comedy of manners which dealt with New York society. *Moorcroft*, also produced by Daly, was not particularly successful, but by this time *Saratoga* had been transferred to English circumstance by Frank Marshall and produced at the Court Theatre as *Brighton*, with Charles Wyndham in the leading role of Bob Sackett. *Brighton* had considerable success on London stages and gave Howard the beginning of a fine reputation which brought him much pleasure during his visits to England. His marriage to Charles Wyndham's sister helped sustain his English popularity; indeed, five of Howard's plays eventually found responsive English audiences, and he was recognized during his lifetime as the first American playwright with a substantial reputation in Great Britain.

Howard's best-remembered play, *The Banker's Daughter*, first produced in 1873 as *Lillian's Last Love*, gained prestige after Howard's 1886 account of its development in his lecture *The Autobiography of a Play*. It was still being produced in 1914. A dozen years after he first came to New York, Howard was an established playwright. *Young Mrs. Winthrop* appeared in 1882; *One of Our Girls*, which stressed the international contrast in social life that was being exploited by Howells and Henry James, opened in 1885 and ran for two hundred nights. In *The Henrietta*, Howard satirized life on the stock exchange, and in *Shenandoah* he provided an exciting sentimental melodrama about love during the Civil War.

Howard wrote fewer plays in his later years. He lessened his stature in the eyes of historians of the drama by writing for the Theatrical Syndicate, an association of businessmen, formed in 1896, which for years controlled most New York theaters and many theaters in other large towns and which gradually exerted a stranglehold over entertainment in the United States. With audiences, however, he remained popular; indeed, Howard was one of the first American playwrights to make a fortune in his profession. A kind and honorable man, wholly without pretense, he enjoyed a long and productive career as a dramatist. When he died on August 4, 1908, at his home in Avon-by-the-Sea, New Jersey, he was widely acknowledged as the dean of American dramatists.

Analysis

Bronson Howard's career as a dramatist developed during that period in American drama when playwrights were turning from dramatizing farcical representations of a stereotyped society, portrayed only in the most obvious ways, to a social comedy in which manners might be clearly distinguished. Prior to this period, the American theater was dominated by spectacles and amusements created either by the person of a star actor or actress or by the ingenuity of a theater manager and his stage carpenter. The Civil War cast a shadow over the American theater, but amid the struggle of social reconstruction the dramatic arts bounced back with astonishing vigor, strengthened by the nationalism of Andrew Jackson's years, stimulated by the social and intellectual revolutions sparked by Karl Marx and Charles Darwin, and tempered by the sorrows of war. By the time Howard stopped writing, the United States had changed, both forcibly and by choice. American society, challenged by the strains upon it, developed its own unique and distinctive character, and the United States was recognized as a nation among nations.

To match these changes, American dramatists needed to create a drama that could both amuse and stimulate the emotions and thoughts of the human mind. Bronson Howard was a major factor in the development of this American drama—as it grew from amusement to art.

Although Howard collaborated on at least three plays—*Baron Rudolph* with David Belasco, *Knave and Queen* with Sir Charles L. Young, and *Peter Stuyvesant* with Brander Matthews—and adapted Molière's *The School for Husbands* (pr. 1661) and *The School for Wives* (pr. 1662) as *Wives*, he is remembered primarily for the originality of his plots and for his sensitivity and insight into American society. Although he was limited by the conventions and requirements of the theater of his time, he was deeply interested in dramatic theory, and he was particularly concerned with questions of dramatic structure. A well-constructed play, for Howard, was a "satisfactory" play—a play that is satisfactory to the audience. Believing that American and English audiences would not accept the death of a heroine in a play, Howard changed the ending of his original version of *The Banker's Daughter*. He made other changes in this play—changes that he claimed were founded on his "laws of dramatic composition." One of these laws, based on Howard's theory of what will satisfy an audience, is that those who do wrong (for example, a wife who has soiled her moral character) must always die before the final curtain falls. Similarly, and for the same reason, a love triangle must always bring disaster.

In the original version of *The Banker's Daughter*, Lillian Westbrook has married an older and wealthy man, John Strebelow, in order to save her father from financial ruin and also as a result of a quarrel with Harold Routledge. Five years later, now living in Paris with her husband and child, Lillian again meets Harold but remains faithful to her husband. The situation is then complicated by the Count de Carojac, who loves Lillian and who forces a duel with Harold. The supposed death of her old lover causes Lillian to reveal her passion and tell Strebelow that she never loved him. As a result, Strebelow takes the child away, and Lillian dies of a broken heart. The revised work shows the influence of Howard's theories of dramaturgy. First, because she has remained faithful, Lillian cannot be allowed to die in the last act, but because a love triangle cannot go unresolved, either Strebelow or Routledge must die. Howard chose Routledge, who is killed in the duel with the Count. Lillian now needs to recognize her own moral strength and save herself through this recognition rather than depend upon her child for that renewed strength. Finally, Strebelow needs to become a much stronger character, the hero of the play, in fact, and an appropriate mate for a mature Lillian, who now recognizes her own love for him.

By the third quarter of the nineteenth century, American society had been strongly affected by the industrial advances that had helped the North to win the Civil War and by the so-called Robber Barons, notorious for their life-style of "conspicuous waste." Howard recognized the growing influence of the businessman in American society, and he foresaw the social pressures that would result. Howard's first play to reveal a conscious use of the social-economic movement against a background of fashionable society was *Young Mrs. Winthrop*. In this play, Howard dramatized the conflict between the world of business and the domestic sphere. The play enjoyed an initial run of 180 performances, and reviews hailed it as a great American dramatic work; indeed, many consider it to be Howard's most important play, if only because it was the first of its kind. Douglas and Constance Winthrop, businessman and society wife, no longer find joy in their married life. When a gossip, Mrs. Chetwyn, arouses Mrs. Winthrop's suspicions concerning Mr. Winthrop's fidelity, Mrs. Winthrop attends a society ball in opposition to the wishes of her husband. Circumstances promote ready suspicions, but Howard added melodrama to social comedy by having the Winthrops' child fall ill and die while they are away. While the early action is enlivened by the careless and amusing Mrs. Chetwyn, the parents' grief in the later stages of the play threatens to overwhelm the initial premise. Mr. and Mrs. Winthrop part, only to be reunited in the final act as Howard superimposes his moral opinion on the problems that can confront the businessman in American society.

In *Young Mrs. Winthrop*, Howard portrayed a businessman but did not present the details of the business world. He would do this most explicitly in *The Henrietta*, which more recent critics have called the first of the American business plays. Linking New York society and the world of finance, Howard created a stage sermon on the vices of commercial gambling and the worship of money. Taking its title from the fictitious Henrietta Railroad, the control of which is the main issue in the melodramatic plot, the play dramatizes the financial rivalry between a father and his son. Nicholas Vanalstyne is known as "the Napoleon of Wall Street"; his son, Nicholas Vanalstyne, Jr., is equally unscrupulous and is monomaniacally concerned with wrenching control of the financial empire from his father— he is even capable of robbing the company safe. To both men, business is "health, religion, friendship, love—everything." Through the activities of a second Vanalstyne son, Bertie, a satiric portrait of the club man of this period, Howard showed that other side of society which looked askance at the feverish and frequently sordid life of moneygrubbers such as the Vanalstynes. The success of young Nicholas is short-lived, and Bertie eventually saves the day for his father, wins the heroine, and, while the villainous son dies of a heart attack, continues his successful operation on the stock exchange, basing his decisions on the flip of a coin. Popular on the American stage for a number of years, *The Henrietta* was revised by Winchell Smith and Victor Mapes in 1913 as *The New Henrietta*. Changed to meet new theater conventions and modern thought, the play was surprisingly successful.

As the international comedy of manners became a strong social theme for American writers, Howard began to plumb its possibilities in his plays. His first such work, *One of Our Girls*, illustrates his mastery of the international theme. *One of Our Girls* ran for two hundred nights after its opening. The action of the play takes place in Paris, where the Fonblanque family is arranging the marriage of their daughter Julie to the Comte de Crebillon, known well as a scoundrel and as a fine duelist. Opposed to this situation is Fonblanque's niece, Kate Shipley, the forthright and confident daughter of an American millionaire, who not only would not tolerate this arranged marriage of her cousin but also finds no good qualities in the Comte. The complications include a British Army captain who falls in love with Kate and Julie's lover, Henri Saint-Hilaire, but these are finally resolved through the good sense and actions of Kate. Julie is united with her lover; Kate and the Captain have a promising future; and the Comte, having confessed that he killed his first wife, is proved to be a villain. There is strong melodramatic action in the duel in which Henri is wounded and in the scene in which Kate protects Julie and allows herself to be caught in an embarrassing situation with Henri. Kate's American speech patterns provide some humor, as do the chatter of the gossips and the witticisms of the doctor. The main subject of the play, however, is the contrasting pictures of French and American marriage customs.

Howard tried again but failed to dramatize an international contrast in *Met by Chance*, in which part of the action takes place in the Adirondack Mountains. In *Aristocracy*, however, he effectually combined his interests in international society and the business world. The hero is Jefferson Stockton, a California capitalist and millionaire whose power and self-confidence precede him into every room. When his young wife reveals her social ambitions, he knows exactly how to satisfy them. Millionaires, he explains to her, are graded according to years and grandfathers, and in New York the newly rich man who thinks himself impressive is a fool. As he once ordered ten thousand tons of iron in New York, he will now order about five tons of good society for his wife, but it must be done carefully. The way to enter New York society is to take a house in London, and this Stockton does—after a few farcical episodes in London among the money-hunting European nobility. Although the caricatures of the financier and of the society he encounters weaken the overall effect of the social melodrama, the play has an interesting basic idea, and it held the stage for a respectable run.

Bronson Howard came into the theater at an opportune time—a time when American rather than English actors and managers were beginning to control American theaters and were looking for American playwrights. As a writer-journalist rather than an actor or manager, Howard tried new approaches in order to learn about the theater. His subsequent comments reveal that literary dramatists and elitist critics tried his patience. This was a transition period—Howard's life in the theater—and when it was over, the writing of drama in the United States had undergone a change. Clyde Fitch was making a fortune in New York and elsewhere; Langdon Mitchell and William Vaughn Moody were successful playwrights, while Rachel Crothers and Edward Sheldon were about to appear on the scene. During that transitional period, other dramatists added to the development of an American drama, but no one matched Howard's accomplishments in social melodrama, dramatic theory, and service to American playwrights.

Other major works

NONFICTION: "American Playwrights on the American Drama," 1889; "Our Schools for the Stage," 1900; "The American Drama," 1906; *The Autobiography of a Play*, 1914.

Bibliography
Bogard, Travis, Richard Moody, and Walter J. Meserve. *The Revels History of Drama in English, Volume VIII: American Drama*, 1977.
Clark, Barrett H. *The British and American Drama of To-Day*, 1915, 1921.
Meserve, Walter J. *An Outline History of American Drama*, 1965.
Moses, Montrose J. *The American Dramatist*, 1925, 1964.
Quinn, Arthur Hobson. *A History of the American Drama from the Civil War to the Present Day*, 1936.
Wilson, Garff B. *Three Hundred Years of American Drama and Theatre*, 1973.

Walter J. Meserve

SIDNEY HOWARD

Born: Oakland, California; June 26, 1891
Died: Tyringham, Massachusetts; August 23, 1939

Principal drama

Swords, pr., pb. 1921; *Casanova*, pb. 1921, pr. 1923 (adaptation of Lorenzo de Azertis' play); *S.S. Tenacity*, pr. 1922, pb. 1929 (adaptation of Charles Vildrac's play *Le Paquebot Tenacity*); *Bewitched*, pr. 1924 (with Edward Sheldon); *They Knew What They Wanted*, pr. 1924, pb. 1925; *Lucky Sam McCarver*, pr. 1925, pb. 1926; *The Last Night of Don Juan*, pr. 1925 (adaptation of Edmond Rostand's play *La Dernière Nuit de Don Juan*); *Morals*, pr. 1925 (with Charles Recht; adaption of Ludwig Thoma's play); *Ned McCobb's Daughter*, pr., pb. 1926; *The Silver Cord*, pr. 1926, pb. 1927; *Salvation*, pr. 1928 (with Charles MacArthur); *Olympia*, pr., pb. 1928 (adaptation of Ferenc Molnár's play); *Half Gods*, pr. 1929, pb. 1930; *The Late Christopher Bean*, pr. 1932, pb. 1933 (adapted from René Fauchois' play *Prenez garde à la peinture*); *Alien Corn*, pr., pb. 1933; *Yellow Jack*, pr., pb. 1934 (with Paul de Kruif; based on de Kruif's book *Microbe Hunters*); *Dodsworth*, pr., pb. 1934 (adaptation of Sinclair Lewis' novel); *Paths of Glory*, pr., pb. 1935 (adaptation of Humphrey Cobb's novel); *The Ghost of Yankee Doodle*, pr. 1937, pb. 1938.

Other literary forms

Although best known for his plays, Sidney Howard also translated and adapted a number of works. In his early years, Howard worked as a literary editor and wrote, with Robert Dunn, a collection of articles on strikebreaking agencies entitled *The Labor Spy* (1921). In 1924, he published four stories under the single title *Three Flights Up*. Like Robert E. Sherwood and Clifford Odets, Howard devoted much of his time to writing screenplays, primarily for Samuel Goldwyn's studio. With Wallace Smith, he wrote the script for *Bulldog Drummond* (1929), based on stories by the British writer H. C. McNeile, who wrote under the pen name "Sapper." Howard also adapted two novels by Sinclair Lewis, *Arrowsmith* (in 1931) and *Dodsworth* (in 1936), to the screen. For his 1939 film adaptation of Margaret Mitchell's *Gone with the Wind*, Howard won an Academy Award.

Achievements

While Sidney Howard contributed little that was unique to American drama, his reputation rests chiefly on his ability to focus on limited, narrow subjects and, in the process, to reveal something essential about the human condition. He created a number of substantial and effective plays, characterized by sound craftsmanship, honesty, and skill. In limiting himself to dramatizing concrete, specific situations, he created sharp, telling vignettes about particular people in varied yet specific settings.

Howard's achievements are seen in his expert characterization and in his emphasis on social perspective, which helped his plays transcend the limitations of contemporary drama. In 1925, his efforts were recognized; he was awarded the Pulitzer Prize for *They Knew What They Wanted.*

Biography

Sidney Coe Howard was the son of John Lawrence Howard and Helen Louise Coe. His paternal grandfather, born of English parents, had emigrated from Antrim, Ireland, in 1848 and had settled in Philadelphia. After attending public schools in Oakland, California, Howard was graduated from the University of California in 1915 and then attended George Pierce Baker's Workshop 47 at Harvard University. During this time, Howard began his early collaborative efforts with Edward Sheldon, who had a great influence on the development of American drama. In 1916, Howard received a master of arts degree from Harvard.

World War I interrupted Howard's creative career; inducted into the service in 1916, he served first as an ambulance driver in France and in the Balkans and then as a captain and fighter pilot in the newly formed Air Service. In 1919, Howard joined the editorial staff of the old humor magazine *Life* in New York. Three years later, he became the literary editor of *Life* and was writing and adapting plays. In 1921, he married Clare Eames, an actress, and they had a child, Clare Jenness Howard.

Howard's determined interest in the daily lives of people led him to work in 1923 as a special investigative reporter and fiction writer for *The New Republic* and *International Magazine*. Before settling into the style of social drama that eventually brought him success, Howard wrote his first play, *Swords*, which failed, and collaborated with Sheldon on *Bewitched*.

Following Howard's recognition as a playwright for *They Knew What They Wanted*, he continued over the next five years to write or translate and adapt several plays. Three of these, *Dodsworth*, *Paths of Glory*, and *The Late Christopher Bean*, are among his best contributions to American drama.

Lucky Sam McCarver opened at the Playhouse Theatre in New York on October 21, 1925, and capitalized on the spectacle of affluent life among New York's socialites. The play is an ironic statement on that society and those who aspire to it. *Ned McCobb's Daughter* and *The Silver Cord* both came to New York theaters in 1926. With its well-drawn characters, *The Silver Cord* is one of the outstanding social-thesis plays in American drama. Neither *Salvation* nor *Half Gods* was successful, and after 1929 Howard concentrated on writing screenplays. During the last ten years of his life, Howard continued to write for the stage and achieved moderate success with his adaptation of *The Late Christopher Bean* and with *Alien Corn*. Active in theater affairs, Howard served from 1935 to 1937 as president of the Dramatists Guild, and in 1938—along with Sherwood, S. N. Behrman, Maxwell Anderson, and Elmer Rice—he formed the Playwrights' Company, organized to produce their plays without interference from commercial producers.

In 1930, following the death of Clare Eames, by that time his former wife, Howard married Leopoldine Blaine Damrosch, the daughter of musician Walter Damrosch. They had two children: a daughter, Sidney Damrosch Howard, and a son, Walter Damrosch Howard. Sidney Howard died on August 23, 1939, as a result of a tractor accident on his Massachusetts farm.

Analysis

Sidney Howard was neither an innovator in dramatic form nor a particularly profound writer, and he readily admitted these facts. He was content to "get a kind of glamour around reality," to dare less and achieve more. He was nevertheless a substantial playwright of considerable theatrical skill and imagination who stepped into the ongoing stream of social drama in America and produced at least two major plays in that genre.

Despite a tendency toward preachiness, *They Knew What They Wanted* is an important play for its humanity and for its insight into social morality. A modern version of Dante's story of the love of Paolo and Francesca, it demonstrated Howard's ability to write a compact, effective play.

Tony, a sixty-year-old Italian winegrower, proposes by mail to Amy, a young waitress, whom he has seen once and admired. They correspond, and Amy asks for a photograph of him. Instead, he sends one of Joe, his handsome young hired hand. On his way to the station to pick up Amy, Tony has an automobile accident and is injured. When Amy arrives at the house, she mistakes Joe for Tony, and on discovering that Tony is to be her husband, she is shocked. After the wedding party, Amy, miserable, is left alone with Joe, and they make love. The discovery three months later that Amy is pregnant, Tony's resultant anger, his struggle with his pride, and his final acceptance of and triumph over the trouble, as well as the resolution for all three characters of this dilemma, comprise the heart of the play. All three characters, in the end, know and get what they want, and all are, in the end, satisfied.

In Tony, Howard created his most successful character. The most appealing and most real figure in the play, Tony is also the one most able to deal with the exigencies of the world. He discovers that he can accept Amy's child, love Amy, and find joy in his new family. He becomes not the most miserable of men but a "most happy fella." The other two characters make similar discoveries: Amy discovers that she really cares for Tony and wants to be his wife, and Joe finds that he really values his freedom. The play ends satisfactorily, for the characters and for the audience.

The Silver Cord, although it also suffers from preachment, has a profound effect upon audiences, delving into a deep and often hidden layer of human emotion. Mrs. Phelps, a domineering mother, is in a struggle to possess the love of her two sons and to exclude from their affections the women whom they love. She successfully destroys the love of Robert and his fiancée, Hester, but fails to break up the marriage of her older son, David, and Christina, a more determined woman than Hester and more of a match for Mrs. Phelps. Howard expresses his antipathy toward filial duty grounded on pathological dependence through Christina, who says, "An embryological accident is no ground for honour," and through Hester, who says of children, "Have 'em. Love 'em. And then leave 'em be."

The play dramatizes this conflict—between a "professional" mother and an independent and ambitious wife. Both deserve some sympathy even as each struggles desperately for the fulfillment of her own selfish needs. Christina, however, is not morally disfigured, as is Mrs. Phelps. Christina's concern for her own career is balanced by her more healthy concern for the life of her unborn child and for the freedom to live that she knows is necessary for her own happiness and for David's.

Mrs. Phelps is singularly diabolical, and this makes her a very interesting character; she stalks her sons like prey, weakening their other loyalties with innuendo and crafty appeals for sympathy, then pouncing when these loyalties have been sufficiently worn down. The play is marred, however, by too much weakness in the sons, by the lack of any real dramatic discovery on Christina's part, by the lack of credibility in David's late and under-motivated decision to leave in the end, and, finally, by the playwright's preachiness. By the end of the play, the audience is satisfied: Christina has defeated the villainess after an intense battle, she has helped to free innocent Hester, and she has gained her own personal objective. Christina, however, seems a bit too much like Mrs. Phelps for comfort, and David may well be merely stepping out of one trap and into another. As a social drama with a Freudian thesis, however—the level on which the play was most generally understood—it was successful and powerfully dramatic on the stage.

During the 1920's, Howard adapted several plays and wrote several more. Both *Lucky Sam McCarver* and *Ned McCobb's Daughter*—one a theatrical failure and the other a success—show elements of the social drama at which Howard excelled. Each is concerned with a strong character who faces a series of frustrating social situations and who reacts powerfully to those conditions and frustrations.

Lucky Sam McCarver starts as an analysis of cold, materialistic Sam McCarver but is more effective as the story of a woman who desperately wants love from a man who has only money to give. Sam, hardened in his worship of money, frankly uses his wife and her name and sees nothing beyond his growing empire. Having lost human compassion and the ability to feel, he can only think and contrive; in Howard's world, which is essentially a world of action and feeling rather than thought, Sam has no value.

Unlike the comedy *Ned McCobb's Daughter*, in which social conditions provide the background for Carrie to show her superiority of character and her Yankee determination, *Lucky Sam McCarver* is an unhappy social drama about irresponsible people: a frustrated woman and a materialistic man who will always be "disappointed in the universe." Howard's characters usually know what they want, but Howard invariably controls their destinies. Although he frequently tempers his moral judgments with true mercy, within his definitions of right and wrong he is completely conventional in meting out rewards and punishments, emphasizing his preference for a "satisfactory" ending to a play.

In the 1930's, Howard wrote and adapted several plays, bringing his total output to more than twenty-five plays. Worthy of mention is *Yellow Jack*, written with Paul de Kruif and based on de Kruif's book *Microbe Hunters* (1926). It was not a popular success when first staged, but it has been frequently revived since that time. Set in and around an army barracks near Havana, Cuba, it follows Major Walter Reed and his colleagues' fight to isolate the cause of yellow fever, quietly tracing the events and highlighting the nobility of the characters involved in the enterprise and the sacrifices they made. Again, Howard keeps the focus of the play narrow, allowing no extraneous "love interest" or other episodes to interfere with the progress of the action.

Howard found his greatest success in creating social drama from a mixture of realism, melodrama, and comedy. His major interest in his plays, however, was his characters. Psychological interpretation of character is an essential part of his best plays. More exuberant than thoughtful, he was frequently satisfied to have his characters simply react emotionally to strong stimuli. In *They Knew What They Wanted*, for example, Tony tells Amy: "What you have done is mistake in da head, not in da heart." For Howard, emotion is more important then intellect. Similarly, Christina in *The Silver Cord* at first relies upon reason to resolve her difficulties with Mrs. Phelps, but her attempts fail; intellect is not enough.

Although he generally followed an established trend in American drama, Howard, in his best plays, created strong, compelling characters, interacting in situations that allowed his drama to transcend the limitations of the merely personal. The individualistic, life-affirming spirit of his work was a welcome addition to the social drama of the 1920's.

Other major works

SHORT FICTION: *Three Flights Up*, 1924.

NONFICTION: *The Labor Spy*, 1921 (with Robert Dunn).

SCREENPLAYS: *Bulldog Drummond*, 1929 (with Wallace Smith; based on stories by H. C. McNeile); *Arrowsmith*, 1931 (based on Sinclair Lewis' novel); *Dodsworth*, 1936 (based on Lewis' novel); *Gone with the Wind*, 1939 (based on Margaret Mitchell's novel).

Bibliography

Downer, Alan. *Fifty Years of American Drama 1900-1950*, 1951.

Kaufman, Alvin S., and Franklin D. Case, eds. *Modern Drama in America, Volume I*, 1982.

Krutch, Joseph Wood. *The American Drama Since 1918*, 1957.

Meserve, Walter J. *An Outline History of American Drama*, 1965.

Quinn, Arthur H. *A History of the American Drama from the Civil War to the Present Day*, 1936.

Wilson, Garff B. *Three Hundred Years of American Drama and Theatre*, 1927.

Walter J. Meserve

WILLIAM INGE

Born: Independence, Kansas; May 3, 1913
Died: Los Angeles, California; June 10, 1973

Principal drama

To Bobolink, for Her Spirit, pb. 1950 (one act); *Come Back, Little Sheba*, pr., pb. 1950; *Picnic*, pr., pb. 1953 (revision of manuscript of *Summer Brave*); *Bus Stop*, pr., pb. 1955 (expanded version of his one-act *People in the Wind*, pb. 1962); *The Dark at the Top of the Stairs*, pr., pb. 1957 (originally as *Farther Off from Heaven*, pr. 1947, pb. 1950); *Four Plays by William Inge*, pb. 1958; *The Tiny Closet*, pr. 1959 (in Italy), pb. 1962 (one act); *A Loss of Roses*, pr. 1959, pb. 1960; *The Boy in the Basement*, pb. 1962 (one act); *Bus Riley's Back in Town*, pb. 1962 (one act); *Summer Brave*, pr., pb. 1962 (expansion of the fragmentary "Front Porch"); *Summer Brave and Eleven Short Plays*, pb. 1962; *Natural Affection*, pr. 1963; *Where's Daddy?*, pr., pb. 1966 (originally as *Family Things*, pr. 1965); *Two Short Plays: The Call, and A Murder*, pb. 1968; *Midwestern Manic*, pb. 1969.

Other literary forms

William Inge was fundamentally a dramatist. Atlantic/Little, Brown published two of his novels, *Good Luck, Miss Wyckoff* (1970) and *My Son Is a Splendid Driver* (1971). Bantam published his earlier scenario for *Splendor in the Grass* (1961). The manuscript of his final novel, "The Boy from the Circus," was found on a table in his living room after his suicide. The manuscript had been rejected by a New York publisher and returned to him; he had not opened the envelope containing it. His two published novels and his first screenplay are set in Kansas and are populated by the same sort of lonely, frustrated people found in his major dramas.

Achievements

Although Inge cannot be said to have advanced the technique of modern drama, as Eugene O'Neill did, for example, he was the first notable American dramatist to write seriously and sensitively about the Midwest, much in the tradition of Theodore Dreiser and Sherwood Anderson among novelists, of Carl Sandburg and Edgar Lee Masters among poets, and of Grant Wood among painters. Inge's first five Broadway plays—*Come Back, Little Sheba*, *Picnic*, *Bus Stop*, *The Dark at the Top of the Stairs*, and *A Loss of Roses*—are set in the Midwest and examine in believable and accurate detail the pent-up frustrations of living in the sort of midwestern small towns that Inge knew intimately from his childhood and youth. The Liberty of some of his plays is the Independence, Kansas, of his childhood; great irony underlies his choice of that place-name.

The decade beginning in 1950 was a remarkable one for Inge. It is unique for an unknown playwright to emerge on Broadway with the sort of critical and commercial success that *Come Back, Little Sheba* commanded and then to be able to produce in rapid-fire succession three more commercial triumphs. Inge did just this, following the 1950 production of *Come Back, Little Sheba* with *Picnic* in 1953, *Bus Stop* in 1955, and *The Dark at the Top of the Stairs* in 1957. *Come Back, Little Sheba* ran for 190 performances; the next three plays ran for more than 450 performances apiece.

Come Back, Little Sheba won for its author an award from the New York critics as the most promising playwright of the season. *Picnic* won the Pulitzer Prize, a New York Drama Critics Circle Award, and the Donaldson Award, which it shared with Arthur Miller's *The Crucible* (1953). Even though Inge's next two plays won no awards, they were highly successful. Inge's reputation as a serious dramatist was assured; in addition, his first four full-length plays were made into films that succeeded both critically and commercially.

In 1958, just as Inge crested the wave of popularity to which his first four Broadway plays had brought him, *Four Plays by William Inge* was issued by Random House, which had previously published each of the plays separately. It was followed by Heinemann's British edition in 1960. Inge's next play, *A Loss of Roses*, into whose production the author put a considerable amount of his own money, reached Broadway in 1959 and was rejected by critics and audiences alike. It closed after twenty-five performances, leaving Inge, who was singularly sensitive, severely depressed as well as financially strained.

The failure of *A Loss of Roses* caused Inge to leave New York permanently. At the strong urging of Elia Kazan, a close friend since he had directed *The Dark at the Top of the Stairs*, Inge moved to the West Coast and turned his talents to screenwriting. His first attempt, *Splendor in the Grass*, which Warner Bros. produced, again focused on small-town midwestern life and was so successful that it received the Academy Award for Best Original Screenplay of 1961.

Splendor in the Grass was to be Inge's last artistic triumph. He followed it in 1963 with *Natural Affection*, which played on Broadway for only thirty-six performances and was the subject of even harsher criticism than *A Loss of Roses* had received. Hurt and distraught, Inge returned to California, where he worked on screenplays. He also did a final original screenplay, based on one of his one-act plays entitled *Bus Riley's Back in Town*, about which he wrote (in a letter to R. Baird Shuman of May 20, 1965): "As for *Bus Riley*, the picture is a loss. I took my name off it. I haven't even seen the version they are showing."

Inge died a broken and defeated man, convinced that he had nothing more to say. His legacy to American drama is nevertheless great. He dealt with the Midwest as had no American playwright before him. As his close friend Tennessee Williams had focused dramatic attention on the South, so had Inge focused dramatic attention on the Midwest. He created a gallery of memorable characters, particularly female characters, because he understood the female mind remarkably well.

Inge's Broadway successes and his screenplay for *Splendor in the Grass* have secured his position as an American dramatist. Although he generally lacked the pioneering genius and willingness to experiment with form of a Eugene O'Neill, a Clifford Odets, or a Tennessee Williams, Inge still ranks high among the significant contributors to American theater in the twentieth century.

Biography

William Inge's understanding of the female personality is not surprising in view of the fact that he came from an emphatically female-dominated home. As the youngest of Luther Clayton and Maude Sarah Gibson Inge's five children, Inge identified more closely with his mother and sisters than he did with males. His father was a traveling salesman who spent little time at home during Inge's formative years. The young Inge, much dominated by his mother, early developed an interest in acting, largely through his initial school experiences with recitation.

Popular as a teenager, Inge was a cheerleader and was active in his high school's dramatic programs. He enjoyed acting and continued his studies after high school at the University of Kansas, where he majored in drama and frequently acted in university productions. Still provincially midwestern at the time of his college graduation, Inge feared going to New York to pursue his first love, acting, and went instead to George Peabody College for Teachers in Nashville to prepare for teacher certification and to take a master's degree in education. Inge taught for one year at the high school level in Columbus, Kansas, where he surely met numerous teachers such as those he depicts with such accuracy in *Picnic* and students such as those in *Splendor in the Grass*. For the next ten years, except for a crucial three years as art, music, book, and drama critic for the St. Louis *Star-Times*, Inge taught English and drama at the college level, first at Stephens College in Columbia, Missouri, and then at Washington University in St. Louis.

It was the crucial years away from teaching, from 1943 to 1946, that led Inge into his career as a playwright. In his position as a three-year replacement for a friend on the *Star-Times* who had been drafted, Inge interviewed Tennessee Williams, who was resting at his parents' home in St. Louis after the 1944 Chicago opening of *The Glass Menagerie*. A friendship blossomed, and Williams persuaded Inge to do some serious writing. *Far-*

ther Off from Heaven, the prototype for *The Dark at the Top of the Stairs*, was the result, and in 1947, Margo Jones, whom Inge had met through Williams, produced the play in her theater in Dallas. The production was well received, and Inge was encouraged by its success to continue writing. By 1949, he had abandoned teaching in order to devote himself fully to his writing.

During this period, Inge had become a heavy drinker, and in 1948, he joined Alcoholics Anonymous. Through his association with this organization, he came to understand much more about alcoholism and about alcoholics, information which finds its way directly into *Come Back, Little Sheba* in the person of Doc Delaney, the play's frustrated protagonist.

Similarly, Inge, continually beset by depression, self-doubt, and concern about his homosexuality, which he was never able to accept, began a course of psychoanalysis in 1949, and he was in and out of analysis through the 1950's. Although one may question whether psychoanalysis made Inge any better able to cope with his own fears and frustrations, its influences and effects are clearly seen throughout his work,. particularly in *A Loss of Roses*, *Natural Affection*, and *Where's Daddy?*

Despite the successes he had known, by 1973 Inge felt that he was "written out," that he had nothing more to say. Although he enjoyed his work in theater workshops at the University of California campuses at Los Angeles and Irvine and was successful in them, he was unable to deal with the artistic frustrations that plagued him, and on June 10, 1973, he took his own life.

Analysis

All of William Inge's best instincts as a playwright are at work in *Come Back, Little Sheba*, the story of Doc and Lola Delaney, who are twenty years into a marriage that was forced upon them when the eighteen-year-old Lola became pregnant while the promising young Doc was a medical student. Their hasty marriage was followed by Doc's dropping out of medical school and becoming a chiropractor as well as by the loss of the baby through the bungling of a midwife, to whom Lola went because she was too embarrassed to go to an obstetrician. Lola ends up sterile and, as the action of the play begins, fat and unattractive. Doc has become an alcoholic, but as the play opens, he has been dry for a year.

Come Back, Little Sheba is a study in contrasts. It presents thesis and antithesis but seldom any satisfying or convincing synthesis, which makes it a sound piece of realistic writing. Little Sheba is Lola's lost puppy, who "just vanished one day—vanished into thin air." More than representing a surrogate child, Little Sheba represents Lola's lost youth, and only when Lola stops looking for Sheba is it clear that some resolution has taken place, even though the resolution is not presented as a cure-all for Doc and

Lola Delaney's problems.

The play revolves largely around four characters: Doc; Lola; Marie, their boarder; and Turk, the recurring priapic figure whom Inge later used to keep the action moving in *Picnic* and in other of his plays. Marie, although she is engaged to someone else, is having a brief affair with Turk (significantly, a javelin thrower) prior to the arrival of her fiancé from out of town. Lola is titillated by this tawdry affair and actively encourages it, even though she is planning to fix a special meal for Marie's fiancé, Bruce, when he arrives. Doc, who sees Marie as the daughter he never had, is appalled by the whole misadventure. He falls off the wagon and gets roaring drunk. His drunk scene, in which he threatens passionately to hack off all of Lola's fat, cut off Marie's ankles, and castrate Turk, is the dramatic climax of the play; but he falls into a drunken stupor before he can accomplish any of these vile deeds and is taken off to the drunk tank. So terrified is he by the drunk tank that he returns home chastened, but not before Lola has attempted to go home to her aging parents, only to be rebuffed when she telephones them with her request that they allow her to come home for a while.

As the play ends, Doc pleads with Lola, "Don't ever leave me. *Please* don't ever leave me. If you do, they'd have to keep me down at that place [the drunk tank] all the time." Doc and Lola are back together, not for very positive reasons, but rather because neither has any real alternative.

The characterization and the timing in this play are superb; the control is sure and steady. The business of the play is well taken care of early in the action as Lola, a lonely woman unhappy with herself and with what she has become, talks compulsively to anyone who will listen—the milkman, the postman, the next-door neighbor, and Mrs. Coffman, who in contrast to Lola is neat, clean, and well-organized, as a woman with seven children needs to be. Lola tells the audience all they need to know about her history while convincing them of her loneliness by reaching out desperately to anyone who comes into her purview. The resolution for Lola comes in the last act, when she begins to clean up the house, pay attention to her appearance, and write a note for the milkman rather than lurk to engage him in conversation.

Lola's dream sequences, which hold up quite well psychologically, are skillfully used to handle more of the necessary business of the play. The final dream has to do with Turk and the javelin, which Turk has already described as "a big, long lance. You hold it like this, erect." In Lola's dream, Turk is disqualified in the javelin throwing contest and Doc picks up the javelin "real careful, like it was awful heavy. But you threw it, Daddy, clear, *clear*, up into the sky. And it never came down." Inge's exposure to Freudian psychoanalysis certainly pervades the dream sequences.

Inge does not give the audience an upbeat or hopeful ending in *Come*

Back, Little Sheba; rather, he presents life as it is. Perhaps Lola has matured a little. Perhaps both she and Doc have gained some insights that will help them to accept their lives with a bit more resignation than they might otherwise have, but nothing drastic is likely to happen for either of them. They will live on, wretchedly dependent upon each other. If their marriage lasts, as it probably will, the mortar that holds it together will be dependence more than love. At least Lola has faced reality sufficiently to say, "I don't think Little Sheba's ever coming back, Doc," and to stop searching for her.

Inge's second Broadway success, *Picnic*, started as a fragmentary play, "Front Porch," that Inge wrote shortly after *Farther Off from Heaven*. The original play consisted of little more than character sketches of five women in a small Kansas town. The play grew into *Summer Brave*, a much more fully developed play, and finally into *Picnic*, which is little different from *Summer Brave* except in the resolution of the Madge-Hal conflict.

Four of the five women in *Picnic* live in one house. They are Flo Owens; her two daughters, Millie, a sixteen-year-old tomboy, and Madge, the prettiest girl in town; and their boarder, Rosemary Sydney, a schoolteacher in her thirties. Madge is engaged to marry Alan Seymour. Their next-door neighbor is sixty-year-old Helen Potts, who also participates in the action of the play. These women are all sexually frustrated; although Madge and Rosemary both have suitors, the relationships are specifically delineated as nonsexual.

Into this tense setting is introduced an incredibly handsome male animal, Hal Carter, who exudes sexuality. As insecure as he is handsome, Hal is down on his luck and has arrived in town looking for his friend Alan Seymour, who might be able to give him a job. Hungry, he exchanges some work in Helen Potts's yard for a meal. He works bare-chested, much to the consternation of the women, whose upbringing decrees that they feign shock at this display but whose natural impulses are in conflict with their conservative upbringing.

Hal, reminiscent of Turk in *Come Back, Little Sheba*, causes chaos, as might be expected. The play focuses on the women, and Hal serves as the catalyst. Inge's ability to draw convincing characters, particularly female characters, is particularly evident in *Picnic*. He maintains his clear focus on the women in the play, using Hal precisely as he needs to in order to reveal these women as the psychologically complex beings they are. Never does the focus slip; never does the control over material and characters waver.

As the action develops toward a climax in the second act, Hal's physical presence more than anything else pushes the conflict to its dramatically necessary outcome. Millie and Rosemary start drinking from Hal's liquor bottle after Hal turns his attention from Millie to her more mature sister. Both Millie and Rosemary are soon drunk. Flo vents her own frustrations by upbraiding the two of them, but not before Rosemary, humiliated that Hal is not available to her and distressed that she finds him so attractive, shrieks at him that he came from the gutter and that he will return to the gutter. This emotional scene heightens Hal's insecurity, which is necessary if the play is to proceed convincingly to a love affair between Hal and Madge, an outcome that seems inevitable.

The screaming fit also forces Rosemary to face reality and to realize that her erstwhile suitor, Howard, is probably her only realistic out if she is not to continue teaching and if she is not to become frustrated and grow old alone. She goes off with Howard and yields to him, after which she asks, then begs him to marry her. In the play's final version, he will go only so far as to say that he will come back in the morning but when he does, Rosemary has already spread the news that she and Howard are going to marry, so that when Howard arrives, everyone congratulates him, and he has no choice but to leave with Rosemary, presumably to marry her. Inge is intrigued by the theme of forced marriage, which recurs in nearly all of his major plays, and *Picnic* offers a striking variation on the theme.

Back at the picnic, Alan and Hal have engaged in fisticuffs and Alan has reported Hal to the police, forcing him to leave town in order to avoid arrest. In *Summer Brave*, Hal leaves and Madge stays behind; at the urging of Joshua Logan, Inge changed the ending of the play, so that in *Picnic*, Madge packs her suitcase and follows Hal a short time after his forced departure.

Bus Stop, despite its popular acceptance, does not have the stature of *Come Back, Little Sheba* or *Picnic*. An expanded version of Inge's one-act *People in the Wind*, *Bus Stop* is set in a small crossroads restaurant between Kansas City and Wichita, where the passengers on a bus are stranded because of a blizzard. Among the passengers is Bo Decker, a twenty-one-year-old cowpoke from Montana who is traveling with Virgil Blessing, a middle-aged father surrogate (suggestive of Pinky in *Where's Daddy?*), and with a brainless little singer, Cherie, whom he met in a Kansas City nightclub, where she was performing. Bo was pure until he met Cherie, but now, in a comical role-reversal, he has lost his virginity to her and is insisting that she return to Montana with him to make him an honest man. Cherie joins Bo and Virgil, and they are on their way west when the bus is forced by the weather to pull off the road.

Cherie has second thoughts about going to Montana, and after thinking the matter over, she accuses Bo of abducting her and the police become involved in the situation. Bo has a fight with the sheriff. He is humiliated and apologizes to everyone in the restaurant, including Cherie. Before the play is over, however, Bo asks Cherie to marry him, she agrees, and they set out for Montana, leaving Virgil Blessing behind and alone.

The development of *Bus Stop* is thin and the characterization, particularly of Bo, is not close to the high level reached in *Come Back, Little Sheba* and *Picnic*. Although Bo is similar in many ways to Turk and Hal, he is made of cardboard and lacks the multidimensional elements that make Turk and Hal convincing.

The play is stronger in the presentation of its minor characters, particularly the lonely, frustrated Grace, a middle-aged woman who lives at the small crossroads where the bus has stopped and who works the night shift in the restaurant. She has sex with a truck driver not because she loves him but because he keeps her from being lonely. In the end, she and Virgil Blessing are left alone in the restaurant. The bus has pulled out, and one might think that Grace and Virgil are the answer to each other's loneliness, but Inge does not provide a double resolution in this play. He permits Bo and Cherie to leave on a somewhat optimistic note, much as he allowed Hal and Madge a future in *Picnic*, but he wisely backs off from providing the pat resolution that a romance between Grace and Virgil would have provided, because the psychological motivation for such a relationship has not been built sufficiently throughout the play.

The original play, *People in the Wind*, contained two characters who were not included in *Bus Stop*. They are two older women, apparently both unmarried and seemingly sisters, who are going to visit their niece. It appears that they want the niece to take them in in their old age, but they are not sure she will do so. They are nervous, drinking bicarbonate of soda to calm their stomachs. They represent the fate that can befall people who do not form close family ties early in their lives. In dropping them from *Bus Stop*, Inge was clearly opting to make the focus of the later play love rather than loneliness, which was the central focus of *People in the Wind*.

The Dark at the Top of the Stairs, the finished version of *Farther Off from Heaven*, is Inge's most autobiographical play. In it, the author returns to a plot centering on a family, and this time, it is clearly Inge's own family that he is writing about. Rubin Flood is a harness salesman who travels a great deal, leaving his children, Sonny and Reenie, in a mother-dominated home. The setting is a small town in Oklahoma.

Inge, who had been in psychoanalysis for several years when he wrote *The Dark at the Top of the Stairs*, paid particular attention to the Oedipal elements of the mother-son relationship in this play and in two subsequent plays, *A Loss of Roses* and *Natural Affection*, although not with the success that he achieved in this earlier presentation.

Rubin Flood and his wife, Cora, were married early, propelled into marriage by Rubin's unmanageable libido. The marriage has encountered difficulties, which come to a head when Rubin, having lost his job—a fact he keeps from his wife—discovers that Cora has bought Reenie an expensive dress for a dance given at the country club by the nouveau riche Ralstons. He demands that the dress be returned for a refund, and a heated argument ensues, during which Cora taunts Rubin to strike her. He obliges and then leaves, vowing never to return. In act 2, Cora's sister, Lottie, and her dentist husband, Morris, have arrived for a visit. Cora hopes that she will be able to persuade Lottie to take her and the children in now that Rubin has abandoned them. In this scene, also, Reenie's blind date for the dance, Sammy Goldenbaum, arrives. A cadet at a nearby military academy, Sammy is meticulously polite and none too secure. His exquisite manners charm Lottie and Morris before he and the pathologically shy Reenie depart for the dance. Once at the dance, Reenie introduces Sammy to the hostess, who is drunk, and Reenie leaves the dance, not telling Sammy she is going. He tries to find her but cannot.

In act 3, Reenie's friend Flirt appears with the news that Sammy took the train to Oklahoma City, rented a hotel room, and killed himself, presumably because the drunken Mrs. Ralston, on discovering that Sammy was Jewish, had asked him to leave the party. Sammy's suicide forces the principal characters to reconsider their lives, and the play ends somewhat on the upbeat. Rubin has returned home. He is tamed, as is evidenced by the fact that he confesses to Cora, "I'm scared. I don't know how I'll make out. I . . . I'm scared," and that he leaves his boots outside, not wanting to dirty up Cora's clean house.

Sonny Flood, who has been an obnoxious child throughout the play, apparently has turned the corner by the end of it. He volunteers to take his distraught sister to the movies, and when his mother tries to kiss him good-bye, he declines to kiss her, giving the audience an indication that his Oedipal tendencies are now coming under control.

Inge tried to do something daring in *The Dark at the Top of the Stairs*, and although he failed, it was a creditable attempt. He juggled two significant conflicts, the Rubin-Cora conflict and the Sammy-society conflict. As the play developed, the conflict involving the suicide was not sufficiently prepared for to be wholly believable. Inge's admitted purpose was to use the suicide subplot to divert the attention of the audience from the conflict between Rubin and Cora, so that they could return to this conflict in the last act with a fresher view.

The suicide subplot has been severely attacked by critics. It is, however, a serious misinterpretation to view the suicide as an event which the author intended to present realistically. It can succeed only as a symbol, serving the useful function of promoting the resolution of the main conflict. This is not to justify the suicide subplot, which is a weakness in the play, but rather to demonstrate the artistic purposes Inge envisioned for it.

None of Inge's later plays achieved the standard of his four Broadway successes. Some of his most interesting work is found in his one-act plays, fourteen of which are available in print. Had Inge lived longer, probably some of the materials in these plays would have lent themselves to further development as full-length dramas; particularly notable are *To Bobolink, for Her Spirit*, *The Tiny Closet*, and *The Boy in the Basement*.

Inge understood both the people and the social order of the Midwest, particularly the matriarchal family structure common to much of the area. Inge's midwestern plays reverberate with authenticity. His first four Broadway plays depict their commonplace characters with extraordinary sensitivity, building through accounts of their prosaic lives toward a pitch of frustration that is communicated to audiences with enormous impact. By capturing so deftly this pervasive sense of frustration, Inge presents the universal which must be a part of any successful drama. Audiences left Inge's early plays with an internalized sense of the gnawing isolation and conflict that his characters experienced. This is his legacy to American drama.

Other major works

NOVELS: *Good Luck, Miss Wyckoff*, 1970; *My Son Is a Splendid Driver*, 1971.

SCREENPLAYS: *Splendor in the Grass*, 1961; *All Fall Down*, 1962; *Bus Riley's Back in Town*, 1964.

Bibliography

Diehl, Digby. "Interview with William Inge," in *Behind the Scenes: Theatre and Film Interviews from the Transatlantic Review*, 1971. Edited by Joseph McCrindle.

Gould, Jean. *Modern American Playwrights*, 1966.

McClure, Arthur F. *William Inge: A Bibliography*, 1982.

Newquist, Roy, ed. *Counterpoint*, 1964.

Shuman, R. Baird. *William Inge*, 1965.

Sievers, Wieder D. *Freud on Broadway: A History of Psychoanalysis and the American Drama*, 1955.

R. Baird Shuman

HENRY JAMES

Born: New York, New York; April 15, 1843
Died: London, England; February 28, 1916

Principal drama

Daisy Miller, pb. 1883 (adaptation of his novel); *The American*, pr. 1891, pb. 1949 (adaptation of his novel); *Theatricals: Tenants and Disengaged*, pb. 1894; *The Reprobate*, pb. 1895, pr. 1919; *Theatricals, Second Series: The Album and The Reprobate*, pb. 1895; *Guy Domville*, pr. 1895, pb. 1949; *The High Bid*, pr. 1908, pb. 1949; *The Other House*, wr. 1909, pb. 1949; *The Outcry*, wr. 1909, pr. 1917, pb. 1949; *The Saloon*, pr. 1911 (one act); *The Complete Plays of Henry James*, pb. 1949 (Leon Edel, editor).

Other literary forms

Henry James was a prolific writer, most lauded for his fiction. His best-known novels, on the intersection of American and European manners and morals, include *The American* (1877), *The Europeans* (1878), *Daisy Miller* (1878), *The Portrait of a Lady* (1881), *The Wings of the Dove* (1902), *The Ambassadors* (1903), and *The Golden Bowl* (1904). He combined his study of mannered society with an evaluation of social and political justice in *The Bostonians* (1886) and *The Princess Casamassima* (1886); in *The Tragic Muse* (1890), he produced his one novel about the theater. James also wrote more than one hundred short stories and tales (now collected in Leon Edel's twelve-volume *The Complete Tales of Henry James*, 1962-1964). James was a perceptive critic of his own fiction as well as that of others; his study *The Art of Fiction* (1884) is a seminal work of its kind. He prefaced many of his novels with long discussions of fiction writing (collected by R. P. Blackmur in *The Art of the Novel: Critical Prefaces*, 1934) and wrote essays on other fiction writers, both contemporaries and predecessors, among them Nathaniel Hawthorne (*Hawthorne*, 1879), Honoré de Balzac, Anthony Trollope, George Eliot, Robert Louis Stevenson, Ivan Turgenev, and Charles Dickens. He also wrote theater reviews and essays on playwrights from William Shakespeare to Henrik Ibsen, which are collected in *The Scenic Art* (1948; Allan Wade, editor). James was a major travel writer of his day, contributing his essays on England and Europe to American publications such as *The Nation*, *Atlantic Monthly*, and the New York *Tribune*. After a return visit to the United States, he wrote *The American Scene* (1907), a reflection on American life. He wrote a biography of his sculptor friend, *William Wetmore Story and His Friends* (1903), and completed two volumes of memoirs, *A Small Boy and Others* (1913) and *Notes of a Son and Brother* (1914). An edition of his letters has been edited by Leon Edel (*Henry James Letters*, 1974-1984).

Achievements

James's novels detail the complexities of human relationships; his exploration of consciousness and of narrative viewpoints led, in his more mature works, to the psychological realism for which his novels are chiefly remembered. James's reputation as a dramatist never equaled his reputation as a novelist. James saw five of his plays professionally produced and five others published, but of his fifteen completed plays, none was both produced and published during his lifetime. Most of James's plays became a part of English dramatic literature only in 1949, some thirty-three years after James's death, when they were collected by Leon Edel in *The Complete Plays of Henry James*. Consequently, James's importance as a playwright stems neither from influential productions nor from timely publications. He is a minor but unique figure in English-language drama, valuable for his ability to treat common turn-of-the-century dramatic themes and forms in an uncommon way. While he borrowed liberally from the French well-made drama he admired, his plays are best understood as English comedies of manners. James took the British stage tradition of William Congreve, William Wycherley, Sir George Etherege, Oliver Goldsmith, and Richard Brinsley Sheridan, refined its upper-class milieu, and in doing so clarified the comedy of manners' conflation of manners and morals. As James's characters struggle for a livable synthesis of manners and morals, James focuses on understanding the special social skills, limitations, and perceptions of women. James realized the full dramatic potential of his innovative comedy of manners only once, in *The High Bid*, a play which stands as an emblem of his successful distillation of the dramatic tradition. While James's plays often suffer from oblique dialogue, melodrama, and flimsy plots, his dramatic works that came after *The American* are generally more graceful and are often more substantial than is the successful West End fare of such contemporaries as Arthur Wing Pinero and Henry Arthur Jones.

James's theater interests were encouraged by such important figures as actresses Elizabeth Robins and Fanny Kemble, writer and producer Harley Granville-Barker, and playwright George Bernard Shaw; his work was commissioned by the actress Ellen Terry and by producer-managers Augustin Daly, Charles Frohman, Edward Compton, Sir John Hare, and Sir Johnston Forbes-Robertson. James's achievements as a playwright, however, remain limited. While his plays are stageable (two were successfully produced in London in the late 1960's), his work has found success on television, stage, and screen only through the adaptations of his fiction by other writers. When he first edited James's plays, Leon Edel suggested that they were most important as experiments in the "dramatic method" which enabled James to write his last novels. Many critics join Edel in finding the plays most important as adjuncts to James's fiction.

Biography

Henry James, Jr., was the second of five children born to Mary Robertson Walsh and Henry James, Sr. A friend of Ralph Waldo Emerson and a follower of the Swedish philosopher-theologian Emanuel Swedenborg, Henry James, Sr., advocated a "sensuous" rearing of his children. This amounted to showering his five children with educational opportunities and encouraging them to adopt an individual morality. While much of the young James's education occurred at home and through extensive foreign travel (his first trip abroad came when he was five months old and was followed by several more stays during his childhood and adolescence), he also had tutors and attended various schools in the United States and in Europe, including Harvard Law School. James's family was of great importance to him throughout his life. He was close to his parents until they died in 1882 and remained close to his siblings—especially William, his older brother and greatest rival, who gained fame as a psychologist and philosopher, and his only sister, Alice, whom James helped care for during her many long illnesses. The frequent, long, newsy, philosophical letters which passed between James and his brother and sister suggest the interests, love, and concern the three shared.

When James traveled to Europe in 1872 at the age of twenty-nine, he began the first of his extended stays abroad. He lived in the United States only for brief stretches of time after this, settling permanently in Europe in 1875. His preference for foreign residency led him, in 1915, the year before his death, to become a naturalized British citizen. James spent the longest stretches of time in England—both in London, where he set up several residences, and in Rye, Sussex, where he took out a long lease on Lamb House. He also paid lengthy visits to France and Italy. James documented such foreign living in the many travel pieces he wrote for American readers but put it to best use in his fiction and drama, where the American abroad and the clash of American and European manners were his special terrain. During his early years in the United States and abroad, James published stories, reviews, essays, and novels while he developed important literary friendships with William Dean Howells, Henry Adams, Robert Louis Stevenson, Ivan Turgenev, Gustave Flaubert, and Émile Zola.

From the publication of his first novel, *Roderick Hudson*, in 1875, the greatest share of James's life was devoted to his fiction writing. Writing was a daily concern, for most of James's work, even his novels, appeared first in magazines such as *Macmillan's Magazine*, *Century Magazine*, *Atlantic Monthly*, and *Harper's Weekly*, which had demanding deadlines. James's preoccupation with his writing was also an aspect of his concern about money; he appears to have had enough money to live comfortably, but he constantly worried about income and expenses. The course of his career has generally been measured by the fluctuating success of his fiction. James gained his early reputation from novels such as *The American*, *Daisy Miller*, and *The Portrait of a Lady*, in which he developed his world of cross-cultural confrontations and integration. During the 1880's, however, with the publication of the more overtly political novels *The Bostonians* and *The Princess Casamassima*, James lost public favor. While production of his stories continued to be prolific, it was in the first decade of the new century, with the publication of his last, long novels—*The Wings of the Dove*, *The Ambassadors*, and *The Golden Bowl*—that he gained his stature as "the Master." James's American tour in 1904, when he returned after a twenty-one-year absence, occasioned *The American Scene*, a volume of essays on his homeland. From 1907 to 1909, James prepared the prefaces and revisions of his life's work for the twenty-four volumes of the New York edition, issued by Scribner's. Although sales of this collected edition disappointed James, his literary reputation had been secured.

While producing novels, stories, travel pieces, reviews, and critical essays, James also managed a full social life. He was a welcome guest at English country-house weekends and a seemingly essential addition to American expatriate households in London, Paris, Rome, Florence, and Venice. His friendships with Americans James Russell Lowell (United States ambassador to Great Britain), Grace Norton and the Curtises (Bostonian socialites), Francis Boott and his daughter Lizzie (Bostonians with European art interests), John Singer Sargent and Edwin Abbey (American artists), and others were cemented by extensive correspondence as well as social visits. Late in life, James traveled and corresponded with American novelist Edith Wharton and was neighbor to H. G. Wells. James's brother and sister, William and Alice, remained James's most life-sustaining connections after their parents died in 1882. James traveled in Europe and to the United States to visit and care for both, and he mourned them deeply when they died (Alice in 1892 and William in 1910). James never married, finding marriage anathema to his art, though he was romantically pursued by Constance Fenimore Woolson, a fellow American writer who was James's close friend from 1880 to her death in 1894. Late in his life, James had close attachments to several of his young admirers, including Jocelyn Persse, Howard Sturgis, and Hendrik Andersen.

James's interest in the theater culminated in the five years from 1890 to 1895, when he considered himself mainly a playwright, but lasted throughout his life. Some of James's most vivid childhood memories include early trips to Broadway and productions of Shakespeare, Dickens, and Harriet Beecher Stowe's *Uncle Tom's Cabin* (1852). As a teenager, he dabbled in playwriting, and one of his first pieces of critical writing was in response to the absorbing performance of an actress. James's several extended stays in Paris in the 1870's convinced him of the vitality of the French theater, and in his essays on the Théâtre Français and on French playwrights such as

Victorien Sardou and Alexandre Dumas, *fils*, he displayed his respect for the well-made play he would use as an early model for his own drama. After James completed *The Tragic Muse*, his novel about the London theater, he devoted the next five years of his life to theatergoing and playwriting; biographer Leon Edel contends that James never wrote with greater intensity. The embarrassment of the opening night of his play *Guy Domville* in 1895 provoked James to declare that he would never write for theater again, but during the remaining years of his life he continued to write plays, attend the theater regularly, and maintain his friendships with actresses, producers, and playwrights. In 1909, James even found himself lobbying the British Parliament for a relaxation of stage censorship.

Some of James's last writings were memoirs of his childhood, in which he recorded his vivid memories of early theater experiences. He continued to write fiction to the last, leaving two unfinished novels at his death. His final years were shadowed by the outbreak of World War I, which James saw as a negation of the world and the art in which he believed. After he had sustained a stroke in 1915, William James's widow, Alice, and her son and daughter, Harry and Peggy, came from the United States to nurse James until his death in February of 1916. The British government bestowed the Order of Merit on James shortly before he died.

Analysis

Henry James's legacy to drama is a perspective on American and British upper- and middle-class social life that no one else could imitate. He brought to his drama the multicultural understanding that was the basis of his best fiction. Onstage, as in a narrative, he tracked turn-of-the-century Americans and their English counterparts through courtship and marriage, leisure and business, money and art. The drama that resulted was not always successful but was an instructive experiment in dramatic style. Concentrating his effort on the creation of a social milieu where manners function as they should, James offered a world where morality is not a matter of right and wrong but a negotiating between individual wants and society's needs. The two most important components of the milieu, or atmosphere, in James's plays are the women who are in control and the missions of social and moral salvation on which they embark.

James was influenced by two dramatic traditions—those of the French and the English theaters. James's intimate knowledge of French theater that he acquired in Paris convinced him that the well-made play was the model to imitate. In his earliest plays, he tried to approximate the neat plots, the series of climaxes, and the easy identification of right and wrong he found in the French drama. As James himself showed in his comparative studies of English and French drama, however, the French model could not be translated neatly into English. James had often complained of the crude morality of English theater audiences, going so far as to label its tastes immoral, yet as he practiced his own playwriting skills in the 1890's, it became clear that he was finding the English tradition of the comedy of manners as useful a model as the French tradition of the well-made play. Borrowing from the English tradition both a striving to balance opposites and a stylized concentration on wit, social artistry, and women, James wrote his best plays.

James's theater career is divided in two by the ill-fated production of *Guy Domville* in 1895. In the first part of his career, while still in his twenties, James wrote three short plays which were published as short stories, "Pyramus and Thisbe," "Still Waters," and "A Change of Heart," which suggest his attraction to witty, comic dialogue and romantic plots. These were followed by adaptations of his novels *Daisy Miller* and *The American*, the first commissioned for an American production with Daniel Frohman in 1882 but never produced, and the second commissioned by British manager Edward Compton in 1889 and produced in 1891. Neither adaptation was successful, but James's lifelong desire to write for the theater had been awakened and he went on to spend the five years from 1890 to 1895 consumed by drama. These years, which Edel has labeled "the dramatic years," are marked in James's letters, notebooks, and life by the great hopes and disappointments tied to the stage. Although James completed at least six plays and parts of several others during these years, only *The American* and *Guy Domville* were produced. When James was hooted offstage during the curtain call of *Guy Domville* in January of 1895, he pronounced himself done with theater. James's letters of early 1895 are full of his feeling that drama (the written product) must be separated from theater (the onstage product), but, as his later involvement with the theater attests, he could not relinquish the hope of seeing his plays produced. While the second half of James's theater career, after 1895, was not marked by the great energy, commitment, and concentration of the earlier period, the plays of this period are more mature and natural. James wrote an early version of *The High Bid* immediately after the *Guy Domville* debacle and completed four plays after 1895, his best among them.

The failures in James's plays are of two extremes, represented by his earliest (*The American*) and latest (*The Outcry*) full-length dramatic works. When James adapted his novel *The American* for the stage in 1890, his decision to use the French well-made play as a model led him to simplify the cultural collisions of the story, so that in the play, the cultured French become everything bad and the innocent American Christopher Newman is everything good. James's imitation of his French model also produced superfluous entrances and exits and melodramatic dialogue and confrontations, and necessitated the addition of a neat, happy ending. Later, James would build a synthesis out of the meeting of European and American morals by borrowing from the comedy of manners, but in this play he offered only a stalemate. By the time of James's last full-length play, *The Outcry* (written in 1909), he had mastered the basics of dramatic construction, but the play is nevertheless a failure, the wit and repartee of its dialogue obscured by oblique references and convoluted thinking. *The Outcry* is too much art and too little life. James's best plays—*The Reprobate, Guy Domville*, and *The High Bid*—offer believable social milieus and delightful characters and dialogue.

   The Reprobate is the best of the four plays James published in 1894 and 1895 in his two-volume series, *Theatricals: Tenants and Disengaged* and *Theatricals, Second Series: The Album and The Reprobate*. The play's two main characters, Mrs. Freshville and Paul Doubleday, are former lovers who meet by chance at the Hampton Court villa of Mr. Bonsor. Mrs. Freshville is there chasing a new love, Captain Chanter, although she eventually ends up with a third man, Pitt Brunt. Doubleday lives there as a ward of Mr. Bonsor; Doubleday is the "reprobate" of the title, whose past indiscretions have necessitated his now being closely guarded. In the course of the play he matures, aided by both Mrs. Freshville and his new love, Blanche Amber. The play is the earliest example of James's mastery of dramatic form. The tight construction of the play is suspenseful, not artificial, and melodrama has become a technique James uses to good effect at the end of his acts. James has also adapted the milieu of the comedy of manners successfully. The dialogues are enticing mixtures of wit, innuendo, and manipulation, and the comedy-of-manners emphasis on social decorum and romance is believable.

   James also developed, in *The Reprobate*, the controlling female character who would become the hallmark of his drama. Mrs. Freshville assumes control of the play's events from her first entrance, displaying her understanding of her social world as one where a person gains power by knowing how to play social games. Blanche Amber is, in many ways, a younger Mrs. Freshville, just learning how her world operates and practicing her newfound social skills. Together, Blanche Amber and Mrs. Freshville direct attention to the issues of the play as they set out to "save" Doubleday. They teach the overprotected Doubleday that social power lies in an understanding of manners, and they teach him how to use that power. By the end of the play, he has learned his lesson well, and his message is James's: Good, bad, and freedom are relative concepts which must be negotiated in the world of manners. The play's first production came in 1919, in London, after James's death. It received both praise and criticism but established the stageworthiness of James's delicate brand of manners comedy.

   Guy Domville is the best known of James's dramas, although it is remembered for its melodramatic stage failure rather than its artistic merits. James wrote the play in 1893 for George Alexander, the popular actor-manager of London's fashionable St. James's Theatre, and worked closely with Alexander and his cast during rehearsals. On the play's opening night, January 5, 1895, however, James was too nervous to watch the production of his own play and spent the evening at a production of Oscar Wilde's *An Ideal Husband*. In his absence, James's first act met with great approval, but his second act was jeered, and the third merely tolerated. When James returned to the St. James's Theatre, he was encouraged by Alexander to acknowledge the curtain-call applause, completely unprepared for the vicious disapproval and hooting with which the audience greeted him. He left the stage "green with dismay" (in the words of actor Franklyn Dyall) and vowed to friends that he would abandon the theater altogether. The play continued its run for four weeks and did not, in the end, mark the conclusion of James's playwriting career, but James's attitude to playwriting had been irrevocably changed. He would never again write plays in which he made such a personal investment.

As even the first-night audience knew, however, the play had its merits. Although *Guy Domville* is not a comedy of manners, James had created for this serious drama a mannered milieu which had a grace, charm, and delicacy rare on the English stage. Reviewers including Arthur B. Walkley and George Bernard Shaw, applauded a dialogue that was witty and playful while allowing the characters to discuss the play's serious issues. While the play, like most of James's other plays, has a love interest, that love is a platonic one between Guy Domville, a young man about to enter the Church, and Mrs. Peverel, a widow whose child Guy is tutoring. Instead of detailing this love, James focuses on the choice Guy must make between entering the Church and accepting his family's call to join them in the fast-paced social world. The play is marred by the melodrama of an unbelievable scene in act 2 in which Guy and another character, George Round, feign drunkenness to trick each other, but generally its topics, seriously expressed, are those of James's other plays: the potential artificiality of mannered life, the saving of individual freedom and morality, and the connection between manners and morals. The play is atypical of his work in that it is not a comedy and is not centered on a powerful woman, but it is the first of James's plays in which his central character is portrayed as a social "artist" who masters the "art" of living.

Also in 1895, shortly after the stage failure of *Guy Domville*, James wrote the one-act "Summersoft" for British actress Ellen Terry. Terry never performed the play, but James expanded it to the full three-act play *The High Bid* in 1907 and saw it successfully performed both in Edinburgh and London by Sir Johnston Forbes-Robertson and his company in 1908. The play is James's best because in it he combined the clean dramatic lines that he mastered in his earlier plays with the cultural insights of his last years. The key to the play's success is Mrs. Gracedew, an American widow who uses her position as a cultural outsider to show the play's Britons why their society's traditions and manners are sacred. Mrs. Gracedew comes to Covering End, the family home of Captain Yule, merely to visit, but finds herself obliged to save the majestic home from the greedy Mr. Prodmore. She also saves Prodmore's daughter, Cora, from a bad love match and successfully engineers her own love match with Yule.

Specific structural techniques James had garnered from his long apprenticeship to the well-made play—suspenseful act closings and ups and downs in a character's fortunes—embellish one of the simplest of James's play plots in *The High Bid*. Such simplicity is balanced by the rich comedy-of-manners milieu, with characters aware of decorum and full of politeness and well-timed deference. Because Mrs. Gracedew—as an American—is an outsider to this mannered world, she has learned its ways almost better than the natives. More than any other character, she commands this world of nuance through innuendo and indirection, wit and wordplay. In her, James created his fullest portrait of the social artist and social savior. What Mrs. Gracedew must save is upper-class British society, a mission accomplished in part through her alliance with young Cora, in part by detailing for others, primarily Yule, the ideals of mannered life, which preserve culture and civilization. While the progressive Yule raises important questions about inequities in this system that Mrs. Gracedew defends, she is successful in her mission: She saves a world where manners are morals and life is a delicate art, as James himself sought to save the comedy of manners as a viable dramatic form. In a series of letters that he exchanged with George Bernard Shaw in 1907, James defended his dramatic art as a rarefied and complex image of life, valuable precisely because it challenges audiences to strive for the most that they can possibly achieve in life. In *The High Bid*, James created such a dramatic world, where life is an art worth saving.

Other major works

NOVELS: *Roderick Hudson*, 1875; *The American*, 1877; *The Europeans*, 1878; *Daisy Miller*, 1878; *Washington Square*, 1880; *The Portrait of a Lady*, 1881; *The Bostonians*, 1886; *The Princess Casamassima*, 1886; *The Tragic Muse*, 1890; *What Maisie Knew*, 1897; *The Awkward Age*, 1899; *The Wings of the Dove*, 1902; *The Ambassadors*, 1903; *The Golden Bowl*, 1904.

SHORT FICTION: *A Passionate Pilgrim*, 1875; *The Madonna of the Future*, 1879; *The Siege of London*, 1883; *Tales of Three Cities*, 1884; *The Author of Beltraffio*, 1885; *The Aspern Papers*, 1888; *The Lesson of the Master*, 1892; *Terminations*, 1895; *Embarrassments*, 1896; *The Real Thing*, 1898; *The Two Magics: The Turn of the Screw and Covering End*, 1898; *The Soft Side*, 1900; *The Better Sort*, 1903; *The Novels and Tales of Henry James*, 1907-1909 (24 volumes); *The Finer Grain*, 1910; *A Landscape Painter*, 1919; *Travelling Companions*, 1919; *Master Eustace*, 1920; *Henry James: Selected*

Short Stories, 1950; *Henry James: Eight Tales from the Major Phase*, 1958; *The Complete Tales of Henry James*, 1962-1964 (12 volumes, Leon Edel).

NONFICTION: *Transatlantic Sketches*, 1875; *French Poets and Novelists*, 1878; *Hawthorne*, 1879; *A Little Tour of France*, 1884; *The Art of Fiction*, 1884; *William Wetmore Story and His Friends*, 1903; *English Hours*, 1905; *The American Scene*, 1907; *Italian Hours*, 1909; *A Small Boy and Others*, 1913 (memoirs); *Notes of a Son and Brother*, 1914 (memoirs); *The Art of the Novel: Critical Prefaces*, 1934 (R. P. Blackmur, editor); *The Notebooks of Henry James*, 1947 (F. O. Matthiessen and Kenneth B. Murdock, editors); *The Scenic Art*, 1948 (Allan Wade, editor); *Henry James Letters*, 1974-1984 (5 volumes; Leon Edel, editor).

Bibliography

Carlson, Susan L. *Women of Grace: James's Plays and the Comedy of Manners*, 1985.

Edel, Leon. "Henry James: The Dramatic Years," in *The Complete Plays of Henry James*, 1949.

———————— . *Henry James*, 1953-1978 (5 volumes).

King, Kimball. "Theory and Practice in the Plays of Henry James," in *Modern Drama*. May, 1967, pp. 24-33.

Kossman, Rudolph. *Henry James: Dramatist*, 1969.

Levy, Leo B. *Versions of Melodrama: A Study of the Fiction and Drama of Henry James, 1865-1897*, 1957.

McElderry, Bruce R., Jr. *Henry James*, 1965.

Peacock, Ronald. "Henry James and the Drama," in *The Poet in the Theatre*, 1946.

Susan Carlson

HENRY ARTHUR JONES

Born: Grandborough, England; September 20, 1851
Died: London, England; January 7, 1929

Principal drama

Hearts of Oak, pr. 1879, pb. 1885 (also known as *Honour Bright*); *A Clerical Error*, pr. 1879, pb. 1904; *The Silver King*, pr. 1882, pb. 1907 (with Henry Herman); *Saints and Sinners*, pr. 1884, pb. 1891; *Wealth*, pr. 1889; *The Middleman*, pr. 1889, pb. 1907; *Judah*, pr. 1890, pb. 1894; *The Crusaders*, pr. 1891, pb. 1893; *The Dancing Girl*, pr. 1891, pb. 1907; *The Bauble Shop*, pr. 1893, pb. 1893(?); *The Tempter*, pr. 1893, pb. 1898; *The Masqueraders*, pr. 1894, pb. 1899; *The Case of Rebellious Susan*, pr. 1894, pb. 1897; *The Triumph of the Philistines*, pr. 1895, pb. 1899; *Michael and His Lost Angel*, pr., pb. 1896; *The Liars*, pr. 1897, pb. 1901; *The Physician*, pr. 1897, pb. 1899; *Carnac Sahib*, pr., pb. 1899; *Mrs. Dane's Defence*, pr. 1900, pb. 1905; *The Lackey's Carnival*, pr., pb. 1900; *The Princess's Nose*, pr., pb. 1902; *Whitewashing Julia*, pr. 1903, pb. 1905; *The Hypocrites*, pr. 1906, pb. 1907; *The Evangelist*, pr. 1907, pb. 1908(?) (also known as *The Galilean's Victory*); *The Lie*, pr. 1914, pb. 1915; *Plays by Henry Arthur Jones*, 1982 (includes *The Silver King*, *The Case of Rebellious Susan*, and *The Liars*).

Other literary forms

Henry Arthur Jones, a prolific dramatist, was also an energetic theatrical critic and polemicist. His prose writings include *The Renascence of the English Drama* (1895), *The Foundations of a National Drama* (1913), and *The Theatre of Ideas* (1915). Jones's polemics are found in his attacks on H. G. Wells and George Bernard Shaw in *Patriotism and Popular Education* (1919) and *My Dear Wells: A Manual for the Haters of England; Being a Series of Letters upon Bolshevism, Collectivism, Internationalism and the Distribution of Wealth, Addressed to Mr. H. G. Wells* (1921, 1922). Jones actively campaigned for the abolition of theatrical censorship. *The Renascence of the English Drama* brings together the essays in which he argues that drama has definite artistic forms, that it is a serious literary genre, and that a national theater should be established. He calls for copyright laws to be reformed and plays printed—at the time, radical ideas meeting with much opposition. *The Foundations of a National Drama* continues Jones's advocacy for the establishment of a national theater, argues for a more intelligent theater, and attacks contemporary theatrical frivolity. Jones believed that art has a social value—that the theater should educate audiences and bring beauty and culture to otherwise impoverished ordinary lives.

Achievements

Jones is regarded as one of the most important English dramatists and men of the theater during the last decades of the nineteenth century. *The Silver King*, hailed as a masterpiece of melodramatic stage craftsmanship, ran for 289 performances—a lengthy run by the standards of the time. In subsequent plays, Jones turned his attention to such serious themes as the exposure of hypocrisy and deceit and the depiction of the emerging "new woman." At his best, Jones was a master craftsman, a superb manipulator of theatrical dialogue and writer of problem plays. After the turn of the century and the success of *Mrs. Dane's Defence* in 1900, Jones, while continuing to write prolifically, began merely to rework well-tried formulas and melodramatic successes. Repetitious melodrama, social comedy, and problem plays made him a theatrical back-number. His energies turned to the attempt to influence the course of subsequent theatrical literature through the dissemination of his ideas in books, pamphlets, and lectures. The 1982 publication by the Cambridge University Press of three of Jones's plays— *The Silver King*, *The Case of Rebellious Susan*, and *The Liars*—demonstrates that he is not an obscure late-Victorian dramatist of merely historical interest. Jones's reputation as a consummate dramatic craftsman stands secure, as does his place in the English theatrical renaissance of the last decades of the nineteenth century.

Biography

Henry Arthur Jones was born on September 20, 1851, in Grandborough, Buckinghamshire. His background was Nonconformist; his father was a farmer, and his mother was a farmer's daughter. Jones's formal education seems to have stopped at the age of twelve, when he was sent to work for his uncle, who had a draper's shop on the Kentish coast at Ramsgate. Jones stayed for three and a half years in Ramsgate before moving to Gravesend, which was nearer to London, and to another draper's shop. In 1869, he moved into London, where he was to remain for most of his life. Self-educated, he read widely; his favorite authors were John Milton, Herbert Spencer, and Samuel Butler, and his favorite works were about scientific advancements. From Milton—a lifetime obsession—Jones learned verse drama techniques and the interweaving of biblical quotation into the texture of his plays. Scientists, explorers, and doctors often appear in his plays, and he makes frequent use of Spencerian and Butlerian ideas. In his first year in London, Jones wrote several unstaged one-act plays and an unpublished novel. *Hearts of Oak*, the first of his plays to be produced, premiered at the Theatre Royal, Exeter, on May 29, 1879, and the production encouraged Jones to devote his whole energies to drama. *A Clerical Error*, his first London play, was performed in October, 1879. Jones's reputation was secured by *The Silver King*, which opened at the Princess's Theatre on November 16, 1882. The success of this play provoked a dispute over its authorship, which Wilson Barrett, an actor-manager, claimed to share with Jones and Henry Herman. A 1905 legal settlement denied Barrett's claim. *The Silver King* gave Jones some degree of financial security. His experience with Barrett soured Jones's attitude toward the prevailing actor-manager theatrical hierarchy of his day, but *The Crusaders*, his self-financed effort, which was produced in November, 1891, proved to be a disastrous financial failure.

In the 1890's Jones's work met with mixed fortune. *The Masqueraders*, *The Tempter*, *The Bauble Shop*, and *The Liars* succeeded, whereas *The Triumph of the Philistines*, *Michael and His Lost Angel*, *Carnac Sahib*, and *The Lackey's Carnival* aroused controversy and lost money. *Mrs. Dane's Defence*, first performed at Wyndham's in October, 1900, was his last real theatrical success. George Bernard Shaw, writing in his regular *Saturday Review* column, denounced *The Princess's Nose* as morally bankrupt, and another hostile critic, Arthur B. Walkley of *The Times* of London, was barred from attending the opening of *Whitewashing Julia* in 1903. *The Hypocrites* was warmly received in America, but Jones's subsequent American theatrical venture, *The Evangelist*, failed. Deeply troubled by World War I, as were so many of his contemporaries, Jones wasted much energy in publically feuding with H. G. Wells and Shaw. He opposed what he regarded as their lack of patriotism in their opposition to the war. The fledgling film industry purchased and produced several of Jones's plays, but he disapproved of the end products. In 1923, he achieved a modest theatrical success in London with *The Lie* (originally produced nearly a decade before in the United States); this drama was prematurely replaced at Wyndham's by Shaw's *Saint Joan*.

Jones's private life is an enigma. With failing health and lack of success in his late years, he retreated from the theatrical world he loved so much. Jones had married Jane Eliza Seeley, the daughter of an artificial flower manufacturer, in 1875; she died in 1924. They had seven children, three sons and four daughters, one of whom, Doris Arthur Jones, produced in 1930 the official biography of her father, *The Life and Letters of Henry Arthur Jones*. A recurring leitmotif in Jones's drama is the conflict among sexual passion, social duty, and respectability. Such a conflict may well have had a foundation in the secrets of his own carefully guarded private life.

Analysis

In 1894, Henry Arthur Jones called for "a school of plays of serious intention, plays that implicitly assert the value and dignity of human life, that it has great passions and great aims, and is full of meaning and importance." He set out to gain respect for the theater as a serious art form, rejecting the sensational melodrama so prevalent on the English stage. In

The Old Drama and the New (1923), William Archer, a distinguished, perceptive critic, looked back at the theatrical world of late-Victorian and Edwardian England. For Archer, Jones was a natural dramatist whose chief aim was to criticize life as he saw it and especially to expose philistinism. Jones's chief weakness, in Archer's view, was his inability to free himself from the melodramatic traditions in which he served his theatrical apprenticeship. Jones's work largely falls into two categories: melodrama and comedy of intrigue. "The pity is" writes Archer, "that the world of his imagination is not sunlit but limelit."

The plot of *The Silver King*, Jones's first major success, provides a good illustration of his manipulation of melodramatic form. The play contains dialogue that is natural without being artificial (a quality of Jones's drama at its best), real passion, and some elements of genuine comedy (a quality sometimes lacking in Jones). *The Silver King* has a wronged hero, a persecuted heroine, a ruthless landlord, a snobbish aristocrat, a faithful family servant, a detective, and a Cockney comic. Wilfred Denver loses his money at the races and, while drowning his sorrows in a London pub, is taunted by his wife's former admirer, Henry Ware. Denver publicly swears to kill Ware. Ware's house is broken into by a gang led by the aristocrat Captain Skinner; Denver is chloroformed. Skinner, using Denver's gun, kills Ware, and Denver, believing that he is the murderer, takes a train north from London—the dramatist not missing the opportunity to throw in a scenically lavish but costly railway scene. Denver gets out at the first station and subsequently discovers that the train he was on has crashed. The police believe him to be dead. Going to the United States, he makes a fortune in the Montana silver mines. Returning to England, Denver discovers that his starving, ailing wife and child are to be ejected from Skinner's land without a roof over their heads. Secretly he gives them money and, in the disguise of an idiot, infiltrates Skinner's gang in order to find out what really happened. Justice triumphs in the end. All the ingredients of classic melodrama are here: an exciting plot, a great deal of action, violence, intrigue, a wronged hero and a suffering heroine, a malignant and devious villain of aristocratic origins, asinine policemen, and the triumph of good over evil. Even Matthew Arnold (not an easy critic to please), writing in the *Pall Mall Gazette*, December 6, 1882, thought that Jones had managed to transcend the limitations of his chosen genre: "throughout the piece the diction and sentiments are natural, they have sobriety, they are literature." In spite of Jones's subsequent attempts to free himself from the shackles of melodrama and to write serious theatrical literature, he is still remembered for *The Silver King*, with its masterly use of well-tried formulas and its invigorating theatricality.

Saints and Sinners is an example of Jones's early attempts to render contemporary social problems dramatically, to write "plays of serious intention." The plot revolves around a village girl's seduction by a handsome, worldly villain—the Little Emily syndrome. The honest fiancé is forced abroad, returning to claim his girl. Jones's aim in *Saints and Sinners*, as stated in his preface to the published text (in which Jones changed his original ending to a happy one), was to expose the "ludicrous want of harmony, or apparently of even the most distant relation of any sort between a man's religious professions and his actions." Letty, the seduced, is the daughter of a pastor in conflict with his materialistic congregation. Pastor Fletcher opposes the attempt of his deacon, a tanner, to throw the widow of his former partner out of his home. The tanner, Hoggard, makes public Letty's seduction, and Fletcher is forced by his congregation to resign. The 1884 theater audience found Jones's exposure of the congregation's hypocrisy too much and strongly reacted to the play, which had a long but controversial London run. After *Saints and Sinners*, Jones had a reputation as an unconventional dramatist who daringly exposed folly. *Saints and Sinners* began his fight for theatrical freedom of expression, and he published the play in book form—not standard practice at the time—in order to give its ideas permanence as serious literature. In the following year, 1885, his one-act play "Welcome Little Stranger" was turned down by the Lord Chamberlain on the grounds that its opening hinted at the mysteries of childbirth. From the viewpoint of the late twentieth century, Jones's depiction in *Saints and Sinners* of seduction, hypocrisy, and the dichotomy between religious belief and private conduct may appear tame and the Victorian public's outcry surprising. "Welcome Little Stranger" provides insight into Victorian attitudes concerning what was permissible onstage and what was not.

Two plays of 1889, *Wealth* and *The Middleman*, demonstrates Jones's theatrical attempt to develop serious themes. *Wealth* revolves around the refusal of its heroine to obey her father and marry the wealthy man he has chosen for her. Turned out into the streets for her disobedience, she marries for love and finally is reconciled with her father on his deathbed. In *Wealth*, Jones deals with the conflict between love and wealth, emotion and filial duty. He was tackling a subject which was increasingly to occupy the attention of his fellow dramatists Arthur Wing Pinero, Oscar Wilde, and Shaw: the emerging modern woman and her aspirations. As theater, however, *Wealth* was not a success—it was believed to lack wit, William Archer's "sunlight." By contrast, *The Middleman* was a stage success and is a very witty play. Humor, love, and social comment are inextricably interwoven into its plot, which has as its focal point a dreamy, exploited porcelain worker turning the tables on his ruthless master. The subplot unites the worker's daughter and the master's son. In terms of the development of Jones's stagecraft, *The Middleman* paved the way for his success with *Judah*; it is with *Judah* that Jones threw off the shackles of melodrama and wrote a genuine problem play.

Reviewing *Judah* in the *Saturday Review*, Shaw objected to it on the ground that it failed to tackle the issues it raised, merely skirting around them. The play, Shaw wrote, "consists of clever preliminaries; and when the real play begins with the matrimonial experiment of Judah and Vashti, down comes the curtain as usual." *Judah*, with its pervasive biblical allusions, its use of allegory, and its hereditary motif, proved to be too ambitious for its author. The plot is not complicated and centers upon a low-church clergyman, Judah, who holds extreme religious beliefs. Judah falls passionately in love with Vashti, a faith healer manipulated by her father into practicing public deceit. Vashti, true to the origin of her name, is torn between loyalty to her father and love. Judah helps her to free herself from her father's deception, and in the final act, after public confession, he resigns his ministry. There appear to be Ibsenite influences at work in the play's treatment of remorse and conscience, even though Jones vigorously denied that he had been influenced by Henrik Ibsen. Contemporary theatergoers were moved by powerful performances in the leading role, but *Judah* is essentially a closet play, more suited to reading than to theatrical performance.

Jones regarded *The Tempter* as one of his finest efforts. A verse play of ideas in five acts, *The Tempter* concentrates on the conflict between duty and passion. The blank verse drama is set in the fourteenth century, with the Devil setting traps for the other characters, especially for a religious man who, despite himself, falls deeply in love with a rebellious, unhappily married girl. The setting is too ambitious and the play too full of Shakespearean and Miltonic echoes and associations to be successful. Jones returned to the theme of the struggle against temptation in *The Masqueraders*, in which one of the leading characters is a scientist, presented as a high-principled but tempted man, devoted to his work and endeavoring to expand the frontiers of knowledge. One woman (a role played for all its worth by one of the leading ladies of the day, Mrs. Patrick Campbell), is caught between two men: her dissolute feckless husband and the scientist. Eventually, the latter chooses the path of research and goes to Africa, but not before he has given the heroine, who has thrown in her lot with him, financial security. The play's attempt to reveal the unhappiness behind the glitter of seemingly successful lives is interesting, but theatrically it does not succeed.

Jones's next play, *The Case of Rebellious Susan*, was a box-office success. Set in high society and wittily focusing upon the new woman and sexual repression, it tackled adultery and sexual discrimination. The play demonstrates in the character of its heroine, Susan, Jones's remarkable ability to create a character whose ideas are basically not in sympathy with his own. *The Case of Rebellious Susan* and *The Triumph of the Philistines* were partly reactions to Shaw's counsel that Jones should write detailed comedies of manners. In *The Triumph of the Philistines*, Jones returned to his earlier theme of attacking English philistinism and resistance to change, while in *The Liars*, he returned to social comedy, the comedy residing in each character's frantic attempts to cover up the "truth" from the others. Lady Jessica Napean weaves a tangled web in order to divert her jealous husband's suspicion concerning what in effect was an innocent meeting. Edward Falkner, a young explorer in love with Lady Jessica, plans an elaborate and complicated elopement, stopped at the last moment by Sir Christopher Deering. Sir Christopher upholds the traditional social conventions and the wisdom that, in English society, pretenses have to be maintained at all costs. Marriage cannot be destroyed. The young explorer goes on an expedition to Africa. Particularly noticeable in *The Liars* is the superb craftsmanship exhibited in the plotting, which reaches a crescendo of Jamesian elaborateness of deceit in the third act. In the brilliant dialogue of *The Liars*, Jones captures the upper-class spirit of his milieu. Even Shaw remarked, when reviewing the play, that Jones gave a "very keen and accurate picture of smart society." Unfortunately, Jones's play ultimately accepts the very conservative values which it seems to have set out to attack.

Today, *Mrs. Dane's Defence* is regarded as Jones's masterpiece. It has been praised for its tightness and economy of construction, its strength of characterization, and its superb dialogue—especially in the third act's cross-examination scene between Sir Daniel (Mr. Justice) Carteret and Mrs. Dane. The ending is not without power. Mrs. Dane is forced into exile to Devonshire, "outside the palings." She and Jones accept that "the world is very hard on a woman," but that is the way of the world. There is no attempt at a happy ending. The dramatist accepts what he regards as inexorable social laws. Jones was a superb craftsman, and his skill reached its consummate height in *Mrs. Dane's Defence*. After this play, he churned out another twenty-six full-length plays, variations on anachronistic themes with settings in a time gone forever. *The Lie*, produced in London in 1923 but written and produced in New York nearly a decade before, became a West End hit. Jones tapped his old melodramatic techniques to produce a drama which revolves around two sisters in love with the same man and which deals with illegitimacy and deceit.

Jones remained a dramatist of the last decades of the nineteenth century, a superb craftsman, the author of a melodrama to outdo all the others, *The Silver King*, and of two brilliantly constructed plays, *The Liars* and *Mrs. Dane's Defence*. He is remembered as a champion of the serious theater, of the theater of ideas, and as an advocate of theatrical freedom. Jones was largely antagonistic toward contemporary theatrical developments, finding, for example, Anton Chekhov's *The Cherry Orchard* (pr. 1904) to be the product of "someone who had visited a lunatic asylum." Even though Jones was eclipsed by Pinero, Shaw, and Wilde, his best plays are still appreciated. After all, as Shaw pointed out, Jones possessed "creative imagination, curious observation, inventive humour, originality, sympathy, and sincerity."

Other major works

NONFICTION: *The Renascence of the English Drama*, 1895; *The Foundations of a National Drama*, 1913; *The Theatre of Ideas*, 1915; *Patriotism and Popular Education*, 1919; *My Dear Wells: A Manual for the Haters of England; Being a Series of Letters upon Bolshevism, Collectivism, Internationalism and the Distribution of Wealth, Addressed to Mr. H. G. Wells*, 1921, 1922.

Bibliography

Archer, William. *The Old Drama and the New: An Essay in Revaluation*, 1923.
Booth, Michael R. *English Melodrama*, 1965.
Cordell, R. A. *Henry Arthur Jones and the Modern Drama*, 1932.
Hunt, Hugh, Kenneth Richards, and John Russell Taylor. *The Revels History of Drama in English, Volume VII: 1880 to the Present Day*, 1978.
Jones, Doris Arthur. *The Life and Letters of Henry Arthur Jones*, 1930.
Rowell, George, ed. *The Victorian Theatre: A Survey*, 1967.
Shaw, [George] Bernard. *Our Theatre in the Nineties*, 1932.
Taylor, John Russell. *The Rise and Fall of the Well-Made Play*, 1967.
Wearing, J. P. "Henry Arthur Jones: An Annotated Bibliography of Writings About Him," in *English Literature in Transition*. XXII, no. 3 (1979), pp. 160-228.

William Baker

PRESTON JONES

Born: Albuquerque, New Mexico; April 7, 1936
Died: Dallas, Texas; September 19, 1979

Principal drama

The Last Meeting of the Knights of the White Magnolia, pr. 1973, pb. 1976; *Lu Ann Hampton Laverty Oberlander*, pr. 1974, pb. 1976; *The Oldest Living Graduate*, pr. 1974, pb. 1976; *A Texas Trilogy*, pr. 1974, pb. 1976 (includes *The Last Meeting of the Knights of the White Magnolia*, *Lu Ann Hampton Laverty Oberlander*, *The Oldest Living Graduate*); *A Place on the Magdalena Flats*, pr. 1976; *Santa Fe Sunshine*, pr., pb. 1977 (one act); *Juneteenth*, pr. 1979 (one act); *Remember*, pr. 1979.

Other literary forms

Preston Jones is known only for his plays.

Achievements

Preston Jones is often labeled a regional playwright, and certainly one of his achievements was his treatment of the American Southwest as a setting for serious drama. His plays capture the idiosyncratic characters, regional language, and unique experience of the rural Southwest at a time of transition for the land and its people. The significance of Jones's work, however, is not limited to his recording of the life of a specific community. The plays are significant commentaries on the way people deal with fundamental human problems: the pain of loneliness, the fear of failure, the effects of time. Like Anton Chekhov, Jones chronicles the passing of a way of life, and he does so with much of the gentle criticism and humorous affection of the Russian playwright. Jones's work also contains an exuberance and rough energy, however, which are uniquely his and which are rooted in the language and energy of his characters. Indeed, Jones's discovery of the value to be found in the lives and troubles of the most ordinary of people and of the lyric poetry embedded in their native idiom constitutes his most important theatrical achievement.

Biography

Preston St. Vrain Jones was born in Albuquerque, New Mexico, on April 7, 1936. His father, a former lieutenant governor of New Mexico, had been a professional military man who at one time had hoped for a career writing Western novels. Jones grew up in New Mexico, attending a Catholic boarding school for boys for a short time before he was graduated from high school in Albuquerque. After a brief period of military service, Jones entered the University of New Mexico, from which he received a bachelor of science degree in speech in 1960. He taught one semester in a high school in Tucumcari, New Mexico, before returning to the University of New Mexico to study drama for a year. During this period, he also spent some time working with the State Highway Department in and around Colorado City, Texas, which later became the model for Bradleyville, Texas, the setting of *A Texas Trilogy*.

In 1961, Jones enrolled in the drama department of Baylor University in Waco, Texas, where he studied with Paul Baker, nationally known as an innovative force in Southwestern theater. Baker quickly became, and remained, a major influence on Jones's life and career; he asked Jones to join the Dallas Theater Center, where Jones continued his studies and worked with the theater's professional company. While there, he married Mary Sue Birkhead, an actress and designer and then assistant director of the Dallas Theater Center. In 1963, the Dallas Theater Center transferred its academic affiliation from Baylor to Trinity University in San Antonio, Texas, from which Jones received a master of arts in drama in 1966. Jones remained in Dallas as a member of the Dallas Theater Center's resident professional company, accumulating experience in all phases of theater, which served him well when he began to develop his interest in playwriting.

Although interested in writing for much of his life, Jones did not emerge as a serious playwright until 1973, with the premiere of *The Last Meeting of the Knights of the White Magnolia*. The previous year, Jones had been appointed producer of the Dallas Theater Center's small, experimental theater. Dissatisfied with the scripts available, particularly with the lack of good regional drama, Jones decided to write something himself, drawing on his knowledge of the Southwest and especially on his experiences in Colorado City. He completed *Lu Ann Hampton Laverty Oberlander* first, following quickly with *The Last Meeting of the Knights of the White Magnolia* and *The Oldest Living Graduate*. In 1974, the three plays were performed in repertory at the Dallas Theater Center. *The Last Meeting of the Knights of the White Magnolia* was selected as the offering of the American Playwright's Theater the following year, and in 1976, the three plays broke all box-office records at the Kennedy Center in Washington and opened on Broadway. Although the reviews of the New York production were mixed, the popular and critical success of the plays across the country established Jones as a major new American playwright.

Following *A Texas Trilogy*, Jones wrote three more full-length plays and a short one-act. All but one of the works premiered at the Dallas Theater Center, where Jones continued to work as an actor and director as well as resident playwright. While the later plays have not received the widespread production and recognition of the first three plays, they show Jones's growing maturity as a writer as well as his continuing interest in the major themes of the trilogy. Unfortunately, Jones's career was cut short when he died unexpectedly on September 19, 1979, following surgery for a bleeding ulcer. The seven plays which he finished, a remarkable feat for the relatively brief span of his writing career, represent an important contribution to American dramatic literature.

Analysis

The plays of Preston Jones are remarkably consistent in their concentration on character over plot, in their exploration of the poetry inherent in ordinary speech, and in their emphasis on certain prominent themes. From the beginning of his literary career, Jones's central theme was time. He explored—sometimes seriously, sometimes humorously, but always sympathetically—the effects of the inexorable march of time on people never quite prepared for the changes it will bring. His characters are usually lonely, isolated, cut off from the mainstream of the world by social changes, by geography, by ghosts from their past. They are often people who would be considered failures by normal standards but in whom Jones finds strength and emotional depth which mitigate their lack of the usual hallmarks of success.

Jones's concerns with the fear of failure, the pain of loneliness, and the effects of time are presented principally through character. Jones's great strength as a dramatist lies in his depiction of original and distinct characters who are able to engage the audience's emotions in a profound way. Like the plays of Chekhov, Jones's theater is often singularly undramatic. If his plotting is sometimes weak or contrived, however, his language never is, and it is primarily through dialogue that his characters are rendered. Jones possessed a sure ear for dialogue, an ability to capture the idiosyncratic phrases, the natural rhythms, the inherent poetry of everyday language. If that language is often rough and profane, it is just as often lyrically beautiful, reverberating with a poetry that transcends its common origins.

Jones is best known for the three plays which make up *A Texas Trilogy*: *The Last Meeting of the Knights of the White Magnolia*, *Lu Ann Hampton Laverty Oberlander*, and *The Oldest Living Graduate*. These plays are not unified by consecutive events, as is typical in dramatic trilogies, but by a single setting, shared characters, and common themes. The action of each play is separate and independent of the others, but each deals in its own way with Jones's themes of failure, isolation, and time. The town of Bradleyville, of which Jones created a map with the locations of various characters' homes and other important landmarks carefully noted, is isolated from the present and the future, bypassed by the new highway, and its people are isolated from one another by racial prejudices, past events, and present needs. The town is a relic of a past way of life, in which most of its characters are trapped by their own pasts: Lu Ann by her marriages, the Colonel by his war experiences, Skip Hampton by his failures and his alcoholism. In the three plays, Jones examines different aspects of the passing rural way of life that Bradleyville represents.

The first of the plays to be produced was *The Last Meeting of the Knights of the White Magnolia*. The plot of the play is very simple: The members of a social lodge gather for their monthly meeting, expecting the usual evening of drinking and playing dominoes, only to find the last remnants of the dying fraternal order disintegrate during the evening as they attempt to initiate their first new member in more than five years. Neither the individual members nor the lodge itself, with its basic ideals of white supremacy and unquestioning patriotism, have been able to adjust to the social changes of the late 1950's and early 1960's.

While Jones ridicules the ludicrous aspects of such fraternal orders—the mystical ceremonies, the pointless rules and regulations—and while he never excuses his characters' basic ignorance and bigotry, he presents sympathetically their need for companionship and sense of community and their fears and confusions at the potential loss of these values. The play is uproariously funny, but it never loses sight of the basic humanity of the characters, each of which is etched with depth and precision. The most memorable figure is that of Colonel J. C. Kincaid, a shell-shocked veteran of World War I whose physical and mental deterioration during the course of the evening graphically parallels the dissolution of the group and, in a broader sense, of the Bradleyville way of life.

While *The Last Meeting of the Knights of the White Magnolia* presents a general view of Bradleyville, Jones's second play concentrates more closely on a single character. *Lu Ann Hampton Laverty Oberlander* begins in 1953, when its title character is a bubbly but dissatisfied eighteen-year-old cheerleader, and traces her life over a twenty-year period. Eager to leave her hometown and see the world, Lu Ann never gets any farther than a trailer park in a nearby town, but she survives a divorce, her second husband's death, her brother's alcoholism, and her mother's debilitating illness, and she achieves a kind of quiet dignity through her acceptance of her fate. A failure by most standards, Lu Ann is seen by Jones as a survivor, worthy of sympathy and praise. *Lu Ann Hampton Laverty Oberlander* also traces the life of Skip Hampton, a character introduced in *The Last Meeting of the Knights of the White Magnolia*. As Lu Ann grows in strength and dignity, her brother degenerates from an optimistic but ineffectual schemer to a painfully dependent alcoholic. The plot of *Lu Ann Hampton Laverty Oberlander*, with its careful symmetry, is perhaps too contrived, but the characters are memorable and the dialogue compares well with that of Jones's other plays. In a typically realistic and poignant sample of Jones's language, Skip notes how ironic it is "when all that stands between a man and the by-God loony bin is his sister's tab down to the Dixie Dinette."

The last play of the trilogy, *The Oldest Living Graduate*, focuses on

Colonel Kincaid, who, as he did in *The Last Meeting of the Knights of the White Magnolia,* reflects the values and attitudes of the past. His distrust of business, his love for the land, and his insistence on salvaging a small part of his past from the ravages of time place him in conflict with his son Floyd, the forward-looking local entrepreneur. The play looks with humor at the foibles and prejudices of Bradleyville's country-club set and its small-town morality, at academic and military folderol, at the values of a lost way of life, at the conflicts between generations, and at death itself. *The Oldest Living Graduate* is the most sophisticated and finely crafted of the three plays which make up the trilogy. In it, Jones combines his skill at characterization with a more complex plot and achieves a level of poetry, particularly in the Colonel's dialogue, that is unmatched in any of the earlier plays. The character of the Colonel is perhaps Jones's finest achievement; it is a portrait that evokes sentiment without being sentimental, a feat achieved principally through the clarity and complexity of the Colonel's language.

While each of the plays of *A Texas Trilogy* stands as a completely independent unit, the three plays have been produced as a single work. In such a production, the events in the three stories are arranged chronologically, beginning with the first act of *Lu Ann Hampton Laverty Oberlander. The Last Meeting of the Knights of the White Magnolia* is played after the first half of *The Oldest Living Graduate.* The performance concludes with the rest of the Colonel's story and the last two acts of *Lu Ann Hampton Laverty Oberlander.* Combining the plays in this way makes clear the intimate connection between the three works, which runs much deeper than the shared locale and characters, and reveals the novelistic aspect of Jones's vision. The details of place and characters give the plays a solid basis in realism which becomes even clearer when the plays are seen together. The town of Bradleyville takes on a level of dense reality akin to that of William Faulkner's Yoknapatawpha County: The lives of the characters interweave with and reflect one another, as they often do in Faulkner's fiction. Lu Ann and Colonel Kincaid, in particular, take on new nuances as their stories are told together; the Colonel, who left Bradleyville and was destroyed by a war he never fully understood, is paralleled by Lu Ann, who remained at home and grew strong and forgiving by facing her troubles there. *A Texas Trilogy,* as a whole, has an import beyond the significance of any of the plays individually.

Jones's later plays have not achieved the success of *A Texas Trilogy*; they share, however, the qualities which characterize that work. *A Place on the Magdalena Flats* was first produced in Dallas in 1976. It underwent substantial revision during later productions in New Mexico and Wisconsin in 1976 and 1979, respectively. The principal changes in the script were alterations in the plot which focused the play more clearly on the older brother,

Carl. While improved, the final version is not completely satisfactory, because of the lack of resolution of the younger brother's story. Although it contains rich humor, *A Place on the Magdalena Flats* is more restrained in mood than any of the trilogy plays. Again, characters deal in isolation with ghosts from their past, this time in the drought-stricken cattle country of New Mexico. The language of the play is particularly rich in poetic imagery and metaphor, marking a growing maturity in Jones's writing.

With *Santa Fe Sunshine* and *Juneteenth*, which was commissioned by the Actors' Theatre of Louisville as one of a series of one-act plays on American holidays, Jones turned to pure comedy. *Juneteenth* is a rather thin play; the plot is weak, and the one-act form does not allow Jones time to develop his characters fully. *Santa Fe Sunshine* is actually an earlier work to which Jones returned after the success of *A Texas Trilogy*. It lacks the depth of Jones's other plays, but it contains some delightfully eccentric characters and very witty dialogue. Set in Santa Fe, New Mexico, during the 1950's, when the city was a growing artist colony, the play gently ridicules the local beatniks, the patrons who know little about art, and the artists themselves, who are all in the business of making art for money's sake, although they like to pretend otherwise.

While Jones drew on his own experiences for all of his plays, his last play, *Remember*, contains the most obviously autobiographical material. Jones, like his leading character Adrian Blair, was graduated from high school in 1954, after spending some time at a Catholic boarding school. Also like Adrian, he began to reexamine his religious roots as he reached middle age. Adrian is a second-rate actor who finds himself playing a dinner theater in his hometown on his fortieth birthday. He has avoided the town, and his past, for twenty years. Now he finds that little of what he remembers is left: His old home is gone, his friends have changed, his former teacher, Brother Anthony, has left the order and become a real-estate salesman. As Adrian tries to go back in time and rediscover values he has lost—religion, friendship, love—he finds that the world he once knew exists, in fact, only in his memory. When his former sweetheart offers the possibility of renewing their love, he rejects her, preferring the past to the present with its shifting values and lack of continuity.

While *Remember* clearly deals with the themes that preoccupied Jones in all of his plays, it also represents a new direction in Jones's writing. Although the geographical location of the play remains the Southwest, the characters are better educated and more self-aware than the inhabitants of Bradleyville. This shift allows Jones a use of literary allusion and metaphor which the more limited experience of his earlier characters prohibited, and his dialogue becomes even richer and more lyric with this addition. This enhanced language, combined with Jones's usual depth of character and his engaging wit, places *Remember* among his finest achievements.

Preston Jones represented a new and important force in American theater. As a successful playwright who lived and worked entirely outside New York, he helped to establish a new acceptance of the work of regional theaters and writers around the country. The weaknesses of his plays, his often thin or contrived plots and an overreliance on the Southwestern setting, are more than balanced by the strength and originality of his characters, the realistic density of his imaginative world, and the natural poetry of his dialogue. His plays grew out of the life of the American Southwest, but they deal with more universal and immediate human problems. In a very short span of time, he created a body of work that should secure his place among the best American playwrights.

Bibliography

Bennet, Patrick. "Preston Jones: In the Jaws of Time," in *Talking with Texas Writers: Twelve Interviews*, 1980.

Cook, Bruce. "Playwright on the Range," in *Saturday Review*. III (May 15, 1976), pp. 40-42.

Marek, Annemarie. *Preston Jones: An Interview*, 1978.

Prideaux, Tom. "The Classic Family Drama Is Revived in *A Texas Trilogy*," in *Smithsonian*. VII (October, 1976), pp. 49-54.

Taitte, W. L. "Keeping Up with Jones," in *Texas Monthly*. III (December, 1975), pp. 50-51.

Kathleen Latimer

BEN JONSON

Born: London, England; June 11, 1573(?)
Died: Westminster, England; August 6, 1637

Principal drama

The Isle of Dogs, pr. 1597 (with Thomas Nashe; no longer extant); *The Case Is Altered*, pr. 1597, pb. 1609; *Every Man in His Humour*, pr. 1598 (revised 1605), pb. 1601 (revised 1616); *Hot Anger Soon Cold*, pr. 1598 (with Henry Chettle and Henry Porter; no longer extant); *Every Man out of His Humour*, pr. 1599, pb. 1600; *The Page of Plymouth*, pr. 1599 (with Thomas Dekker; no longer extant); *Robert the Second, King of Scots*, pr. 1599 (with Henry Chettle and Thomas Dekker; no longer extant); *Cynthia's Revels: Or, The Fountain of Self-Love*, pr. 1600-1601, pb. 1601; *Poetaster: Or, His Arraignment*, pr. 1601, pb. 1602; *Sejanus His Fall*, pr. 1603, pb. 1605 (commonly known as *Sejanus*); *Eastward Ho!*, pr., pb. 1605 (with George Chapman and John Marston); *Volpone: Or, The Fox*, pr. 1606, pb. 1607; *Epicoene: Or, The Silent Woman*, pr. 1609, pb. 1616; *The Alchemist*, pr. 1610, pb. 1612; *Catiline His Conspiracy*, pr., pb. 1611 (commonly known as *Catiline*); *Bartholomew Fair*, pr. 1614, pb. 1631; *The Devil Is an Ass*, pr. 1616, pb. 1631; *The Staple of News*, pr. 1626, pb. 1631; *The New Inn: Or, The Light Hart*, pr. 1629, pb. 1631; *The Magnetic Lady: Or, Humours Reconciled*, pr. 1632, pb. 1640; *A Tale of a Tub*, pr. 1633, pb. 1640; *The Sad Shepherd: Or, A Tale of Robin Hood*, pb. 1640 (fragment).

Other literary forms

Ben Jonson was a masterful poet as well as a dramatist. His poetry, with some justification, has the reputation of being remote from modern readers. A dedicated classicist, Jonson emphasized clarity of form and phrase over expression of emotion, and many of his poems seem to be exercises in cleverness and wit rather than attempts to express an idea or image well. Other of his poems, however, retain their power and vision: "To Celia," for example, has given the English language the phrase "Drink to me only with thine eyes."

The difficulty of Jonson's poetry originates in large part in his very mastery of poetic form. Jonson was a student of literature; he was a man of letters with few equals in any era. He studied the poetic forms of classical Greek and Latin literature as well as those of later European literature, and he used what he learned in his own work. The result is a body of poetry that is very diverse, including salutations and love poems, homilies and satires, epigrams and lyrics. Much of the poetry appeals primarily to academics because of its experimental qualities and its displays of technical virtuosity. Yet those who allow themselves to be put off by Jonson's prodigious intellectualism miss some of the finest verse in English.

Jonson was also a prodigious writer of masques—dramatic allegorical entertainments, usually prepared to celebrate special occasions and presented at court. Jonson's masques have in common with his poetry technical achievement and with much of his occasional verse a focus on the virtues, real and reputed, of nobility and royalty. Although the emphasis was on spectacle and celebration of the aristocracy, Jonson tried to make his masques legitimate works of literature, and they have enjoyed increasing critical attention in recent years.

Achievements

Ben Jonson was the foremost man of letters of his time. His knowledge of literature was combined with a passionate personality and a desire to be respected; the combination resulted in his efforts to elevate authors in the estimation of society. He endeavored to demonstrate the importance of literature in the lives of people and in their culture. Although he regarded his dramatic work as merely one facet of his literary life, he was determined that the playwright should receive the esteemed title of "poet." In the Elizabethan era, plays were regarded as unimportant public amusements; satires, sonnets, and narrative verse were expected to carry the heavy freight of ideas and art. Jonson worked to establish drama as a legitimate literary form by showing that it could be a conscious art with rules of organization that were as valid as those of more esteemed literary genres.

In 1616, Jonson published *The Workes of Benjamin Jonson*, including in the volume nine of his plays in addition to other writings. Never before had any author dared to give his plays the title "Works." The term "works" was usually reserved for profound philosophical treatises. Jonson was derided by some writers for being conceited and for trying to make plays seem important; even after his death, some traditionalists found his title difficult to accept. Further, Jonson promoted the cause of drama as high art by devoting much care to the publishing of the texts of his plays, thereby establishing a higher standard for published texts of dramas than had existed before. The publication of *The Workes of Benjamin Jonson* led at least indirectly to the important First Folio edition of William Shakespeare's plays.

Jonson's reputation as a dramatist is inextricably bound with that of Shakespeare. Although Jonson was esteemed above Shakespeare by most of his contemporaries, subsequent eras have elevated Shakespeare at Jonson's expense. Thus, although Jonson's comedies are wonderful and are well received by modern audiences, they are rarely performed. Shakespeare's poetry is better than Jonson's; his tragedies are more moving; his comedies are more diverse and have superior characterizations. To acknowledge Shakespeare's superiority is not to derogate Jonson's achievement; Shakespeare is alone atop the world's authors, but Jonson is not far below. In addition, Jonson's plays are superior to Shakespeare's in consistency of plot and structure. Had there been no William Shakespeare, there might today be Jonson festivals, and *Volpone* and *The Alchemist* might be the revered standards for college drama productions.

Biography

Tradition has it that Benjamin Jonson was born in 1572; literary historians put his birth in 1573, probably on June 11. His father, an Anglican minister, died about a month before Jonson was born. His mother married a master bricklayer in 1574; the family lived in Westminster. While growing up, Jonson attended Westminster School and became a student of William Camden, who was perhaps the greatest classicist and antiquarian of the Elizabethan and Jacobean ages. Jonson's interest in classical literature, his care in constructing what he wrote, and his respect for learning all have their origins in the teachings of Camden. Techniques for writing that Jonson used throughout his life were first learned from Camden, including the practice of writing out a prospective poem first in prose and then converting the prose to verse.

In about 1588, Jonson became an apprentice bricklayer. This part of his life became the subject of jokes and gibes in his later years, but he seems to have taken pride in his humble origins. His respect for achievement and general lack of respect for claims of importance based solely on heredity or accident may have had their roots in his own struggles as a lower-class laborer. He left his bricklaying work to join the army in its war against the Spanish in the Lowlands in 1591 or 1592. During his tenure in the army, he apparently served with some distinction; he claimed that he was the English champion in single combat against a Spanish champion and that he slew his opponent while the assembled armies watched. He was handy with swords and knives and was, when young, quite combative and physically intimidating.

Jonson eventually returned to England. Little is known of his activities until 1597, save that he married Anne Lewis on November 14, 1594. The marriage seems to have been unhappy. Before 1597, Jonson might have been an actor with a traveling troupe, many of whose members eked out marginal livings in the towns and hamlets of England. He was imprisoned in 1597 for having finished a play begun by Thomas Nashe; *The Isle of Dogs* was declared seditious by the Privy Council of the queen. The play, like most of Jonson's collaborations, has not been preserved. After a few weeks, Jonson was released from prison.

Jonson's career as a playwright began in earnest in 1598 after the production of *The Case Is Altered*, which was performed by a troupe of boys from the Chapel Royal. In that same year, *Every Man in His Humour*, the first of Jonson's important plays, was performed by William Shakespeare's company, the Lord Chamberlain's Men. Tradition has it that Shakespeare recognized Jonson's talent and persuaded the Lord Chamberlain's Men to stage the play. Although he admired Shakespeare, Jonson never regarded himself as principally a playwright, and thus he never became a permanent shareholder in an acting company, as did Shakespeare. This enabled Jonson to maintain his artistic freedom but prevented him from earning the good living that Shakespeare and other shareholders enjoyed.

The year 1598 was a busy one for Jonson; he was again imprisoned, this time for killing an actor, Gabriel Spencer, in a duel on September 22. Jonson's property was confiscated, he was branded on the thumb, and he was to be executed, but he saved his life by pleading benefit of clergy, which he could do under ancient English law because he could read. While in prison, he was converted to Roman Catholicism, a faith he practiced until about 1608. In 1606, he was charged with seducing young people into Roman Catholicism; the charges were dropped when he converted back to Anglicanism.

Jonson pursued an active life as an author of plays, poetry, and treatises. His comedies were successful, but his tragedies were badly received. In 1603, Queen Elizabeth died and King James assumed the English throne. Jonson's *Entertainment at Athorpe* helped to launch him on a long career as a court poet. Also that year, his son Benjamin died at the age of six. Though Jonson was finding public acclaim and honor, his private life was miserable. He and his wife lived apart from 1602 to 1607, he lost his namesake son, and he grew obese. In 1605, he collaborated with John Marston and George Chapman on the rollicking comedy *Eastward Ho!* and was again imprisoned for a supposed slight to King James; the play made fun of Scots.

Jonson's plays *Volpone*, *Epicoene*, and *The Alchemist* enhanced his reputation among his literary peers; his court poetry and masques enhanced his status with King James. In 1616, he published *The Workes of Benjamin Jonson* and was awarded a pension by the king. The pension and Jonson's position as the leading literary figure in England in 1616 have encouraged many historians to call him an unofficial poet laureate, and he is usually honored as the first to fill that role in England. Until the death of King James in 1625, Jonson enjoyed his role as a favorite of the king and a respected author; his honors included a master of arts degree from Oxford University.

When Charles I assumed the throne, Jonson's status at court declined. The pension of wine and money was haphazardly delivered, and Jonson had difficulty pursuing his scholarly career because his lodgings burned down in 1623, and his books and papers were destroyed. He returned to playwriting with *The Staple of News* in 1626; the play was not as well received as his earlier comedies. In 1628, he suffered a stroke and was partially paralyzed. In 1629, his play *The New Inn* was staged by the King's Men and was a disaster. He continued to write until his death on August 6, 1637. He left unfinished the play *The Sad Shepherd*, which some critics admire. Although cranky, egotistical, and homely, Jonson retained much of his hold on the leading literary people of his time and was esteemed by younger authors even after his death. He is one of literature's most colorful figures. Combative, robust, and dedicated to his art, Jonson made major contributions to the development of English literature.

Analysis

Ben Jonson's dramatic canon is large, and most of the plays in it are worthy of long and careful study. He is best remembered for his comedies, which influenced comedy-writing well into the eighteenth century and which remain entertaining. Jonson took Horace's maxim to heart—that to teach, a writer must first entertain—and he followed literary rules only so far as they enabled him to instruct and entertain his audience. By observing the neoclassical unities of time and space in his plays, Jonson gave his works a coherence often lacking in the comedies of his contemporaries: Loose ends are resolved, subplot and main plot are interwoven so that each enhances the other, and the conclusion of each play resolves the basic issues brought up during the action. Jonson's concern with entertaining makes most of his comedies delightful and attractive to modern audiences; his effort to instruct makes his plays substantial and meaningful.

From the beginning of his career as a playwright, Jonson was successful with comedy. His two attempts at tragedies are interesting as experiments but are unlikely to be successful with general audiences. His comedies are varied, ranging from the city to the countryside and including satires, comedies of manners, and farces. He was most successful when writing about city life, moralizing with good-natured humor.

Of his early comedies, *Every Man in His Humour* is the most important. Jonson's first significant popular success, it best represents those qualities that make some of his later plays great works of literature. Typical of a Jonsonian comedy, *Every Man in His Humour* has a complex interweaving of plots that creates an atmosphere of comic frenzy. Fools are duped, husbands fear cuckolding, wives suspect their husbands of having mistresses, fathers spy on sons, a servant plays tricks on everyone, and myriad disguises and social games confuse the characters. The audience is not left in confusion, but is carefully let in on the nuances of the various plots.

The plot features Edward Knowell, who journeys to London to visit Wellbred, a wit whose devil-may-care behavior might get Edward into trouble. Old Knowell, Edward's father, follows his son to London in order to spy on him; his servant Brainworm connives and plays tricks—as much to amuse himself as to gain anything. Subplots involve Captain Bobadill, a braggart soldier; Cob and Tib, the landlords of Bobadill; Kitely, a merchant; and Downright, Wellbred's plainspoken brother. The almost bewildering multiplicity of characters is typical of many of Jonson's plays. He borrows the plot of unwarranted suspicions from classical dramatists. Captain Bobadill is the miles gloriosus, the braggart soldier (usually a coward), a stock character in classical comedies. Brainworm is the conniving servant, another stock figure from classical comedies. Other characters also serve specific purposes: Downright is a shatterer of illusions—he points out the falseness in others. Edward Knowell is the romantic lead—a hero who retains his innocence in the middle of the turmoil of the plot. Kitely, Dame Kitely, Cob, and Tib provide much of the low comedy and serve to reflect the ridiculousness of the behavior of the main characters.

Although it shares many of the characteristics that typify Jonson's later comedies, *Every Man in His Humour* shows the dramatist still in the process of forging his mature style. He is still trying to reconcile his classical models to the traditions of English drama and to the tastes of his audience. The plot is loose, almost chaotic, and not as tightly controlled as those of *The Alchemist* and *Volpone*.

"What a rare punishment/ Is avarice to itself," declares Volpone. At the heart of the complex play *Volpone* is the straightforward moral judgment that the evil one commits brings with it a suitable punishment. In *Volpone*, Jonson satirizes human nature and the baser impulses of humanity.

The play's characters pursue basely materialistic ideals, and in attaining their goals, they ensure their own downfall. Volpone begins the play with a monologue that is in itself a classic: "Good morning to the day; and next, my gold!/ Open the shrine that I may see my saint." His servant and partner in crime, Mosca, draws open a curtain and reveals piles of gold. Volpone has called the repository a "shrine" and the gold a "saint." As the rest of the monologue reveals, Volpone regards wealth with a religious fervor; gold, he asserts, is the "son of Sol"; it "giv'st all men tongues"; it "mak'st men do all things."

Volpone is not merely a clever faker, nor is his servant, Mosca. He is a devotee of an ideal, and as such he is at once more likable and more dangerous than an ordinary thief. He has the excuse that confidence men traditionally have had: that the greed of his victims is their undoing; if they were good people, he would be unable to cheat them. As long as he sticks to victimizing greedy people, he is spectacularly successful; the victims eagerly give him gold and jewels in the hope of gaining his fortune by having it left to them when he dies. When he seeks to "bed" innocent Celia, however, his empire of gold and deceit begins to crumble into its component parts of venality, lust, and spiritual morbidity.

Volpone is a captivating character. He is capable of wonderful flights of language and of clever intrigue, and he is a consummate actor; his strength is his knowledge of how much he can manipulate people into doing what he wants done; his weakness is his overweening pride—he revels too much in his ability to dupe his victims. By pretending to be an old, dying man, he helps convince his victims of his imminent death and of the possibility that one of them will inherit his wealth. They give him expensive gifts in order to ingratiate themselves with him. His accomplice, Mosca, is also a skilled actor, who can be obsequious one moment, gallant the next—all things to all people. Mosca convinces each victim that he is favored above all others in Volpone's will. The scheme is very successful, and there is much hilarity in the gulling of the lawyer Voltore (the vulture), the elderly Corbaccio (the crow), and the merchant and husband of Celia, Corvino (the raven). The actors should resemble their roles: Voltore is craven and menacing; Corbaccio is thin and leggy; and Corvino is quick-eyed and aggressive. There is exuberance in Volpone's shifts from boisterous and athletic man to bedridden old cripple, in Mosca's cheerful conniving, and in the duping of three socially prominent and nasty men. The subplot of Lord and Lady Politic Would-be heightens the comedy as Volpone, in his guise as cripple, endures Lady Would-be's endless talking and her willingness to surrender her virtue for his favor. Volpone's gold-centered world would be thoroughly jolly if he were not right about gold's ability to influence people. His victims include innocents, such as Bonario, who is disinherited by his father, Corbaccio, so that Corbaccio can leave his wealth to Volpone in the hope that Volpone will reciprocate. Corvino values wealth above all else; he is a fitting worshiper at the shrine of gold, and he would sacrifice anything to the high priest Volpone in exchange for the promise of acquiring more wealth: Corvino even gives his jealously guarded and naïve wife, Celia, to the supposedly impotent Volpone; she is expected to sleep with him.

Underlying the gold-centered world is ugliness; under Volpone's dashing personality is bestiality; under Mosca's wit is spiritual paucity. Jonson shows this graphically. Volpone must pretend to be physically degenerated, yet the pretense mirrors the spiritual reality. As the play progresses, his performance becomes more extreme; eventually, he pretends to be nearly a corpse. The more complex his scheming becomes, the more wretched he must show himself to be. He is trapped in his world of gold; when he wants to leave his home to see what Celia looks like, he must disguise himself as a lowly mountebank. The physically vibrant Volpone is restricted to his gold and Mosca. When he reveals himself as ardent lover to the trapped Celia, his feigned physical degeneration emerges in his spiritual self, and he is doomed.

Volpone is a great play because it is a nearly perfect meshing of comedy, symbolism, suspense, and moralizing. Each change in any of its aspects is matched by changes in all. Its satiric targets are universals, including greed, moral idiocy, and the replacement of spiritual ideals with materialistic ones. Greed brings down most of the principal characters, including Mosca. Pride brings down Volpone; he cannot resist one more chance to display his brilliance. He pretends to be dead and to have left his fortune to Mosca, simply for the sake of seeing how his victims respond when they learn that he has left them nothing. Mosca, loyal only to the money, wants to keep all for himself. Gold turns the world upside down when made the focus of human endeavor: A husband gives his wife to another man; a father displaces his son; the just are made to look false; and a servant becomes master. Gold should serve its owner, and when Volpone enshrines it, he upsets the proper order of society.

The carnality of Volpone is discovered by Bonario, who was accidentally present during Volpone's near-rape of Celia because of one of Mosca's plots involving Corbaccio. In the ensuing trial, Volpone is presented to the court as a nearly dead old man who is incapable of molesting anyone. Voltore puts on his public mask of respectability and argues to the court that Bonario and Celia are liars and worse, and that those accused by them are honest and innocent. An important theme in the play is that of performance versus reality. Corbaccio properly *acts* the part of the kindly old gentleman. Corvino *plays* the honest merchant. Both are respected members of society. Yet, just as the exuberant exterior of Volpone covers a decayed spirit, so, too, do the public personalities of Corbaccio, Corvino, and Voltore belie their evil. In a world where gold is of paramount importance, such people can seem good; likewise, the truly honest and chaste Bonario and Celia can be made to seem conniving, greedy, and concupiscent.

Mosca almost gets the money. Corbaccio and Corvino almost escape with their reputations intact. Voltore almost wins a false case with his skillful arguments. Volpone cannot stand to lose his gold and cannot stand to see his victims succeed where he has failed. He reveals all to the court. The conclusion seems contrived—after all, the clever Volpone could start over and find new victims to gull—but it is thematically apt. No matter how often Volpone were to start over, his plotting would end the same way, because he worships a base and false god that cannot enrich his soul. The ending reveals the falseness in the principal characters and lays bare the emptiness of Volpone's world.

The use of the villain as protagonist can be found in the tragedies of Jonson's contemporaries. Shakespeare's Macbeth, for example, remains one of literature's most interesting villainous heroes. The use of a villain as protagonist in a comedy was more rare and may have come from classical comedies, in which conniving servants were often the most entertaining characters. Jonson created for himself a distinctive literary voice by using villains such as Volpone to carry his moral ideas; in *The Alchemist*, he exploited the same tension with equal success.

Samuel Taylor Coleridge ranked the plot of *The Alchemist* among the three best in literature, along with those of Sophocles' *Oedipus Tyrannus* (c. 429 B. C.) and Henry Fielding's *Tom Jones* (1749). Like *Volpone*, the play is about people pretending to be what they are not. *The Alchemist*, however, goes a step further: Its characters seek to be transformed, to be made over into new people. The three characters who gull the others operate out of a house, and as in *Volpone*, the victims are brought to the house for fleecing. In contrast to the action of *Volpone*, however, the action of *The Alchemist* remains tightly focused on the house; society at large comes to the Blackfriars house to be duped and cheated. Jeremy, the butler, goes by various names—usually Face, the conspirator. When his master leaves on a trip, he takes in Subtle, a down-on-his-luck swindler, and Doll Common, a prostitute. There is little pretense of a noble alliance, as in *Volpone*; these are criminals whose ignoble characters are never in doubt, although they, like their victims, aspire to become what they are not.

Part of the genius of the play is the fooling of the victimizers even as they prey upon their victims. Doll Common plays the Queen of Faery for the stupid Dapper and a noblewoman for Sir Epicure Mammon; she throws herself into her roles with the hope that she will become—not simply pretend to be—a lady of noble character. Subtle forgets his recent destitution and begins to believe in his ability to transmute human character, even if his alchemical tricks cannot change matter. Face retains some sense of proportion as he shifts from one role to another, but even he hopes to become the important man in society that he cannot be while he remains a butler. These three quarrelsome rogues are laughable, but they also carry Jonson's moral freight: One must know oneself before a change in character is possible. All except the house's master, Lovewit, hope to be what they are not yet cannot change because they do not know themselves.

Dapper is a clerk who hopes to be a successful gambler; he hopes that Subtle, who poses as an alchemist, will be able to guarantee him good luck. Drugger is a silly shopkeeper who wants a guarantee of good business. Kastril is a country squire who wishes to become an urban wit. His sister, Dame Pliant, is an empty-headed, wealthy widow whose beautiful body hides an almost nonexistent personality. Tribulation, Wholesome, and Ananias are hypocritical Puritans who hope that Subtle will give them the philosophers' stone—which is reputed to have great alchemical powers to transmute—so that they will be able to rule the world. Sir Epicure Mammon (regarded by many critics as one of Jonson's greatest dramatic creations), egotistical and blind to his own weaknesses, wants the philosophers' stone so that he can become a kind of Volpone, ruling a materialistic realm in which he would be wonderful in his generosity and terrible in his appetites. Mammon is already living a fantasy, and he needs little encouragement from Subtle, Face, and Doll Common. The victims are motivated by greed and lust; their desires dictate the nature of their cozening.

The fun is in the increasingly complex machinations of the resourceful schemers. The satire is in the social roles of the victims, who range from clerk and shopkeeper to religious leader and gentleman. By the play's end, Surly, the friend of Mammon, has tried to reveal the schemers for what they are, but only Pliant believes him, and she believes whatever she is told. Mammon is in ardent pursuit of a prostitute in whom he sees noble ancestry; Wholesome and his aide Ananias are fearful of losing their chance to transform the world; Dapper is bound, gagged, and locked in a closet; and Subtle and Face are hopping from one deceit to another in order to keep their schemes balanced. Their small world is based on false understandings of self; no one understands who he really is. The hilarious confusion ends when Lovewit returns home and refuses to be fooled by Face's explanations.

Some critics argue that Lovewit is every bit as deluded as the other characters. They argue that the world of *The Alchemist* remains disordered at the play's finish. Yet Lovewit seems to see through Face's lies and games; he seems to know perfectly well what he is doing when he takes Pliant and her fortune for himself. While his remark to Face, "I will be rul'd by thee in any thing," can be taken to mean that master has yielded to servant, which would be a representation of disorder, it is more likely that Lovewit is expressing gratitude for the deliverance to him of Pliant, as his subsequent remarks suggest. He puts Face back in his place as servant; he puts Kastril in his proper place as his brother-in-law; and he handles the officers of the law and Tribulation and Mammon with confidence. He is in command of the problems created by Face, Subtle, and Doll Common almost from the moment he enters his home. Given the moral themes of the play, Lovewit's commanding presence provides a satisfying conclusion by showing a character who knows himself bringing order to the chaos brought on by fools.

Between *Volpone* and *The Alchemist*, Jonson wrote *Epicoene*, and after *The Alchemist* he wrote *Bartholomew Fair* and *The Devil Is an Ass*. The last-named work is an amusing play but not one of Jonson's best. The other two, however, rank among his most successful comedies. Unlike *Volpone* and *The Alchemist*, they involve broad social milieus. *Volpone* and *The Alchemist* present tight little worlds that parody reality; Volpone and Mosca rule theirs at the shrine of gold; Subtle, Face, and Doll Common are minor deities in the world encompassed by their house. In both plays, the outer world intrudes only to resolve their plots. In *Epicoene* and *Bartholomew Fair*, the larger world of Jacobean society appears on the stage.

Epicoene was written for a theatrical company made up entirely of boys, and the central conceit of the play turns on that aspect of its first performance, much as Shakespeare's *As You Like It* (pr. c. 1599-1600) has the young man playing Rosalind, a woman, pretend to be a woman pretending to be a man pretending to be a woman. Jonson's trick is to have Epicoene, played by a boy, turn out at play's end to be a boy. As in his other great comedies, false pretenses form one of the play's major themes. The duping of Morose, who loathes noise, draws in braggarts, pretentious women, and urbane wits. Coarse language, persistent lying, and brutality are revealed as the underlying traits of the supposedly refined and sophisticated members of polite society. In addition, Jonson calls into question the validity of sexual roles; Epicoene is called everything from the ideal woman to an Amazon—the boy who plays her fits easily into the society of women and is readily accepted by women until revealed as a boy.

Bartholomew Fair also deals in disguises and confused identities, but is more cheerful than Jonson's other great comedies. The setting of a fair encourages varied action and characters, and Jonson evokes the robust nature of the fair by providing vigorous action and scenes that would be typical of the fairs of his day. The character Ursula is representative of the fair: She is the pig-woman, the operator of a stall that sells roast pig. Big, loud, and sweaty, she embodies the earthiness of the fair, which is noisy and hot with crowding people. The language of the characters is coarse, and they often use vulgarities. The effect is one of down-to-earth good humor and the happy-ending plot. This effect contrasts with *Epicoene*, which also features grossly vulgar language; its characters are supposedly refined, but they reflect their gutter minds in gutter language. Instead of being down-to-earth, much of the humor seems dirty.

Jonson's stature as a playwright is greater than popular knowledge of him would indicate. Had Shakespeare lived at another time, Jonson would be the dramatic giant of his era. His comedies deserve to be performed more often than they are; his masterpieces play well before modern audiences, and even his minor plays have wit and ideas to recommend them. Jonson is a dramatist of the first rank.

Other major works

POETRY: *Poems*, 1601; *Epigrams*, 1616; *The Forest*, 1616; *The Underwood*, 1640; *Execration Against Vulcan*, 1640.

NONFICTION: *The English Grammar*, 1640; *Horace His Art of Poetry*, 1640; *Timber: Or, Discoveries Made upon Men and Matter*, 1641.

MISCELLANEOUS: *The Workes of Benjamin Jonson*, 1616; *The Works of Benjamin Jonson*, 1640-1641 (2 volumes).

Bibliography
Barish, Jonas A. *Ben Jonson and the Language of Prose Comedy*, 1960.
Barton, Anne. *Ben Jonson, Dramatist*, 1984.

Beaurline, L. A. *Jonson and Elizabethan Comedy: Essays in Dramatic Rhetoric*, 1978.

Brock, D. Heyward, and James M. Welsh. *Ben Jonson: A Quadricentennial Bibliography, 1947-1972*, 1974.

Chute, Marchette. *Ben Jonson of Westminster*, 1953.

Dessen, Alan C. *Jonson's Moral Comedy*, 1971.

Partridge, Edward B. *The Broken Compass: A Study of the Major Comedies of Ben Jonson*, 1958.

Summers, Claude J., and Ted-Larry Pebworth. *Ben Jonson*, 1979.

Swinburne, Algernon Charles. *A Study of Ben Jonson*, 1889.

Kirk H. Beetz

GEORGE S. KAUFMAN

Born: Pittsburgh, Pennsylvania; November 16, 1889
Died: New York, New York; June 2, 1961

Principal drama

Someone in the House, pr. 1918 (with Larry Evans and Walter Percival; originally as *Among Those Present*, pr. 1917); *Dulcy*, pr., pb. 1921 (with Marc Connelly); *To the Ladies*, pr. 1922, pb. 1923 (with Connelly); *Merton of the Movies*, pr. 1922, pb. 1925 (with Connelly; based on Harry Leon Wilson's novel); *Helen of Troy, N.Y.*, pr. 1923 (musical comedy with Connelly; music and lyrics by Bert Kalmar and Harry Ruby); *The Deep Tangled Wildwood*, pr. 1923 (with Connelly); *Beggar on Horseback*, pr. 1924, pb. 1925 (with Connelly); *Be Yourself*, pr. 1924 (musical comedy with Connelly; music by Lewis Gensler and Milton Schwartzwald); *Minick*, pr., pb. 1924 (with Edna Ferber); *The Butter and Egg Man*, pr., pb. 1925; *The Cocoanuts*, pr. 1925 (musical comedy; music and lyrics by Irving Berlin); *The Good Fellow*, pr. 1926, pb. 1931 (with Herman J. Mankiewicz); *If Men Played Cards as Women Do*, pr., pb. 1926; *The Royal Family*, pr. 1927, pb. 1928 (with Ferber); *Animal Crackers*, pr. 1928 (musical comedy with Morrie Ryskind; music and lyrics by Kalmar and Ruby); *June Moon*, pr. 1929, pb. 1931 (with Ring Lardner); *The Channel Road*, pr. 1929 (with Alexander Woollcott); *Strike Up the Band*, pr. 1930 (musical comedy with Morrie Ryskind; music by George Gershwin and lyrics by Ira Gershwin); *Once in a Lifetime*, pr., pb. 1930 (with Moss Hart); *The Band Wagon*, pr. 1931 (musical revue with Howard Dietz; music by Arthur Schwartz and lyrics by Dietz); *Of Thee I Sing*, pr. 1931, pb. 1932 (musical comedy with Ryskind; music by George Gershwin and lyrics by Ira Gershwin); *Dinner at Eight*, pr., pb. 1932 (with Ferber); *Let 'em Eat Cake*, pr., pb. 1933 (musical comedy with Ryskind; music by George Gershwin and lyrics by Ira Gershwin); *The Dark Tower*, pr. 1933, pb,. 1934 (with Woollcott; based on Guy de Maupassant's story "Boule de suif"); *Merrily We Roll Along*, pr., pb. 1934 (with Moss Hart); *First Lady*, pr. 1935, pb. 1936 (with Katherine Dayton); *Stage Door*, pr., pb. 1936 (with Ferber); *You Can't Take It with You*, pr. 1936, pb. 1937 (with Moss Hart); *I'd Rather Be Right*, pr., pb. 1937 (musical revue with Moss Hart; music by Richard Rodgers and lyrics by Lorenz Hart); *The Fabulous Invalid*, pr., pb. 1938 (with Moss Hart); *The American Way*, pr., pb. 1939 (with Moss Hart); *The Man Who Came to Dinner*, pr., pb. 1939 (with Moss Hart); *George Washington Slept Here*, pr., pb. 1940 (with Moss Hart); *The Land Is Bright*, pr., pb. 1941 (with Ferber); *The Late George Apley*, pr. 1944, pb. 1946 (with John P. Marquand; based on Marquand's novel); *Park Avenue*, pr. 1946 (musical comedy with Nunnally Johnson; music by Arthur Schwartz and lyrics by

Ira Gershwin); *Bravo!*, pr. 1948, pb. 1949 (with Ferber); *The Small Hours*, pr., pb. 1951 (with Leueen MacGrath); *The Solid Gold Cadillac*, pb. 1951, pr. 1953 (with Howard Teichmann); *Fancy Meeting You Again*, pr., pb. 1952 (with MacGrath); *Silk Stockings*, pr. 1955 (musical comedy with MacGrath and Abe Burrows; music and lyrics by Cole Porter; based on Menyhért Lengyel's film *Ninotchka*).

Other literary forms

George S. Kaufman began his literary career by voluntarily writing humorous verse and prose for Franklin P. Adams' column in the New York *Evening Mail*. Later, he was hired to write his own column in the Washington *Times*. Kaufman then replaced Adams at the *Evening Mail* for a short time, was fired, and took a job as a reporter on the New York *Tribune*. Shortly thereafter, he was made drama editor, only to leave the *Tribune* in 1917 for the same position at *The New York Times*. He held on to his relationship with *The New York Times*, despite his success as a playwright, until 1930, when he was asked to resign because his career as a playwright was taking too much of his time. Throughout his life he contributed short sketches, prose humor, and light verse to such magazines as *Saturday Review*, *The Nation*, *Life*, *Theatre* magazine, *Playbill*, and *The New Yorker* (founded by his friend Harold Ross), as well as various newspapers.

Kaufman also wrote several screenplays, although he disliked Hollywood and, as a rule, avoided long-term relationships with the film industry. The Marx Brothers' films *The Cocoanuts* (1929) and *Animal Crackers* (1931), which Kaufman wrote in collaboration with Morrie Ryskind, were adapted from their plays and filmed in New York. Later, Samuel Goldwyn hired Kaufman and Robert E. Sherwood to write the screenplay for *Roman Scandals* (1933); a disagreement with star Eddie Cantor caused Kaufman to invoke the clause of his contract which stipulated that he would not have to work with Cantor. In 1935, Irving Thalberg of Metro-Goldwyn-Mayer guaranteed Kaufman $100,000 to write (with Ryskind) the Marx Brothers' classic *A Night at the Opera* (1935). By 1936, his distaste for Hollywood was such that he refused to adapt his and Moss Hart's Pulitzer Prize-winning play *You Can't Take It with You* for the screen. Ironically, the film later won the 1938 Academy Award for Best Picture.

Achievements

Although George S. Kaufman is generally considered to be one of the greatest geniuses of the Broadway theater, it is difficult to assess his individual talents because he wrote nearly all of his plays in collaboration. *The Butter and Egg Man*, his only full-length comedy written solo, was composed early in his career and shows his talent; nevertheless, apparently never fully confident of his talent even after dozens of successful plays, he continued, until his death, to work with collaborators, some of whom were among the major literary figures of his period. From 1918 to 1955, Kaufman's name appeared as author or coauthor on more than forty productions, some of which were unsuccessful and many of which were successful. Forty-eight full-length motion pictures from 1920 to 1961 were based on plays Kaufman had either written or directed. He directed some forty-five plays, many by notable authors other than himself. As a result, perhaps no one had more influence on the shape and direction of popular drama in the 1920's through the 1950's than Kaufman. He was considered a master of stage technique, an incomparable wit, and an extraordinary satirist. His record of success on the Broadway stage is without equal.

Biography

George S[imon]. Kaufman was born to Joseph S. Kaufman and Henrietta Myers, both members of the German-Jewish community of Pittsburgh. Joseph Kaufman had once worked as a deputy sheriff in Leadville, Colorado, and participated in one of the Ute Indian wars, but returned to Pittsburgh poorer than when he had left. Marrying the wealthiest woman in his social circle was no help, as he soon brought his family to the brink of poverty. Mrs. Kaufman was a hypochondriac, and young George, who had been overprotected because of the infant death of his older brother, became an introverted, skinny adolescent who read adventure stories in *Argosy* magazine. (He even attempted to write for *Argosy* but had nothing accepted.) His father determined to toughen him up by sending him to an old family friend's ranch in Idaho, but the boy was only confirmed in his reclusive tendencies.

In his teens, Kaufman became interested in theater. Encouraged by a rabbi, he first acted the part of a Scotsman in a religious production, and thereafter he was hooked for life. He collaborated on a play in 1903 with another boy, Irving Pichel, who would later become a Hollywood actor-director. The play was entitled *The Failure*, and both boys acted in it.

Kaufman studied law for three months, then gave it up, and on the advice of a physician took a job on a surveying team in West Virginia. That job did not last either, and other jobs followed. He went to secretarial school and became a stenographer for the Pittsburgh Coal Company. He became a window clerk for the Allegheny County tax office. In 1909, Joseph Kaufman got a job with the Columbia Ribbon Manufacturing Company in Paterson, New Jersey, and George became a traveling salesman for the company. It was in Paterson and on his trips into New York City selling ribbons that Kaufman began reading Franklin P. Adams' column "Always in Good Humor" in the New York *Evening Mail*. The column consisted of humorous contributions from throughout the area, as well as Adams' witticisms, and Kaufman began submitting pieces under the initials "G.S.K." to mimic Adams' use of "F.P.A." (only later in his life did Kaufman, who did not have a middle name, decide that the "S" represented "Simon," his grandfather's name.)

Adams recognized Kaufman's talent and urged him to take acting lessons at the Alveine School of Dramatic Art, as well as a playwriting course at Columbia University. In 1912, Adams maneuvered Kaufman into a position on the Washington *Times*, where he wrote a column entitled "This & That," similar to Adams'. He became familiar with the works of Mark Twain while there and honed his staccato writing style and ability to play poker. Within a year, however, the owner of the paper, who had never seen Kaufman face-to-face, noticed him in the office and remarked, "What is that Jew doing in my city room?" After several words were exchanged, Kaufman was fired and returned to New York, where he succeeded Adams at the *Evening Mail*, only to be dismissed. Adams then got him a job on the *Tribune*, where he covered local news. While reporting on incoming ships and other insignificant events, he began cadging free admission into the theaters, and eventually got himself assigned to the drama desk. In 1914, he became the drama editor. Three years later, after losing out to Heywood Broun for the position of top drama critic, he became drama editor of *The New York Times*.

In March of 1917, Kaufman married Beatrice Bakrow, whose ambitions and contacts helped thrust him into the theatrical world. She provided emotional support and critical and social guidance for the always uncertain Kaufman for most of his long career, despite the deterioration of their marital relationship after the stillbirth of a deformed child. They later adopted a daughter, Anne, but, as part of their "arrangement" sought sexual relationships outside the marriage. They remained married until Beatrice's death in 1945.

In 1917, John Peter Toohey noticed a play submitted by Kaufman to the Joseph W. Stern Music Company. The play was never produced, but Toohey introduced Kaufman to impresario George C. Tyler, who offered Kaufman the task of revising a play by Larry Evans and Walter Percival. Though produced, *Among Those Present*, which finally reached Broadway after still more revisions as *Someone in the House*, was never a success. Kaufman next tried to adapt Hans Miller's *Jacques Duval*, a European hit. Although George Arliss played the lead, it, too, failed. Tyler, however, continued to have faith in Kaufman, and put him to work on *Dulcy* with Marc Connelly. Based on a character, Dulcinea, created by Kaufman's friend Adams, the play opened in New York on August 13, 1921, and became an immediate hit.

Connelly and Kaufman worked together until 1924, when each decided to write a play on his own. Connelly became successful on his own and would eventually write the remarkable *The Green Pastures* (pb. 1929).

After the breakup, Kaufman did write *The Butter and Egg Man*, a rare solo effort, but working alone was not to his liking, and he spent most of the rest of his life collaborating. Through the rest of his career, his collaborators included some of the most successful writers of the time, including Edna Ferber, Alexander Woollcott, Herman J. Mankiewicz, Ring Lardner, John P. Marquand, Moss Hart, and Abe Burrows. He also collaborated with Morrie Ryskind, Howard Dietz, Katherine Dayton, Nunnally Johnson, his second wife, Leueen MacGrath, and his biographer, Howard Teichmann. Although he was never much interested in music, Kaufman was associated with George and Ira Gershwin and Cole Porter, and he rewrote Gilbert and Sullivan's *H.M.S. Pinafore*. He served as a "play doctor" for an unknown number of plays for which he got no credit, and he advised John Steinbeck on adapting *Of Mice and Men* for the stage.

After having codirected *The Good Fellow* with Howard Lindsay in 1926, Kaufman was persuaded by producer Jed Harris in 1928 to direct *The Front Page* by Ben Hecht and Charles MacArthur. After he had overcome his shy way of sending notes to the stage, Kaufman also had a remarkable career as a director. Besides his own plays, which he felt might be botched by another director, Kaufman directed *Joseph* (pr. 1930) by Bertram Bloch, *Here Today* (pr. 1932) by George Oppenheimer, *Of Mice and Men* (pr. 1937) by John Steinbeck, *My Sister Eileen* (pr. 1940) by Jerome Chodorov and Joseph Fields, *Mr. Big* (pr. 1941) by Arthur Sheekman and Margaret Shane, *The Naked Genius* (1943) by Gypsy Rose Lee, *Over Twenty-One* (1944) by Ruth Gordon, *While the Sun Shines* (pr. 1943) by Terence Rattigan, *The Next Half Hour* (pr. 1945) by Mary Chase, *Town House* (pr. 1948) by Gertrude Tonkonogy (based on short stories by John Cheever), *Metropole* (pr. 1949) by William Walden, *The Enchanted* (pr. 1950) by Jean Giraudoux, *Guys and Dolls* (pr. 1950) by Abe Burrows and Jo Swerling, and *Romanoff and Juliet* (pr. 1957) by Peter Ustinov. This extraordinary list ought to have been more than enough for one man's lifetime, but when one includes the list of plays he wrote, one sees exactly how inexhaustible Kaufman was.

Yet the anxieties of Kaufman's childhood drove him to do even more. He adapted two of his plays (with Ryskind) for the Marx Brothers for the screen, and then (also with Ryskind) wrote *A Night at the Opera* for them. He directed the movie *The Senator Was Indiscreet* with William Powell and Ella Raines in 1947, but—basically uninterested in the mechanics of filmmaking and disappointed with the way Hollywood was handling McCarthyism—he returned to the theater. He also acted in productions of *Once in a Lifetime* and *The Man Who Came to Dinner* and served as a panelist on an early television show, *This Is Show Business*. Given his extraordinarily productive working life, the legends portraying Kaufman as an incessant womanizer, a skilled poker player, and a regular member of the Algonquin

Round Table may seem exaggerated, but the sheer number of these stories testifies to their probable basis in fact, to his incredible capacity for unceasing activity, and perhaps to a neurotic inability to relax.

The least productive period of Kaufman's life followed the death of Beatrice in October, 1945, and lasted until he married actress Leueen Emily MacGrath in May, 1949. The disparity in their ages led to an eventual separation in 1957, but even after their divorce, Leueen spent much time helping him in various ways as his health declined. Small strokes hindered his ability to work, so much so that he was a mere shadow of himself when directing *Romanoff and Juliet*. In the last few years of his life, his mind deteriorated, and, among other things, he would wander onto Park and Madison Avenues in his nightshirt. After he fell against a radiator in 1961 and was badly burned, he rarely left his bed, and he died peacefully in June, 1961.

Analysis

As a practical man of the theater, George S. Kaufman concerned himself with the meticulous details of whatever project he was working on and gave little consideration to his place in the literary world or posterity. If he was writing, he would badger his collaborators to write better exit lines, to add more humor, to refine every sentence. When directing, he acidly chastized the slightest carelessness of an actor. As a literary figure, though, he was peculiarly unconcerned with plays or productions he had done in the past, eschewing the role of an author of drama, ignoring the possibility that what he had written with his collaborators had literary merit. Only once was he active in the revival of one of his plays, *Of Thee I Sing*. Indeed, his own attitude toward his art has contributed to the critical neglect of his work.

Primary among Kaufman's talents was his wit. The only weapon of a slim, shy boy and honed by his association with Adams, Woollcott, Dorothy Parker, Groucho Marx, and others of the Algonquin Round Table, "wisecracks" became characteristic of a Kaufman play and are obvious in every play on which he worked, from *Dulcy*, his first success, to *The Solid Gold Cadillac*. After three failures on Broadway, the success of *Dulcy*, with Lynn Fontanne in the title role, surprised Kaufman as much as anyone else (he always seemed to see his success as undeserved and always expected a disaster). As Malcolm Goldstein observes, *Dulcy* was basically a rehash of materials used by dozens of writers; what made it different from other plays was its flow of wit.

Although Kaufman would use any form of humor or stage technique to achieve his desired effect—in his plays there are many examples of slapstick, parody, nonsense, and various levels of verbal humor—satire is a recurring element. Ironically, one of the most famous quotations of Kaufman is "Satire is what closes Saturday night," as if he wished to ignore his own use of it. His wit could be quite vicious, particularly toward those who he felt had crossed him in some way. Even Dorothy Parker, the master of the acid quip, was severely wounded by Kaufman's barbs on more than one occasion. Earl Wilson once commented that Kaufman had been "blasting away at somebody or something all his life." It was only natural that such wit would be turned to satiric purpose against the pompous, the pretentious, the rich, and the powerful.

Little in society escaped his satire. *Beggar on Horseback* (written with Marc Connelly), the only commercially successful American expressionist play, satirized the American obsession with success, as if Kaufman were trying to exorcise the ghosts of failure from his own childhood. *Merton of the Movies* (also with Connelly) and *Once in a Lifetime* (with Hart) mocked Hollywood. *June Moon* (with Ring Lardner) satirized Tin Pan Alley. *I'd Rather Be Right* (with Hart) satirized Franklin D. Roosevelt, while *Of Thee I Sing* (with Ryskind) took on the presidential election process and vice-presidency. *The Solid Gold Cadillac* (with Teichmann) poked fun at big business. One of his more curious satiric vehicles is *The Man Who Came to Dinner* (with Hart), in which the major character was based on Kaufman's pompous friend Alexander Woollcott, who even good-humoredly agreed to play the title role in one production. It was perhaps convenient, even wise, for Kaufman to deny that he had satiric intent, particularly when he was more concerned with giving an audience a pleasant evening, but the moral outrage, sarcasm, and derision that is characteristic of satire is present to an extraordinary degree in his work.

Yet another element which can be observed in many of Kaufman's plays is the struggle and eventual triumph of the "little man" against the forces which oppress him, particularly big government and big business. In play after play, regardless of his collaborators, people in low social positions turn the tables on their social superiors. In his early plays, there is usually a relatively innocent young man who is ambitious but not intelligent enough to carry out his plans for advancement without the help of a more intelligent, maternal young woman in love with him. In Kaufman's last play, *The Solid Gold Cadillac*, an old woman triumphs over the executives of General Motors. It is a pattern observed in many of the plays and films of the 1920's and 1930's, such as in Frank Capra's *Mr. Deeds Goes to Town*, and, particularly in the Depression, seemed to draw much of its appeal from the general feeling that the titans of business and their governmental allies had let down or betrayed the common man.

Despite the popularity of Kaufman's plays and their nearly predictable success, only two of his works were taken seriously enough to win the Pulitzer Prize. The first play to win was *Of Thee I Sing*, written with Morrie Ryskind, with music and lyrics by George and Ira Gershwin. Although Kaufman had been forced to soften the satire of *Strike Up the Band* only a few years previously, he believed that the country was weary of the Depression and the Republican platitudes of prosperity being "just around the corner," and might just be serious-minded enough to accept a play that satirized American politics, especially presidential elections. He invited Ryskind to join him on the project. Ryskind, who never believed such a scathing play would ever be produced, thought it might be fun to write. They began with the working title "Tweedledee" to refer to two virtually indistinguishable parties, and the plot of a presidential election hinging on the selection of a national anthem ("The Star-Spangled Banner" was not made the official national anthem until March 3, 1931). The Gershwins, who were attracted by the musical possibilities, were immediately interested and quickly began composing.

Ryskind and Kaufman soon realized the abstractness of their plot and decided to put a romantic interest into it, even though Kaufman maintained an absolute abhorrence of romantic scenes and generally refused to write them, leaving them to his collaborators. In the play, presidential candidate John P. Wintergreen uses the notion of marriage to a "typical American girl" as a device to win votes: He agrees to marry the winner of an Atlantic City beauty contest arranged by his managers. Once elected, however, he rejects the winner, marries his secretary, and causes international turmoil (she is of French descent). Facing impeachment, he is finally saved by his wife's delivery of twins and by a curious interpretation of the Constitution which forces the Vice President to marry the contest winner.

In August, 1931, over a period of seventeen days, the collaborators completed the book, turning the harmless fluff of their plot into withering satire. It opened to rave reviews in Boston and became an extraordinary hit on its opening in New York, when George Gershwin conducted the orchestra and the audience was filled with such luminaries as Mayor Jimmy Walker, ex-presidential candidate Al Smith, Florenz Ziegfeld, Beatrice Lillie, Ethel Barrymore, Condé Nast, and Samuel Goldwyn. The play was praised in every way possible, although critic Robert Benchley dissented. It was compared to Gilbert and Sullivan's *Iolanthe* (pr. 1882) and called a new departure from the musical comedy style. The songs were considered so well integrated that some critics went to the extreme of calling *Of Thee I Sing* more an "operetta" than a "musical," particularly ironic praise, since Kaufman would later do an unsuccessful updating of *H.M.S. Pinafore* called *Hollywood Pinafore* (pr. 1945); he was not much interested in music and often resented the intrusions of songs into his comic plots. In 1932, when the Pulitzer Prize committee astounded the theater world by awarding the prize to a musical for the first time in its history, it caused much controversy, because such plays as *Mourning Becomes Electra* by Eugene O'Neill and Robert E. Sherwood's *Reunion in Vienna* were passed over. The critic of *Commonweal* defended the decision, however, when he wrote that *Of Thee I Sing* ". . . is much closer to Aristophanes than O'Neill ever came to Euripides."

The remark was particularly well-founded. A. Cleveland Harrison has commented extensively on what he perceives as the revival of Aristophanic Old Comedy in the Kaufman-Ryskind play, noting how the episodes of the plot are linked less by a cause-effect relationship than by the development of aspects of the central topic. Extreme characters and situations are used to put ideals into conflict. The ideal of democracy, for example, is in conflict with the reality of it, where politicians use side issues to get themselves elected. The stereotyped characters themselves are less important than the allegorical concepts they represented. Furthermore a wide range of societal types is represented, from Irish and Jewish power-brokers, to newspapermen and Southern pork-barrel senators, each using their particular slang, with many of society's institutions, such as the beauty contest and the vice presidency, subjected to ridicule. The satire was sufficiently irreverent to lead Victor Moore, who played Vice President Throttlebottom, to wonder if he would be arrested on opening night. Today, however, *Of Thee I Sing*, like many of Kaufman's works, seems somewhat dated. The Aristophanic nature of most of his comedies may indeed contribute to the general current impression of them as extremely amusing, cleverly written, brilliantly constructed period pieces.

Other major works

SCREENPLAYS: *Business Is Business*, 1925 (with Dorothy Parker); *The Cocoanuts*, 1929 (with Morrie Ryskind); *Animal Crackers*, 1931 (with Ryskind); *Roman Scandals*, 1933 (with Robert E. Sherwood, George Oppenheimer, Arthur Sheekman, Nat Perrin, and W. A. McGuire); *A Night at the Opera*, 1935 (with Ryskind); *Star-Spangled Rhythm*, 1943.

Bibliography

Freedley, George. "George S. Kaufman, 1889-1962," in *Modern Drama*. VI (1963), pp. 241-244.

Goldstein, Malcolm. *George S. Kaufman: His Life, His Theater*, 1979.

Harrison, A. Cleveland. "Of Thee I Sing, Baby!" in *Players*. XLVII (1972), pp. 275-279.

Hart, Moss. *Act One*, 1959.

Krutch, Joseph Wood. *The American Drama Since 1918*, 1939.

Meredith, Scott. *George S. Kaufman and His Friends*, 1974.

Nannes, Caspar H. *Politics in the American Drama as Revealed by Plays Produced on the New York Stage, 1890-1945*, 1960.

Teichmann, Howard. *George S. Kaufman: An Intimate Portrait*, 1972.

J. Madison Davis

SIDNEY KINGSLEY
Sidney Kirshner

Born: New York, New York; October 22, 1906

Principal drama

Men in White, pr., pb. 1933; *Dead End*, pr. 1935, pb. 1936; *Ten Million Ghosts*, pr. 1936; *The World We Make*, pr., pb. 1939 (adaptation of Millen Brand's novel *The Outward Room*); *The Patriots*, pr., pb. 1943; *Detective Story*, pr., pb. 1949; *Darkness at Noon*, pr., pb. 1951 (adaptation of Arthur Koestler's novel); *Lunatics and Lovers*, pr. 1954; *Night Life*, pr. 1962, pb. 1964.

Other literary forms

Sidney Kingsley is known exclusively for his plays.

Achievements

Kingsley is generally regarded as a social dramatist, one who made the social and political problems of his age the subject matter of his plays. Because his early work was done in the 1930's, a time of economic depression and of a crisis for capitalism, there are strong liberal (at times leftist) perspectives in his dramas. Invariably his characters struggle with a fate not simply personal but, in a very explicit sense, social as well. George Ferguson in *Men in White*, Thomas Jefferson in *The Patriots*, Nicolai Rubashov in *Darkness at Noon*, and Will Kazar in *Night Life* are very different as characters, yet all of them, in Kingsley's plays, must weigh their personal desires and private dreams against their social responsibilities and public ambitions.

Kingsley's plays demonstrate his interaction with the world of his day: its politics, its institutions, its social issues, its technologies. The movies inspired by three of his plays—*Men in White* (1934), *Dead End* (1937), *Detective Story* (1951)—expanded his already strong influence on the popular culture of his day.

By concentrating on the interaction between the idealist and the community in which he functions, Kingsley was able to project the tensions and dynamics of society in the midst of industrial transformation. Although the actions in Kingsley's plays are often melodramatic, they serve to illuminate the struggle between materialism and idealism, between the structures of a society and the people trying to adjust to their social institutions. Few twentieth century writers have been more thorough in examining the dedicated professional and the meaning of work to those whose work is the property of others.

Kingsley is also significant because he has interacted with many of the major talents of his age. The varied list of prominent theatrical people associated with his productions is impressive in itself: Luther Adler, Morris Carnovsky, Elia Kazan, Clifford Odets, Lee Strasberg, Norman Bel Geddes, the Dead End Kids, Lee Grant, Ralph Bellamy, Orson Welles, Howard Lindsay, Russel Crouse, Claude Rains, Jack Palance, Kim Hunter, Buddy Hackett, and Kingsley's wife, Madge Evans. In addition to pursuing his own active career as a creative artist, Kingsley has attempted to encourage the creativity of others, particularly in his work with the Dramatists Guild. Playing many different roles, Sidney Kingsley has been a major figure in American theatrical history.

Kingsley has received extensive recognition for his accomplishments. He received a Pulitzer Prize for *Men in White* as well as New York Theatre Club Medals for it, for *Dead End*, and for *The Patriots*. Kingsley also received New York Drama Critics Circle Awards for *The Patriots* and for *Darkness at Noon*. *The Patriots* also earned for him the New York Newspaper Guild Front Page Award, and for *Detective Story*, he earned a Newspaper Guild Page One Citation and an Edgar Allan Poe Award. *Darkness at Noon* also won a Donaldson Award for Outstanding Achievement and an American Academy of Arts and Letters Award of Merit Medal. Finally, Kingsley has received a Yeshiva University Award for Achievement in the Theatre (1965), a doctor of letters degree from Monmouth College (1978), and an induction into the Theatre Hall of Fame (1983).

Biography

Sidney Kingsley was born Sidney Kirshner on October 22, 1906, in New York City; he has spent most of his life in the New York area. Involved in the drama from an early age, he was already writing, directing, and acting in one-act plays at Townsend Harris Hall in New York City. After he was graduated from high school in 1924, Kingsley attended Cornell University, where he was a member of the Dramatic Club and acted with Franchot Tone. At Cornell, he continued to write plays: His play "Wonder-Dark Epilogue" won a prize for the best one-act play written by a student. After receiving his bachelor of arts degree in 1928, Kingsley did some acting with the Tremont Stock Company in the Bronx. Although he had a role in the 1929 Broadway production *Subway Express*, he decided at that time that acting was not the career for him.

That year, Kingsley went to California where he worked for Columbia Pictures as a play reader and scenario writer, but he soon returned to New York. At this time he was working on his own play, originally entitled "Crisis," later to be *Men in White*. During the writing he began to research the subject matter systematically, a procedure he would employ during the composition of several other plays. Since his play was to be about doctors, he visited various hospitals in the New York City area—Bellevue, Beth Israel, Lebanon—to gather material and to render as accurate a social picture as he could. (One story has it that he once masqueraded as an intern.) While several would-be producers had options on the play, it was finally presented by the soon-to-be-famous Group Theatre. It was their first major success, and the play established Kingsley as a prominent American playwright, winning for him the Pulitzer Prize (in a controversial decision) and the Theatre Club Award. It was also a financial success; Kingsley reportedly received forty-six thousand dollars for the motion picture rights. Kingsley had become a principal figure in the theatrical community of New York.

Kingsley has directed all of his plays except *The Patriots*. Perhaps because he is himself an amateur painter and sculptor, he has shown great concern throughout his career for the physical appearance of his plays onstage. His second drama, *Dead End*, owed its immediate impact in no small part to a spectacular New York setting created by Bel Geddes. Animated by the energetic argot of his New York boys, the Dead End Kids, Kingsley's second play was even more popular and critically acclaimed than his first effort. Although the next two plays, *Ten Million Ghosts* and *The World We Make*, were not the popular hits his first two had been, they also featured memorable visual effects. By this time, Kingsley was regarded as a dramatist of social realism and spectacular staging effects, one whose plots inclined to melodrama and whose sympathies were clearly with the less fortunate.

In July, 1939, Kingsley married actress Madge Evans, a marriage that would last until her death in 1981. She retired from her film career soon after the marriage and assisted Kingsley in the historical research for his new play, tentatively entitled "Thomas Jefferson." She later appeared in the 1943 production version, *The Patriots*. Kingsley found himself inducted into the United States Army in March, 1941, about the time he finished the first version. He spent his free time polishing the play and was rewarded by largely favorable notices, most of which found Sergeant Kingsley's dramatization of the precarious nature of freedom in the early republic pertinent to the contemporary struggle of the United States in World War II. Later in 1943, Kingsley was promoted to lieutenant.

After his discharge from the army, Kingsley spent some time working for Metro-Goldwyn-Mayer on the movie scripts for *Cass Timberlane* (1947) and *Homecoming* (1946). Much of the time in the late 1940's, however, he was back in New York, haunting detective squad rooms to gather material for his new production, *Detective Story*. Even though it did not win the great awards some of his earlier efforts received, *Detective Story*, with its harsh, intense drama and convincing factual setting, is considered by many critics to be Kingsley's best play. Like *Men in White* and *Dead End*, it was made into a successful motion picture.

Kingsley's next drama, *Darkness at Noon*, was based on Arthur Koestler's 1941 novel of the same title. The production, featuring Claude Rains, Jack Palance, and Kim Hunter, was successful enough to win for Kingsley the Donaldson Award and the New York Drama Critics Circle Award. Kingsley and Koestler, however, quarreled publicly about the play; indeed, Koestler threatened to take Kingsley to court for what he thought were distortions of his text. In addition, Brooks Atkinson, the reviewer for *The New York Times*, raised similar unfavorable comparisons between the novel and the play. Produced in 1951, a time of strong anti-Communist feeling (and of reaction against that feeling), the play may have been a victim of its era. In spite of inspiring some harsh criticism, the play ran for almost two hundred performances.

For his next effort, *Lunatics and Lovers*, Kingsley shifted to totally different dramatic material, presenting the mid-1950's in a farce complete with lots of noise, various con games, and a plethora of sexual comedy. Although most critics were not fond of the play, it had a respectable run of more than three hundred performances. *Night Life*, presented in 1962, focuses on a labor racketeer, but in its frenzied surreal quality it reflects an era's growing emphasis on style rather than on social or political issues, an emphasis not suited to Kingsley's talents.

Since *Night Life*, much of Kingsley's creative energy has gone into the writing of a dramatic trilogy, "The Art Scene," which would examine the phenomenon of radical change in the contemporary world as reflected in graphic arts, modern dance, and the theater. Kingsley finished the first part, "Man with a Corpse on His Back," in the early 1970's.

When not involved with his own work, Kingsley has been concerned with encouraging and improving the artistic endeavors of others. Convinced that television was going to set the intellectual and spiritual climate of the age, he was briefly in the 1950's a television consultant to the Columbia Broadcasting System. As president of the Dramatists Guild, he was active in efforts to help young playwrights and to preserve Off-Broadway theater. In the late 1970's, as chairman of New Jersey's Motion Picture and TV Authority, he was able to encourage film companies to shoot movies in the New Jersey area.

In recognition of his many contributions to the cultural scene, Kingsley was inducted into the Theatre Hall of Fame in May, 1983. Few lives have been more intimately involved in the American theater at such a crucial period of its development.

Analysis

As a dramatist, Sidney Kingsley is noted for being a theater technician— not a surprising reputation, since he has spent all of his life in the theater and has directed all of his plays except *The Patriots*. Typically, the characters in his plays represent a social spectrum and dramatize sharp, overt ideological differences. Within this pattern there are also more subtly contrasting pairs of individuals: Gimpty and "Baby-Face," former members of the same youth gang in *Dead End*; the two proletarian brothers in *The World We Make*; the two women who love George Ferguson in *Men in White*; Rubashov and his inquisitor in *Darkness at Noon*.

Kingsley's plays have invariably displayed his fondness for spectacle. His settings are obviously the result of studied decisions, and they appear in virtually every production to be an indispensable element in the play. Bel Geddes' stunning set for *Dead End* articulated the social contrasts at the heart of the play as much as did its plot. The prison set in *Darkness at Noon*, with its spectacular tapping out of communication from one cell to another, starkly defined Soviet Russia for Kingsley's audience. The operating room in *Men in White* and the squad room of *Detective Story* anticipated in their powerful immediacy the television series of a later era. Indeed, Kingsley's sets have sometimes been disproportionately powerful: The expressionistic set of *Ten Million Ghosts* may in fact have been too heavy for the play, and the first two settings in *The World We Make* convey such a sharp, deterministic insistence that the rest of the play, set in John's room, seems too sequestered.

Dr. Schiller's statement in *The World We Make*, that no normal human being lives alone in the world, is a basic truth for Kingsley's plays, which stress the working out of the necessary difficulties in social existence. His characters tend to be types, figures who seem vibrantly alive only when struggling with the idea of their social duties. In this respect, it is society which animates them. Like other social realists, Kingsley has the gift of evoking a sense of community, the feeling that his characters are bound, for better or worse, by a system of deeply felt values. When this system breaks down, as it does in Kingsley's later work, the basic unity of the plays begins to fragment.

The title of Kingsley's first play, *Men in White*, indicates the play's focus on the profession of medicine itself. Throughout, Kingsley is concerned with what a doctor's life is and what it should be, examining the ethics, economics, and the dedication of the medical community. The entire play is confined to various parts of St. George's Hospital, and in one of the most crucial scenes, Kingsley takes the audience into the operating room, where the real and the melodramatic mingle. As Laura prepares to witness her fiancé operating, she suddenly discovers that the case, a botched abortion, is the result of her fiancé's affair. As this is happening, the visual dimension of the play emphasizes the ritual, the impersonal element, of medicine, so much so that the scene becomes an ironic comment on the plot and the action, a measure of the personal frustrations of the characters. The efficiency and sterility of the operating room conveys an atmosphere of professional mystery: The putting on of the gloves, the scrubbing, and the masks all blend to suggest the distinct, new nature of this community and the people in it, and the scientific impersonality of its activities.

Two doctors, one mature and one at the beginning of his career, are at the center of the action. The older man, Dr. Hochberg, is a model for those around him. While he seems casual in his initial appearance, it is soon apparent that he is a very disciplined, confident practitioner, the expert to whom everyone turns for advice and direction. He is a man of principle, informing the rich Mr. Hudson that doctors are more interested in working and learning than in making money, yet he is practical enough at board meetings to realize that the hospital's economy requires wealthy friends. In explaining his profession, he states that success in medicine is essentially a kind of glory, that one lifetime is not long enough to get at all the problems that confront medicine.

The younger man, Dr. George Ferguson, is more dynamically involved in the plot. At a position in life where he must make many crucial career decisions, George finds himself torn between Hochberg's demand for dedication—ten more years of hard work—and the insistence of Laura that he devote more time to her and to his personal life. Despite George's genuine respect for the master professional, Hochberg, his fiancée's request does not seem unreasonable. The conflict here defined between the responsibilities and ambitions inherent in public life and the demands of private life is a recurrent situation in Kingsley's drama.

George seems to acquiesce to Laura's wishes, though he wants to compromise with Hochberg rather than reject him. At this point, the plot is complicated by the botched abortion, a problem, the play suggests, resulting from a thoughtless moment between George and a sympathetic nurse. When Laura discovers the situation, she rejects George, saying that there is no excuse for what he did. Hochberg is much more tolerant and objective, noting that human bodies are human bodies and that the pregnancy was an accident. George seems about to marry the nurse, but she conveniently dies. In the conclusion, George explains to a more forgiving Laura that the hospital is where he belongs and where she ought to leave him. In terms of what the play has presented, he seems to be right.

Kingsley's most popular play, *Dead End*, owed its success to its theatrical boldness and to its projection of the mood of the 1930's. The spectacular set by Bel Geddes emphasized the contrasts of a New York neighborhood by placing a tenement house opposite the exclusive East River Terrace Apartment. For the river, a play area for the boys of the neighborhood, Bel Geddes flooded the orchestra pit. To give the flavor of the working city, a huge, red sand hopper stood prominently in the right center of the stage and a Caterpillar steam shovel stood farther back, up the street.

The boys of the neighborhood—later to be known in motion pictures as the Dead End Kids—carry much of the action of the play. Eager and energetic, they project vividly the communal intimacy of the neighborhood and define the kind of life that is nurtured by such surroundings. Kingsley's transcription of the lower-class New York dialect ("Howza wawda?"— "How's the water?") and his ethnic mixing adds local color to his cultural portrait.

Insistent in its emphasis on economic desperation, *Dead End* is one of the representative literary documents of the 1930's. Like other literary works that examine the social problems of the era, it romanticizes the inner goodness of the poor and treats the rich with contempt. The play is a grim speculation about the power of social conditions to define the fate of the individual.

Two former residents of the neighborhood, Gimpty and "Baby-Face" Martin, have been marked by growing up in this environment, each in his own way. Gimpty, a lame but resourceful slum-boy who has become an architect but cannot find work in the barren economy of the day, suggests the inability of his generation to build a new world, having been deprived of the chance to make its own future; his physical disability symbolizes his socially disadvantaged state. Gimpty is in love with Kay, who has overcome poverty by becoming a rich man's mistress.

Martin, a criminal on the run, serves to trace a more disastrous path for a tenement boy, from the ranks of the underprivileged to the criminal class. He advises the kids to become more violent in their gang wars, to forget about fighting fair. His corruption is certified when even his mother rejects him. Gimpty turns Martin in just when he seems on the verge of hatching a kidnaping scheme, and the G-men kill Martin. In one sense, Gimpty's action is a betrayal of a neighborhood code—indeed he is filled with anguish over his part in Martin's death, but by this time Martin can be seen as one who has gone too far to be saved. In the end, Kay declares her love for Gimpty but will not give up her luxurious life for him.

In the subplot, a Dead End Kid, Tommy, gets into trouble when he plays a trick on a rich boy and then stabs the boy's father in a struggle. This situation opens the possibility that he will go Martin's way. The boys enthusiastically point out that he can pick up all kinds of criminal know-how in reform school; in contrast, his sister Drina is horrified by what seems an inevitable direction for his life. Her plea for the forgiveness of Tommy proves not a strong argument with the rich, but because Gimpty now has the reward money he got from turning in Baby-Face, the two can hire a good lawyer and work to make the social system operate for their benefit.

The conclusion of the play moves back, appropriately, to focus on the rest of the Dead End Kids and their innocent (and ignorant) energy. As they play around with the song "If I Had the Wings of an Angel," the audience is reminded that the boys must fly over the walls of a social prison if they are to have a chance in life.

As a play, *The Patriots* is a skillfully crafted historical drama centered on the conflict in early American history between Jeffersonian democracy and Hamiltonian conservatism. It is also Kingsley's warning about the precarious nature of freedom, a warning that prompted many reviewers to call attention to the play's relevance to World War II and the struggle to preserve democratic institutions. The action begins with Thomas Jefferson's return from France to accept, albeit reluctantly, President George Washington's offer to make him his secretary of state and concludes with Jefferson's election as president. Throughout the play, the three historical giants—Washington, Jefferson, and Hamilton—dominate the stage. Kingsley did extensive research for the play, and he succeeded in introducing much material from original documents, but the strength of *The Patriots* lies in Kingsley's talent for endowing these historical characters with believable personalities.

Throughout the conflict between Jefferson and Hamilton, Washington represents a middle ground, the understanding of two American political extremes. In his concise portrait of the first president, Kingsley brings out a struggle between Washington's weariness with politics and his sense of public responsibility. It is this conflict treated on a larger dramatic scale that animates, as well, the character of Jefferson. Kingsley's Jefferson is a private doer, an inventor and architect who would rather retire to the comforts of private life than deal with Hamilton's petty political intrigues.

Hamilton is more completely the politician, one who will connive but who is also statesman enough to compromise for the better candidate when his side cannot win. The play treats neither Hamilton's ambitions nor his ideas kindly; in fact, Kingsley seems to have gone out of his way to bring in a nasty case involving Hamilton's philandering, perhaps to contrast Hamilton's sense of private pleasures with Jefferson's pastoralism. Although Hamilton is not simply a villain in this version of American history, there is no question that Kingsley's sympathies are with Jefferson, the man who trusts the people. At the end, it is Jefferson who has come to be in the middle, standing between the extremes of anarchy (the excesses of the French Revolution) and monarchy (Hamilton's desire for an aristocratic America). The conclusion places Jefferson's election in the context of progressive history. Hamilton laments that he lacks Jefferson's faith in the people, and both he and Jefferson conclude finally that their particular portion of American history has been fashioned by an irresistible destiny, the people's need for freedom.

In preparation for the writing of *Detective Story*, Kingsley spent two years haunting detective squad rooms in Manhattan, gathering the naturalistic details which would give his dramatization of New York police work a searing authenticity. The resulting production featured a combination of the contemporary and the timeless, a blending of the texture of realism with a structure drawn from dramatic tradition.

The opening of the play features a symphonic blending of the varied characters of the police world and suggests immediately the richness and flexibility of the social interaction in this place of emerging good and evil. The initial dialogue presents the quotidian nature of police work—even its monotony. More idiosyncratic elements appear with Keogh, the singing policeman, and the paranoid Mrs. Farragut. These elements help to sketch out the varied nature of humanity's furtive desperations, an idea basic to Kingsley's vision.

The play focuses on the character of Detective James McLeod and the series of events that combine to destroy him. Although he seems a good man, committed to justice and integrity, McLeod's cruelty and his tendency to make absolute judgments are his tragic flaws. His understandable impatience with the criminal justice system lures him into a false confidence in his own instinctive sense of the evil in people. Although his superior tells him that he has a messianic complex, McLeod sees himself as a man of principle fighting both criminals, whom he believes are a separate species, and the justice system, which he sees as hopelessly flawed by loopholes for criminals. The plot centers on his search for evidence to convict an abortionist, the notorious Dr. Schneider. McLeod is also interrogating a shoplifter and a burglar, Arthur, who is a young first offender. Even though the complainant is willing to drop the charges against Arthur, McLeod refuses to release him, and he also beats Schneider severely during questioning, seriously injuring him. Ironically, McLeod's relentless quest for truth leads to the discovery that his own wife, Mary, whom he has idealized, has had an abortion performed by Dr. Schneider.

Kingsley's stage directions refer to the squad room as "ghost-ridden," and the play reveals McLeod as a prisoner of an unexamined past. His wife's accusation that he is cruel and vengeful, like the father he has despised, rings true: Though torn by his love for Mary, McLeod cannot help but condemn her. For him, forgiveness is too great a price to pay to a flawed world. His whole existence is at stake, yet he is unable to take the action—the act of forgiveness—that would save him. Indeed, his inflexibility is so inherent in his character that when, dying from wounds he received when the burglar tried to escape, he relents—letting young Arthur go and forgiving his wife—this final insistence on the possibility of change seems implausible and melodramatic.

Because McLeod's attitudes are tied to the social system, tragic form and cultural realism blend rather smoothly. The other characters contribute to the tragic dimension as well. The uncooperative attitude of the suborned witness, Miss Hatch, gives credence to McLeod's view that his instincts are more reliable than the system of courts and juries. Both Schneider's lawyer and McLeod's own lieutenant warn him not to act as judge and jury, and Joe Feinson, a journalist, advises him to humble himself before he digs his own grave. Arthur represents the essential goodness McLeod would deny, and Pritchett's willingness to forgive Arthur stands out as one alternative for the detective-accuser. Detective Brody, who has been humanized by the death of his son, makes the strongest case for a belief in the fundamental goodness of man.

Few dramatists have more consistently articulated in their works the liberal political philosophy than has Kingsley. Keenly attentive to the social and political events of his day, Kingsley's plays demonstrate his faith in the essential goodness of people, his suspicion of authority and power, his belief in progress, and his admiration for the life of reason. Thomas Jefferson, the hero of *The Patriots*, is Kingsley's ideal intellectual; those who work with dedication and integrity are the cornerstones of his hope for the future. At times, Kingsley tends to be sentimental about the working class, and frequently his idealism and his belief in the value of work for its own sake lead him into melodramatic conflicts and facile resolutions. At his best, however, he powerfully embodies the virtues of liberal humanism.

Bibliography

Bailey, Paul M. "Sidney Kingsley," in *Dictionary of Literary Biography, Volume VII: Twentieth Century Dramatists*, 1981. Edited by John Mac-Nichols.

Clark, Richard McConnell. *A Critical Analysis of Eight Selected Plays of Sidney Kingsley*, 1976 (dissertation).

Clurman, Harold. "From Lorca Down," in *The New Republic*. CXXIV (February 5, 1951), pp. 22-23.

_____. "Theatre: Good Show," in *The New Republic*. CXX (April 11, 1949), pp. 25-26.

Gassner, John. *Theatre at the Crossroads*, 1960.

Gibbs, Wolcott. "Standard Brands," in *The New Yorker*. XXX (December 25, 1954), pp. 38-40.

Gilder, Rosamond. "The Worlds They Make," in *Theatre Arts*. XXIV (January, 1940), pp. 11-20.

Isaacs, Edith J. R. "Unwritten Plays," in *Theatre Arts*. XX (December, 1936), pp. 919-936.

Krutch, Joseph Wood. "Drama: An Event," in *The Nation*. CXXXVII (1933), pp. 419-420.

Mantle, Burns. *Contemporary American Playwrights*, 1938.

Walter Shear

JACK KIRKLAND

Born: St. Louis, Missouri; July 25, 1901(?)
Died: New York, New York; February 22, 1969

Principal drama

Frankie and Johnnie, pr. 1928; *Tobacco Road*, pr. 1933, pb. 1952 (adaptation of Erskine Caldwell's novel); *Tortilla Flat*, pr. 1938 (adaptation of John Steinbeck's novel); *I Must Love Somebody*, pr. 1939 (with Leyla George); *Suds in Your Eye*, pr., pb. 1944 (adaptation of Mary Lasswell's novel); *Georgia Boy*, pr. 1945 (with Haila Steddard; adaptation of Caldwell's novel); *Mr. Adam*, pr. 1949 (adaptation of Pat Frank's novel); *The Man with the Golden Arm*, pr. 1956 (adaptation of Nelson Algren's novel); *Mandingo*, pr. 1961 (adaptation of Kyle Onstott's novel).

Other literary forms

Although Jack Kirkland wrote or worked on a number of screenplays, he is best known for his stage plays.

Achievements

Kirkland is remembered less for the literary or dramatic quality of his plays than for their social impact. From his first play, *Frankie and Johnnie*, to his last, *Mandingo*, he challenged the accepted standards of the American stage. His plays never won awards and were often castigated by critics for their perceived crudeness, artlessness, and obscenity. Kirkland, in fact, consistently received some of the worst reviews accorded to any major playwright. Nevertheless, his dramatization of Erskine Caldwell's *Tobacco Road*, which premiered on December 4, 1933, became at the time the longest-running play in the history of the Broadway stage, a veritable institution for seven and a half years in the New York theaters. Deplored by most first-night critics, it won influential fans and supporters, who rallied to it as something more than a shocking, brutal (though often humorous) portrait of poor Georgian sharecroppers. Over the years, the play earned a grudging admiration for its frankness, vitality, and dramatic power. From a social standpoint, it led the battle against outdated, unfair, often arbitrary and conflicting censorship laws across the country. None of Kirkland's other works achieved such success (nor did they deserve it), although they did provoke similar indignation and outrage (often justified). Thus, Kirkland's fame rests primarily on the reputation of *Tobacco Road*, which forever changed the state of modern drama.

Biography

Jack Kirkland was a member of the hard-living, no-nonsense school of professional writers (as opposed to artists) epitomized by such figures as Ben Hecht and Charles MacArthur. Like them, he began his career as a reporter, working for such papers as *The Detroit News*, the *St. Louis Times*, and the *New York Daily News*, and like them, he turned his talents to both film and the stage. From this background, he brought to his drama a scorn for sentimentality, a tendency toward sensationalism, and a penchant for a kind of vulgar, black comedy which seems to have characterized his view of the world. He was not so much interested in art as in effect, and the subjects he chose often came from the demimonde familiar to any streetwise reporter.

Kirkland was born in St. Louis, Missouri, on July 25, 1901 (or possibly 1902, since there was no official birth record and other sources conflict on these dates); he was the son of William Thomas and Julia Woodward Kirkland. In his teens, he roamed about the country, working from state to state at odd jobs and often living with and observing the kind of people about whom he would later write. He claimed to have developed a kinship with the poor and homeless which enabled him to understand and sympathize with them in such works as *Tobacco Road*. Soon thereafter he began his newspaper career and made his way to New York, where he attended Columbia University and worked at the *New York Daily News*. In 1924, he married Nancy Carroll, the first of his five wives. (His subsequent wives were Jayne Shadduck, Julia Laird, Haila Stoddard, and Nancy Hoadley.) Carroll was a noted Broadway chorine, and when she was called to Hollywood, Kirkland accompanied her and began to write films, among them *Fast and Loose* (1930), with Miriam Hopkins, and *Now and Forever* (1934), with Gary Cooper, Shirley Temple, and Carole Lombard. Nancy Carroll became one of the most popular stars of the 1930's and was nominated for an Academy Award for her performance in *The Devil's Holiday* in 1930. She and Kirkland were divorced in 1935.

Kirkland's main interest, however, lay in the theater. His first play was *Frankie and Johnnie*, which he wrote in 1928. In 1929, during its Chicago performance, it was attacked as obscene and was closed. Kirkland brought the play to New York in 1930 where, once again, it was closed on charges of obscenity, and Kirkland was arrested. He and the theater owners took the case to court, and in 1932, in a landmark ruling, the play was judged not to be obscene. Kirkland would be involved in many such court cases throughout his career.

In 1931, while in Hollywood, Kirkland was given a copy of Erskine Caldwell's scandalous new novel *Tobacco Road*, which dealt with the almost subhuman existence of a family of Georgian sharecroppers. In the spring of 1933, Kirkland (having spent much of his film earnings on the legal battles surrounding *Frankie and Johnnie*) retreated to the island of Majorca to write a dramatic treatment of the book. He took the play to New

York, where it was turned down by every Broadway producer whom Kirkland approached. Finally, producer Harry Oshrin agreed to cosponsor the play. Kirkland put up his last six thousand dollars as investment and went into partnership with Oshrin and Sam H. Grisman, who became his lawyer and personal representative. The play, directed by Anthony Brown, opened at the Masque Theatre in New York on December 4, 1933, the day Prohibition ended. Despite praise of the acting, initial reviews were generally negative (although not as awful as theater lore has it), and the play lost thirty-eight hundred dollars in the first five weeks. To keep the play alive, ticket prices were reduced, the cast took pay cuts, and Kirkland and the others (except Caldwell) waived their royalties. "I had a hunch after that first night at the Masque that the show would click," Kirkland later remembered. "It left me all in a heap." After this shaky start, *Tobacco Road* established itself as a crowd-pleaser, and its popularity continued largely unabated during its record run of 3,180 performances. Since Kirkland held more than half ownership (approximately sixty-six percent) and sold the film rights to Twentieth Century-Fox for $200,000 plus a percentage of the earnings (Kirkland and Oshrin were listed as associate producers of the film, which was directed by John Ford), he became a rich man. "I hate to think how much money I made," he said shortly before his death, "because so much isn't there any more."

Kirkland never repeated the success he achieved with *Tobacco Road*, but he remained active on the New York theater scene for the next thirty years. In 1936, he coproduced two unsuccessful plays, *Forbidden Melody* and *Bright Hour*. In 1938, he adapted and coproduced John Steinbeck's short novel *Tortilla Flat* (1935) for the stage, but the play quickly failed. Kirkland, furious at the reviews, threw a punch at the New York *Herald Tribune* drama critic Dick Watts, causing *The New York Times* critic Brooks Atkinson to call him "Killer" Kirkland in his review of Kirkland's next play, *I Must Love Somebody*, which Kirkland cowrote (with Leyla George) and produced in 1939. *I Must Love Somebody* proved to be Kirkland's second hit, although its run of 191 performances did not challenge the success of *Tobacco Road*. From 1940 to 1943, Kirkland produced three other plays—*Suzanna and the Elders* (1940), *Tanyard Street* (1941), and *The Moon Vine* (1943)—but the longest run of any was only thirty performances.

In 1944, Kirkland wrote *Suds in Your Eye*, based on Mary Lasswell's popular 1942 novel about the American homefront during World War II. The play was an inoffensive comedy, but it failed to equal the success of the book and closed after thirty-seven performances. The following year, Kirkland returned to the work of Erskine Caldwell with a dramatization of Caldwell's 1943 novel *Georgia Boy*, which Kirkland cowrote with his third wife, Haila Stoddard. He also directed and coproduced this effort, which opened and closed in Boston. In 1949, he wrote, produced, and directed *Mr. Adam*, based on a novel by Pat Frank concerning life after a nuclear explosion. It was savaged by every critic who bothered to review it, called the worst play of the year, and quickly disappeared. *The Man with the Golden Arm*, taken from Nelson Algren's novel about drug addiction, met with more favorable reviews and ran for seventy-three performances, but Kirkland's last play, *Mandingo*, inspired by Kyle Onstott's pulp novel of slavery in the antebellum South, was howled off the stage after only eight performances.

When Kirkland died of heart trouble at the age of sixty-six, he was remembered primarily for *Tobacco Road*. Indeed, he never wrote anything as good, and he returned to the material at various times in his career, through revivals (in 1950 it was revived with an all-black cast) or revisions (at his death he had recently completed a musical version called "Jeeter").

Analysis

Most of Jack Kirkland's work was derived from other sources, usually popular novels, and it would probably be pushing matters to discuss too intently the overriding themes or concerns in his plays. His works reflected not so much a personal philosophy as a desire to entertain. Kirkland did speak of the social significance of *Tobacco Road*, noting that the play realistically illustrated the plight of poor Southern sharecroppers caught in an economic and cultural dead end. He also spoke of Jeeter Lester, his most enduring character, in terms of his universal qualities, stating that his "tolerance for the sins and beliefs of others makes him a man apart, a man whose one great virtue is more important than his lack of lesser ones. . . . " In his other plays, Kirkland dealt with such problems as nuclear war, slavery, and drug addiction, but rarely did he aim for more than a superficial treatment of complex issues. In *Mr. Adam*, for example, the bomb is nothing more than a pretext for a series of dirty jokes, and *Mandingo* uses its historical setting as an excuse to indulge in sexual titillation and sadistic violence. Kirkland was a competent playwright who, with *Tobacco Road*, did achieve a dramatic power above the average, but who all too often appealed to the lowest common denominator among his audiences.

As a professional man of the theater, Kirkland believed strongly in the need for artistic freedom. His willingness to challenge, through lengthy and costly legal battles, the prevailing concepts of obscenity changed the standards of what could be presented on the legitimate stage. For example, Kirkland's first play, *Frankie and Johnnie*, was based on the popular and racy American folk song, which told of love, betrayal, and murder. Kirkland's drama was set in 1849, in the red-light district of St. Louis among the waterfront dens and gambling houses. Like the couple of the song, Frankie is a prostitute and Johnnie a gambler. When Johnnie has a run of luck, he is secretly stolen from Frankie by a rival prostitute, Nellie Bly, on whom he spends all of his money. Meanwhile, to maintain his life-style, Johnnie acts as pimp for Frankie, who works for him out of love. When Frankie discovers that Johnnie has "done her wrong," she shoots and kills him.

Reviewers of the play found it to be coarse, vulgar, and clumsy. As Atkinson put it, "A gaudy lithograph, dramatizing literally the song . . . it has moments of theatrical effectiveness, split seconds of amusement. But it does not sustain itself or what it attempts in the way that Mae West did in *Diamond Lil. . . .* " When first performed, the play was ruled obscene and closed in Chicago, only the second time the city had taken such action. When it opened Off-Broadway at the Carlton Theatre in New York in September of 1930, it was raided following the third performance by plainclothes policemen who arrested Kirkland, the cast, and others connected with the play. Found guilty of obscenity, Kirkland fought for the next two years to have the judgment overturned. In a landmark decision made in March, 1932, Judge Cuthbert W. Pound of the New York Court of Appeals wrote that although the play was "indecent" and "degrades the stage," it "does not counsel or invite to vice or voluptuousness" and, therefore, could not be considered obscene. The play itself had opened on Broadway at the Republic Theatre on September 25, 1930, where it ran for sixty-one performances. By the time of the court ruling, the play was long forgotten.

The *Frankie and Johnnie* ruling, however, set the precedent for the legal maneuverings surrounding Kirkland's second play, *Tobacco Road*, which became a *cause célèbre* for the defenders of free speech and a public event which reached beyond the merits of the play itself. When the play was accepted by the Masque Theatre in New York, its acceptance was contingent on a special clause which allowed either party to break the contract at the end of the first three weeks. Rehearsals started without an actress to play Jeeter's wife Ada (Fay Bainter, Jessie Royce Landis, and Dorothy and Lillian Gish had all refused the role, which was finally taken by Margaret Wycherly). The initial reviews praised the acting of Henry Hull as Jeeter Lester, but they found the play offensive, although infused with a kind of brutal realism. As *The New York Times* review put it, "Although *Tobacco Road* reels around the stage like a drunken stranger to the theatre, it has spasmodic moments of merciless power when truth is flung into your face with all the slime that truth contains." When, after poor business, the Masque Theatre owners exercised their option, the play moved to the Forty-eighth Street Theatre, where it was nursed along with cut-rate prices until it had built an audience largely through word-of-mouth. In the summer, Henry Hull left the show to try his luck in films. As a result, the play was once again asked to move. The owners leased the Forrest Theatre, where, in September of 1934 (with James Barton as Jeeter), the play settled in for its record-setting run. There would be five Broadway Jeeters in all (James Bell, Eddie Garr, and Will Geer all played the role, which became known as "the American Hamlet") in addition to other Jeeters in the three road-show companies that traversed the country.

When the play opened, it was considered a serious portrayal of social dehumanization. *Theatre Arts Monthly* called it "one of the bitterest plays ever produced in New York, but one of the most compelling." Most thought it too brutal for the average audience. Like Caldwell's novel, the play deals with the Lesters, a family of impoverished sharecroppers abandoned on a worn-out farm, which had once belonged to Jeeter's people. Kirkland focused the play on Jeeter's sincere love of the land and, conversely, his basic shiftlessness and immorality. In truth, Kirkland had toned down the more outrageous and shocking episodes found in the book. For example, he had Ada tell Jeeter that Pearl (the daughter Jeeter sold in marriage to Lov Bensey for seven dollars) was not really his child, thus diluting the incestuous nature of Jeeter's desire for her. Grandmother Lester simply disappears in the woods rather than being run over and left to die while the family ignores her, as occurs in the book. Jeeter and Ada are no longer burned to death at the story's end; instead, it is Ada who is killed by Sister Bessie's car as she tries to help Pearl escape to a better life in Augusta. The play thus ends with Jeeter facing an uncertain future, alone but still alive.

Moreover, the longer the play ran, the more its tone began to shift, and soon it was staged more for its comedy than for its supposed realism. Caldwell's novel, to be sure, has many moments of dark humor throughout, but overriding them is a sense of intense outrage. When James Barton, a former vaudevillian, took over the role of Jeeter, he played the character as a reprobate and rascal; lost was the sense of despair and doom which Caldwell's characterization of Jeeter evokes. By the end of its run, the play had become a rollicking and bawdy good time, having long since lost its original seriousness.

Despite its shocking nature, *Tobacco Road* aroused little legal opposition until it began to tour the country. In October of 1935, after it had played for seven weeks without protest in Chicago, its license was suddenly revoked by Mayor Edward H. Kelly, who proclaimed the play "an insult to decent people." Kirkland immediately responded. "I am opposed to arbitrary censorship, particularly when it affects something which has been accepted nationally and possesses a definite social purpose," he said, asking for an injunction against the mayor's ban. Following Chicago's lead, other cities, such as Detroit, Boston, St. Paul, Tulsa, Albany, and even New Orleans, also stopped production of the play, while still other cities allowed only expurgated versions to be performed. In each case, Kirkland and his co-owners went to court. A permanent legal staff was kept busy following the road shows from place to place. By 1939, Kirkland had won thirty-two out of thirty-five court cases. Many celebrities and advocates of free speech had spoken out in favor of the work; even Eleanor Roosevelt defended it as a play of fundamental seriousness and social importance.

By the time *Tobacco Road* closed, it had permanently changed the American stage. *The New York Times* ran an article on May 31, 1941, which colorfully captured the effect of the play: "*Tobacco Road* Retires Tonight Undefeated; Champ of All Plays Beat Critics 3,180 Rounds." More important, it had altered the acceptable moral standards of the stage throughout the country. Cities that had originally banned the play during its first tour accepted it without protest in following years. The play itself was reevaluated as well. As George R. Kernodle observed in a 1947 retrospective article, "The Audience Was Right," in *Theatre Arts Monthly*, the play illustrated man's ability to endure and thus offered reassurance during the Depression years of its run. Kirkland himself believed that the play was an "American classic," as, in fact, it has proved to be.

In his next play, *Tortilla Flat*, Kirkland tried once again to adapt a book by a leading American writer, but John Steinbeck's short episodic novel of Danny and the other *paisanos* living on the outskirts of Monterey, California, had less substance than Caldwell's work, and none of the characters was as original or fascinating as Jeeter Lester. Moreover, whereas *Tobacco Road* had starkly portrayed the grinding effects of poverty on the human will, *Tortilla Flat* tried to make its impoverished inhabitants seem comic and charming free spirits in rebellion against the soul-killing inducements of the materialistic world. As long as Danny and his companions are poor, they are happy, but when Danny inherits two shacks, the responsibility of ownership comes between him and the others. Only by burning down the shacks in an act of deliberate repudiation can Danny recapture the good and easy life. Compared to *Tobacco Road* (however burlesque the play had become), *Tortilla Flat* seemed an abrupt turnabout for Kirkland, and the play lasted only five performances after its premiere on January 12, 1938.

With his next play, *I Must Love Somebody*, Kirkland returned to sexually suggestive material and to the legal arena. He coauthored the play with Leyla George, a former actress who had originated the role of Charmaine in Maxwell Anderson's *What Price Glory?* (pr. 1924). *I Must Love Somebody* is a fictionalized account of the Florodora Girls, six chorines who had appeared in the play *Florodora*, a musical imported from London to the Broadway stage in 1900, where it ran for 505 performances (only the second musical to break the five-hundred-performance mark). The girls, according to legend, all married millionaires. Kirkland and George's version concentrates on the backstage affairs of these high-living women and their top-hatted stagedoor Johnnies, with scenes in the dressing rooms of the Casino Theatre, in private rooms of Canfield's gambling establishment, and in the girls' apartments. Like *Frankie and Johnnie*, the play emphasizes atmosphere more than story. One of the girls, Birdie Carr, falls in love and decides to give up the fast life. Another of the girls, Ann Gibson, discovers that her "protector" has infected her with a venereal disease and kills him. While Birdie and her friends try to keep Ann out of jail, Birdie learns that her lover, Bob Goesling, has no intention of marrying her as he has promised but plans only to set her up as his mistress. The play was judged poorly written and poorly acted when it opened on February 7, 1939, at the Longacre Theatre in New York. It moved, on April 24, from the Longacre to the Vanderbilt Theatre. There, the owners claimed that Kirkland had added salacious material to the show and demanded that it vacate by May 6. Kirkland asked for an injunction against the owners but lost. Nevertheless, the play ran for 191 performances, making it Kirkland's second most successful show.

Kirkland's next work (which he both wrote and directed) was *Suds in Your Eye*, an inoffensive and rather frothy comedy based on a popular novel by Mary Lasswell. When Kirkland adapted it to the stage, the book had sold more than seventy thousand copies since its publication in 1942. Like the book, the play relies heavily on the Irish charm of the main character, Mrs. Nora Feeley (portrayed by Jane Darwell, famed as Ma Joad in the film version of John Steinbeck's *The Grapes of Wrath*). Mrs. Feeley, a type of Tugboat Annie in drydock, owns a junkyard in San Diego, California, during World War II. Living with her is a small Oriental boy named Chinatown, who actually runs the business; Miss Tinkham, a refined, retired music teacher; and Mrs. Rasmussen, a neighbor who can no longer abide to stay with her daughter and her daughter's crass husband. What plot there is revolves around the efforts of this unusual group to save the junkyard from the tax collector and to fix up Mrs. Feeley's nephew, a sailor home from the war, with a local teacher. The play is pure escapism, sweet, sentimental, and silly enough to make it an anomaly among Kirkland's works. It closed on February 12, 1944, after thirty-seven performances.

With *Mr. Adam*, which Kirkland wrote and directed in 1949, he reached the nadir of his career. The play was inspired by a novel by Pat Frank concerning the last sexually competent male on earth after an atomic explosion has left all other men sterile. Homer Adam (who was in a lead mine at the time of the accident) is called upon by the National Refertilization Program to perpetuate the race with a number of desperately willing women. The play was set to premiere at the Lobero Theatre in Santa Barbara, California, on March 12, 1949, but was banned by the city council. After playing in San Francisco, Chicago, and Detroit, *Mr. Adam* opened at the Royale Theatre in New York on May 25, 1949, to the most devastating reviews received by any of Kirkland's works. Both *The New York Times* and *Theatre Arts Monthly* deemed it the worst play of the year. Words such as "gruesome," "loathsome," "tasteless," and "stupid" were used to describe it, and *Mr. Adam* closed after five performances, much to Kirkland's anger and bafflement.

Kirkland's next play was a redemption of sorts and remains one of his most interesting works. *The Man with the Golden Arm*, based on the novel by Nelson Algren, opened at the Cherry Lane Theatre on May 21, 1956. The book had been made into a hit film by Otto Preminger during the previous year, and the film had provided Frank Sinatra with one of his best dramatic roles as Frankie, the small-time Chicago gambler who becomes addicted to drugs. In the opening run of Kirkland's play, Frankie was compellingly portrayed by Robert Loggia. His downfall, leading to murder and suicide, is dispassionately shown through a series of short episodes, chronologically arranged, making the play more impressionistic than realistic. In one sense, the play was a return to the underworld that Kirkland had romantically portrayed in *Frankie and Johnnie*, but in *The Man with the Golden Arm*, the tone is stark and darkly shaded. The dialogue is rough and accurate, and Frankie's doom is inevitable. It is a hard play to like, one that challenges an audience, but it enjoyed a first run of seventy-three performances.

Kirkland's last play was *Mandingo*, a ludicrous and sensationalized reworking of a ludicrous and sensationalized novel by Kyle Onstott. Ostensibly a study of the evils of slavery in antebellum Alabama, the play (like the book and the later film) revels in violence, racism, and sexual perversity. *Mandingo* opened at the Lyceum Theatre on May 22, 1961, with Franchot Tone as the vile plantation owner Warren Maxwell, Dennis Hopper as his crippled son Hammond, Brooke Hayward as Hammond's wife Blanche, and Rockne Tarkington as the Mandingo slave Mede. The play uses every racial and sexual stereotype imaginable: the alcoholic Warren Maxwell beats his slaves, breeds them to sell, and keeps a special one as his mistress. His son, who believes in more humane treatment of slaves, marries a Southern belle who has been her brother's lover and who develops an insatiable craving for the proud slave Mede. Disgusted by his wife, Hammond Maxwell falls in love with a beautiful octoroon, much to his father's outrage. The play ends with Blanche flogging the pregnant octoroon to death and the elder Maxwell shooting his son and the Mandingo in order to preserve the old Southern way of life. A critic in the July, 1961, issue of *Theatre Arts* aptly put it, "The play is so offensively ill-written, wantonly violent, pointless and immoral that everyone connected with it should be ashamed." It closed after eight performances.

Of Kirkland's plays, only *Tobacco Road* is likely to be remembered. It is a better work than its reputation suggests, more important than is suggested by the popular hoopla and controversy which surrounded it. In its original form, before it became a parody of itself, it was a brave dramatization of a serious novel. It affected its audiences (both in this country and abroad) because it acknowledged man's universal suffering and celebrated man's ability to endure. In Jeeter Lester, Kirkland (albeit greatly indebted to Caldwell) gave the modern stage one of its classic roles. Finally, through his willingness to defend his work against censorship, Kirkland expanded the range and depth to which other and better artists could explore the human condition. For these reasons, Kirkland deserves to be remembered as an important figure of twentieth century American drama.

Other major works

NONFICTION: "How Long *Tobacco Road*," 1939 (in *The New York Times*).
SCREENPLAYS: *Fast and Loose*, 1930; *Zoo in Budapest*, 1933; *Now and Forever*, 1934; *Adventures in Manhattan*, 1936; *Sutter's Gold*, 1936.

Bibliography

Caldwell, Erskine. "Introduction," in Kirkland's *Tobacco Road: A Three Act Play*, 1952.
──────── . "Two Years on the Road," in *The New York Times*. XII (December 1, 1935), sec. 11, p. 7.
Crowther, Bosley. "It Paid to Hold a Hot Potatoe," in *The New York Times*. XIV (November 29, 1936), sec. 12, p. 1.
"Jack Kirkland Is Dead at 66; Was *Tobacco Road* Adapter," in *The New York Times*. LX (February 23, 1969), sec. 1, p. 73.
Loney, Glen. *Twentieth Century Theatre*, 1983.
Who's Who in the Theatre, 1967 (14th edition). Edited by Freda Gaye.

Edwin T. Arnold

JAMES SHERIDAN KNOWLES

Born: Cork, Ireland; May 12, 1784
Died: Torquay, England; November 30, 1862

Principal drama

Leo: Or, The Gypsy, pr. 1810, pb. 1873; *Caius Gracchus*, pr. 1815, pb. 1823; *Virginius: Or, The Liberation of Rome*, pr., pb. 1820; *William Tell*, pr., pb. 1825 (based on Friedrich Schiller's play); *The Beggar's Daughter of Bethnel Green*, pr., pb. 1828 (revised as *The Beggar of Bethnel Green*, pr., pb. 1834); *Alfred the Great: Or, The Patriot King*, pr., pb. 1831; *The Hunchback*, pr., pb. 1832; *The Vision of the Bard*, pr., pb. 1832; *The Wife: A Tale of Mantua*, pr., pb. 1833; *The Daughter*, pr. 1836, pb. 1837; *The Love Chase*, pr., pb. 1837; *Woman's Wit: Or, Love's Disguises*, pr., pb. 1838; *Love*, pr. 1839, pb. 1840; *John of Procida: Or, The Bridals of Messina*, pr., pb. 1840; *Old Maids*, pr., pb. 1841; *The Secretary*, pr., pb. 1843.

Other literary forms

Though James Sheridan Knowles is now remembered almost exclusively for his drama, he wrote several other works which were highly regarded in his own time. At the beginning of his literary career, he wrote a popular ballad, *The Welch Harper* (1796), which the critic William Hazlitt praised in his critical volume *The Spirit of the Age* (1825). In 1810, Knowles published (by subscription) a collection of his best early verses entitled *Fugitive Pieces*; this work received little acclaim, and Knowles subsequently wrote little nondramatic poetry.

Knowles's most significant nondramatic writings concerned oratory and theater. The most famous and influential of these was *The Elocutionist* (1823), a textbook on debate that he wrote for his students while teaching at Belfast. This book expresses Knowles's view that the effective speaker must avoid artificiality and be in earnest, and it contains one of his most popular model debates, "Was Julius Caesar a Great Man?" *The Elocutionist* became a very popular textbook in both English and American schools and went through many editions during Knowles's lifetime. His writings and lectures on poetry were also well received by his contemporaries, and his *Lectures on Oratory, Gesture and Poetry*, published posthumously in 1873, considered the adaptability of poetry for elocutionary purposes. Though these discourses often concerned poetry by important writers, such as Sir Walter Scott and Lord Byron, they were neither profound nor influential as literary criticism.

Knowles's *Lectures on Dramatic Literature*, also posthumously published in 1873, reveals the depth of his practical knowledge of stagecraft. These discourses consider important dramatic subjects, such as Greek drama and William Shakespeare's plays, and address significant technical questions of unity, plot, and characterization. Typically, Knowles concentrated more on issues relating to acting than to literary criticism, but his critical judgments were often sound. For example, his view that the unity of action is more essential to successful drama than are the unities of time and place reflects a significant departure from neoclassical dramatic theories. Knowles realized how much his audience valued carefully developed climactic action and powerful characterizations.

Knowles was not a sophisticated theologian, and the religious writings he produced after 1843 were zealous but unsophisticated. These tracts, such as *The Rock of Rome: Or, The Arch Heresy* (1849), were published during a period of great religious controversy in England involving the Oxford Movement, which sought to ally the Anglican Church with Roman Catholicism. In an age during which religious inquiry occupied some of England's greatest minds, Knowles's contribution was negligible. As a preacher, his elocutionary training served him well, but, though he could keep his congregation's attention, his published sermons were undistinguished.

In his youth, Knowles wrote several operas and adaptations of plays written by others, but these are of little significance. His two novels, *Fortesque* (1846) and *George Lovell* (1847), though somewhat more successful in the United States than in England, have now been largely forgotten. Knowles's fame rests primarily on his plays.

Achievements

During the course of the nineteenth century, England's population quadrupled, and the nation became increasingly democratic. The rapidly growing theater audience of the time was largely uneducated; they had little use for either the poetry of Shakespeare or the numerous imitations of Jacobean drama which writers such as Samuel Taylor Coleridge—and a host of lesser talents—inflicted upon them. Instead, they favored the melodrama, with its sentimentalized faith in justice and moral purity and its thrilling, often spectacularly staged, plots.

Though Knowles followed the traditional Aristotelian model in writing his tragedies, he consciously tried to write a less ornate poetic language that would be more appealing to his audience. The critic Hazlitt praised Knowles's avoidance of artificial poetic language, and a reviewer in *The London Magazine* wrote in June, 1820, that the diction of his play *Virginius* was "colloquial and high-spirited; in short it is the true language of life." Though Knowles's attempt to write tragedy in a more realistic style was not always so well received by more conservative critics, his prosaic blank verse was the product of a conscious attempt to reconceive drama in the realistic terms required by his audience. Furthermore, Knowles's concern for English domestic, patriarchal values, a theme which recurs frequently in his plays, touched the lives of his audience and contributed significantly to the success of *Virginius* and that of many of his later dramas. Though critics have complained that Knowles's anachronisms and stilted verse result in inferior tragedy, his attempt to make his drama more realistic and contemporary suited the tastes of his audience. It also can be seen as a significant transition between the obsolete pseudo-Elizabethan style of the late eighteenth and early nineteenth century tragedies and Gothic dramas and the more carefully crafted, satiric, and socially conscious dramas of W. S. Gilbert, Arthur Wing Pinero, and Henry Arthur Jones.

A further ground of Knowles's achievement lay in his collaborations with the greatest actor of his day, William Charles Macready, who played the title role in Knowles's *Virginius*. The great success of *Virginius* launched Knowles's career as a playwright; at the same time, the success of *Virginius* also helped establish Macready as, in Harry M. Ritchie's words, "the leading actor in England, confirming the supremacy of a new [acting] style based on 'domesticity' and 'humanity.'" Until this time, Edmund Kean, another of Knowles's acquaintances, had been the most celebrated actor in England, largely praised for his declamatory—some would say ranting—portrayals of Shakespeare's tragic heroes. When Kean opened in his own version of the Virginius story a few days after the first performance of Knowles's play, he failed completely.

This was Kean's first London defeat, and as such it can be considered the beginning of the decline of the exaggerated, romantic acting style for which he was so famous. From this point on, Kean's acting career declined, while Macready's flourished. *Virginius* not only established Macready as a powerful figure in the London theater but also marked his debut as the leading practitioner of a more natural style of tragic acting. More than one-third of Knowles's subsequent plays were written for Macready or at his suggestion, and their symbiotic relationship enabled both to achieve considerable success and to influence the development of nineteenth century English drama.

Though Knowles was an actor as well as a playwright, his own performances were generally not very successful in England. He lacked the physical stature and intensity required of a great performer, and he had an Irish brogue which many English critics found objectionable. Nevertheless, in September, 1833, he was elected an honorary member of the Cambridge Garrick Club. Knowles's English audience recognized him primarily for his playwriting, but when he toured America in 1834, he was phenomenally successful as an actor and as a lecturer with the less sophisticated American audiences.

Perhaps the most eloquent testimony to the English public's esteem of

Knowles as a playwright is the fact that, in 1850, he was one of four writers nominated to succeed William Wordsworth as poet laureate of England. The other nominees were John Wilson, Sir Henry Taylor, and Alfred, Lord Tennyson; the latter was finally chosen by Queen Victoria, largely because of Prince Albert's liking for Tennyson's great elegy *In Memoriam* (1850). The fact that a writer of Knowles's limited poetic talents could be seriously considered for such an honor might now seem peculiar—even ludicrous— but it shows how highly Knowles's contemporaries regarded his dramas.

Biography

James Sheridan Knowles was born on May 12, 1784, in the city of Cork, Ireland. His father, James Knowles, a somewhat well-known Protestant schoolmaster and lexicographer, was also a first cousin of the great playwright Richard Brinsley Sheridan, for whom he named his son. Knowles was such a frail child that his parents frequently feared for his life, until he finally recovered his health at about the age of six. When he was twelve years old, he made his first visit to the theater; it was at that point that he resolved to be a dramatist.

Knowles's parents had originally intended that he study medicine, but, when his mother died in 1800, his father remarried, and young James, who disliked his stepmother, left home. When he finally did begin to study medicine in 1806, his heart was not in it. Instead, he became interested in the ministry and spent considerable time listening to sermons and yearning to preach to vagrants in the streets of London. Knowles still longed to be a dramatist, and the moral and didactic fervor which he had inherited from his father found expression in the plays which he soon began to write. After receiving his medical degree and practicing for three years, Knowles abandoned his medical career and joined a professional acting company in 1808.

Knowles's acting debut, in which he ill-advisedly attempted the demanding role of Hamlet, was a total failure, and he soon joined another company at Wexford. There, in July of 1809, he met Catherine Charteris, a young Edinburgh actress, whom he married, after a rather tempestuous courtship, on October 15 of the same year. The newlyweds moved to Waterford and joined Cherry's acting company. At Waterford, Knowles first met the as yet unknown actor Edmund Kean, who encouraged him to complete a play entitled *Leo: Or, The Gypsy*, which became a minor hit. Knowles was also improving as an actor, and by the time he and his wife moved to Swansea in 1811, he had acted successfully in operas, comedies, and tragedies. His first child, James, was born the same year, and the young family moved to Belfast.

At this point, Knowles's budding stage career was temporarily halted when his depleted finances forced him to accept a teaching position.

Knowles enjoyed teaching, and his love of oratory made him so successful at it that he opened his own school in Belfast. A short time later he joined his father, who was then headmaster at the Belfast Academical Institution, as his assistant. When the two quarreled violently over the son's theory of elocution, the father was fired and the son resigned his post. Then, in 1815, the success of Knowles's first mature play, the tragedy *Caius Gracchus*, rekindled his theatrical ambitions, and the family moved to Glasgow, where Knowles was teaching in 1820 when the success of *Virginius* made him famous.

Following the triumph of *Virginius*, Knowles established a Whig newspaper, *The Free Press*, in Glasgow, but the enterprise collapsed after three years. In 1825, Knowles was rescued from financial problems by the success of his historical drama *William Tell*, but his first comedy, *The Beggar's Daughter of Bethnel Green*, performed in 1828, failed miserably. Beset again by financial problems, Knowles lectured publicly to supplement his income. His lectures on poetry, elocution, and drama were generally admired, and his financial situation improved accordingly.

In 1832, Knowles presented a petition to Parliament which sought greater protection for author's rights through a copyright bill. In 1833, he supported an actors' movement which opposed the monopoly theaters. Neither enterprise produced results, and Knowles continued to increase his acting roles both in his own dramas and in productions of Shakespeare's plays. Because his stage activities had become full-time, the Knowles family had settled in London, but by that time Knowles had ten children, and, when an acting tour of Ireland in April and May of 1834 was unsuccessful, he resolved to travel to the United States, where his dramas had been much more widely acclaimed than in England.

When Knowles arrived in New York on September 6, 1834, he was hailed as the greatest living English playwright. The tour was a resounding success; Knowles himself was thoroughly surprised by the warmth and praise of the American audiences. He captivated them with dramatic performances in his own plays, lectures, and readings from his poems; indeed, so great was his American success that he formed a lasting friendship with President Andrew Jackson, and, as a farewell gesture, a huge dramatic festival was held in his honor on April 8, 1835. Knowles understandably retained a warm regard for the United States until his death and continued to correspond with his many American friends.

During the eight years following his return to England in 1835, Knowles continued to act in his own plays and wrote several more dramas. He toured Dublin and Edinburgh in 1836 and acted in *William Tell*, *The Hunchback*, *The Wife*, *Virginius*, *The Beggar of Bethnel Green* (his revised version of the earlier, failed effort), and *Alfred the Great*; later that year, he performed in several plays by Shakespeare. Though he announced in

November, 1837, that he would retire from acting, he continued to perform from time to time and to manage his own plays until as late as 1849. *The Secretary* was produced in 1843, but he continued to write plays until 1846. Nevertheless, by 1843, Knowles, for all practical purposes, was no longer actively involved with the stage.

Knowles's retirement from the stage and his subsequent ordination as a Baptist minister can be at least partly explained by certain character traits which he had always possessed. Throughout his life, he had been a man of strong moral principles, and his plays often reflected his convictions. His love of oratory and elocution, combined with his concern with matters of conscience, had almost turned him to preaching in the streets earlier in his life, so Knowles's conversion from the boards to the pulpit was not so radical a change as it might at first appear. Knowles himself was not comfortable preaching against acting and drama, as his new calling required him to do; in fact, he wrote two novels after being ordained and continued to present friends with copies of his plays.

Though his American tour had made him wealthy, Knowles was both generous and careless with his earnings. He continued to realize some income from his popular plays, but not nearly what he would have received if copyright laws had been more stringent. His financial state, therefore, became so critical that in 1846 a group of his friends tried to obtain a pension for him, finally succeeding in establishing a fund for his benefit in 1848. Knowles himself succeeded in securing a pension of two hundred pounds a year. This, with his earnings as curator of Shakespeare's house at Stratford—a post he was awarded in 1848—enabled him to support himself until his death on November 30, 1862.

Analysis

Though critics have maintained that James Sheridan Knowles's tragedy *Virginius* is his greatest play, many of Knowles's most characteristic themes find their earliest expression in his first mature and original play, the tragedy *Caius Gracchus*. *Caius Gracchus* is not a great play, but in spite of its flaws, it is in some respects both intense and compelling. Knowles's radical political attitudes were crudely but vividly presented in some of the title character's speeches, and the prosaic quality of the blank verse reflects Knowles's intention of writing dialogue in a language that would be more accessible to his audience. The play also seeks to combine elements of the popular melodrama with the more traditional themes of political intrigue and ambition which characterize Shakespearean and Jacobean tragedy. *Caius Gracchus* is, in fact, modeled on Shakespeare's *Coriolanus*, and Knowles's title character closely resembles Shakespeare's protagonist, particularly in his self-destructive devotion to the state. *Caius Gracchus* was Knowles's first attempt to synthesize different dramatic influences into a popular form, the domestic tragedy. The later success of *Virginius* can largely be attributed to the fact that in that play Knowles achieved a more natural synthesis of these disparate influences than he did in *Caius Gracchus*. Therefore, the earlier play is interesting as a precursor of the values and techniques which Knowles tried to refine in his later tragedies.

Part of the problem with *Caius Gracchus* was that Knowles had selected an inappropriate story on which to graft his rather mundane and sentimental values. His choice of the traditional and popular story of Virginius, the noble Roman who kills his own daughter, Virginia, rather than allow her to be defiled by the tyrant Appius, was a much more appropriate vehicle to express his ideals of virtue, honor, and liberty. Knowles probably based his tragedy on the version of the story told by Livy, the Roman historian, though he often departs significantly from that model. In *Virginius*, as in his other tragedies, Knowles used the classical five-act structure and emphasized many of the themes he had developed in *Caius Gracchus*: oppression of the common people, the purity of familial (domestic) love, and the importance of justice and liberty.

The villain, Appius, is a deceitful Roman senator who has turned against the citizens who elected him, and Knowles's characterization of him is effective. Appius' evil machinations, though somewhat improbable, are cleverly conceived, and the audience certainly appreciated the malice, if not the psychological subtlety, of his character. Appius is reminiscent of Shakespeare's Richard III, and, though he lacks Richard's complexity, his absolute depravity generates an exciting plot. Appius' character was clearly conceived in the tradition of the "fall of princes" tragedy, and Knowles obviously intended his audience to rejoice loudly at his demise. In fact, the playwright seems consciously to have sacrificed psychological complexity for moral effect.

Virginius, on the other hand, is as noble as Appius is evil. In act 4, Virginius reviles Appius for his treachery and incites the crowd to attack him. After leading the charge, Virginius is deserted by the cowardly citizens; realizing that he can no longer save his daughter from Appius, Virginius stabs her to death and races, mad with grief, from the Forum. Knowles conceived the daughter's character along typically sentimental Victorian lines. She is beautiful and pathetic in her innocence and vulnerability, but she lacks any deeper qualities. Thus, her death has no real tragic impact. Though it is Virginia who dies, Knowles directs our real pity toward her father, forced by circumstances to kill his only child.

Like *Caius Gracchus* and *Virginius*, Knowles's next tragedy, *William Tell*, has civic liberty as its main theme. *William Tell* is based on a play by the great German playwright, Friedrich Schiller, but it lacks the philosophical depth of its model. By modern standards it also suffers considerably from the excessive ranting of the protagonist. Knowles was probably influenced by the work of Lord Byron in this regard, but while the Byronic hero is driven by some mysterious obsession, the emotions of Knowles's hero are superficial. The addition of humorous episodes and lyrics also tends to detract from the play's unity, and it was later revised from five to three acts, which improved it greatly. Next to *Virginius*, *William Tell* was Knowles's most popular tragedy. Its romantic excesses and volatile speeches were well suited to Macready's acting style and thus made it successful onstage.

Knowles's comedies are somewhat less competent than are his tragedies. Though his tragedies frequently suffered from shallow characterizations and unimpressive poetry, they often succeeded in terms of presenting an exciting plot that could keep an audience involved. Furthermore, both *Caius Gracchus* and *Virginius* combine contemporary, Renaissance, and classical dramatic influences into a compelling whole. In his comedies, however, Knowles's characters are often poorly conceived, while the complex plots and subplots, inspired by Elizabethan comedies, are poorly integrated. Knowles's penchant for the five-act structure caused him to include considerable extraneous material in his comedies. In fact, one of his best comedies, *The Beggar of Bethnel Green*, is a three-act revision of the earlier, unsuccessful five-act play *The Beggar's Daughter of Bethnel Green*. Knowles's most popular comedy, *The Hunchback*, was also much improved by revision from five to three acts. None of his comedies, however, showed the artistic consistency of *Virginius*.

As a dramatist, Knowles was trying to achieve two conflicting goals. He wanted to reach his audience by banishing artificiality from dramatic poetry and by using more natural cadences of speech, yet he could not help but aspire to the traditional poetic standards of the greatest Renaissance writers. Both Knowles's tragedies and his comedies reflected the taste of his time as well as the limitations of his creative abilities. Nevertheless, they are often superior to the dramas of his contemporaries, many of whom gave themselves up to writing facile and sensationalized melodramas. Knowles's drama has its share of such elements, but their presence is always counterbalanced by the playwright's attempt to restore the grandeur of the Renaissance tradition to the nineteenth century stage.

Other major works

NOVELS: *Fortesque*, 1846; *George Lovell*, 1847 (3 volumes).

SHORT FICTION: *The Magdalen and Other Tales*, 1832; *The Letter-de-Cachet*, 1835; *Tales and Novelettes*, 1874.

POETRY: *The Welch Harper*, 1796; *Fugitive Pieces*, 1810.

NONFICTION: *The Senate: Or, Social Villagers of a Kentish Town*, 1817; *The Elocutionist*, 1823; *The Rock of Rome: Or, The Arch Heresy*, 1849; *The Idol Demolished by Its Own Priest*, 1851; *The Gospel Attributed to Matthew Is the Record of the Whole Original Apostlehood*, 1855; *A Debate upon the Character of Julius Caesar*, 1856; *Lectures on Dramatic Literature*, 1873; *Lectures on Oratory, Gesture and Poetry*, 1873; *Lectures on Dramatic Literature: Macbeth*, 1875; *Sheridan Knowles' Conception and Mrs. Irving's Performance of Macbeth*, 1876.

Bibliography

Fletcher, Richard M. *English Romantic Drama, 1795-1843*, 1967.

Hasberg, Ludwig. *James Sheridan Knowles' Leben und Dramatische Werke*, 1883.

Horne, Richard Hengist. *A New Spirit of the Age*, 1844.

Knowles, Richard Brinsley. *The Life of James Sheridan Knowles*, 1872.

Macready, William Charles. *Diaries*, 1912. Edited by William Toynbee.

——————. *Reminiscences*, 1875. Edited by Sir Frederick Pollock.

Meeks, Leslie Howard. *Sheridan Knowles and the Theatre of His Time*, 1933.

Nicoll, Allardyce. *History of English Drama, Volume V: Early Nineteenth Century Drama*, 1959.

Michael McCully

ARTHUR KOPIT

Born: New York, New York; May 10, 1937

Principal drama

The Questioning of Nick, pr. 1957 (staged), pr. 1959 (televised), pb. 1965 (one act); *Gemini*, pr. 1957; *Don Juan in Texas*, pr. 1957 (with Wally Lawrence); *On the Runway of Life, You Never Know What's Coming Off Next*, pr. 1957; *Across the River and into the Jungle*, pr. 1958; *Aubade*, pr. 1959; *Sing to Me Through Open Windows*, pr. 1959, pr. 1965 (revised), pb. 1965; *To Dwell in a Palace of Strangers*, pb. 1959; *Oh Dad, Poor Dad, Mamma's Hung You in the Closet and I'm Feelin' So Sad: A Pseudoclassical Tragifarce in a Bastard French Tradition*, pr., pb. 1960; *Mhil'daiim*, pr. 1963 (one act); *Asylum: Or, What the Gentlemen Are Up To, Not to Mention the Ladies*, pr. 1963 (also as *Chamber Music*, pb. 1965, pr. 1971); *The Conquest of Everest*, pr. 1964, pb. 1965; *The Hero*, pr. 1964, pb. 1965; *The Day the Whores Came Out to Play Tennis*, pr., pb. 1965 (one act); *The Day the Whores Came Out to Play Tennis and Other Plays*, pb. 1965 (includes *Sing to Me Through Open Windows*, *Chamber Music*, *The Conquest of Everest*, *The Hero*, *The Questioning of Nick*; reissued as *Chamber Music and Other Plays*, pb. 1969); *An Incident in the Park*, pb. 1967; *Indians*, pr. 1968, pb. 1969; *What Happened to the Thorne's House*, pr. 1972; *Louisiana Territory*, pr. 1975; *Secrets of the Rich*, pr. 1976, pb. 1978; *Wings*, pr. 1977 (radio play), pr., pb. 1978 (staged), pr. 1983 (televised); *Nine*, pr. 1982 (music, libretto, and lyrics by Maury Yeston; adaptation of Federico Fellini's film *8½*); *End of the World*, pr. 1984.

Other literary forms

Arthur Kopit has written *The Conquest of Television* (1966) and *Promontory Point Revisited* (1969) for television. In addition, an article by Kopit entitled "The Vital Matter of Environment" was published in *Theatre Arts* in April, 1961.

Achievements

Critics have applied labels to Kopit based on his first successful work, *Oh Dad, Poor Dad, Mamma's Hung You in the Closet and I'm Feelin' So Sad*, and while his work has continued to evolve, the labels have stuck. Reviewers called the play an unsuccessful example of the Theater of the Absurd and Kopit an Absurdist whose extraordinary titles have been far more enticing than his plays. In spite of these charges, *Oh Dad, Poor Dad, Mamma's Hung You in the Closet and I'm Feelin' So Sad* won the Vernon Rice Award and the Outer Circle Award in 1962 and was popular enough to be made into a motion picture (directed by Richard Quine and Alexander Mackendrick) in 1967.

While Kopit's titles certainly attract attention, he is more than a clever deviser of titles. *Indians*, for example, must be considered one of the major American plays written in the 1960's, and *Wings*, one of the major dramas of the 1970's. Furthermore, he has displayed a diversity of style and a range of theme uncommon among his contemporaries. Kopit has publicly criticized the American theatrical tradition, especially as embodied by Broadway—a stance which may in part account for his lack of critical recognition. Subsidized by a Harvard University Shaw Traveling Fellowship, Kopit toured Europe and studied continental theater in 1959, and his essay "The Vital Matter of Environment" summed up his feelings about the mediocrity and lack of vitality of the American theater in comparison to European drama. "One can never wholly dissociate a work of art from its creative environment," he wrote, "Tradition has always been the basis of all innovation. . . . Style is related to tradition to the extent that it is representative of a cultural or social characteristic of its creative environment, and is itself characteristic to the extent that it has evolved from or rebelled against any of these." Consequently, Kopit charged, the lack of tradition in the American theater forces American playwrights to rely on European dramatic innovations. Clearly, Kopit has used his knowledge of European traditions to bring innovations to the American stage. Although some of his work is obviously and even consciously derivative, he has gone beyond his models to produce distinctive plays of great strength.

In 1964, Tyrone Guthrie, with the help of a Rockefeller Foundation grant of seventy thousand dollars, offered to mount Kopit's one-act plays *The Day the Whores Came Out to Play Tennis* and *Mhil'daiim* in connection with the University of Minnesota, but a problem arose with university officials. The university's position was that the intent of the grant was to provide playwrights with an opportunity to revise scripts under experimental conditions, and that the plays were not meant to be performed publicly, in spite of Kopit's assumption to the contrary. Kopit withdrew his plays from rehearsal, and in a scathing interview in the January 13, 1964, issue of *The New York Times*, he accused the university of "deceit" and "censorship in its most insidious form" in denying him the benefit of an audience.

Like all successful playwrights, Kopit roots his plays in performance. His recognition of the importance of producing an effect on his audience is central to his writing, yet his intellectual approach to his themes keeps his dramas from degenerating into melodramas. The combination of powerfully emotional theatrical moments and significant subject matter is a staple in Kopit's drama.

Kopit is sensitive both to the dignity of mankind and to the absurdity of the human condition. To explore this tension between dignity and absurdity, Kopit has utilized a number of different formats and techniques; *The Questioning of Nick* is realistic, *Oh Dad, Poor Dad, Mamma's Hung You in the Closet and I'm Feelin' So Sad* contains Absurdist elements, *Indians* owes some of its structure to Bertolt Brecht's concept of epic theater, and *Wings* is surreal, impressionistic, psychological realism.

Biography

Arthur Lee Kopit was born in New York City, New York, on May 10, 1937, the son of George Kopit, a jeweler, and Maxine (née Dubkin) Kopit. He married Leslie Ann Garis, a concert pianist from Amherst, Massachusetts, on March 14, 1968; they have a son, Alexander Garis Kopit, who was born in 1971.

During an "uneventful" childhood, living in a prosperous suburb in which he found himself to be the "victim of a healthy family life," Kopit demonstrated an interest in dramatics by entertaining his friends with puppet shows. Radio was an important element in his development; he says, "It's a much more exciting medium than TV because it involves your creative faculties." Although he wrote for the school newspaper while attending Lawrence (Long Island) High School, Kopit showed little inclination toward a career in the arts when he was graduated in 1955, and he entered Harvard University with a scholarship to study electrical engineering. After taking some creative writing courses, however, he decided that he wanted to become a playwright, and he was graduated cum laude and Phi Beta Kappa with a bachelor of arts degree in June, 1959.

Kopit's first theatrical experiences at Harvard took place during his sophomore year; as he reports in the introduction to *The Day the Whores Came Out to Play Tennis and Other Plays*, "My career was determined." His class work with Robert Chapman and his success under the tutelage of Gaynor Bradish, a tutor in Dunster House who was in charge of its Drama Workshop, stimulated Kopit's interest in the stage and introduced him to the fundamentals of playwriting. Over a period of three or four days during his spring vacation, the aspiring dramatist wrote *The Questioning of Nick*, a one-act play which won a collegewide playwriting contest the following fall; it was subsequently performed on television in New Haven, Connecticut, in June, 1959. The seven other dramas that Kopit wrote while studying at Harvard include *Don Juan in Texas*, written in collaboration with Wally Lawrence; *On the Runway of Life, You Never Know What's Coming Off Next*; *Across the River and into the Jungle*; "Through a Labyrinth"; and the productions of his senior year, *Aubade, Sing to Me Through Open Windows*, and *To Dwell in a Palace of Strangers*, the first act of a projected three-act drama that was published in the *Harvard Advocate* in May, 1959. A revised version of *Sing to Me Through Open Windows* was produced Off-Broadway in New York in 1965 and in London in 1976.

During a tour of Western Europe in 1959, Kopit wrote *Oh Dad, Poor Dad, Mamma's Hung You in the Closet and I'm Feelin' So Sad* "to enter [in another] playwriting contest at Harvard," this time in the Adams House competition. Again Kopit's work won a prize, and the reaction when the play was mounted as a major undergraduate production was so overwhelming that, with the aid of a Ford Foundation grant, it was moved to the Agassiz Theatre in Cambridge, Massachusetts, in January, 1960. Kopit had cast a young woman from Radcliffe College in one of his Harvard productions, and through his friendship with her, he was introduced to the Broadway producer Roger L. Stevens. *Oh Dad, Poor Dad, Mamma's Hung You in the Closet and I'm Feelin' So Sad* opened at the Phoenix Theatre in New York City on February 26, 1962, as part of their repertory offerings, produced by Stevens and directed by famed choreographer Jerome Robbins. The play ran for 454 performances before it closed on March 31, 1963, and it then toured for eleven weeks. On August 27, 1963, it returned to the Morosco Theatre in New York for a brief revival (forty-seven performances). *Oh Dad, Poor Dad, Mamma's Hung You in the Closet and I'm Feelin' So Sad* was the first of Kopit's plays to be published by a major house, Hill and Wang, and it has been performed in London, Paris, Australia, Belgium, Canada, Italy, Mexico, the Scandinavian countries, Turkey, and West Berlin. Kopit also received the Vernon Rice Award and the Outer Circle Award in 1962, and a film version was released by Paramount in 1967. The motion picture did not repeat the success of the stage play.

Asylum: Or, What the Gentlemen Are Up To, Not to Mention the Ladies, was scheduled to open at the Off-Broadway Theatre de Lys in March, 1963, but after five preview performances, Kopit decided to cancel the production. The dramatist reports that the bill was actually composed of two one-act plays, *Chamber Music* and a companion piece that he intended to expand into a three-act play later. The concept for *Chamber Music* occurred to Kopit sometime in 1959, though he did not begin writing the play until late in the spring of 1962, finishing it that summer. The author withdrew the plays because he "wanted to do more work on them." *Chamber Music* was revised and rewritten during the summer of 1964 and staged in London in 1971. With *The Day the Whores Came Out to Play Tennis, Sing to Me Through Open Windows, The Hero, The Conquest of Everest*, and *The Questioning of Nick*, it was collected in *The Day the Whores Came Out to Play and Other Plays*, the second of Kopit's five volumes to be published by Hill and Wang. The collection was published under the title *Chamber Music and Other Plays* in England four years later.

The Hero and *The Conquest of Everest* were both written in March, 1964. Kopit explains that *The Hero* contains no dialogue because he was "struck dumb by the prospect of writing two plays in a single day." *The Conquest of Everest* was produced in New York in 1964 and in London in

1980; *The Hero* was produced in New York in 1964 and in London in 1972.

As part of a Rockefeller Foundation grant, two other one-act plays, *The Day the Whores Came Out to Play Tennis* and *Mhil'daiim*, were to be staged at the Tyrone Guthrie Theatre in Minneapolis, Minnesota, in February, 1964, but, as mentioned above, Kopit withdrew the plays because of a disagreement with the University of Minnesota. On March 15, 1965, director Gerald Freeman opened *The Day the Whores Came Out to Play Tennis* on a double bill with *Sing to Me Through Open Windows* (directed by Joseph Chaikin) at the Player's Theatre in Greenwich Village. *Sing to Me Through Open Windows*, written while Kopit was at Harvard, had actually served as a curtain raiser for *Oh Dad, Poor Dad, Mamma's Hung You in the Closet and I'm Feelin' So Sad* in the New York previews in 1962, but because of production difficulties, it, too, had been canceled before opening night. The revised version also played in London in 1976. Next came *An Incident in the Park*, published in Bob Booker and George Foster's *Pardon Me, Sir, but Is My Eye Hurting Your Elbow?* in 1968; in 1969, one of his television plays, *Promontory Point Revisited*, a segment of the series *Foul* on the New York Television Theatre, followed.

Kopit's next major play, *Indians*, was written with the aid of a Rockefeller Foundation grant. It premiered as part of the Royal Shakespeare Company's repertory at the Aldwych Theatre in London under Jack Gelber's direction on July 4, 1968, a symbolically appropriate date for this play. On May 6, 1969, the play was transferred to the Arena Stage in Washington, D.C., and on October 13 of the same year, it was moved again to the Brooks Atkinson Theatre in New York under the direction of Gene Frankel (ninety-six performances). High production costs were blamed when the play, cited by Otis L. Guernsey, Jr., as one of the "best plays of 1969-1970," closed on January 3, 1970. *Indians* was met with critical acclaim and has been performed in France, Germany, Japan, and the Scandinavian countries. In 1976, Robert Altman, working from a script suggested by Kopit's play, directed a film entitled *Buffalo Bill and the Indians: Or, Sitting Bull's History Lesson*. Kopit received $500,000 for the screen rights to *Indians*.

Between 1969 and 1977, Kopit's output diminished, and he wrote nothing of great significance for the stage. The Impossible Time Theatre held a Kopit Festival in 1977; in the same year, Kopit wrote *Wings*, which had been commissioned in the fall of 1976 by Earplay, the drama project of National Public Radio. John Madden directed the version of *Wings* broadcast on National Public Radio in 1977, and when Kopit, at the urging of Robert Brustein, then dean of the Yale School of Drama, rewrote the work for a stage presentation during the Yale Repertory Theatre's 1978 season, Madden again served as director. *Wings* was produced at the New York Shakespeare Festival in 1978 (sixteen performances at the Public/

Newman Theatre), at the Lyceum Theatre in 1979 (113 performances), and in London in 1979; it was published simultaneously in America and Canada in 1978, with British publication coming the following year. *Wings* was televised on the Public Broadcasting System in 1983.

Like many contemporary American playwrights, Kopit has subsisted at least in part through the support of foundation grants, supplemented by academic positions. He was awarded a Guggenheim Fellowship in 1967 and a Rockefeller grant in 1968; he was a National Endowment for the Arts grantee and a Fellow at the Center for the Humanities at Wesleyan University from 1974 to 1975; he served as playwright-in-residence at Wesleyan from 1975 to 1976; he was a CBS fellow at Yale University from 1976 to 1977; and he has been an adjunct professor of playwriting at the Yale School of Drama since 1979. In addition to the awards already noted, Kopit was the recipient of a National Institute of Arts and Letters Award and was elected to the American Academy of Arts and Letters in 1971; in 1979, he won both the Italia Prize for his radio version of *Wings* and the Pulitzer Prize for the stage version.

Kopit prefers to live and work away from people ("any holiday resort in the off-season . . . Majorca . . . [in] a huge hotel almost empty"). A man of the theater, he has also directed some of his own works, including the 1959 television production of *The Questioning of Nick*, and the stage productions of *Oh Dad, Poor Dad, Mamma's Hung You in the Closet and I'm Feelin' So Sad* in Paris, in 1963, and of *Louisiana Territory* in Middletown, Connecticut, in 1975.

Analysis

There has been relatively little scholarly attention paid to the works of playwright Arthur Kopit, with almost nothing written about his entire can, and most of the criticism that has been published is not very impressive. Furthermore, those critics who attempt an overview of the plays usually devote a fair amount of time to discussing the plays that he wrote as an undergraduate at Harvard. While Sherwood Anderson, Robert Sherwood, Eugene O'Neill, and other playwrights have moved from Harvard to Broadway in the past, critical studies of their works have focused on what they wrote as professional playwrights. There are three related reasons that justify a different approach to Kopit. First, the Harvard plays represent nearly half of the author's output; second, the majority of his twelve later plays have been short and relatively insignificant; and third, as a result of these first two points combined with the reputation established by his major plays, several of the Harvard pieces have been published and are thus easily accessible.

The best of Kopit's early plays is *Sing to Me Through Open Windows*. Clearly not meant to be realistic (the set is a bare stage hung with black curtains), the drama is in the tradition of Theater of the Absurd and shows the influence of Samuel Beckett in its setting, language, pauses, minimal plot, and mysterious characters. In spite of Kopit's statement that Beckett "has had no influence on me as far as I know," critics have pointed out structural and linguistic resemblances between this play and Beckett's *Endgame* (pr. 1957).

The protagonist of the play is a boy, Andrew Linden, who visits the home of a magician, Ottoman Jud, and his helper, Loveless the Clown, in the middle of a dark forest. Ottoman and the Clown have entertained Andrew on the first day of spring every year for five years. This year, however, Ottoman's illusions fail, and Andrew is exposed to the games that Ottoman and the Clown play, mysterious games that also prove unsuccessful. This year, too, Andrew announces that he wants to stay with Ottoman, but the announcement is made in the third person, answering a "Distant Voice of Ottoman," as though the event is being recalled even while the present action continues: "And although I say them, some time later I will ask myself, Now what was it again that you said to him . . . back there? . . . And the boy said yes, he wanted to stay there. . . . I love you, Mr. Jud." The play ends with Ottoman apparently dead and Andrew gone.

The format of the work combines with its symbolism to depict a transitional moment in life. Memory and the present intermix as Andrew must leave the unworried, love-filled, exciting, circuslike atmosphere of his childhood and move into manhood. Ottoman, a symbolic father figure, is failing, certainly growing old and perhaps even dying (another transition), and while he can put his arm around the boy's shoulder to encourage him, the youngster must continue his journey through life alone. Symbolically, the time of year during which the action takes place represents hope, birth, and renewal, but it is cold, and snow is falling as the play ends, negating the positive aspects of spring and suggesting the fear that both old man and young man feel as they approach the unknown. Kopit has said that *Sing to Me Through Open Windows* is "about the necessity of certain things dying to enable certain things to live. It deals with memory and time. . . . "

Oh Dad, Poor Dad, Mamma's Hung You in the Closet and I'm Feelin' So Sad caught theatergoing audiences in America by surprise, and a summary of the action provides a clue as to why this happened. The three-scene production, subtitled *A Pseudoclassical Tragifarce in a Bastard French Tradition*, is set in a Caribbean island hotel where Madame Rosepettle, her son Jonathan, two large Venus flytraps, and a cat-eating, talking piranha fish named Rosalinda (after Rosepettle's husband's former secretary) are in transit. Also traveling with the family is the stuffed body of Rosepettle's husband, which is kept in a coffin when traveling and hangs from a hook in Rosepettle's bedroom closet the rest of the time: "He's my favorite trophy. I take him with me wherever I go," she chortles. In scene 1, Rosepettle harangues the bellboys and dominates her son. Scene 2, set two weeks later, brings Jonathan together with a young governess, Rosalie, who tries to seduce him, but who is run off by his mother. One week later, in scene 3, Rosepettle is courted by elderly Commodore Roseabove, but her story of how she brought about her husband's death (a description that paints men as bestial and women as virginal) unnerves him. She proclaims that her goal in life is to protect her son (he was delivered after a twelve-month term, so she obviously began her campaign early): "My son shall have only Light!" Later, while Rosepettle is out on her habitual round, searching for couples making love on the beach so she can kick sand in their faces, Rosalie returns to try to persuade Jonathan to run off with her, but she is so self-centered and insensitive that her sexual desire arouses only terror in Jonathan. When his father's corpse falls on them, Rosalie commands, "Forget about your father. Drop your pants on top of him, then you won't see his face." The play concludes when Rosepettle returns to find that Jonathan has killed the girl by smothering her.

There are many Freudian and Oedipal overtones to *Oh Dad, Poor Dad, Mamma's Hung You in the Closet and I'm Feelin' So Sad*, with its theme of a domineering mother and Milquetoast son. The theme is not a new one, having been dealt with in Sidney Howard's *The Silver Cord*, (pr. 1926), and more recently in Harold Pinter's *A Night Out*, (pr. 1960), and Philip Roth's *Portnoy's Complaint*, (1969), yet Kopit's embroidering of the theme with man-eating plants (symbolic of the emasculating wife/mother), maniacal cuckoo clocks, uncontrollable tape recorders (as in Arthur Miller's *Death of a Salesman*, pr. 1949), and self-propelled chairs, spiced with a loved one's body (as in Joe Orton's *Loot*, pr. 1965), results in a unique creation.

Some critics claim that Kopit is metaphorically portraying the neurosis brought about by the tensions of the nuclear age. This reading is certainly reinforced by the dramatist's use of Absurdist techniques, though this interpretation is not completely convincing. The play is not really an Absurdist play, in spite of Kopit's use of Absurdist techniques—a careful examination of Rosepettle's dialogue, for example, reveals the psychological realism which underlies the bizarre surface of the action. There are flashes of brilliance in the grotesque humor, but they are not sustained throughout the play. Some critics called the work a satire that mimics avant-garde conventions, while others dismissed it as an unsuccessful example of the Theater of the Absurd. In any case, the play conclusively established Kopit's theatrical talent.

After a series of lesser works, Kopit surprised audiences again with *Indians*, his second major play. *Indians* fuses the principal themes and techniques of Kopit's previous works. The conception of the play dates to March, 1966, when Kopit read a statement made by General William Westmoreland, the commander-in-chief of American forces in Vietnam, regarding incidents in which American soldiers had killed Vietnamese civilians: "Of course innocent people have been killed. In war they always are. And of course our hearts go out to the innocent victims of this." Realizing that this sentiment could be traced throughout American history, Kopit put Westmoreland's exact words in the mouth of a character in *Indians*, Colonel Forsythe, who speaks them while looking over the site on which a group of Indians have been massacred the day before. The casual dismissal of the action is overwhelming. At the moment that he read Westmoreland's quote, Kopit has recalled, he "was listening to Charles Ives' Fourth Symphony. There are two orchestras playing counterpoint. The orchestras play completely opposing pieces of music based on American Folk songs— 'Shenendoah,' 'Columbia the Gem of the Ocean.' . . . You have this serene, seraphic music based on these folk songs, and then the violent opposition of a marching band drowning it out." The dramatist admits that when the Westmoreland quote was juxtaposed to the music, "I just sort of went berserk."

Another ingredient that contributed to the play's success was the tempering influence of Kopit's intellectual approach to his material. In both *Don Juan in Texas* and *Across the River and into the Jungle*, he had touched on the source of mythic heroes. In *Indians*, he complemented this interest with research. The emotional content and the research came together in the composition process to create interwoven subtexts: "Most of the scenes in the play are based on real incidents that were then distorted." For example, Kopit notes, "The scene on the Plains is based upon a famous expedition of the Grand Duke Alexis. Spotted Tail was not killed then, but he could have been." He goes on to observe that "in a way he was killed; he was made to play the stage Indian for the Grand Duke."

The play is composed of thirteen scenes, alternating between Buffalo Bill's Wild West Show and an 1886 Indian Commission hearing. The extravagant Wild West Show segments illustrate American prejudices, reveal Buffalo Bill's character, comment on historical events, and develop Kopit's theme that Americans create heroes through a mythmaking process that lets their society justify the destruction of other less powerful societies. The commission scenes demonstrate how alien the white and Indian societies appear to each other. The whites do not understand why Indians will neither abide by their treaties nor recognize the innate inferiority of their race. The Indians do not understand how the treaties can be valid, since land cannot be owned, and also why, if there are treaties, the whites do not abide by the agreed-upon terms. Neither side understands, respects, or grants dignity to the opposing side.

The conflict between basic cultural instincts is emphasized by the tension between the alternating scenes and epitomized by the contrast between Westmoreland's words and the noble, moving surrender speech given by

Chief Joseph in 1877, which Kopit incorporates into the play twice, the second time as the concluding speech in the play:

> . . . I am tired of fighting. Our chiefs have been killed. . . . The old men are all dead. It is cold and we have no blankets. The children are freezing. My people, some of them, have fled to the hills and have no food. . . . No one knows where they are—perhaps frozen. I want to have time to look for my children and see how many of them I can find. Maybe I shall find them among the dead. Hear me, my chiefs. I am tired. My heart is sick and sad! From where the sun now stands, I will fight no more, forever.

For his part, Buffalo Bill is trapped by his own nature, by historical events, and by America's need to create heroes. He is instrumental in destroying a people and a way of life he admires.

Kopit does not intend his play to be taken on a literal level. The chronology (referred to as a "Chronology for a Dreamer") that is supplied in the printed version of the play is not the chronology followed in the drama. Spotted Tail rises after his death to make a speech. The opening, in which the figures of Buffalo Bill and Sitting Bull are seen as though they are in museum cases, is intended to alert the viewer immediately that the play is not to be taken realistically. Instead, Kopit offers an emotional gestalt, an impressionistic, surreal representation of his theme. By means of a deliberately confusing Brechtian production through which the spectators are made aware of historical processes, the playwright forces them to realize that those processes are man-made, not natural elements, and that they are alterable. The play gets off to a weak start, but after the first three or four scenes, the cumulative effect of Kopit's dramatic structure begins to build, and the play gathers power as it progresses, each scene taking its strength from the scenes that precede it while simultaneously adding to their impact.

As impressive as *Indians* was, *Wings* was the product of an even more mature dramatist and is probably Kopit's finest work. Again he combined a strong emotional expression with an intellectual context, and again he relied on the themes and techniques that had served him well in the past, but he explored new material as well. Stylistically there is an impressive distance between the realism of *The Questioning of Nick* and the impressionism of *Wings*; there is also an interesting thematic progression from the commonplace subject matter of the early plays to the public, social impulse behind *Indians* and then to the personal, individual content of *Wings*.

In the spring of 1976, Kopit's father suffered a massive stroke that rendered him incapable of speech. This event became the source of *Wings*'s emotional content. During his visits to the Burke Rehabilitation Center in White Plains, New York, as he explains in a Shavian preface to the published script, Kopit formulated what became the operative or controlling questions for the play, going beyond a mere exploration of the problems of communication and of the nature of language: "To what extent was [his father] still intact? To what extent was he aware of what had befallen him? *What was it like inside?*" In addition to his father, the dramatist observed several other patients, upon whom the protagonist, Emily Stilson, was to be modeled. Kopit not only became involved in trying to convey what it would be like to undergo the personal and terrifying catastrophe of a stroke but also began examining the nature of identity and of reality itself, for to the disoriented victim, reality is confused and unverifiable, and the resultant terror must be faced in virtual isolation.

To supplement his own observations, Kopit once more turned to exhaustive research. The published text of the play has an epigraph from Charles Lindbergh's *The Spirit of St. Louis* (1953), which describes the pilot's feeling of being cut off and unsure of what is real; ironically, the feeling is similar to that experienced by a stroke victim, and Lindbergh's words are later echoed in Emily's dialogue. Kopit also drew on two books concerning brain damage, Howard Gardner's *The Shattered Mind* (1975) and A. R. Luria's *The Man with a Shattered World* (1972), and on the experience of the center's therapist, Jacqueline Doolittle, herself a former stroke victim.

The effective representation of the mind of the victim is what sets this drama apart from most of its contemporaries and supplies a strength that would be missing if the playwright had adopted a documentary approach. The ninety-minute play moves from fragmentation to integration, a movement synchronized with stage effects—live and recorded sound, colored and flashing lights, shifting points of view, a minimal set conveying a sense of limbo, overlapping dialogue, loudspeakers situated throughout the theater, and other such devices, which exercise the potential of the theater to the maximum.

The play is open-ended in that it comes to no climax or conclusion. Performed without intermission, it is composed of four segments. In "Prelude," Emily suffers her stroke. In "Catastrophe," she realizes that something has happened, but she cannot determine what or identify her status. "Awakening" traces Emily's transition from a total lack of understanding to the dawning of understanding. In "Explorations," the final segment, she begins to sort out her identity and starts to appreciate the significance of her condition. Although these states of being are distinct, the person progressively experiencing them cannot perceive either edge of the transition, a condition that Kopit reproduces nicely while still managing to maintain a sense of Emily's gradual reconstruction of her personality and of reality itself.

The dramatist's careful combination of logic and nonsense, of articulate speech and babble, parallels his stage effects to depict an extraordinary, nonverbal sequence of events. There is not much action in *Wings*, and what there is seems confusing and unstructured. The audience, however, soon becomes deeply involved with Emily; tension is created not by dramatic action, but by the audience's effort to decipher what is happening in the play and what is real, and by their concern for Emily. The charge that *Wings* is not interesting because it lacks sufficient rising action is similar to the criticism leveled against Eugene O'Neill's *Long Day's Journey into Night* (pb. 1955) and is equally invalid. *Wings* is not meant to entertain superficially in the way that Lanford Wilson's *Talley's Folley* (pr. 1979), or Neil Simon's plays do; like *Long Day's Journey into Night*, it sheds light on the perennial human condition.

Ironically, Kopit's reputation currently rests on *Oh Dad, Poor Dad, Mamma's Hung You in the Closet and I'm Feelin' So Sad*, the weakest of his major works. In *Indians* and *Wings*, Kopit has proved himself a master craftsman, and the seriousness of his subject matter establishes his credentials as potentially the most important American playwright of his generation. Kopit has fulfilled some of that great promise, and he has demonstrated an ability to develop his technical skills and to apply those skills to significant topics. If his evolution continues at the same rate, he will become one of the major playwrights of the twentieth century.

Other major works

NONFICTION: "The Vital Matter of Environment," pb. 1961 (in *Theatre Arts*).

TELEPLAYS: *The Conquest of Television*, 1966; *Promontory Point Revisited*, 1969.

Bibliography

Auerbach, Doris. *Sam Shepard, Arthur Kopit, and the Off Broadway Theatre*, 1982.

Brustein, Robert. *The Culture Watch: Essays on Theatre and Society, 1969-1974*, 1975.

_____. "The New American Playwrights," in *Modern Occasions*, 1966. Edited by Philip Rahv.

_____. *Seasons of Discontent: Dramatic Opinions, 1959-1965*, 1967.

_____. *The Third Theatre*, 1970.

Cohn, Ruby. "Camp, Cruelty, Colloquialism," in *Comic Relief: Humor in Contemporary American Literature*, 1978. Edited by Sarah B. Cohen.

Gilman, Richard. *Common and Uncommon Mask*, 1971.

Greenberger, Howard. *The Off Broadway Experience*, 1971.

Hennessey, Brendan. "Interview with Arthur Kopit," in *Transatlantic Review*. XXX (Autumn, 1968), pp. 68-73.

Kauffmann, Stanley. *Persons of the Drama*, 1976.

Kostelanetz, Richard. *The Theatre of Mixed Means*, 1971.

Wellwarth, George E. *The Theatre of Protest and Paradox*, 1964.

Wolter, Jürgen. "Arthur Kopit: Dreams and Nightmares," in *Essays on Contemporary American Theatre*, 1981. Edited by Hedwig Bock and Albert Wertheim.

Steven H. Gale

BERNARD KOPS

Born: London, England; November 28, 1926

Principal drama

The Hamlet of Stepney Green, pr. 1957, pb. 1959; *Good-Bye World*, pr. 1959; *Change for the Angel*, pr. 1960; *The Dream of Peter Mann*, pr., pb. 1960; *Enter Solly Gold*, pb. 1961, pr. 1962 (music by Stanley Myers); *Stray Cats and Empty Bottles*, pr. 1964 (televised), pr. 1967 (staged); *The Boy Who Wouldn't Play Jesus*, pr., pb. 1965 (children's play); *David, It Is Getting Dark*, pr., pb. 1970; *It's a Lovely Day Tomorrow*, pr. 1975 (televised), pr. 1976 (staged) (with John Goldschmidt); *More Out than In*, pr. 1980; *Ezra*, pr. 1981.

Other literary forms

Bernard Kops is a prolific writer. He has published numerous novels, including *Awake for Mourning* (1958), *Motorbike* (1962), *Yes from No-Man's Land* (1965), *The Dissent of Dominick Shapiro* (1966), *By the Waters of Whitechapel* (1969), *The Passionate Past of Gloria Gaye* (1971), *Settle Down Simon Katz* (1973), *Partners* (1975), and *On Margate Sands* (1978). His books of poetry include *Poems* (1955), *Poems and Songs* (1958), *An Anemone for Antigone* (1959), *Erica, I Want to Read You Something* (1967), and *For the Record* (1971). Kops's powerful autobiography, *The World Is a Wedding*, was published in 1963. His dramatic writing includes work for television and radio as well as for the stage; much of it is unpublished, but available in typescript form from David Higham Associates, a London literary agency.

Achievements

First and foremost, Kops is a lyric poet who uses the theater, television, and radio as vehicles for poetry. Theatrically, he is an innovator in his use of music and songs and in his often successful attempts to restore vitality to hackneyed themes. Kops's exploration of fantasy, of inner states of being, and of schizophrenia is juxtaposed to the presentation of realistic, sordid surroundings. His handling of dream logic is superb and explains why he is so attracted to the radio as a dramatic form. Radio drama depends upon pauses, sounds, words, silences, and the intimate relationship between the listeners (the unseen audience) and the unseen performers in the studio. Such a form is ideally suited to Kops's synthesis of past and present, actuality and fantasy.

Kops's plays have been hailed as triumphs of sordid realism much in the kitchen-sink mold, as imaginative explorations of psychic worlds, and as politically charged allegories. Kops was at first bracketed with Harold Pinter and Arnold Wesker, two other East End Jewish dramatists who emerged in the new wave of British drama heralded by the 1956 Royal Court Theatre performance of John Osborne's *Look Back in Anger*. Each has since gone his own way, the differences being greater than the similarities. Unlike Pinter's work, Kops's theater is frequently overtly Jewish. While hostility in Pinter is characterized by innuendo and body movement sometimes erupting into violence, hostility in Kops is overt; it does not simmer. Unlike Wesker, Kops does not preach. Most of Kops's drama, even when focusing upon old age and death, has a vitality, an instinctive sense of life, and often a coarse humor which are lacking in Wesker.

The relative critical neglect of Kops may result in part from his extensive work in nontheatrical dramatic forms such as radio and television; his prolific activity as a novelist may have further distracted attention from his dramatic achievements. Nevertheless, following the widespread publicity given to his brilliant evocation of Ezra Pound's insanity in *Ezra*, Kops is beginning to be recognized in England as a supreme master of dramatic dream poetry.

Biography

Bernard Kops's work is intensely autobiographical. Details of his early life may be found in *The World Is a Wedding*. He was born in Stepney in the East End of London in 1926. His father was a Dutch Jewish immigrant cobbler who came to London's East End in 1904, and his mother was born in London of Dutch Jewish parents. Kops was the youngest of a family of four sisters and two brothers. Although his family was very poor, Kops grew up in an intense, colorful, and cosmopolitan environment. The English Fascist demonstrations and counterdemonstrations of the late 1930's in the East End of London provided a personal background for the awareness of anti-Semitism which pervades Kops's work.

Kops left school when he was only thirteen to earn a living as best he could—as a docker, chef, salesman, waiter, liftman, and barrow boy, selling books in street markets. Already writing and reading intensely, he was particularly moved by Eugene O'Neill's *Mourning Becomes Electra* and its depiction of family conflicts and fantasy states. T. S. Eliot was another early literary influence, from whom Kops gained insight into the theatrical use of popular songs. The foundations for Kops's dramatic methodology were formed at the evening drama classes he attended at Toynbee Hall in London's East End.

During World War II, Kops's family moved around England in frequent evacuations and return trips to the badly blitzed East End. The postwar years saw Kops acting in repertory theater; traveling through France, Spain, and Tangier; living in a caravan in Camden Town, North London;

and taking drugs. Following the death of his mother in 1951, Kops was committed to a psychiatric hospital. Kops has twice been institutionalized; the concern with extreme mental states in his work clearly has a personal genesis. Kops's meeting with and marriage in 1956 to Erica Gordon, a doctor's daughter, eased his bereavement and transformed his life, giving him the support he so desperately needed. They had four children, and, beginning in the late 1950's, he earned his living as a professional writer.

Kops's first play, *The Hamlet of Stepney Green*, was produced by Frank Hauser at the Oxford Playhouse in 1957, subsequently moving to London's Lyric Theatre and then to New York. With the success of this play, Kops arrived on the theatrical scene. Kops was the first person to be awarded the C. Day Lewis fellowship (1980), was the recipient of several Arts Council bursaries, and has been writer-in-residence in Bristol and the London Borough of Hounslow.

Analysis

Much of Bernard Kops's work revolves around family situations, the basic conflict he sees in such situations, and the individual's doomed attempt to free himself from the family and its nets. He is obsessed with family themes, with people tied together in intense love-hate relationships. Like O'Neill, Kops uses the theater to express the inner life of human beings. All of his plays are shadowed by the streets and sounds of the London of his childhood, by his Jewishness, by his family, and by his wild, anarchic, surrealistic inner life.

The plot of *The Hamlet of Stepney Green* provides a good illustration of the nature of Kops's drama. Kops transforms William Shakespeare's *Hamlet* into an East End London Jewish lyric fantasy. Hamlet becomes David Levy, twenty-two years old, tall, and intelligent, who wants to be a singer like Frank Sinatra. He refuses to see his future in terms of inheriting his aging father's small pickled-herring street stall. Kops describes two ways in which David Levy can be played—as someone who can sing, or as someone who cannot: "The crucial thing about David is that although he is bored with the life around him he is waiting for something to happen." Hava Segal, the daughter of Solly Segal, David's father's best friend, becomes Ophelia and dotes on David. Throughout the first act, Sam, David's father, is dying; the curtain to the first act falls as he dies. At the moment of death, father and son are united. Like so many of Kops's subsequent creations, the old man is unwilling to relinquish his hold on life. He is sad because there is a gulf between him and his son and because there is no love in his relationship with Bessy, his young and still quite attractive wife.

In the second act, Sam returns to the stage as a ghostly figment of his son's imagination, calling upon David to avenge his death. In David's heightened imagination, his mother has poisoned his father. Bessy is going to marry Solly Segal. David, imitating Hamlet, dresses in black and is treated as though he were insane by relatives and a chorus of salesman. Meanwhile the ghost attempts to dampen David's vengeful desires. Sam, aware that only good can come through Bessy's marriage to Solly, arranges, through a séance, for the marriage to take place.

In the final act, the ghost persuades David to mix a seemingly deadly potion to be used on the wedding day, but the potion is actually life-giving. The drama concludes on a frenzied note of love and reconciliation, and the ghosts haunting David's mind are liberated and disappear into nothingness.

Throughout *The Hamlet of Stepney Green*, realism and fantasy interweave. The play, like much of Kops's work, is rooted in the East End of London (the equivalent of New York's Lower East Side)—its characters, noise, bustle, rhythms, and songs. Music is used to great effect by Kops, to re-create the East End ambience, to evoke nostalgia, and to provide a sad, ironic commentary on the action. During the mourning period at the end of the first scene of the second act, for example, Sam's family and friends gather around the home in the traditional Jewish way to remember him. David, in black, disrupts tradition by singing "My Yiddisher Father" to the tune of Sophie Tucker's famous "My Yiddishe Mamma." The "shiva" rituals (for mourning the dead) are parodied by transforming the gender of popular song lyrics. Reviewers noted that the play was far too long, especially when it indulged in lyric fantasies concerning the past—a reflection of Kops's lack of discipline. Kops often forgets his plot, forgets the limitations of the stage, and even forgets the patience of an audience; Sam takes a long time to die. In spite of these defects, the play generates a tremendous sense of life and bustle, brilliantly rendering ordinary London Jewish existence with its hopes, fears, music, and tears.

Good-Bye World, performed in Guildford Surrey in 1959, has long, rambling dream sequences which make it theatrically unsatisfactory. Kops enjoys conveying the details of low-life London. His setting is a Paddington boardinghouse, and the protagonist is a thuggish, obsessive dreamer, a hardened criminal of twenty-two who breaks out of prison because his mother has committed suicide. The play contains three of Kops's basic dramatic ingredients: London rhythms and atmosphere, dreams and fantasies, and mothers and their influence upon their sons. The protagonist, John, has two objectives: to find out if his mother left him a message, and to give her a decent burial. In his room, the characters who knew his mother—a landlady, a drunken Irishman, and a blind circus clown—come and talk to him. While John listens, the police wait outside to recapture him. The long personal monologues of each character reveal Kops's fascination with the poetry of the inner mind, his handling of dream logic, his sudden switches of mood and tone, and his exploration of schizophrenia. These dramatic elements achieve their summit in his mature drama, *Ezra*.

Kops's next play, *Change for the Angel*, which had a limited run at the Arts Theatre in London in March, 1960, develops many of the ideas introduced in *The Hamlet of Stepney Green* and *Good-Bye World*. Paul Jones is a teenager in search of a meaningful life; his sister, Helen, is a machinist; and his brother, Martin, is the leader of a local gang of Fascist youths. Paul's father, Joe, is a baker whose business has been adversely affected by a supermarket. He takes to drinking in the pub to escape from work and the family. Paul wants to be a writer and resists his father's efforts to turn him into an engineer. By the end of the first act, Paul is praying for his father's death, and Helen has been seduced by an American serviceman.

The second act introduces the first of a long line of Kopsian characters, just released from mental institutions, who have to face a hostile world. In this instance, the former mental patient is the victim of Joe's attempted rape.

In the third act, Paul hates his father so much that he invokes the Angel of Death, who takes the wrong life—his mother's instead of his father's. The audience is treated to a very lengthy deathbed scene and to frenetic, hysterical reactions. Paul leaves home and, in a manner reminiscent of the ending of D. H. Lawrence's *Sons and Lovers*, goes into a hostile world after his beloved mother, rather than the detested father, dies.

The name of the family in *Change for the Angel* may be Jenkins, but the cadences are those of East End Jewish family life. The play contains Kops's recurrent ingredients, but there is also an overt political conviction not so evident in his earlier plays. The threat of nuclear disaster dominates the play, as does the continual fear of anti-Semitism.

Oedipal elements, the bomb, and lyric fantasy are the essential ingredients of *The Dream of Peter Mann*, which suffered the insult, on its Edinburgh Festival premiere early in September, 1960, of having half the first-night audience walk out. The play proved to be too expensive to perform satisfactorily and too much goes on in it; nevertheless, it remains one of Kops's most interesting works. The author reflected in a personal communication that he "wanted to write a play about a man who was up with progress but got mixed up in power and in so doing helped to create the destruction of the world." The protagonist, Peter Mann, dominated by his strong Jewish mother, has grown up in a London street of run-down small shops. A small, cunning tramp named Alex persuades Peter to travel the world to make his fortune. After he robs his mother's safe, Peter's fantasies take over most of the remainder of the play. The people in the street become robots compulsively digging for uranium, then change into savages prepared to lynch Peter on his return from his travels, into slaves working twenty-four hours a day preparing shrouds for the next war, into rebels, and finally back into themselves. During the action of the play, Peter is defeated, victorious, penniless, and enormously wealthy. Clearly, Peter Mann is Everyman, a leader and a victim, hopeful and despairing, generous and selfish, shrewd and simple. The fantasy is an enlargement of reality, another dimension of the everyday. Kops keeps the play in control by grounding its frenetic fantasy in the sounds of London Jewish life, conveyed through colloquial dialogue, Cockney backchat, dance-hall rhythms, catchy songs, and contemporary political references.

Superficially, *Enter Solly Gold* may appear to be different from Kops's earlier working-class-oriented plays; nevertheless, it has much in common with them. It won a competition organized by Centre 42, an early 1960's movement designed to bring the theater to people outside London and to factory districts where little if any theater had been performed. The hero of the drama is a carpetbagger, Solly Gold, who informs the audience within the first few minutes that "work is all right for workers . . . but for Solly Gold?" Solly is scavenging in London's East End, trying to get enough money to emigrate to America, his "spiritual home," where he believes "dog eats dog" and ". . . that's the way [he] like[s] it."

The opening scene is Rabelaisian. Solly fiddles money out of a tailor, carries on with the tailor's wife, sleeps with a hard-bitten prostitute, and dons the clothes of a widow's deceased husband, a rabbi, in order to cheat her out of a bunch of large chickens.

In the second scene, Solly, still disguised as a rabbi, has gate-crashed a wealthy home where a wedding is taking place. Solly announces the start of "Rabbinical Chicken Sunday" and gradually takes over the household, making himself indispensable to Morry Swartz, head of the house and king of a shoe business, a melancholy millionaire. Solly sets about making Morry the Messiah so that Morry will find the peace of mind he lacks and Solly will get the cash he needs.

In the course of the drama, Kops lashes out at bar mitzvahs, weddings, and big business, writing some of his most sustained and brilliant comic lines. Many of these reflect the love-hate attitude he has toward his own Anglo-Jewish background. The play's warm reception in non-Jewish communities is evidence, however, of its universality: Carpetbaggers exist everywhere, and Kops's depiction of greed and hypocrisy speaks to audiences of all kinds, as does his blend of slapstick comedy and exuberant verbal wit.

David, It Is Getting Dark, produced and performed in France in 1970 by the distinguished French actor Laurant Jerzieff, depicts the conflict between a right-wing English writer and a Socialist English Jewish writer. In this play, Kops tackles an issue which has continued to absorb him: how to reconcile great writing with inhuman political theories. The play also examines the relationship between victim and victor. While *David, It Is Getting Dark* can be viewed as a trial run for *Ezra*, it is a valuable work in its own right. Success and failure, the need to love and be loved, loneliness and the need to communicate, Jewishness and anti-Semitism, the need for God, the way human beings use and are used in turn by one another, sterility, and creativity, the dark forces within the self transcending political conviction—all these themes swirl together in the play. The long final scene, which depicts David, the Jewish poet, returning to his room and dancing with his mistress, Bella, while Edward, the reactionary artist, pleads with him to look at his manuscript, is made unforgettable by Kops's powerful, haunting, and evocative poetry.

David, It Is Getting Dark is intensely autobiographical: David's sense of failure is Kops's. There is superb irony in the fact that nearly a decade after its composition, Kops decided to restore Ezra Pound to life. A seemingly failed English Jewish writer uses a great anti-Semitic writer's last, sad years to show how human that writer was and, in the process, achieves fame for himself. In *David, It Is Getting Dark*, Edward Nichols appropriates David's autobiography; Kops transforms Pound's last years in *Ezra*.

Ezra explores the relationship between insanity, political extremism, and poetic power. Kops has long been obsessed with the question of how great poetry can be written by a man holding vicious political opinions and insidious economic ideas. At the same time, *Ezra* continues his exploration of extreme mental states. Kops gets inside Pound's mind by creating a world in which all things coexist at the same time: the past and the present, the living and the dead, fact and fantasy, truth and illusion. Once again, Kops's drama inhabits the territory of fantastic juxtapositions. Benito Mussolini and Antonio Vivaldi are as real for Pound as his wife, his mistress, and the officials who put him into a cage and then into a Washington, D.C., asylum. Kops's Pound is sensitive, learned, egotistical, and eccentric. Onstage he is exhibited as a gorilla in a large cage, all the while producing poetry for his seminal work, *The Cantos*. Kops intertwines snatches of poetry, dialogue, ranting, animal sounds, contemporary popular songs, and fragments of great lyric insight. The effect is profoundly moving—the summit of Kops's theatrical achievement. Using stream-of-consciousness techniques, Kops enters Pound's mind, developing surreal scenic juxtapositions to structure the text and convey the howling sounds of genius at bay. *Ezra* encapsulates all of Kops's recurring themes and techniques: his social and political awareness, his obsession with down-and-outs, with the antisocial and the insane, with the victim-predator relationship, and with the family. Pound is caught in a love-hate relationship with his wife, his mistress, his country—and himself. Theatrically, the power of the play lies in the visual presentation of entrapment. Kops uses a wooden set with protruding nails. The prison and the cage are projections of the entangled web of Pound's mind. Ian McDiarmid played Pound in the London performance. His long white hair hung from his head like that of an Old Testament prophet.

Accompanied by the music of Antonio Vivaldi and Richard Wagner in the background, McDiarmid switched in mood from King Lear to his Fool in less than a second.

Kops is a supreme dramatist of frenetic states. The distinguished English theater critic Irving Wardle, in a 1980 review in *The Times* (London), wrote that "no other living playwright matches" Kops "in the virtuoso handling of dream logic." Kops has progressed from the often undisciplined rendering of Oedipal fantasies and dreamy young poetic rebels and confidence tricksters to the exploration of the subconscious mind, where reality and illusion intertwine and provide the vehicle for richly resonant dramatic poetry. Kops is a writer aware of the drama inherent in the sudden shifts in perception and changes of mood he has always found so natural. In *Ezra*, the London working-class Jewish poet has found his métier: *Ezra* places Kops in stature and achievement with the best dramatists of his generation.

Other major works

NOVELS: *Awake for Mourning*, 1958; *Motorbike*, 1962; *Yes from No-Man's Land*, 1965; *The Dissent of Dominick Shapiro*, 1966; *By the Waters of Whitechapel*, 1969; *The Passionate Past of Gloria Gaye*, 1971; *Settle Down Simon Katz*, 1973; *Partners*, 1975; *On Margate Sands*, 1978.

POETRY: *Poems*, 1955; *Poems and Songs*, 1958; *An Anemone for Antigone*, 1959; *Erica, I Want to Read You Something*, 1967; *For the Record*, 1971.

NONFICTION: *The World Is a Wedding*, 1963.

RADIO PLAYS: *Home Sweet Honeycomb*, 1962; *The Lemmings*, 1963; *The Dark Ages*, 1964.

Bibliography

Cohn, Ruby. *Modern Shakespeare Offshoots*, 1975.

Hill, Douglas. "Bernard Kops," in *Contemporary Poets*, 1980. Edited by J. Vinson.

Knight, G. Wilson. "The Kitchen Sink," in *Encounter*. XXI (December, 1963), pp. 48-54.

Kustow, Michael. "Note from the Road," in *Plays & Players*. XI (December, 1962), pp. 26-27.

Limb, Sue. "The Modest Muse: Bernard Kops," in *The Listener*. CVII (April, 1982), pp. 32.

Lumley, Frederick. *New Trends in Twentieth Century Drama*, 1972.

MacInnes, Colin. "Bernard Kops," in *Encounter*. XIV (May, 1960), pp. 62-64.

Nightingale, Benedict. "Bernard Kops," in *Contemporary Dramatists*, 1982. Edited by J. Vinson.

Taylor, John Russell. *The Angry Theatre: New British Drama*, 1969.

Wellwarth, G. *The Theatre of Protest and Paradox: Developments in the Avant-Garde Drama*, 1964.

William Baker

THOMAS KYD

Born: London, England; November 6, 1558 (baptized)
Died: London, England; August, 1594

Principal drama

The Spanish Tragedy, pr. c. 1585-1589, pb. 1594(?); *Soliman and Perseda*, pr. c. 1588-1592, pb. 1599; *Cornelia*, pr. c. 1593, pb. 1594 (translation of Robert Garnier's *Cornélie*; also known as *Pompey the Great: His Fair Cornelia's Tragedy*, pb. 1595).

Other literary forms

Although Thomas Kyd was cited by Francis Meres for commendation not only for tragedy but also for poetry, no verse remains that can with certainty be ascribed to him. The translation of Torquato Tasso's *Il padre di famiglia* (pr. 1583), published in English in 1588 as *The Householder's Philosophy*, is the only nondramatic work now generally attributed to Kyd.

Achievements

Probably no one questions Kyd's historical importance in the development of Elizabethan English drama, and few who read *The Spanish Tragedy* doubt his power to move audiences even today. Though he has, inevitably, been damned for his failure to be William Shakespeare, modern critics and historians have generally regarded Kyd, along with Christopher Marlowe, as one of Shakespeare's most important forerunners. Kyd entered the theatrical world of Elizabethan London at a time when medieval popular drama had run its course and classical drama, though influencing such plays as Thomas Norton and Thomas Sackville's *Gorboduc* (pr. 1562), had not effected a reshaping of contemporary English drama. Kyd brought the traditions together in *The Spanish Tragedy*, probably the most famous play of the sixteenth century. He combined an intrigue plot worthy of the comic machinations of Plautus or Terence with the revenge motif and violence suggested by Seneca's closet dramas and presented it all with spectacular theatricality. He rescued blank verse from the boredom of discourse and used it to create the excitement of psychological realism. He exploited the possibilities of the theater by employing imaginative staging techniques. Although his reputation rests safely on *The Spanish Tragedy* alone, the fact that scholars have so easily believed through the years that Kyd may be responsible for a pre-Shakespearean version of *Hamlet* suggests the imaginative power most readers attribute to him.

Biography

What is known of Thomas Kyd is based on a very few public documents and a handful of allusions and references to him, most of them occurring after his death. Contemporary biographical accounts of Kyd, including this one, are indebted to Arthur Freeman's careful investigation of Kyd's life in *Thomas Kyd: Facts and Problems* (1967). Records show that Kyd was baptized in London on November 6, 1558. Though there is no documentary identification of his parentage, scholars generally believe that his father was Francis Kyd the scrivener. If one may judge by other scriveners (John Milton's father was a scrivener), Francis Kyd was educated and reasonably well-to-do. Records also show that Kyd was enrolled at the Merchant Taylors' School in October, 1565. There—like Edmund Spenser, who was an older pupil in the school when Kyd entered—Kyd came under the influence of the school's well-known headmaster, the Humanist Richard Mulcaster. The date of Kyd's leaving the Merchant Taylors' School is not recorded; indeed, nothing is known "for fact," Freeman says, about Kyd for the decade after he should have left school. Although some have conjectured that Kyd may have entered a university or traveled abroad, there is no evidence for either. The curriculum of the Merchant Taylors' School was sufficient to have taught him the Latin he used in *The Spanish Tragedy* and in the translations he made.

In a tantalizing allusion that most scholars have interpreted as a reference to Kyd, Thomas Nashe, in his preface to Robert Greene's *Menaphon* (1589), complains of someone who has left the trade of scrivener, to which he was born, and is busying himself with the "indevors of Art," apparently writing imitations of Senecan tragedy and dabbling in translations. Though much has been made of this passage, especially in an effort to link Kyd with an early version of *Hamlet* (also mentioned in the passage), the allusion, if it does in fact refer to Kyd, yields very little biographical information other than that Kyd was active in the theater by, and probably before, 1589. T. W. Baldwin has shown in "Thomas Kyd's Early Company Connections" (1927) that a reference by Thomas Dekker in a 1607 pamphlet to "industrious Kyd" and his associates at that time indicates clearly that Kyd was writing for the theater as early as 1585. It was probably during these years, 1583 to 1589, that he wrote *The Spanish Tragedy* as well as *Soliman and Perseda* and translated a dialogue by Tasso, *Il padre di famiglia*, as *The Householder's Philosophy*. If he was truly "industrious Kyd," as Dekker labeled him, and if he was of real concern to Nashe, it must be assumed that he wrote, or had a hand in, many other plays.

Kyd's career came to an inglorious end; he died, apparently abject and desolate, in 1594 after a period of imprisonment and a seemingly unsuccessful effort to stage a comeback. In a letter to Sir John Puckering, an important member of the Privy Council, Kyd recounts some of the circumstances surrounding his arrest, defends himself against the charges, and pleads for assistance in regaining the favor of his former patron. Since the letter was written shortly after Kyd's release from prison and refers to Marlowe as already dead, it was probably written in the summer of 1593. Kyd was arrested earlier that year under suspicion of having written some libelous attacks on foreign residents of London. A search of his quarters revealed even more incriminating papers, containing "vile hereticall Conceiptes." Kyd was jailed and tortured, although the papers were not written by him and belonged, he said, to Marlowe, having by mistake been mixed with some of his own when they were "wrytinge in one chambere twoe yeares synce."

After his release, Kyd apparently hoped to regain favor with his former lord; when he was not reinstated to that service, he wrote to Puckering asking for help. From the letter it is clear that Kyd had been for some years in the service of a patron, that he at one time had shared quarters— or at least had written in the same chamber—with Marlowe, that he had been arrested, imprisoned, and released, and that he found life after imprisonment difficult without assistance from his patron. A reference to "bitter times and privie broken passions" in the dedication to *Cornelia*, published early the next year, suggests that his suit was unsuccessful and that he had resumed his writing in an effort to regain favor. In only a few months, however, Thomas Kyd was dead. The parish register of St. Mary Colchurch, London, records his burial on August 15, 1594. The final public document relating to Kyd is a formal renunciation by Anna and Francis Kyd of the administration of their son's estate, a legal means of dissociating themselves not from their son but from his debts.

Analysis

Thomas Kyd is best known for a play not specifically attributed to him during his lifetime. Although the early editions of *The Spanish Tragedy* are anonymous, few readers have seriously disputed Kyd's authorship, since the play was first attributed to him by Thomas Heywood (in his *An Apology for Actors*) in 1612. Most readers of *Cornelia*, ascribed to Kyd in the original edition, and of *Soliman and Perseda*, presumed by most to be by Kyd, point to similarities which suggest common authorship with *The Spanish Tragedy*. The play has traditionally been dated between 1582 (when a work by Thomas Watson, which it seems to echo, was published) and 1592, the date the play was first entered in the Stationers' Register. Modern biographers do not agree when they attempt to narrow the limits, but the lack of any reference in the play to the famous English victory over the Spanish Armada and the suggestion in Ben Jonson's *Bartholomew Fair* (pr. 1614) that the play had been around for twenty-five or thirty years make the period from 1585 to 1589 more likely. Kyd's influence on the development of Elizabethan drama could be more surely assessed if the date of *The Spanish Tragedy* were certain, but, whether it or Marlowe's *Tamburlaine the Great* (pr. c. 1587) came first, *The Spanish Tragedy* holds a place of high importance in English dramatic history.

Critical assessment of *The Spanish Tragedy* has been made difficult by a perplexing textual problem. Scholars who have sorted out the extant texts from the 1590's are able to agree that the authoritative text is the unique copy of the undated octavo printed by Edward Allde for Edward White. What has baffled researchers, however, is the presence of about 320 lines of additions deriving from a quarto of 1602. Most editors, though they assume that the lines are by a later hand, include them nevertheless, set in a different typeface, within the text of the play, so that the additions have, in effect, become a part of most modern readers' experience of the play. It is possible, as Andrew S. Cairncross notes in his Regents edition of the play (1967), that the so-called additions were originally written by Kyd, later cut, and still later restored as "additions." Much scholarly effort has gone into trying to identify the author of the additions. *Henslowe's Diary* records payment in 1601 and 1602 to Ben Jonson for "adicyons" to "Jeronymo." If the reference is to *The Spanish Tragedy*, Jonson was employed to rework to some degree a play which he ridiculed in other places. Without further evidence, modern readers have no way of knowing who wrote the additions. It is probably safest to believe that they were not written by Kyd and to attempt to see the play whole without them, in spite of the fact that some of them, especially the "Painter Scene," are interesting both in their own right and as they are integrated into the play.

Coming at the outset of Elizabethan drama, *The Spanish Tragedy* is inevitably seen in historical perspective, but what is remarkable about the play is its own interest apart from historical considerations. Although it is clear that Kyd is doing some things either for the first time or quite crudely in comparison to later dramas, it is possible to understand how *The Spanish Tragedy* enthralled audiences in Kyd's day and to read it with pleasure even today.

The play opens with a long speech by the Ghost of Andrea, but if there is little that is dramatic in that technique, the vividly descriptive speech illustrates the theatricality that characterizes this play from start to finish. From "dreadful shades of ever-glooming night," Revenge and the Ghost of Andrea have come to witness the working out of vengeance for Andrea's death at the hand of Balthazar on the battlefield. They remain to "serve for Chorus in this tragedy" and return after each act to reestablish this infernal atmosphere and to comment on the progress—or the apparent lack of progress—toward the goal of revenge.

Kyd plants the seeds of a psychological conflict between Andrea's friend Horatio and Lorenzo, son of the Duke of Castile and brother of Horatio's beloved Bel-imperia, in scene 1, when Lorenzo claims credit for capturing Balthazar and when the King of Spain, Lorenzo's uncle, rewards him with the captive prince's horse and weapons. Because Horatio had bested Balthazar in single combat, he feels cheated of spoils and honor that should have been his. When he submits to the king's decision, a spectator might wonder how the conflict, here seemingly prepared for, is going to effect Andrea's revenge. In truth, the play shifts even more radically in the next act to reveal not Horatio but his father, Hieronimo, as the inheritor of his son's conflict and as the chief character in the developing tragedy. Though Kyd does not fully develop the psychological conflict he sets up here, it is characteristic of *The Spanish Tragedy* to get beneath the surface of events to that psychological level, and it is this tendency to get at the heart of human action that sets Kyd's work apart from the plays of the previous two decades which he might have chosen to follow as models.

The following scene has proved a problem for critics. The action shifts abruptly to the Portuguese court, where the nobleman Villuppo forges a tale about how his enemy Alexandro (another nobleman) shot Balthazar in the back and caused Portugal to lose the battle. Some readers believe that Kyd introduces essentially extraneous material in this second plot line. The similarity of the situations, however—each turning on a vicious man's deception of his ruler to the hurt of another—suggests that Kyd may have intended that the subplot amplify and comment on the main plot. If so, the Portuguese viceroy's decision to investigate before taking action against Villuppo may suggest to the audience that Hieronimo, who will soon have cause to act, must also be sure before he moves.

At this point, there is still no hint of how Andrea's revenge is to be effected. To make Horatio, and ultimately Hieronimo, the instrument of Andrea's revenge, Kyd must provide a greater reason for the involvement of Horatio with Bel-imperia. In the next scene, without very much regard for consistency in Bel-imperia's character, Kyd reveals that she has chosen Horatio not only as the agent of her revenge but also as her "second love." The action has come back to the subject announced by the Ghost and Revenge, but the real subject of the play has not yet been broached. Though spectators are reminded at the end of each act that Andrea's revenge is the true concern of the tragedy, the play takes a turn in the next act that puts Hieronimo at the center. As yet, this central figure has appeared in only a minor role. His next appearance is in scene 5, where—again with no suggestion of his later importance—he presents at court a dumb show depicting England's conquest of Portugal and Spain. Remarkably, this spectacle pleases both the Spanish king and the Portuguese ambassador (and doubtless appealed to the patriotism of Kyd's English audience as well). The first act ends with the Ghost of Andrea complaining bitterly about this "league, love, and banqueting" between the Spanish and the Portuguese. He wants vengeance. Revenge promises to turn it all sour in due time. Essentially that is what happens: It all turns sour, and Andrea is revenged after a fashion, but Andrea is never the focus of the play. In the second act, Hieronimo assumes that position.

A new cry of revenge is heard as act 2 begins. Upon learning that Bel-imperia loves Horatio, Balthazar vows to take revenge against this man who first took his body captive and now would "captivate" his soul. He is encouraged by Lorenzo, who—without an apparent motive for his evil deeds—manipulates much of the action in the second act. Kyd's early development of a character reflecting the popular notion of a Machiavellian villain suggests once again his importance as a forerunner of the creator of Iago. As manipulator of the action, Lorenzo arranges for Balthazar to spy on Horatio and Bel-imperia as they make an assignation to meet in her father's "pleasant bower." The staging of this scene reveals Kyd's skill in using several levels of the stage at once. Balthazar and Lorenzo observe the conversation between Horatio and Bel-imperia from "above," while the Ghost of Andrea and Revenge, from their vantage point, watch the couple being watched.

When in the third scene a state marriage is arranged for Balthazar and Bel-imperia (the Spanish king's niece), it seems certain that the direction of the play is fixed: Bel-imperia has succeeded in involving Horatio so intimately in her life that this announced marriage will be the spark that triggers Horatio's anger toward Balthazar, and Andrea, through that anger, will be revenged. The play, however, here moves structurally, as a Roman comedy might, and introduces a significant bit of action that will provide a basis for the intrigue worked out in the double-length third act. When Horatio and Bel-imperia meet and wage a poetic "war" of love, they are surprised by Lorenzo, Balthazar, and his servant Serberine. Horatio is hanged and stabbed, and Bel-imperia is taken away as their captive. Hieronimo hears Bel-imperia's cry and finds Horatio's body; the play now becomes the story of Hieronimo's revenge. In what surely must have been both visually and aurally a spectacular moment, Hieronimo, in fourteen lines of Latin and with a dramatic sword-to-breast gesture, vows revenge. Modern critics, following Alfred Harbage's observation in his essay "Intrigue in Elizabethan Tragedy" (1962), recognize the significance of Kyd's innovation in this development of tragic materials with comic methods and within a comic structure.

It is not surprising that the Ghost of Andrea renews his complaint that events are not moving very directly toward his revenge: His friend, not his enemy, has been slain. Telling him that he must not expect harvest "when the corn is green" and promising to please him, Revenge allows act 3 to begin. The sudden reappearance, after seven scenes, of the matter of Alexandro and Villuppo is doubtless the reason some critics regard this "subplot" as an intrusion. Others, calling attention to the parallel between the Portuguese viceroy and Hieronimo, see this scene as a warning to

Hieronimo not to be too hasty in reacting to his son's murder. The intrigue plot that feeds Hieronimo's delay is set in motion when a letter written in blood (the stage direction specifies "red ink") falls into Hieronimo's hands. It is a message from Bel-imperia revealing that Lorenzo and Balthazar are Horatio's murderers. Lorenzo suspects that Serberine has talked. One intrigue leads to another: He hires Pedringano to kill Serberine and then sets up a time for them to meet when the watch, whom he has alerted, will be able to catch Pedringano in the act of murder. Serberine will be murdered, Pedringano will be executed, and Lorenzo will be rid of them both. When, after Pedringano is arrested, he sends to Lorenzo for help, the action—in keeping with the structure—becomes darkly comic. Lorenzo plays a cruel joke on Pedringano; he sends him word that he will save him and then sends a page to him bearing a box that supposedly contains a pardon. Despite instructions to the contrary, the page opens the box and sees that it is empty, but he decides to go along with the deception. The comedy with the cloud of death louring over it continues as Pedringano, certain that he will be saved, confesses recklessly in Hieronimo's court of justice and jests with the hangman even as he is turned off the scaffold.

With this third death onstage, spectators may begin to suspect that Kyd is exploiting in action the horrors only reported in Seneca. Neither the horror nor the comedy of the situation can obscure the painful irony of Hieronimo's position as minister of justice, himself crying out for justice. This theme, introduced near the midpoint of the long third act, grows to major significance in the second half. When in scene 7 the hangman brings to Hieronimo Pedringano's letter, written to reveal all in death if Lorenzo has failed to deliver him, Hieronimo has the evidence he needs to confirm Bel-imperia's identification of Horatio's murderers. Still able to believe that justice exists, he resolves to "go plain me to my lord the king,/ And cry aloud for justice, through the court. . . ."

This theme of justice, placed for development in close juxtaposition to the darkly comic, promises to shift the play from a mere revenge intrigue to an exploration of a genuinely tragic experience. Not all critics agree that Kyd is successful in bringing the play from mere sensational display of horror and intrigue into the realm of tragedy, but most readers will agree that the play takes on that potential at this point. The revenge theme that has informed the play up to this point will inevitably clash with the theme of justice. Hieronimo will cry out for both. Critics lament that Kyd's control of this conflict is uncertain. It is not clear exactly what Kyd intends when he has a minister of justice desert his own quest for justice and resort to private revenge, as Hieronimo does in the final act. Perhaps Kyd—among the first to attempt to reconcile this pagan theme of revenge, which he and his contemporaries found so attractive in Seneca, with the Christian conscience of his audience—was not careful enough with the consistent development of his central character. Modern readers, at least, are left unsure of his intent. Perhaps Kyd was also.

The remainder of this long third act is given over to two things: taking care of plot necessities in order to set up Hieronimo's revenge in act 4 and exhibiting Hieronimo in various states of calm or distraction, always searching for justice. The plans for the marriage of Balthazar and Bel-imperia proceed; the Portuguese viceroy arrives and announces that he intends to give his son Balthazar his crown upon Balthazar's marriage to Bel-imperia. It is this royal wedding which later provides the occasion, in act 4, for Hieronimo's revenge. Hieronimo, meanwhile, confronts the Spanish king and demands justice, but his wild manner of doing so makes it easy for Lorenzo to persuade the king that he is "helplessly distract." An entire scene is given to exhibiting Hieronimo distraught and to underscoring the reason: his failure to find justice in his own cause. The man who had been the best advocate in Spain is now so distracted by his own frustrated efforts to find justice for himself that he is incapable of doing his duty. In the final scene of act 3, Kyd—his eye always on the theatrical—has Lorenzo's father demand to know why the relationship between Lorenzo and Hieronimo is so strained. The Duke of Castile accepts his son's explanation and requires the two to embrace. Hieronimo, on the verge of executing his revenge, accedes, and the Ghost of Andrea labors the irony by his furious reaction to seeing "Hieronimo with Lorenzo . . . joined in league." To calm Andrea down, Revenge shows him an ominous dumb show—another Kyd spectacular—revealing two bearing nuptial torches burning brightly, followed by a sable-clad Hymen, who puts them out.

In act 4, Hieronimo moves swiftly to act on his plan for revenge. He confides his plan to Bel-imperia and asks her to cooperate in whatever way he asks. When Hieronimo is asked for an entertainment for the court on the first night of the wedding feast, he agrees, provided the courtiers themselves consent to act in his tragedy of Soliman and Perseda. They agree also to the strange request that they speak their lines in different languages. Hieronimo promises to explain all in a final speech and "wondrous show" which he will have concealed behind the curtain. Before the entertainment can begin, Isabella cuts down the arbor in which Horatio was hanged and stabs herself. Her death, the fourth in this tragedy, is only the beginning. With all locked in the room and with the keys securely in Hieronimo's possession, the play begins. What seems to be a play within a play, which is itself being watched by two who have been an onstage audience throughout, turns out to be all too real for those who think they are acting. The Bashaw (Hieronimo) stabs Erasto (Lorenzo); Perseda (Bel-imperia) stabs Soliman (Balthazar) and herself. Hieronimo reveals the "wondrous show" behind the curtain (his dead son) and explains his "play" as revenge for Horatio. He then runs off to hang himself but is stopped.

Though it is not perfectly clear what more they want to know, the king and Castile try to force Hieronimo to give further explanation. Kyd's taste for the spectacular is not yet satiated: Hieronimo bites out his tongue rather than talk. Then, calling for a knife to mend his pen in order to write an answer, he stabs Castile and finally himself.

A dead march ends the action except for the chorus. Finally, the Ghost of Andrea is happy, though his own death is avenged only in the fact that Balthazar has died in Hieronimo's revenge for Horatio. The final chorus, like all the others, recalls the ostensible subject of the play, but even more it points up the fact that Andrea's primary function has been to provide atmosphere. If spectators have come to accept him and Revenge as a touch of atmosphere, they are not shocked to hear him say that "these were spectacles to please my soul." To be pleased by these "spectacles," which include the death of his lover, his best friend, and his friend's father and mother, is certainly to go beyond his function as a real character. As a bit of spectacle, however, and as a means of providing both atmosphere and obvious structural links for the various revenges in the play, the chorus serves well.

The ambiguity of Hieronimo's portrayal precludes the possibility of a confident assessment of the meaning of the play. A more certain hand might have drawn Hieronimo clearly as one who tragically fails to wait for God's justice and destroys himself in the process or, alternatively, as one who seeks diligently and finds the world void of justice and in despair seeks his own redress. Hieronimo is probably best understood as a person destroyed by the tragic dilemma of being a minister of justice who is forced—or feels that he is forced—to take justice into his own hands. On reflection, this looks very much like private revenge, but there is little doubt that even Kyd's first audience, constantly reminded from the pulpit that God claims vengeance for his own, would fail to make allowances for a man so sorely abused and so faithful in his own administration of justice to others. The tragedy is that he destroys himself and his own faith in justice in the process.

Kyd's other works are of lesser interest. The only play ascribed to Kyd in the first edition is *Cornelia*, his translation of Robert Garnier's *Cornélie* (pb. 1574), which had appeared in a collected edition of Garnier's works in 1585. Kyd was trying to recover from the disgrace of imprisonment by offering to a potential patron this translation, done under the influence of an earlier translation by the Countess of Pembroke (*Antonius*, 1592) of Garnier's *Marc Antoine* (pr. 1578). He excuses the flaws in his translation by reference to "those bitter times and privie broken passions that I endured in the writing of it." To read *Cornelia* after reading *The Spanish Tragedy* is to understand the originality of the latter. One coming to *Cornelia* from *The Spanish Tragedy* would be surprised to find a play filled with talk rather than action—talk voiced in rather uninspired blank verse. *Cornelia* preserves Garnier's brand of French Senecanism in its quiet, reflective, and very long speeches. Act 1, for example, consists of one long speech by Cicero, lamenting Rome's war-torn state, followed by further lamentation and reflection by the chorus. In act 2, Cornelia debates with Cicero whether she should take her own life; having lost two husbands, she believes that she is a plague on any who love her. Much of the middle part of the play is about Caesar's tyranny; the focus returns to Cornelia in act 5 when a messenger, in a speech of nearly three hundred lines, provides a detailed account of the defeat of her father, Scipio, and his decision to take his own life rather than submit to captivity. Lamenting, Cornelia, who has longed for death throughout the play, wonders if the time has now come for her to die. She decides against suicide, however, because no one would be left to provide proper burial and tombs for Scipio and her husband, Pompey. The play ends with her quiet resolve to live. For all of its quiet manner, however, *Cornelia* was, as Freeman notes, Kyd's "most celebrated work for nearly two centuries."

Soliman and Perseda, published anonymously in 1599 by the same publisher who issued *The Spanish Tragedy*, is ascribed to Kyd by most literary historians because of the plot relationship to Hieronimo's final "entertainment" in *The Spanish Tragedy* as well as other parallels, echoes, and stylistic considerations. If it is indeed Kyd's, he probably wrote it during the same period when he was writing *The Spanish Tragedy* and Marlowe was writing *Tamburlaine the Great*, another play of death and destruction set in the Near East. Critics have paid little attention to *Soliman and Perseda*, but Kyd's mingling of the comic and tragic, evident in *The Spanish Tragedy*, is given such full development here that *Soliman and Perseda* should surely be seen as a forerunner of a long line of Elizabethan plays which integrate the two modes. Freeman believes that Kyd may have been the first to effect a "true confrontation of comic and tragic themes within mixed scenes," a confrontation which goes beyond the mere mixing of tragic matter with unrelated buffoonery. Like *The Spanish Tragedy*, *Soliman and Perseda* employs a chorus to preside over a bloody story. Love, Fortune, and Death vie for position as chorus, each claiming a major role in causing the story. In the end, Death lists twelve dead, brutally murdered onstage, as evidence of his power. (At that, Death must have lost count, for the toll is even larger.) The play also offers the beautiful love of Erastus and Perseda, the comic pursuit of Perseda by the boastful but cowardly Basilisco, and the murderous obsession of Soliman for Perseda—a desire so strong that he is persuaded to kill Erastus, whom he loves and admires, for her. In the final scene, Soliman kills Perseda herself. Having disguised herself as a man and vowed to defend Rhodes against Soliman's attack, Perseda challenges Soliman to single combat, promising to yield

Perseda to him if he wins the duel. When she is mortally wounded, she reveals herself, and Soliman asks for a kiss before she dies. Perseda, having earlier poisoned her lips, grants his request, and Soliman dies giving orders that his soldiers take Rhodes ("Spoil all, kill all. . . .") but that he and Perseda be buried with his friend and her husband, Erastus.

Of several other plays that have been attributed to Kyd, the most difficult attribution to prove or refute is that of the *Ur-Hamlet*. Assuming that Nashe was referring to Kyd as the "English Seneca" who would, "if you intreate him faire in a frostie morning, . . . affoord you whole *Hamlets*," many scholars have concluded that there was some pre-Shakespearean dramatic version of *Hamlet* and that Kyd was probably the author of it. Kyd's obvious interest in the revenge theme has fed this suspicion. No such play is extant, however, and it seems fruitless to try to reconstruct the lost play—if one ever existed—unless further evidence comes to light. *The First Part of Jeronimo* (pb. 1605), though it has been advanced as a first part of *The Spanish Tragedy*, was probably not by Kyd but, like the *Spanish Comedy* (mentioned in *Henslowe's Diary*), a spin-off from Kyd's extremely popular play.

Whatever is said of Kyd's other works, *The Spanish Tragedy* is an enduring achievement. Kyd adapted to his own purposes the horrors, the theme of revenge, the trappings of ghosts and chorus, the long speeches, and the rhetoric of Senecan drama. He pointed the way to a new form merging the impulses of the popular drama with the structure and methods of classical drama—both tragedy and comedy. He demonstrated that what gives life to a play is not argument or idea so much as psychological reality—characters that develop naturally out of the action of the play. He brought together in one play, perhaps not with perfect success, a variety of styles ranging from the sententiousness of his Senecan models to the lyric love combat between Bel-imperia and Horatio and the anguished cries of a distraught father. The extravagance Kyd permitted himself in Hieronimo's raving ("O eyes! no eyes, but fountains fraught with tears. . . .") made the play a byword in Ben Jonson's day, but Kyd's sense of dramatic propriety helped rescue blank verse from monotony for use in genuine dramatic expression. Kyd's flair for the theatrical allowed him to pave the way for an exciting and meaningful use of the stage; later developments in stagecraft may have proved more subtle, but few have surpassed the power of the final scene of *The Spanish Tragedy*. If the play could be dated with exactness, *The Spanish Tragedy* might well prove to be historically the most important play written before Shakespeare's. Even without exact dating, however, the play makes Kyd, with Marlowe, one of the two most significant predecessors of Shakespeare. Whatever its historical importance, the play retains, even today, its own intrinsic power.

Other major work

TRANSLATION: *The Householder's Philosophy*, 1588 (of Torquato Tasso's *Il padre di famiglia*).

Bibliography

Baldwin, T. W. "Thomas Kyd's Early Company Connections," in *Philological Quarterly*. VI (1927), pp. 311-313.

Boas, Frederick S. "Introduction," in Kyd's *The Spanish Tragedy*, 1901.

Cairncross, Andrew S. "Introduction," in Kyd's *The First Part of Hieronimo and The Spanish Tragedy*, 1967.

Edwards, Philip. "Introduction," in Kyd's *The Spanish Tragedy*, 1959.

_____ . *Thomas Kyd and Early Elizabethan Tragedy*, 1966.

Freeman, Arthur. *Thomas Kyd: Facts and Problems*, 1967.

Harbage, Alfred. "Intrigue in Elizabethan Tragedy," in *Essays on Shakespeare and Elizabethan Drama in Honor of Hardin Craig*, 1962. Edited by Richard Hosley.

Murray, Peter B. *Thomas Kyd*, 1969.

E. Bryan Gillespie

ARTHUR LAURENTS

Born: Brooklyn, New York; July 14, 1918

Principal drama

Home of the Brave, pr. 1945, pb. 1946; *The Bird Cage*, pr., pb. 1950; *The Time of the Cuckoo*, pr. 1952, pb. 1953; *A Clearing in the Woods*, pr., pb. 1957; *West Side Story*, pr. 1957, pb. 1958 (libretto; lyrics by Stephen Sondheim, music by Leonard Bernstein); *Gypsy*, pr. 1959, pb. 1960 (libretto; adaptation of Gypsy Rose Lee's autobiography; lyrics by Stephen Sondheim, music by Jule Styne); *Invitation to a March*, pr. 1960, pb. 1961; *Anyone Can Whistle*, pr. 1964, pb. 1965 (music by Stephen Sondheim); *Do I Hear a Waltz?*, pr. 1965, pb. 1966 (libretto; lyrics by Stephen Sondheim, music by Richard Rodgers); *Hallelujah, Baby!*, pr., pb. 1967 (libretto; lyrics and music by Styne, Betty Comden, and Adolph Green); *The Enclave*, pr. 1973, pb. 1974; *A Loss of Memory*, pr. 1981, pb. 1983.

Other literary forms

Although primarily a playwright and author of librettos for several musicals, Arthur Laurents has also written for both radio and the movies. Shortly after his first Broadway success, he began writing screenplays as well, producing eight over the next thirty years: *The Snake Pit* (1948, with Frank Partos and Millen Brand), *Rope* (1948, with Hume Cronyn), *Caught* (1949), *Anna Lucasta* (1949, with Philip Yordan), *Anastasia* (1956), *Bonjour Tristesse* (1958), *The Way We Were* (1973), and *The Turning Point* (1977). Because of their wide popularity with moviegoers, Laurents wrote novelizations of both *The Way We Were* and *The Turning Point*. His one foray into work for television came in 1967, with the script for *The Light Fantastic: How to Tell Your Past, Present, and Future Through Social Dancing*.

Achievements

Among American dramatists of his generation, Laurents certainly stands out as one of the more versatile: He is the author of plays that have received New York productions, as well as of Broadway musicals, several radio plays and one-act plays, Hollywood screenplays, novels based on screenplays, and a teleplay. Other plays or musicals have been given minor productions—all this while Laurents himself has become involved in directing, both his own works and those of others, and even in coproducing a film. A few of his radio plays, including *Western Electric Communicade* (1944) and *The Face* (1945), have been selected for inclusion in collections of "best" one-act plays. His first Broadway success, *Home of the Brave*, won for him the Sidney Howard Memorial Award in 1946; this was followed in the next decade by three additional Broadway productions: *The Bird Cage*, *The Time of the Cuckoo*, and *A Clearing in the Woods*.

In the mid-1950's, Laurents began his collaboration with Stephen Sondheim, writing the librettos for a series of musicals—an association that would last a decade and result in two of the most important works in the genre, *West Side Story* and *Gypsy*. The libretto for the latter work is so strong that it could almost stand on its own, without the songs, as a serious play, making it both the culmination and the epitome of a long line of book musicals. Little wonder that Sondheim singled out Laurents as one of the best book writers in the musical theater, or that he collaborated with him on two further works, the original *Anyone Can Whistle* and the book, *Hallelujah, Baby!*, which won the Tony Award as Best Musical of 1967. Sandwiched in between the musicals with Sondheim was Laurents' last Broadway play *Invitation to a March*, although his full-length work *The Enclave* did receive an Off-Broadway production in 1973.

Ever since the late 1940's, Laurents has lent variety to his writing career by work in film, providing screenplays for a number of well-received movies, including *Anastasia*, *Bonjour Tristesse*, *The Way We Were*, and *The Turning Point*, the last of which he coproduced and which won the Writers Guild of America Award, the Golden Globe Award, and the National Board of Review Best Picture Award. The 1960's and 1970's saw Laurents extend his expertise to yet another area of theatrical activity when he began to direct a number of his own works, including the highly successful London and New York revival of *Gypsy* during the 1973-1974 season. Most recently, he directed the Broadway blockbuster *La Cage aux Folles*, which won the 1984 Tony Award for Best Musical.

Biography

The son of a lawyer, Arthur Laurents was born on July 14, 1918, in Brooklyn, New York. After receiving his bachelor of arts degree from Cornell University in 1937, he began writing scripts for radio. For the five years from 1940 to 1945, he served in the United States Army. By the time he left the armed forces, having attained the rank of sergeant, several of his radio plays had been included in collections of "best" one-act plays. Considered one of the most promising dramatists to appear after World War II, he wrote several serious plays in the fifteen years that followed, then turned to writing musical comedy, with considerable success.

Analysis

If Arthur Laurents can be said to belong to any group of post-World War II American dramatists, his closest affinity is surely with those who might be called psychological realists and who came into maturity in the late 1940's and early 1950's, especially William Inge and Robert Anderson. Like them, Laurents is primarily a playwright who focuses upon character. He often, though not always, portrays women caught up in the age of anxiety, beset by self-doubt or even self-loathing. Yet unlike either Inge or Anderson, Laurents reveals a solid measure of Thornton Wilder's influence, both in the generally optimistic philosophy as well as in the nonrealistic stylistic techniques of some of his later plays and musical books. Although he has, like Anderson, decried those playwrights, particularly of the late 1960's and 1970's, who value experiments in form and style over content, who make the manner rather than the matter count most, Laurents will depart from strict realism and from a linear method of dramatizing his story when a legitimate reason exists for doing so, as he does in his use of narrators in *Invitation to a March* and *Anyone Can Whistle*, in his use of characters to change sets in *The Enclave*, and in his use of variations on the flashback technique in *Home of the Brave* and *A Clearing in the Woods*. As he says in the preface to *A Clearing in the Woods*, he willingly embraces greater theatricality if it brings with it a greater ability to illuminate the truth.

In that same preface, Laurents provides perhaps his clearest statement of the central insight into the human condition that pervades all of his writing for the theater: If men and women are lonely, and they are, it is because they cannot accept themselves for the flawed, imperfect creatures that they are; and until they achieve such self-acceptance, they will be unable to feel sufficiently, or to give of themselves sufficiently, to experience a sense of completion and fulfillment. When Laurents' characters are unhappy in this way, when they are hurting within themselves, they lash out and, attempting to deflect their own misery, hurt others. The pattern is as applicable to Peter Coen (*Home of the Brave*), Leona Samish (*Time of the Cuckoo*), and Virginia (*Clearing in the Woods*) as it is to Wally Williams (*The Bird Cage*), Mama Rose (*Gypsy*), or Ben (*The Enclave*). Wally, for example, is a sexually disturbed egomaniac who destroys others and eventually himself, while Ben has been hurting for so long from having to keep his homosexuality hidden that he finally decides to hurt his friends back by shocking them into recognition, if not acceptance, of his lover Wyman. Rose is the archetypal stage mother, seeking in her daughter's accomplishments a substitute for the success she never had. (The influence of parents in Laurents' work, it should be noted, is not invariably restrictive; for every Rose who uses a child to gain something for herself, there is a Camilla Jablonski— *Invitation to a March*—who, by example and urging, liberates the child.)

The diminished sense of self-worth exemplified by so many of Laurents' characters has an individual psychological basis, but it can also be greatly exacerbated by social forces, such as prejudicial attitudes and the drive to conform. The prejudice may be racial, as in *Home of the Brave*, *West Side*

Story, and *Hallelujah, Baby!*, or sexual, as in *The Enclave*, while the conformity may be either in the area of perpetuating the success syndrome through seeking a comfortable economic status, as in *A Clearing in the Woods* and *Invitation to a March*, or in the inability to break free of repressive sexual mores and conventions, as in *The Time of the Cuckoo* and *Invitation to a March*. Finally, Laurents' characters are often plagued by an impossible dream, by a desire to find magic in their lives. Sometimes the magic is short-lived, as it is for Leona in *The Time of the Cuckoo* or for the young lovers in *West Side Story*; at other times, it endures, as it does for Camilla, Norma, and Aaron in *Invitation to a March* or for Fay Apple in *Anyone Can Whistle*. Indeed, characters such as Camilla and Fay (complicated women who need and, luckily, find heroes) come closest to embodying Laurents' ideal of being free and wholly alive, of enjoying each and every moment, an ideal that he seems to have inherited from Wilder. If Laurents' upbeat endings sometimes seem slightly forced, and if his sentiment once in a while veers over into sentimentality, he remains an intelligent, sensitive, and thoroughly professional man of the theater.

A taut drama about prejudice during World War II, Arthur Laurents' *Home of the Brave* dramatizes how the experience of being condemned as an outsider, being made to feel different from others, affects the victim. Although not as theatrically elaborate as Peter Shaffer's *Equus* (pr. 1973) three decades later, *Home of the Brave* employs a surprisingly similar dramatic strategy: A doctor attempts to uncover the cause of a patient's symptoms by having the patient, under the influence of drugs, abreact, or therapeutically act out traumatic events from the past; what might appear to be flashbacks, then, are more accurately considered as deeply embedded memories now reenacted. Private first class Peter Coen (nicknamed "Coney") suffers from paralysis and amnesia brought on when, of necessity, he left behind his friend Finch during a dangerous reconnaissance mission on a Japanese island. For a long time, the sensitive Finch (he retches after having to kill an enemy soldier) had been one of the few to refrain from— and even physically defend Coney against—the anti-Semitic remarks rampant among the other soldiers. Especially guilty is Colonel T. J. Everitt, a former company vice-president who makes Coney the butt of his resentment over finding himself at war, not seeing any connection between his attitudes and those of the enemy.

Coney has been on the receiving end of such hatred ever since grade school, and Doctor Bitterger counsels that for his own good Coney must, to a degree, become desensitized to such unthinking prejudice. Under the pressure of their fatal wartime mission, Finch had hesitatingly called him a "lousy yellow . . . jerk," and Coney sensed then that Finch had caught himself just in time to prevent "Jew bastard" from slipping out. When Finch died and Coney's gut reaction was to be glad that it was not he who was killed, he felt shame and guilt, and he continues to imagine that there was some connection between the momentary hatred he experienced for Finch and his not staying behind and dying with him. Although Bitterger helps his patient understand intellectually that he acted in much the same way in which anyone else might have under the same circumstances, this realization does not sink into Coney's heart until another soldier, Mingo, recounts a similar experience.

Coney is not the only soldier whom Mingo tutors. Their commander, Major Robinson, though—like Mingo and Finch—essentially free of judging others in terms of racial distinctions, still experiences some difficulty in knowing how to command a group of men. Younger than some of the soldiers under him, Robinson attempts to compensate for lack of experience through an excess of enthusiasm, seeing war metaphorically as a game to be won. He cannot easily admit that his men might instinctively know more than he does—he fails, for example, to see T. J. for the bigot he is—nor does he fully understand that they deserve respect as men just as much as he does as an officer. Mingo, already overly sensitive to the fact that his poet-wife is better educated than he, has recently received a "Dear John" letter telling him she is leaving him for another man. When, as a result of the mission on which Finch was killed, Mingo loses an arm, he feels doubly afraid to return home, since as a cripple he will now be one of society's outsiders.

When Coney discovers that Mingo, too, despite his crippling injury, felt glad to be alive when he saw comrades die, he has a vision of his communion with all of humanity: Despite differences, all men are fundamentally the same. Two frightened individuals can now go home from the war brave enough to start life again. Together Coney and Mingo will open the bar that Coney had originally planned to run with Finch. The land they will return to is not yet free of the prejudice that wounds men like Coney and Mingo, and this helps keep Laurents' ending from being too saccharine. If the revelation that Coney receives seems perhaps too meager to effect much in the way of a permanent cure, Laurents' play is for that very reason both honest and understated.

Perhaps because of the perennially popular 1955 Katharine Hepburn movie *Summertime* that was adapted from it, *The Time of the Cuckoo* will probably remain the best remembered of Laurents' plays. This bittersweet romance concerns a clash of cultures, of life-styles, that occurs when Leona Samish, a thirtyish American spinster, has a brief affair in Venice with the somewhat older and attractively silver-haired Renato Di Rossi. As Leona remarks, Americans abroad carry with them "more than a suitcase": They bring a whole trunk load of attitudes and values, manners and mores. New World brashness confronts Old World charm; money—in the person of the boorish Lloyd McIlhenny on a hop-skip-and-a-jump tour with his wife—

meets culture; and puritan guilt and repression come up against an instinctive lust for life. Partly under the tutelage of Signora Fioria, at whose pensione the action occurs, Leona can overcome her initial qualms and experience her night of love with Di Rossi, a devoted father enduring a now loveless marriage.

Signora Fioria and Di Rossi both serve as foils to the American tourist in matters of sexual morality. Di Rossi, regarding himself as a kind of spokesman for Mediterranean culture, believes that abstract notions of right and wrong simply do not exist; to live life fully and to make contact with others is the only good, and so he bemoans the tendency of Americans to always "feel bad" and wallow in sexual guilt. Signora Fioria, who had an affair while her husband was alive and is having another now, also deems as "impractical" any morality except discretion, urging others to live life as it is, being certain only to leave it a little "sweeter" than they found it by entering a giving relationship from which they do not necessarily get anything in return. The values of these two Italians gain added weight when Laurents shows the shortcomings of the traditional notions of sexual morality by which another American couple, the young, beautiful, blond Yaegers, live and love. Eddie Yaeger, an artist whose later work has never measured up to his first exhibit, suffers from painter's block; his wife June, earlier married to a musician, suffers from something even less tangible but equally destructive: the romantic ideal that a wife must be her husband's complete life. She attributes Eddie's infidelities with Signora Fioria to his temporary inability to create, and she reconciles with him—albeit in an uneasy truce—only after he comes around to her strict notion that love cannot be love without complete fidelity. Into this subplot, Laurents introduces as well a staple theme of the 1950's, lack of communication, through Eddie's comment that language is often a method of "excommunication" and June's observation that people without the ability to talk might feel less alone.

What finally prevents Leona and Di Rossi from achieving even a shaky truce is not so much their differing attitudes toward sexual morality and the need for love as a failure within Leona herself. A woman who prides herself on independence but who is increasingly hiding her insecurities behind drink, she underestimates her attractiveness to Di Rossi; if she at first acts insulted by his forwardness, she later thinks he must want her only for her money. What finally brings her around to Di Rossi is not, however, his and Signora Fioria's accusations that she actually insults herself by having so little self-esteem, but rather his gift of a garnet necklace, a gesture so overwhelming that she—together with the audience—hears a waltz. When it appears that he has made money off her by exchanging her dollars for counterfeit on the black market, however, she rejects him. Emotionally bruised herself, she must hurt others by telling

June about Eddie and Signora Fioria. The "wonderful mystical magical miracle," the impossibly romantic ideal she had hoped to and did fleetingly meet in Italy, evaporates quickly, yet it leaves Leona with a new awareness of her limitations: her inability to love herself; her need for someone outside herself to confirm her value and self-worth by wanting her.

Her souvenirs of Venice—two wine-red eighteenth century goblets that she buys in Di Rossi's shop and the longed-for garnet necklace which he gives her—suggest by their color her long repressed passion. That she insists on keeping the necklace, that she must take something tangible home with her, indicates her insecurity, her need for things as a proof of feelings. Leona has not yet outgrown her inability to give of herself without getting something in return, and she finds it difficult to believe that others can either: When the street urchin Mauro, who has been trying to swindle her all along, offers a souvenir for free, she still instinctively wonders why, rather than simply saying thank you. It is not clear whether she will return to America any the wiser, but at least she stays in Venice to complete her vacation rather than fleeing further experiences that might test her conventional moral code.

A Clearing in the Woods concerns a woman who must confront the past in order to move into the future, thus continuing Laurents' exploration of the need for psychological wholeness. The most theatrically intricate—and, according to the playwright's own testimony, the most difficult yet satisfying of his plays to write—it does not lend itself to simple categorization. Laurents himself discounts all the formulas—flashback, dream, nightmare, hallucination, psychoanalysis, psychodrama—that might readily describe this play in which not only the woman Virginia but also her three former selves all appear onstage. Even stream of consciousness does not seem an accurate enough classification; perhaps nonrealistic fantasy, with a dose of Expressionism, comes closest. Each of Virginia's three earlier selves is seen mainly in the way she interacts with a man—father, teenage "lover," husband—in acted out fragments of her past experience.

Jigee, Virginia as a little girl of nine or ten, rebels against both the restraints and lack of attention of her father Barney; she feels, in fact, cut off from both her parents—distant from a mother too absorbed in her father, as well as jealous of her mother's hold over him. In a plea that he pay attention to her, she cuts off his necktie, wishing it were the tongue that had lashed out. Virginia's initiation into sexuality is seen through Nora, her seventeen-year-old self who goes off with a woodchopper, as, simultaneously in the present, Virginia enters the cottage for an abortive assignation with George, a suspect homespun philosopher who counsels enjoying the pleasures of today that lead to pleasant memories tomorrow while he advocates a belief in "Nothing," for then there can be no risk of disappointment and disillusionment. Virginia's lack of success in marriage is seen through twenty-six-year-old Ginna's relationship with Pete. The big man on campus, he had married her thinking she was pregnant; he never reaches his potential, and his life seems to have peaked at twenty. No longer sexually excited by her and believing not only that she has given up on him but also that she actually feels glad when he fails, Pete is temporarily impotent, effectively emasculated by Ginna.

Like Virginia now, neither Nora nor Ginna wanted to be ordinary; each wanted a life somehow special and set apart from that of ordinary people. This same desire stands in the way of Virginia's marrying Andy. Two years before the present time of the play, she called off their engagement on their wedding day, knowing that he would always be simply a competent researcher rather than a brilliant discoverer. Virginia now invites him to cross over the magic circle and enter the fantasy world of the clearing in the woods with her, hoping to erase that day as if it never happened, but, like Ginna with Pete, Virginia demands that Andy live up to her goals for him, and will be angry if he fails, while he is happier accepting and living within his limitations. Because Virginia has never been satisfied with herself, she has placed unhealthy, destructive expectations upon others. As Bitterger does for Coney in *Home of the Brave*, Andy acts as a kind of therapist for Virginia, helping her see that she has never really loved anyone, even herself, and that she has consequently destroyed the men in her life. Yet as each of the men returns in the present, she discovers that her impact upon them has not been wholly negative: The boy in the woods, who actually thought Nora pretty and not ordinary, surreptitiously left a bouquet of flowers behind; Pete, now remarried, reveals that Ginna actually provided color and excitement in his rather ordinary existence; and Barney, now on the wagon, can be reconciled with his adult daughter by their mutual understanding that a parent sometimes needs more love than a resentful child is willing to offer. Virginia, by becoming content with herself as she is rather than seeking a false image that could never be, can finally accommodate her former selves rather than deny their existence. By accepting them for what they can teach her about herself, she can reach integration and move freely and with hope into the future.

Invitation to a March is a charming romantic comedy about people's need to march to no drummer at all, even to break out and dance. Deedee and Tucker Grogan have come East to the Long Island coast to see their son Schuyler married to Norma Brown. Deedee and Norma's mother, Lily, the widow of a General who starts each day with a flag ceremony complete with toy bugle, are conventional, status-happy women: Deedee has wealth, Lily, social position, and both are morally proper; yet their limited lives are dull, dreary, without adventure, and it annoys them even to think that others might have something more. The bride-to-be's one peculiarity is her propensity to fall asleep for no apparent reason; this odd habit is her quiet revolt against the conformity and complacency that surround her. She sleeps because life is not worth staying awake for—that is, until Aaron Jablonski, riding on a horse in the rose-colored light, arrives to fix the plumbing and wakes her with a kiss. If Schuyler's mother, Deedee, is literary cousin to Lloyd McIlhenny from *The Time of the Cuckoo*, Aaron's mother, Camilla, is drawn in the same mold as Signora Fioria and Renato Di Rossi.

Although many of the characters in *Invitation to a March* at times face front and unselfconsciously and ingratiatingly address the audience, taking them into their confidence and interpreting for them, Camilla is the chief of these narrators—and the playwright's mouthpiece. There is more than a little of the down-to-earth philosophizing of Wilder's Stage Manager about her, and more than a bit of Wilder's point of view within the play. A wacky individualist, a free spirit who treasures the adventures life offers, Camilla knows that one can deaden life by not living it the way one wants to; since time passes and one does not have many chances, one must take the opportunities that present themselves, as she did twenty years earlier during a summer romance with Aaron's father—who turns out to be Tucker Grogan and thus will be the father of the groom no matter what. Tucker had made Camilla feel attractive simply by wanting her, and for all these years the memory of that time, nurtured by imagination, has sustained her so that she has wanted no other man. She found her magic.

Norma's similarity to Camilla reveals itself in her penchant for tearing up calendar pages, an act symbolic of her desire to break free from the restrictions of a confined, regimented life. In the play's title passage, Camilla warns about all the marchers in the world who try to take away one's individuality, who want one to toe the line, to move in lockstep, as do those in the military. It is easier and safer to submit than to assert one's difference, but it is finally deadly dull to do so. Although Norma feels no guilt after her first night with Aaron, it takes some time before she can break free and dance by giving up the prospects of a secure and success-oriented life in suburbia with a lawyer-husband and replace that goal with her love for Aaron. Eventually, though, they do hear their waltz, and they do dance off.

Camilla makes no excuses for her conduct; what she did was right for her. If she has any guilt, it stems from her selfishness in letting Aaron love her so much that he finds it temporarily difficult to love another. Tucker is not perfect either; finding it awkward to communicate with other men, he has never made enough effort until now to reach out to Schuyler. Although Schuyler, so much the prisoner of conventionality that he cannot respond to feelings, finds the shoe Norma kicks off before she dances away, he is no Prince Charming—in fact, he confesses to not believing in princes anymore—and so he symbolically falls asleep, a victim of the march, while his fully awakened and alive beauty waltzes off with another.

Since Laurents has turned increasingly from writing to directing, it appears that his career as a dramatist is virtually complete and that his position among American dramatists is now open to some overall assessment. No one would claim that Laurents belongs among the indisputably first rank (with Eugene O'Neill and Tennessee Williams, for example). Still, he has produced, along with librettos for two of the best works of the musical theater—*West Side Story* and *Gypsy*—one or two memorable plays that readers will return to and little theaters will revive: *The Time of the Cuckoo* and *Invitation to a March*. The latter work, in fact, with its deft handling of tone and comfortable assimilation of Wilder's philosophical outlook and stage techniques to Laurents' own purpose, may finally be seen as his most significant play.

Because Laurents' major efforts are so varied in form and structure, he remains difficult to categorize. He resembles both Lillian Hellman and Arthur Miller in his hatred of prejudice and his compassion for those who must hide a facet of themselves, whether racial or sexual, to avoid rejection. In Laurents, however, it is not only, or even primarily, the other person or society which seeks to limit his characters' world; rather, the central characters themselves, through their psychological inhibitions and moral or sexual repression, circumscribe their own existence. Like several other playwrights from the decade immediately following World War II, Laurents has not always escaped criticism for his "group therapy session" or "pop psychologizing" plays, which have, admittedly, sometimes ended with victories too contrived or too easily won: Simply recognizing one's own frailties does not always assure a newfound freedom and integration and maturity. Laurents' accurate reading of modern man's injured psyche, awash in the anxiety and self-doubt that inevitably accompany any search for an ethical system running counter to traditional social and sexual mores, remains in somewhat uneasy balance with his innately positive view that the individual can win through to a sense of personal wholeness. Yet Laurents dramatizes this tension with such honesty and in such understated terms that Coney's and Leona's and Norma's victories seem to be the audience's own; the illusion complete, they, too, at least momentarily hear a waltz. Like his spokeswoman Camilla in *Invitation to a March*, Laurents at his best can be an adroit stage manager, gently pulling the strings that have always moved audiences in the theater.

Other major works

NOVELS: *The Way We Were*, 1972 (novelization of his screenplay); *The Turning Point*, 1977 (novelization of his screenplay).

SCREENPLAYS: *The Snake Pit*, 1948 (with Frank Partos and Millen Brand); *Rope*, 1948 (with Hume Cronyn); *Caught*, 1949; *Anna Lucasta*, 1949 (with

Philip Yordan); *Anastasia*, 1956; *Bonjour Tristesse*, 1958; *The Way We Were*, 1973; *The Turning Point*, 1977.

TELEPLAY: *The Light Fantastic: How to Tell Your Past, Present, and Future Through Social Dancing*, 1967.

RADIO PLAYS: *Now Playing Tomorrow*, 1939; *Western Electric Communicade*, 1944; *The Face*, 1945; *The Last Day of the War*, 1945.

Bibliography

Bordman, Gerald. *American Musical Theatre: A Chronicle*, 1978.

Lewis, Allan. *American Plays and Playwrights of the Contemporary Theatre*, 1970.

Meserve, Walter J. "Arthur Laurents," in *Contemporary Dramatists*, 1982. Edited by James Vinson.

Sievers, W. David. *Freud on Broadway: A History of Psychoanalysis and the American Drama*, 1955.

Weales, Gerald. *American Drama Since World War II*, 1962.

Thomas P. Adler

RAY LAWLER

Born: Melbourne, Australia; May 23, 1921

Principal drama

Cradle of Thunder, pr. 1949; *Summer of the Seventeenth Doll*, pr. 1955, pb. 1957 (commonly known as *The Doll*); *The Piccadilly Bushman*, pr. 1959, pb. 1961; *The Unshaven Cheek*, pr. 1963; *The Man Who Shot the Albatross*, pr. 1971; *Kid Stakes*, pr. 1975, pb. 1978; *Other Times*, pr. 1976, pb. 1978; *The Doll Trilogy*, pr. 1977, pb. 1978 (includes *Kid Stakes*, *Other Times*, *Summer of the Seventeenth Doll*).

Other literary forms

Although Ray Lawler has written and adapted works for the British Broadcasting Corporation, he is known primarily for his playwriting.

Achievements

Lawler won first prize in a minor play competition in Melbourne, Australia, for his *Cradle of Thunder* and wrote nine plays before becoming internationally famous with *Summer of the Seventeenth Doll*. He shared first prize, worth about two hundred dollars, for *Summer of the Seventeenth Doll* in a competition sponsored by the Playwrights Advisory Board in 1955. *The Doll*, as it is known among Australian theater aficionados, was one of 130 plays submitted for judging. It shared first prize with a play by Oriel Gray, *The Torrents*, and served as Lawler's catapult to fame. With this play, he almost single-handedly revolutionized Australian theater, bringing it out of its previous lethargy.

Prior to the production of *Summer of the Seventeenth Doll*, there had been a feeling in Australia that the homegrown dramatic product was inferior to foreign drama. It was largely because of the unparalleled international success of *Summer of the Seventeenth Doll* that Australian theater enjoyed a spectacular period of growth throughout the late 1950's and during the next two decades. Today, Australian theater is produced throughout the English-speaking world, and even in non-English-speaking countries. With his play, which won the *Evening Standard* Award for Best Play in 1957, Lawler helped to stimulate Australians to a fuller appreciation of their own culture, not only in terms of theater but also in other fields of artistic endeavor, such as literature, music, and the plastic arts.

Biography

Raymond Evenor Lawler was one of eight children born to a tradesman in Melbourne, Australia. At the age of thirteen, Lawler started work in an engineering plant and took lessons in acting in his spare time. When he was twenty-three, he sold his first play, which was never produced, to J. C. Williamson's theatrical company, known in Australia simply as "the Firm." Lawler acted and wrote pantomimes and scripts for revues, and when he was in his mid-thirties, he became manager and director of the Union Theatre Repertory Company. While in that position, he worked on the script of his masterpiece, *Summer of the Seventeenth Doll*, in which he had written a part for himself, that of Barney.

Lawler appeared in the original Australian production and in both the London West End and New York Broadway productions, and his work as an actor received high praise. After the early closing of the Broadway production, he moved to Denmark; later, he returned to London, then moved to Ireland in 1966. These moves were indirectly prompted by the success of *Summer of the Seventeenth Doll*: Lawler could not return to Australia, nor could he live in London or New York, because of a tax situation resulting from productions of his play and the sale of film rights. He took up residence in Ireland after learning that he could obtain an income exemption granted to writers in that country. Lawler is of Irish descent and admires Irish writers. Lawler's wife, Jacqueline Kelleher, is an actress originally from Brisbane; they have twin sons, born in 1957, and a daughter, Kylie, born in 1959.

Lawler returned briefly to Australia in 1971, after a lengthy absence, to assist with the production of *The Man Who Shot the Albatross*, a play about Captain William Bligh's rule as Governor of New South Wales. He moved back to Australia in 1975, and in 1977 assisted with the production of *The Doll Trilogy*, comprising *Kid Stakes*, *Other Times*, and *Summer of the Seventeenth Doll*. *The Doll Trilogy* relates the history of the protagonists of *Summer of the Seventeenth Doll* in the sixteen years prior to the time frame of that play. Both *Kid Stakes* and *Other Times* were written in the 1970's, some twenty years after Lawler's success with *Summer of the Seventeenth Doll*.

Analysis

Summer of the Seventeenth Doll is by far Ray Lawler's most important work. His early plays have not been published, and his subsequent plays do not have the same verve, although two of them, *The Piccadilly Bushman* and *The Man Who Shot the Albatross*, have both received critical acclaim.

Summer of the Seventeenth Doll is a seminal play in the development of contemporary Australian drama. It was written at a time when Australia was emerging from the domination of Great Britain and the United States, although both countries have retained a strong influence on the Australian way of life. Australia was subjected to a veritable invasion of British immigrants after World War II. By the time the play was written, more than one million Britons had moved to Australia. British and American films dominated the Australian market, and the most popular stage productions were from the West End or Broadway, often with second-rate British or American actors in the main roles and Australians in the secondary roles.

This problem had been recognized in Australia since at least 1938, when a number of Australians joined together to start the Playwrights Advisory Board (PAB), with a view to promoting the work of indigenous playwrights. The PAB was to have a lasting effect on Australian theater. One of its aims was to circulate plays among Australian producers, thereby seeking outlets for the playwrights, and it was responsible, during its existence from 1938 to 1963, for nurturing a great number of Australian playwrights. One of its methods for encouraging Australian writers was to develop competitions for Australian works. It was in one of these competitions that Lawler won first prize in 1955.

While Lawler was writing *Summer of the Seventeenth Doll*, the Australian Elizabethan Theatre Trust—"the Trust," for short—was being formed. This organization was begun at the instigation of H. C. Coombs, Governor of the Commonwealth Bank of Australia. The Trust was to be formed as a private enterprise, with the support of the public in the form of subscriptions. As Coombs wrote in 1954, in the literary magazine *Meanjin*, "The ultimate aims must be to establish a native drama, opera and ballet which will give professional employment to Australian actors, singers and dancers and furnish opportunities for those such as writers, composers and artists whose creative work is related to the theatre." The Trust was to encourage such activities by offering financial support and guarantees to those producing Australian works. The initial appeal was for $200,000, and it was hoped that, once the Trust was established, the Australian federal government would lend its support to the cause of theater subsidies—which is precisely what happened. The federal government matched grants on a one-to-three basis, contributing one dollar for every three dollars raised by the Trust.

Both the PAB and the Trust played immensely important roles in Lawler's career. His sharing of first prize in the 1955 PAB-sponsored competition was a turning point for all involved. By 1954, the Trust had its own home, a former theater in the industrial Sydney suburb of Newtown, converted to a movie house and then restored to a theater. In January, 1955, it produced its first play, and then three more, not one of which was Australian. This was contrary to its founders' philosophy. On January 11, 1955, however, according to the official publication of the Australian Elizabethan Theatre Trust, *The First Year*, "a new page of theatrical history was written. . . . An Australian play by an Australian author, with an all-Australian cast, achieved at once a complete and resounding success." *Summer of the Seventeenth Doll* was the play, and with that success, Lawler's career was launched.

On November 28, 1955, Lawler's play opened at the Union Theatre at the University of Melbourne, where he was director. Although Lawler had felt somewhat diffident about having his play produced in the theater in which he was employed, fearing the production would lead to charges of favoritism, both the PAB and the executive director of the Trust prevailed on the vice-chancellor of the University of Melbourne to encourage the production.

The play opened to critical acclaim in Melbourne newspapers, as well as in other Australian and even British papers. It played for three weeks at the Union, earning for that theater the princely sum of $3,735.50, probably more money than the theater had hitherto made from any one play.

Once the play had gone through its tryout period as an experimental, university-produced play and had proved a success, the Trust was confronted with the problem of where to stage it in Sydney. The Trust owned the theater in Newtown, newly opened and renamed The Elizabethan. It was an immense barn of a theater, with some fifteen hundred seats, and it was almost solidly booked for its first year of operation. There was, however, a three-week gap in its bookings, starting in mid-January: This period falls right in the middle of Australian summer, and the theater had no air-conditioning. Lawler's play was booked for this slot and once again received universal praise; Lawler's pioneering work was compared to that of Eugene O'Neill in the United States and John Millington Synge in Ireland, establishing a first-rate national theater.

After it completed its three-week booking at the Elizabethan, *Summer of the Seventeenth Doll* was taken on tour throughout New South Wales by the Arts Council of Australia. Other touring companies were formed, and some amusing anecdotes relate to those tours. Australia has vast distances, and the play was touring the Northern Territory. One playgoer saw the production and thought that his wife should see it also. The following night, however, it had moved some six hundred miles, to the "neighboring" community. The man took his wife to that community for the production and then returned home—a trip of twelve hundred miles to see a play.

After eighteen months, negotiations were under way to present the play in London, where Sir Laurence Olivier, who had read the script, became involved. It opened on the West End in April, 1957, with most of its original Australian cast from the Elizabethan, after tryouts in Edinburgh, Nottingham, and Newcastle. Lawler made a curtain speech in which he said: "The first play was produced in Australia in 1789. It was a convict production—and, need I add, it had an all-English cast. It has taken 168 years for an Australian company to pay a return visit."

During its run at the New Theatre in London, the film rights for the play were sold to an American company. Lawler shared in the profits, together with the Trust, Olivier, and a Broadway management firm. Arrangements were also made for a Broadway production, and after seven months at the New Theatre, the play was moved to New York. On opening night, there were seven curtain calls, but the press reviews were largely negative, and the production closed after three and a half weeks. Nevertheless, *Summer of the Seventeenth Doll* did find American success: Ernest Borgnine played the part of Roo in the film adaptation, and the play was very popular with summer stock companies. It was also presented in translation in Germany and Finland and was even translated into Russian.

Summer of the Seventeenth Doll relates the story of two sugarcane cutters, Roo and Barney, who work seven months of the year in the Australian north and then have a five-month summer layoff in Melbourne, in the Australian south. Thus, they follow the sun. For the previous sixteen years, during their Melbourne sojourns, Roo and Barney have stayed in a boardinghouse, where they have taken up with Olive and Nancy, two barmaids whom they have known for the entire sixteen years. The play derives its title from Roo's habit of bringing Olive a Kewpie doll each time he arrives for the layoff. Olive has collected and kept all of these dolls as symbols of the good times the foursome have had during the sixteen previous years.

This summer, the seventeenth, Nancy is no longer at the boardinghouse. She has decided to marry, and Olive has tried to replace her with a fellow barmaid, Pearl. Unfortunately, Pearl does not have the same disposition as Nancy, and Barney and Pearl do not hit it off. Matters are further complicated by the fact that Roo and Barney are getting old. Roo had a disastrous season and left the cane cutting early, being supplanted as the chief of his gang (the "ganger" in Australian idiom) by a younger man, Johnny Dowd. For his part, Barney has always had the reputation of being a "lady's man," having sired a number of illegitimate children, yet halfway into the play, the audience discovers that he had a disappointing season with women up north. This discovery is reinforced by his singular lack of success with Pearl.

Because Roo left the cane fields early, he was forced to seek employment in Melbourne, where he found work in a nearby paint factory. This is a vital point, for it is a complete loss of face for Roo to have to work in the city during the layoff. Barney brings Johnny, the new ganger, to the house and they discover Roo asleep in his paint-spattered clothes after a hard day's work. Roo is humiliated into making peace with Johnny but cannot forgive Barney for the humiliation, and this eventually leads to a fight between the two old friends.

Olive, meanwhile, has realized that the layoff romance has come to an end. Her "eagle, flying out of the sun to mate," has feet of clay. Still, she resists this realization, and when Roo offers to marry her, she has a tantrum and rages against the inevitability of the situation.

Summer of the Seventeenth Doll is a play about ordinary people. It is very simple in its construction. Its language is plain, studded with everyday expressions; it is not strained, and does not strive for eloquence. The play develops in the customary three-act manner: exposition, development, a second-act climax, and a third-act resolution. There are no earth-shattering events, nothing startlingly out of the ordinary. It is a play that examines an Australian situation—a play that depends for its universality on the inter-relations of men and women, ordinary working people who choose to live in a somewhat unorthodox manner but who have all the same needs and desires as the rest of the world: friendship, love, comfort, companionship.

Lawler recognizes Olive's need when Roo offers her marriage. Roo says tenderly: "Look, I know this is seventeen years too late, and what I'm offering is not much chop, but . . . I want to marry you, Ol." Olive responds emphatically: "No!" She says: "You can't get out of it like that—I won't let you." Roo is appalled. "Olive, what the hell's wrong?" Olive replies: "You've got to go back [to cane cutting]. It's the only hope we've got." "Give me back what you've taken," she says, to which Roo replies: "It's gone—can't you understand? Every little scrap of it—gone. No more flyin' down out of the sun—no more eagles. . . . This is the dust we're in and we're gunna walk through it like everyone else for the rest of our lives." Olive stumbles out of the house, and Roo, too inarticulate to weep, sees the seventeenth doll lying on a piano and crushes it. Barney leads him out of the house, their friendship perhaps restored, and the curtain falls.

Summer of the Seventeenth Doll is a truly indigenous play, firmly rooted in the Australian ethos, and it illustrates a world that was disappearing, even as the play was being written. The "mateship" that it espouses was eroding as rapidly as Australia was becoming an urban society, and it is this realization, more than any other, that shocks Roo into offering to marry Olive. Still, Lawler does indicate that life is cyclical. Johnny Dowd is intro-duced to Bubba, a neighbor in her twenties who has been friendly with Ol-ive and Nancy all of her life. Bubba is determined to follow the same life-style, except that "things will be different"; she is sure that she will not suffer the same fate as Roo, Olive, Barney, and Nancy.

Lawler's mastery of the Australian vernacular was certainly responsible in part for the play's instant success with Australian audiences. Before the triumph of this play, most Australian playwrights had been careful to use a "cultured" or "refined" dialogue, with very few slang terms and little curs-ing. With one or two notable exceptions, such as Sumner Locke-Elliott's play *Rusty Bugles* (pr. 1948), which had audiences shocked by its use of the word "bloody," playwrights had eschewed the strong language so character-istic of everyday Australian speech. This caution was a reflection of the power wielded by the various State Chief Secretaries, analogous to the British Lord Chamberlain, with the right to remove plays from the stage because of perceived immoralities or offenses to public decency. Thus, Lawler's use of street language—which is employed in the play in the most natural way, not intrusively—had a great impact on Australian drama. Indeed, it has been suggested that the play failed on Broadway because of its use of Australian vernacular and dialect: The reviewer in the *New York Daily News* spoke of a "great invisible barrier of language between the United States and Australia."

Lawler's next play was *The Piccadilly Bushman*. The term "Piccadilly Bushman" is a derogatory one and refers to a wealthy Australian who lives in the West End of London, in Earl's Court, known as "Kangaroo Court," not in the judicial sense but because of the large numbers of Australians ("kangaroos") living there. It was presented in 1959 in Melbourne, and in 1961 in Adelaide.

A savage portrait of a bitter man who has been unable to find his place in his homeland, the play examines the Australian feeling of inferiority that was instilled while Australia was a British colony. Australia was settled at the close of the eighteenth century as a substitute for the American colonies, at a time when Great Britain needed an outlet for the hundreds of convicts imprisoned in rotting hulks on British rivers. There were two classes of settler: On the one hand, there was the convict, and on the other, his supervisors and those who, for one reason or another, believed that they would have a better chance at a new life in a new land. These two classes, the penal and the free, maintained a certain distance from each other for nearly two hundred years, and both classes always referred to Great Britain as "home." The supervisory and free-settler class looked down on the emancipists, and British visitors looked down on the free settlers as colonials. By the end of the nineteenth century, when wealthier Australians began visiting Great Britain, they were lumped together with the descendants of the convicts and patronized by the British.

It was only in 1901, upon federation, that Australia became independent, although retaining the status of membership in the British Commonwealth of Nations and recognizing the British monarch as titular head of the nation. The feeling of inferiority was pervasive in Australia, and it manifested itself in many different ways. The typical Australian referred to the Englishman as a "bloody Pommie," but he still regarded himself as of British stock. It was only with the vast postwar immigration to Australia, at which time two million Britons as well as many hundreds of thousands of European migrants were attracted to the vastness of Australia from their own war-ravaged countries, that Australian attitudes began to change, and Australia began to come to terms with its own national ethos.

Lawler, who was himself an expatriate at the time of writing *The Piccadilly Bushman*, examines the motivations and feelings of an expatriate film actor who returns to Australia to star in a film and to try to save his marriage, or, if that is not possible, to take his son back to England with him. The play is written in three acts and is set in Sydney, in a spacious house overlooking Sydney Harbour. Alec, the protagonist, left Australia at the age of twenty-five, and he considers that his life up to that time had been a prison sentence. He has become successful and famous in Britain but has never overcome his sense of inferiority.

One of the secondary characters, O'Shea, is the writer of the film in which Alec is to star, and he is the foil to the expatriate. He realizes that Meg, Alec's wife, must stay with Alec. Meg has had a history of alcoholism and infidelity in England. It emerges that the men with whom she has been having affairs are the type categorized by O'Shea as misfits, that type of person who goes overseas but does not succeed in his chosen field. Meg does not understand that, while Alec is successful, he, too, is a misfit, and she consoles these other men rather than her husband. O'Shea points out to her that it is Alec who is the greatest misfit of all.

Lawler tries, without much success, to address a number of questions in *The Piccadilly Bushman*. The play's central themes—the patronizing attitude of the British toward "colonials," homesickness, and the ambivalent attitudes of Australians toward Britain—were aimed at a rather small audience, and while the play attracted some praise, it was largely a failure, critically as well as financially.

Neither Alec nor O'Shea is drawn with great sympathy. Alec is shown to be something of an opportunist; he has used his wife as a stepping-stone in his career, and his attitudes throughout the play are essentially negative. O'Shea, supposedly the voice of reason, is long-winded and unpretentious almost to the point of naïveté.

Of greater interest are the first two plays of *The Doll Trilogy*: *Kid Stakes* and *Other Times*. Though written many years after *Summer of the Seventeenth Doll*, as noted above, these two plays precede it in the internal chronology of the trilogy. Interestingly enough, the three plays worked very well together when first performed as a trilogy. After having been written separately and produced as self-contained plays, they were presented in repertory for two weeks in February, 1977, with two Saturdays devoted to productions in which all three plays were presented in sequence. The general slide from the joyous youth of *Kid Stakes* into the disillusionment of postwar Australia in *Other Times* and thence into the devastating finale of *Summer of the Seventeenth Doll* was accomplished with style and great success.

Kid Stakes had been presented for the first time in Melbourne in November of 1975. Reviews were not encouraging, and the play probably suffered because of comparisons with, and distant memories of, *Summer of the Seventeenth Doll*. Nevertheless, Lawler was encouraged to proceed with *Other Times* while *Kid Stakes* toured Australia. *Other Times* opened in

December, 1976, at the Russell Street Theatre, to favorable reviews.

Kid Stakes begins immediately after the Depression. Barney and Roo have arrived in Melbourne for their first layoff, and they meet Olive and Nancy at the Aquarium. Also appearing is Bubba, here five years old, and the stage is set for the following sixteen years. Olive and Nancy quit their jobs as milliners to become barmaids, and Roo and Barney establish the pattern of the years to come. Olive's mother, Emma, is the owner of the boardinghouse where Olive and Nancy live. Emma is a crusty, middle-aged woman who accepts her daughter's life-style with some misgivings, feeling herself powerless to change things.

The setting for *Other Times* is the same boardinghouse, at the end of World War II. Barney and Roo have served in the Australian Army and are about to be demobilized. They are waiting to return north to resume their jobs as cane cutters, and they look forward to continuing their relationships with Olive and Nancy during layoffs. *Other Times* is the pivotal play in the series. In it, the characters become mature adults, whereas in *Kid Stakes* they were in their early twenties. Life is portrayed as no longer a game; Barney's practical jokes backfire for the first time during a poignant scene in which Emma's dreams of black-market profiteering are ridiculed.

Indeed, probably the turning point of the entire trilogy is the scene at the end of the second act of *Other Times*, which foreshadows the eventual breakup of the foursome. Nancy points out to Olive exactly what it has meant for Roo to stay together with Barney throughout the war. Roo rejected promotions; first, so that he and Barney would not be separated, and second, so that he and Barney could go on leaves together and visit the girls. The audience understands that Nancy has outgrown the good-times philosophy of the layoffs and needs to put down more permanent roots. At the close of the play, her departure seems inevitable. *Other Times* is a melancholy and somber play, dramatizing a process of disillusionment that is thoroughly Australian in its particulars but universal in its import.

Bibliography

Fitzpatrick, Peter. *After "The Doll,"* 1979.
Holloway, Peter, ed. *Contemporary Australian Drama: Perspectives Since 1955*, 1981.
Lord, Mary. "Ray Lawler," in *Contemporary Dramatists*, 1982. Edited by James Vinson.
Rees, Leslie. *The Making of Australian Drama: A Historical and Critical Survey from the 1830's to the 1970's*, 1973.

Peter Goslett

NATHANIEL LEE

Born: Hatfield (?), England; c. 1653
Died: London, England; May, 1692

Principal drama

The Tragedy of Nero, Emperor of Rome, pr. 1674, pb. 1675; *Sophonisba: Or, Hannibal's Overthrow*, pr., pb. 1675; *Gloriana: Or, The Court of Augustus Caesar*, pr., pb. 1676; *The Rival Queens: Or, The Death of Alexander the Great*, pr., pb. 1677; *Mithridates, King of Pontus*, pr., pb. 1678; *Oedipus*, pr. 1678, pb. 1679 (with John Dryden); *The Massacre of Paris*, wr. 1679, pr., pb. 1689; *Caesar Borgia: Son of Pope Alexander the Sixth*, pr. 1679, pb. 1680; *The Princess of Cleve*, pr. 1680 (?), pb. 1689 (based on Madame de La Fayette's romance *La Princesse de Clèves*); *Theodosius: Or, The Force of Love*, pr., pb. 1680; *Lucius Junius Brutus: Father of His Country*, pr. 1680, pb. 1681; *The Duke of Guise*, pr. 1682, pb. 1683 (with Dryden); *Constantine the Great*, pr. 1683, pb. 1684.

Other literary forms

While Nathaniel Lee published a few occasional poems, he is known primarily for his drama.

Achievements

Nathaniel Lee was an extremely popular dramatist of his time; many of his plays, including *Sophonisba*, *The Rival Queens*, *Mithridates, King of Pontus*, *Theodosius*, and *Oedipus* (written with John Dryden) were frequently revived and reprinted. These plays, five of the most popular Restoration dramas, were produced through the seventeenth century and occasionally revived in the next.

Lee wrote primarily heroic tragedy, characterized by superhuman heroes torn between passion and honor, a struggle that usually results in the hero's death. Spectacle, battles, processions, and bombastic language in rhymed couplets are common to this form. Moreover, along with Dryden, with whom he collaborated on two plays, *Oedipus* and *The Duke of Guise*, Lee abandoned the use of rhymed couplets and employed blank verse, which allowed for greater expressiveness, realism, and emotive force.

Like the quality of his work, critical estimation of Lee as a dramatist varies. Lee has been criticized for his lack of balance and control, for allowing his scenes to degenerate into mere spectacle and his dialogue, into rant. Nevertheless, he created individual scenes of great effect and passages of compelling beauty and dramatic power. Many critics and historians of English drama have placed him in the first rank of English dramatists and some have called him great. Unfortunately, very little attention has been paid to his work, which, according to the famous critic George Saintsbury, has been "shamefully neglected."

Biography

Little is known about the early life of Nathaniel Lee. The playwright was born to Richard and Elizabeth Lee about 1653. A minister thoroughly engaged in the religious and political issues of the day, Richard Lee tended to the intellectual development of his children, sending five of his six surviving sons to Oxford or Cambridge University. Thus, Lee was educated at the Charterhouse School in preparation for Trinity College, Cambridge, where he received his bachelor of arts degree in 1668-1669.

At the beginning of the next decade, Lee became an actor, playing the Captain of the Watch in Nevil Payne's *Fatal Jealousie* (pr. 1672) and Duncan in Sir William Davenant's *Macbeth* (pr. 1663). Although Lee was handsome and had a powerful voice, he apparently suffered from stage fright, so he retired and began playwriting. Lee's first play, *The Tragedy of Nero, Emperor of Rome*, failed, but *Sophonisba* was a success. *Gloriana* also failed, but Lee recovered with *The Rival Queens*, which achieved a popularity that lasted into the eighteenth century. In the next few years, Lee saw plays such as *Mithridates, King of Pontus*, *Oedipus*, and *Theodosius* become successes.

Lee's last three plays did not match the success of *Theodosius*, and on November 11, 1684, he was admitted to the Bethlehem Royal Hospital, the insane asylum popularly known as Bedlam. The reasons for Lee's "distraction," as it was called, are not clear. He was evidently a heavy drinker and had a rather mercurial temperament; it is possible that, at the time of his confinement, he was suffering from the effects of poverty. Whatever the origins of his illness, Lee spent the next four years in Bedlam. He was discharged from the hospital in 1688, taking up residence on Duke Street. There is no solid evidence that Lee wrote any plays either during or after his stay at Bedlam, although he did compose some poetry. In the spring of 1692, he was found dead in the street and was buried on May 6, 1692, in an unmarked grave.

Analysis

Nathaniel Lee consistently used historical figures and events as his dramatic subjects. In *The Rival Queens*, Lee dramatized the fall of Alexander the Great, a larger-than-life figure who succumbs to his own passions and to the plots of others. His fall is truly tragic. When the play opens, Alexander is returning from his most recent exploits and is about to enter Babylon. Having committed some personal and political indiscretions, Alexander may not be warmly received by everyone. He has executed some of his most respected generals, imagining that they were trying to stage a coup. He publicly insulted Polyperchon, commander of the Phalanx, and Cassander, son the the Macedonian governor, Antipater. Breaking a promise to his devoted Babylonian queen, Statira, he has returned to the bed of his hot-blooded first wife, Roxana. Finally, he has sanctioned the match between Parisatis, sister to Statira, and Hephestion, an unctuous courtier. Parisatis, however, is the lover of Lysimachus, a fearless soldier loyal to Alexander. Lysimachus believes that he is more deserving than Hephestion of Alexander's favor, as does Clytus, the conqueror's old and faithful adviser, who also served under Philip of Macedonia, Alexander's father.

Alexander enters Babylon triumphantly, but he is soon embroiled in the conflict between Hephestion and Lysimachus. Alexander tries to settle the issue by having Lysimachus thrown to a lion. The doughty warrior slays the lion with his bare hands, however, and Alexander, who cannot overlook such a marvelous feat, lets Lysimachus compete for the hand of Parisatis, deciding that the woman will go to the soldier who serves most impressively in battle.

At the same time, the rival queens are contending for Alexander's affections. Upon hearing that Alexander had bedded Roxana, Statira decides to remove herself from him. By this ploy, however, she risks losing him to Roxana, so she later entertains his impassioned lovemaking and forgives his recent intrigue with Roxana. Roxana witnesses the reunion and seeks revenge. Cassander convinces her to murder Statira as she awaits the conqueror's return from the banquet. Cassander, however, has arranged for Alexander to be poisoned at the feast.

At the banquet, a drunken Alexander becomes enraged at Clytus for his satiric barbs, and he kills the old man on the spot. Alexander's maudlin remorse for the impulsive deed is cut short by the news that Roxana and her band of thugs are threatening Statira. Alexander arrives just in time to see Roxana stab the queen. As she dies, Statira begs Alexander not to kill Roxana; he resists taking revenge, but only because his first wife is pregnant. The audience now discovers that Hephestion drank himself to death at the banquet. Alexander then begins to stagger from the poison poured into his drink. After hallucinating about his heroic past, the conqueror dies, leaving Lysimachus to apprehend the assassins and to claim, at last, Parisatis.

This play dramatizes the story and spectacle of a great man brought down by his own failures. If Alexander were merely the victim of an unfortunate series of events, as are many heroes of the Restoration's serious drama, the audience would not care about his fate, but Lee's Alexander is a tragic figure because he had the power to save himself. Poor judgment, not inescapable fate, causes him to fall. The play is made even more tragic because the audience can see his fall coming. The audience has more information than Alexander and knows that, by the conventions of tragedy, seemingly small lapses in judgment at the beginning of a play have large and damnable consequences toward the end.

Alexander's mistakes result from his letting passion overrule reason. Throughout the play, Alexander increasingly becomes the tool of his own passions. One of his first acts is to favor Hephestion by supporting his suit for Parisatis over that of Lysimachus. Like King Lear, Alexander elevates those who flatter him the most, rather than those who display quiet virtue: The glib court favorite is preferred over the silent but dutiful soldier. As the play continues, mistakes become misdeeds: At the banquet, Clytus is not merely ignored, he is slain. In the last scene of the play, Alexander loses his reason entirely and goes mad under the poison's influence.

The tension between Alexander's affective and intellectual faculties is dramatized by opposing pairs of characters. Roxana is a lusty, sensuous woman, intent on satisfying her sexual desires; Statira, in contrast, is a model of selfless devotion, ethereal, rather than earthy. On the side of passion is Hephestion, the sot; on the side of reason, Lysimachus, the soldier. Cassander is a scheming, sinister malcontent, willing to say what Alexander wants to hear, while he plots the conqueror's destruction; Clytus is a blunt, stoical adviser, who risks Alexander's wrath to criticize his indulgence in Persian luxuries. Lee polarizes the selfish character and the selfless, the scheming, and the honest. The spiritual land of the first group is Babylon, the lap of decadent luxury; the spiritual land of the second group is Macedonia, the seat of austerity and other martial virtues. Thus, the characterization and the very structure of the play reflect Alexander's inner conflict.

If *The Rival Queens* is quite clearly a tragedy, *The Princess of Cleve* defies precise generic description; Lee himself called the play "Farce, Comedy, Tragedy or meer Play." Set in Paris, the play focuses on the amorous exploits of Duke Nemours, a nobleman with a penchant and talent for seducing the wives of his compatriots. Despite his appetite for sexual sport, Nemours is betrothed to Marguerite, Princess of Jainville. Queen Catherine de Medici, however, wants to end the match so that the princess can marry the Dauphin, soon to be King Francis II.

To achieve her political ends, Catherine, who never appears in the play, persuades one of her ladies, Tournon, to sleep with Nemours and to find him other women to bed as well. Presumably, Marguerite will discover Nemours' faithlessness and welcome the Dauphin's attentions. In her campaign, Tournon first suggests to Marguerite that an amorous letter from a whore to her anonymous lover belongs to Nemours. She next attempts to involve Nemours with Celia and Elianor, the lusty wives of two fops, St. Andre and Poltrot. Tournon then spreads the news that the newly married Princess of Cleve is accepting Nemours' adulterous advances.

The action involving the two fops and their wives soon takes off without Nemours. St. Andre and Poltrot try intensely to be in style—which, by

Restoration standards, meant betraying one's wife in a cavalier, offhand manner. Celia and Elianor, for their part, also engage in flirtations. All receive their proper reward: Celia and Elianor run off with Nemours (under the eye of Marguerite) and are eventually debauched by his cronies, Bellamore and Vidam; the husbands are unsuccessful in their own attempts, in effect receiving no compensation for the privilege of being cuckolded.

When the Prince notes a certain malaise in his wife, he implores her to reveal the origin of her low spirits, suspecting that she has taken a lover. She reluctantly confesses her passion for Nemours—a confession which eventually causes the Prince to die from heartbreak.

Nemours' association with the wives of the fops and with the Princess of Cleve arouses Marguerite's suspicion that he has not been faithful. She attends the ball in disguise and tries to arouse Nemours' passions as another woman. She succeeds, and when she doffs her disguise, Nemours can hardly deny his infidelity. Nemours, then, has presumably lost Marguerite, whose last words are "Monster of a Man," and he has lost the Princess of Cleve as well, even though she is now technically available: She has given him up forever. No sooner has she left the stage, however, when Nemours predicts that "I Bed her eighteen months three weeks hence, at half an hour past two in the Morning."

Nemours' prediction suggests the sleazy atmosphere and ethos of the play. He does not believe that the Princess of Cleve is as good as her word, but he does believe in his own sexual prowess. Indeed, any kind of oath in the universe of this play is meaningless. The Princess, Celia, Elianor, St. Andre, and Poltrot all do their best to violate their marriage vows. Since no character in the play is untainted by sin, the audience tends to judge them not by ethical standards but by sheer performance. Since there are no saints and no sinners, only winners and losers, the most impressive performer is Nemours.

Lee wanted to show his audience sexual libertinism unvarnished by witty rationalizations. When this play was composed, in about 1680, sexual promiscuity was almost a way of life for the English courtiers and their king, Charles II; George Villiers, the second Duke of Buckingham and John Wilmot, the Earl of Rochester, in particular, were infamous for their sexual adventures. The English court's rakish ways were reflected in plays such as John Dryden's *Marriage à la Mode* (pr. 1672), William Wycherley's *The Country Wife* (pr. 1675), and Sir George Etherege's *The Man of Mode: Or, Sir Fopling Flutter* (pr. 1676). Lee's intention in *The Princess of Cleve* was to provide a corrective to the tacit acceptance of promiscuity often found in such works, whatever their explicit moral.

The plays of Nathaniel Lee are, for Allardyce Nicoll, "of inestimable importance in any attempt to divine the quality of tragedy of his age."

From this glimpse into Lee's tragedy we can perhaps see at work a serious search for a more comprehensive ethical perspective, despite staginess, special effects, and sensational events.

Other major works

POETRY: "On the Death of the Duke of Albemarle," 1670; "To Mr. Dryden, on His Poem of Paradice," 1677; *To the Duke on His Return*, 1682; *On Their Majesties Coronation*, 1689; *On the Death of Mrs. Behn*, 1689; "To the Prince and Princess of Orange, upon Their Marriage," 1693.

Bibliography

Armistead, J. M. *Nathaniel Lee*, 1979.

Birley, Robert. "Nathaniel Lee: *The Rival Queens*," in *Sunk Without a Trace: Some Forgotten Masterpieces Reconsidered*, 1962.

Ham, Roswell Gray. *Otway and Lee: Biography from a Baroque Age*, 1931.

Hume, Robert D. *The Development of English Drama in the Late Seventeenth Century*, 1976.

_____. "The Satiric Design of Nathaniel Lee's *The Princess of Cleve*," in *Journal of English and Germanic Philology*. LXXV (1976), pp. 117-138.

Nicoll, Allardyce. *A History of English Drama: Restoration Drama, 1660-1700*, 1952.

Douglas R. Butler

MATTHEW GREGORY LEWIS

Born: London, England; July 9, 1775
Died: At sea, near Jamaica; May 14, 1818

Principal drama

Village Virtues, pb. 1796; *The Minister*, pb. 1797 (translation of Friedrich Schiller's play *Kabale und Liebe*); *The Castle Spectre*, pr. 1797, pb. 1798; *Rolla: Or, The Peruvian Hero*, pb. 1799 (translation of August von Kotzebue's play *Die Spanier in Peru: Oder, Rollas Tod*); *The Twins: Or, Is It He or His Brother?*, pr. 1799, pb. 1962 (adaptation of Jean François Regnard's *Les Ménechmes: Ou, Les Jumeaux*); *The East Indian*, pr. 1799, pb. 1800; *Adelmorn, the Outlaw*, pr., pb. 1801; *Alfonso, King of Castile*, pb. 1801, pr. 1802; *The Captive*, pr. 1803 (dramatic monologue); *The Harper's Daughter: Or, Love and Ambition*, pr. 1803 (adaptation of Lewis' play *The Minister*); *Rugantino: Or, The Bravo of Venice*, pr., pb. 1805 (two acts; adaptation of Lewis' *The Bravo of Venice*); *Adelgitha: Or, The Fruits of a Single Error*, pb. 1806, pr. 1807; *The Wood Daemon: Or, "The Clock Has Struck,"* pr. 1807; *Venoni: Or, The Novice of St. Mark's*, pr. 1808, pb. 1809 (adaptation of Jacques Marie de Monvel's play *Les Victimes cloîtrées*); *Temper: Or, The Domestic Tyrant*, pr. 1809 (adaptation of Sir Charles Sedley's translation, *The Grumbler*, of David Augustin Brueys and Jean Palaprat's play *Le Grondeur*); *Timour the Tartar*, pr., pb. 1811; *One O'Clock: Or, The Knight and the Wood Daemon*, pr., pb. 1811 (music by Michael Kelly and Matthew Peter King; adaptation of Lewis' *The Wood Daemon*); *Rich and Poor*, pr., pb. 1812 (music by Charles Edward Horn; adaptation of Lewis' *The East Indian*).

Other literary forms

Although Matthew Gregory Lewis was one of the most successful British dramatists of the Romantic era, his primary claim to fame today is his authorship of that most extravagant of Gothic novels, *The Monk: A Romance*, which was originally published, in 1796, as *Ambrosio: Or, The Monk*. This was Lewis' first significant published work, and it created such a sensation among his contemporaries that he is still referred to more often by his nickname of "Monk" Lewis than by his given name. Despite the objections of moralists and literary critics alike, this lurid tale of human perversity, with its seductive demons and bleeding ghosts, sold prodigiously during Lewis' lifetime and remains standard reading for anyone studying the development of the English novel.

Two of Lewis' nondramatic publications were *The Love of Gain* (1799), written in imitation of the Thirteenth Satire of Juvenal, and *Tales of Wonder* (1801), an anthology of horror poems. The former, an insignificant throwback to the subject matter and the style of the Age of Johnson, attracted little attention, but the latter stirred considerable interest, some of it admiring but much of it amused. *Tales of Wonder* was compiled in response to a vogue for Gothic ballads which occurred after the publication in the 1790's of several translations of G. A. Bürger's *Lenore* (1773). Unfortunately, the vogue had begun to wane by the time the anthology appeared, and it was unmercifully parodied during the months following its publication. Nevertheless, it remains a work of considerable historical interest because of its inclusion of some of the early poetry of Robert Southey and Sir Walter Scott and because of its influence throughout the nineteenth century on poetic Gothicism.

Much of Lewis' work was derived from or was influenced by German sources, and in 1805 and 1806, he published translations of a pair of German romances, one of which he subsequently dramatized. The first, *The Bravo of Venice*, was based on J. H. D. Zschokke's *Aböllino der Grosse Bandit*, and the second, *Feudal Tyrants: Or, The Counts of Carlsheim and Sargans*, was a somewhat freer rendering of Christiane Benedicte Eugénie Naubert's *Elisabeth, Erbin von Toggenburg: Oder, Geschichte der Frauen in der Schweiz*. Suffice it to say of these works that they again show Lewis' fascination with the sensational and that both, especially *The Bravo of Venice*, achieved popular success.

Lewis was also an important writer of popular songs, many of which appeared first in his plays and a number of which were Lewis' original contributions to the works of his fellow playwrights. His nondramatic poetry, too, was sometimes set to music, and, collaborating with such people as Charles Edward Horn, Michael Kelly, and Harriet Abrams, Lewis was frequently able to catch the public's musical fancy. Such songs as "The Banks of Allan Water" (from *Rich and Poor*), "The Wind It Blows Cold" (from *Adelmorn, the Outlaw*—both words and music by Lewis), "The Wife's Farewell: Or, Oh No My Love No!" and "The Orphan's Prayer" are unknown today, but in the early nineteenth century they were sung *ad nauseam*. Lewis himself was a reasonably skillful melodist, and as the title of his most substantial song collection, *Twelve Ballads, the Words and Music by M. G. Lewis* (1808), indicates, he occasionally composed his own tunes.

Lewis published a mixed collection of poetry and prose, *Romantic Tales*, in 1808. This four-volume work contained one long narrative poem, five short stories, and seven ballads. Much of the material was translated or adapted from Continental originals, some of it again from the German. Although *Romantic Tales* shows frequent Gothic touches reminiscent of much of Lewis' other work, the individual works vary considerably in tone and subject matter and belie the usual exclusive association of Lewis' name with the wondrous and the horrifying. Two other publications, *Monody on the Death of Sir John Moore* (1809) and *Poems* (1812), are even more remote from Gothic extravagance and exhibit a neoclassical polish that would startle those who know Lewis only through *The Monk*, *Tales of Wonder*, and *The Castle Spectre*.

Poems was the last volume of Lewis' work to be published during his lifetime, but two others appeared posthumously, *The Isle of Devils: A Metrical Tale* (1827) and *Journal of a West India Proprietor* (1834). The former is a narrative poem in heroic couplets concerning a young woman who is pursued and victimized by monsters after a shipwreck. Critics have not treated it well. *Journal of a West India Proprietor*, on the other hand, has been praised more consistently than any of Lewis' other writings. It gives an engaging and unpretentious account of Lewis' two voyages to his estates in the West Indies, an account which Samuel Taylor Coleridge, generally one of Lewis' severest critics, found impressively well written.

Also of interest are Lewis' letters, many of which appeared in Margaret Baron-Wilson's *The Life and Correspondence of M. G. Lewis* (1839). Although he was not an important epistolary stylist, Lewis wrote letters which exhibit considerable charm and which, because of his extensive acquaintance with prominent men, are sometimes of significance to the literary biographer and the historian.

Achievements

Lewis is one of those delightful literary figures whose ability to appeal to the bad taste of the public brings them immense popularity during their own day and critical damnation forever after. In an age when most of Britain's greatest writers found themselves incapable of pleasing London audiences, Lewis brought immense sums into the coffers of the Drury Lane and Covent Garden theaters. He was a master of the sentimental and the sensational, and sentiment and sensation were what London audiences clamored for. Although not all of his plays, referred to by his biographer Louis F. Peck as "brainless stories," were popular successes, enough of them were to make Lewis the darling of the theater managers.

As one might expect of the author of *The Monk*, Lewis is primarily important for his contributions to dramatic Gothicism. Indeed, Bertrand Evans, author of *Gothic Drama from Walpole to Shelley* (1947), writes that "the name of Matthew Gregory Lewis is perhaps the most important in the history of Gothic drama." Lewis, Evans observes, drew together the "materials of his predecessors and contemporaries, English and German, and out-Gothicized them all." He did this most triumphantly in *The Castle Spectre*, which was an immediate and overwhelming theatrical sensation. According to Evans, its forty-seven performances made it "the most successful play of its time," a success achieved by ruthlessly sacrificing "consistency of character, probability of action, and forward movement of plot . . .

to immediate sensational effect."

In order to appraise Lewis' approach fairly, however, it is necessary to know what was considered to be the height of fashion and of entertainment in his day—just at the beginning of the Regency period. The royal establishments at Blenheim and Bath set the tone for outrageous combinations of exaggerated Oriental borrowings mixed with every new fad that the empire builders had brought home from around the world. People went to playhouses more to see and be seen by others than to pay attention to the story line of any play. The audiences in general were so preoccupied with finery and social scandals and made so blasé by experience at places such as Astley's Amphitheatre with fireworks, lakes filled with boats on which naval engagements were reenacted, and the like that it took a lot to get even a moment of their attention.

A man well suited to his time, Lewis was more skillful as an entertainer than as a dramatic artist, and his theatrical creations were so well attended because he had the capacity of engaging his audience's interest, often through unsubtle means. Whether by means of music, melodrama, or shameless spectacle, Lewis made his works impossible to ignore.

Biography

Matthew Gregory Lewis, the first child of Matthew Lewis and the former Frances Maria Sewell, was born in London, England, on July 9, 1775. His father served for a number of years as both Chief Clerk in the War Office and as Deputy-Secretary at War, positions whose salaries, in combination with the revenues from estates owned by the elder Lewis in Jamaica, rendered the Lewis household financially prosperous. Prosperity did not assure marital harmony, however, and his parents agreed to a permanent separation when young Matthew Gregory was seven or eight years old. According to a bill of divorcement which was never brought to enactment, the primary cause of his parents' estrangement was an adulterous affair carried on by Mrs. Lewis, which resulted in her giving birth to a child.

In addition to this illegitimate sibling, Lewis had two sisters, Maria and Sophia, and a brother, Barrington, all of whom lived with their father. Young Matthew Gregory, who had begun his education at Marylebone Seminary, resided at Westminster College and Christ Church College, Oxford, during much of his childhood and adolescence and maintained affectionate contact with both of his parents. Throughout his lifetime, in fact, whatever slight cohesiveness existed within the Lewis family was largely the result of Matthew Gregory's efforts.

Although young Lewis was not a systematic, self-disciplined scholar, he did exhibit considerable talent in foreign languages, music, and literature, and by age sixteen, largely through the stimulation of a summer spent in Paris, he was busily at work as both writer and translator. His earliest efforts, about which he carried on a regular correspondence with his mother, who also had literary ambitions, were refused publication. Of the works which eventually made Lewis famous, however, a surprising number were completed, or at least begun, during his teens—a genesis that goes far to explain the adolescent feverishness of many of his most characteristic productions.

In Paris, Lewis became familiar with French drama, and there he may also have encountered translations of contemporary German literature. At any rate, he became thoroughly imbued with the spirit of the German *Sturm und Drang* movement during a stay in Weimar which began in July of 1792 when Lewis was seventeen. His father had sent him there to learn German so that he might enter the diplomatic service, and during his stay, he met Johann Wolfgang von Goethe and Christoph Martin Wieland, spent many hours translating German literary works, and continued to fashion a literary style of his own, a style heavily influenced by his experiences in both Paris and Weimar.

Lewis returned to Oxford in the early months of 1793 and was graduated in the spring of 1794, shortly before his nineteenth birthday. Between May and December of 1794, he held a minor diplomatic post at The Hague, where he found ample time to complete the novel which was to assure his fame. That novel, *The Monk*, was published in 1796 and made Lewis an immediate, and slightly infamous, celebrity. His presence was very much in demand at London social gatherings, a fact which delighted the gregarious young author.

In this same eventful year, Lewis became the parliamentary representative for Hindon in Wiltshire, a position he retained until 1802. His parliamentary duties and his literary fame brought him the acquaintance, during these and subsequent years, of many of the prominent men of England, a number of whom mention Lewis in their correspondence and other writings. The impression which these accounts give of Lewis is of a physically unattractive, dreadfully nearsighted man, whose kindliness and affability made him difficult to dislike but whose boring garrulousness often made his company difficult to enjoy. A tone of amused, sometimes exasperated, affection suffuses many of these verbal portraits, especially those by Lord Byron.

As he had at The Hague, Lewis found sufficient time while a Member of Parliament to carry forward his literary projects. He was occasionally instrumental, too, in advancing the careers of other literary men, the most important of whom was Sir Walter Scott. In addition to inviting Scott, whom he had met in 1798, to contribute to *Tales of Wonder*, Lewis helped to arrange for the publication of Scott's 1799 translation of Goethe's *Goetz von Berlichingen*. It is amusing to read Scott's account of the deference with which he, then almost entirely unknown as a writer, received Lewis' often imperious pronouncements concerning literary style.

During this same period, Lewis' talents as a playwright came to the public's attention, with *The Castle Spectre*, the third of his plays to be published but the first to be staged. *Village Virtues*, a social farce, and *The Minister*, a translation of Friedrich Schiller's *Kabale und Liebe*, had attracted little attention to Lewis' dramatic skills, but *The Castle Spectre*, which opened on December 14, 1797, earned eighteen thousand pounds for Drury Lane Theater in less than three months.

Lewis' next dramatic project, a translation of August von Kotzebue's 1794 play *Die Spanier in Peru*, appears originally to have been intended as a collaboration with Richard Brinsley Sheridan, but the pair found it impossible to work together, and Sheridan turned to another translator for assistance. Sheridan's version of the play, *Pizarro: A Tragedy in Five Acts*, opened in May, 1799, without acknowledgment of Lewis' initial contributions to the production, and achieved spectacular success. Lewis' version, *Rolla*, was published but not performed, and the ill will generated by this incident and by various other difficulties experienced by Lewis at Drury Lane eventually led to a temporary shift of his loyalties to Covent Garden.

Before this occurred, however, three more of his plays were presented at Drury Lane, *The Twins* and *The East Indian* in 1799 and *Adelmorn, the Outlaw* in 1801, but none achieved any extraordinary success. The first two, a social farce and a sentimental comedy, were originally acted as benefit presentations for a pair of Drury Lane's veteran performers; although they served that purpose adequately, the critical and popular reception of the plays was at best lukewarm. Like his other attempts at comedy, they were neither great triumphs nor notable catastrophes. *Adelmorn, the Outlaw* on the other hand, threatened to become an embarrassment of the first order. The stage set and the incidental music were well received, but the play itself was a critical failure. *Adelmorn, the Outlaw* included many of the same melodramatic plot elements and Gothic flourishes that had attracted enthusiastic audiences to *The Castle Spectre*, but *Adelmorn, the Outlaw* was so absurdly and, at times, so tastelessly constructed that Lewis' utmost exertions were able to sustain it through a first run of only nine performances.

The reviewers treated Lewis' first Covent Garden production, *Alfonso, King of Castile*, with considerably more kindness. Although praise was not universal, some reviewers thought *Alfonso, King of Castile* the greatest tragic play of its age, and it was certainly Lewis' most concerted attempt at high dramatic art. The play is written in blank verse, occasionally with impressive poetic effect, but the plot is marred by a melodramatic intensity that makes it difficult for a twentieth century reader to take seriously. *Alfonso, King of Castile* was published several weeks before its January 15, 1802, premiere, and though its first run of only ten performances suggests that it was a very modest popular success, it remained the play in which

Lewis took the greatest artistic pride.

During 1803, Lewis' only new theatrical productions were *The Captive*, a dramatic monologue, and *The Harper's Daughter*, a shortened version of *The Minister*. They both appeared at Covent Garden, on March 22 and May 4, respectively, and each was successful after its own fashion. *The Harper's Daughter* was a benefit presentation and drew a large enough audience to provide a tidy sum. *The Captive*, billed as a "mono-drama," was an extended speech by a young wife who had been consigned to a madhouse by her cruel husband. So effective was its presentation of the wife's gradual loss of sanity that several spectators experienced hysterical fits during and after the performance and the drama was withdrawn in order to preserve the mental health of Covent Garden's customers.

Lewis' next play, a melodrama in two acts entitled *Rugantino*, opened at Covent Garden on October 18, 1805, and was performed thirty times before enthusiastic houses. Lewis again caught the public's fancy by relying on spectacle rather than subtle art, and though an occasional viewer might complain of headaches brought on by the play's many pistol shots and thunderclaps, most were enthralled, nor did the dazzling costume changes and the gorgeous Venice scenery hurt the play's attendance. Lewis knew his audience well and gave it what it wanted.

Rugantino was followed on April 1, 1807, this time at Drury Lane, by the even more spectacular *The Wood Daemon*. Full of more Gothic paraphernalia than any of Lewis' previous dramatic creations, *The Wood Daemon* is more truly a play of special effects than of plot and dialogue, and it was judged in such terms by contemporary reviewers: There was considerable praise for the production's visual impact but very little positive comment on the play as literary art. The visual impact was enough, however, to assure *The Wood Daemon* a first run of thirty-four performances.

Lewis' next three productions met with a more modest reception. *Adelgitha*, a play which Lewis had published in 1806, opened at Drury Lane in April of 1807 to favorable reviews. Centering on a character whose tragic life was meant to illustrate the fatal consequences of youthful sin, the play relies for its effect on melodramatic plot complication rather than visual spectacle, and although its nine first-run performances compare unfavorably with the thirty-four of *The Wood Daemon*, it was not nearly so ambitious a theatrical project and seems fully to have satisfied the expectations of those involved in its staging.

Venoni did not, at first, fare so well. The play, whose plot Lewis adapted from a French original, premiered at Drury Lane on December 1, 1808, and was immediately attacked by the reviewers. One scene in particular, in which a pair of lovers, unaware of each other's presence, speak alternating soliloquies from their adjoining dungeon cells, was judged especially ludicrous. The play required extensive rewriting, which Lewis undertook with some success, and *Venoni* had reached its eighteenth performance when a fire destroyed the theater. Lewis then provided the Drury Lane troupe, temporarily housed at the Lyceum Theater, with a farce entitled *Temper*, which opened on May 1, 1809, attracting so little attention that it was lost from Lewis' dramatic canon until 1942.

At this point, Lewis announced that he would write no more plays, a decision which, if he had adhered to it, would have denied posterity his most dubious contribution to British theater, the grand equestrian drama *Timour the Tartar*. *Timour the Tartar* was not the first play to introduce horses onto the British stage; that honor belongs to *Blue Beard*, whose cast of characters was horseless until February 18, 1811. On that date, the Covent Garden management made its initial test of the public's readiness to accept equestrian performers. The popular response was gratifying, and *Timour the Tartar*, whose equestrian elements were not extraneous inter- polations but integral parts of the plot, was awaited with considerable anticipation. The play opened on April 29, 1811, to the howls of the critics and the applause of the paying customers. In the ensuing months, parodies and imitations abounded, one featuring a performing elephant, and *Timour the Tartar* itself was staged a profitable forty-four times.

Lewis' final two theatrical offerings were reworkings of old material. They do, however, illustrate Lewis' frequent use of songs to increase the entertainment value of his plays. Working with Michael Kelly and Matthew Peter King, Lewis transformed *The Wood Daemon* into "a grand musical romance" with the slightly altered title, *One O'Clock: Or, The Knight and the Wood Daemon*; collaborating with Charles Edward Horn, he extensively revised *The East Indian*, turning it into a comic opera entitled *Rich and Poor*. The musical romance premiered on August 1, 1811, and was per- formed twenty-five times during its first season by the company of the En- glish Opera House; the comic opera opened on July 22, 1812, and was per- formed twenty-seven times by the same organization.

Lewis' literary endeavors had been made possible largely by a yearly allowance of a thousand pounds granted him by his father. This allowance was reduced for a time as a result of an argument between father and son over a sexual affair in which the elder Lewis had become involved, but the two managed to reconcile their differences before the father's death in May of 1812, and Lewis inherited all of his father's considerable wealth. Very soon thereafter, he used a portion of the money to purchase a permanent home for his mother.

Another consequence of the inheritance was the first of Lewis' two voy- ages to Jamaica to inspect his island properties. The primary purpose of his visit, which occurred during the first three months of 1816, was to ascertain that slaves on his plantations were properly treated. Although Lewis made no provision for the freeing of these slaves, he did establish strict rules intended to make their lives more bearable. Also, to prevent a deterioration in their living conditions after his death, he added a codicil to his will insisting that any future heir to his estates visit the plantations every third year for the purpose of looking after the slaves' welfare. In addition, no slaves were to be put up for sale.

The alterations in Lewis' will were witnessed on August 20, 1816, by Lord Byron, Percy Bysshe Shelley, and Dr. John W. Polidori during a trip Lewis took to the Continent, a trip which lasted for more than a year. The most noteworthy literary events of that tour were his oral translation of Goethe's *Faust* (1808, 1833) for Byron, the latter's first direct experience with that work, and Lewis' telling ghost stories for the entertainment of Byron and the Shelleys. Although Lewis cannot be claimed to have inspired Mary Shelley's *Frankenstein* (1818), since she had begun her novel several weeks before Lewis' arrival in Geneva, his enthusiasm for the Gothic is likely to have encouraged her to continue the project.

After a short stay in England following his wanderings on the Continent, Lewis again set sail for Jamaica on November 5, 1817. During this second visit, he introduced further reforms to improve the plight of his slaves, and having assured himself that he had done what he could for them, he embarked for England on May 4, 1818. He was ill with yellow fever when the voyage began, and within two weeks, he was dead.

Analysis

Despite considerable diversity in style and content, Matthew Gregory Lewis' plays are generally characterized by a melodramatic intensity that is often reinforced by visual spectacle. Dramatic subtlety was difficult to achieve in the huge theaters for which Lewis wrote, and Lewis' unsubtle ways were peculiarly suited to the physical environment in which his plays were performed. This is not to say, however, that Lewis presents no unified dramatic vision, that he has nothing to say about the state of man. On the contrary, his plays are surprisingly consistent in their expression of one particular theme—that the sanctity of human relationships should and must not be violated.

The Castle Spectre, for example, relates the tale of the villainous Earl Osmond, who has sinned against the bonds of love at every opportunity and who pays the ultimate price for his crimes. Long before the action of the play begins, Osmond has already launched his egocentric career by overthrowing his own brother, the benevolent Earl Reginald, and inadvertently killing Lady Evelina, the woman whom he had hoped to marry but who had married his brother instead. Evelina has martyred herself to love by throwing her body in the path of a dagger-thrust which Osmond intended for Reginald. Her sacrifice has not prevented the usurpation of her husband's power, but it has, as the audience is eventually informed, preserved her husband's life.

As one might expect of such a man, Osmond has shown no more respect for the relationship between a ruler and his subjects than he has for the ties of blood, and though he conceals the guilty secret of his rise to power, Osmond is universally hated as a tyrant. He surrounds himself with brutal henchmen who deal efficiently and savagely with any who would oppose their master. At the beginning of the play, there are no obvious threats to Osmond's continued dominion, but the isolation and loneliness which his actions have brought upon him are soon to lead to his downfall.

Appropriately enough, the undoing of this sinner against the bonds of affection is the direct result of his falling in love. The unwilling object of his amorous attentions is his niece, the beautiful and virtuous Angela, daughter of Reginald and Evelina. To minimize Angela's threat to his power (as heir to the rightful lord), Osmond has placed her with a peasant couple who have reared her as their own child. He makes the fateful decision to call her back to the court, however, when her resemblance to Evelina inspires his passion. To legitimate Evelina's sudden change in status, Osmond invents a story affirming her noble birth while concealing her actual parentage.

Like his obsession with Evelina, though, his interest in Angela is doomed to failure—again because the woman he has chosen has already selected a worthier man. During the last weeks of her peasant existence, she has fallen in love with the lowly Edric, whom she had met while she was living as a peasant, and even the opportunity to marry an earl is not temptation enough to shake her fidelity to this humble swain. Neither sweet words nor threats of imprisonment are sufficient to win her consent to become Osmond's wife.

As the audience soon discovers, Angela has chosen more wisely than she knows, because Edric is actually Percy, Earl of Northumberland, whose benevolent rule has earned for him the respect and affection of his people and whose purity of heart is suggested by the circumstances of his falling in love. Neither Percy nor Angela had been aware of the other's noble birth, but each has recognized the other's nobility of character. Percy and Osmond are spiritual opposites, and their rivalry for Angela is a clash between codes of behavior, between the ways of sentiment and the ways of selfishness.

One manifestation of this opposition is the method each uses to form alliances. Osmond surrounds himself with men who are motivated by fear and hatred or by self-interest. He enslaves his henchmen and awes them with his power, or he entices them with the hope of illusory rewards. His black slaves, like Hassan, have been stolen from their homelands and welcome every opportunity to wreak vengeance on the race which separated them from their loved ones. Others, like Kenric, have been promised worldly wealth and release from service in exchange for their fidelity, only to discover Osmond's intention to betray them. Percy's followers, on the other hand, eagerly join his effort to rescue Angela; they are motivated by love and remain faithful to their master at moments when Osmond's followers are most likely to become undependable. One in particular, Gilbert the Knave, has been the object of Percy's generosity during a period of personal crisis and shows his gratitude through his courageous support of his master at several key points in the play. As Percy himself says, "Instead of looking with scorn on those whom a smile would attract, and a favor bind forever, how many firm friends might our nobles gain, if they would but reflect that their vassals are men as they are, and have hearts whose feelings can be grateful as their own."

Osmond refuses to recognize this sentimental truth, and as a result, he loses the loyalty of a man who is in a position to reveal more about Osmond's perfidious nature than that noble cares for the world to know. When Kenric discovers that his master is plotting to kill him, he tells Angela the secret of her birth and that her father Reginald is alive, hidden away in a dungeon by Kenric himself so that he might blackmail Osmond if the need should ever arise. Unfortunately, Osmond overhears this conversation and goes in search of his hated brother, intending to carry to completion the fratricide which he had thought he had already committed.

Before the climactic arrival of the principal characters at Reginald's dungeon, the sympathy of the supernatural with the defenders of sentiment has been implied by the spectacular appearance to Angela of her mother's ghost. The specter of Evelina blesses Angela and directs her to rescue her father; elements in this scene suggest the triumph of love over hatred, a triumph which occurs in the play's busy final moments. Osmond and Angela come upon her father's darkened cell at almost the same time, and Osmond uses the occasion to threaten her with Reginald's death unless she acquiesces to their immediate marriage. This she is about to do when Reginald stops her by saying that he will take his own life rather than see his daughter dishonored. Enraged by this declaration and by news that Percy's forces have taken the castle, Osmond prepares to kill his brother but falls back in horror when Evelina's ghost repeats the self-sacrificing gesture of the living Evelina. Angela then strikes Osmond with the same dagger with which her mother had been stabbed, and the sinner against sentiment is carried away to die.

As one might imagine, despite the extraordinary commercial success of *The Castle Spectre*, it was not a universal favorite of the critics. This fact seems not to have concerned Lewis, however, who was especially cavalier in his response to one very particular objection to his play. When the critics pointed out that his inclusion of black slaves in the cast of characters of a Gothic story was a patent absurdity, he defended himself by saying that he had done it to "give a pleasing variety to the characters and dresses" and that if he could "have produced the same effect by making my heroine blue, blue I should have made her."

Obviously, Lewis did not take *The Castle Spectre* seriously as a work of art, but he did feel considerable artistic pride in *Alfonso, King of Castile*. Nevertheless, the two plays have essentially the same theme: The forces of sentiment are pitted against the forces of selfish ambition, and after the moral superiority of sentiment has been clearly displayed, ambition is defeated. In *Alfonso, King of Castile*, however, there are surprising twists of plot and characterization which create a greater sense of dramatic sophistication than is evident in the earlier play.

The curtain rises on a narrative situation that is already quite complex. Alfonso has been a good king, but he has been duped into committing one act of injustice. He has imprisoned his best friend, Orsino, on the basis of evidence fabricated by Orsino's enemies. As a result, Orsino's wife, Victoria, has died in poverty-stricken exile after swearing her son, Caesario, to avenge his father. Concealing his identity, Caesario has insinuated his way into the good graces of the king and has so successfully encouraged the rebellious spirit of the king's son that the son has defected to the king's foes. Caesario has also secretly won the love of and married the king's daughter, Amelrosa, but he has not managed, as the play begins, to break the filial bond between Alfonso and his daughter.

Ironically, it is love—for his parents—that causes Caesario to become filled with hatred. His hatred is directed against a man whose only fault is gullibility, and he attempts to make use of the innocent love of a virtuous woman to further his despicable ends. Like Osmond, Caesario is a sinner against the dictates of sentiment, and he, too, will pay with his life for his crimes.

That Caesario's actions are crimes is made clear in a number of ways. First, while courting Amelrosa, Caesario has shown his duplicitous nature by carrying on an illicit liaison with Ottilia, the vicious wife of Marquis Guzman, the man primarily responsible for his father's fall from grace. The difficulties of this situation cause him to weave a web of lies which suggest that his feelings toward neither woman are genuine. Furthermore, as the moment of Caesario's final vengeance against Alfonso approaches, it becomes increasingly obvious that a desire for personal power is at least as important in motivating Caesario as any wish to punish his father's persecutor. In fact, the killing of Alfonso is to be carried out in a way intended to alert any English audience to his murderer's villainy; a cache of explosives is to be detonated beneath Alfonso's palace, an obvious allusion to the infamous Gunpowder Plot.

During the course of the play, Orsino is discovered to be alive, and, despite his bitterness over the sufferings of himself and his family, he condemns Caesario's plans for the overthrow of Alfonso. When Alfonso has come to beg his forgiveness, his resentment has been too great to allow a reconciliation to occur, but when his son reveals his dastardly plotting, Orsino affirms the basic goodness of his former friend and allies himself with Alfonso rather than with Caesario. In a speech which summarizes the central idea of the play, he tries to draw his son back to the paths of virtue:

> True glory
> Is not to wear a crown but to *deserve* one.
> The peasant swain who leads a good man's life,
> And dies at last a good man's death, obtains
> In Wisdom's eye wreaths of far brighter splendour
> Than he whose wanton pride and thirst for empire
> Make kings his captives, and lay waste a world.

Unfortunately, Caesario's hatred and ambition blind him to the truth of his father's statement.

As they generally are in a Lewis play, the final scenes of *Alfonso, King of Castile* are almost overburdened with action. When the play ends, all the principals, with the exception of Alfonso himself, are either dead or dying, and Orsino, mortally wounded, has been forced to choose between killing his vicious son and watching the flawed but virtuous Alfonso be murdered. He chooses, in an odd affirmation of the laws of sentiment, to save the friend who had once betrayed him and to sacrifice the son.

Although it does call for the simulated detonation of a cache of gunpowder, *Alfonso, King of Castile* is less dependent for its success on sensational stage effects than are most of Lewis' plays. *Timour the Tartar*, for example, is unashamed stage spectacle from beginning to end. A play in which live horses take part in elaborate battle scenes and in which one particular equine performer leaps with its rider over a parapet into the sea could hardly be anything else. Nevertheless, the same thematic material which gives *Alfonso, King of Castile* some semblance of high seriousness is also to be found in *Timour the Tartar*, another tale of the triumph of sentimental virtue over egocentric vice.

Timour himself is the ruthless villain whose selfishness threatens the very existence of those whose actions are motivated by selfless love. Even his father, Oglou, fears for his life when in Timour's presence. As the code of sentiment dictates, however, he loves his son despite being afraid of him. Throughout the play, Oglou struggles to act in accordance with this love for his son while at the same time behaving properly toward two of his dearest friends, Agib and Zorilda, the most dangerous of Timour's enemies.

Agib is the son and Zorilda the widow of the murdered Prince of Mingrelia, and when the play opens, Agib is Timour's captive. Fortunately, Agib's jailer is the kindly Oglou, whose life was once saved by Zorilda.

Oglou will protect Agib as best he can, but he lacks the courage to defy his son by setting Agib free. In a display of the deepest maternal fortitude, that task is undertaken instead by Zorilda.

Zorilda boldly enters Timour's palace disguised as his fiancée, the Princess of Georgia, a woman to whom Timour has become engaged without having met her. Her intention is to demand that Agib, a threat to their united power, be placed with her countrymen for safekeeping. Unfortunately, just as this plot is about to succeed, Oglou is forced to reveal Zorilda's true identity because he anticipates a similar revelation by Octar, Timour's messenger to the Georgian court.

In defiance of every rule of sentiment and decency, Timour proceeds to demand that the spirited Zorilda become his bride despite her obvious distaste for her husband's barbaric murderer; her son, Agib, is to be killed if she refuses. The necessity of making such a choice is obviated, however, when the faithful Oglou assists in getting Agib out of the palace. He asks only, as paternal sentiment demands, that mercy be shown to Timour if Agib and his allies succeed in overthrowing the tyrant. Out of respect for their friend's fatherly feelings, Zorilda and Agib agree.

By this point in the play, there have been illustrations of the sentiments appropriate to a number of human relationships: widow to deceased husband, son to deceased father, mother to son, father to son, and friend to friend. The play's final scene portrays, in rather spectacular fashion, the courageous love of a son for his mother. As Agib and his troops gather for their attack on Timour's stronghold, Timour, in full sight of the massed armies, attempts to kill the captive Zorilda. She flees and is forced to leap into the sea, at which point Agib spurs his horse over a parapet and rescues his mother from a death by drowning. The stage then becomes a battleground where the forces of virtuous sentiment defeat the forces of self-serving oppression with convincing finality.

For his next theatrical effort, Lewis turned from the comparatively new equestrian drama to the more familiar Gothic drama. He transformed his earlier *The Wood Daemon* into *One O'Clock: Or, The Knight and the Wood Daemon*, advertising this extraordinary concoction as "a grand musical romance." In keeping with this designation, it contains considerable singing and dancing, and its costumes, sets, and stage machinery are more extravagant than anything used in Lewis' previous productions. Nevertheless, *One O'Clock* is thematically consistent with Lewis' other plays in that it deals with the corrupting influence of egocentric ambition and the saving grace of sentimental virtue.

The power-mad villain of this particular piece is Hardyknute, a former peasant who has become the Count of Holstein by forming a pact with Sangrida, the Wood Daemon. Sangrida has granted him wealth, beauty, eternal youth, and invulnerability in battle in exchange for an annual sacri-

fice of a child. Each year, on the seventh of August, Hardyknute must spill
innocent blood or become the Wood Daemon's perpetual slave. If he fails
to accomplish his hideous task before Sangrida's clock strikes one in the
morning, he will be subjected to everlasting torment. The play centers on
Hardyknute's attempt to sacrifice a ninth child, Leolyn, and take possession of his reward, the beautiful peasant girl Una.

The representatives of virtuous innocence within the play are Leolyn,
Clotilda, Oswy, and Una. Leolyn is the long-lost son of the former count,
Ruric, whom Hardyknute clandestinely murdered in order to seize power.
Leolyn, who had been entrusted to Una's sister, Clotilda, was stolen by
marauding Gypsies and reappears as the play opens, struck dumb and rec-
ognizable only by a birthmark on his wrist. Una, whose name suggests
(among other things) the dreaded hour of sacrifice, is a young peasant
maiden who has been so confounded by the magic of Sangrida that she
is on the brink of marrying Hardyknute; her heart, however, belongs to
Oswy. Oswy is the poor but faithful peasant who loves Una to distraction
and would unhesitatingly lay down his life for her.

To an even greater extent than usual, Lewis concentrates the significant
action of the play in the final scenes. The first two acts contain a painfully
slow exposition of the plot, the introduction of sentimental subplots which
are never satisfactorily integrated with the main plot, and the insertion of
various entertainments and spectacles that are obviously intended to dazzle
and divert the audience. Storms, secret passages, disappearing statues, and
a miraculous bed are only a few of the special effects, with other diversions
including a chorus of spirits, a procession of Gypsies, a triumphal march of
troops leading a captured giant and dwarfs, a prophetic dream, and a ballet of the seasons, as well as intermittent outbursts of ballad-singing and
guitar-playing. By the end of act 2, however, Hardyknute has come to realize, through the venerable device of the birthmark, that his predecessor's
son is within the castle and that he must act if he is to preserve his power.
He has also been reminded, by the terrifying voice of Sangrida, that only a
few hours remain before he must make his annual sacrifice.

In the final act, the allegiance of the central characters to the laws of
sentiment is tested, and only Hardyknute is found wanting. Clotilda, suspicious of Hardyknute's murderous intentions, guards Leolyn's bedchamber
and is foiled in her vigilance only by a treacherous mechanism that lowers
Leolyn's bed into a subterranean dungeon. At this point, Oswy is called
upon to seek help from the King of Denmark, a task he undertakes despite
his worries concerning the wavering fidelity of his beloved Una. Una
herself is tried most severely of all. After gaining access to the dungeon
into which Leolyn has been caged and releasing him from his chains, she is
confronted by Hardyknute, who reveals his dreadful secret and makes clear
that he will spill her blood in place of Leolyn's if he can save himself from

Sangrida in no other way. His love for her will make the murder difficult, but his self-love, being greater, will steel him to commit the crime. Faced with the choice of becoming Hardyknute's accomplice by revealing Leolyn's hiding place or of jeopardizing her own life, Una hesitates for a moment but then chooses to save the innocent young boy. Leolyn, in turn, proves himself worthy of Una's courageous selflessness by remaining in the dungeon and by finding a means of preventing her death. In full sight of Hardyknute, he climbs to Sangrida's clock and pushes the hands forward to the hour of one, thereby calling up the demon before Una can be killed. Sangrida appears immediately and, in a scene that is reminiscent of the conclusion of *The Monk*, four fiends drag Hardyknute away to his eternal punishment.

Although the artistic merit of Lewis' plays is minimal, his contemporaries enjoyed them. The sensationalism and the melodramatic moralizing of his dramatic works are symptomatic of the bad taste which produced one of the most sterile periods in British theatrical history, and if Lewis cannot be accused of creating this bad taste, he can justly be said to have been the most adept playwright of his age at exploiting it.

Other major works

NOVEL: *Ambrosio: Or, The Monk*, 1796 (also as *The Monk: A Romance*).

POETRY: *The Love of Gain: A Poem Imitated from Juvenal*, 1799; *Monody on the Death of Sir John Moore*, 1809; *Poems*, 1812; *The Isle of Devils: A Metrical Tale*, 1827.

NONFICTION: *Journal of a West India Proprietor, Kept During a Residence in the Island of Jamaica*, 1834 (also as *Journal of a Residence Among the Negroes in the West Indies*, 1861).

ANTHOLOGIES: *Tales of Terror*, 1799 (also as *An Apology for Tales of Terror*; includes work by Sir Walter Scott and Robert Southey); *Tales of Wonder*, 1801 (2 volumes; includes work by Scott, Southey, Robert Burns, Thomas Gray, John Dryden, and others).

TRANSLATIONS: *The Bravo of Venice: A Romance*, 1805 (of J. H. D. Zschokke's novel *Aballino der Grosse Bandit*); *Feudal Tyrants: Or, The Counts of Carlsheim and Sargans: A Romance, Taken from the German*, 1806 (4 volumes; of Christiane Benedicte Eugénie Naubert's novel *Elisabeth, Erbin von Toggenburg: Oder, Geschichte der Frauen in der Schweiz*).

MISCELLANEOUS: *Romantic Tales*, 1808 (4 volumes; includes poem, short stories, and ballads); *Twelve Ballads, the Words and Music by M. G. Lewis*, 1808; *The Life and Correspondence of M. G. Lewis, with Many Pieces Never Before Published*, 1839 (2 volumes; Margaret Baron-Wilson, editor).

Bibliography

Booth, Michael R., et al. *The Revels History of Drama in English. Volume VI: 1750-1880*, 1975.

Brawley, Benjamin. "Early Nineteenth Century Drama," in *A Short History of the English Drama*, 1921.

Conolly, L. W., and J. P. Wearing. *English Drama and Theatre. 1800-1900*, 1978.

Donohue, Joseph W., Jr. *Dramatic Character in the English Romantic Age*, 1970.

Evans, Bertrand. *Gothic Drama from Walpole to Shelley*, 1947.

Nicoll, Allardyce. *A History of English Drama, 1660-1900, Volume III: Late Eighteenth Century Drama, 1750-1800*, 1955.

_____ . *A History of English Drama, 1660-1900, Volume IV: Early Nineteenth Century Drama, 1800-1850*, 1955.

Peck, Louis F. *A Life of Matthew G. Lewis*, 1961.

Stephen, Leslie. "Matthew Gregory Lewis," in *Dictionary of National Biography*, 1909.

Robert H. O'Connor

GEORGE LILLO

Born: London, England; February 4, 1693
Died: London, England; September 3, 1739

Principal drama

Silvia: Or, The Country Burial, pr., pb. 1730; *The London Merchant: Or, The History of George Barnwell*, pr., pb. 1731; *The Christian Hero*, pr., pb. 1735; *Guilt Its Own Punishment: Or, Fatal Curiosity*, pr. 1736, pb. 1737 (commonly known as *Fatal Curiosity*); *Marina*, pr., pb. 1738; *Britannia and Batavia*, pb. 1740 (masque); *Elmerick: Or, Justice Triumphant*, pr., pb. 1740; *Arden of Feversham*, pr. 1759, pb. 1762 (with John Hoadly); *The Works of Mr. George Lillo*, pb. 1775, 1810 (2 volumes; Thomas Davies, editor).

Other literary forms

George Lillo is known only for his plays.

Achievements

Of George Lillo's seven plays, only *The London Merchant* was both a popular and critical success when first presented, and only it and *Fatal Curiosity* continued to be performed long after most plays of their period had been forgotten. These homiletic domestic tragedies, which reflect their author's creed as a Dissenter, had a profound effect upon the Continental drama of the late eighteenth century and early nineteenth century.

During a playwriting career that spanned less than a decade, Lillo tried his hand at most popular dramatic forms: ballad opera, heroic drama, masque, prose tragedy, blank-verse tragedy, even adaptations of Elizabethan domestic tragedy (*Arden of Feversham*) and Shakespearean romance (*Marina*, a reworking of the last two acts of William Shakespeare's *Pericles*). Lillo worked within the bounds of tradition but at the same time went beyond past practice. For example, his first play, *Silvia*, is a ballad opera of the sort that had become popular in the wake of John Gay's success with *The Beggar's Opera* in 1728. In it, Lillo follows Gay's pattern of punctuating the action with dozens of familiar tunes, and he includes burlesque and seriocomic elements. The pastoral motif dominates, however, and Lillo's announced intention—"to inculcate the love of truth and virtue and a hatred of vice and falsehood"—foreshadows the strong didacticism and sentimentalism of his two major plays which were to follow.

Lillo was a relatively inexperienced playwright when he offered *The London Merchant* to Theophilus Cibber, manager of a summer company acting at the Drury Lane. Though the famous actor David Garrick credited Lillo with "the invention of a new species of dramatic poetry, which may properly be termed the inferior or lesser tragedy," the drama of hapless George Barnwell is actually in the tradition of such Elizabethan domestic tragedies as the anonymously authored *Arden of Feversham* (1592) and *A Yorkshire Tragedy* (c. 1606). Further, earlier in the eighteenth century there were such middle-class forebears as Lewis Theobald's *The Perfidious Brothers* (pb. 1715) and Aaron Hill's *The Fatal Extravagance* (pb. 1720), the latter based on *A Yorkshire Tragedy*; Thomas Otway during the Restoration and Nicholas Rowe early in the eighteenth century also wrote plays whose sentimentalism and pathos verged on the melodramatic. Despite these predecessors, Lillo's achievement in *The London Merchant* is notable, for it is a realistic prose drama that consciously celebrates the virtues of middle-class life. It offered theatergoers (in its day, and for more than a century thereafter, as a Christmas and Easter entertainment for London apprentices) not a tale of "prinses distrest and scenes of royal woe," but the story of an honest merchant, his errant apprentice, and a conniving woman, characters with whom middle-class Londoners could identify and whose emotions they could share. Eschewing blank verse, Lillo chose to write in "artless strains," which emphasized both the realism and the bourgeois subject matter of the play and successfully accommodated his work "to the circumstances of the generality of mankind." Young men about town came to the first performance ready to scoff (having purchased from street hawkers copies of the Elizabethan ballad on which the play was based), but they soon "were drawn in to drop their ballads and pull out their handkerchiefs." Alexander Pope was at the first performance and reacted favorably; Queen Caroline asked for a copy of the play, and the royal family went to see it; and both *The Weekly Register* and *The Gentleman's Magazine* defended it enthusiastically against charges that its characters, "so low and familiar in Life," were therefore "too low for the Stage."

Enduringly popular as the play was, it did not start a trend on the London stage; there were some imitations, but only Edward Moore's *The Gamester* (pr. 1753) is noteworthy. On the Continent, however, it was both popular and influential. It was translated into French, German, and Dutch, and it was praised by Denis Diderot and Gotthold Ephraim Lessing, the latter of whom wrote, "I should infinitely prefer to be the creator of *The London Merchant* than the creator of *Der sterbende Cato*." Indeed, Lillo's play is a clear ancestor of Lessing's *Miss Sara Samson* (pr. 1755), an early *Schicksaltragödie*, or German domestic drama.

Fatal Curiosity, another mercantile domestic drama but in blank verse, has been described by Allardyce Nicoll as the only tragic masterpiece produced between 1700 and 1750 and by William H. McBurney as a landmark play: "at once a climax to Restoration tragedy written according to 'the rules,' and a dramatic protest against the 'frigid caution' of an age in which 'Declamation roar'd whilst Passion slept.'" When first presented in 1736 at

Henry Fielding's theater, it ran only seven nights, but when it was revived the following March as a curtain raiser for Fielding's *The Historical Register for the Year 1736*, it lasted for eleven nights. The play was revived again in 1741, 1742, and 1755; George Colman's pre-Romantic version was done in 1782; and Henry MacKenzie's reworking (called *The Shipwreck*) was presented in 1784. *Fatal Curiosity* clearly had continuing appeal to eighteenth century audiences, and its characterizations, moral sentiments, and theatricality withstood changing dramatic fashions. (Mrs. Elizabeth Inchbald, in *The British Theatre*, 1808, described a performance of Colman's version at which "a certain horror seized the audience, and was manifested by a kind of stifled scream.") In addition to its continuing presence on the English stage, the play was widely read, particularly in the aftermath of James Harris' enthusiastic comparison (in *Philological Inquiries*, 1781) of it to Sophocles' *Oedipus Rex*, to Shakespeare's *Othello* and *King Lear* and to John Milton's *Samson Agonistes*, and his description of it as "the model of a Perfect Fable." As in the case of *The London Merchant*, however, the enduring popularity of the play had very little effect on subsequent English tragedy. In Germany, however, where imitations, adaptations, and translations abounded between 1781 and 1817, it was as influential a forerunner of the *Schicksaltragödie* as was *The London Merchant*.

Though Lillo's other works were failures on the stage, and even though *The London Merchant* and *Fatal Curiosity* sometimes are dismissed as little more than sentimental melodramas, both are of lasting interest not only because they obviously addressed a need felt by audiences in England and on the Continent but also because they significantly influenced the course of German tragic drama.

Biography

George Lillo was born in London near Moorgate on February 4, 1693; his father was Dutch, his mother English. He was reared as a Puritan Dissenter. Lillo learned his father's trade as a jeweler, and the two were partners in London for some years until the son decided to become a playwright. Little else is known about Lillo's life; contemporary accounts by Thomas Davies and Theophilus Cibber are still the primary sources.

Davies says that though Lillo was a Dissenter, he was "not of that sour cast which distinguishes some of our sectaries." He further describes him as being "lusty, but not tall, of a pleasing aspect, though unhappily deprived of the sight of one eye." Of a meeting with Lillo during a rehearsal of *Fatal Curiosity* in 1736, Davies recalls:

> Plain and simple as he was in his address, his manner of conversing was modest, affable and engaging. When invited to give his opinion of how a particular sentiment should be uttered by the actor, he exprest himself in the gentlest and most obliging terms, and conveyed instruction and conviction with good nature and good manners.

Soon after the death of Lillo, Fielding wrote in tribute to him the following words of eulogy:

> He had the gentlest and honestest Manners, and, at the same Time, the most friendly and obliging. He had a perfect Knowledge of Human Nature, though his Contempt for all base Means of Application, which are the necessary Steps to great Acquaintance, restrained his Conversation within very narrow Bounds. He had the Spirit of an old Roman, joined to the Innocence of a primitive Christian.

On the evidence of these statements, one can conclude that Lillo patterned the character Thorowgood in *The London Merchant* after himself.

The prologue to *Elmerick*, his last completed play, suggests that near the close of his life Lillo was "Deprest by want, afflicted by disease...," and the third performance of the play, at Drury Lane on February 26, 1740, was said to be "for the benefit of the author's poor relations...." The evidence of his will, however, indicates otherwise (his primary beneficiary was a nephew, John Underwood, also a jeweler), and Davies reports that Lillo had accumulated a considerable estate from productions of his plays (*The London Merchant* alone was done seventy times between 1731 and his death) and through their publication by his friend John Gray, a London bookseller to whom Lillo sold the rights to all of his works.

Lillo died on September 3, 1739, and was buried three days later in the vault of St. Leonard's Church, in London's Shoreditch.

Analysis

"The Ballad of George Barnwell" (which was sung to the tune of "The Merchant"), the late Elizabethan song which became the source of George Lillo's masterpiece, *The London Merchant*, was said to have been inspired by an actual murder case in Shropshire. The case concerned an apprentice who was seduced by an unscrupulous woman, embezzled funds from his master and gave them to the seductress, and then murdered an uncle in order to rob him. The authors of Elizabethan domestic tragedies often turned to accounts of murder cases for their sources, and Lillo was familiar with these sixteenth and seventeenth century middle-class plays (he wrote his own version of one, *Arden of Feversham*), so it is easy to understand the appeal of such a moralistic ballad to a young playwright who had been a shopkeeper and was a Calvinist Dissenter. It provided him with a substantive basis for a dramatized sermon on loyalty, honor, greed, and sexual morality—all of which he had touched upon in his first play, *Silvia*.

Allusions early in *The London Merchant* date the action prior to the defeat of the Spanish Armada, but there is nothing else to detract from its contemporary realism (its original title included the words "A True History"), and Lillo's addition of the characters of Maria, Trueman, and Millwood's servants to the four in his source increased the possibilities for thematic development as well as dramatic conflict. He also made Millwood, the seductress, into a tragic figure through passages that recall Cleopatra and Lady Macbeth and by focusing upon the reasons for her misanthropy.

The play opens with a dialogue between Thorowgood, the merchant, and Trueman, an apprentice, in which the master praises his country, its queen, and his fellow merchants, who "sometimes contribute to the safety of their country as they do at all times to its happiness." Thorowgood warns Trueman that if he "should be tempted to any action that has the appearance of vice or meanness in it," he should reflect "on the dignity of our profession," and then "may with honest scorn reject whatever is unworthy of it." When his only child, Maria, enters, the merchant recalls her many suitors, but she discounts "high birth and titles"; her melancholia, one suspects, is the result of unrequited love (for Barnwell, as it turns out).

The scene shifts to the home of Millwood, a malcontent who labels men "selfish hypocrites," hates other women, and supports herself by taking advantage "only of the young and innocent part of the sex who, having never injured women, apprehend no injury from them." Eighteen-year-old Barnwell, whom she has observed in financial transactions, is her latest intended victim, and Lillo prepares the audience well for his naïveté and easy distraction in the face of her advances. When she asks what he thinks about love, he talks about "the general love we owe to mankind" and his attachment for his uncle, master, and fellow apprentices. First addled and then smitten, Barnwell almost as quickly is miserable, having bought "a moment's pleasure with an age of pain." Conscience-stricken, he returns home, unable to reveal his transgression even to Trueman, his fellow apprentice and closest friend, but he is convinced that Millwood loves him. Thorowgood confronts but quickly pardons Barnwell for his unexplained absence ("That modest blush, the confusion so visible in your face, speak grief and shame") and then warns his charge: "Now, when the sense of pleasure's quick and passion high, the voluptuous appetites, raging and fierce, demand the strongest curb." Barnwell, though, is tempted anew, this time by Millwood's story of poverty. He seals his fate by giving her money taken from Thorowgood, but again is immediately tormented by remorse.

Asides and soliloquies are the means by which Lillo reveals Barnwell's recurring bouts of conscience, and they serve not only to develop his character but also to advance Lillo's didactic purposes, for almost all such speeches are brief exempla, parts of a play that Stephen L. Trainor, Jr., describes as structured "according to the prescribed format for a Dissenting sermon."

Trueman, not present in Lillo's source, is a moral counterpart of the fallen Barnwell. He remains Thorowgood's willing student and loyal apprentice and illustrates the highest ideals of lasting friendship. Shaken as he is by Barnwell's flight and confession of embezzlement in a letter to him, Trueman plans with Maria to make up the losses and thus conceal all from her father. During their plotting, Maria turns to the audience: "In attempting to save from shame one whom we hope may yet return to virtue, to Heaven and you, the judges of this action, I appeal whether I have done anything misbecoming my sex and character." Lillo apparently wanted theatergoers to wrestle with the moral implications of the action not only after a play but also during it. Millwood's servants, like Trueman and Maria creations of Lillo, are the traditional helpmates and coconspirators of their mistress at the start, but they quickly become disillusioned and decide that " 'Tis time the world was rid of such a monster" when Millwood convinces Barnwell to kill his uncle, for "there is something so horrid in murder that all other crimes seem nothing when compared to that." They resolve, therefore, to prevent the crime. The four characters Lillo has created thus dedicate themselves to saving a soul and eradicating evil. Representing several walks of life—apprentice, servants, daughter of a well-to-do merchant—they are role models for Lillo's audience, a substantial portion of which had been sent to the theater by masters and elders for edification as well as for entertainment.

The longest speech in the play is Barnwell's third-act soliloquy prior to the murder. Aware as he is of the "impiety" of his "bloody purpose" and sensing that nature itself trembles because of his "accursed design," he cannot fail to do Millwood's bidding: "She's got such firm possession of my heart and governs there with such despotic sway. . . . In vain does nature, reason, conscience, all oppose it." Hesitant to act, he finally stabs his uncle, who in his dying words asks the "choicest blessings" for his "dearest nephew" and forgiveness for his murderer. Barnwell's self-serving laments over the body have led many to echo Millwood's characterization of him as a "whining, preposterous, canting villain" who fails to evoke sympathy and lacks tragic stature. Lillo, however, was not influenced solely by classical tradition; his Calvinistic background also was likely a determining force in Barnwell's course of action. When he is seized as a result of Millwood's treachery, Barnwell complains: "The hand of Heaven is in it. . . . Yet Heaven, that justly cuts me off, still suffers her to live, perhaps to punish others. Tremendous mercy!" On the other hand, he recognizes the heinous nature of his crime ("This execrable act of mine's without a parallel") and accepts responsibility for what he has done: "I now am—what I've made myself." He also warns youths in the audience to "Avoid lewd women, false as they are fair. . . . By my example, learn to shun my fate. . . ." Such statements support Trainor's thesis that "Lillo seeks to bring the theatregoer to a sentient realization of the evil that exists within him for the purposes of confession and correction of that evil" and that this tragic concept evolved "from Puritan homiletic theory, which also seeks to achieve reformation by affective means. . . ."

The play as first presented and published has Millwood make her final appearance at the end of the fourth act as she is taken to prison, having been denounced by her servants. She lashes out at "men of all degrees and all professions . . . alike wicked to the utmost of their power," and as for religion, "War, plague, and famine have not destroyed so many of the human race as this pretended piety has done. . . ." Warped though her self-justification may be, she sees herself as a victim of society and is utterly unrepentant, as bitterly and uncompromisingly defiant as she was earlier in the play. There is not even a last expression of despair in the manner of Macbeth or Faustus.

Lillo originally had reunited Barnwell and Millwood at the gallows in a closing scene, "but by the advice of some friends it was left out in the representation," and not until the fifth edition (1735) was it included with the rest of the text. In addition to the highly charged drama of a meeting at the scaffold, the scene also softens a bit the sharp edges of Millwood's character, since she laments the end of her "flattering hopes," admits to having "sinned beyond the reach of mercy," echoes Barnwell's Calvinism with her statement "And I was doomed before the world began to endless pains . . .," and tells Barnwell that his prayers for her "are lost in air, or else returned perhaps with double blessing to your bosom, but they help me not." Her plaintive final cry recalls Christopher Marlowe's Faustus: "Encompassed with horror, whither must I go? I would not live—nor die! That I could cease to be—or ne'er had been!" These expressed doubts notwithstanding, Millwood remains unrepentant at the end, and as McBurney notes, "Millwood, rather than Barnwell, enacts the 'tragic' role of the Christian drama by dying in blasphemous despair."

The London Merchant is a play that must be considered from several vantage points. While the primary reason for its contemporary success was its middle-class realism and bourgeois morality, its newness was primarily a matter of degree and style, for Elizabethan domestic tragedies were equally homiletic and journalistically true to life. Lillo's occasional rhetorical excesses, however, tie it to the classical tradition, and his background as a Dissenter also is apparent.

His only other noteworthy play is *Guilt Its Own Punishment: Or, Fatal Curiosity*, which was first presented in 1736 (when printed by Gray in 1737, its title was given as *Fatal Curiosity: A True Tragedy*). On this occasion as in 1731, Lillo based his domestic tragedy upon an Elizabethan crime. Originally reported in a 1618 pamphlet, *Newes from Perin in Cornwall of a most Bloody and un-exampled Murther very lately committed by a Father on his owne Sonne (who was lately returned from the Indyes) at the Instigation of a mercilesse Step-mother . . .*, the event was later recounted in Sir William Sanderson's *Compleat History of the Lives and Reigns of Mary Queen of Scotland, And of Her Son and Successor, James the Sixth, King of Scot-*

land . . . (1656), and this condensation of the pamphlet was included in *The Annals of King James and King Charles the First* (1681), known as *Frankland's Annals*. Lillo probably did not use the pamphlet as his source; he likely was familiar with one or both of the compendiums. In each of them, the wicked stepmother of the original has become the real mother of the victim, and preceding the murder account in each there is a discussion of Sir Walter Raleigh's fall from grace. In *Fatal Curiosity*, the real mother is the murderer, and early in the play, Old Wilmot and Randal, his young servant, discuss Raleigh's arrest.

Fielding's prologue spoken at the first performance was intended to justify this tragedy of "lower life," which also stood apart from most other plays of the period in that it had only three acts. Its pervasive didacticism, with love for country and the honorable nature of commerce again expressed, recalls *The London Merchant*. Loyalty to one's master and selfless love are also portrayed.

The action opens at the Cornwall home of Old Wilmot. Ruined by poverty and saddened by his son's failure to return from a voyage to India, the old man moves to discharge his loyal servant Randal from his "unprofitable service." Randal objects, but to no avail, and Old Wilmot suggests that he renounce "books and the unprofitable search/ Of wisdom there, and study humankind," for doing so will teach him how to "wear the face of probity and honor" as he proceeds to deceive people in order to take advantage of them for his own ends. The old man cynically instructs Randal: "Be a knave and prosper!" His own ruin, he says, has come about through his failure to treat mankind as they deserve; the world, he claims, "is all a scene of deep deceit," and the man "who deals with mankind on the square/ Is his own bubble and undoes himself." The lesson in villainy concluded, Randal bemoans the fall of his "High-minded . . . pitiful and generous" master, who once had honor as his idol. At the same time, though, Randal refers to Wilmot as improvident and pleasure-loving, the first of several such inconsistent and conflicting views of the protagonist of the play, whose tragic flaw is his misguided and untempered reason. The scene shifts to the home of Charlot, who is engaged to the missing Young Wilmot. Charlot rejects overtures by other men and supports his parents, whom Maria, Charlot's maid, describes as gloomy, proud, and impatient. When Agnes, the mother, enters, Maria says that the old lady's "pride seems to increase with her misfortunes" and also refers to "her haughty, swelling heart." Thus, one is prepared for the emergence of Agnes as a villain who is destroyed by hubris and greed. Further, in conversation with Charlot, Agnes is scornful of "the common herd," to whose level she has been reduced by poverty. She is equally disdainful of her "wretched husband," whose "fixed love for me" is all that "withholds his hand" from "foul self-murder," a blasphemous desire that reveals the old man's loss of faith. Charlot attempts to counter Agnes' miseries by telling of a possibly prescient dream she had the night before in which Patience and Contemplation were joined by Young Wilmot and his parents. In the first two scenes, then, Lillo sets the stage for the return of the long-lost son and sows the seeds of the catastrophes to come.

Young Wilmot's appearance in the next scene is punctuated by a patriotic paean to England and a tedious speech of devotion to Charlot, to whose home he then repairs. Their reunion is marked by rhetorical bombast that the blank verse fails to ameliorate. Charlot, though a sentimental heroine in the tradition of Otway's Belvidera is the most fully realized and believable person in *Fatal Curiosity*.

Soon after his reunion with Charlot, Young Wilmot has a chance meeting with Randal, and they scheme to hide the son's identity from his parents (his features having sufficiently changed during his long absence so they would not recognize him) to enable him to satisfy his curiosity by first meeting with them as a stranger. Lillo thus portrays him not only as a virtuous, loving, brave, and successful merchant but also as a self-indulgent adventurer who is very much his parents' son and is as much his own victim as he is Agnes'. He arrives at their home just as Agnes is leaving to sell a volume of Seneca to get money for bread. He gives them a letter of introduction ostensibly from Charlot, and they welcome him, talking of their lost son and listening to an account of his adventures. Fearful that his emotions will betray him into revealing his identity before Charlot arrives, he feigns a need for sleep and retires, giving into Agnes' care a casket with "contents of value." Alone, she is overtaken by curiosity and opens the box, which is filled with jewels, treasures that would end their "Base poverty and all its abject train. . . ." Old Wilmot enters; she shows him the jewels; and he senses her purpose: "Th' inhospitable murder of our guest!" What ensues is the most exciting dialogue in the play, as wife urges husband on, first gaining his tacit assent and eventually convincing him to commit the act. Her determination, persistence, and success are reminiscent of Lady Macbeth, while his reluctance and malleability recall Macbeth himself. No sooner is the deed committed than Agnes reacts in a manner that also recalls Shakespeare's play: "Inconstant, wretched woman!/ What, doth my heart recoil and bleed with him/ Whose murder you contrived?" When Charlot and Randal arrive in the wake of the stabbing, the parents learn the full horror of their act, and Wilmot resolves that "Our guilt and desolation must be told/ From age to age to teach desponding mortals/ How far beyond the reach of human thought/ Heaven, when incensed, can punish." he then stabs Agnes, who asks forgiveness from her son and vows: "Had I ten thousand lives/ I'd give them all to speak my penitence,/ Deep, and sincere, and equal to my crime." Wilmot stabs himself, and before he dies proclaims that he and Agnes brought their ruin upon themselves with their pride and impatience. "Mankind may learn . . .," he says as he dies.

However serious the weaknesses of the first two acts may be, the tragic intensity of the third is overwhelming. While the action of the entire play spans a period no greater than the time of presentation, there is a startling rapidity to the final progression toward the terrible catastrophes. This classical compression of time is as important to the effect as is Lillo's decision to have the murder done offstage, with Young Wilmot's muted "Oh, Father! Father!" and Agnes' reports and urgings providing all the immediacy that is needed. To avoid diluting the emotional impact, Lillo wisely brings the play to a rapid close after the father dies, while Randal delivers a choruslike coda: "Let us at least be wiser, nor complain/ Of Heaven's mysterious ways and awful reign."

Largely because of *The London Merchant*, George Lillo is a playwright to be reckoned with in any consideration of middle-class or domestic tragedy, not only in England but also on the Continent, where his influence was more generally felt. He demonstrated once and for all that tragedy was not the exclusive province of princes, but that middle-class men and women possessed the necessary stature for tragic action. While his plays are not of the first rank, they are worthy progenitors of a large body of later drama.

Bibliography

Davis, Thomas. "Introduction," in *The Works of Mr. George Lillo*, 1775, 1810.

Havens, Raymond D. "The Sentimentalism of *The London Merchant*," in *Journal of English Literary History*. XII (1945), pp. 183-187.

McBurney, William H. "Introduction," in Lillo's *Fatal Curiosity*, 1967.

Rodman, George Bush. "Sentimentalism in Lillo's *The London Merchant*," in *Journal of English Literary History*. XII (1945), pp. 45-61.

Trainor, Stephen L., Jr. "Tears Abounding: *The London Merchant* as Puritan Tragedy," in *Studies in English Literature*. XVIII (1978), pp. 509-521.

Gerald H. Strauss

HENRY LIVINGS

Born: Prestwich, England; September 20, 1929

Principal drama

Stop It, Whoever You Are, pr. 1961, pb. 1962; *Big Soft Nellie*, pr. 1961, pb. 1964; *Nil Carborundum*, pr. 1962, pb. 1963; *Kelly's Eye*, pr. 1963, pb. 1964; *The Day Dumbfounded Got His Pylon*, pr. 1963 (radio play), pr. 1965 (staged), pb. 1967; *Kelly's Eye and Other Plays* (includes *Big Soft Nellie*), pb. 1964; *Eh?*, pr. 1964, pb. 1965; *The Little Mrs. Foster Show*, pr. 1966, pb. 1969; *Good Grief!*, pr. 1967, pb. 1968 (one-acts and sketches: *After the Last Lamp*, *You're Free*, *Variable Lengths*, *Pie-eating Contest*, *Does It Make Your Cheeks Ache?*, *The Reasons for Flying*); *Honour and Offer*, pr. 1968, pb. 1969; *The Gamecock*, pr. 1969, pb. 1971; *Rattel*, pr. 1969, pb. 1971; *Variable Lengths and Longer: An Hour of Embarrassment*, pr. 1969 (includes *The Reasons for Flying*, *Does It Make Your Cheeks Ache?*); *The Boggart*, pr. 1970, pb. 1971; *Conciliation*, pr. 1970, pb. 1971; *The Rifle Volunteer*, pr. 1970, pb. 1971; *Beewine*, pr. 1970, pb. 1971; *The ffinest ffamily in the Land*, pr. 1970, pb. 1973; *You're Free*, pr. 1970; *Mushrooms and Toadstools*, pr. 1970, pb. 1974; *Tiddles*, pr. 1970, pb. 1974; *Pongo Plays 1-6*, pb. 1971 (includes *The Gamecock*, *Rattel*, *The Boggart*, *Beewine*, *The Rifle Volunteer*, *Conciliation*); *This Jockey Drives Late Nights*, pr. 1972, pb. 1972, 1976 (adaptation of Leo Tolstoy's play *The Power of Darkness*); *Draft Sam*, pr. 1972 (televised), pb. 1974, pr. 1976 (staged); *The Rent Man*, pr. 1972, pb. 1974; *Cinderella: A Likely Tale*, pr. 1972, pb. 1976 (adaptation of Charles Perrault's story); *The Tailor's Britches*, pr. 1973, pb. 1974; *Glorious Miles*, pr. 1973 (televised), pr. 1975 (staged); *Jonah*, pr. 1974, pb. 1975; *Six More Pongo Plays Including Two for Children*, pb. 1974 (includes *Tiddles*, *The Rent Man*, *The Ink-Smeared Lady*, *The Tailor's Britches*, *Daft Sam*, *Mushrooms and Toadstools*); *Jack and the Beanstalk*, pr. 1974 (music by Alan Glasgow); *Jug*, pr. 1975 (adaptation of Heinrich von Kleist's play *The Broken Jug*); *The Astounding Adventures of Tom Thumb*, pr. 1979 (children's play).

Other literary forms

In addition to his plays for the stage, Henry Livings is known for his screenplay adaptation of *Eh?—Work Is a Four-Letter Word*—and for his work as a television writer.

Achievements

Usually clustered uncomfortably with the post-Osborne playwrights of Great Britain, Livings is perhaps more popular in the regional theaters than in London itself. An actor influenced by Joan Littlewood and her presentational approach to theater, Livings first confounded London audiences with *Stop It, Whoever You Are*, especially the industrial lavatory scene, the beginning of Livings' career-long interest in the workingman *in situ*. Along with successes at the Royal Court Theatre, London, Livings' plays have been successful in Stratford, Manchester, Oxford, Lincoln, Birmingham, and Stoke-on-Trent. This appeal to the less sophisticated audience is what separates Livings from both critical approval and big-name notoriety in London theatrical circles. As for American productions, only the Cincinnati Playhouse in the Park has shown continuing interest in Livings' work, having produced *Honour and Offer* as well as *Eh?*, his best-known play in America, which won a 1966 Obie Award for its production at New York's Circle in the Square Theatre. The value of Livings' contribution lies in his concentration on the fairly short entertainment segment, appealing directly to the working-class audience of every age, without concessions to more traditional dramatic considerations such as structure and psychological character studies. Combining the vaudevillian *lazzi* (the stock-in-trade of the British comic actor) with an uncanny insight into the real problems and delights of the British working class, Livings manages to make an evening at the theater the robust, titillating, hugely entertaining experience it was meant to be. His work adds humor and linguistic virtuosity to the otherwise sober, even whining, "kitchen sink" school of British drama.

Biography

Born in Prestwich, Lancashire, on September 20, 1929, Henry Livings was not, as might be suspected from his work, reared in a working-class family, but in a white-collar family. Perhaps from visits to his father's place of work (George Livings was a shop manager), he began to look carefully at the lives of men at work. Livings' grammar-school years at Park View Primary School (1935-1939) and Stand Grammar School (1940-1945) put him in contact with the lives of his sturdy public-school classmates from Lancashire during the war years. After a brief enrollment (on scholarship) at Liverpool University (1945-1947), where he concentrated on Hispanic studies, Livings served as a cook in the Royal Air Force until 1950, when a series of jobs finally brought him to an acting career with the Century Mobile Theatre, in Leicestershire. Livings' association with Joan Littlewood's company at the Theatre Royal, Stratford East, London, began with a role in Brendan Behan's *The Quare Fellow* (pr. 1954). It was Joan Littlewood who encouraged Livings to continue writing, and, having married Fanny Carter, an actress with the company, in 1957, he wrote his first successful play, *Stop It, Whoever You Are*, produced at the Arts Theatre in London in 1961. Despite the furor it raised, and encouraged by the *Evening Standard* Award in 1961, Livings wrote busily during the next five years, a period which produced *Eh?*, *The Little Mrs. Foster Show*, *Kelly's Eye*, and several other plays. His audience, he found, was not in London but in the shires, where a more solidly working-class audience understood the world Livings was creating onstage, the language with which the characters communicated and failed to communicate, and the special defeats and triumphs of their social class. The anti-intellectual bias of Livings' vision naturally led him to radio and television; he was associated with the British Broadcasting Corporation's program *Northern Drift* and wrote several short radio works collected and published under the title *Worth a Hearing*. After 1970, Livings worked in shorter forms, writing short sketches centering largely on a picaresque but British working-class Scapin named Pongo. The Pongo plays have been collected in two volumes to date (1971 and 1974); the latter contains two plays for children, an important part of Livings' work. Livings finds his voice in the gathering places of the common workman, the lodge halls and Rotary clubs that recognize the veracity of his imagination and comprehend the language and life of his characters.

Analysis

Quite a few of Henry Livings' plays begin with the entrance of a man at work or just from it, who addresses the audience directly, setting up the first confrontation, either with his environment or with the scabrous social system that put him somehow beneath the station he deserves, if wit and perception were the criteria. Henry Cash, beekeeper and bookkeeper in *Honour and Offer*, is typical: "HENRY (*sombre and intense, to us*): This is where I contemplate. Later in the day, the bees murmur, and I'm able to contemplate even better." This kind of opening, which violates traditional rules against addressing the audience directly, typifies the nature of Livings' relationship with the theater: It is a place where he goes to present himself in various disguises, to discuss in theatrical and humorous ways the dilemma of being in this world and happy at the same time. The signature of Livings' characters is whatever is opposite passivity, helplessness, anguish, and defeat. What separates the workingman from his pitiable superiors is that he works, while they merely swot at the free enterprise system as it is oddly practiced in England. Stanley, the lisping hero in *Big Soft Nellie*, defends his entire existence with the simple statement, "I am a man and I do a job."

The corollary to the dignity of work is the sanctity of the workplace. In Livings' world, a man's shop is his castle, and no interfering foreman or supervisor is going to taint it. Livings' best-known play, *Eh?*, takes place in the boiler-room of a mammoth dye factory, where someone upstairs shovels coal into the boiler while the hero, Valentine Brose, watches the gauges, at least in theory. Instead, Val commands his fortress like a baron, growing hallucinogenic mushrooms in the moist heat; bedding his new bride in the double bunk; confounding the works manager, the personnel officer, and the local environmentalist with startling vigor. Winning them over with his mushrooms does not save his castle, however, which is destroyed from within by a vigor of its own. "Once upon a time. There was a boiler. Once upon a time," recites Val as the boiler explodes, making the connection between children's tales and working-class life that Livings has claimed as his own invention.

For exploding or confounding, the best tool available to Livings' characters is the language. Just as Federico García Lorca captures the naturally poetic diction of the Spanish peasant and John Millington Synge re-creates the rhythms and cadences inherent in the Western Irish tongue, Livings reproduces the amazing language patterns of the working-class families of Liverpool, Yorkshire, Manchester, and Birmingham. It is a difficult tangle of near-communication, lost threads, subjective references, internal arguments going on underneath the normative conversation, subtexts overpowering the superficially civil correspondences, vague antecedents, and private vocabularies hinting at metaphoric connections long lost to logic. Miraculously, they understand each other—in fact, they are bonded by the commonality of their language, so that an argument shouted in the presence of strangers has all the secrecy of a family code. The reader may wish for more signposts through the labyrinth of utterances that seem to be attacks and ripostes but whose meaning is just out of reach; the signposts are there, but they are obscured by the lush undergrowth of Livings' imagination. If his characters are rather more loquacious than those of Harold Pinter, David Mamet, or Samuel Beckett, they share the same uneasy distrust of oversimplified exposition.

The comparison with Beckett does not end with the language. Livings finds great resources in the vaudeville skits and sight gags that find their way into Beckett's *Waiting for Godot* (pb. 1952). In the opening scene of Livings' *The ffinest ffamily in the Land*, Mr. Harris spends a good five minutes at the elevator looking for his key in every possible nook and cranny of his outfit, while his wife and son look on. When Mrs. Harris takes a try, her hand goes through a hole in Mr. Harris' pocket and her wedding ring gets caught in the hair on his leg. Trapped in this ridiculous position, the Harrises take several elevator rides trying to avoid being seen by their lodger and her male companion. The short sketches collected as the Pongo plays (1971 and 1974) are essentially music-hall skits, featuring such visual tricks as walking in place, miming puddles and other impediments, exaggerated playing at saber and pistols, and mugging reactions. The broad appeal of this kind of humor calls upon the talents of the actor, who must do considerably more than memorize his lines in order to bring the theatrical moment to life. Songs often introduce the plays, sung by a "Musician" visible onstage, who often takes a small part in the stage business as well, as though the fictive stage intrudes on the real world at every turn. When, in *The Boggart*, the monster succeeds in scaring Pongo into wrestling with his daughter, the Musician joins in the fun with a song sung in harmony with the Boggart. In *Beewine*, however, an angry master, foiled in his pursuit of Pongo, takes out his wrath on the Musician, who must flee for his life as the skit ends.

While critics generally acknowledge Livings' debt to vaudeville and other popular forms, they find fault with his dramatic structure. Plots moving in one direction suddenly shift; pieces of business elaborately constructed are abandoned; characters introduced are left behind. Livings explains that he writes in short bursts, keyed to the attention span he perceives in the theater, and otherwise gives little attention to structure. A case in point is his first success, *Stop It, Whoever You Are*, actually a five-scene vehicle for a series of slapstick routines involving Perkin Warbeck and his attempts at simple survival. The play begins with a harmless flirtation between Warbeck (recently retired) and a buxom fourteen-year-old, and ends, after several visits to the factory lavatory, with the explosion of the leaking gas in the Warbeck household, peopled with Warbeck's ghost and Mrs. Harbuckle, medium extraordinaire, now bald and looking "like Warbeck in drag." The play resembles a meandering Sunday drive; it steps from point to point, and the sights are worth the trip.

More serious in tone and more structurally sound is *The Little Mrs. Foster Show*, a nightmarish look not only at the decolonialization of Africa but also at the madness of war without zeal. Presented in the format of a touring lecture-with-slides on the adventures of Mrs. Foster's missionary work in Africa, the play deals with her relationship to a mercenary, Hook, who has been abandoned by his comrade, Orara, after his leg has been injured in a grenade blast. Stumbling on Hook in the jungle, Mrs. Foster submits to his charms but denounces him on their return to civilization, to save her reputation as a maiden. Orara imprisons and tortures Hook, but when an enterprising Mr. Clive convinces Mrs. Foster to take her story on the lecture circuit, they need Hook to help them dramatize those months together. Now sporting an artificial leg (but keeping the original one in a handy package on his lap), Hook joins the show. In an attempt to avoid the smell of the leg, Mrs. Foster splits her dress in half; now exposed, she "abandons the ruined dress and takes her place, brave and breathless, by HOOK, to wave to us." Thus, her earlier modesty and refusal to face her own sensuality, which began Hook's troubles, now are abandoned in favor of a more honest admission of her complicity in the seduction. For critics who seek thematic consistency and structural integrity in Livings' work, this play provides a sufficiency of both.

The Hook-Mrs. Foster seduction contains a kind of vigor that typifies all the romances in Livings' work, expecially those between husband and wife.

Women here are demonstrative, even aggressive; they like to be tickled and chased; any sort of terrain will do, whether garden or workshop, and vows must be renewed and reinforced with deeds. Perhaps Livings' only purely serious full-length play, *Kelly's Eye*, is at base a love story. Fleeing the automobile of a young seducer, Anna finds the beach hut of Kelly, fugitive from the law for the murder of his best friend. Responding to their sudden attraction for each other, but not wanting to reduce it to a simple sexual one, they agree to sleep apart, Kelly protecting Anna while she reexamines her values. When Anna's father, Brierly, a typical Livings antagonist from the world of high finance, tries to return Anna to her country-club life, Kelly takes her away to a small seaside room, giving up his own anonymity and obscurity. A prying landlady and a nosy reporter ruin Kelly and Anna's substitute "honeymoon" by showing Brierly where they are hidden, and, in one of the most gruesome scenes in Livings' generally optimistic theater, Kelly swallows disinfectant and dies. Reminiscent of Eugene O'Neill or D. H. Lawrence, the play confused critics who expected the same kind of farce that Livings had produced before, and it did not receive favorable reviews. The starkness of the landscape in which this bizarre but honest love affair grows and the suddenness of the characters' willingness to expose themselves to one another mark this play as a significant work waiting only to be refound by a sensitive director.

For the reader, however, the delights of Livings' plays lie in their humor. This humor is almost always subtle when embedded in the language, but it is broad in the action. There is a kind of tension set up between the obvious, even childish, silliness of the stage business and the droll and obtuse humor of the dialogue, often understated, sardonic, in the ironic mode, and consequently available only to the careful reader. A particular habit of Livings is the elaborate stage direction, not unlike George Bernard Shaw's: Highly literate prose is inserted into the dialogue not only as a signal to the actor but also as a parenthetical comment by the playwright to the reader. As is always the case with irony, the sense of the line is apparent not necessarily in the words but in the tone, and Livings sees fit to assist the reader or actor in those moments. In a scene of conjugal bliss *al fresco*, from *Honour and Offer*, Livings prescribes this stage direction: "Doris shrieks with shocked glee, claps her hand to her mouth, glances toward the bench, and flees on tiptoe. They tiptoe hazardously round the savage beehive, excited as much by the need for silence and the danger of the malignant bees as by the prospect of one catching hold of the other." This sort of rhetorical insertion is not meant to get in the way of the director's task but to help the reader grasp the texture of the scene.

Conversely, Livings' ostensibly prose works contain the same theatrical flair that identifies his stage pieces. His work for the British Broadcasting Corporation, some of which is gathered in the collection entitled *Pennine*

Tales (1983), straddles the boundary between prose and drama; their personal style and their obviously autobiographical content render them a sort of continuation of Livings' dramatic work, but reduced to words without pictures. "Twice-Nightly, Thursday Off to Learn It," "Fit-Up Touring, Also to Help in Kitchen," and "Will the Demon King Please Wear the Hat Provided?" all reflect Livings' early struggles as an actor. While it is a mistake to take these short radio pieces as pure autobiography, it can be said, as a narrator admits in one of the stories about childhood, "The boy was me."

Taken together, Livings' plays constitute something more than just a variation on the "kitchen sink" or "dustbin" drama of the 1960's and 1970's. Livings' distinct contribution is a heartiness in the people dramatized in that era. They are harder-working, prouder, more robust than their counterparts in the hands of John Osborne, Arnold Wesker, or John Arden. They are more loving, more open, and more insistent that life give them their share. And, like Livings himself, they are more content with being themselves and less charmed with the prospect of trying to be something they are not.

Other major works

SHORT FICTION: *Pennine Tales*, 1983.

NONFICTION: *That the Medals and the Baton Be Put on View: The Story of a Village Band 1875-1975*, 1975.

SCREENPLAY: *Work Is a Four-Letter Word*, 1968 (adaptation of *Eh?*).

TELEPLAYS: *The Arson Squad*, 1961; *Jack's Horrible Luck*, 1961; *There's No Room for You Here for a Start*, 1963; *A Right Crusader*, 1963; *Brainscrew*, 1966; *GRUP*, 1970; *Shuttlecock*, 1976; *The Game*, 1977 (adaptation of Harold Brighouse's play); *The Mayor's Charity*, 1977; *Two Days That Shook the Branch*, 1978; *We Had Some Happy Hours*, 1981.

RADIO PLAYS: *Worth a Hearing: A Collection of Radio Plays*, 1967.

Bibliography

Bigsby, C. W. E. "Henry Livings," in *Contemporary Dramatists*, 1982.

Giannetti, Louis D. "Henry Livings: A Neglected Voice in the New Drama," in *Modern Drama*. XII (1969), pp. 38-48.

Hunt, Hugh, et al., eds. *The Revels History of Drama in English, Volume VII*, 1978.

Taylor, John Russell. *Anger and After*, 1962.

Thompson, Peter. "Henry Livings and the Accessible Theatre," in *Western Popular Theatre*, 1977.

Wakeman, John, ed. *World Authors 1950-1970*, 1975.

Weimer, Michael J. "Henry Livings," in *Dictionary of Literary Biography, Volume XIII: British Dramatists Since World War II, Part 1*, 1982.

Thomas J. Taylor

THOMAS LODGE

Born: London or West Ham, England; 1558(?)
Died: London, England; September, 1625

Principal drama

The Wounds of Civill War, pr. c. 1586, pb. 1594; *A Looking Glass for London and England*, pr. c. 1588-1589, pb. 1594 (with Robert Greene).

Other literary forms

Thomas Lodge is best known for his prose romances, which are among the precursors of the novel. The most famous of these prose romances, *Rosalynde: Or, Euphues Golden Legacy* (1590), was William Shakespeare's major source for *As You Like It* (pr. c. 1599-1600). Lodge also published several collections of poetry, a volume of poetic satire (*A Fig for Momus*, 1595), translations of Josephus (1602) and Seneca (1614), and a commentary on du Bartas (1621). Most of Lodge's works are available in the four-volume *The Works of Thomas Lodge* (1875-1888, reprinted 1963).

Achievements

Although Thomas Lodge is better known for his lyric poetry and his romances than for his drama, his two extant plays have an important place in the history of the English drama. Lodge was a competent if not a brilliant writer, and, more important, he was an innovative one. *The Wounds of Civill War* is one of the earliest dramas to be written principally in blank verse and may be the earliest extant example of an English drama based on classical history, a mode which became very popular with later Elizabethan playwrights. *A Looking Glass for London and England* provides almost a summary of the various strands of drama being woven together by Lodge and his contemporaries to form the framework of the drama of the Elizabethan period. Elements from both of the plays were borrowed by more successful playwrights whose works eventually overshadowed Lodge's. Lodge's drama remains important, however, from a historical standpoint and for its influence on his more brilliant contemporaries.

Biography

Because of the wide range of his abilities and interests, Thomas Lodge's biography is often offered as an example of the life of a typical Elizabethan gentleman and man of letters. Neither the date nor the place of his birth is known definitely, but he was probably born in 1558. He was the second son of a Lord Mayor of London. Lodge studied at the Merchant Taylors' School in London and entered Trinity College, Oxford, in 1573, completing his bachelor's degree in 1577. In April of 1578, he was admitted to study law at Lincoln's Inn, London.

Lodge's early years in London were marked by personal problems, the exact nature of which is unknown, but which led to an appearance in court and a brief period of imprisonment. He may have had some problems with debts, which may have led to the criticism of usury that appears in some of his works, including *A Looking Glass for London and England*, but it is unlikely that he was ever truly profligate. More likely, his personal difficulties resulted from his leanings toward and eventual conversion to Catholicism. Lodge's literary career began in 1579 with the publication of an epitaph for his mother. The next year, he became widely known for his reply to Stephen Gosson's *School of Abuse* (1579), a pamphlet attacking the arts on moral grounds. The quarrel between Lodge and Gosson continued for some years, with Lodge's final reply appearing in an epistle published with his *An Alarum Against Usurers* (1584).

Around 1585, Lodge made a voyage to the Canaries, during which he wrote his famous romance *Rosalynde*. Little is known of his activities during the next four years, but it is likely that he spent part of his time writing for the theater and that his two extant plays date from this period. He seems to have renounced the theater about 1589. In August of 1591, Lodge sailed to South America with Sir Thomas Cavendish. The expedition was plagued by misfortune, and Lodge was one of the few survivors to return safely to England.

Lodge continued to produce and publish a variety of nondramatic literature until 1596, when he turned to the study of medicine, receiving a degree from Avignon in 1598; the degree was recognized by Oxford in 1602. After studying law, enjoying a modestly successful literary career, and experiencing a brief stint as an adventurer, Lodge seems to have found his place in life as a physician. He married about 1601 and apparently developed a large practice in London, particularly among the Catholic population. Although the date of his conversion in unknown, he was definitely a professed Catholic by this time and had some difficulties with the law over his recusancy. He died in September, 1625, perhaps of the plague, which he may have caught while attending the poor in London.

Analysis

Despite attempts to credit him with a number of early Elizabethan plays, especially the highly successful *Mucedorus* (pr. 1598), Thomas Lodge can be definitely identified as the author of only two extant plays, *The Wounds of Civill War* and *A Looking Glass for London and England*, the latter written with Robert Greene. Neither play has received much critical attention, nor has either play remained a living part of the English theatrical repertory. Lodge had considerable talent as a lyric poet, a gift that can be glimpsed in the verse of his plays. His sense of dramatic structure was unsure, but his works were innovative, breaking new ground for the English theater. Lodge's plays are important as examples of early stages in the development of the drama and as plays that had a strong influence on his contemporaries.

Neither of Lodge's plays can be dated with any precision, but both were probably written between 1585, when he made his first voyage to the Americas, and 1589, when he seems to have given up writing for the theater. Both *A Looking Glass for London and England* and *The Wounds of Civill War* were first published in 1594. Although published slightly later, *The Wounds of Civill War* is believed to be the earlier of the two. Little is known of the stage history of either play. The title page of *The Wounds of Civill War* indicates that the play was performed by the Admiral's Men, but the records of the company do not mention the play. The early history of *A Looking Glass for London and England* is similarly blank, but there are records of a revival in 1592 and other indications that the play was successful. Allusions to Jonah and the whale and the story of Nineveh became popular on the puppet stage, and the influence of the play may have reached as far as Germany.

The exact date of Lodge's first play, *The Wounds of Civill War*, is matter of considerable critical discussion, principally because of its possible relationship with Christopher Marlowe's *Tamburlaine the Great*, Parts I and II (pr. c. 1587). *The Wounds of Civill War* has traditionally been dated later than Marlowe's tragedy. The two plays show a number of striking similarities, but while it seems probable that one play influenced the other, it is impossible to determine in which direction the influence moved. The argument for dating *The Wounds of Civill War* after 1587 is based primarily on the questionable assumption that the weaker playwright, Lodge, must have been influenced by the stronger writer, Marlowe. This assumption has been challenged by critics who offer strong evidence for an earlier date for Lodge's play. In his *Thomas Lodge: The History of an Elizabethan* (1931), N. Burton Paradise notes that similar scenes which have been noted in the two plays could easily have begun with Lodge rather than with Marlowe, or could have been borrowed by both playwrights from other sources. The often-mentioned chariot scene in each play, for example—in which the hero enters in a chariot pulled by men—could have been derived from a similar scene in *Jocasta* (pr. 1566), an earlier play that is a translation by George Gascoigne and Francis Kinwelmershe, which might have been familiar to both writers. It has also been noted that there are no verbal parallels between the two plays. It seems unlikely that Lodge, who shows in his other works a particularly sensitive ear for language, would have borrowed details from Marlowe's drama without picking up some of Marlowe's dynamic verse style. The verse in *The Wounds of Civill War* tends to be monotonous, with little flexibility or variety; most of the lines are end-stopped, with few feminine endings, suggesting that the play was written before Marlowe's important advances in the handling of dramatic blank verse. Finally, Lodge's play shows no influence of *The Spanish Tragedy* (pr. c. 1585-1589) by Thomas Kyd. Kyd's bloody tragedy seems to have initiated the Elizabethan interest in spectacular and often brutal special effects and had an immediate impact on the developing English drama. *The Wounds of Civill War* contains many possibilities for such action. Had Lodge's chronicle been written after *The Spanish Tragedy*, one would expect its influence to appear in the staging of the battle scenes, at least, but Lodge's play makes little use of such sensational effects. The available evidence, then, suggests that *The Wounds of Civill War* might have been written about 1586, soon after Lodge's return from the Canaries but before the productions of Marlowe's and Kyd's popular and highly influential works.

If *The Wounds of Civill War* was written this early, it is the earliest English play based in classical history still extant. Even if it was written a few years later, it remains one of the first of a long series of history plays that were popular during the last years of Queen Elizabeth's reign. Lodge apparently used at least two sources for his chronicle: Appian's *Roman History* (second century A.D.), translated in 1578, and Sir Thomas North's translation (1579) of the *Parallel Lives* (105-115), by Plutarch. In turning to the latter work, Lodge pointed the way for Shakespeare, who later used Plutarch as his major source for his Roman plays.

Although the title page of the first edition of *The Wounds of Civill War* identifies it as a tragedy, the play is more properly described as a chronicle or history play. It concerns the continuing conflict between Marius and Sulla during the Roman Civil Wars, beginning in 88 B.C. The story is episodic, covering a ten-year period of Roman history, and the play lacks unity, chiefly because Lodge followed his sources too closely. Although Lodge concentrates on the clash of personal ambitions between the major characters, the incidents are never quite drawn together with a central dramatic focus. The central conflict is one of ambition rather than of character, and the play lacks psychological depth, a fact that is particularly clear in the final act, when Sulla's remorse and subsequent death seem sudden and unmotivated. Despite numerous battle scenes, Lodge's chronicle remains rather static; its emphasis is on language rather than action. Fortunately, Lodge was a talented poet, and the verse, though often monotonous, is well-crafted and sometimes melodious.

The Wounds of Civill War, while imperfect, represents an important step in English dramatic history. The play is innovative and experimental rather than a polished achievement, and it should be judged accordingly. Lodge's writing tended to be better when he followed an established form, as in his prose romances. Lodge's experimentation with classical history may have produced a somewhat flawed work, but it provided other writers with an indication of the dramatic potential of the material.

A Looking Glass for London and England is similarly experimental and similarly flawed, but it is, for the most part, a tighter and more interesting drama than *The Wounds of Civill War*. Whether this is at all attributable to the influence of Lodge's collaborator, Robert Greene, is impossible to determine. The styles of the two writers are very similar, and in this play, they blend so smoothly that it is impossible to identify the authorship of the various parts.

The date of composition of *A Looking Glass for London and England* is most frequently given as 1588 or 1589. The play shows some influence of *Tamburlaine the Great* and *The Spanish Tragedy*, which suggests that it was written after 1587. The greater variety and flexibility of the verse suggests the influence of Marlowe, while the spectacular effects may have been designed to appeal to the taste for sensationalism primed by Kyd's tragedy. Lodge's renouncement of the theater in 1589 sets the latest possible date for the play, but it is likely that it was composed earlier, since despite frequent references to contemporary events, it makes no mention of the Spanish Armada. This fact suggests that the play could have been written as early as 1587, just after the appearance of Marlowe's tragedy but before the threat of invasion by Spain.

A Looking Glass for London and England is a highly didactic work based loosely on the Old Testament book of Jonah. Lodge and Greene also probably used Josephus' history of the Jews, a work Lodge later translated. The authors exercised considerable freedom in expanding the story, particularly in the development of the character of Rasni, the King of Nineveh, who does not appear in the sources, and in the addition and elaboration of a clown plot involving a smith and his servant.

Like *The Wounds of Civill War*, *A Looking Glass for London and England* is episodic, but it is held together by a clearer sense of dramatic purpose. Although the play's moralizing often seems naïve, it provides a central focus that holds the many disparate elements of the drama together. The final turn toward romantic comedy at the end is sudden, but it is prepared for by the biblical story and the basic moral stance of the work. *A Looking Glass for London and England* is innovative and traditional at the same time, blending together a variety of theatrical traditions into an original work. Its heavy didacticism suggests the influence of morality interludes. The basic story of the conversion of Nineveh is reminiscent of the plays of the mystery cycles, while the clown plot, with its devils, echoes the vice episodes of the morality plays. John Lyly's euphuistic style, which Lodge used quite seriously in his romances, is parodied in one scene. The characterization of the despot Rasni may be derived from Marlowe's *Tamburlaine the Great*, and the spectacular and sometimes violent effects suggest a debt to Kyd's *The Spanish Tragedy* as well as to the elaborate stage machinery of the mystery cycles. All of these elements are brought together in a kaleidoscopic form which possesses a surprising degree of unity and a distinct charm.

Both of Lodge's dramatic works are experimental, which is at once their strength and their weakness. Like the other University Wits, Lodge was a dramatic pioneer, experimenting with new forms or with new uses for old theatrical materials. Unfortunately, he does not seem to have had the sense of dramatic form that allowed other writers, such as Shakespeare, to take the basic idea of the history play and create from it a much tighter and richer drama. Lodge's chief talent seems to have been as a lyric poet, but the verse of his plays shows his full lyric genius only rarely. Written at a time when blank verse first began to appear on the stage, Lodge's lines tend to be monotonous. He depends heavily on long set speeches rather than on true dialogue, which makes the plays seem rather stiff and some-times unemotional. The plays also suffer from Lodge's tendency to moral-ize rather than let the action carry his moral concerns. Many of these weaknesses come from the experimental nature of Lodge's work, however, and he should not be judged too harshly. While he was not a Shakespeare or a Marlowe, Lodge was a competent and sometimes daring dramatist. Despite his weaknesses, his influence on the English theater is significant and undeniable. *The Wounds of Civill War* and *A Looking Glass for London and England* remain important texts, the first for its pioneering role in the development of the history play and the second for its sophisticated combination of widely diverse literary elements, providing almost a sum-mary of the most significant influences on the early English theater.

Other major works

NOVELS: *The Delectable History of Forbonius and Prisceria*, 1584; *Rosalynde: Or, Euphues Golden Legacy*, 1590; *Euphues Shadow*, 1592; *The Life and Death of William Longbeard*, 1593; *A Margarite of America*, 1596.

POETRY: *Phillis with the Tragical Complaynt of Elstred*, 1593; *A Spider's Webbe*, 1594; *A Fig for Momus*, 1595.

NONFICTION: *A Defence of Poetry, Music, and Stage Plays*, c. 1579; *An Alarum Against Usurers*, 1584; *The Famous, True, and Historical Life of Robert Second Duke of Normandy*, 1591; *The Diuel Coniured*, 1596; *Prosopopeia*, 1596; *Wits Miserie and Worlds Madnesse*, 1596; *The Flowers of Lodowicke of Granada*, 1601 (translation); *The Famous and Memorable Works of Josephus*, 1602 (translation); *A Treatise on the Plague*, 1603; *The Works, both Morall and Natural, of Lucius Annaeus Seneca*, 1614 (transla-tion); *The Poore Mans Talentt*, 1621; *A Learned Summary upon the Fam-ous Poem of William of Saluste, Lord of Bartas*, 1625.

Bibliography

Logan, Terence B., and Danzell S. Smith, eds. *The Predecessors of Shakespeare*, 1972.

Paradise, N. Burton. *Thomas Lodge: The History of an Elizabethan*, 1931.

Rae, Wesley D. *Thomas Lodge*, 1967.

Sisson, Charles J., ed. *Thomas Lodge and Other Elizabethans*, 1933.

Whitman, C. W. "*The Wounds of Civil War* and *Tamburlaine*: Lodge's Alleged Imitation," in *Notes & Queries*. XXII (June, 1975), pp. 245-247.

Kathleen Latimer

FREDERICK LONSDALE
Lionel Frederick Leonard

Born: St. Helier, Jersey, Channel Islands; February 5, 1881
Died: London, England; April 4, 1954

Principal drama

Who's Hamilton?, pr. 1903; *The Early Worm*, pr. 1908; *The King of Cadonia*, pr. 1908 (libretto; music by Sidney Jones; based on Anthony Hope's novel *The Prisoner of Zenda*); *The Best People*, pr. 1909; *The Balkan Princess*, pr. 1910 (libretto, with Frank Curzon; music by Paul Rubens); *Betty*, pr. 1914 (libretto, with Gladys Unger; music by Rubens); *The Patriot*, pr. 1915; *High Jinks*, pr. 1916 (libretto; music by Rudolph Friml); *Waiting at the Church*, pr. 1916; *The Maid of the Mountains*, pr. 1917, pb. 1949 (libretto; music by Harold Fraser-Simson, lyrics by Harry Graham); *Monsieur Beaucaire*, pr. 1919 (libretto; music by André Messager, based on a French libretto); *The Lady of the Rose*, pr. 1921 (libretto; music by Jean Gilbert); *Aren't We All?*, pr. 1923, pb. 1924 (originally as *The Best People*); *Spring Cleaning*, pr. 1923, pb. 1925; *The Fake*, pr. 1924, pb. 1927; *Katja the Dancer*, pr. 1924 (libretto, with Graham; music by Gilbert); *The Street Singer*, pr., pb. 1924 (libretto; music by Fraser-Simson); *The Last of Mrs. Cheyney*, pr., pb. 1925; *On Approval*, pr. 1926 (staged), pb. 1927, pr. 1982 (televised) (originally as "The Follies of the Foolish"); *The High Road*, pr., pb. 1927; *Lady Mary*, pr. 1928 (libretto, with John Hastings Turner; music by Albert Sirmay and Philip Craig); *Canaries Sometimes Sing*, pr., pb. 1929; *Never Come Back*, pr. 1932; *Once Is Enough*, pr., pb. 1938 (originally as *Half a Loaf*, wr. 1937, pr. 1958); *The Foreigners*, pr. 1939; *Another Love Story*, pr. 1943, pb. 1948; *But for the Grace of God*, pr. 1946; *The Way Things Go*, pr. 1950, pb. 1951 (revised as *Day After Tomorrow*, pr. 1950); *Let Them Eat Cake*, pr., pb. 1959 (revision of *Once Is Enough*).

Other literary forms

Frederick Lonsdale's success as a librettist for musical comedies and operettas was equal to his success as a playwright. His libretto for *The King of Cadonia* was clearly inspired by Anthony Hope's novel *The Prisoner of Zenda* (1894) and in its turn influenced Ivor Novello's operetta *King's Rhapsody* (pr. 1950). Lonsdale's most popular work in this vein was *The Maid of the Mountains*, which ran at Daly's Theatre, London, for a total of 1,352 performances. Lonsdale collaborated with other leading musical theater composers of the early twentieth century English stage, including Paul Rubens, who did the music for *The Balkan Princess* (written with Frank Curzon) and *Betty* (written with Gladys Unger). He also had a hand in a number of adaptations of European successes, such as *The Lady of the*

Rose and *Katja the Dancer*, both with music by the German composer Jean Gilbert (pseudonym of Max Winterfield); *High Jinks*, with a score by the Hungarian-born Rudolf Friml; and *Monsieur Beaucaire*, with music composed by André Messager, the last major writer of French operetta. Lonsdale's last effort as a librettist was *Lady Mary*, which he coauthored with John Hastings Turner to a score by Albert Sirmay and Philip Craig.

Generally, Lonsdale seems to have been sought out by the impresarios of musical theater for his ability to supply sprightly, well-constructed books which blended wit and sentimentality. The most convincing testimony to his skill in this area is *The Maid of the Mountains*, which was second only to Oscar Asche and Frederic Norton's *Chu Chin Chow* (pr. 1916) as the major musical success of London's West End theater during World War I.

After his major drawing-room comedies had achieved success in New York, Lonsdale's talents were also recognized and recruited by the film industry. He wrote, or had a hand in, several screenplays, including Alexander Korda's vehicle for Douglas Fairbanks, *The Private Life of Don Juan* (1934; with Lajos Biro), and Metro-Goldwyn-Mayer's episodic World War II tribute to British patriotism, *Forever and a Day* (1943; with Charles Bennett, C. S. Forester, John Van Druten, Christopher Isherwood, R. C. Sherriff, and many others too numerous to mention). That he wrote so little for the screen can be attributed partly to his dislike of Hollywood ("I could never live in a film city because there is no conversation") and partly to his habit of breaking contracts. Certainly such of his work as reached the screen displayed the same skill and charm that marked his stage plays.

Achievements

Lonsdale reached his peak of acclaim in the 1920's and early 1930's, when his name was as closely associated with sophisticated drawing-room comedies, such as those of Noël Coward, S. N. Behrman, and Philip Barry. During Lonsdale's long career as a playwright, which extended from the staging of *Who's Hamilton?* at the New Theatre, Ealing, in 1903, to the posthumous production of *Let Them Eat Cake* at the Cambridge Theatre, London, in 1959, his work was praised by such diverse theater critics as Henrik Ibsens archenemy Clement Scott of *The Daily Telegraph*, Arthur B. Walkley of *The Times* (London), *The Sunday Times*' convivial James Agate, Heywood Broun of *New York World*, *The New Yorker*'s resident wit, Robert Benchley, and the British eccentric, Hannen Swaffer of the *Daily Express*. Typical of such critics' comments was Benchley's on *Spring Cleaning*'s New York production in 1923: "It is written with a respect for the audience's intelligence and has an easy humor which brought a pleasant glow to this sin-hardened heart." In the same vein, Agate, reviewing a revival of *On Approval* in London in 1933, observed that "time is powerless against true wit and diversion."

Lonsdale's reputation declined in the 1940's and 1950's, and indeed, in 1953, almost at the end of his life, he experienced the bitterness of an old established author being goaded by a critical wunderkind when Kenneth Tynan, writing in the *Evening Standard* about a revival of *Aren't We All?*, said: "Frederick Lonsdale's comedy, first produced thirty years ago, is what some would call gentle, others toothless: where Somerset Maugham chews and digests his characters, Lonsdale merely mumbles them." More recently, however, there has been an upsurge of interest in Lonsdale's work. A successful revival of *The Last of Mrs. Cheyney* was presented at the Chichester Festival in 1980, and in 1982, a polished and hard-edged British Broadcasting Corporation television production of *On Approval* with Jeremy Brett and Penelope Keith proved that the years have not eroded its quality. Though no innovator, Lonsdale was one of those artists who take a particular form and handle it with consummate skill and flair.

Biography

Unlike the heroes and heroines of his own plays, Frederick Lonsdale came from a decidedly humble background. Lonsdale was born Lionel Frederick Leonard on February 5, 1881, in St. Helier, the capital of Jersey in the Channel Islands. The third son of a local tobacconist and his wife, Frederick and Susan Leonard, Lonsdale was an unruly child who disappointed his family by refusing to attend school and by running off to Canada in his late teens on a romantic impulse. There he seems to have lived by his wits and, according to his own account, was not above perpetrating fraud to finance his passage back to England. On his return, he worked for some time on the Southampton docks and wrote plays in his spare time. When he moved back to Jersey in 1903, his first play had already been produced at a suburban London theater and had been noticed favorably by one of the leading British critics, Clement Scott, who had entered the theater by chance to shelter himself from the rain. The producing company brought the play to St. Helier that same year, and from that point Lonsdale began to be accepted into the more elevated reaches of Jersey society. His transformation from the "villainous and undisciplined child" of a small-town shopkeeper into an international celebrity whose smallest sartorial innovations made instant newspaper copy seems to have begun at about this time. Lonsdale was obviously a keen observer and a gifted mimic, and he rapidly assumed the manners and accent of the upper class, about which he was to spend much of his life writing.

In 1904, Lonsdale—still known in private life as Frederick Leonard—married Leslie Hoggan, the daughter of a retired colonel. For the first four years of their marriage, the young couple spent much of their time apart. Lonsdale had returned to England to pursue his career as a playwright and was not making sufficient income to provide a home for both of them there. Finally, however, he attracted the attention of a London impresario, Frank Curzon, who staged Lonsdale's first successful work, *The King of Cadonia*, at the Prince of Wales Theatre in September, 1908. The young couple were reunited and soon afterward changed their names by deed poll from Mr. and Mrs. Frederick Leonard to Mr. and Mrs. Frederick Lonsdale, the name which the playwright had adopted as his nom de plume. From that time onward, Lonsdale's success was assured, and with *The Maid of the Mountains* in 1917, he achieved sufficient financial security to enable him to play the man-about-town for the next two decades.

By the mid-1920's, Lonsdale was equally celebrated in England and the United States. His marriage had failed, and he had separated from his wife and family. In the 1930's, he was invited to Hollywood to write screenplays, chiefly for Metro-Goldwyn-Mayer. In that decade, his productivity as a playwright declined, and only three new works were staged between 1930 and 1940. With the advent of World War II, Lonsdale's criticism of the war effort and his voluntary exile in the United States lost him the respect of many of his countrymen. Nevertheless, when the war ended, he returned to England and resumed his career as a West End playwright. From 1950 onward, he spent much of his time in France, but by that time, his particular brand of witty drawing-room comedy had begun to fall out of favor, and his income declined steeply. Furthermore, age brought with it an increasing uncertainty of temper which made him unpopular with many members of the theatrical profession. Lonsdale died in London in 1954. He was survived by his wife, Leslie, and three daughters.

Analysis

Frederick Lonsdale's plays were the product of an almost fatally facile talent. He wrote so easily and on the whole so successfully that he seems to have begun to regard his achievement as a species of confidence trick, similar to the one he claimed to have perpetrated as an adolescent in Canada. Peter Daubeney, the English director who staged *But for the Grace of God* in 1946, has spoken of Lonsdale's "Olympian contempt for the theatre," calling him "an outstanding example of a man who despises the very medium where he excels." Clearly, though Lonsdale rivaled both Coward and Maugham in his ability to devise effective and amusing drawing-room comedies, he rarely attempted to extend his range. When he did—as in *The Fake* and *The Foreigners*—the result was invariably one of his rare failures at the box office. Maugham, on the other hand, though best in such high comedy as *The Circle* (pr. 1921) and *The Constant Wife* (pr. 1926), was able to write sardonic domestic comedies such as *The Breadwinner* (pr. 1930) and effective melodramas such as *The Letter* (pr. 1927). Coward, in whom sentimentality and romantic patriotism coexisted with cynicism and outrageousness, also stretched his talents to encompass not only the comedy of manners of *Private Lives* (pr. 1930) but also the lower-class realism of *This Happy Breed* (pr. 1942), the suburban pathos of *Still Life* (pr. 1936), and the epic social history of *Cavalcade* (pr. 1931). In itself, to be sure, such a narrow social range does not invalidate Lonsdale's work, any more than it does the work of Jane Austen, Henry James, Ivy Compton-Burnett, or, for that matter, of William Congreve, Marivaux, or Anton Chekhov. The question that remains is how far Lonsdale succeeded in using the essentially atypical milieu of the English upper class to reflect something beyond itself.

A close examination of Lonsdale's plays reveals not merely a fascination with the lives and manners of members of the English upper class but also a deeply divided attitude toward them. On the one hand, there is the apparent disdain for certain types who do not belong to the charmed circle—as in his occasional disparaging references to shop girls, Socialist politicians who never bathe, and illiterate Jewish theater managers; on the other hand, there is a moralizing tone in several of the plays in which the palms of honesty and worthiness are awarded to ex-chorus girls and women who live by their wits rather than to the aristocrats who patronize or exclude them. Another theme which emerges almost as consistently is that of the pleasures and perils of disguise. It is difficult to resist the temptation to speculate that both of these themes attracted Lonsdale so powerfully because he had emerged from a world of shop girls, advanced by living on his wits, succeeded finally in making London society accept him by adopting an upper-class persona, and ever after feared that some day he would be unmasked.

Lonsdale's love-hate relationship with the aristocracy and his preoccupation with disguise predate his first successful West End comedies. They go back, indeed, to his days as the librettist of such works as *The King of Cadonia* and *The Balkan Princess*. *Monsieur Beaucaire*, though an adaptation of a French libretto based on Booth Tarkington's novella (1900), illustrates the point almost perfectly. Lonsdale must have found it an appealing project, since it attacks the hypocrisy and snobbishness of the upper class by unfolding the tale of a mysterious young French nobleman, the Marquis de Chateaurien, who is in love with an English noblewoman, Lady Mary Carlisle. His rival for Lady Mary's love, Lord Winterset, unmasks him as Monsieur Beaucaire, a common barber. Lady Mary then rejects him, only to discover to her chagrin that the common barber is, in reality, under the multiplicity of disguises, Louis XV's cousin, the Duc d'Orléans. Translated into the idiom of Lonsdale's later work, its message becomes that it is unwise to snub a shop girl, for she may turn out to have the soul of a duchess. Other possible propositions which might spring from this—that a duchess may turn out to have the soul of a shop girl, or that the souls of both duchesses and shop girls could be equally worthy of consideration—

seem not to have interested Lonsdale to the same degree.

In his first really successful West End comedy, *Aren't We All?*, Lonsdale was still in his first flush of infatuation with the peerage. His depiction of Lord Grenham and his heir, Willie Tatham, of Lady Frinton, and of such representatives of the *jeunesse dorée* as Arthur Wells and Martin Steele is on the whole benign. Quite untypically, in fact, Lonsdale reserves his sharpest barbs for a Church of England clergyman who is married to Grenham's sister, Angela. Pompous, narrow-minded, hypocritical, and defensive, the Reverend Ernest Lynton is not so much a character as a caricature from *Punch*, and he clearly belongs to a world about which Lonsdale shows little knowledge or interest. His presence in the play, like that of his wife, is not essential to the main plot; he is there to provide an easily shocked target for Grenham's worldly cynicism and to set up the curtain line, which is also the title of the play:

> VICAR: . . . In answer to a simple remark I made last night, Grenham, you called me a bloody old fool! (*Puts his head in his hands as if crying.*)
> LORD GRENHAM: (*Puts his arm around his shoulder.*) But aren't we all, old friend?

To the degree that they are unable to separate appearance from reality, to penetrate disguises, or to refrain from leaping to conclusions, they are all indeed fools.

The play turns upon a misunderstanding between two characters: Willie Tatham, Grenham's son, and Margot Tatham, Willie's wife. Willie is forced to wear the disguise of guilt, while Margot assumes the disguise of innocence. When the play opens, Willie has agreed to let Lady Frinton use his house to give a dance. Willie is worried and lonely. His wife has gone on a trip to Egypt, and he has not heard from her for more than a week. At the dance, a former actress with whom Willie is acquainted, Kitty Lake, is sympathetic to him, and they exchange a consoling kiss. Margot arrives home unexpectedly at that very moment and assumes immediately that Willie and Kitty are having an affair. Margot is unforgiving and proposes to leave Willie, but her very intransigence arouses the suspicions of her father-in-law, Lord Grenham. In an attempt to save his son's marriage, he unearths a secret alliance that Margot has formed in Egypt and arranges a confrontation between her and the young man concerned. His plan fails, however, when the young man gallantly pretends not to know Margot. Margot's mask remains secure, but her own confidence in her behavior toward her husband is shaken. Their peccadilloes cancel each other out, and at the end they go away together, reconciled.

The slightness of the plot is bolstered by two other concurrent actions: one in which Lord Grenham's sister, Angela, is gradually humanized as she learns to discard the appearance of grim, repressive "virtue" and to appreciate her brother's more flexible attitude toward life; the other in which

Grenham is trapped into marriage with Lady Frinton by Margot, who, to revenge herself for his attempt to unmask her, places an announcement of their engagement in *The Times*. As in the main plot, changes are brought about in the circumstances of the characters as they are compelled to relinquish one set of attitudes for another.

Lonsdale's reputation for wit is not, on the whole, reinforced by the dialogue of this play. Lonsdale clearly intended Lord Grenham to be the main conduit of this quality, but at best he is able to rise to the sub-Wildean: "All my life I have found it very difficult to refuse a woman anything; except marriage." On the other hand, the dialogue generally is efficient, uncluttered, and has the rhythm, if not the content, of wit. Spoken, as it originally was, by first-rate light comedians, it seems to have persuaded audiences and critics alike that they had experienced the sensations of surprise and delight which true wit brings.

In 1925, two years after the premiere of *Aren't We All?*, Lonsdale's most successful nonmusical play was staged. *The Last of Mrs. Cheyney* is, in a sense, an anomalous play since it resurrects the atmosphere and many of the devices of nineteenth century society melodrama. The echoes of, for example, Oscar Wilde's *Lady Windermere's Fan* (pr. 1892) are very strong, particularly during the second-act climax, which involves a woman being trapped in compromising circumstances with a man of dubious reputation. Lonsdale, however, amusingly inverts the formula to create a comedy-drama with several well-placed *coups de théâtre*. The one which ends the first act is particularly effective. Mrs. Cheyney, apparently a wealthy widow from Australia, is holding a charity concert in the garden of her house. The concert is attended by various representatives of London society, including the upright Lord Elton, the disreputable Lord Dilling, and Mrs. Ebley, a woman who has grown rich on the attentions of other women's husbands. Lord Elton and Lord Dilling are both attracted to Mrs. Cheyney, but Elton's intentions are honorable whereas Dilling's are not. Rather unusually, Mrs. Cheyney's establishment seems to be staffed entirely by menservants; one of them, Charles the butler, strikes a chord in Dilling's memory. The butler is suspiciously gentlemanly, and Dilling suspects that they were at Oxford together. When the guests leave at the end of the concert, Mrs. Cheyney, who has represented herself as someone who neither smokes nor drinks nor swears, immediately lights a cigarette, burns her fingers on the match, and curses. Then, as she sits at the piano and begins to play, her menservants enter, sprawl on the furniture, and smoke. It becomes clear that they and Mrs. Cheyney are a gang of jewel thieves bent on relieving Mrs. Ebley of her pearls.

The play's second act builds to a similar bravura climax. It is set in Mrs. Ebley's house, where the characters from act 1 have assembled for the weekend. The plot to rob Mrs. Ebley is foiled by Lord Dilling, who, having recognized Charles as a jewel thief whom he had once encountered in Paris, switches bedrooms with Mrs. Ebley and catches Mrs. Cheyney as she comes in to steal the pearls. Dilling presents a proposition: Either Mrs. Cheyney can submit to him and remain undiscovered or he will ring the bell and turn her over to the police. Instead, Mrs. Cheyney rings the bell herself and, in front of Dilling, Elton, and the rest, hands back the pearls to Mrs. Ebley.

Act 3, adding a touch of Augustin Scribe and Victorien Sardou to the Wildean mix, revolves around a letter. Written by Elton to Mrs. Cheyney and containing a proposal of marriage, it also includes a number of painfully accurate pen portraits of the upper-class set in which Mrs. Cheyney has been moving and of which the stiff-necked Elton intensely disapproves. The possibility that Mrs. Cheyney might use this letter to cause a scandal prompts heavy bidding for its return. Elton writes Mrs. Cheyney a check for ten thousand pounds, and Mrs. Ebley promises to drop the charges of theft. Mrs. Cheyney accepts the check but then tears it up and informs them that she has already torn up the letter. The members of the house party, amazed by this, are even more amazed when they learn that it was she and not Dilling who rang the bell in Mrs. Ebley's bedroom. Their attitude toward her changes; they see her as someone with a sense of good sportsmanship, which is their equivalent of honor. Somewhat surprisingly, she is willing to be reabsorbed into the set which has shown itself so eager to reject her, and, as the play closes, she agrees to become Dilling's wife.

Lonsdale's two chief themes echo throughout this play. Mrs. Cheyney is clearly more interested in being accepted by society than in thieving from it. As she says to Charles, her butler and coconspirator, toward the end of the first act: "I'm sorry, but I didn't realise when I adopted this profession that the people I would have to take things from would be quite so nice." Even when they have proved themselves not "quite so nice," she is willing to forgive and be forgiven by them. On the other hand, the flaws of the play's three main representatives of high society are repeatedly exposed to the audience. Lord Elton is priggish and pompous; Lord Dilling is a wastrel and a womanizer; Mrs. Ebley exploits her appeal for men. At the climax of the play, the unmasking of Mrs. Cheyney is paralleled by the unmasking of society itself. Lonsdale's ambivalence is amply demonstrated.

The pleasures and perils of disguise are illustrated chiefly in the characters of Mrs. Cheyney and Charles, though William the footman, Jim the chauffeur, and George the page boy are also implicated in the masquerade. Mrs. Cheyney and Charles, however, unlike the latter three, who are lower-class "Cockney" types, are represented as people of grace, wit, and charm, educated people who might well have made their way into society by legitimate means but who have chosen a more adventurous course. At the same time, their actions are given a moral color which verges on Lincoln green, inasmuch as the people they rob deserve it, having in their turn, morally speaking, robbed others:

> CHARLES: I'm not trying to persuade you, my sweet, but there is this to be remembered, the pearls we want from Mrs. Ebley were taken by that lady, without a scruple, from the wives of the men who gave them to her.

Mrs. Cheyney is persuaded, and she goes on to play a bold and dangerous game, seemingly courting exposure and disaster but winning through to acceptance and marriage into the peerage.

The Last of Mrs. Cheyney is a very skillful theatrical piece, with cleverly placed reversals, recognitions, crises, and climaxes. It is an admirable mechanism, like a fine example of a Swiss clockmaker's art, and as such it can still be persuasive on the stage. Yet in *The Last of Mrs. Cheyney*, Lonsdale had not yet achieved as sure a grasp of his themes as he did in his next play, *On Approval*.

On Approval is in many respects the most economical of Lonsdale's comedies. It has only four characters, dispensing with the clutter of minor figures which in the earlier plays give substance and color to the milieu but contribute little to the action. The premise of the play is as self-consciously daring as that of Coward's *Private Lives*, to which it also bears a certain structural resemblance. The principal characters, Maria Wislak and the Duke of Bristol, are as monstrously egotistical as Coward's Eliot and Amanda, though they belong not so much to the smart set who honeymoon on the Riviera as to the landed gentry who grouse-shoot in Scotland. Like *Private Lives*, *On Approval* is a minuet of changing alliances. The action is initiated by the wealthy Maria, who decides that the pleasant but penniless Richard Halton may be a suitable candidate for her next husband. To try him out, she proposes to take him to her house in Scotland for a month. Her longtime enemy, the Duke of Bristol, decides that he will go, too, ostensibly to lend Richard moral support but actually to escape his creditors. The fourth member of the group is an attractive, good-natured pickle heiress, Helen Hayle, who follows in pursuit of the duke, with whom she is in love.

In the course of the action, Lonsdale leaves the audience in no doubt that the representatives of the ruling class are outrageously and comically tiresome. Not only do Maria and the duke berate and abuse each other incessantly, but also they treat the penniless Richard and Helen, the pickle-profiteer's daughter, like servants. The effect of this is to draw Richard and Helen closer together, and finally they conspire to sneak away in the only available automobile, just as a massive snowstorm is beginning—a snowstorm which threatens to trap the monstrous Maria and the appalling duke together for several weeks. As Richard says: "It's the kindest thing that has ever been done for them. Such hell as a month alone here together will make them the nicest people in the world." This denouement recalls that of *Private Lives*, in which Eliot and Amanda tiptoe out of the Paris apartment to which they have eloped, leaving their respective spouses, Victor and Sybil, quarreling violently. Because *Private Lives* appeared two years later than *On Approval*, it is more than probable that Coward learned something from Lonsdale about the construction of sophisticated drawing-room comedies.

Clearly, in *On Approval*, Lonsdale has resolved his conflict with respect to acceptance/rejection by society. In this play, it is the upwardly mobile who are the "nice" people, unequivocally; the established members of society may yet become "nice" but only through undergoing an ordeal of isolation in uncongenial company. There is no falsely sentimental juxtaposition of gentlemen and jewel thieves, or duchesses and ex-chorus girls, with Lonsdale judiciously trying to hold the balance; here he rightly identifies with the aspiring middle class and asserts his own niceness against the arrogance of the upper class.

Lonsdale's other perennial theme, of masks and unmasking, is also present, though in a subtler form than in *The Last of Mrs. Cheyney*. Maria Wislak takes Richard Halton "on approval" to find out if he is as pleasant and congenial as he appears to be. She decides that he is, but meanwhile Richard has found out that Maria is not as she has appeared to him for twenty years, "too good, too beautiful, too noble" for him; indeed, she is "one of the most unpleasant of God's creatures." Like Lady Mary Carlisle in *Monsieur Beaucaire*, Maria is deeply chagrined at this turn of events: "To think I brought the brute here to find out if I like him, and he has the audacity the moment I tell him I do, to tell me he doesn't like me!" Similarly, Helen sees through the Duke of Bristol's charm to the spoiled schoolboy underneath: "To make him a decent man he needs six months before the mast as a common sailor." The misunderstandings and deceits that complicate the lives of the four characters in *On Approval* are much more character-based than in the somewhat mechanically contrived *Aren't We All?* and *The Last of Mrs. Cheyney*.

The dialogue, too, is more distinctive, more deft and more plausible. Instead of the secondhand epigrams of Lord Grenham and Lord Dilling, there is the genuine crackle and tension of strong-willed people using language as a weapon to penetrate their opponents' armor of conceit and self-absorption. The play's witty lines cannot be taken out of context to survive as freestanding aphorisms; their humor depends entirely on the audience's understanding of the characters of Maria, the duke, Richard, and Helen, and of the conflicts between them.

On Approval is the high point of Lonsdale's achievement as a comic playwright. Though he continued to write sporadically for another quarter of a century and though none of the plays he wrote in that period (except

The Foreigners) lost money, he never quite repeated the artistic and popular success he reached with his comedies of the mid-1920's. A typical example of his later work is *Let Them Eat Cake*, which like many of Lonsdale's plays is a revision, or a renaming at least, of an earlier one. *On Approval*, for example, was a substantial revision of an early, unproduced work, "The Follies of the Foolish," and *Aren't We All?* was a reworking of *The Best People*. *Let Them Eat Cake* was first titled *Half a Loaf* (written in 1937); was produced in 1938 as *Once Is Enough*; reappeared as *Half a Loaf* at the Theatre Royal, Windsor, in 1958, four years after Lonsdale's death; and finally opened at the Cambridge Theatre, London, in 1959, again as *Let Them Eat Cake*. In it, Lonsdale reverts to the pattern of earlier plays such as *Aren't We All?* Indeed, its theme of marital misunderstanding is not dissimilar, and its cast list is even more replete with titled characters, including the Duke and Duchess of Hampshire, Lord and Lady Plynne, Lord and Lady Whitehall, Lord Rayne, and Lady Bletchley. The main action involves Johnny, the Duke of Hampshire, who becomes infatuated with Liz Pleydell, the wife of his friend Charles, and Nancy, the Duchess of Hampshire, who attempts to save their marriage. Johnny is prepared to leave his wife and run away with Mrs. Pleydell to her orange plantation in South Africa. Nancy prevents them by the simple expedient of telling Mrs. Pleydell that she will not divorce Johnny, thereby rendering Mrs. Pleydell's social status, if she persists in going off to live with him, uncomfortably precarious. In the rather unconvincing denouement, Johnny realizes that Mrs. Pleydell's real object is not him, but his title, and that he has been suffering from the "temporary disease" of infatuation.

The main characters are even less attractive than those in *On Approval*, but in this case unintentionally so. There is also, as in *Aren't We All?* and *The Last of Mrs. Cheyney*, a superfluity of minor figures who have little function other than to provide a sort of living decor. Furthermore, the dialogue has the secondhand ring of reach-me-down epigrams, common in the earlier plays, as in this exchange:

> LADY BLETCHLEY: What actually is cirrhosis of the liver?
> REGGIE [LORD RAYNE]: A tribute nature pays to men who have completely conquered Teetotalism!

All in all, the play marks a regression in Lonsdale's technique: less economical and integrated than *On Approval* and less splendidly theatrical than *The Last of Mrs. Cheyney*.

Lonsdale's work, placed in historical perspective, occupies the midpoint in what might be called "the rise and fall of the drawing-room comedy," beginning not so much with Wilde as with Thomas William Robertson in the 1860's, continuing through such work in the late nineteenth and early twentieth centuries as Arthur Wing Pinero's *The Gay Lord Quex* (pr. 1899) and Maugham's *Lady Frederick* (pr. 1907), reaching a peak in the 1920's with *Private Lives* and *On Approval* and declining in the 1950's with such works as Terence Rattigan's *The Sleeping Prince* (pr. 1953), William Douglas Home's *The Reluctant Debutante* (pr. 1955), and Hugh and Margaret Williams' *The Grass Is Greener* (pr. 1958). The shock waves that John Osborne's *Look Back in Anger* (pr. 1956) sent reverberating through the British theater made it difficult for any playwright thereafter to practice the art of light badinage among the denizens of Mayfair and Belgravia with quite such unself-conscious insouciance.

Comedy seldom gets a fair hearing from literary critics and historians, and writers who specialize in comedy must often be content with only the most condescending of acknowledgments. To point to Aristophanes and Molière, to Congreve, W. S. Gilbert, and George Bernard Shaw, will give pause only temporarily to those who regard comic playwriting as an inferior vocation. Yet, if one weighs Lonsdale's work against the "serious" work of his British contemporaries, the comparison is not altogether in Lonsdale's disfavor. J. B. Priestley's time plays and expressionist experiments, the attempts of W. H. Auden, Christopher Isherwood, Ronald Duncan, T. S. Eliot, and Christopher Fry to revive poetic drama, the bourgeois realism of R. C. Sherriff, John Galsworthy, St. John Ervine, and John Van Druten seem no likelier to hold the attention of future audiences and readers than Lonsdale's best comedies. The only British playwrights of the first half of the twentieth century who clearly surpass him are not the "serious" playwrights but other writers of comedy: Sir James Barrie, Shaw, and Coward.

With all of his failing, his laziness, his self-plagiarism, his too-easy cynicism, and his occasional sentimentality, Lonsdale at his best possessed some distinct countervailing virtues, not least among them being a consummate sense of theater and a keen eye for the foibles of the upper class. Above all, his basic respect for human honesty and decency raised his most assured work to the level of critical comedy, an achievement that might very well have earned for him a nod of approval from both Aristophanes and Molière.

Other major works

SCREENPLAYS: *The Devil to Pay*, 1930; *Lovers Courageous*, 1932; *The Private Life of Don Juan*, 1934 (with Lajos Biro); *Forever and a Day*, 1943 (with Charles Bennett, C. S. Forester, John Van Druten, Christopher Isherwood, R. C. Sherriff, and others).

Bibliography
Donaldson, Frances. *Freddy Lonsdale*, 1957.
Hudson, L. *The English Stage, 1850-1950*, 1951.

Nicoll, Allardyce. *English Drama, 1900-1930*, 1973.
Reynolds, E. *Modern English Drama*, 1949.
Taylor, John Russell. *The Rise and Fall of the Well-Made Play*, 1967.

Anthony Stephenson

JOHN LYLY

Born: Canterbury (?), England; 1554 (?)
Died: London, England; November, 1606

Principal drama

Campaspe, wr. 1579-1580, pr., pb. 1584 (also known as *Alexander, Campaspe and Diogenes*); *Sapho and Phao*, pr., pb. 1584; *Galathea*, pr. c. 1585, pb. 1592; *Endymion, the Man in the Moon*, pr. 1588, pb. 1591; *Midas*, pr. c. 1589, pb. 1592; *Mother Bombie*, pr. c. 1589, pb. 1594; *Love's Metamorphosis*, pr. c. 1589, pb. 1601; *The Woman in the Moon*, pr. c. 1593, pb. 1597; *Dramatic Works*, 1858 (2 volumes; F. W. Fairholt, editor).

Other literary forms

John Lyly continues, unfortunately, to be most remembered for his early prose works, *Euphues, the Anatomy of Wit* (1578) and *Euphues and His England* (1580). These works uneasily combine the values of moralistic Humanism with the erotic subject matter and psychological potential of the Italian novella; these two elements are overlaid and indeed overwhelmed by the famous style, subsequently labeled "euphuism." Both Lyly's own contemporaries and scholars have also assigned Lyly the authorship of *Pap with an Hatchet* (1589), a turgid religious tract published anonymously in the course of the Martin Marprelate controversy.

Achievements

Twentieth century readings have led to recognition of John Lyly as more than a quaint writer. Since the initial work of Jonas Barish in 1956, Lyly's prose style has been more highly (though still variously) valued, and both Barish and, in 1962, G. K. Hunter helped to enhance appreciation of Lyly's plays. Lyly has been served by the freeing of Elizabethan drama criticism in modern times from its earlier compulsion to consider its material in the light of William Shakespeare. Lyly can be seen now as, at his best, a highly intelligent writer of comic psychological and philosophical allegory. He is important not merely for his historical position or for his constructive skill, but also for his insight—which is part of the general Renaissance insight into human personality, informed by the newly experienced classics, often expressed in a symbolic rather than a purely realistic mode.

Biography

Unsurprisingly for an Elizabethan, John Lyly's date of birth cannot be ascertained. From college records, it can be extrapolated back to some time in the early 1550's, probably between late 1553 and late 1554. Lyly was brought up, perhaps also born, in Canterbury, where his father was a cleric attached to the official service of the archbishops. Lyly's near ances-tors and family included central figures in the tradition of Humanism in England.

In the early 1570's, John Lyly appears on the books of Magdalen Col-lege, Oxford. There is evidence that Lyly intended to pursue an academic career. On the other hand, some rather problematic testimony suggests that Lyly at Oxford was most noted for his interest in the fashionable life and recreations accessible to young men there. By the end of the 1570's, he had moved out of the academic setting and was living in London. His two Euphues books, which he wrote around this time, seem to reflect both an affinity for a Humanistically colored academic world and a certain distance from such a world. The two books were immediately immensely popular, and with their publication, Lyly's life rose clearly into a new orbit, around the court of Queen Elizabeth I.

Lyly became attached to the household of Edward de Vere, Earl of Ox-ford, an important courtier; Lyly may have been the earl's secretary. The connection led into another one, crucial to Lyly's creative life. Oxford pa-tronized the troupes of choirboy actors that were based on the Chapel Royal and St. Paul's Cathedral. These troupes, carefully recruited and trained, entertained the court during the major winter holidays, such as New Year's, and also, from the 1570's on, performed for paying audiences at the indoor "private" theater of Blackfriars in London. The semicourtly, semiprofessional boys' theater was the highly specialized medium in which Lyly worked throughout the 1580's. Seven of his eight known plays were written for boys; six of the eight are heralded on the title pages of their quarto editions as having been performed before the queen.

Lyly's first play, *Campaspe*, had almost the same phenomenal early popularity as his fiction. Lyly clearly believed he was given reason during the 1580's to hope for regular employment under the queen. As the decade wore on, however, Lyly's court and theatrical career lost its promising rhythm.

The boys' companies' obstreperous participation in the Martin Marpre-late controversy of 1588-1590 led to a ban on their productions throughout the 1590's, which all but shut down Lyly's theatrical work. His euphuistic style went rapidly from being in vogue to being the target of sophisticated ridicule. Although Lyly did serve in various parliaments throughout the 1590's, he never achieved the court office to which he aspired. At the time of his death in 1606, Lyly was burdened with a family whom he could not support and suits from his creditors which he failed to answer.

Analysis

Campaspe, John Lyly's first play, is closely related to the Euphues works in several respects, first of all in its Humanism. It shares with segments of the Euphues writings a typical Humanistic source, Plutarch. The work is to a large extent one of ethical counsel, specifically of counsel to the ruler. The boy actors produced the play before Queen Elizabeth, and much of it constitutes an image of wise conduct by an exemplary ruler from the past, Alexander the Great.

For critics such as Hunter and Peter Saccio, *Campaspe* is a major instance of lack of plot development or even sequence in Lyly's dramaturgy. Some scenes in the play, such as a meeting of Alexander with the philosophers of Athens, are detached set pieces not meant to advance any plot line, and involve characters who appear nowhere else in the play. Lyly regularly breaks the continuity of such actions as do develop in the play and thus denies the audience any steadily growing involvement with them. An action begun in one scene will not be resumed until several scenes later, after one's attention has been diverted and diverted again by different bits of other material. Characters' motives shift without explanation from one scene to another.

The point seems to be that Lyly's sense of construction is not based on the wholeness of a realistic action but, in this case, on a doctrinal picture. The interrelatedness of many of *Campaspe*'s scenes arises not from their placement in a plot but rather from their function as sections of the image of Alexander which the play is putting together. The scenes show the different characteristics (or characteristic modes of behavior) of Alexander as the good king: his benevolence toward the weak, his regard for the learned, and so on. Much of the play builds less by a process of sequential development, in which each new scene depends on previous ones for its full significance, than by additive composition, in which each scene is discrete, making its separate contribution to the total construction.

To the extent that *Campaspe* is more Humanistic picture than plot, it resembles the many images of model human figures in Renaissance literature such as Desiderius Erasmus' Christian knight in the *Enchiridion militis christiani* (1503), Baldassare Castiglione's *The Courtier* (1528), and Sir Thomas Elyot's *The Boke Named the Governour* (1531). Like much Humanistic writing, *Campaspe* is concerned with the function of the prince but also, as an important corollary, with the prince's relationship to his counselors (in Renaissance terms, to Humanistically educated subjects). *Campaspe*'s picture of Alexander is complemented by its picture of the Cynic Diogenes, an embodiment of an extreme claim for the virtuous counselor's status in the polity. One of Alexander's most exemplary decisions is his drafting of Diogenes for attachment to the court: Alexander wants to listen to a voice that speaks only for virtue, without regard for power.

In addition to these model figures, the Humanistic aspect of *Campaspe* involves sketches of moral tales. The prodigal-son narrative structure that critics have recognized in *Euphues, the Anatomy of Wit* also seems related to the rather minimal sustained sequence of actions in which Alexander does become directly involved: his experience of love for Campaspe, the realization that she loves the painter Apelles, and Alexander's final renunciation of her. Campaspe, humbly born, is clearly inappropriate as a match for Alexander; Hephastion moralizes upon Alexander's love for her as a tempting detour from the course of honor.

Campaspe's resemblance to the Euphues books involves factors besides Humanism. Much of the play is overlaid by a euphuistic style; the style sometimes works positively to give dialogue epigrammatic pointedness. The love of Apelles and Campaspe is a very different matter from that of Alexander, and one that can be related not to the Humanistic but to the novella pattern lying behind *Euphues, the Anatomy of Wit.* Apelles and Campaspe's scenes, though other kinds of scenes are interspersed between them, themselves follow a perfectly regular rhythm, in which scenes of dialogue alternate with soliloquies by the two lovers; dialogue and soliloquy were the major frameworks in which emotion could be explored in the Euphues books and the narrative tradition anterior to them. The love portrayed in the scenes is not a distraction from honor or serious matters; rather, it is personal feeling which seems to be central to the psychic lives of the two people involved, and it grows. Unlike the Humanistic picture scenes with their additive interrelation, the scenes of Apelles and Campaspe dramatize an intelligible development, through which the characters move continuously from the first sense of love toward more ample realization and expression of it.

As in the Euphues books, Humanism and this other narrative component coexist uneasily in *Campaspe*. The motif of Apelles and Campaspe's kind of love, virtually absent from the play's first two acts, weighs heavily in the last three, receiving about eight of their thirteen scenes. The large influx of romantic feeling produces an unbalancing shift in the whole mood of the play.

Along with the pictures of Alexander and Diogenes and the love story of Apelles and Campaspe, there is one further set of scenes in the play, which is of a kind different from anything in the Euphues books and which became increasingly important in Lyly's playwriting as it progressed. In *Campaspe*, there are only two or three scenes of high-spirited page comedy, in which servants of the play's major figures meet on some pretext, exchange jokes, mock their masters, and express unflagging appetites for food and drink. Such scenes sometimes culminate in the singing of drinking songs. It seems reasonable to relate this kind of material to two circumstances of the production of Lyly's plays. As court entertainment for holidays such as Christmas and Twelfth Night, Lyly's plays belonged to the Saturnalian context that C. L. Barber described in *Shakespeare's Festive Comedy* (1959), in which rule for the moment was to be made light of and appetite gratified even to excess. As plays performed by choirboys, Lyly's works gained dimensions when their comedy projected standard boys' appetites and smart-aleckism, and when they exploited the boys' musical talents. Among the other constituents of *Campaspe*, the festive, disrespectful page comedy attaches itself most strongly to the characterization of Diogenes, the disrespectful satirist, but the pages completely lack Diogenes' will to make moral judgments; their mockery is for the sake of having a good time. In fact, the page comedy seems extraneous both to the play's nobler Humanistic themes and, certainly, to Apelles and Campaspe's love.

Campaspe is a rich combination, but the continued lack of integration of the work's elements makes it a noticeably less impressive play than Lyly's more mature and mythic works. The play's proportion of success is connected with the appeal or impact of certain moments—bits of incisive dialogue such as that between Parmenio and Timoclea in the play's first scene, which, even more than the language of Diogenes, has the excitement of truth spoken to force; the last line, in which Alexander charmingly warns Hephestion that when he has no more worlds to conquer, then he may yet fall in love.

Sapho and Phao involved a new source for Lyly, Ovid, whose potential impact, however, was not fully realized until *Galathea*. Lyly was remarkably successful in adapting his source material to a generally Humanistic pattern. The Sappho of Ovid's *Heroides* (before A.D. 8), whose whole character is that of a passionate lover, becomes in Lyly's play the queen of Syracuse, controlling a court and herself conditioned by social and political duties and norms. Phao becomes a figure like Campaspe, an inferior love; the play ultimately dramatizes Sapho's taking control of erotic power (personified as Venus and Cupid), which had sought to rule her. The parallel between Queen Elizabeth's chastity and Sapho's is obvious; the triumphant establishment of the latter becomes clear praise of the former.

Roman mythography became a potent influence in Lyly's work in *Galathea*. Ovid was Lyly's source for this symbolic drama in which actions clearly have significance as they refer to an underlying dynamic pattern. Ovid's *Metamorphoses* (c. A.D. 8) comprise many incidents, through each and all of which the reader looks toward the underlying universal process of metamorphosis itself, the reality of change. Both *Galathea* and Lyly's later play, *Love's Metamorphosis*, consist of plots that are discontinuous—inconsequential if taken strictly on their own terms—but that imply a continuous line of allegorical meaning. This kind of writing clearly differs in several ways from the Humanistic modes that had more or less dominated Lyly's first two plays. It is truly dynamic, never static or additive as *Campaspe* was, even though the dynamic continuity does not appear on the literal plot level. It embodies truths (or visions) instead of encouraging conduct; thus, it presents human life in a psychological rather than a hortatory manner, concerning itself with growth and health rather than with virtue and vice. Lyly's Ovidian drama is not set in an arena of social or political action, a historical or pseudohistorical court or city. The plots of *Galathea* and *Love's Metamorphosis* occur in the pastoral world, which traditionally has had symbolic value. Setting and symbolic purpose also differentiate this drama from the more realistic novella.

Love appears in *Galathea* not as a temptation countervailed by honor, but as a psychic presence experienced and accepted differently at different stages in a process of human growth. In other words, the play is a vision of adolescence. It takes its name from its adolescent girl heroine and ultimately from the nymph in *Metamorphoses* 13 whose lover changes before her eyes. As the play opens, young virgins are exposed to rumors of an incomprehensible savage force bent on attacking them. The allegorical progression begins as the play moves into the next scene, in which a better-understood, less terrifying, clearly erotic power, Cupid, is incited to show his power over virgins who are more mature at least in understanding. Thereafter, as the play meanders engagingly back and forth between its two main plots, love is presented in guise after different guise, but changing fairly steadily in a determinate direction, appearing in embodiments that are less frightening: Cupid descends to the disguise of a shepherd, is captured, and exercises his nature in a disarmed (and less external) state, as love develops as an emotion Galathea and Phyllida feel within themselves.

As love becomes understood as more acceptable, it also becomes more accepted. Through the course of the play, Galathea, Phyllida, and Diana's nymphs all succumb and come to enjoy this new part of their beings. The process is happy in its result. Neptune, who has become a mediator, effects a resolution in which love's power is recognized, not repressed, but in which it can be incorporated into intact human personalities rather than destroying them. Galathea and Phyllida are ready for healthy, mature, emotional life. With lovely precision, the play leaves them just ready, just at the verge, still within a semi-sexual stage which Lyly (like Shakespeare) dramatizes as involvement with someone not fully identifiable as one's sexual complement. As in *Twelfth Night* and *As You Like It*, produced about five years later, girls disguise themselves as boys and are fallen in love with as such: Galathea and Phyllida fall in love with each other, each under the misapprehension that the other is a boy. One is left uncertain at the end of the play which of the two a generous Venus is about to metamorphose into a male, to make full sexual life for them possible.

The delighted, smooth comic feeling of the play's ending is a point around which Lyly manages to orient a remarkable number of elements. *Galathea* is typical of Lyly's work inasmuch as it is a hybrid of diverse constituents—Lyly's first fully successful work in that these elements are fully integrated and mutually responsive. There is a good deal of euphuism in the style, but now delight in its neat working-out of syntax and sound can be subsumed in delight at the economy of growth which the play symbolizes (instead of jarring against a Humanistic message). Like the euphuistic aspects, the festive servant boys' subplot can now work to expand and prepare the audience for the joy to which the main plots are leading. In mood, the comedy of Rafe, Robin, and Dick represents a distinctive modulation away from Lyly's norm for such scenes: Instead of Lyly's usually loud, rambunctious, prank-playing boys, *Galathea*'s boys are gulls, and the resulting humor is somewhat quieter and very much in keeping with the whole play's trend, which is to settle into a smile more than to explode in laughter. At the end of the play, Venus welcomes the boys into direct contact with the main action. They are to serve as entertainers, enhancing the joy of the forthcoming marriage—which is exactly the role they have been performing throughout the play.

Galathea is in some ways Lyly's most characteristic success; it involves tendencies that were important in many of his other works. Like Ovid's *Metamorphoses*, it achieves a smooth unity among a diversity of coequal factors. The play marks the beginning of a mature phase of not invariably but usually unified dramatic works.

Endymion dramatizes a Neoplatonic ascent through various levels of love and being to transcendent knowledge. Important details make the play's process congruent also with the general Christian concept of redemption.

The protagonist first appears caught in involvement with his immediate physical world, but also drawn by a reality beyond it. He loves Cynthia, with whom he is not yet in direct contact. The attraction seems bizarre and out of order, both to his friend Eumenides and to himself. Endymion's situation is complicated by his difficult and ambivalent relationship with Tellus. Low metaphysical status is represented here not only through the drama of Endymion's attitudes and problems, but also in the modes of description used: Cynthia at this point is, to all intents and purposes, the actual physical moon; Tellus is a very material, fecund earth goddess. Endymion's persistence on the earthly level appears in Tellus' power over him, which, however, has its limits. She cannot force Endymion's love back to herself, but she can hinder his rise. Through her agent Dipsas, she holds Endymion in sleep; he rests suspended, out of the worldly consciousness that has prevailed to this point in the play but unable to waken to the life which appears around his sleeping figure and which includes Cynthia as a directly present character.

As in *Galathea*, Lyly's allegorical line passes unbroken from one plot medium to another. As Endymion is sleeping, two surrogates, Corsites and Eumenides, act out the position that he occupies between two worlds. Both are deputized by Cynthia, Corsites to control Tellus, which he fails to do, thus continuing the dramatization of human weakness. Eumenides' mission is to find a way to help Endymion. He does so and reaches the height of purely human potential when, at some emotional cost, he puts aside the claims of human sexual love in favor of those of more purely spiritual friendship and of duty to Cynthia. The discovery he makes at this level is that further progress, in the form of the main protagonist's recovery from his trance, can come only through an act of condescension by Cynthia in the form of an act of love, a kiss. This is one of the points clearly suggestive of Christianity in the play, specifically of the Christian doctrine of man's need for God's loving gift of grace.

Cynthia's kiss arouses an Endymion who definitely has surpassed the passionate love in which he began. His altered language is noticeable, especially when one comes to this play from Lyly's earlier works. By the time *Endymion* was written, euphuism, certainly of the kind found in the early narratives, was receding as a factor in Lyly's writing. By the play's end, Endymion is speaking in relatively even, straightforward sentences, reflecting his arrival at a definitely rational frame of mind. No longer so committed to a set style, Lyly could make language flexibly project action.

Endymion's appearances as an old man toward his play's end have a clear philosophical association. He resembles the old Platonic lover described by Pietro Bembo in Castiglione's *The Courtier*. Like the old lover, Endymion is no longer interested in physical love; instead, he is happy with the position he has achieved as a purified attendant in Cynthia's immediate presence. Endymion's final metamorphosis, back into a young man (he has slept and aged for forty years), may imply a Christian step beyond a philosophical one, a putting off of the old man and entry into a new life of redemption. Cynthia herself emerges as a benevolent supernatural figure near the play's close.

As a final image of hierarchy, Cynthia in the last scene brings love to fulfillment for several couples: herself and Endymion on down through pairs representing less exalted levels. The lowest in the line is the impersonal mating instinct of Sir Tophas, who earlier had wanted Dipsas, but— now that she is unavailable—reaches for her servant Bagoa. The play's low comedy is one of its liveliest elements. Sir Tophas is a new feature in such writing by Lyly—a sustained, gradually developed, low-comic character. His place in the play is somewhat indeterminate until he forces himself on the other characters' attention in the last scene, as the lowest level from which the hierarchical structure they have elaborated rises.

Endymion is Lyly's most ambitious play. With its reach toward philosophy and religion, it embodies the continued expansiveness of Lyly's mind as well as the extent of his mature control.

Much of *Midas* is topical, political, and Humanistic. It is quite clear in the play, and accepted in the critical tradition, that discussion of an unsuccessful war by Midas' Phrygia against the island of Lesbos allegorically refers to Philip of Spain's attack on England with his Armada. Like its predecessors from *Sapho and Phao* on, *Midas* has its source in Ovid. The lighthearted Ovidian fables which provide *Midas'* plot coexist rather uneasily with much of the dialogue's serious moral tone. The Humanistic lessons delivered by Midas' counselors are not responsive to the developing Ovidian plot. They stand apart as set pieces and tend simply to be repeated in one debate scene after another, instead of changing in any way corresponding to plot changes. In several respects, *Midas* is a rather unsatisfying reversion to Lyly's early dramatic pattern.

Neither hortatory nor Ovidian, *Mother Bombie* is instead a very pure experiment in neoclassic secular comedy. It is witty New Comedy of clever servants helping young people to overcome obstacles raised by their selfish elders; its ultimate ancestor is the Roman comedy of Terence. Within Lyly's work, there is a connection not to the kinds of dramatic writing that dominate his other plays as wholes, but instead to the usually secondary element of page comedy. In tone and action, the play is fairly firmly and neatly unified, although it seems thinner in meaning and less inventive than Lyly's plays based on mythography.

Love's Metamorphosis is the most interesting of Lyly's later works, and probably his most underrated play. It is close to *Galathea* in several ways. As its title suggests, the whole play is Ovidian in feeling, although the main plots are actually not drawn from Ovid or from any other source. The play is a sequential allegory: It presents not only physical metamorphoses performed by the god Cupid but also, and much more important, like *Galathea*, changing visions of love (and of human relationships in general). The allegory is organized somewhat differently from that of *Galathea*. A distinct major vision is localized in each of the play's plots. The plot which gets first exposure, that of three amorous foresters' love for three nymphs, could be interpreted as a sane psychological critique of traditions of courtly love and Petrarchianism. The three lovers are met with refusals to love from the ladies to whom they are drawn. The ladies' refusals, instead of being idealized, are analyzed as various forms of sexual egotism. The ladies are punished by being metamorphosed into items of subhuman nature—a stone, a flower, a bird—symbolic of their different kinds of detachment from human involvement. Punishment in itself is not a solacing ending. The audience is left with a picture of one-sided adoration as a type of failed relationship.

On the other hand, instead of being an opposing figure who withdraws into himself and refuses contact (as the ladies themselves do to the foresters), Erisichthon emerges to attack the nymphs' own space, their sacred grove, and to prevent them from carrying out the activities proper to their natures. Relationships here are not exclusively erotic, but rather more well-rounded. The divinity to whom the maidens can appeal is Ceres, who suggests a broader (but less exalted, literally more down-to-earth) image of human experience than does the foresters' Cupid. Erisichthon is punished with famine, although again punishment is not resolution; he is brought before the audience later in the play, repentant of his actions but caught in punishment, unable to escape his actions' consequences.

The play's movement toward resolution begins when a third, clearly different vision of human relationships comes about, one that involves mutuality. Its protagonist, Protea, is constantly helping others and being helped by them. The pattern began in the character's past, when she yielded her virginity to Neptune and received his promise of future help in return. Neptune keeps faith, and Protea is saved through supernatural power in the various situations in which she finds herself during the play's course. At the same time, she is saving her father and her lover. She first avoids a relationship of pure (and not specifically erotic) dominance when she escapes from enslavement by a merchant. Then she destroys the alluring power of the selfish, isolated Siren over her lover Petulius. Thus, she has managed to eliminate from her life both of the dilemmas that the play's first two plots embody. Mutuality is allied to flexibility. Protea's name indicates her ability to change, and she defeats the bad versions of relationship through magical metamorphoses of her person. At the play's end, the vision associated with Protea expands over the play and redeems the other characters from their symbolic entrapment.

Although similar to *Galathea* as highly sophisticated psychological allegory, *Love's Metamorphosis* differs in tone. The play certainly remains a comedy, but it is a darker one than *Galathea* and allows at least as much awareness of difficulties and problems as any of Lyly's other works. The three ladies continue to resist love even in the play's last scene, long after (in the progress of the allegory) the benign concept of mutual, flexible interaction has become available. There is the suggestion of an egotism so profound that it cannot be brought into relationship to the external world except through coercion. *Love's Metamorphosis* does not include the page comedy which lightens up *Galathea* and tonally predicts a happy ending; one reaches the happy ending of *Love's Metamorphosis* with some feeling of relief, not through a play full of light or bland emotional ease. *Love's Metamorphosis* is also not very euphuistic. Instead of continuously providing symmetry, the play's language often conspicuously evades it. The description of the famine that will attack Erisichthon has some of the ruggedness and irregularity of seventeenth century "anti-Ciceronian" prose. The play in general experiments with asymmetry as a medium for its emotional, psychological conceptions.

The characterization of Protea involves a successful modulation for Lyly in the direction of genuine pathos. *Love's Metamorphosis* represents human beings' achievement of love against odds within themselves that must be taken seriously. Along with *Galathea* and *Endymion*, this is one of the works by which Lyly ought to be remembered.

A sense of the Elizabethan literary environment suggests one appropriate overall comment on Lyly's work. The 1580's, the decade of Lyly's principal achievements on the stage, were years of extraordinary literary ferment. Sir Philip Sidney and Edmund Spenser were decisively altering values in poetry. Almost doctrinaire neoclassic drama lingering from the 1560's gave way not only to Lyly but also to the violent tragedy of Thomas Kyd and Christopher Marlowe. Lyly's drama corresponds to its transitional, eclectic times: His work made use of change as a chance for variety, instead of suffering from it as disorienting or disintegrating. Juxtapositions of Lyly to Shakespeare are likely to be odious, but Lyly may not be harmed by the recognition that, like Shakespeare, he profited from his historical moment. Lyly, like Shakespeare, grew toward a capacity to merge diverse elements in his plays and to hold together in suspension tints of different kinds of awareness and experience—Humanistic and Neoplatonic, lightly comic and seriously problematic. In Lyly's earlier works, the multiplicity of available influences helps create disunified writing; later, it yields writing that is rich and experimental.

Linking this literary-historical pattern mechanically with the content of the work would be a mistake, in Lyly's case as much as in Shakespeare's. Still, Lyly's greatest works celebrate change and greet it as comic growth through which people become more fully human. *Galathea*, *Endymion*, and *Love's Metamorphosis* especially should still be enjoyed for their adult gentleness, consciousness, and openness.

Other major works

NONFICTION: *Euphues, the Anatomy of Wit*, 1578; *Euphues and His England*, 1580; *Pap with an Hatchet*, 1589.

MISCELLANEOUS: *The Complete Works of John Lyly*, 1902, 1967 (3 volumes; R. Warwick Bond, editor).

Bibliography
Barish, Jonas. "The Prose Style of John Lyly," in *Journal of English Literary History*. XXIII (1956), pp. 14-35.

Croll, Morris W. "The Sources of the Euphuistic Rhetoric," in *Style, Rhetoric and Rhythm: Essays by Morris W. Croll*, 1966. Edited by J. Max Patrick et al.

Hunter, G. K. *John Lyly: The Humanist as Courtier*, 1962.

Jeffrey, U. M. *John Lyly and the Italian Renaissance*, 1929.

Knapp, Robert S. "The Monarchy of Love in Lyly's *Endimion*," in *Modern Philology*. LXXIII (1976), pp. 353-367.

Saccio, Peter. *The Court Comedies of John Lyly: A Study in Allegorical Dramaturgy*, 1969.

Sandbank, Shimon. "Euphuistic Symmetry and the Image," in *Studies in English Literature*. XI (1971), pp. 1-13.

John F. McDiarmid

CARSON McCULLERS

Born: Columbus, Georgia; February 19, 1917
Died: Nyack, New York; September 29, 1967

Principal drama

The Member of the Wedding, pr. 1950, pb. 1951 (adaptation of her novel); *The Square Root of Wonderful*, pr. 1957, pb. 1958.

Other literary forms

Carson McCullers will be remembered primarily as a writer of fiction who experimented, with varying degrees of success, in the genres of drama, poetry, and the essay. She was one of the foremost of the remarkable generation of Southern women writers that included, in addition to McCullers herself, Flannery O'Connor, Eudora Welty, and Katherine Anne Porter. With her fellow women writers, and with such Southern male writers as William Faulkner, Truman Capote, and Tennessee Williams, McCullers shares an uncanny talent for capturing the grotesque. Her fictional world is peopled with the freaks of society: the physically handicapped, the emotionally disturbed, the alienated, the disenfranchised. This preoccupation with the bizarre earned for her a major place in the literary tradition known as the "Southern Gothic," a phrase used to describe the writers mentioned above and others who use Gothic techniques and sensibilities in describing the South of the twentieth century.

Few have created a fictional South as successfully as has McCullers in her best fiction. Hers is a small-town South of mills and factories, of barren main streets lined with sad little shops and cafés, of intolerable summer heat and oppressive boredom. In her first and perhaps best novel, *The Heart Is a Lonely Hunter* (1940), she portrays a small Southern town from the points of view of five of its residents: Mick Kelly, the confused adolescent heroine; Doctor Copeland, an embittered black physician whose youthful idealism has been destroyed; Jake Blount, an alcoholic drifter with Marxist leanings; Biff Brannon, the sexually disturbed owner of the café, where much of the novel's action takes place; and John Singer, the deaf-mute whose kindness, patience, and humanity to the other characters provide the moral center of the novel.

The themes of *The Heart Is a Lonely Hunter* are ones that McCullers never completely abandoned in her subsequent fiction and drama: the loneliness and isolation inherent in the human condition; the impossibility of complete reciprocity in a love relationship; the social injustice of a racially segregated South; adolescence as a time of horrifying emotional and sexual confusion. In *Reflections in a Golden Eye* (1941), she explored sexual tension and jealousy among the denizens of a Southern army post. *The Mem-*

ber of the Wedding (1946), the novel which she later adapted into the successful play of the same title, treats the delicate symbiotic relationship
between a lonely adolescent girl, her seven-year-old cousin, and a black
domestic. *The Ballad of the Sad Café*, first published in *Harper's Bazaar* in
1943 and later in a collection of McCullers' short works, is justifiably called
one of the finest pieces of short fiction in American literature. It deals with
another bizarre triangle, this one involving a masculine, sexually frigid,
small-town heiress; her cousin, a hunchback dwarf; and her former husband, a worthless ex-convict with an old score to settle.

The four works of fiction mentioned above guarantee McCullers a permanent place among American writers of the World War II and postwar
era. She also published more than a dozen short stories, most of which are
not specifically set in the South. The best of them—"Wunderkind" (1936)
and "A Tree. A Rock. A Cloud." (1942), for example—are proficiently executed exercises that demonstrate the sure control and balance so crucial to
McCullers' longer fiction.

McCullers also wrote critical essays that betray a deep emotional and
technical understanding of imaginative literature. Her small body of poetry,
heavily influenced by the seventeenth century Metaphysicals, is consistently
interesting. After McCullers' death, her sister, Margarita G. Smith, collected her previously uncollected short fiction, her literary criticism, and
her poetry and essays in *The Mortgaged Heart* (1971).

Achievements

McCullers' reputation as a playwright rests solely upon the phenomenal
success of one play, *The Member of the Wedding*, which she based on her
novel of the same title. Her only other play, *The Square Root of Wonderful*,
was a critical and popular failure and a professional disappointment from
which McCullers never quite recovered. The very critics and theatergoers
who hailed McCullers as a brilliant innovator in 1950 turned their backs on
her in 1958. Flawed and uneven as her theatrical career was, however,
McCullers deserves a special place among modern American playwrights,
not only for what she achieved but also for what she attempted. With her
friend Tennessee Williams, she was one of the first American playwrights
to parlay a fragile, moody, nearly static vision of human frailty into solid
commercial theater.

No one was more surprised by the success of *The Member of the Wedding* than McCullers herself. She had seen but a handful of plays in her life
when Williams, with whom she was spending the summer of 1946 on Nan-
tucket, suggested that she turn her novel into a play. Excited by the idea of
writing in a new and unfamiliar genre and intrigued by Williams' sense that
the novel had strong dramatic possibilities, McCullers spent that June
calmly and steadily composing a draft of the play. Across the dining room

table from her sat Williams, who was working on *Summer and Smoke*—it was the only time either of them was able to work with anyone else in the room. Despite Williams' willingness to help, McCullers steadfastly rejected her friend's advice, following instead her own creative instincts.

Though all odds were against it, the play was an immediate success when it opened on Broadway in January, 1950. Audiences gave the cast standing ovations, and the critics almost unanimously praised the work's grace, beauty, and timing. In the spring, *The Member of the Wedding* won two Donaldson Awards—as the best play of the season and as the best first Broadway play by an author—and the New York Drama Critics Circle Award for Best Play. McCullers was named Best Playwright of the Year and given a gold medal by the Theatre Club. *The Member of the Wedding* ran for 501 performances and grossed more than one million dollars on Broadway before enjoying a successful national tour.

This great acclaim, remarkable enough for a more conventional drama, is even more remarkable when one considers that *The Member of the Wedding* is a "mood play," dependent upon emotion and feeling rather than upon a standard plot. All three acts take place on one deliberately confining set, and much of the play's significant action happens offstage, "between acts," as it were. Indeed, even while praising the play, reviewers questioned whether it was a genuine drama at all. Like Williams' *The Glass Menagerie* (pr. 1944) and Arthur Miller's *Death of a Salesman* (pr. 1949)— significantly, the only two plays Carson McCullers had seen produced on Broadway prior to writing her hit—*The Member of the Wedding* is a play that subordinates plot to characterization, action to the almost poetic accretion of psychic detail. That audiences would even sit through, let alone cheer, such a slow-moving piece of drama was a revelation to the theater world of 1950.

The success of *The Member of the Wedding* solved McCullers' chronic financial problems and earned for her a reputation as a gifted and innovative dramatist, but six years of ill health and personal tragedy ensued before her next play, *The Square Root of Wonderful*, opened on Broadway in October, 1957. Plagued from the outset by personnel changes and by McCullers' incompetence at the kind of last-minute rewriting required by the theater, the play failed almost immediately. Neither McCullers nor director Jose Quintero could do anything to save it, and it closed after only forty-five performances. The disaster of *The Square Root of Wonderful* left McCullers severely depressed, so anxious had she been to repeat the triumph of *The Member of the Wedding*. Various physical ailments by then made it difficult for her to write at all, and she never again attempted writing for the theater.

Though McCullers' reputation as a playwright will never approach her reputation as a writer of fiction, it is her uniqueness in both genres that accounts for both her successes and her failures. Her first play succeeded because it defied conventions of plot and action; her second play failed in part because it too often mixed the modes of tragedy, comedy, and romance. It is no accident that three of her novels have been made into successful films, nor is it accidental that no less a playwright than Edward Albee adapted her novella *The Ballad of the Sad Café* for the stage. Carson McCullers' dramatic sense was in every way original, and both her hit play and her failure demand acceptance on their own terms, quite apart from the whims of current theatrical convention and popular tastes.

Biography

Carson McCullers' life was one beset by intolerable illnesses and complex personal relationships. The last twenty years of her life were spent in the shadow of constant physical pain, but, like her fellow Southerner Flannery O'Connor, she continued working in spite of her handicaps, seldom complaining. She was married twice to the same man, an emotional cripple who drained her financially and psychically and who ultimately killed himself. That she left behind her a magnificent body of work and any number of devoted friends when she died at the tragically young age of fifty is a testament to the courage with which overwhelming obstacles can be overcome.

McCullers knew at first hand the small-town South that figures so prominently in her best writing. As the eldest of the three children of Lamar and Marguerite (Waters) Smith, Lula Carson Smith spent a normal middle-class childhood in the racially segregated mill town of Columbus, Georgia. Her father, like Mr. Kelly in *The Heart Is a Lonely Hunter* and Mr. Addams in *The Member of the Wedding*, was a jeweler who spent much of his time at work. Her mother, a lively, cultured woman and a strong influence throughout McCullers' life, encouraged her daughter's intellectual and artistic pursuits. By the age of fourteen, Carson Smith had dropped the Lula from her name and had announced her intention to become a concert pianist. She was by then practicing the piano several hours a day and taking lessons from Mary Tucker, the wife of an army colonel stationed at nearby Fort Benning. Her complex relationship with the Tucker family, at once giving her a sense of belonging and of estrangement, was later to provide material for the triangle theme of *The Member of the Wedding*. Like her heroine Frankie Addams, McCullers was fond of writing plays, casting them with family and friends, and staging them in her living room.

By the time she was graduated from high school, McCullers had already privately decided to become a writer rather than a musician. Inspired by the Russian realists and by the plays of Eugene O'Neill, McCullers had already tried her hand at both drama and fiction. The seventeen-year-old McCullers set out for New York City in September, 1934, with vague plans both to study music at the Juilliard School of Music and to study creative writing at Columbia University. By February, 1935, she had enrolled at Columbia, and the following September she enrolled in Sylvia Chatfield Bates's writing class at New York University.

During the summer of 1935, while she was vacationing in Georgia, a mutual friend introduced her to James Reeves McCullers, an army corporal stationed at Fort Benning. Reeves McCullers, like Carson, was interested in a career in letters. That he had neither the motivation nor the talent that enabled Carson to become a successful author was to be the source of much friction between them and a contributing factor to Reeves's eventual mental collapse. In 1936, Reeves left the army to join Carson in New York, and in September of 1937, they were married in the Smith home in Columbus.

By this time, McCullers had begun to undergo the cycles of illness and creativity that would characterize the rest of her life. Fatigued by the hectic pace of New York, she was forced to return to Georgia from time to time for peace and quiet, but her writing career had also taken off. Whit Burnett, with whom she had worked at Columbia, had published her story "Wunderkind" in the December, 1936, issue of his magazine *Story*, and she had begun to outline the plot of what would become her first novel, *The Heart Is a Lonely Hunter*. In the spring of 1939, while she was living with Reeves in Fayetteville, North Carolina, "The Mute" (as the novel was then called) was accepted by Houghton Mifflin. By autumn, she had completed a second manuscript, "Army Post" (later published as *Reflections in a Golden Eye*).

McCullers had long before vowed that when she became a famous author, she would make New York her home. Feeling stifled in the South, their marriage in trouble, the McCullerses moved to New York only a few days after the publication of *The Heart Is a Lonely Hunter*, in June, 1940. The move, however, did nothing to improve their relationship. Carson, a sudden celebrity, was being courted by the literary world and making distinguished friends, among them W. H. Auden; that summer, as recipient of a fellowship to the Bread Loaf Writers Conference in Middlebury, Vermont, she came to know Wallace Stegner, Louis Untermeyer, and Eudora Welty. It was not only Carson's increasing fame and Reeves's continued obscurity that placed stress on their relationship. Both were sexually naïve at the time of their marriage, and both were given to infatuations with members of their own sex. Though most of their homosexual relationships remained unconsummated, Carson's crush on the brilliant young Swiss emigrant Annemarie Clarac-Schwarzenbach was difficult for Reeves to tolerate. In September, 1940, Carson and Reeves separated. They were later divorced, only to remarry in 1945 when Reeves returned from action in World War II. For the rest of Reeves's life, they were to be alternately separated and reconciled. Their long and stormy relationship was ended only by Reeves's suicide in France in 1953.

When she separated from Reeves in the autumn of 1940, Carson accepted an invitation from her friend George Davis to move into a restored brownstone located in Brooklyn Heights. Upon establishing residence at 7 Middagh Street, she found herself in the midst of an unusual experiment in group housing; it later came to be known as February House. Besides her and Davis, the inhabitants included W. H. Auden, the striptease artist Gypsy Rose Lee, and, later, the composer Benjamin Britten and the writer Richard Wright and his family. McCullers made her home in this strange household intermittently for the next five years. When not traveling abroad, resting in Georgia, or spending time at Yaddo, the artists' colony in Upstate New York, she played hostess in Brooklyn Heights to a distinguished group of celebrities from the literary and entertainment worlds, including Janet Flanner, Christopher Isherwood, Salvador Dalí, and Aaron Copland.

While in Georgia in February, 1941, McCullers suffered a stroke that left her partially blind and unable to walk for weeks. She would be victimized by such attacks for the rest of her life, and even after the first one, she never quite regained the kind of creative fervor of which she had once been capable. She was not to finish her next novel, *The Member of the Wedding*, until 1946, six years after she first started drafting it. Her final novel, *Clock Without Hands*, took her ten years to complete, not appearing until 1961. After 1947, as a result of the second severe stroke in a year, her left side was permanently paralyzed, and even the physical act of sitting at a typewriter was a challenge for her.

McCullers' Broadway career of the 1950's was, as has been noted, a source both of exhilaration and of disappointment for her. Nevertheless, her uneven career as a playwright brought her financial security, greater exposure than she had ever had before, and the fame she had craved since childhood. By the end of her life, she was an international literary celebrity, able to count among her friends the English poet Edith Sitwell and the Danish-born writer Isak Dinesen.

In 1958, severely depressed by Reeves's suicide in 1953, her mother's death in 1955, and the failure of her second play, McCullers sought professional psychiatric help from Dr. Mary Mercer, a therapist who was to care for McCullers until the author's death. Through the 1960's, McCullers was progressively less able and willing to leave the Nyack, New York, house that she had bought in 1951. She died there on September 29, 1967, of a cerebral hemorrhage.

Analysis

Like the novel from which it was adapted, *The Member of the Wedding*,

Carson McCullers' first play, is a masterpiece of timing, mood, and character delineation. Insofar as there is a plot, it can be summarized as follows: Somewhere in the South, twelve-year-old Frankie Addams, a rebellious loner and a tomboy, secretly longs to belong to a group. Rejected by the girls at school, having recently lost her best friend, Frankie has no one to talk to except Berenice Sadie Brown, the black woman who cooks for Frankie and her father, and a seven-year-old cousin, John Henry. When she discovers that her brother, Jarvis, is going to be married, Frankie decides to join him and his bride on their honeymoon and make her home with them in nearby Winter Hill, thus becoming once and for all a member—a member of the wedding. Though Berenice tries to make her come to her senses, Frankie persists in her plan and makes a scene during the ceremony, begging the couple to take her with them. When they refuse, an agonized Frankie vows to run away from home. Sticking her father's pistol into the suitcase that she has already packed for the honeymoon, Frankie does leave, but it is later disclosed that she has spent the night in the alley behind her father's store. Chastened and somewhat resigned, she returns home, admitting that she had thought of committing suicide but then had changed her mind.

By the end of the play, which takes place several months after the wedding, life has changed for all three main characters. John Henry has died of meningitis; Berenice has given notice to Mr. Addams; and Frankie, having largely outgrown the adolescent identity crisis of the previous summer, has acquired a best friend and a beau, both of whom she had earlier hated. While Frankie is undoubtedly much happier than she was at the beginning of the play, she has become a pretentious teenager, bereft of the poetry and passion of childhood. Berenice has lost not only John Henry but also her foster brother, Honey, who has hanged himself in jail. As the curtain falls on the third act, Berenice is alone onstage, quietly singing "His Eye Is on the Sparrow," the song that she had sung earlier to calm the tortured Frankie.

Most of the "action" of the play takes place offstage and is only later recounted through dialogue. The wedding and Frankie's tantrum occur in the living room of the Addams house, but the scene never moves from the kitchen: The audience is told about the wedding and about Frankie's disgrace by characters who move back and forth between the two rooms. Both Honey's and John Henry's deaths occur between scenes, as does Frankie's night in the alley. By thus deemphasizing dramatic action, McCullers is able to concentrate on the real issue of the play, the relationship among Frankie, Berenice, and John Henry. By confining the action to one set, the kitchen and backyard of the Addams residence, the author effectively forces the audience to empathize with Frankie's desperate boredom and sense of confinement (and, perhaps, with Berenice's position in society as a black domestic). For much of the play, the three main characters are seated at the kitchen table, and this lack of movement lends the work the sense of paralysis, of inertia, that McCullers learned from the plays of Anton Chekhov and applied to the South of her childhood.

Frankie Addams is one of the most memorable adolescents in literature, at the same time an embodiment of the frustrations and contradictions inherent in adolescence and a strongly individual character. She yearns to belong to a group even as she shouts obscenities and threats to the members of the neighborhood girls' club. She is both masculine and feminine, a tomboy with a boy's haircut and dirty elbows who chooses a painfully vampish gown for her brother's wedding. McCullers skillfully exploits alternately comic and tragic aspects of Frankie's character. The audience must laugh at her histrionic declarations ("I am sick unto death!") but must also experience a strong identification with her sense of vulnerability and isolation ("I feel just exactly like somebody has peeled all the skin off me"). Caught between childhood and womanhood, she is curious about both sexual and spiritual love. She claims to have been asked for a date by a soldier, only to wonder aloud "what you do on dates," and she is still capable of climbing into Berenice's lap to hear a lullaby. Frankie's body is fast maturing, but her emotions are slow in catching up.

Berenice Sadie Brown serves in the play as Frankie's main female role model (Frankie's own mother has died in childbirth), an embodiment of fully realized adult sexuality. As complex a character as Frankie, Berenice is much more than a servant: She is confessor, nurse, and storyteller. At forty-five, Berenice has been married four times but truly loved only her first husband—the remaining three she married in vain attempts to regain the bliss she enjoyed with Ludie Maxwell Freeman. Her search for love closely parallels Frankie's own, and despite their often antagonistic relationship, they share moments of spiritual harmony, as when they discuss the nature of love, a "thing known and not spoken."

Berenice also represents the position of the black in a segregated South; indeed, the issue of racism is very much present in *The Member of the Wedding* (as it is in *The Heart Is a Lonely Hunter* and *Clock Without Hands*), a fact that has often been overlooked by critics of both the novel and the play. Though she is the most influential adult in the world of the two white children, she is treated as a servant by the white adults. Berenice must deal not only with Frankie's growing pains but also with problems ultimately more grave: the funeral of an old black vegetable vendor and the arrest, imprisonment, and suicide of her foster brother, Honey. Both Berenice and T. T. Williams, her beau, behave noticeably differently around white adults, while Honey, in a sense representative of a new generation of Southern blacks, refuses even to call Mr. Addams "sir." He is eventually jailed for knifing a white bartender who will not serve him.

Honey's flight in the third act coincides with Frankie's own. Like Frankie, Honey is rebellious and frustrated, but unlike her, he is unable to find a place for himself in a hostile society. Death for Honey is preferable to confinement in the "nigger hole" or more "bowing and scraping" to white people.

If Honey's death in the third act symbolizes the end of Frankie the rebel, the death of John Henry represents the end of Frankie's childhood. Throughout the play, John Henry acts as a sort of idiot savant, uttering lines of great insight and demanding the plain truth from a hypocritical adult world. He asks Berenice why Mr. Addams has called Honey a nigger, and seems, ironically, incapable of understanding the nature of death. He is a link between Frankie and her childhood, a constant reminder of how recently she played with dolls (he gratefully accepts the doll that Jarvis has given Frankie as a gift after she rejects it). Frankie wants at once to be John Henry's playmate and to outgrow him. Though the transformed Frankie reacts coldly to John Henry's death, Berenice is devastated by it. She truly loved her "little boy," and she blames herself for having ignored his complaints of headaches in the first stages of his disease. John Henry dies a painful death, a victim who has done nothing to deserve his cruel fate.

The Member of the Wedding is a play about growing up, but it is also about the sacrifices that must be made before one can enter the adult world. Frankie is composed and even confident at the end of the play, but she has lost whatever sympathy she had for Berenice. Berenice is severely depressed by two deaths whose logic defies her. John Henry and Honey are dead, and the newlyweds are stationed in occupied Germany. When Berenice is left alone onstage at the end of the third act, holding John Henry's doll and singing a song whose truth the play has seriously questioned, the audience is forced to wonder with her whether the adult world of compromise and responsibility is worth entering.

McCullers stated in the author's preface to the published version of *The Square Root of Wonderful* that the lives and deaths of her mother and her husband in part compelled her to write the play. Marguerite Smith's grace, charm, and love of life emerge in the character of Mollie Lovejoy, while Phillip Lovejoy embodies all the tragic contradictions that led Reeves McCullers to alcoholism and suicide. Like so much of McCullers' work, the play concerns a love triangle: Mollie Lovejoy, who lives on an apple farm in suburban New York with her twelve-year-old son, Paris, has twice been married to Phillip Lovejoy, an alcoholic writer now confined to a sanatorium. As the play opens, Mollie has only recently met John Tucker, a no-nonsense architect who is determined to wed her. Complications arise when Phillip Lovejoy unexpectedly returns to the farm, intent on a reconciliation with Mollie. His mother and his spinster sister are also on the scene, having come to New York from the South to visit Mollie and Paris and to see Phillip's new play (ironically, a failure).

The relationship between Phillip and Mollie has been a stormy one. The sexual attraction between them remains strong, and they sleep together on the night of Phillip's return, much to the chagrin of John Tucker. Still, Mollie cannot forget the years of drunken abuse she suffered at Phillip's hands. Physical abuse she could tolerate, but she decided to divorce him finally when he humiliated her by telling her that she used clichés. Mollie is clearly in a dilemma. In one of the play's most successful scenes, she admits to Paris that she loves both John and Phillip.

Phillip's problems, however, are manifold and insoluble. Clearly, he wants a reunion with Mollie so that she will protect him, as she once did, from his own self-destructive tendencies. When he at length realizes that Mollie will not return to him and, perhaps more important, that he will never again be able to write, he commits suicide by driving his car into a pond. With Phillip's death, Mollie is free to leave the apple farm and move to New York, and there is every reason to believe that she will eventually marry John Tucker.

Despite its commercial and critical failure, the play is perhaps worthy of more attention than it has received. At its best, it is a meditation on the nature of love. Mollie Lovejoy has always conceived of love as a sort of magic spell that is divorced from logic and free will. Her love for Phillip has brought her as much humiliation as happiness. From John Tucker, she learns that love can also be a matter of choice among mature adults. He uses the language of mathematics in describing his view of love to Paris: For John, humiliation is the square root of sin, while love is the square root of wonderful. The minor characters also provide interesting commentaries on the nature of love. Sister Lovejoy, the spinster librarian, lives in a world of fictional lovers drawn from the pages of books. Mother Lovejoy, while often a comic character, is at base a loveless woman who has spent her life humiliating her daughter.

The play's weaknesses, however, are many. The sure sense of timing that characterizes *The Member of the Wedding* is largely absent from *The Square Root of Wonderful*. The shifts in mood are less subtle than in the earlier play, and tragedy often follows too closely on the heels of comedy. The superb early morning scene in which Phillip Lovejoy says goodbye to his son, for example, is too rapidly undercut by a comic scene between Mother and Sister Lovejoy as they discuss Phillip's death. This tragicomic mixture of modes that McCullers executes so well in *The Member of the Wedding* goes awry in *The Square Root of Wonderful*, in part because none of the characters—except, perhaps, Phillip Lovejoy—is carefully enough drawn to elicit an audience's sympathy.

McCullers' best work is set in the South, not in Upstate New York farmhouses. Her best work is also fiercely individual, completely defiant of convention and popular tastes. *The Square Root of Wonderful* fails largely because its author, in her eagerness to produce a second Broadway triumph, allowed producers, directors, and script doctors to strip it of the brilliant idiosyncracies that make *The Member of the Wedding* an American classic.

Other major works

NOVELS: *The Heart Is a Lonely Hunter*, 1940; *Reflections in a Golden Eye*, 1941; *The Member of the Wedding*, 1946; *Clock Without Hands*, 1961.

SHORT FICTION: *The Ballad of the Sad Café and Other Works*, 1951; *The Ballad of the Sad Café and Collected Short Stories*, 1952, 1955.

CHILDREN'S LITERATURE: *Sweet as a Pickle and Clean as a Pig*, 1964.

MISCELLANEOUS: *The Mortgaged Heart*, 1971 (short fiction, poetry, and essays; Margarita G. Smith, editor).

Bibliography
Carr, Virginia Spencer. *The Lonely Hunter: A Biography of Carson McCullers*, 1975.

Clurman, Harold. "The American Playwrights—Carson McCullers," in *Lies Like Truth—Theatre Reviews and Essays*, 1958.

Gianetti, Louis D. "*The Member of the Wedding*," in *Literature/Film Quarterly*. IV (Winter, 1976), pp. 28-38.

McDowell, Margaret B. *Carson McCullers*, 1980.

Phillips, Louis. "The Novelist as Playwright: Baldwin, McCullers, and Bellow," in *Modern American Drama: Essays in Criticism*, 1968. Edited by William E. Taylor.

J. D. Daubs

DONAGH MacDONAGH

Born: Dublin, Ireland; November 22, 1912
Died: Dublin, Ireland; January 1, 1968

Principal drama

Happy as Larry, wr. 1941, pr., pb. 1946; *God's Gentry*, pr. 1951; *Step-in-the-Hollow*, pr. 1957, pb. 1959; *Lady Spider*, pb. 1980.

Other literary forms

In addition to writing plays, Donagh MacDonagh collaborated with A. J. Potter in a ballet, *Careless Love*, and an opera, *Patrick*, neither of which has been published. MacDonagh published two essays—one on his father, Thomas MacDonagh, in 1945, and one on James Joyce, in 1957—and was the author of several short stories. He often wrote new lyrics for old Irish ballads, some of which are collected in *The Hungry Grass* (1947) and *A Warning to Conquerors* (1968), two volumes of his poetry. With Lennox Robinson, MacDonagh coedited *The Oxford Book of Irish Verse* (1958) and, at the time of his death, was working on a dictionary of Dublin slang, which remains unfinished. The dictionary and the rest of MacDonagh's personal library and papers are now the property of the Irish University Press.

Most important is MacDonagh's poetry, published in four volumes: *Twenty Poems* (1933), *Veterans and Other Poems* (1941), *The Hungry Grass*, and *A Warning to Conquerors*. Even his earliest poems are essentially dramatic and therefore foreshadow his later plays. Some, like "Dublin Made Me" and "The Hungry Grass," are essentially mood pieces calculated to evoke in the reader precise feelings, such as patriotic allegiance to a proud, unbowed city or the nameless, all-encompassing fear of straying into a cursed area. Other poems are character sketches or dramatic dialogues apparently indebted to Alfred, Lord Tennyson.

Major themes of MacDonagh's drama also appear in his early poetry. In "Alleged Cruelty," for example, MacDonagh writes that we are all torn "with longings/ For something undefinable and wild," a recurrent thought in both the author's poems and his plays, often symbolized by the beauty of an unattainable woman. In contrast to such longings, our real lives, the poet asserts, are more like a horse, freighted with each passing year, endlessly running around the same track, or like "the changeless sound/ Of an engine running." This view leads MacDonagh to see past, present, and future as the same and therefore to accept and make the most of an inherently flawed world. Allied with this perception is a strong note of resignation, perhaps even fatalism, that creeps into MacDonagh's poetry from time to time, most notably in "The Veterans," one of his best poems. Like William Butler Yeats's "Easter 1916," "The Veterans" examines the famous

Easter Rising of 1916. For his part in this rebellion, Donagh MacDonagh's father, Thomas MacDonagh, was executed on May 3, 1916. Whereas Yeats questions the human cost of this Irish rebellion, MacDonagh, one generation later, questions its legacy. Domesticated by time and history, the Easter Rising has become "petrified" and academic, at best a shadowy memory of what it once was.

Two other themes are worth mentioning, one traditional and the other radically modern. Like the Elizabethan sonneteers, especially William Shakespeare, MacDonagh sometimes envisioned life as a struggle between love and the ravages of time. In his poems and some of his best plays, "Joy" and "the heart's extravagance" are offered as experiences that temporarily halt the inexorable corrosion of time. More contemporary is MacDonagh's recognition that culture, knowledge, and thought are all "varnish," under which lurks the primitive beast in all of us, from which springs "all wild desirable barbarities" and "time's rat teeth."

Achievements

Although MacDonagh was a poet, playwright, and scholar, a writer of ballads and short stories, the coauthor of a ballet and an opera, and a skillful and knowledgeable editor of Irish poetry, his real achievements are hard to gauge. This is true for two reasons. First, modern scholars have not yet focused sufficiently on the Irish playwrights and poets who followed William Butler Yeats, John Millington Synge, George Russell (Æ), and Sean O'Casey. Consequently, no complete history of modern Irish drama, no adequate bibliography, and few good anthologies exist. Indeed, many important plays of this period, at least one of which is by MacDonagh, remain unedited and unpublished. With the exception of a brief but trenchant study by Robert Hogan, the dean of modern Irish studies, no scholarly evaluations of MacDonagh have appeared. The second reason for the neglect of MacDonagh's work is more personal. His father, Thomas MacDonagh, has been the subject of numerous articles and two critical biographies, and the political and historical importance of the father has tended to overshadow the literary achievements of the son.

Some tentative judgments of Donagh MacDonagh, however, can be made. He was a better poet and playwright than his more famous father, and he, along with T. S. Eliot, deserves pride of place for attempting to resurrect poetic drama in the modern theater. In fact, MacDonagh's verse is more flexible and lively than Eliot's, and it has a much broader range, from ballad forms to rhyming couplets, from blank verse to colloquial Irish expressions, à la Synge. *Happy as Larry* is the best-known Irish verse play of recent memory, and some of MacDonagh's other plays, though almost completely unknown, are even better. His plays are notable for their deft characterization, whether sketched in detail or painted with a broad brush.

Fame largely eluded MacDonagh during his lifetime, although he was elected to the Irish Academy of Letters, saw his verse play *Happy as Larry* translated into twelve European languages, and gained great popularity as a broadcaster on Radio Éireann, where he sang and recited folk ballads and ballad operas, often his own, and where he explained the significance and importance of Irish songs and poetry to a large and enthusiastic listening audience. Selected by Lennox Robinson to help edit *The Oxford Book of Irish Verse*, MacDonagh also contributed a learned and insightful introduction to the collection.

Biography

Born in Dublin on November 22, 1912, Donagh MacDonagh made the most of a life that was singularly unlucky and troubled. His father Thomas MacDonagh, the great Irish patriot, was executed when Donagh was only three years old, and shortly afterward the young boy contracted tuberculosis, a disease that greatly hampered him for the rest of his life. On July 9, 1917, only fifteen months after his father's death, Muriel MacDonagh, Donagh's mother, drowned while attempting to swim to an island off the shore of Skerries, an ocean resort close to Dublin. Thereafter, the custody of Donagh and his sister Barbara was contested for some time by the families of their father and mother, apparently in part because of a disagreement about whether the children should be reared as Catholics.

In time, Donagh was sent off to school, first to Belvedere College, where James Joyce had been a student some years earlier, and then to University College, Dublin, where he was part of a brilliant student generation that included such future notables as Niall Sheridan, Brian O'Nolan (who is best known under his pen names, Flann O'Brien and Myles na gCopaleen), Denis Devlin, Charles Donnelly—MacDonagh's close friend who died in 1937 during the Spanish Civil War—and Cyril Cusack, who later became an accomplished actor.

MacDonagh took both his bachelor of arts and master of arts degrees at University College, Dublin, and became a barrister in 1935. He practiced law until 1941, when he was named as a district justice for County Dublin, a post that required much traveling in the countryside.

At the time of his death on New Year's Day, 1968, MacDonagh was serving as a justice for the Dublin Metropolitan Courts. MacDonagh was twice married: His first wife drowned while she was taking a bath, and his second wife, who survived him, later choked to death on a chicken bone.

Analysis

Donagh MacDonagh's plays derive from three distinct sources. The first of these is the double heritage of the early Abbey Theatre: on the one hand, Yeats's romantic, poetic drama, and, on the other hand, the more realistic plays of Edward Martyn. All of MacDonagh's major works are comedies—even *Lady Spider* is technically a comedy—but in each one, the author offers a particular blend of realism and fantasy, with one or the other usually predominating. Another important source for MacDonagh's drama is his deep love of poetry and various verse forms. As a practicing poet, he attempted to revive the marriage of poetry and drama, experimenting with different types of verse that he thought were appropriate for and pleasing to theater audiences. The third source of MacDonagh's art is his great learning, above all his familiarity with Elizabethan and Jacobean drama, especially Shakespeare, and his scholar's interest in old Irish poetry and ballads and in various Irish dialects and slang.

All of these influences are present in MacDonagh's first published drama, *Happy as Larry*, his most popular and successful play. Technically accomplished, *Happy as Larry* has been described as "a ballad opera without music," and the definition is a good one. The rhythms of well-known Irish ballads and the use of homey Irish words and phrases provide a constant undercurrent of familiar patterns that make the verse easy to read or listen to. MacDonagh employs short, medium, and long lines of verse, together with musical repetitions and refrains, to which he adds simplicity and clarity of diction. The result is a verse play of uncommon pleasure.

The plot of *Happy as Larry* is highly fanciful and melodramatic. Six tailors, one of whom is Larry's grandson, are located on the outer stage and introduce the story. Larry, a hard-drinking, fast-talking Irishman, happens upon a young girl of about twenty who is kneeling by the grave of Johnny, her recently deceased husband. She is fanning the dirt on Johnny's grave, for her late husband made her promise not to marry again until the clay on his grave is dry. Intrigued and amused, Larry invites the young widow home to have a cup of tea. Meanwhile, at Larry's house, the local Doctor is attempting to seduce Mrs. Larry. Soon after Larry and the widow arrive, Seamus, the pharmacist, enters with a vial of poison, ordered by the evil Doctor, who puts it in Larry's drink. Poor Larry dies from the poison, and the shocked and bereaved Mrs. Larry quickly plans a wake, during which the nefarious Doctor presses his suit. Soon Mrs. Larry weakens and agrees to marry the Doctor, even though her husband's corpse is not yet cold. Outraged, the six tailors, with the help of the three Fates, travel back in time to join the party at Larry's wake, where they decide to take a hand in events by using the Doctor's own poison against him. The unsuspecting Doctor toasts his future happiness and promptly dies. Seamus convinces Mrs. Larry to draw some blood from Larry's corpse in order to give the Doctor a transfusion which, according to the pharmacist, will bring the Doctor back to life. Mrs. Larry agrees but faints and dies when she sees Larry's blood. Incredibly, the blood she drains from Larry contains the poison that killed him, so Larry revives, believing that he is the victim of a monumental hangover. The young widow consoles Larry over the loss of his wife and talks him out of a life of debauchery and dissipation. The second tailor ends the play by telling the audience that Larry will marry the young widow and live happily ever after.

MacDonagh provides a cast of wonderfully drawn comic types to complement his fantastic plot. Mrs. Larry talks too much, bosses her poor husband around, and is somehow capable of delivering a highly metaphysical eulogy for her dead husband: "Empty on their racks the suits are hanging,/ Mere foolish cloth whose meaning was their wearer." Still, she is a loving and faithful wife until Larry's death. The Gravedigger, wholly superfluous to the plot, is right out of Shakespeare's *Hamlet*; he is a comic reductionist and a walking, talking *memento mori* whose every line reminds us that death is both unpredictable and unconquerable. The young widow is the Gravedigger's opposite number, healthy and buxom, good-humored and witty, and convinced that she can conquer death—as, in a way, she does, by marrying again and refusing to be a widow for the rest of her life. Larry is the archetypal henpecked husband, decent enough and faithful to his wife, but not above a little flirting on the side.

The star of the show is MacDonagh's evil Doctor, a hilarious combination of Oil Can Harry and Groucho Marx. MacDonagh endows the Doctor with the spurious eloquence of a first-class rake and with the persuasive powers of John Donne. Arguing at one point that love is religion because God is love, the Doctor slyly turns to Mrs. Larry and croons, "Let us pray/ Together, Mrs. Larry." Later, this schemer touts the virtues of friendship to Mrs. Larry, arguing that since friendship transcends passion, his kiss should be allowed to linger. When the six tailors succeed in poisoning him, the audience is sure to cheer: He has been hoist with his own petard.

The Doctor's fellow in crime, the unctuous pharmacist, spotlights MacDonagh's major theme in the play. Seamus' presence in this comedy is a kind of learned joke: The Greek *pharmakos* means both remedy and poison, just as the word "drug" even today carries both a positive and a negative sense. Thus, infusing this delightful comedy is a vision of the world in which nearly everything cuts two ways, and in which rigid views, either of proper conduct or of the opposite sex, need to be broadened and softened. Except for the Doctor and his henchman Seamus, everyone in *Happy as Larry* is a mingled yarn—both good and bad together.

The play gently asks us to support a widow's right to remarry. According to custom, especially in Catholic Ireland, widows do better to honor the memory of their dead husbands by not remarrying—Mrs. Larry makes exactly this point to the young widow—yet such expectations are both unrealistic and cruel, as Mrs. Larry discovers in the course of the play. MacDonagh endorses the young widow's wish to marry again rather than follow the outdated suicide of Dido or the self-immolation of Indian wives, both mentioned at the start of the play.

Allied to the theme of remarriage is MacDonagh's attempt to adjust male attitudes toward women. Though written twenty years before the rebirth of feminism in the 1960's, the play poses a key question about Larry's two wives: Which is bad and which is good? The answer is that both are essentially good. The play approves of Mrs. Larry's wish for companionship after Larry's death, though it does not approve of the way the Doctor manipulates her, and Mrs. Larry's attempt to save the Doctor, though it fails, stems from the reasonable premise that it is better to save a life than to let someone die. Likewise, the lusty young widow's wish to dry her husband's grave quickly is rewarded at the end of the play when MacDonagh allows her to marry Larry.

The second tailor, Larry's grandson, begins as a misogynist—"Woman curses every plan"—but ends by praising the many virtues of the young widow and by wishing that his own son "may be as happy as Larry." Like the second tailor, the audience learns the need for tolerance and empathy in an imperfect world.

Step-in-the-Hollow, like *Happy as Larry*, is an experimental play. Local dialects and lively, contemporary turns of phrase energize this comedy, which, again like its predecessor, contains a wide variety of verse forms. In both technique and construction, however, *Step-in-the-Hollow* is superior to *Happy as Larry* and was a great success when it premiered at the Gaiety Theatre, Dublin, on March 11, 1957. Parts of the play are written in rhyming couplets, a difficult and demanding form that MacDonagh uses with great skill and to good effect. The verse is flexible enough for the actors to avoid the singsong monotony that can vitiate a long series of couplets, and MacDonagh also employs the couplet form wisely: to highlight important moments in the play, and as a device to underscore the character of Julia O'Sullivan, the local harridan who threatens to destroy Justice Redmond O'Hanlon, the title character.

The play is so well constructed that it moves along with great speed, full of interest and crackling with life and vitality. MacDonagh deftly uses the first act to introduce the main complications one by one. First, the audience learns that a government inspector is on his way to evaluate the courtroom procedures of Justice O'Hanlon. Then Julia O'Sullivan appears, with her daughter, aptly named Teazie, in tow, demanding that the Justice try Crilly Duffy, a local boy, for compromising her daughter's virtue. Throughout, the reactions of the Justice's cohorts—Molly, the Sergeant, and the Clerk—establish their essential characters for the audience, while MacDonagh holds back the main antagonists, Justice Redmond O'Hanlon and Sean O'Fenetic, the government inspector. When the Judge finally enters, MacDonagh adds a third complication: An old man, much like Redmond O'Hanlon, was in Teazie's room before Crilly Duffy entered.

Act 2 consists of two short scenes in which the case of O'Sullivan versus Duffy is argued and almost resolved. With the Inspector watching every move, Justice O'Hanlon tries as hard as he can to prevent the truth from being discovered, but Julia O'Sullivan discovers that O'Hanlon, not Duffy, is the real villain and storms into the courtroom to accuse the Justice. Overcome with emotion and gin, she builds to a climax at great length, allowing O'Hanlon to adjourn the court and whisk away the Inspector before Julia can name the man who compromised her little Teazie.

Act 3 belongs wholly to Molly Nolan, who conceives and executes a plan that saves the Justice, the Sergeant, and the Clerk, while ensuring her own future as the heir of Redmond O'Hanlon and the new wife of the Inspector. Skillful, effective, and satisfying, the conclusion to *Step-in-the-Hollow* is both unexpected and delightful.

The twin themes of this play are love and justice. The symbol of playful, worldly love is Sandro Botticelli's *The Birth of Venus*, prominently displayed in Justice Redmond O'Hanlon's apartment, the location for acts 1 and 3. During the play, MacDonagh examines different kinds of love: the May-December infatuation of the Justice for Teazie; the young love of Crilly and Teazie, who are to be married by the end of the play; the romantic, yet imprudent, love of the Sergeant for Molly; the lascivious love of the Justice for Molly; the liquor-induced love of the Clerk for Molly; and, finally, the birth of the Inspector's love for Molly, which she both induces and accepts in act 3.

In some ways, Molly is an unlikely heroine—as clever and resourceful as Shakespeare's comic heroines, which she clearly resembles, but much less chaste. She took a tumble in the hay with the Sergeant once, and the full extent of her duties for the Justice clearly exceed those of a paid housekeeper. Moreover, Molly is no starry-eyed, empty-headed girl, such as Teazie; rather, she wants respectability and a good fortune, as well as the passion of first love, all of which the Inspector finally provides. Molly is not above asking, "What's in it for me?" and her mixture of love and prudence wins the day for herself and for others.

Molly's attitude toward love is highly practical, not extreme. The need for a practical, reasonable approach to justice is the play's complementary theme. Justice Redmond O'Hanlon and Inspector Sean O'Fenetic represent radical attitudes toward the law, neither of which can be accepted. Once a good scholar and student of the law, Justice O'Hanlon has been worn down by thirty years on the bench and has become the very embodiment of the Seven Deadly Sins that justice seeks to prevent and punish. On the other hand, the God-fearing Inspector, sworn to temperance, is an essentially innocent and sterile advocate of governmental rules and regulations that often hinder instead of promote the impartial administration of justice. Molly, rather than the Justice or the Inspector, leads the audience to a better understanding of justice and the law. She puts the Inspector in the same compromising position in which Crilly Duffy found Justice Redmond O'Hanlon. The point is simple and clear: Let him who is without sin cast the first stone. Thus, mercy and forgiveness, and a second chance, are the better parts of justice.

As in his other plays, MacDonagh's characters are exceptionally well drawn—from the gin-soaked Julia O'Sullivan and the voyeuristic Mary Margaret Allen to the inhibited Inspector, who, with Molly's help, discovers at the end of the play that he has always been afraid of women. Above all, there is Justice Redmond O'Hanlon, an authentic triumph of the literary imagination. Old in years yet young at heart, limping after his last exploit with Teazie yet still chasing after women, this fat Justice is a liar, a cheat, and a scoundrel, but his cleverness and humor are endearing qualities that help him retain audience sympathy. He derives from Sir John Falstaff, as does the basic conflict of *Step-in-the-Hollow*: The clash between the Inspector and the Justice is an Irish version of the contest between the Lord Chief Justice and Falstaff in Shakespeare's *Henry IV, Part II*. Moreover, some of the pathos and melancholy of Shakespeare's work creep into MacDonagh's play: Justice O'Hanlon's startling admission, "An old man knows what's lost," echoes Falstaff's frank confession in *Henry IV, Part II*, "I am old, I am old."

In part, however, O'Hanlon is an alter ego of the author himself, who also spent many years on the bench in Ireland. Though obvious differences exist between the playwright and his creation, a Justice who quotes T. S. Eliot and who displays above his bench the harp of Ireland, the symbol of old Irish poetry and music, shares something with MacDonagh. One suspects, for example, that O'Hanlon's wish to replace the rules of evidence with common sense echoes the wish of his creator, and the Justice's view that the law seems bent on mystifying common people may also have been shared by MacDonagh.

The Justice provides a sobering counterpoint to an otherwise happy ending. As the curtain is about to fall, O'Hanlon stands alone, looking out the window at Molly and the Inspector as they leave to get married. To grow old, the Justice muses, is to gain money, place, and power but to lose forever carefree youth and the chance to be in love again. "I can't complain" is O'Hanlon's last line, but the audience knows better.

Lady Spider is MacDonagh's most daring and ambitious play, in which he offers his version of the Deirdre legend that has obsessed Irish poets and playwrights for more than one hundred years. The tragedy of Deirdre is to the Irish imagination as Homer's *Iliad* is to the English, and it is fair to say that MacDonagh handles the love of Deirdre and Naoise much as Shakespeare treats the story of Troilus and Cressida; *Lady Spider* minimizes romance and fantasy by pushing comedy to the limits of realism. In short,

MacDonagh demythologizes myth by making it modern, psychological, and political. The result is as brilliant as it is unsettling, a fable for modern times.

The story of Deirdre is part of the Red Branch Cycle of ancient Irish tales. During the reign of Conor, King of Ulster, a female child named Deirdre is born who, according to prophecy, will bring down the House of Usna and Emain Macha, the palace of King Conor. Conor refuses to kill the child; instead, he sends her into the wilderness to be brought up by Leabharcham, a nurse. Deirdre, whose name means "alarm" or "troubler," grows up to be so desirable that Conor intends to marry her, but she meets Naoise, a son of the House of Usna, and runs away with him and his two brothers, Ardan and Ainnle. After a few years, Conor sends Fergus to convince the lovers that all is forgiven. They accept Conor's offer to return to Ireland, whereupon the still lovesick king uses stealth and guile to kill Naoise and his brothers once they arrive at his palace. Three variant endings exist: Deirdre immediately kills herself, she quickly dies of sorrow, or Conor keeps her for a year, after which she commits suicide.

Three great Irish plays before MacDonagh's were based on the Deirdre legend, and each in its own way interprets Deirdre as a romantic symbol of female heroism and as a model of support, inspiration, and companionship for the Irish hero. In his *Deirdre* (1902), Æ depicts the heroine as the incarnation of the ancient Irish gods, who will one day return to validate the sacrifice of Deirdre and Naoise, made immortal by their escape into death. Images of sleep, dreams, and vision help establish a mystical context in which the world of myth and magic, not the everyday world, is the deepest reality and the most true. Yeats's *Deirdre* (pr. 1906) is an exercise in concentrated poetic imagery that accentuates the passion of the lovers and invites them to live forever in the Byzantium of art. The greatest of these three plays is Synge's *Deirdre of the Sorrows* (pr. 1910), written in simple, direct prose with a peasant dialect. Synge's version establishes a sympathetic connection between the lovers and nature; the lovers triumph over age and the mutability of earthly love by choosing the timeless immortality of death.

Just as Shakespeare wrote his *Troilus and Cressida* with Geoffrey Chaucer and Homer in mind, so MacDonagh composed his play as both a contribution to and a comment on the great plays that preceded his. He deromanticizes the story by using the technique of inversion. Unlike Æ, MacDonagh refers to no gods who wait in the wings, and mysticism gives way to a hard-nosed, deeply flawed world. Unlike Yeats, MacDonagh refuses to glorify the passion of Deirdre and Naoise; in fact, he purposefully degrades it into a sexual obsession that Deirdre must overcome. Like Synge, MacDonagh fills his play with nature imagery, but the effect is very different. Images of nature, animals, and food in *Lady Spider* accentuate the bestial side of man and his subjugation to appetites of all kinds. The blank verse that contains these images is tough, lean, and elemental, stunningly beautiful in its starkness.

The central purpose of *Lady Spider* is to criticize earlier versions of the Deirdre legend and to recover the basic meaning of the myth, which proves to be startlingly modern. This purpose may be seen by examining closely the way in which MacDonagh changes a scene that first appears in Synge's play. Synge invented the character of Owen, a grotesque peasant who values nothing but Deirdre's love. MacDonagh replaces Owen with Art, a Scottish king who promises Deirdre "honey words" and "truth," and who wishes to take her to the Palace of Art, the home of "sweet poetry," where all the bards and harpers will sing of Deirdre. She is singularly unimpressed with Art and threatens to cut out his tongue, the traditional punishment for poets who lie.

Literally, this exchange emphasizes Deirdre's desirability—wherever she goes, men lust after her. The scene also foreshadows the real reason that Conor wants her back in Ireland: Like King Art, King Conor is a lustful, unprincipled old man, as drawn to Deirdre as any young man. Symbolically, however, the ugly little Scottish king represents literary art, which has tried to appropriate Deirdre for its own purposes, oblivious to the beauty of the original myth. As MacDonagh sees it, Æ, Yeats, Synge, and many others are guilty of attempted rape, of forcing the legend into wholly alien significance. Soon after Deirdre first meets Art, he is killed while attempting to flee and lies sprawling in the middle of the stage at the end of act 2. This is poetic justice, so to speak, and the end, MacDonagh implies, of all of this romantic Deirdre nonsense in Irish art.

As this short explication illustrates, *Lady Spider* is richly artistic, despite its attitude toward art and poetry, and its characters are superbly realized. Naoise, Deirdre's lover, is the playboy of the Western world, cynical about women and sex and unable to get enough of either, a sort of Hotspur without young Percy's charm. Naoise is full of empty idealism and self-interest but unable to develop into anything better. His rival Conor is shrewder and more intelligent but has grown old without wisdom. A superb manipulator of men, he is in turn manipulated by his own glands, which make him as lecherous as a monkey. Buffeted between these two men, Deirdre is a quintessentially modern woman, blamed for being the source of all trouble yet in reality the victim of men's appetites and of her own.

Deirdre's development is the center of interest in the play. At first, MacDonagh's Deirdre dreams romantically about men. It is love she wants, but in Naoise she gets animal lust that makes her his sexual thrawl. Desperate, she puts Naoise under *geasa*—magical bonds that are supposed to force consent—in an attempt to make Naoise marry her. After the couple flees to Scotland, Deirdre hardens with time, still sexually captivated by her lover but increasingly aware of his faults, especially his promiscuity. Lured back to Ireland, Deirdre has outgrown Naoise, both mentally and physically, and she has frank admiration for the way in which Conor outwits and outmanipulates her and Naoise, causing the death of the latter. Seeing that manipulation is the necessary means to any end in this brutal, political world, Deirdre resolves to become Conor's wife, not out of love or even pity but to torment him with his sexual inadequacy, thereby becoming his master, driving him to despair, and securing his crown for her son, who is safe in Scotland. Deirdre's final goal will elude her, for the audience knows in advance that she will be the one to commit suicide.

The world of *Lady Spider* turns on negatives, on false hopes and Pyrrhic victories. MacDonagh has revealed the modern world in an ancient mirror, and it is a world in which all value has drained away, a world in which love is reduced to sex, in which supernature is replaced by nature, in which wisdom gives way to craft and guile, and in which human virtues are supplanted by animal appetites. This kind of world cannot support real tragedy, and so Deirdre remains alive at the play's end—doomed but denied the dignity of death. Paradoxically, however, the play itself is captivating, possessed of a hard, gemlike brilliance that simply overpowers the audience with the force of MacDonagh's vision. For all of these reasons, *Lady Spider* is the best of the Deirdre plays.

Yet it may not be MacDonagh's best play. Surprisingly, *God's Gentry* remains unpublished despite the fact that Robert Hogan, one of the few scholars to have seen it acted, calls *God's Gentry* "a much more colorful and theatrical show than *Happy as Larry*." The exact opposite of *Lady Spider*, *God's Gentry* pushes romance and fantasy to their limits in a story about a band of tinkers who invoke the help of an Irish god to turn County Mayo upside down. Tinkers and gentry trade places for a year until the god's power wears off. According to Hogan, *God's Gentry* is a perfectly delightful play, full of "dancing, singing, spectacle, and high spirits." It remains for some enterprising scholar to edit and publish this play—and other inaccessible or unpublished plays by MacDonagh—so that this neglected modern playwright can begin to receive the critical attention and the wide audience that he deserves.

Other major works

POETRY: *Twenty Poems*, 1933; *Veterans and Other Poems*, 1941; *The Hungry Grass*, 1947; *A Warning to Conquerors*, 1968.

ANTHOLOGY: *The Oxford Book of Irish Verse*, 1958 (editor, with Lennox Robinson).

Bibliography

Browne, E. Martin. "Introduction," in *Four Modern Verse Plays*, 1959.

Coffin, Rachel W. *New York Theatre Critics Reviews*. XI (January 9, 1950), pp. 394-396.

Colum, Padraic. "MacDonagh of Dublin," in *Saturday Review of Literature*. March 19, 1948, pp. 12-14.

Hogan, Robert. *After the Irish Renaissance*, 1967.

Wickstrom, Gordon M. "Introduction to *Lady Spider*," in *Journal of Irish Literature*. IX, no. 3 (1980), pp. 4-8.

Edmund M. Taft

ARCHIBALD MacLEISH

Born: Glencoe, Illinois; May 7, 1892
Died: Boston, Massachusetts; April 20, 1982

Principal drama

The Pot of Earth, pb. 1925; *Nobodaddy: A Play*, pb. 1926; *Panic: A Play in Verse*, pr., pb. 1935; *The Fall of the City: A Verse Play for Radio*, pr., pb. 1937; *Air Raid: A Verse Play for Radio*, pr., pb. 1938; *The Trojan Horse: A Play*, pr. 1952 (broadcast), pb. 1952, pr. 1953 (staged); *This Music Crept by Me upon the Waters*, pr., pb. 1953 (one act); *J.B.: A Play in Verse*, pr., pb. 1958; *Herakles: A Play in Verse*, pr. 1965, pb. 1967; *Scratch*, pr., pb. 1971 (inspired by Stephen Vincent Benét's short story "The Devil and Daniel Webster").

Other literary forms

Critics concerned with the achievements of Archibald MacLeish unite in warning literary taxonomists against differentiating between his work as poet and as dramatist, for with only one exception, all his plays are composed in verse. Nevertheless, his poetic dramas form a group that can be considered separately from his poetry. Indeed, MacLeish's output in both genres is considerable; of the three Pulitzer Prizes he received, two were awarded for his poems.

As early as 1917, MacLeish published his collection of verse *Tower of Ivory*, bringing together his undergraduate efforts from his years at Yale, detached poems derivative in both tone and technique of the powerful nineteenth century British Romantic lyric tradition. The volume is significant, however, for introducing MacLeish's ubiquitous artistic themes: man's relation to God and the reality of human existence. No more of his poetry appeared until 1924, when *The Happy Marriage* was published. Here, MacLeish appears more influenced by the Metaphysical poets of the seventeenth century, and here he experimented with a number of more complex verse forms as well as with the difficulties inherent in paradox. Two other works of the 1920's, *The Pot of Earth* and *Nobodaddy*, have been included variously in discussions of either MacLeish's poetry or drama. In truth, they are embryonic verse plays, despite the author's reference to them as poems; since they prefigure and resemble his fully developed plays, they should be included with that genre.

After continued exclusive attention to poetry, especially during his sojourn in France, MacLeish received his first major recognition as a poet for *Conquistador* (1932), a powerful lyric and descriptive epic in free terza rima form. Chronicling the heroic exploits of Hernando Cortés, as seen through the eyes of a Spanish soldier, the narrative poem was awarded the

1933 Pulitzer Prize for poetry. MacLeish had personally visited Mexico in 1929, retracing by mule and on foot the route of the sixteenth century Spanish explorer and conqueror of Montezuma's Aztec empire. The poem expresses the ultimate hollowness of heroism, as both adversaries, Cortés and Montezuma, fall victim to corruption. Only the majestic landscape remains, the scene of monumental waste and loss.

Yet another facet of MacLeish's talent became evident in 1934, for then the poet was librettist for a ballet, *Union Pacific*, celebrating the completion of the transcontinental railroad in 1869. A resounding critical and artistic success, the ballet was performed in New York and on extensive tours in both the United States and Europe by the Ballet Russe de Monte Carlo company, providing the rapidly maturing writer with his first experience on the professional stage.

Escapism into a more joyous and optimistic past was not, however, Mac-Leish's primary artistic thrust in the increasingly troubled 1930's, a decade which marked the poet's increased concern with social and political issues and his recognition of both the rapidly developing crisis in Europe and the infiltration into the United States of foreign ideologies, particularly Marxism. To give voice to his fears for America's ability to withstand these threats, MacLeish turned to prose, and by the time of World War II, he had published a number of volumes of patriotic political essays; among the most influential was *A Time to Speak* (1941), followed by *A Time to Act* in 1943.

Since the early days of Franklin D. Roosevelt's New Deal, MacLeish had been an editor of *Fortune* magazine, using that journalistic forum to express his views on contemporary issues. Wartime public service claimed most of his creative energies, and it was not until 1948 that his next collection of poetry, *Actfive and Other Poems*, appeared. Although written as a play in three scenes and using the language of stagecraft, "Actfive" is usually considered a poem, one expressing disillusionment with American politics in action, for MacLeish had believed very strongly in Roosevelt's idealistic program for economic and social reforms.

In 1950, the first of MacLeish's two theoretical analyses of poetry appeared, *Poetry and Opinion*, followed eleven years later by *Poetry and Experience* (1961). In these essay collections, MacLeish expanded on his theories of "private" and "public" poetic worlds, extending his classroom work as a professor at Harvard to a larger reading audience. As if being a literary essayist, poet, playwright, and journalist were not challenge enough, MacLeish at this time in his career also wrote several screenplays and television scripts and innumerable contributions to periodicals both in the United States and abroad. In 1966, he won an Academy Award for Best Feature Documentary for his 1965 screenplay *The Eleanor Roosevelt Story*.

Achievements

Throughout his long and distinguished career, MacLeish's seemingly unlimited energies were spent in an amazingly broad range of activities directed at the reconciliation of literature and public service, far more so than any other modern American poet. He was an indefatigable lecturer in halls and on university campuses throughout the United States, exemplifying his informing belief that an artist cannot indulge himself by retreating exclusively to a private "tower of ivory" (the title of his first poetry collection), but must use his "gifts" (the title of his first published poem) by addressing himself to current public issues in the larger world in which all men live.

In both his prose and poetry, MacLeish drew on his wide-ranging intellectual and aesthetic resources to recast the American legacy of myth, history, and folklore into powerful and moving parables for troubled times. The British critic John Wain has observed that "MacLeish . . . has certainly made it a central part of his business to 'manipulate a continuous parallel' between the immemorial and the modern." This tendency is most evident in MacLeish's verse drama, and it is here that his achievement in twentieth century American literature is most significant. Until the appearance of *J.B.*, there had been little work of any importance in this genre, and the success of this monumental epic of philosophic rationalism encouraged others to explore new possibilities for poetic drama.

The popularity and critical acclaim earned by MacLeish's exemplary *J.B.* proves that he not only mastered the techniques of stagecraft, but also, and more important, created a responsive, humanistic, yet classically theatrical work that speaks to common experience while at the same time engaging each member of his audience personally. In an age geared to mass audiences and noncontroversial, often mindless yet commercially successful productions, MacLeish's courage in refusing to compromise his beliefs and values is remarkable in itself.

Biography

The son of upper-middle-class parents, Archibald MacLeish was born in 1892 in Glencoe, Illinois, where he attended grammar school. His father, a Scotchman, was a prosperous department-store executive whose wealth allowed his son the privilege of a preparatory-school education at Hotchkiss School before his entrance into Yale University, where he took a B.A. degree in 1915. His mother, his father's third wife, was graduated from and taught at Vassar College and, before the birth of the poet, was president of Rockford College in Illinois. The young MacLeish was active in both literary and athletic groups at Yale, and was elected to Phi Beta Kappa his junior year.

He enlisted for military duty in World War I, entering as a private in an army hospital unit and serving as a volunteer ambulance driver. After transferral to the artillery, he saw active duty at the front in France; he was discharged in 1918 with the rank of captain. In 1916, he married his childhood sweetheart, Ada Hitchcock, a singer. Four children were born to the couple, although one son died in childhood. After the war, he returned to Harvard Law School, which he had attended briefly before his military service. He taught government there for a year after he was graduated first in his class in 1919. Although avidly concerned with his developing poetic career, he practiced three years with a prestigious law firm in Boston.

By 1923, MacLeish had decided to give up the law, despite his election as a member of the firm. With his wife and children, he left for a five-year sojourn in France and Persia, and there he cultivated his artistic taste and talents by steeping himself in French literary culture. He also associated with the coterie of American expatriates then in Paris, among them Gertrude Stein, Ezra Pound, and Ernest Hemingway. MacLeish, however, had no intention of leaving his homeland permanently, and in 1929, he and his family returned, settling in the small New England village of Conway, Massachusetts, where the poet lived as a "gentleman farmer" for the rest of his life.

During these formative years abroad, the years MacLeish considered "the beginning of my more or less adult life," he matured rapidly as a poet and began to gain an audience for his work as well as critical acclaim. To support his family after his return, he joined the editorial board of *Fortune*, a new business magazine, work which brought him into intimate contact with influential leaders of business and government. This position provided him with a sense of focus for his increasingly liberal views concerning the destiny of the United States during the New Deal years of the Great Depression and the eve of global war.

In 1939, after holding office as the first curator of the Neiman Collection of Contemporary Journalism at Harvard, MacLeish accepted his first position in public life, serving as Librarian of Congress until 1944. During the early war years, he also was a director of various branches of governmental information services, and spoke and wrote effectively about the crucial issues of the day. In 1944-1945, he served as Assistant Secretary of State. After the war, he was one of the founders of the United Nations Educational Scientific and Cultural Organization (UNESCO) and, in 1946, was chairman of the American delegation at its first conference in Paris.

In 1949, MacLeish accepted an appointment as Boylston Professor of Rhetoric and Oratory at Harvard, holding this honored position until his retirement in 1962. In 1953, he received for *Collected Poems 1917-1952* his second Pulitzer Prize for Poetry, and he was elected president of the American Academy of Arts and Letters. In 1959, he received another Pulitzer Prize for his verse drama *J.B.*, and in 1963, was named Simpson Lecturer at Amherst College, remaining there for four years.

Less than a month before his ninetieth birthday, MacLeish died in a Boston hospital. Even in the final months of his life, he was actively engaged in both writing and granting interviews, continuing to express both his unquenchable passion for art and his concern for justice.

Analysis

A critic observed in 1910 that "we cannot expect a rebirth of the poetic drama until our poets turn playwrights"; such an extended generic transition is obvious in the career of Archibald MacLeish. After publishing two early volumes of verse, he wrote two embryonic verse plays in the mid-1920's, *The Pot of Earth* and *Nobodaddy*, works often regarded as long poems. MacLeish himself included *The Pot of Earth* in his first anthology, *Poems 1924-1933* (1933). All of this creative output resulted from his five-year sojourn in Paris.

Its title taken from William Blake's derisory name for the Old Testament God of vengeance and mystery, *Nobodaddy* was written before *The Pot of Earth* but published a year after it. A short philosophical verse play in three acts, sometimes classed as a poetic essay or closet drama, *Nobodaddy* treats the Genesis story of the first family and prefigures MacLeish's use in *J.B.* of modernized Old Testament material to illuminate universal human dilemmas. In *Nobodaddy*, Cain and Abel struggle as adversaries, representing the conflict between the independent mind and the dogma of orthodoxy, a theme to which the poet would return in *J.B.*, three decades later.

The Pot of Earth is also significant as a precursor of *J.B.*, for here too MacLeish used ancient myth as a vehicle for suggesting a reinterpretation of values—in this case Sir James Frazer's description, in *The Golden Bough*, of fertility rites in the garden of Adonis as a metaphor for the disillusionment of a representative human being. In a series of dramatic scenes, an anonymous modern young girl realizes the lack of meaning and lack of free will in her existence as she, like the mythic symbolic plants, rapidly grows to sexual maturity, marries, reproduces, and dies, sacrificed in the endless pattern of ruthless natural forces directed by an indifferent and invisible Gardener, a figure previously evoked in *Nobodaddy*. Technically, *The Pot of Earth* offers evidence of MacLeish's mastery of a variety of verse patterns and other techniques of prosody such as complex assonance and alliteration, and has often been compared to T. S. Eliot's *The Waste Land* which was published three years earlier. The two works do resemble each other in their mythic basis, although MacLeish's work is far more conservative stylistically; each emphasizes, in a manner typical of the 1920's, the transience of life.

Returning to poetry, including *Conquistador*, MacLeish did not attempt drama for another decade, when *Panic* appeared. Together with two half-hour radio scripts provoked by MacLeish's concern for the seeming indifference of Americans toward the threatening world crisis, these plays were his only dramatic work until 1952, and they demonstrate the poet's exploration of the "underlying reality" beneath surface events. Shortly before his death, MacLeish recalled that he had "never seen anything that even remotely approached the misery and anguish and horror of the Great Depression"; this dark epoch in America's history was the background for *Panic*, his first play performed in a theater.

As in all of his poetry and prose during this period, MacLeish's theme in *Panic* is a warning against mindless acceptance of authoritarianism, and a reminder of the threat to personal freedom in time of crisis. Here, the protagonist, McGafferty, a powerful and wealthy New York industrialist and financier finds himself at the height of the American financial crisis, in February, 1933, elevated beyond his leadership abilities by the blind fear of those who look to him as their savior. These people, including his bank colleagues and the poor unemployed, perish; in the end, in the classical tradition, McGafferty perishes helplessly along with them. The play, which has been seen as a hybrid—both Aristotelian tragedy and proletarian drama—drew heavily on the then voguish expressionist techniques. MacLeish was encouraged by the play's acceptance: When both workers and the unemployed responded enthusiastically, MacLeish exalted "Now I have found my audience."

This period piece of the Depression is highly significant in MacLeish's dramaturgic development, for in *Panic*, he experimented with a new verse form, accentual meter, responsive to the contemporary American speech rhythms. He continued to use this form, and not the popular blank verse, in all of his subsequent plays, with one exception, the prose *Scratch*. Briefly, accentual meter is a type of sprung rhythm; rather than counting syllables, one counts the number of stresses or accented syllables in a line. MacLeish's choice was a combination of five-accent lines (but unlimited syllables) and three-beat lines, both to underline conflict inherent in his plots and to avoid monotony.

MacLeish's two vivid half-hour radio dramas in verse, *The Fall of the City* and *Air Raid*, followed his next poetry collection. Along with *Panic*, all three of his verse plays of the 1930's were evidence of his "public" poetry, generalizations of philosophical truths about human behavior focused on timely political issues. In the radio plays, which featured a collective protagonist, the seductive dangers of rampant totalitarianism as well as isolationism were presented by expressionist techniques. *The Fall of the City*, broadcast on the Columbia Broadcasting System (CBS) in 1937, included in its published version a foreword in which the playwright remarked upon the effectiveness of radio for the presentation of verse drama to attract large audiences, claiming that "the imagination works better through the ear than through the eye." Here, MacLeish recalls that poetry is meant primarily to be heard, and thereby to stimulate the undistracted "word-excited imagination" into evocation of the depicted action. The advent of television eclipsed radio presentations of this sort, however, and MacLeish's advocacy came to little, as graphically visualized action rapidly captured popular taste.

In MacLeish's play *The Fall of the City*, the disembodied voice of an Announcer (as in classic Expressionism, the characters lack personal names) objectively and dispassionately describes the collapse and destruction of a metropolis. A demoralized and terrified population has mindlessly refused to defend itself against the attack of the Conqueror, who promised a strong leadership for which they are willing to sacrifice personal freedom ("Freedom's for fools: Force is the certainty!"). The more digressive *Air Raid* does not exemplify the unity of place evident in the other radio drama, and therefore lacks the total immediacy and impact so vivid there but gains its effect by its topicality: Two years prior to *Air Raid*'s presentation on CBS, the ancient Basque town of Guernica had been destroyed by Nazi planes in a cruel demonstration of the blitzkrieg strategy of modern warfare. Again, in this play, MacLeish employed a callous and impersonal Announcer to describe the attack, underlining the grave dangers inherent in refusal by Americans to denounce this massacre of the innocent and the vulnerability of those who refuse to protect themselves against aggression. Ruthless and impersonal technical "progress" is thereby measured ironically against its price in human suffering. Together, these two verse plays, *The Fall of the City* and *Air Raid*, constitute American radio's major contribution to dramatic literature.

Not until the 1950's did MacLeish turn again to poetic drama. In six years, three plays appeared—*The Trojan Horse, This Music Crept by Me upon the Waters*, and his masterpiece in the genre, *J.B.*—each increasingly more complex both poetically and dramaturgically than anything he had previously attempted. *The Trojan Horse* continued MacLeish's indictment of mindless collective consent to self-destructive fear, in this case generated by the accusations of Joseph McCarthy. Recognizing that in the age of television, poetic drama written for radio was all but moribund, MacLeish indicated that his new one-act play would be performed on the stage, without scenery or other elements of stagecraft that might detract from the impact of the spoken word, as well as on radio. Indeed, the play was presented in both forms, broadcast by BBC radio and included in a double bill with *This Music Crept by Me upon the Waters* by the Poets' Theatre in Cambridge, Massachusetts.

The Trojan Horse continued MacLeish's use of mythology as a vehicle for social criticism. Here he varied somewhat his use of accentual meter, combining a verse line of three accents with blank verse. MacLeish continued his expressionist technique of de-emphasis on individual characters by using nameless type characters, thereby focusing on the theme rather than on fully rounded characterization.

MacLeish's other one-act verse drama of this period, *This Music Crept by Me upon the Waters* (the title is from William Shakespeare's *The Tempest*), uses the more conventional pattern of ten named cast characters to focus on an American proclivity to spoil whatever dreams and plans one has for achieving happiness. Because of the large cast, emphasis is on conversation, much in the manner of Eliot's *The Cocktail Party*. Living on a contemporary paradisiacal Caribbean island, a group has gathered for dinner and falls into a discussion of what might constitute the good life— peace, order, simplicity—but each speaker reveals an inability to sustain such an idyllic existence. MacLeish implies that such idlers dream of the prelapsarian Edenic state without the willingness to assume the efforts that would earn it; in their despair, the antithesis of Job's fortitude, they inevitably "fumble happiness."

MacLeish's major achievement in poetic drama, *J.B.*, fulfilled his own exhortation to poets to discover a metaphor for the truth they were moved to communicate. In the poetry of the Old Testament book of Job, Mac-Leish found a metaphor for the eternal human dilemma: man's compulsion to know the meaning and cause of his afflictions and to be able to justify the works of God.

From one point of view, *J.B.* is two plays: the original script (the basis of the popular published version) produced at Yale University in April, 1958, and the revision that was produced and directed by Elia Kazan on Broadway in December of that year. The original is far more austere and poetic, although critics generally agree that the verse in *J.B.* does not represent MacLeish's finest poetry. When the drama was mounted for New York, a largely rewritten version developed during rehearsals, one which not only altered the play's structure (from eleven continuing scenes to two acts with an intermission) but also introduced new characters (such as the roustabouts), deleted others, and altered the roles of still others. Dramatically effective episodes of stage business were also developed in the Kazan production. Many of these changes resulted in little more than clarification for the stage of MacLeish's original ideas, but in the play's final scene, the entire philosophic resolution is altered by a shift in the protagonist's rationalization of his ordeal. In the New York version, as he is reunited with his wife, Sarah, he recognizes the value of his experience and affirms an almost Shelleyan belief in the strength and efficacy of love as a requisite for survival. In the original script, the play ends with Sarah's conviction that eventually the couple will achieve knowledge ("Blow on the coal of the heart and we'll know. . . . We'll know. . . ."). In the Kazan version, however, J.B. refutes her claim ("We can never *know*"), proclaiming that only by his suffering has he learned that one can "still live . . . still love."

Structurally also, *J.B.* is two plays, for the trials of the protagonist, the wealthy, powerful, and satisfied industrialist and banker, J.B., form a play within a play. J.B.'s story is framed by the drama of Zuss and Nickles, who appear to be "two broken-down actors" (MacLeish's own description of them) reduced to hawking balloons and popcorn at "a side show of some kind." As Zuss gradually assumes the role of a god (Zeus), metamorphosing into the imposing God of the biblical Job, Nickles assumes the role of the taunting Satan (Old Nick); together these two characters function as a Greek chorus, commenting upon and participating in the trials of J.B. (Job).

MacLeish himself pointed out yet another aspect of duality in *J.B.*: He saw his accomplishment as the construction of "a modern play inside the ancient majesty of the Book of Job," rather than as a distinct freestanding reconstruction, for he admitted the questions he probed in the play were "too large" to be handled without the strong undergirding structure of the biblical story. Thus, many of the original situations and characters appear in MacLeish's modernization: the specific details of Job's suffering (loss of fortune and family, as well as his physical afflictions), and the parade of his comforters, the ostensibly supportive Bildad, Eliphaz, and Zophar, who jargonize respectively Marxist, Freudian, and theological arguments that leave J.B., like his earlier counterpart, suffering even more acutely.

The original version of *J.B.* opens with a prologue: The elderly actors Zuss and Nickles are inspired to play an impromptu dialogue between "God in Job" and Satan, and they wear appropriate masks to facilitate their performance under the circus tent. By nature, Zuss is reluctant to attempt such a lofty role, but during the repartee with the cynical wit Nickles, he eventually assumes a highly orthodox religious posture which only goads his adversary to more audacious taunts. As they prepare for their "performance," they realize the need for someone to play Job, but foresee no difficulty, for, as Nickles observes, "Job is everywhere we go."

Now that the casting is complete, with Zuss as God and Nickles as "opposite to God," and mindful of the "they" who are the originals, the two actors gradually and unconsciously assume the actualities behind the roles they are playing. In effect, their play becomes the Book of Job. The satanic Nickles accuses God of being a creator who "fumbles Job" by giving him a mind that could "learn to wish" and be concerned with justice. As they continue, they discover that their masks have transformed them into the characters they have assumed; Nickles asks, "You really think I'm playing?" and from the darkness comes "A Distant Voice" that affirms their transformation into more than two seedy actors. The prologue ends with the voice beneath the Godmask speaking the words from the Bible that ask of Satan when he seeks a subject for his test of power "Hast thou considered my servant Job?" and the two begin their rivalry for supremacy over a contemporary counterpart.

Scene 1 follows with a joyful Thanksgiving dinner under way at J.B.'s house, where the family considers their good fortune ("we have so much!"). J.B. asserts seriously that "never . . . have I doubted God was on my side, was good to me," although his prescient wife, Sarah, is frightened: "It's not so simple as all that," for "God rewards and God can punish," because He is just, and J.B. agrees that indeed "a man can count on Him." Scene 2 returns to Zuss and Nickles, now controlled by their assumed roles, who rejoice that in the complacent J.B. they have found their "pigeon," and gloat that he will soon find out "what the world is like" as he becomes God's "victim of the spinning joke!"

In scenes 3 and 4, callous messengers come to the home of J.B. to tell him and his wife of the deaths of three of their five children in senseless accidents. In scene 5, Zuss and Nickles, who have been silently watching, return to centerstage to prophesy that J.B. is learning God's purpose for him—to suffer. The light on them fades as another messenger enters to report that J.B.'s youngest daughter has been abducted, sexually abused, and murdered by a psychopath, and Zuss and Nickles allude to the universality of their dramatized actions by recognizing that actually J.B. "isn't in the play at all," but is "where we all are—in our suffering."

Zuss and Nickles peer down in scene 6 as J.B. discovers that a bomb has destroyed his bank, taking with it his fortune as well as killing his last child. By now, Sarah is rebellious and hysterical and shrieks that God not only gives but also takes and "Kills! Kills! Kills! Kills!" Despite everything, J.B. continues to bless "the name of the Lord." In scene 7, Zuss and Nickles review the trials of J.B. and ridicule his endurance and refusal to despair. Zuss, as God, feels that he has triumphed over Nickles in J.B.'s test, but Satan refuses to concede, even though J.B.'s acceptance is "the way it ends" in the Bible. The two decide to continue his trials.

Scene 8 reveals that a worldwide nuclear holocaust has destroyed all but a few pitiful survivors, a rag-clad J.B. and his wife among them. His skin is blistered by the fire, the modern counterpart of Job's boils, but even now J.B. refuses to join Sarah in condemning God as their enemy, although he agonizes over why God is continuing their persecution. Sarah refuses to accept her husband's adamant defense of God as just, and she vows to leave him, seeing his position as a betrayal of the innocence of their children. When he responds that he has "no choice but to be guilty," she challenges him to "curse God and die," and runs from him. Now totally alone, J.B. pleads "Show me my guilt, O God!" but experiences only an agonizing silence, just as Adam and Eve did after their Edenic transgression in *Nobodaddy*. Nickles, who has been watching, decides that this is the time to bring to J.B. the "cold comforters" who also appeared in the Book of

Job, those dogmatists "who justify the ways of God to Job by making Job responsible."

The three appear in scene 9, with the same names as their biblical counterparts. When J.B. asks "My God! What have I done?" (to justify such suffering), Bildad, a Marxist, cries, "Screw your justice!" and praises collectivism as the ultimate solution to man's pain ("One man's suffering won't count"). J.B. insists that guilt matters, or all else is meaningless, but Bildad rants that "guilt is a sociological accident." The Freudian Eliphaz sees guilt as "a psychophenomenal situation," inciting Zophar, a religionist to proclaim his belief that "All mankind are guilty always!", thereby negating any place for individual will in the matter. J.B. chides them all for squabbling and for mocking his misery, asserting that only in his suffering could he have found affirmation of his identity, by knowing it was "I that acted, I that chose."

J.B. again cries, "What have I done?" but there is still no answer from Heaven. Suddenly he hears the Distant Voice in a whirlwind; it rebukes and humiliates him for his arrogance in challenging God, and in the familiar biblical catechism reminds J.B. of His many powers and accomplishments. The three glib comforters depart as J.B. is accused of desiring to instruct God. Not answered, only silenced, the humbled J.B. nevertheless proclaims that his eye has now seen God, and that because of this experience, "I abhor myself . . . and repent. . . ."

As scene 10 opens, Nickles and Zuss decide that they have had enough; Zuss is particularly distressed because, as Nickles observes, although he won the argument and was right about J.B., "being magnificent and being right don't go together in this universe." Together they ridicule what they see as J.B.'s impotence, because he has "misconceived the part" and because he has given in and whimpered before the omnipotent voice of God. Outraged by his refusal to despair and by his utter subjection to God's will, the two old actors prepare to resume their circus jobs but recall that there is one more scene "no matter who plays Job or how he plays it," the restoration of his fortunes. Zuss reminds Nickles that when he is released from his suffering, J.B./Job will again assume his life, just as those of all generations do, so Nickles confronts J.B. directly to inform him of the resolution of his fate; signs of his deliverance appear, for J.B.'s blistered skin is healed and Sarah returns.

In the final lyric reconciliation scene, a new beginning from the ashes of destruction is evident as Sarah convinces J.B. that indeed there is no justice in the world, but there is nevertheless conjugal love, which, if strong enough, can triumph over heavenly tyranny. Even if God does not love, J.B. asserts, His existence suffices. In a final declaration, Sarah prophesies that when the heart is warmed by love, despite the loss of religious and societal support, "we'll see where we are" and "we'll know." They have no assurance of the truth of this claim yet no alternative but to accept its challenging promise, affirming, in MacLeish's words, "the worth of life in spite of life."

J.B. ran for 364 performances on Broadway. In its published form (the original version), it became a best-seller and was translated into several foreign languages. Some critics faulted MacLeish's attempt to portray modern people "in terms of a cosmic myth," while others pointed to excessive rhetoric. Although critical interpretations differed, all agreed that MacLeish's controversial modern morality play was a rarity on the American stage—a religious poetic drama that was a commercial and artistic success.

MacLeish followed the triumph of *J.B.* with another verse play, *Herakles*, in 1965, and with the prose *Scratch* in 1971, in addition to the short *The Secret of Freedom* (1960), which was published together with two poetic radio dramas of the 1930's, *The Fall of the City* and *Air Raid*. *Herakles* ran for fourteen performances at the University of Michigan theater, and *Scratch* ran for four in New York. *The Secret of Freedom* was written for television and was televised by the National Broadcasting Company (NBC).

Returning to Greek heroic myth and to Euripides for inspiration, MacLeish sought in *Herakles* to achieve the moral resonance of *J.B.* In this new parable, a monomaniacal American physicist is awarded the Nobel Prize for his Promethean achievement in finding new sources of energy but fails both as a humanist and as a husband and father in his mad pursuit of even greater glory and accomplishment. Like the labors of Herakles, Professor Hoadley's work benefits mankind, but he is an irresponsible individual and is forced to recognize the limits of his humanity. Less lyric than the original version of *J.B.*, *Herakles* is more tragically realistic in its portrayal of yet another victim of the sin of excessive pride. Whereas the essentially passive Job endured seemingly endless, meaningless suffering, the anti-Job Hoadley is a dynamic achiever, willing to sacrifice everything for the palpable rewards of his efforts.

In *Scratch*, a drama suggested by Stephen Vincent Benét's popular short story "The Devil and Daniel Webster," MacLeish once again warned against the willingness to sacrifice personal freedom in exchange for controlled lives of comfort and stifling "law and order." Although relevant to the turmoil of the 1960's, *Scratch* was an artistic failure, dismissed by critics as ambiguous, too abstract, talky, and even tedious and incomprehensible. MacLeish never attempted full-length theatrical drama again. *The Great American Fourth of July Parade* (1975) was his final, somewhat nostalgic return to the form he had so ardently defended and so skillfully practiced.

Other major works

POETRY: *Songs for a Summer's Day*, 1915; *Tower of Ivory*, 1917; *The Happy Marriage*, 1924; *Streets in the Moon*, 1926; *The Hamlet of A. Mac-*

Leish, 1928; *Einstein*, 1929; *New Found Land: Fourteen Poems*, 1930; *Conquistador*, 1932; *Poems 1924-1933*, 1933; *Frescoes for Mr. Rockefeller's City*, 1933; *Public Speech*, 1936; *Land of the Free*, 1939; *America Was Promises*, 1939; *Brave New World*, 1948; *Actfive and Other Poems*, 1948; *Collected Poems 1917-1952*, 1952; *New Poems 1951-1952*, 1952; *Songs for Eve*, 1954; *The Collected Poems of Archibald MacLeish*, 1962; *The Wild Old Wicked Man and Other Poems*, 1968; *The Human Season: Selected Poems 1926-1972*, 1972; *New and Collected Poems, 1917-1976*, 1976; *On the Beaches of the Moon*, 1978.

NONFICTION: *Housing America*, 1932; *Jews in America*, 1936; *Background of War*, 1937; *The Irresponsibles: A Declaration*, 1940; *The American Cause*, 1941; *A Time to Speak: The Selected Prose of Archibald MacLeish*, 1941; *American Opinion and the War*, 1942; *A Time to Act: Selected Addresses*, 1943; *Poetry and Opinion: The "Pisan Cantos" of Ezra Pound*, 1950; *Freedom Is the Right to Choose: An Inquiry into the Battle for the American Future*, 1951; *Poetry and Experience*, 1961; *The Dialogues of Archibald MacLeish and Mark Van Doren*, 1964; *A Continuing Journey*, 1968; *The Great American Frustration*, 1968; *Champion of a Cause: Essays and Addresses on Librarianship*, 1971; *Riders on the Earth: Essays and Reminiscences*, 1978; *Letters of Archibald MacLeish: 1907–1982*, 1983 (R. H. Winnick, editor).

SCREENPLAYS: *Grandma Moses*, 1950; *The Eleanor Roosevelt Story*, 1965.
TELEPLAY: *The Secret of Freedom*, 1960.
RADIO PLAYS: *The States of Talking*, 1941; *The American Story: Ten Radio Scripts*, 1944; *The Great American Fourth of July Parade: A Verse Play for Radio*, 1975.

Bibliography

Ciardi, John. "The Birth of a Classic," in *Saturday Review*. XLI (March, 1958), pp. 11-12, 48.

Falk, Signi Lenea. *Archibald MacLeish*, 1965.

Lutyens, David Bulwer. "Archibald MacLeish," in *The Creative Encounter*, 1960.

Morgan, Charles. "The Poet in the Theatre," in *The Yale Review*. XXIV (Summer, 1935), pp. 834-841.

Smith, Grover. *Archibald MacLeish*, 1971.

Maryhelen C. Harmon

TERRENCE McNALLY

Born: Saint Petersburg, Florida; November 3, 1939

Principal drama

The Lady of the Camellias, pr. 1963 (adaptation of Giles Cooper's play based on the novel by Alexandre Dumas, *fils*); *And Things That Go Bump in the Night,* pr. 1964, pb. 1966 (originally as *This Side of the Door,* pr. 1962); *Next,* pr. 1967, pb. 1969; *Tour,* pr. 1967, pb. 1968; *Botticelli,* pr. 1968 (televised), pb. 1969, pr. 1971 (staged); *¡Cuba Si!,* pr. 1968, pb. 1969 (one act); *Noon,* pr., pb. 1968; *Sweet Eros,* pr. 1968, pb. 1969 (one act); *Witness,* pr. 1968, pb. 1969 (one act); *Apple Pie,* pb. 1969 (includes *Next, Tour, Botticelli*); *Bringing It All Back Home,* pr. 1969, pb. 1970; *Last Gasps,* pr. 1969 (televised), pb. 1970; *Sweet Eros, Next, and Other Plays,* pb. 1969 (includes *Sweet Eros, Next, Botticelli, ¡Cuba Si!, Witness*); *Three Plays: ¡Cuba Si!, Bringing It All Back Home, Last Gasps,* pb. 1970; *Bad Habits: Ravenswood and Dunelawn,* pr. 1971, pb. 1974 (2 one-acts); *Where Has Tommy Flowers Gone?,* pr. 1971, pb. 1972; *Whiskey,* pr., pb. 1973 (one act); *The Ritz,* pr. 1975, pb. 1976 (as *The Tubs,* pr. 1973); *The Ritz and Other Plays,* pb. 1976 (includes *Bad Habits, Where Has Tommy Flowers Gone?, And Things That Go Bump in the Night, Whiskey, Bringing It All Back Home*); *Broadway, Broadway,* pr. 1978.

Other literary forms

Terrence McNally is also known for his screenplays *The Ritz* (1976) and *The 5:48* (1980).

Achievements

McNally achieved prominence as a comic playwright who satirized the controversial issues of popular culture in the 1960's and 1970's. Targets for his satire were the Vietnam War, Fascism, middle-class values, popular culture, and sexual codes. McNally is skillful at creating antiheroic protagonists who, in spite of their nonconformist qualities, appeal to a wide audience. McNally's typical protagonist is driven to express himself, protect his individuality, and develop a community of friends who will tolerate his irresponsible urges. His characters are outraged at a world that twists personality and that corrupts motives through its insistence on convention. McNally's drama forces the audience to acknowledge the sometimes bizarre variety of human needs and to see that the infinite variety of human qualities cannot be defined and limited by social convention.

Through his portrayal of social misfits, McNally not only dances the rebellious spirit of the 1960's across the stage, but also evokes the isolation of the rebel and conveys the fear of abandonment that is masked by defiance. Repeatedly, McNally addresses the problem of understanding and preserving identity in a world where social conventions and political trends are in constant change. He dramatizes the need to manipulate identity by often having characters change their names and assume varied roles. McNally's theatrical chaos makes an exciting evening of drama, and his images of identity in flux also evoke the anxiety and loneliness of the rebellious spirit who, like a clown, uses his roles to satirize himself and those around him. The audience laughs at McNally's ragged misfits much as it laughs at the Chaplinesque waif who struggles to preserve himself in an indifferent and demanding world. McNally takes that charming and pathetic figure from the Depression era—where hardship was primarily economic—and places him in the 1960's, in a society whose demands are more complex and therefore more difficult to meet.

McNally's chaotic characters and plots rebel against the traditional rules of drama that require motive, action, and consequence to develop along a clear line; his shuffling of scenes, characters, and audience expectations dramatizes the difficult, sometimes violent metamorphoses of popular culture. Indeed, his deliberately incoherent plots provide a metaphor for a culture in conflict with itself: American culture, which since its revolutionary birth has simultaneously called for traditional values and individual freedom. McNally's plays often seem illogical, but the method to his madness resides in his desire to portray a schizophrenic society that makes impossible demands on its citizens.

Although McNally draws on experimental techniques pioneered by Samuel Beckett and Bertolt Brecht, his achievement lies in his ability to make sophisticated theatrical techniques accessible to the average American audience. Although his characters do not merely embody philosophical statements, they are clearly unreal caricatures: He startles his audience to prevent them from being lulled into an illusion that gains its power from verisimilitude. As eccentric as McNally's characters may be, however, they always have a pathetic humanity which allows the audience to identify with their condition.

Biography

Terrence McNally was born in Saint Petersburg, Florida, and he grew up in Corpus Christi, Texas. His parents, both native New Yorkers, introduced him to the theater at the age of seven by taking him to see *Annie Get Your Gun* (1946), starring Ethel Merman. In 1956, after he was graduated from high school, McNally left Corpus Christi to attend Columbia University, where in his senior year he collaborated on a college variety show. He was graduated from Columbia Phi Beta Kappa in 1960 with a bachelor's degree in English. After graduation, McNally went to Mexico on a Henry Evans

Traveling Fellowship, awarded for his work in a creative writing class. In Mexico, he wrote a long one-act play which he sent to the Actors' Studio in New York. Molly Kazan, wife of director Elia Kazan, saw promise in the script but deduced that McNally had no theatrical experience. She offered him a job as a stage manager at the Actors' Studio, and as a result he became acquainted with the Kazans, Lee Strasberg, and Kim Hunter, while learning how plays are produced. Through the Studio's connections, McNally was offered a job as a tutor for John Steinbeck's children, who were living in Europe. In the next year, he developed a close relationship with the Steinbeck family as he toured the world with them.

In 1962, McNally received the Stanley Award for the best original play at the New York City Writers' Convention with *This Side of the Door*, which, after revisions, became *And Things That Go Bump in the Night*. Also in 1962, Susan Strasberg introduced him to director Franco Zeffirelli, who was interested in staging *The Lady of the Camellias*, by Alexandre Dumas, *fils*. Zeffirelli asked McNally to rework an adaptation written by English dramatist Giles Cooper. Although Zeffirelli's production, which opened in March, 1963, closed after thirteen performances, McNally had received his first Broadway credit. During this period, McNally shared an apartment with Edward Albee. The two exchanged ideas and commented on each other's work, but McNally did not rely on the already well-known Albee to have his plays produced.

McNally's first recognition for an independent production came in 1964, when he received a grant from the Rockefeller Foundation to produce *And Things That Go Bump in the Night*. The play was scheduled to be produced along with two of Arthur Kopit's one-act plays at the Tyrone Guthrie Theatre in Minneapolis. McNally and Kopit became the center of a sensational scandal when the University of Minnesota removed the production from the list of plays to be seen by their season-ticket subscribers on the grounds that it was offensive to public taste. Both playwrights were indignant at this censorship, but while Kopit withdrew his plays, McNally went ahead with the production. The censorship battle brought the unknown McNally a great deal of publicity, and reviewers from New York were present at the premiere on February 4, 1964. When the play came to the attention of producer Theodore Mann, he decided to produce it in New York. While he was in New York, McNally became an active supporter of Off-Off-Broadway as he struggled to become known as a playwright. In his April, 1974, article, "Theatre Isn't All on Broadway," in *The New York Times*, McNally argues that Off-Off-Broadway has replaced the university as the true conservatory of American theater because it allows actors and playwrights to take chances and thus develop their art. In spite of his early Broadway credit, McNally relied on Off-Off-Broadway to gain an audience for his early work.

Analysis

Terrence McNally's plays reflect the anxieties of the 1960's. A member of the generation of children who were drilled to duck under their school desks and cover their eyes to protect themselves from nuclear fallout, McNally grew to develop a sharp sense of the conflict between the individual and his world, the conflict between self and other. In McNally's plays, the "other" may take the form of family expectations, sexual codes, social conventions, or the threat of war. In his early play, *And Things That Go Bump in the Night*, McNally dramatizes the anxiety that resulted from widespread fear of the atom bomb. Through this nightmarish play, McNally evokes the deep yet vague fear of a society that hoped to protect itself from a menace it could not comprehend.

And Things That Go Bump in the Night presents a family of characters who function as symbols of perverted humanity. Through bizarre characters who live in fear, McNally explores the corruption that occurs when man is threatened too long by an oppressive and destructive force. Hiding from some omnipresent menace that could be a fantastic beast or nuclear fallout, the family has lived too long in paranoia, and as a result its members survive through constant battles for power. Each member has lost the human qualities of compassion and faith. Such noble characteristics have been replaced by cynicism and the animal instincts of fear and aggression. Through the grandfather, who is ridiculed while he waits to be committed as insane, McNally criticizes man's cruelty toward the helpless. Through the father, who sleeps while his family plays sadistic games, McNally dramatizes the modern male as indifferent by nature and impotent by choice. Ruby, the mother, thrives on paranoid domination, and she heads McNally's symbolic family as they continually fight, plead, and wrestle with both animalistic drives and philosophical urges to justify their behavior.

McNally has suggested that prolonged oppression not only perverts the individual but also corrupts the human drive to perpetuate and improve the race, an instinct that helped primitive man evolve into a civilized and intelligent social creature. Ruby pronounces that "we shall *not* inherit the earth! . . . it has already disinherited us." She reasons that as people are without faith, they must find their way in darkness, which is light enough, and as people are without hope, they must turn to despair which has its own consolations. Through the menacing and violent action of the play, McNally demonstrates the grim consolations of despair.

McNally has created these abnormal characters to symbolize the abnormal qualities of a world that runs on aggression. When a contemporary family is reduced to living on primitive fear, its members resort to macabre rituals which provide a catharsis for their fears and a controlled opportunity for power. After the egotistical Ruby and her sadistic children have exhausted themselves by victimizing one another, they send out for fresh prey, a school friend with homosexual inclinations, and they brutally exploit his innocence and weakness.

McNally's characters express their primitive instincts while using a variety of technological gadgetry, and thus the audience is reminded of the dangers of technological power when in the hands of impulsive, often cruel and irrational people. The children use slides and recordings first to destroy psychologically and then, eventually, to kill their guest, McNally's multimedia techniques punctuating the sadistic action. Although the play lacks logic, its visceral impact forces the audience to acknowledge the bestial side of humanity and to experience the guilt and fear that is usually limited to nightmares.

The ambiguous ending is a McNally trademark, and in this play it serves to remind the audience that the playwright has no solution. As the action closes with the sounds of a menacing thumping noise which has been present but ignored throughout most of the play, the audience is as threatened and confused as are the characters. Ruby's fear of the unknown menace is verified as the mystery and the danger are evoked for the audience. Whether the oppressor is the atom bomb or a tyrannical social convention, McNally's message is clear: Fear breeds aggression, and stifled aggression results in perversion. McNally's vivid portrayal of life lived in fear is a horror story few want to hear.

In a later play, *Where Has Tommy Flowers Gone?*, McNally once again addresses the problem of oppression, but with a lighter touch. Here, McNally draws on the techniques of Brecht's epic theater, with an episodic structure and characters who continually remind the audience that they are watching a play which provides images of the world, not reproductions of it. Like Brecht's, McNally's technique forces the audience to think about rather than merely identify with the play. While general American taste often finds Brecht's methods a bit short on dramatic action and long on diatribe, McNally, with his understanding of the American audience's taste for action and colorful characters, has satisfied that need.

Without any attempt at realism, McNally presents a series of rapidly changing scenes, direct addresses to the audience, and a protagonist who continually changes roles throughout the play to dramatize the way a world shapes, restricts, and inspires an individual who tries to assert his will against an army of influences. Tommy Flowers, one of McNally's charming antiheroes, has both a passionate urge for self-expression and a need for community appreciation of his rebellious attempts to right the world.

In spite of his guerrilla tactics directed against American cultural institutions, and in spite of his tremendous ego, Tommy wins the audience's sympathy—not only through his Huck Finn-ish good spirits, but also because of his sensitivity, which compels him to create a family from the misfits he encounters on the streets of New York. Like those archetypal American wanderers Mark Twain's Huck Finn and Herman Melville's Ishmael, Tommy is a self-proclaimed social outcast who must suppress his occasional feelings of abandonment.

As Tommy wanders through New York City with his red shopping bag containing a bomb, he charms everyone with his individuality and his urge to sabotage convention by shoplifting, using drugs, and aggressively engaging in casual sex. In *Tommy Flowers*, all this recklessness seems little more than a harmless game which is probably good for the soul. Nevertheless, Tommy's rebellious journey suggests to the audience that he loses something each time he hurries forward to a new scene and a new love. Intent on rebellion, Tommy is unaware that he feeds on a society he hates; obsessed with freedom, he fails to realize that he destroys the community which he instinctively craves.

The play's episodic, discontinuous plot theatrically conveys the contradictions that bedevil Tommy, but McNally wisely takes into account the average theatergoer's tolerance for confusion, pacing manic and obscure actions with engaging dramatic scenes and evocative monologues which draw the audience into the strangely beautiful and sadly confused world of his well-intentioned characters.

Although Tommy never fully articulates his values, the audience understands that he rebels against convention because he knows that society abhors individuality. His refusal to compromise with authority, however, finally deprives him of both his natural and self-made families. In the end, McNally depicts the loneliness of a rebel who on one hand joyfully revels in his defiance and on the other hand longs for community.

McNally easily could have become merely another angry young artist who used the stage as a soapbox to launch his attack on moral complacency, convention, and mindless acquiescence to authority, but through his sharp and somewhat zany sense of humor, he has avoided didacticism. It is a great achievement for an artist with passionate convictions not to take himself too seriously. As a satirist, McNally remembers the theater's invitation to escape, and he provides an occasion for the audience to laugh at the absurd gyrations which the individual must perform to be socially acceptable.

McNally's farcical satires *Next* and *The Ritz* invite audiences to laugh their way to a revelation. The premise of *Next* is a metaphor for an unreasonable and authoritarian society. Because of a bureaucratic mistake, Marion Cheever, an overweight theater manager in his forties, has been called to the draft and must undergo an examination to determine whether he is acceptable. Forced to strip by an implacable asexual bulldog of a nurse, he is physically and psychologically humiliated. As the nurse ignores Marion's reasoned argument against being drafted, McNally comments on an inhumane governmental system that makes demands without logic or justification, but McNally's bitter message is understated throughout most of the play. McNally is more concerned with distracting the audience with the comedy of a fat man in a tight spot than with making a statement. *Next* illustrates McNally's gift for disguising statement through engaging drama: The protagonist wraps himself in a flag to hide his massive nudity; standard sexual roles are reversed as the aggressive and callous nurse pokes, prods, and pricks a man who is openly sensitive to psychological and physical pain; and reasoned discussion is reduced to a slapstick tug-of-war.

The conflict draws on vaudevillian sight gags and thus tricks the audience into believing they are seeing a familiar comic situation: the story of a lovable and pathetic victim who must use his wits to win safety. Once Marion has been labeled unacceptable and has failed his exam, the audience expects him to rejoice in his success, but here McNally surprises expectations. Abandoned in the sterile examination room, Marion develops from a clown into a real man, and he shocks the audience with his passionate humanity and pain. As he plays out the role of the nurse, he forces the audience to understand the cruelty of the examination, which was simply a routine job for the nurse and a source of entertainment for the audience. Through Marion's role reversal, McNally also comments on the fragility' of personality. If one's identity can be so easily manipulated, McNally warns, the self may be lost to adopted roles.

McNally uses comedy to move even farther from didacticism in *The Ritz*. Drawing on the controversial issue of changing sexual codes, McNally does not challenge conventional sexual values; instead, he makes sexual preference grounds for comedy. Set in a New York city gay bathhouse, *The Ritz* uses a formula similar to that of *Next*. Like Marion, heterosexual Gaetano Proclo is forced into a threatening and bewildering situation. His Mafia-connected in-laws want to kill him because his graceless and somewhat dull personality does not accord with the family's pretentious perception of themselves as the operators of a reputable sanitation business. Gaetano hides out in a gay bathhouse because he believes that it is the only safe place in town; ironically and comically, he discovers there a variety of threats. Forced to flee the amorous intentions of a "chubby chaser" and to pacify a third-rate cabaret singer, Gaetano tries to insist on his true married and heterosexual identity, but at the same time he must wear a clownish disguise and pretend that he is a regular patron in order to mislead the detective hired by his in-laws. The slapstick hide-and-seek games, the confused identities, the constant comic misunderstandings make for great theatrical scenes, and the audience is so entertained that they are hardly aware of McNally's message: Conventions require the individual to undergo constant contortions in order to be accepted and safe.

In the comic tradition, McNally reveals all true identities at the end of the play. Conflicts are resolved, and Gaetano's marriage and safety are restored when the predatory brother-in-law is exposed as the bathhouse landlord. Again, McNally dramatizes the hypocrisy that permeates all of society.

McNally's message is so well hidden behind the farce, it may not be seen, and for those who perceive his social criticism, it hardly seems worth challenging. His instinctive sense for entertainment allows the audience to enjoy the manic action and the witty arguments even when his message is unclear. His talent for creating sharply original characters, raucous yet sensitive dialogue, and engaging action, makes it possible to enjoy the play without having any idea what it all means.

While McNally's early plays suggest that he is out to indict a hypocritical society, his later work suggests that he is a playwright willing to laugh away his cares. Close reading, however, reveals that McNally, like his comic and futile revolutionary in *¡Cuba Si!*, always knows where he is, and that, in spite of his humor, he clings to his opinions. After the protagonist, Cuba, has dispatched one of her enemies, she turns to a shocked observer and says, "That's revolutionary politics, sweetheart. You think because I laugh, I play games?" In spite of his gift for farce, McNally is not simply playing games.

Other major works

SCREENPLAYS: *The Ritz*, 1976; *The 5:48*, 1980.

Bibliography

MacNicholas, John, ed. *Dictionary of Literary Biography, Volume VII: Twentieth-Century American Dramatists, Part 2*, 1981.

Shepard, Richard. "Three Young Playwrights Talk Shop," in *The New York Times*. LIX (December 10, 1968), p. 54.

Jane Falco

DAVID MAMET

Born: Chicago, Illinois; November 30, 1947

Principal drama

Lakeboat, pr. 1970, 1980 (revised), pb. 1981; *Duck Variations*, pr. 1972, pb. 1978; *Squirrels*, pr. 1974; *Sexual Perversity in Chicago*, pr. 1974, pb. 1978; *American Buffalo*, pr. 1975, pb. 1977; *Reunion*, pr. 1976, pb. 1979; *The Revenge of the Space Pandas: Or, Binky Rudich and the Two-Speed Clock*, pr. 1977; *The Water Engine*, pr. 1977, pb. 1978; *Dark Pony*, pr. 1977, pb. 1979; *A Life in the Theater*, pr. 1977, pb. 1978; *The Woods*, pr. 1977, pb. 1979; *Mr. Happiness*, pr., pb. 1978; *Lone Canoe*, pr. 1979 (music and lyrics by Alaric Jans); *The Sanctity of Marriage*, pr. 1979; *Sermon*, pr. 1979; *Edmond: A Play*, pr. 1980; *Donny March*, pr. 1981; *The Poet and the Rent*, pr. 1981; *Glengarry Glen Ross*, pr. 1983, pb. 1984.

Other literary forms

Besides brief essays on the theater and screenplays for *The Postman Always Rings Twice* (1981) and *The Verdict* (1983), David Mamet is known only for his plays.

Achievements

Critical acclaim for Mamet's work centers on his extraordinary use of speech and on his satiric but sympathetic awareness of contemporary American life. For Mamet, as for Harold Pinter, Samuel Beckett, and other modern playwrights, language is both an obstacle to understanding and, in rarer moments, a medium of true communication. His characters often stumble and repeat themselves, voice profanities with alacrity (and fervor), mumble incoherent "hmmms" or "uhhhs," and lapse into awkward silences. Critics do not always appreciate this technique; Mamet has been called an "enemy of words," a writer of "robot language," and a purveyor of "scatalogical or obscene street language . . . attempting in vain to perform the office of eloquence." Most have observed in him, however, a talent for dialogue that precisely renders American vocabulary, including the everyday obscenities of common speech. Mamet believes his dialogue does more than advance plot or situation; it must be "poetic"—must support and help create the atmosphere and the idea of the play. In one sense, characters on the stage are what they say, and the "realism" of Mamet's urban, lower-class settings demands a certain level of diction. The actual range of this language is quite broad, however, including not only clichés, B-grade adventure-film phrasing, newspaper reportage, and slang, but also flawed echoes of biblical eloquence, reflective musings, and metaphoric or elevated language, such as that of *Dark Pony*. As Robert Storey suggests in "The Making of David Mamet" (written for *The Hollins Critic* in 1979), Mamet's America is founded upon people who reflect a "verbal busyness, glib, deft, quick; the parenthetical asides that lace his dialogue . . . suggest minds that abhor verbal vacuums, that operate, at all levels, on the energy of language itself." Yet, when silences or pauses occur, as they frequently do in Mamet's plays, these silences may communicate more about the characters than do the surrounding torrents of words. The playwright has said, quoting Voltaire, that words typically are invented to hide real feelings. Fear, vulnerability, and sympathy, which he finds everywhere in modern life, are masked in aggressive, even vicious exchanges of language, which in turn influence what people think of one another. Mamet's job as a dramatist is to allow audiences to hear the nuances of loneliness and need that lurk behind the verbal fireworks.

Mamet finds loneliness to be typical of contemporary America. Most of his plays depict the dilemma of a people inundated with media messages, crowded into physical contact with others in urban communities, yet incapable of connecting with one another. His characters often manipulate and prey upon each other, generally isolating or destroying themselves in the process. To a great degree, Mamet blames the modern business ethic for this dilemma, since people take their cues from the success-oriented, manipulative, sometimes merciless methods of American business. Mamet is certainly not original in this criticism, but he does have a keen perception of how this ethical perversity carries over into private relationships. His work details the subtle manifestations of competition, trade, and the drive to acquire that he believes have nearly overwhelmed America.

Biography

David Alan Mamet was born in Chicago, Illinois, on November 30, 1947, the son of Lenore Silver, a teacher, and Bernard Mamet, a prominent Chicago labor attorney. Mamet grew up in a Jewish neighborhood on the city's South Side, from which he has drawn much of the dialogue and background for his best plays. After his parents' divorce in the late 1950's, he attended high schools in both Chicago and suburban Olympia Fields. To some extent, he lived a disciplined and structured childhood. His father was especially exacting. In a November, 1979, interview with Linda Witt for *People Weekly*, however, Mamet remembers "hamming it up" and being silly even at the dinner table, as well as spending most of his Saturdays like other kids: "watching two double features and about eighty cartoons." He also recalls spending many afternoons during these formative years at his father's law office, where he would type letters, make phone calls, play with rubber stamps, and type out notes on a variety of ideas. He attributes his awareness of the "music of language" to his father's influence, for

Mamet's father was an "amateur semanticist" as well as an attorney. Piano lessons, early backstage experience at a neighborhood playhouse, a stint as a busboy at Second City (Chicago's improvisational comedy cabaret), and later training in dance all contributed to his understanding of rhythm in action and speech.

Mamet resisted his father's wish that he become a lawyer, choosing instead a liberal education at Goddard College in Plainfield, Vermont. He studied literature and theater, wrote a satiric revue entitled "Camel" to fulfill degree requirements, and received his bachelor of arts degree in 1969. For about eighteen months during this period, he studied acting at the Neighborhood Playhouse School of the Theater in New York City, as well as working evenings as lighting man and house manager in Tom Jones and Harvey Schmidt's Off-Broadway musical *The Fantasticks* (pr. 1960). His dream of becoming a professional actor, however, was not realized. Although he did repertory work in New England following graduation from Goddard, he candidly admitted he was "terrible" at it, and he turned instead to teaching acting for a brief period at Marlboro College in Marlboro, Vermont. A few months later, he returned to Chicago, where he worked as a cabdriver, short-order cook, truck-factory and canning-plant worker, and telephone salesman for a real-estate firm that sold worthless land in Florida or Arizona. These experiences, along with his propensity for hanging around and playing pool or poker with friends in the city, made him acutely aware of working-class attitudes and language. His primary work, though, was to be teaching, writing, and directing drama.

In 1971, Mamet returned to Goddard College to become a drama instructor and artist-in-residence. While there, he wrote several short plays for his acting classes and recruited his best students to form an acting ensemble called the St. Nicholas Theatre Company. Amateur in scope, these productions nevertheless helped Mamet to see his plays performed and therefore sharpened his playwriting abilities. Increasingly confident of his skills, he returned to Chicago in 1973 and began to get his plays produced at local theaters. He supplemented his income by teaching theater classes at the University of Chicago and at the State Prison in Pontiac, Illinois. For a time, he lived at the decrepit Hotel Lincoln, which his sister Lynn describes as "downwind from the zoo." He also lived for a short time at a complex for the elderly because, Mamet jokes, his father always told him to get it out of the way while he was young. His first real break came when the Organic Theater production of *Sexual Perversity in Chicago* gained for him the Joseph Jefferson Award, given annually to the best new Chicago play. Although his career flourished in Chicago, he was unknown in New York until the Off-Broadway Cherry Lane Theatre opened *Sexual Perversity in Chicago* and *Duck Variations* in June of 1976. Critics and audiences made these two plays an immediate hit, leading eventually to an

Obie Award from *The Village Voice* and a ranking on *Time* magazine's "ten best plays" list for 1976. During this time, Mamet's *American Buffalo* broke box-office records at the Goodman Theater in Chicago (where many of Mamet's plays were first produced) and won for him an Obie Award as best new playwright of the year. When *American Buffalo* appeared on Broadway, it was voted best play of 1976-1977 by the New York Drama Critics.

At one point in 1977, Mamet had ten plays simultaneously in production around the country. Since then, he has branched out into serious musical drama with *Lone Canoe* and into film with exceptional screenplays for a 1981 adaptation of James M. Cain's 1934 novel *The Postman Always Rings Twice* and for *The Verdict*, a 1983 production starring Paul Newman and directed by Sidney Lumet. Despite these forays into film, however, Mamet is devoted to the theater as a craft and as an instrument for social reform. His filing cabinets are stuffed with scraps of conversations and scenes, which he eventually sifts and puts together to form his plays. Although several of these efforts are one-act companion pieces for longer works, full-length productions such as *A Life in the Theater*, *The Woods*, and *Glengarry Glen Ross*, which won the 1984 Pulitzer Prize, have cemented Mamet's reputation as "one of the bright rays of hope" on the American theater scene.

Analysis

Since David Mamet has written many plays in a relatively short period, it would be artificial to divide his work into periods or to try to show more than tentative growth in his thinking. Two representative plays—*Sexual Perversity in Chicago* and *American Buffalo*—provide excellent examples for analysis. Generally speaking, all of Mamet's works reveal his facility for urban speech, his satiric view of media-oriented, commercialized life, and his belief that "under all this very cynical vision is a crying need for human contact in a bad, bad world."

Mamet's first play to achieve national success, *Sexual Perversity in Chicago*, is also a good starting point for a study of his career. It illustrates his tendency to block action into short scenes rather than fully developed acts, and to strip the stage of props and setting in order to throw dramatic emphasis on the language itself. Originally produced with *Duck Variations* as a companion piece, the play is normally staged for continuous, fluid presentation, often on multilevel platforms, with a shifting spotlight and blackouts to mark scenes. All of these techniques suggest Mamet's debt to improvisational theater, such as the satiric revues of Chicago's Second City troupe. In any case, the method is perfect for *Sexual Perversity in Chicago*, because the play concerns the fractionalized, disconnected lives of "swinging singles." Their lives are in fact a succession of unpromising scenes, or events, which lead to uncertainty and posturing rather than to fulfillment.

Mamet centers the play on a potential relationship between two young singles, Danny and Deborah, who fight unsuccessfully against their own misconceptions about love and the meddling of two older friends, Bernie and Joan. Bernie's influence on coworker Danny is especially devastating, because his macho posturing makes any real relationship with women impossible. He uses language to type women so that he will not be vulnerable to his emotions, and he fabricates bizarre, sadomasochistic stories to show Danny that women are despicable and deserve their position of social inferiority. In fact, the play opens with one of these stories, a wildly comical fantasy, but at the same time an expression of Bernie's anger and fear. He tells Danny that a woman at the Commonwealth Hotel lobby invited him to her room, wanted to be slapped around and have things thrown at her, and liked to "do it" wearing a World War II flak suit while Bernie yelled "Boom" every thirty seconds and she screamed over and over, "Red Dog One to Red Dog Squadron." Finally, when she pours five gallons of gasoline from a jerrican onto the floor and sets the room on fire, Bernie reaches his limit and leaves. Above the flames, he hears her singing "Off We Go, into the Wild Blue Yonder." This image of sex-as-war reveals much about Bernie's own attitude, but it is laced so obviously with blarney that Danny ought to see it as a transparent lie. Yet all he can say when the story ends is, "Nobody does it normally anymore." Throughout the play, Bernie's views fascinate Danny, because Danny is trying to sort out his own sexuality, and Bernie is more than equal to the task of supplying him with possibilities. Bernie's unending stream of name-calling, antifeminist jokes, kinky sex stories, and advice boil down essentially to two things that make men sexually attractive to "broads": treating them as badly as possible and having intercourse as often as one is capable of it. Mamet neatly intersperses scenes that show Bernie watching television or attending pornographic movies night after night until the wee hours, trying out unsuccessful lines at singles bars, and watching women at the beach from a distance. In other words, his experience is completely at odds with his language. He hides his fear and loneliness in violent speech, hoping that it will somehow compensate him for the loss of real companionship.

Just as Bernie controls the male view in *Sexual Perversity in Chicago*, Deborah's roommate, Joan, contaminates the young couple's relationship with her jaded vision. Joan believes that love between the sexes is a "dirty joke," dominated by patterns which people neither understand nor truly try to investigate. She sees Deborah's "possession" by Danny as ownership and sets out to undermine their feeling for each other in order to "save" Deborah from his tyranny. She does not acknowledge that her own attitude toward Deborah is equally possessive and that her lesbian attachment renders Deborah an object as much as a heterosexual relationship would.

Although Mamet does suggest latent homosexual tendencies in all four characters, these leanings are a result of sexual confusion and fear rather than psychological orientation. Joan has had an unsatisfying association with a man who, she believes, prematurely ejaculated to punish her. She surmises that people must come to grips with themselves by overcoming the "finite puzzle" of life, by controlling energies in the form of lust and desire and hope, and then trying to pound the "pieces into places where they do not fit at all." It is this confusion that allows her to see men as the enemy, so she can keep the opposite sex distant, as Bernie does.

With these kinds of influences, one might guess that Danny and Deborah are doomed from the start. Indeed, their first meeting reflects the attitudes and snappy, aggressive speech of their mentors:

> DAN: . . . Is someone taking up a lot of your time these days?
> DEB: You mean a man?
> DAN: Yes, a man.
> DEB: I'm a Lesbian. (*Pause.*)
> DAN: As a physical preference, or from political beliefs?

Even after their relationship becomes fact, Bernie constantly tries to undercut its seriousness and hopes Dan will drop Deborah like a hot potato. Joan predicts that it will last "two months." Yet, for nearly two-thirds of the play, Dan and Deborah resist these influences and happily explore their growing love for each other. Dan is finally able to say, fearfully, "I love you," and Deborah commits herself by moving out of Joan's apartment to live with him. Eventually, however, their negative images and uncertainties begin to predominate. Petty arguments arise over personal habits and the use of each other's property. They stop communicating for a time, then replace the silence with verbal violence and name-calling. Deborah believes Dan cannot distinguish love and affection from physical sex. To Dan, Deborah is cold and manipulative. The play ends as it begins—with Deborah back in Joan's apartment and Dan reflecting Bernie's macho attitudes. In the last scene, Bernie and Dan lie on the beach watching women in bathing suits. They enjoy themselves until Dan believes he can "see" one woman right through her suit. Strangely offended by this flaunting, Bernie honors her with a stream of epithets and says that there is really little difference between a "knockout broad" and a "pig." Finally, when an attractive woman passes by and refuses to speak to them, Bernie says she is "probably deaf."

> DAN: She did *look* deaf, didn't she?
> BERNIE: Yeah. (*Pause.*)
> DAN: Deaf*bitch*.

It is fitting that *Sexual Perversity in Chicago*, which depends so much on language for understanding, should demonstrate Dan's calcifying vision in its final word.

Many of Mamet's plays echo the human failures of *Sexual Perversity in Chicago*: People wish to live together in companionship or love, but stereotypical thinking, jealousy, fear, and ingrained competitiveness block their attempts and cast them into isolation and loneliness. Often, they hope in vain that conventions or forms of behavior alone will establish an etiquette that encourages civilized life. For example, *A Life in the Theater* presents a fading actor, Robert, who believes that the aesthetic structure of the theater will somehow help him avoid the way of all society, in which people "take too much for granted, fall away and die." Mamet once said in a February, 1977, interview with Mel Gussow of *The New York Times*, however, that "law is chimerical. Rules are anarchistic. People make up rules to meet a necessary situation, rules that won't bind them in future." Certainly, Robert's rules of order in *A Life in the Theater* do not keep him from vicious attacks on an actress who is stealing scenes; from jealousy of John, a fellow actor whose reputation is eclipsing his own; from rampages against the "leeches, sots, and boors" who fail to appreciate his performances; and finally, from breaking down completely onstage and cutting his wrists near the play's end.

Despite his feeling that rules and laws of behavior are chimerical, Mamet does believe in the need for friendship, love, and respect. *Duck Variations*, the companion piece to *Sexual Perversity in Chicago*, clearly embodies this answer to the former's scenes of frustration and despair. The two old men in *Duck Variations* disagree violently on many things, including the ultimate meaning of life and death, but both face their own impending deaths secure in the bond of their friendship. When George Aronovitz says he has read that the cactus lives alone, Emil will not accept the idea: "I don't want to hear it. If it's false, don't waste my time and if it's true I don't want to know." Living alone, Mamet appears to say, is not living at all. If urban culture is to be successful in forming communities rather than masses of strangers, people must find a way to communicate.

American Buffalo is also about language, loneliness, and friendship, but it is more explicit in its antibusiness bias. Its three characters are small-time crooks who plan to burglarize the home of a coin collector. One of the three, junk-shop owner Don Dubrow, has sold a buffalo nickel to the collector for ninety dollars, but when he realizes it is probably worth much more than that, he wants revenge on the man who "stole" it from him. Taking the rest of the collector's rarities will simply sweeten the pot. On the surface, then, *American Buffalo* concerns the characters' abortive plan to commit robbery, but its actual focus is on their rules of behavior. Mamet draws his characters from the fringes of society, suggesting that, like the buffalo, they are a shabby remainder of the American Dream. It would therefore be easy to dismiss them as atypical of American life, if the play-wright had not specifically identified them as stand-ins for the corporate classes. In an interview in January, 1978, with Richard Gottlieb of *The New York Times*, Mamet said: "There's really no difference between the *lumpenproletariat* and stockbrokers or corporate lawyers who are the lack-eys of business. Part of the American myth is that a difference exists, that at a certain point vicious behavior becomes laudable." Indeed, the central issue of *American Buffalo* is whether vicious competition will outweigh per-sonal attachments. Don Dubrow is poised between acceptance of the busi-ness ethic espoused by Walter Cole, who counsels him to eschew friendship for the sake of success, and loyalty to Bobby, an ex-junkie friend who works at his shop. As the play progresses, Dubrow discovers that friend-ship and loyalty are more important than the business of stealing in which they are engaged.

Walter Cole, called "Teach" by the other characters, consistently deter-mines to keep business separate from personal relationships. His nickname (short for teacher) suggests that he is to be the voice of conventional busi-ness wisdom, although his frenetic, foulmouthed language is anything but conventional. He enters the play agitated, apparently because two card-playing women friends have accused him of mooching toast at breakfast. When he says of the woman, Grace, that there "is not one loyal bone in that bitch's body," he appears to believe in lasting relationships. Yet, within a few lines, he asserts that money and friendship do not mix. Friendship is friendship, and he is all for it as long as it is kept separate from the busi-ness of playing cards. Only then, he says ironically, can people "deal with each other like some human beings." In another example, Teach tells Dubrow that he should not allow Bobby to take part in the robbery. He admits Bob is a "great kid" and loyalty is admirable, but "a guy can be too loyal" if he starts confusing business with pleasure. Instead, of course, he recommends himself for the job at forty-five percent of the take, then gets upset with Dubrow when the latter suggests they bring in Fletcher to en-sure success. It hurts him, Teach says, to have his own ability to "pull the job" questioned this way. When Dubrow insists that he thinks it is "good business" to call Fletcher in, however, Teach tells him reluctantly to do what he thinks is right. The lesson seems to be that friendship is fine as long as it benefits Teach, but otherwise it is subordinate to the ethics of commerce.

Mamet is able to bring this misuse of business into sharper focus by con-centrating on the developing character of Don Dubrow. Initially, Dubrow is drawn toward Teach's philosophy of free enterprise, which Teach emphati-cally defines as the freedom of the individual to embark on any course that he sees fit "in order to secure his honest chance to make a profit." Thus, Dubrow admires Fletcher, whose consistent winning at cards and sharp dealing make him a model for "good businessmen." Dubrow teaches Bobby that people like Fletcher "stand for something," because they have skill and talent and the courage to arrive at their own conclusions. In business, he says, it is action that counts—not intentions or feelings. Yet, Bobby and Teach both know that Fletcher stole some pig iron from their mutual friend Ruthie, and Teach later reveals that Fletcher probably cheats at cards. When Bobby tells Dubrow that Ruthie was "real mad" about the pig iron, Dubrow first says, "It was *business*. That's what business *is*. . . . People taking *care* of themselves." As he goes on to define business and friendship, however, Dubrow haltingly reveals the real meaning of both terms in the play: "When you walk around you *hear* a lot of things, and what you got to do is keep clear who your friends are, and who treated you like what. Or else the rest is garbage, Bob, because . . . things are not always what they seem to be."

Eventually, Dubrow is able to take his own advice. Near the end of the play, Bobby comes to the shop with a buffalo nickel of his own to sell to Dubrow. He also brings Dubrow and Teach the news that Fletcher is in the hospital with a broken jaw and therefore will not be able to help them out with the burglary. The appearance of a buffalo nickel, combined with Fletcher's convenient absence, immediately makes them suspect Bobby of having double-crossed them. Teach interrogates him about the nickel, finally striking him viciously with a nearby object to force the truth out of him. Bobby reveals not the betrayal of which Teach suspects him, but rather loyalty to Dubrow. He had bought the buffalo nickel at a coin shop for fifty dollars so Don could have one to replace the one he had lost, figuring that Don would eventually get much more for it from a collector. About this sort of friendship, Teach can only say, "You people make my flesh crawl," but Dubrow tells Teach that he is through with him, that he makes life garbage with his stinking deals and his poisonous views. In other words, Dubrow begins to "keep clear" who his friends are. As Dubrow turns on Teach to drive him out of the shop, however, Bobby reveals that he had lied about seeing their victim leave home with a suitcase that morning (ostensibly, on an out-of-town trip). He had missed seeing the collector leave, so he tried to make amends for disappointing Don by saying he went back in time to catch the man's departure, thus allowing them to steal back "Don's nickel." To Teach, this revelation signifies betrayal and lies. He rampages destructively through the junk shop, shouting: "There Is No Law. There Is No Right and Wrong. The World Is Lies. There Is No Friendship." Dubrow draws the opposite conclusion, because he realizes that Bobby values his friendship so much that he would lie and take the risk of breaking into the dealer's house to secure it. As Robert Storey points out in "The Making of David Mamet," these characters have "instincts that transcend both the values and imperatives of their language." Although

Teach is unable to penetrate the world of emotion and loyalty that exists between Bobby and Dubrow, even he is not unaware of the demands of such a world. Despite feeling betrayed, he goes out in the rain for his car to take Bobby to the hospital, and his chief concern at the play's end is that Dubrow not be mad at him. Far from ending with the "message that life, rotten as it is, is all we have," as Brendan Gill pronounced in the February 28, 1977, issue of *The New Yorker, American Buffalo* insists on the positive value of human relationships, which must supersede the predatory credo of American business.

The instincts for loyalty and emotional commitment, obliterated by myths of the popular media in *Sexual Perversity in Chicago* and emerging tentatively in *American Buffalo*, appear more frequently and insistently in Mamet's later plays. For example, *Reunion* deals with the effort to overcome loneliness through mutual commitment. After a twenty-one-year separation, an unhappily married daughter seeks out her lonely and feckless father. Together, they discover that they can communicate and build toward the future, despite the disappointments of their past. *Dark Pony* is a brief, lyric tale of the loyalty between an Indian boy and his horse, told by a father to his daughter as they drive home one evening. It served in production as an appropriate companion piece to *Reunion. The Woods* returns in part to the questions of distrust and fear in human relationships explored in *Sexual Perversity in Chicago*. It is a story of two young lovers, Ruth and Nick, who spend a night in the family's cabin in the woods. They both appear to be euphorically in love, believing that they need not be afraid of anything, because they have each other. As sexual desire is appeased, however, their intimacy becomes a trap for Nick, who turns fretful and fearful. Ruth says he has no idea of the limitless possibilities of their friendship, but he appears troubled by her willingness to come to the cabin with him, as though it somehow demeans her. Their argument turns finally to an exchange of blows, but physical violence leads Nick to assess himself honestly. He has been full of dreams and myths and fears from his childhood. Eventually, however, he realizes that he needs someone to "hold back death," to fend off the loneliness that eats at him, and to "lead him out of the dark woods" of his visions into the reality of love and caring. Mamet continues to believe that society's salvation lies in two equally important events: People must shed their cultural conditioning in order to cast off the neurotic drive for fame and power which appears to govern the contemporary world, and they must seek to build honest, intimate human relationships in order to achieve personal fulfillment.

Glengarry Glen Ross continues Mamet's themes and techniques. Business comes even more directly under fire, though, because his characters are small-time real-estate salesmen, trying to sell lots in distant Florida developments. The champion salesman of past years, Shelly "the Machine"

Levene, is this year's bum. He is given the worst leads and ridiculed by the office manager, John Williamson, who has never gone on the street to sell. In other words, the salesmen are essentially grist for the corporate mill; if their sales fall below a certain percentage, their leads go "cold," which forces lower sales—a treadmill existence that Mamet would see as disguised slave labor. Meanwhile, the salesmen parcel out the American Dream in plots of ground, to be sold by any means possible to anyone who cannot resist their sales line. As Levene puts it: "This is now. This is that thing that you've been dreaming of, you're going to find that suitcase on the train, the guy comes in the door, the bag that's full of money. This is it. The time is now." Or as Richard Roma, the number-one salesman of the year, says to a client: "I trust myself. And if security concerns me, I do that which *today* I think will make me secure. . . . According to the dictates of my mind." He sells a perverted version of the early exploration and settlement of America: land as opportunity for success and status.

The consequences of this blighted vision are petty competition and isolation of all the characters from one another. Attempts at companionship or friendship are tainted by coercion, backbiting, outright stealing, and self-deception. Dave Moss, the number-two salesman, tries to force hapless George Aronow into joining him in a robbery of their own real-estate office, with an eye to selling the leads they steal to a competitor. Eventually, he is able to "sell" Levene on the idea, largely because they deceive themselves that they will not be caught and that the money will be enough to stake them somewhere else. At the end of the play, they have lost both dreams. The most revealing character, however, is Roma. He chides Ross for slighting Levene, fusses with Williamson about trying to get the older man fired, and claims that he admires Levene's salesmanship. Yet, in fact, he is poised to take a fifty-percent cut of Levene's sales through a special deal with Williamson. David Mamet appears to be saying, once again, that the rules of the real-estate game serve only as a convenience to the players. Rules, like much of the dialogue, are simply exercises in deception, binding only long enough for the most adept salesman to gain an advantage over others. As long as they are motivated by power, status on the sales board, and promotional gifts such as trips and fancy cars, they appear to have little hope of escaping the rat race.

A young playwright with considerable early success, Mamet is often nagged by the question of future directions in his work. Some critics, notably John Simon of *New York* magazine, have consistently claimed that his verbal fireworks are brought to bear on static or trivial subjects. Even his celebrated *American Buffalo* has drawn criticism as an inactive and plotless play, which entertains without challenging its viewers or provoking them to thought. Mamet conceded the deficiency of plotlessness in a 1980 interview for *The New York Times*, admitting that dramatists too often write bad plots and then fill in the spaces with verbiage. The lesson he learned from scriptwriting for Hollywood, he said, was to concentrate on plot and "not to cheat." Concerning the charge of triviality, however, he concedes nothing. He has repeatedly called for the theater to eschew wish fulfillment, the mundane, and the personal politics of individual artists. Rather, as he said in an article for the Autumn, 1978, issue of *Dramatists Guild Quarterly*, the nation should have a theater that "both heralds and promotes the possibility of the greatest benefit of the reasoned self-view, an individual contentment born of balance." He calls for devotion to theatrical ethics, which demand action, beauty, economy, artistic unity, and above all, commitment to the idea of a play, without desire for praise or fear of censure.

Other major works

SCREENPLAYS: *The Postman Always Rings Twice*, pr. 1981 (adaptation of James M. Cain's novel); *The Verdict*, 1983 (based on Barry Reed's novel).
RADIO PLAY: *Prairie du Chien: A Radio Play*, 1978.

Bibliography

Barbera, Jack V. "Ethical Perversity in America: Some Observations on David Mamet's *American Buffalo*," in *Modern Drama*. XXIV, no. 3 (September, 1981), pp. 270-275.
"David Alan Mamet," in *Current Biography*, 1978.
Gottlieb, Richard. "The 'Engine' That Drives David Mamet," in *The New York Times*. January, 1978, sec. 2, p. 1.
Storey, Robert. "The Making of David Mamet," in *The Hollins Critic*. XVI, no. 4 (October, 1979), pp. 1-11.
Witt, Linda. "Bio: Playwright David Mamet Fashions a Life in the Theatre Out of Scavenged Speech," in *People Weekly*. November, 1979, p. 58.

Perry Luckett

CHRISTOPHER MARLOWE

Born: Canterbury, England; February 6, 1564
Died: Deptford, England; May 30, 1593

Principal drama

Dido, Queen of Carthage, pr. 1586-1587, pb. 1594 (with Thomas Nashe); *Tamburlaine the Great, Part I*, pr. c. 1587, pb. 1590; (commonly known as *Tamburlaine*); *Tamburlaine the Great, Part II*, pr. 1587, pb. 1590; *Doctor Faustus*, pr. c. 1588, pb. 1604; *The Jew of Malta*, pr. c. 1589, pb. 1633; *Edward II*, pr. c. 1592, pb. 1594; *The Massacre at Paris*, pr. 1593, pb. 1594 (?).

Other literary forms

Christopher Marlowe translated Lucan's *Pharsalia* (1600) and Ovid's *Elegies* (*Amores*, 1595-1600) while still attending Cambridge (c. 1584-1587). The renderings of the *Elegies* are notable for their imaginative liveliness and rhetorical strength. They provide as well the earliest examples of the heroic couplet in English. *Hero and Leander* (1598), a long, erotic poem composed before 1593, is also indebted to Ovid. It is the best narrative of a group that includes William Shakespeare's *Venus and Adonis* (1593) and John Marston's *Metamorphosis of Pygmalion's Image* (1598). The vogue for these Ovidian epyllions lasted for more than a decade, and Marlowe's reputation as a poet was confirmed on the basis of his contribution. He completed only the first two sestiads before his death, after which George Chapman continued and finished the poem. Marlowe's brilliant heroic couplets create a world, in Eugene Ruoff's words, of "moonlight and mushrooms"; his lovers are the idealized figures of pastoral, chanting lush and sensual hymns or laments. A sophisticated narrator—viewed by most critics as representing Marlowe's satiric viewpoint—manages to balance the sentimentalism of the lovers, giving the poem an ironic quality that is sustained throughout. This tone, however, is not a feature of Marlowe's famous lyric, "The Passionate Shepherd to His Love." First published in an anthology—entitled *The Passionate Pilgrim* (1599) the poem is a beautiful evocation of the attractions of the pastoral world, a place where "melodious birds sing madrigals." Technically called an "invitation," "The Passionate Shepherd to His Love" became an extremely popular idyll and was often imitated or parodied by other writers. One of the most intriguing responses, "The Nymph's Reply," was composed by Sir Walter Raleigh and published in *The Passionate Pilgrim*. Its worldly, skeptical attitude offers a contrast to the exuberance of Marlowe's lyric. Without a doubt, this pastoral piece, along with *Hero and Leander*, would have ensured Marlowe's reputation as a major literary figure even if he had never written a work intended for the stage.

Achievements

It is difficult to underestimate the poetic and dramatic achievement of Marlowe. Although his career was short (about six years), Marlowe wrote plays that appealed to an emerging popular audience and that strongly influenced other dramatists. The heroes of the plays have been called "overreachers" and "apostates," figures whom many critics believe reveal the defiance and cynicism of Marlowe himself. In addition to introducing these controversial, larger-than-life protagonists, Marlowe was also instrumental in fusing the elements of classical—and especially Senecan—drama and native morality plays, thereby establishing a style that would be followed by many subsequent playwrights. *Doctor Faustus* is the prime example of Marlowe's talent for combining classical satire and a conventional Elizabethan theme of man in a middle state, torn between the angel and the beast. The vitality of *Doctor Faustus*, *Tamburlaine the Great*, and Marlowe's other works can be traced as well to his facility for writing powerful yet musical blank verse. Indeed, so regular and forceful is his style that his verse has been described as "Marlowe's mighty line," and his achievement in blank verse no doubt influenced Shakespeare. It is apparent in such plays as *Richard II*, *The Merchant of Venice*, and *Othello* that Shakespeare was also inspired by certain of Marlowe's themes and plots.

Marlowe did not possess a patriotic spirit; his heroes are not Prince Hals but rather men similar to Shakespeare's Richard III. Yet he was sensitive to the range of passion in human nature. Many of Marlowe's characters reflect a true-to-life, even psychological complexity that preceding English playwrights had been incapable of demonstrating. Doctor Faustus' fear on the night he will lose his soul is beautifully portrayed in the memorable Latin line, adapted from Ovid's *Amores*, "O lente, lente currite noctis equi!" ("O slowly, slowly, run you horses of the night"). Barabas, villain-hero of *The Jew of Malta*, displays almost the same intensity of feeling as he rhapsodizes over his gold, his "infinite riches in a little room." Over the short span of his career, Marlowe moved away from the extravagant declamatory style of *Tamburlaine the Great* to a blank verse—notably in *Edward II*—that echoed the rhythm of elevated speech. It is difficult to predict what further advances there would have been in his style had he lived as long as Shakespeare. It is doubtful, however, that he would have changed so radically as to achieve universal popularity. His vision was satiric and therefore narrow; the themes and characters that he chose to write about lacked widespread appeal. Nevertheless, "Kit" Marlowe transformed the English stage from a platform for allegorical interludes or homespun slapstick into a forum for exploring the most controversial of human and social issues. Marlowe also established the poetic medium— vigorous blank verse—that would prove to be the dominant form of dramatic expression until the close of the theaters.

Biography

Christopher Marlowe was born in Canterbury, England, in February, 1564. His father was a respected member of the tanners' and shoemakers' guild. Marlowe attended the King's School of Canterbury in 1579 and 1580, leaving in 1581 to study at Corpus Christi College, Cambridge. He was the recipient of a scholarship funded by Matthew Parker, Archbishop of Canterbury; as a foundation scholar, Marlowe was expected to prepare for a post in the Church. In 1584, he took his bachelor of arts degree, after which he continued to hold his scholarship while studying for his master of arts degree. It appears that he would not have been granted his degree in 1587 except for the intervention of the queen's Privy Council. This body declared that Marlowe had done the government some service—probably as a spy in Reims, home of exiled English Catholics—and ordered that he be granted his M.A. at the "next commencement." Marlowe had no doubt been writing poetry while at Cambridge, and he probably decided to make his way in this profession in London. It is certain that he was there in 1589, because he was a resident of Newgate Prison during that year. He and a man named Thomas Watson were jailed for having murdered another man, although it appears that Watson actually did the killing. Three years later, in 1592, Marlowe was again in trouble with the law, being placed under a peace bond by two London constables. Clearly, the young writer and scholar did not move in the best of social circles, even though his patron was Thomas Walsingham and Sir Walter Raleigh was his close friend. One of Marlowe's colleagues, a man with whom he once shared a room, was Thomas Kyd, who in May of 1593 was arrested, charged with atheism, and tortured. Kyd accused Marlowe of atheism, claiming that the heretical documents found in their room belonged to the latter. The Privy Council sent out an order for Marlowe's arrest (he was staying at the Walsingham estate), but instead of imprisoning him, the Council simply required that he report every day until the hearing.

That hearing never took place: Marlowe died within two weeks after his detainment. On May 30, after a bout of drinking at a tavern in Deptford, Marlowe quarreled with a companion named Ingram Frizer, who settled the account by stabbing the playwright. Those who believed the charge of atheism brought against him saw Marlowe's end as an example of God's justice. Others, however, speculated on the possibility that he was the victim of an assassination plot, spawned to eliminate a spy who may have known too much. This theory seems fanciful, but it had many contemporary adherents; the details surrounding the murder do not adequately explain the facts. Whatever the cause, Marlowe's death marked the tragic end of a meteoric career on the public stage. As an innovator—and rebel—he challenged his fellow playwrights to achieve greater heights of creativity while he himself left behind a rich legacy of plays and poems.

Analysis

Christopher Marlowe probably began writing plays while he was a student at Cambridge. *Dido, Queen of Carthage*, which appeared in quarto form in 1594, was composed in collaboration with Thomas Nashe and was first performed by the children's company at the Chapel Royal. How much Nashe actually had to do with the work is conjectural; he may have only edited it for publication. The tragedy shows little evidence, however, of the playwright's later genius. It is closely tied to Vergil's *Aeneid*, with much of its blank verse qualifying as direct translation from the Latin. The characters are wooden and the action highly stylized, the result of an attempt to translate the material of epic into drama. The play impresses mainly through the force of its imagery.

Sections of Marlowe's first popular theater success, *Tamburlaine the Great, Part I*, were probably sketched at Cambridge as well. First produced around 1587 (probably at an innyard), this exotic, bombastic piece won for its author considerable fame. His name was quickly cataloged with other so-called University Wits—men such as Robert Greene, John Lyly, and George Peele, whose dramas dominated the Elizabethan stage in the late 1580's. Marlowe's great dramatic epic was roughly based on the career of Timur Lenk (1336-1405), a Mongolian fighter who had led an army that defeated the Turks at Ankara in 1402. The defeat meant the salvation of Europe, an event that doubtless stimulated Marlowe's ironic vision. The playwright could have found the account of the audacious Scythian's career in many Latin and Italian sources, but his interest may have been first aroused after reading George Whetstone's *The English Mirror* (1586).

Tamburlaine emerges as an Olympian figure in Marlowe's hands. He begins as a lowly shepherd whose physical courage and captivating, defiant rhetoric take him to victories over apparently superior opponents. Although episodic, the plot does achieve a degree of tension as each successive opponent proves more difficult to overcome. Tamburlaine's first victim is a hereditary king named Mycetes, who underrates his adversary's strength and persuasiveness. The lieutenant who is sent to capture the upstart is suddenly and decisively won over to the rebel's side. Tamburlaine next outwits Cosroe, Mycetes' brother, who thinks he can use this untutored fighter to consolidate his own power. As the "bloody and insatiate Tamburlaine" kills him, Cosroe curses the turn of Fortune's Wheel that has cast him down. Even so, Marlowe believes not in the capricious goddess as the chief ruler of men but in a kind of Machiavellian system directed by the will of his larger-than-life hero.

A major test of Tamburlaine's will comes in his confrontation with Bajazeth, Emperor of the Turks. Before the battle between the two warriors, there is a boasting bout between their two mistresses, Zenocrate and Zabina. The former, daughter to the Soldan of Egypt and in love with

Tamburlaine, praises her beloved's strength and his destined glory. Both women also pray for the victory of their men, parallel actions that invite a comparison between the pairs of lovers. When Tamburlaine defeats Bajazeth, he takes the crown from Zabina's head and gives it to his queen—and "conqueror." Marlowe thereby demonstrates that the play qualifies as a monumental love story as well. Bajazeth is bound up and later thrown into a cage with his defeated queen; this contraption is then towed across the stage as part of Tamburlaine's victory procession. Before the final siege of Damascus, the city that houses Zenocrate's father, the Soldan, Tamburlaine unveils a magnificent banquet. During the festivities, he releases Bajazeth from his cage in order to use him as a footstool from which he will step onto his throne. This audacious touch of spectacle verifies Marlowe's aim of shocking his audience and displays contempt for the pride of rulers.

In the midst of this banquet, Tamburlaine orders his lieutenants to "hang our bloody colors by Damascus,/ Reflexing hues of blood upon their heads,/ While they walk quivering on their walls,/ Half dead for fear before they feel my wrath!" These threatening, boastful words are followed quickly by a change of colors to black, which signifies Tamburlaine's intention to destroy the city. He underscores this purpose by condemning four virgins, supplicants sent to assuage his anger, to their deaths on the spears of his horsemen. The destruction of the city soon follows, although the Soldan and the King of Arabia (to whom Zenocrate is still betrothed) lead out an army to do battle with their oppressor. While this battle takes place offstage, Bajazeth and Zabina are rolled in to deliver curses against their torturers. Wild from hunger and despair, Bajazeth asks his queen to fetch him something to drink; while she is away, he brains himself against the bars of the cage. Zabina, returning from her errand, finds her husband's battered corpse and follows his lead. The horror of this double suicide no doubt satisfied the popular audience's appetite for gore, an appetite that Marlowe fed lavishly in this play.

The finale of the first part depicts Tamburlaine's victory over the Soldan, who is spared because the victor plans to crown Zenocrate Queen of Persia. Meanwhile, her betrothed, the King of Arabia, dies from battle wounds; his death causes little conflict, however, in Zenocrate, who follows Tamburlaine as if he were indeed her conqueror, too. Now the lowly shepherd-turned-king declares a truce, buries his noble opponents with solemn rites, and prepares to marry his beloved in pomp and splendor. He appears to stand atop Fortune's Wheel, a startling example of the Machiavellian man of iron will to whom no leader or law is sacrosanct. There is little sense here that Tamburlaine is intended as an example of pride going before a fall. He has achieved stunning victories over foes who are as immoral as he is; most of them, including Bajazeth, emerge as fools who miscalculate or underrate Tamburlaine with fearful consequences. No doubt the popularity of the play is traceable to this fact and to the truth that most people nurture an amoral desire for fame or power that this hero fulfills with startling success.

Part II shows Tamburlaine continuing on his road to conquest, securely characterizing himself as the Scourge of God. As the play opens, Sigismund, Christian King of Hungary, and the pagan monarch Orcanes agree to a truce. This ceremony strikes one as ironic, as pagans and Christians swallow their pride in order to challenge and defeat the half-god who threatens them. In the meantime, Tamburlaine proudly surveys the fruits of Zenocrate's womb: three sons through whom he hopes to win immortality. One of the brood, however, is weak and unattracted by war; Calyphas seems devoted to his mother and to the blandishments of peace. His effeminate nature foreshadows Tamburlaine's decline and fall, revealing that his empire cannot survive his own death. Even though his two other sons exhibit natures cruel enough to match their father's, the flawed seed has obviously been planted.

The hastily forged truce is suddenly broken when Sigismund tears the document and turns his forces on Orcanes. Though Marlowe appears to be attacking the integrity of Christianity, he was in fact appealing to his audience's anti-Catholic sentiments. When Sigismund is wounded and dies, moreover, Orcanes announces that Christ has won a victory in defeating one so treacherous as Sigismund. While these events transpire on the battlefield, another death is about to take place in Tamburlaine's tent. Zenocrate has been in failing health, and her imminent death causes her husband to contemplate joining her. That he should entertain such a gesture at the height of his power confirms the depth of his love for Zenocrate. Her imploring words—"Live still, my lord! O, let my sovereign live!"—manage to stay his hand, but his pent-up rage cannot be restrained at her death. Shifting from a figure of gentleness and compassion in a moment's time, Tamburlaine orders the town in which she dies to be burned to the ground.

With the defeat of Sigismund, Orcanes emerges as a kingmaker, leading the grand procession at which Callapine, the avenging son of Bajazeth, vows to use his new crown as the means to conquer the lowly Scythian. This scene is succeeded by another ceremonial pageant, this one led by the mournful Tamburlaine and his sons carrying the coffin of Zenocrate. Her body will remain with the company wherever they go in battle. Determined to teach his sons the arts of war, Tamburlaine commences a lesson in besieging a fort. When Calyphas balks, afraid of wounding or death, an angry father lances his own arm and orders his sons to dip their hands in his blood. All of them comply, although Calyphas is moved to pity at this horrid sight. With this ritual, Marlowe underscores the tribal nature of his hero's family but at the same time implies that the letting of blood by Tamburlaine will not necessarily cure the "defect" in it.

The central battle in the second part pits Tamburlaine and his sons against Callapine and his crowned kings before Aleppo. In a preliminary verbal skirmish, Tamburlaine belittles Almeda, a traitor, who cowers behind Callapine's back when invited to take his crown. The scene is serio-comic as Almeda proves himself a coward before his kingly followers; his weakness is meant to parallel that of Calyphas, Tamburlaine's son. The latter remains behind in a tent playing cards while his two brothers earn martial honors on the battlefield. When they and their father enter, trailing the conquered Turkish monarchs behind them, Tamburlaine seizes his weakling son and stabs him. Among the many scenes of bloodshed Marlowe presents in the play, this is probably the most shocking and repulsive. Although he cites his role as God's scourge and this deed as "war's justice," Tamburlaine here reveals a self-destructive side of his nature that has not been evident before.

The audience does not have long to ponder the murder; the scene of horror is quickly followed by one of pageantry. Trebizon and Soria, two pagan kings, enter the stage drawing a chariot with Tamburlaine holding the reins. This spectacle is accompanied by the superhero's disdaining words: "Holla, ye pamper'd jades of Asia!/ What can ye draw but twenty miles a day,/ And have so proud a chariot at your heels,/ And such a coachman as great Tamburlaine?" The monarch-prisoners hurl curses at their captors as, like Bajazeth and Zabina, they are taunted unmercifully. Tamburlaine's soldiers are rewarded with Turkish concubines, after which the royal train heads toward Babylon for yet another bloody siege.

Before the walls of this ancient city, Tamburlaine calls upon its governor to yield. (The scene recalls the negotiations before the walls of Damascus in Part I.) When he refuses, the lieutenants Techelles and Theridamas lead their soldiers in scaling the city's walls. The victory is quickly won, and Tamburlaine, dressed in black and driving his chariot, proudly announces the city's defeat. A quaking governor promises Tamburlaine abundant treasure if he will spare his life, but the conqueror disdains such bribes and has his victim hanged in chains from the walls. Theridamas shoots the governor while Tamburlaine proceeds to burn Muhammadan books in an open pit. Defying Mahomet to avenge his sacrilege if he has any power, Tamburlaine suddenly feels "distempered"; he recovers quickly, however, when he hears of Callapine's army advancing. Does Marlowe mean to imply that his hero's unexpected illness is punishment for his act of defiance? Although such an explicit moral lesson seems uncharacteristic, the connection between the two events appears to be more than a passing one.

The weakened Tamburlaine manages a final victory over Bajazeth's son, after which he produces a map that represents the extent of his conquests. With a trembling finger, he also directs his sons' attention to the remaining countries that they will be expected to conquer. Giving his crown to Theridamas (who later bestows it on Amyras) and turning his chariot over to his sons, Tamburlaine then calls for Zenocrate's hearse, beside which he stretches out to die. Before the mighty general's body is carried off, Amyras delivers the fitting eulogy: "Meet heaven and earth, and here let all things end,/ For earth hath spent the pride of all her fruit,/ And heaven consum'd his choicest living fire:/ Let earth and heaven his timeless death deplore,/ For both their worths will equal him no more." The death of the Scourge of Heaven follows no particular event; its suddenness only serves to underscore Tamburlaine's mortality. The audience is reminded of Alexander's demise in the midst of his glory. Because the chariot becomes such a dominant prop in the second part, Marlow may have likewise meant to suggest a parallel between his hero and Phaëthon, who in his pride fell from Jove's chariot because he could not control its course. Whatever the interpretation of this hero's fall, there can be little doubt that his mighty feats and his Senecan bombast made him an extremely popular—and awesome—figure on the Elizabethan stage.

For his next play, *The Jew of Malta*, Marlowe also chose an antihero who poses a threat to the orderly rule of European society. As Tamburlaine had ruled by martial strength, Barabas (named to recall the thief whose place on the Cross was taken by Christ) hopes to dominate the world by his wealth. Although Marlowe depicts him as a grasping, evil man (to the delight of the anti-Semitic Elizabethan audience), Barabas holds one's interest as Richard III does—by the resourcefulness of his scheming. Just as Tamburlaine's audacity appeals to an unconscious desire for power, so Barabas' scorn for Christian morality probably appealed to the audience's wish to defy authority. He is not portrayed, however, as a sympathetic character, even though in the early stages of the play, the behavior of his Christian opponents toward him reveals their hypocrisy. Faced with a threat from the powerful Turkish fleet, Ferneze, the Maltese governor, turns to Barabas for help in raising tribute money. While three of his colleagues agree to give up half of their estates and consent to baptism, Barabas refuses this arrangement, miscalculating the power and determination of the governor. Accompanied by a chorus of anti-Semitic remarks by the knights, Ferenze announces that he has already sent men to seize Barabas' property. He also declares that he intends to transform the Jew's mansion into a nunnery; this news further enrages Barabas, who curses them: "Take it to you, i' th' Devil's name." This scene highlights the hypocrisy of the Maltese; it also reveals the extent of Barabas' hatred for those among whom he has lived and worked. The audience has learned from the prologue spoken by Machiavel that the hero is one of his disciples and soon realizes that the subsequent action will show him "practicing" on his enemies.

When his daughter Abigail comes to recount angrily the takeover of their house, Barabas counsels patience, reminding her that he has hidden a fortune beneath its floorboards. In order to recover the money, he spawns a daring plan that requires his daughter to take vows as a means of entering the newly founded nunnery. In a heavily theatrical confrontation staged by Barabas, father accuses daughter of deserting him and their religion, while in an aside he tells her where to find the money. As Abigail is hurried into the mansion, she is spied by two young men, Mathias and Lodowick, both of whom fall in love with her—a rivalry that Barabas will later turn to his advantage. Later that night, Abigail appears on a balcony with Barabas' bags in her hands; she throws these down to him as he sees her and shouts: "O girl! O gold! O beauty! O my bliss!" This outburst illustrates the Jew's seriocomic nature, as he employs such impassioned speech to praise his gold. Eight years later, Shakespeare incorporated this trait into his characterization of Shylock in *The Merchant of Venice*.

In the square the next day, Barabas begins to practice in earnest against Ferneze. Ferneze's son Lodowick expresses his love for Abigail and is invited by Barabas to supper for a meeting with his "jewel." This dinner will prove Lodowick's undoing, as Barabas tells the audience in an aside. The Jew then proceeds to purchase the slave Ithamore, who will serve his master's will no matter what the command. In order to test the fellow, Barabas lists a remarkable catalog of evil deeds—including poisoning wells in nunneries—that he has supposedly committed. Ithamore responds by declaring himself in a league of villainy with the Jew: "We are villains both!—Both circumcised, we hate Christians both!" The slave aids his master by taking a forged challenge from Lodowick to Mathias, with whom Abigail is truly in love, even though her father has forced her to display affection for Lodowick. When the rivals meet to engage in a duel, Barabas is positioned above them, watching with pleasure as they kill each other.

Now, however, Ithamore and Abigail, whom he has told of the feigned challenge, know the extent of Barabas' treachery. In melodramatic fashion, the Jew decides that his daughter must die or she will reveal his deed; to kill her, he has Ithamore prepare a poisoned pot of rice to be "enjoyed" by all the nuns. To secure Ithamore's loyalty, Barabas promises him the whole of his inheritance, and he seems to adopt him as his son. The audience, however, knows from another aside that Barabas intends to kill his slave as well when the time is right. Ithamore does his master's bidding, but before Abigail dies, she gives proof of her father's guilt to Friar Bernardine (depicted as a lustful clown), who vows to confront the Jew with it, accompanied by Friar Jacomo. Barabas outwits these two fellows, assuring them that he wishes to be converted; as he did with Lodowick and Mathias, he starts the two men quarreling with each other. By means of a clever ruse devised with the aid of Ithamore, he also eliminates these potential enemies. As each of his schemes proves successful, Barabas celebrates more openly and melodramatically. In this play, unlike *Tamburlaine the Great*, the audience senses that the hero-villain will soon go too far, tripping up on some unforeseen obstacle. The audience is meant to experience this sense of impending doom, especially after the murder of the innocent Abigail, who converted to Christianity before her death. This deed establishes a parallel between Barabas and the biblical Herod, another murderer of innocents.

Meanwhile, Ithamore, aided by a pimp and his whore, tries to blackmail his master to feed the whore's expensive tastes. Barabas resolves to kill them all. Disguised as a French musician, he comes to the party at which Ithamore and the others are drunkenly planning to destroy the Jew. Barabas plays and sings, then tosses to the revelers a bouquet that he has dusted with poison. They smell it and they go ahead boldly in their plan to expose the Jew's actions. Before they die, they manage to tell Ferneze of Barabas' treachery; he and the others are led offstage, from where an officer quickly comes to tell of *all* of their deaths. The audience quickly learns, however, that Barabas has taken a sleeping potion and thus has deceived his enemies. Now intent upon revenge, he joins forces with the besieging Turks, showing them a way into the city through a hidden tunnel.

With a suddenness of movement that imitates the Wheel of Fortune, Ferneze is defeated and Barabas is appointed governor of the island by the Turks. Rather than torturing and killing the former governor, as might be expected, Barabas offers to return his power and destroy the Turks if Ferneze will pay him, which Ferneze agrees to do. The Jew then invites Calymath to a feast in celebration of their great victory. Hard at work in the hall, Barabas constructs an elaborate trap that he plans to spring on Calymath with Ferneze's help. When the moment arrives, however, the Maltese governor cuts a rope that causes Barabas to fall into the trap, a large cauldron filled with boiling liquid. Ferneze then arrests the Turkish leader, telling him that his troops have been surprised and killed in the monastery where they were housed. Amid the shouts and curses of the Jew—"Damn'd Christians, dogs, and Turkish infidels!"—the play ends in triumph for the Maltese citizens.

The Jew of Malta ends in the defeat of Machiavellian plotting. Even though he is a scheming villain throughout most of the action, however, Barabas might also be considered a near-tragic figure if one regards him as a man who degenerates in reaction to the evil done to him. In part, this reaction must follow from the behavior of Ferneze and Calymath; neither is morally superior to Barabas. He must honestly be described as the Elizabethan stereotype of a Jew, given to melodrama and sardonic humor. The audience feels no sympathy for him in his death, only a kind of relief that his destructive will has been defeated by someone capable of outwitting him. Although he finally overreaches himself, Barabas emerges as a totally fascinating villain, matched only by Shakespeare's Iago and Richard III.

In *The Massacre at Paris*, Marlowe depicts the episodic adventures of another antihero, the Guise, who is distinguishable from his predecessors only in representing the power of the Papacy. The character is based on a historical figure who was assassinated in 1588; the action recounts the infamous Saint Bartholomew's Day debacle of 1572, when hundreds of Huguenots were murdered by Catholic forces. The succession of victims, whom the Guise orders murdered ostensibly to please the Church, makes the audience recoil from the character and his motives. Lacking any comic element in his nature, he qualifies as a parodied Machiavel intent on disrupting the reign of Henry III, a lecherous and inept leader. The Guise's soliloquies show him to be in quest of an "earthly crown," which he believes he deserves because of his superior will and intelligence. What makes him different from Tamburlaine is his inability to control his passions and the behavior of those closest to him. In critical situations, his rhetoric fails him. His wife's affair with the king's favorite cuckolds the Guise; Henry delights in making the sign of the horns at him in public. Enraged at being made a figure of public ridicule, he arranges to kill his rival, an act that all but ensures his fall.

The man who stands in opposition to both the Guise and Henry III is King Henry of Navarre. Although his speeches lack the fire and melodrama that mark the Guise's outbursts, Navarre champions a Catholicism that is anticlerical, even fundamentalist. He also defends the principle of king and country, which the Guise and Henry seem to have forgotten in their quest for power. To prove his antipapal views, Navarre joins forces with Queen Elizabeth in an alliance the rightness of which Marlowe underscores by having a dying Henry III embrace it. This bit of manipulation has led some critics to argue that with this play, Marlowe was returning to his own Christian faith and was rejecting the amoral position taken by Tamburlaine. It is dangerous, however, to infer an author's beliefs from those held by his characters; there is no corroborating evidence in this case. There can be little doubt that Navarre is intended to be seen as a heroic character unlike any encountered in the other plays. If he is not Prince Hal, he is certainly Bolingbroke, a man who acts on principle and proves effective.

Even though the confrontation between Navarre and the Guise has about it all the elements of exciting drama, *The Massacre at Paris* is ultimately disappointing. The Guise's philosophy of seeking out perilous situations in order to test his strength of will does hold one's attention for a while, but the play offers none of the heroic bombast of a Tamburlaine or witty audacity of a Barabas. There is a great deal of bloodshed on the stage and off, but there is no clear purpose for the murders, no sense in which they forward some particular end in the plot. To complicate matters, the text that has survived is garbled; no amount of reconstructing can account for the missing links. While Marlowe may have been attempting a new dramatic design (some textual critics suggest that the original version was twice as long), *The Massacre at Paris* in its present form cannot be regarded as achieving the degree of pathos necessary to call it a successful tragedy.

In *Edward II*, however, such pathos can be found in the fateful careers of two men whose wills and hearts are sorely tested. Edward is presented as a man who is required to rule as king even though his weak nature disqualifies him from the task. As misfortune hounds him, he acquires humility and insight, which help to give him a more sympathetic personality than he had at the play's opening. He progresses toward self-understanding, and this transformation distinguishes him from more static characters such as Tamburlaine and Barabas. On the other hand, Mortimer, a man like Navarre who starts out professing deep concern for the destiny of his country, gradually loses the audience's sympathy as he becomes driven by ambition for the crown. This pattern of characterization charges *Edward II* with pathos of the kind Shakespeare would achieve in his tragedy *Richard II*, which was based on Marlowe's play and appeared a year after it.

Like Shakespeare, Marlowe turned to Raphael Holinshed's *Chronicles* (1577) to find the source material for *Edward II*. While earlier playwrights had attempted to transform the stuff of chronicle history into drama, Marlowe was the first to forge a dramatic design that is coherent and progressive. He presents a single theme—the struggle between Edward and his nobles—modulating it by means of the hero's victories and defeats. When Edward is finally overcome and the crown falls to his heir, he pursues Mortimer and his deceitful queen until revenge is won. In an ending unlike those of Marlowe's earlier plays, the accession of Edward III brings with it the promise of happier, more prosperous days. This exuberance at the close is a far cry from the condition of the state when the action begins. Gaveston, Edward's minion, seeks to divide his lover from the nobles not only for sexual reasons. He shows that he is ambitious and disdainful of his superiors. In an opening-scene confrontation (which Gaveston overhears), Edward defies the lords, announcing his intention to appoint Gaveston Lord High-Chamberlain. Edward's brother Kent at first supports him, telling the king to cut off the heads of those who challenge his authority. Yet by the close of the scene, when Edward has alienated the lords, the commons, and the bishops, Kent begins to wonder openly about his brother's ability to rule.

Mortimer, a man possessed by brashness, stands as the chief opponent to the king. He is begged by Queen Isabella not to move against the crown, even though she has been displaced by Gaveston. Mortimer is not alone in his opposition to the king's behavior; the Archbishop of Canterbury joins the peers in composing a document that officially banishes Gaveston. Although Edward rages against this rebellious act, he soon realizes that to resist might well lead to his own deposing. He is trapped because he has placed love for his minion above his concern for England. It is significant in this regard that Gaveston is both low-born and a Frenchman, which qualified him as a true villain in the eyes of Elizabethan Englishmen. Before the two men part, expressing vows that sound like those of heterosexual lovers, Edward turns to Isabella, accusing her (at Gaveston's prompting) of being involved in an affair with Mortimer. Tortured by her husband's harsh, and for the moment untrue, words, Isabella approaches the lords and, with Mortimer's aid, convinces them to rescind the banishment order. Edward rejoices, suddenly announcing plans to marry Gaveston to his niece; his enthusiasm is not shared by Mortimer and his father, who see this as another move to entrench Gaveston in royal favor. The minion's success also breeds Machiavellian ambition in younger courtiers, the audience learns from a short interlude involving Young Spencer and Baldock. This mirroring technique, by which lesser characters are observed copying the traits of the central figures, serves Marlowe's moral or instructive purposes in other plays as well.

When Gaveston returns in triumph, he expresses contempt for the "base, leaden earls" who greet him with a mocking recital of his newly acquired titles. Lancaster, then Mortimer and others, draw their swords and threaten Gaveston, an action that prompts Edward to order Mortimer from his court. A shouting match follows, sides are taken, and the earls set about planning how they will murder Gaveston. Fuel is added to the fire when Edward childishly refuses to ransom Mortimer's uncle, who has been captured by the Scots. (One can see in this episode parallels with the Hotspur-Henry IV quarrel in Shakespeare's *Henry IV, Part I*.) Rejecting his brother Kent's sound advice to seek a truce with the lords, Edward declares his intention to be revenged on them all, plotting openly with Gaveston to be rid of his enemies. By allowing himself to be driven by anger, Edward exhibits his political naïveté: His threat against Mortimer also alienates the people, to whom he is a hero. Furthermore, as Marlowe makes clear, the lords frequently express their desire to expel the king's favorite, not the king. It is important to realize that the playwright does not present the homosexual affair in an exploitative way; rather, he wants the audience to understand how Edward's blind defense of his "friendship" makes it easy for his enemies to rally to the cause.

The lords finally decide to move openly against Gaveston, whose whereabouts Isabella reluctantly reveals. Isabella's position has been made increasingly difficult by the king's claim that she and young Mortimer are lovers. Now her action seems to confirm Edward's suspicions, even though she affirms her love for the king and her son. When Gaveston is overtaken by his enemies—one of whom compares him to Helen of Troy—he is accused of being a common thief then given over to Warwick's custody, an act that assures his death. Rather than solving the country's problems, however, the removal of Gaveston exacerbates them. Edward quickly embraces the support of Young Spencer and Baldock, his new favorites, while continuing to ignore the incursions of Scots marauders and of the French King Valois, who has invaded Normandy. Marlowe here paints a vivid picture of the collapse of the body politic from internal and external forces. Yet when the inevitable civil war breaks out, Edward wins, proceeding quickly to take revenge against those "traitors" who opposed him. In his rage, however, he makes another mistake; rather than killing Mortimer, he imprisons him in the Tower, where his ambition (or *virtu*) has an opportunity to flower. With the aid of Edward's disgruntled brother Kent, Mortimer escapes to France to seek aid—along with Isabella—to restore England to her former health. It now appears that Isabella and Mortimer have joined forces to place Prince Edward on the throne. Yet as they leave the French court with promises of support, the queen and the young climber appear to have their own interests, not those of the king-dom, at heart.

Not surprisingly, Edward is easily defeated in a second encounter with the lords, bolstered as they are by the troops of Mortimer and Isabella. Isabella immediately proclaims Prince Edward the new "warden" of the realm, then turns the question of Edward's fate over to the lords. It is at this point that Marlowe begins portraying the deposed king in a more sym-pathetic light. When he is captured by Leicester, Edward, along with Young Spencer and Baldock, is disguised and begging sanctuary from an abbot. In these perilous straits, he still refuses to denounce his friendship with obvious parasites. As the Bishop of Winchester asks for his crown, deeming the act for "England's good," Edward suddenly refuses to take it from his head, accusing Isabella and Mortimer of outright rebellion. What makes Edward such a pitiful figure here is his inability to comprehend his part in creating the circumstances of his fall. He regards himself as a wronged innocent surrounded by wolfish traitors; this self-blindness pre-vents him from acting wisely and in the country's best interests. Although he lacks the spiritual dimensions of Shakespeare's King Lear, his jealous possession of the crown represents the same childlike faith in the object, not in the qualities which it represents. This attitude and the behavior that it engenders—a self-dramatizing resignation—lead to Edward's death.

References to the Wheel of Fortune fill the final scenes of *Edward II*. Mortimer and Isabella appear to have reached the Wheel's top, as both ac-tively plot Edward's death. Isabella emerges, however, as a mother deter-mined to see her son ascend the throne, while Mortimer clearly plots to seize power for himself. He determines that the deposed king must die, but he will act through subordinates rather than directly. Mortimer's tactics represent the victory of Machiavellianism, as he proceeds to rule through plotting and hypocrisy. He has Prince Edward crowned, declaring himself to be protector, then sends Lightborn and Matrevis to murder Edward. In a sad yet gruesome scene, the disheveled Edward is murdered in his jail bed when Lightborn places a table on top of him and jumps up and down on it. This horrible deed is quickly answered by Edward III, who arrests Mortimer, has him hanged and beheaded, and then places the head on his father's hearse. Isabella is sent to the Tower as the new king demonstrates the traits of strength and decisiveness that assure England's future glory. Edward III is a monarch who, like Shakespeare's Henry V, restores not only peace but also the values of patriotism and justice, which are necessary to the peaceful progress of the state.

In *Edward II*, Marlowe scores several successes. He creates a coherent play out of strands of historical material, lending pathos and poetic strength to the main character. He explores the depths of human emotions and depicts skillfully the ambiguous personalities of figures such as Isabella with consummate talent. He also reveals the effects of Machiavellianism in a personage, Mortimer, whose nature is more believable, less stereotyped, than those of Barabas or the Guise. These advances in dramaturgy not only lent tragic potency to *Edward II* but also prepared the way for Marlowe's most spectacular tragic achievement, *Doctor Faustus*.

A major obstacle in the path of critics of Marlowe's most popular melodrama, however, is the state of the text. Not published until eleven years after the playwright's death, the play was modified by "doctors" who were paid to add certain effects and delete others. To complicate matters further, an enlarged quarto edition was published in 1616; this version features alterations that suggest it may have been printed from the promptbook. Today's text is largely the work of Sir Walter Greg, who attempted a reconstruction of the play based on the extant quartos. The tragedy bears some resemblance to English morality interludes dealing with damnation and salvation. By selecting the Faustus myth, however, Marlowe was committed to portraying a story of damnation alone, with a hero who realizes too late the terrible consequences of selling his soul to the Devil. Indeed, the most impressive aspect of *Doctor Faustus* is its incisive treatment of the protagonist's tortured state of mind, which could easily be construed as an object lesson to sinners in the Elizabethan audience. Yet Marlowe was not preparing an interlude for the edification and instruction of simpleminded rustics. He was a daring, provocative artist exploring the character of a man who was legendary for his intellectual curiosity, for his intense desire to break the bonds of human knowledge and experience. As Irving Ribner so persuasively puts it (in his introduction to *The Complete Plays of Christopher Marlowe*, 1963): "*Doctor Faustus* is not a Christian morality play because it contains no affirmation of the goodness or justice of the religious system it portrays." This statement indicates how intimately related Doctor Faustus is to Tamburlaine, another Marlovian hero whose desire for knowledge and power sent him on a spectacular quest. While Tamburlaine, however, is able to win the prize—if only for a brief time—Doctor Faustus in fact falls from the position of social and spiritual prominence he holds at the play's opening. He is a victim of a system he chooses to defy; in that act of defiance, he begins almost immediately to deteriorate into a fool. The stages of that decline are carefully, ironically traced by Marlowe, who seems to want the audience to regard his hero's striving as a futile gesture. The play's ending, with Faustus being led away by devils who torture and then dismember him, offers no optimistic vision to the audience. *Doctor Faustus* thus stands as Marlowe's most pessimistic play, a tragedy that instructs its spectators in the dangers and ultimate limitations of the human imagination.

The play's opening (after an induction by a Senecan Chorus) finds Faustus in his study rejecting the orthodox or conventional disciplines and hungering for the demigod status of a magician. Even though he is cautioned against incurring God's anger by the Good Angel, Faustus invites two magicians, Valdes and Cornelius, to dine with him. In an effective bit of mirroring, Marlowe invents a servant named Wagner, who mimics the behavior of his master by behaving condescendingly toward two scholars who have come to warn Faustus about practicing the "damn'd art." One is struck throughout the play by the concern shown for the hero by his friends.

When Doctor Faustus manages to cast a spell and call up his servant Mephostophilis, the audience should quickly realize that he has made a bad bargain. Lucifer's messenger tells him directly that he desires the magician's soul and that Faustus will possess only the power the devils choose to give him. Unfortunately, Faustus' pride blinds him to the reality of the contract, which he signs with his own blood. He must forfeit his soul after twenty-four years of magic. In a humorous parallel scene, Wagner, too, calls up spirits and purchases the services of a clown, the burlesque counterpart of Mephostophilis. The slapstick underplot makes clear the ironic point: The servants control their masters and not vice versa.

While the Good Angel urges Faustus to repent, he instead boldly defies God and mocks the existence of Hell. His haughtiness begins to weaken, however, when second thoughts about the contract start to plague him. Supposing himself to be beyond salvation, Faustus instead turns to Mephostophilis for answers to questions about the creation of man and the world. In place of answers, Mephostophilis offers evasions and sideshows, such as the procession of the Seven Deadly Sins. Again a comic scene echoes the main action as Robin the Clown steals his master's conjuring books and invites Dick to turn invisible with him, in which state they plan to visit the tavern and drink all they wish without paying. References to bills and nonpayment throw into relief the predicament of the hero, whose "bill" must be paid with his life. When the audience next encounters Faustus, he is in fact supposed to be invisible as he visits a papal banquet, where he daringly strikes the pope and plays sophomoric tricks on the cardinals. The appeal of such anti-Catholic skits to a Protestant audience is obvious; Marlowe reinforces that point when he has Faustus help rescue the rival Pope Bruno from imprisonment. Yet even though he succeeds in puncturing the vanity of Rome, Faustus also reveals himself to be a second-rate showman rather than the demigod he had hoped to become. Marlowe accomplishes this effect by depicting his hero first in the papal setting; then in Emperor Charles' court, placing the cuckold's horns on the heads of three courtiers; and finally in a tavern, where he tricks a horse-courser into believing he has pulled off Faustus' leg.

This foolery has been heavily criticized by commentators as nothing more than an attempt to divert the mechanicals. Some have argued that the scenes involving Robin and the other clowns were in fact added by subsequent playwrights. There can be little doubt, however, that many of these scenes are intended to underscore the hero's decline and to foreshadow later events. The horse-courser's pulling off of Faustus' "leg" and the subsequent purchase of a mare that turns out to be a bale of hay foreshadow the hero's final dismemberment and comment on the bad bargain that Faustus has made with Lucifer. As in plays such as Shakespeare's *Henry IV, Part I*, burlesque business in the underplot of *Doctor Faustus* provides a more informal way of appreciating the thematic significance of the main action.

Marlowe also exhibits his expertise in using conventions of the Elizabethan stage to reinforce his main themes. At the court of Emperor Charles, Faustus creates a dumb show that depicts Alexander defeating Darius, then giving the defeated king's crown to his paramour. (While this action is taking place, Mephostophilis places the cuckold's horns on the head of Benvolio, one of the courtiers who has challenged Faustus' authority.) The dumb show celebrates the victory of a great warrior and is obviously intended as an elaborate compliment to the Emperor. Yet it also suggests how distant Faustus himself is from the noble stature of an Alexander; instead of performing great deeds—his original purpose—he can function only in the medium's role. This identity is reinforced in the climactic scene of the play, when Faustus requires Mephostophilis to conjure up Helen of Troy. She crosses the stage quickly, leaving Faustus unsatisfied. He is then approached by an old man who urges him to repent before it is too late. Stricken by these words and by his conscience, Faustus nearly commits suicide with a dagger that the invisible Mephostophilis conveniently places in his hand. The old man returns to stop him, but when he leaves the stage, Mephostophilis materializes and berates Faustus for his desperate attempt. Now believing himself beyond redemption and driven by desire, the magician calls again for Helen of Troy, whom he praises, kisses, and then leads away.

Several commentators believe this act of intercourse with a spirit (a succuba) damns Faustus unequivocally. His soul has become so corrupted as a result that it shares the demoniac spirit with the other devils. Marlowe, however, clearly wants his audience to believe that Faustus could save himself at any time should he decide to repent and ask forgiveness. The dilemma he faces is that he is torn between despair and faint hope; he never manages to decide on a course of action and take it. This depiction of man as a battleground for the forces of good and evil looks back to the morality plays and ahead to plays of psychological complexity such as Shakespeare's *Hamlet*. In the case of Doctor Faustus, the failure to repent allows Lucifer, Mephostophilis, and other devils to conjure up yet another vision, this time of a horror-filled Hell. Left alone on the stage, Faustus makes a pitiful attempt to slow the passage of time—"O, lente, lente, currite noctis equi!"—but now his magic has left him. This speech highlights one of the play's chief ironies: Twenty-four years have passed as quickly as twenty-four hours, the last one ticking away toward Faustus' doom. When the scholars who were Faustus' friends next enter, they find only his limbs, the grim remains of a man who thought himself to be a god. Hell turns out to be no fable for the damned hero.

Doctor Faustus certainly qualifies as Marlowe's major artistic and popular success. Its hero belongs with Marlowe's others by virtue of his defiance and his compelling rhetorical style. Taken as a whole, Marlowe's canon represents a crucial step forward in the development of Elizabethan dramaturgy. Without him, there could not have been a Shakespeare or a John Webster, both of whom learned something of the art of popular melodrama from this master. It is lamentable that Marlowe's early death deprived audiences and subsequent critics of more examples of his poetic drama, drama that stirs both the heart and the mind.

Other major works

POETRY: *Hero and Leander*, 1598 (completed by Chapman); "The Passionate Shepherd to His Love," 1599 (in *The Passionate Pilgrim*).

TRANSLATIONS: *Elegies*, 1595-1600 (of Ovid's *Amores*); *Pharsalia*, 1600 (of Lucan's *Pharsalia*).

Bibliography

Bakeless, John. *The Tragicall History of Christopher Marlowe*, 1942 (2 volumes).

Bevington, David. *From Mankind to Marlowe*, 1962.

Cole, Douglas W. *Suffering and Evil in the Plays of Marlowe*, 1962.

Ellis-Fermor, Una. *Christopher Marlowe*, 1927.

Godshalk, William L. *The Marlowe World Picture*, 1974.

Kocher, Paul H. *Christopher Marlowe: A Study of his Thought, Learning, and Character*, 1946.
Levin, Harry. *The Overreacher: A Study of Christopher Marlowe*, 1952.
Waith, Eugene. *The Herculean Hero in Marlowe, Chapman, Shakespeare, and Dryden*, 1962.
Wilson, F. P. *Marlowe and the Early Shakespeare*, 1954.

Robert F. Willson, Jr.

JOHN MARSTON

Born: Near Coventry, England; October 7, 1576 (baptized)
Died: London, England; June 25, 1634

Principal drama

Histriomastix: Or, The Player Whipt, pr. 1599, pb. 1610; *Antonio and Mellida*, pr. 1599, pb. 1602; *Antonio's Revenge*, pr. 1599, pb. 1602; *Jack Drum's Entertainment*, pr. 1600, pb. 1601; *What You Will*, pr. 1601, pb. 1607; *The Dutch Courtesan*, pr. 1603-1604, pb. 1605; *The Malcontent*, pr., pb. 1604; *Parasitaster: Or, The Fawn*, pr. 1604, pb. 1606 (commonly known as *The Fawn*); *Eastward Ho!*, pr., pb. 1605 (with George Chapman and Ben Jonson); *The Wonder of Women: Or, The Tragedie of Sophonisba*, pr., pb. 1606 (commonly known as *Sophonisba*); *The Insatiate Countess*, pr. c. 1610, pb. 1613 (completed by William Barksted).

Other literary forms

John Marston's satiric bent is apparent in his first publications: *The Metamorphosis of Pigmalion's Image and Certaine Satyres* (1598) and *The Scourge of Villainie* (1598). Indeed, the Pigmalion poem, ostensibly in the Ovidian amatory mode fashionable in the 1590's, is most interesting and effective as a satiric commentary on the very tradition that it purports to embrace. Underlying the familiar romantic paradigm of the sculptor's infatuation with his creation is the portrayal of an artist beset by what Marston calls a "fond dotage," a form of insanity. Pigmalion's inability to separate shade from substance is an obvious target for the unremitting satire that informs nearly all of Marston's work. Moreover, the poem's lurching oscillations between the genres of erotic epyllion and verse satire point to the stylistic confusion that mars several of Marston's plays.

Certaine Satyres and *The Scourge of Villainie* broaden the field of satire to include an entire world of corruption and decay, of dissolving social ties and religious values. Emotionally forceful, if not always structurally coherent, the satires parade a motley cast of characters representative of the assorted vices and foibles of fallen man. This dramatization of moral states, as well as an overriding obsession with sexual depravity and hypocrisy, carries over into Marston's plays.

Achievements

A ceaseless experimenter, Marston invested a variety of dramatic forms with the satiric, even mordant, worldview that originated in the late 1590's and came to define Jacobean drama. To study Marston, therefore, is to study the structural varieties of Elizabethan and Jacobean drama: the morality play in *Histriomastix*, revenge conventions in the Antonio plays, romantic comedy in *Jack Drum's Entertainment*, tragicomedy in *The Malcontent*, classical tragedy in *Sophonisba*. Marston's recurring dramatic strategy pits individual integrity against worldly corruption under hysterically theatrical conditions. His protagonists are often conscious role players, gambling for survival in a world not of their making, which they bitterly condemn. Fascinated by theatrical artifice, by shadings of illusion and reality, and by the interplay between actor and role, Marston speaks to the twentieth century as clearly as he did to his own. Despite the relatively infrequent performance of his plays, even in his own day, Marston's influence upon his contemporaries was profound, his uniquely strident voice echoing through the plays of John Webster, Cyril Tourneur, and John Ford, among others. A judicious assessment of his achievement must at least acknowledge, with Una Ellis-Fermor's *The Jacobean Drama* (1936, 1958), that Marston passed "on to the hands of masters the vision he himself could not express, transmitting to them images, phrases, situations which just fail in his hands of becoming poetry and with them become inevitable and immortal."

Biography

John Marston, the son of a prominent and prosperous lawyer, was christened on October 7, 1576. The exact date and place of his birth are unknown, although he surely passed his youth in Coventry, where his father, a distinguished member of the Middle Temple, was town steward from 1588 until his death in 1599. Little is known of Marston's early life until he matriculated at Brasenose College, Oxford, in 1592. Completing his bachelor of arts degree in 1594, he assumed residence in London at the Middle Temple, sharing his father's chambers and beginning to study law. That Marston would never practice law was apparent by 1599, when his father cautioned him "to foregoe his delighte in playes, vayne studdyes, and fooleryes." A resigned yet plaintive note creeps into the final version of his father's will, when, leaving his law books to his son, the dying man recalls his hope "that my sonne would have proffetted in the studdye of the lawe wherein I bestowed my uttermost indevor but man proposeth and God disposeth." Marston nevertheless continued to live in the Middle Temple, a not uncommon practice at a time when fewer than fifteen percent of the residents actually embraced law as a profession. No better place for witty companionship, lively debate, and satiric mockery could have been found; the influence of Middle Temple life was to shape Marston's entire literary output.

That output, as well as its early cessation, was perhaps regulated by the religious and political climate of the era. The bishops' ban on satiric and erotic poems in 1599 may have prompted Marston's shift to playwriting in the same year. In 1605, Jonson and Chapman were jailed for their jibes in

Eastward Ho! against James I and the Scots, although the offending material might as easily have been Marston's. When the king, insulted by attacks against him in two plays, one of which may have been Marston's *The Fawn*, closed all London theaters in March, 1608, he vowed that the offending playwrights should "never play more but should first begg their bred and he wold have his vow performed." This time Marston could not avoid the punishment he had luckily escaped in 1605; he was committed to Newgate Prison. He wrote no plays thereafter.

From the time of his 1606 marriage to Mary, daughter of the Reverend William Wilkes, one of King James's favorite chaplains, Marston had given up his Middle Temple lodgings to reside at the Wiltshire living of his father-in-law. Whether it was that churchman's influence, the fear of the king's wrath, or the natural evolution of a moral habit of mind that led Marston into holy orders is unclear. In any event, the playwright severed his theatrical connections in 1608 by selling his shares in the Blackfriars Theatre. He was ordained as a deacon in September, 1609, and as an Anglican priest later that year, on Christmas Eve. Thereafter, Marston surfaced from his provincial clerical duties only briefly in 1633 to demand the withdrawal of an unauthorized collection of six of his plays. Marston died in London on June 25, 1634; his epitaph, *Oblivioni Sacrum*, recalls his early dedication "To Everlasting Oblivion" from *The Scourge of Villainie*. By the time of his death, Marston had long since put behind him that "delighte in plays, vayne studdyes and fooleryes" of which his father had despaired.

Analysis

John Marston's entire dramatic career can be read as an attempt to adapt the materials of Renaissance formal satire to the stage. While his output reveals no neat gradations of development, it falls conveniently into two general divisions: those plays from *Histriomastix* through *What You Will*, crowded into the years between 1599 and 1601, and those that followed, ending with Marston's retirement from the theater. Perhaps the 1601-1604 hiatus constituted a period of artistic reflection and consolidation for Marston; in any event, the later plays seem clearly more successful in their integration of satiric materials and dramatic form.

Whatever their relative success as dramatic vehicles, Marston's plays characteristically advance his moral vision by means of a potent mixture of satiric denunciation and exaggerated theatricality; the grotesque savagery of his early imagery was remarkable even in an age when harsh rhetoric was the norm. While Marston's satirists never lose their hard-edged scorn, they are gradually transformed from irresponsible railers lashing out at anyone or anything that angers them into responsible critics of men and manners. Marston's targets are legion, but they all inhabit the world of city or court, "of perverted or wasted work, ruins and catacombs, instruments of torture and monuments of folly," as Northrop Frye describes the typical satiric world in *The Anatomy of Criticism* (1957).

The crucial task for Marston the dramatist is to find appropriate modes of theatrical expression for his essentially mordant worldview. Since no single attitude is proof against the rapacious onslaughts of human wickedness, the playwright is forced into constant shifts of rhetoric and tone. These, in turn, produce a drama of wrenching extremes in which tragedy is forever collapsing into melodrama and comedy into farce. At the heart of the drama is usually found Marston's mouthpiece, a satiric commentator living painfully in a fallen world whose vices he condemns and whose values he rejects. Often disguised, the satirist proceeds by seeming to embrace, even to prompt, the very crimes and foibles which he savagely denounces. His disguise symbolizes the chasm between being and seeming wherein lies the hypocrisy to be discovered and exposed; moreover, it allows the fitful starts and stops, the aesthetic and moral twists embodied in the deliberate theatricality of Marston's seriocomic vision.

The dangerously insecure and deceptive worldview of the plays invites the growing misanthropy of Marston's satire. Feelings of guilt and revulsion define bodily functions and poison sensual delights. Una Ellis-Fermor argues in *The Jacobean Drama*:

> There proves, upon analysis, to be an almost overwhelming preponderance of images from the body and its functions, sometimes normal but more often images of disease, deformation or maiming; these make up more than a third of the total imagery of one play [*Antonio and Mellida*] and give a clue, if not to Marston's conscious thought, at least to his unconscious preoccupations.

Dramatic action takes place in a nightmare world of brutal lust and violent intrigue where darkness cloaks venal and shameful deeds. Women, once incidental factors in man's degeneracy, increasingly become repositories of perverted desire, culminating in the animalistic Francischina of *The Dutch Courtesan*. Social intercourse consists mainly of manipulations and betrayals from which Marston's dramatic persona finds refuge only in the impassive self-containment of stoicism. When neither stoicism nor withdrawal can protect Sophonisba from the spreading stain of worldly corruption, Marston's last heroine elects the only remaining moral refuge: suicide. It is an ironically apt solution to the problem of acting in a depraved world, and it highlights the central theme of Marston's plays: the moral cost of living in such a world.

Marston's early plays experiment with various dramatic forms: the morality play in *Histriomastix*, romantic comedy in *Jack Drum's Entertainment*, the revenge play in *Antonio's Revenge*. Chiefly interesting as attempts to find appropriate vehicles for satiric commentary, they contain many of the theatrical ingredients but little of the dramatic power of Marston's master-piece, *The Malcontent*.

The Malcontent depicts the morally debilitated world of *What You Will* and the Antonio plays; here, however, the characters are neither the mere labels for the commonplace ideas of *What You Will* nor the tenuous projections of the satiric background of the Antonio plays. In the central figure of Malevole-Altofronto, Marston has created the perfect objective correlative for his worldview. That view is embedded in the structure of *The Malcontent*, which continues and amalgamates *Antonio and Mellida* and *Antonio's Revenge*. Eddying between comedy and tragedy, *The Malcontent* employs all the Senecan sordidness, theatrical self-consciousness, and satiric commentary of its predecessors. Ostensibly, *The Malcontent* is a revenge play at the heart of which Altofronto, deposed Duke of Genoa, assumes the disguise of Malevole in order to regain his dukedom from the usurper Pietro, who, in turn, is the tool by which the scheming Mendoza advances his own ducal ambitions. Unlike the typical revenge play, which culminates in the hero's bloody reprisals, *The Malcontent* achieves a fragile harmony based upon the hero's modified goals, for this revenger seeks to reform rather than to destroy. Undeniably bitter at his dispossession, Altofronto is nevertheless driven as much by the will to rejuvenate his enemies as to reclaim his rule. A victim of deception and intrigue, Altofronto must learn to deceive his deceivers. The mask of Malevole becomes a strategy for survival in the ridiculous yet hazardous world created by fallen man. That world is defined by the sexual corruption of Aurelia, Pietro's unfaithful wife; of Ferneze, her lustful lover, who competes with Mendoza for her favor; of Biancha, who distributes her favors wholesale; and of Maquerelle, the overripe procuress, no less than by the sinister plotting of Pietro and Mendoza.

Altofronto's mask is so firmly in place from the outset that a considerable portion of the first act transpires before Malevole reveals his true identity to the "constant lord," Celso. By this time, he has already tortured Pietro by disclosing Aurelia's adultery with Mendoza. Liberated by the traditional role of the malcontent, Malevole will continue to castigate the corruption which he exposes. Malevole shapes the play even as he is shaped by its demands: It is in the service of reform that he spotlights human vice and folly. The essentially passive satirist, periodically intruding into other characters' stories, now emerges as the hero of the play whose still biting commentary is crucial to its action. When Malevole, who has been hired by Mendoza to solicit Altofronto's "widow," Maria, and to murder Pietro, reveals the depth of Mendoza's perfidy to the horrified Pietro, the latter disguises himself as a hermit and returns to court to announce his own death. Mendoza now moves swiftly to consolidate his rule, banishing Aurelia, sending Malevole off to urge his case to the imprisoned Maria, and hiring the hermit to poison Malevole, who in turn is ordered to poison the hermit. Forced into a horrified recognition of the depraved world that he has helped create, Pietro is not even permitted the solace of Aurelia's sincere repentance before Malevole's savage castigation of earth as "the very muckhill on which the sublunarie orbs cast their excrement" and man as "the slime of this dongue-pit." This episode at court and its aftermath typify Malevole's practice of moral surgery: positioning characters first to confront their own depravity, then to repent of it, and finally to excise it. Malevole's manipulations fittingly culminate in the court masque that ends the play. Ordered by Mendoza to celebrate his accession to power, the masque becomes the vehicle of his undoing. The masquers reveal themselves as Mendoza's apparent murder victims and Malevole, again Altofronto, reclaims Maria and his dukedom. Such characters as Pietro, Aurelia, and Ferneze, truly contrite and repentant, are freely pardoned; others, such as Maquerelle and the knavish old courtier, Bilioso, are banished from court. Mendoza, reduced to cravenly begging for his life, is contemptuously, and literally, kicked out.

Altofronto's intricate role-playing and manipulations have brought concord out of discord. By consciously delimiting his revenge, by constantly pointing to the absurdity of human action, and by the consummate theatricality not only of his gestures but also of his double role, he transforms the revenge play into a vehicle for social conciliation.

In *The Dutch Courtesan*, Marston abandons the satiric furor and Italianate intrigues of *The Malcontent* for exuberant comedy. While its dramatic material is undeniably lighter, *The Dutch Courtesan* is equally successful in its depiction and analysis of human nature. The play's moral center is Freevill, who plans one last visit to Francischina, the courtesan of the title, before settling down to married life with the angelic Beatrice. Outraged by Freevill's loose conduct, Malheureux goes along in order to admonish Francischina and dissuade his friend. A chilly, puritanical, and inexperienced young man, Malheureux is jolted from his moral complacency at first sight of the courtesan, whom he immediately longs to possess. When Francischina demands Freevill's murder as the price of her favors, the distressed Malheureux confesses his plight to his friend. Concluding that only strong medicine can restore Malheureux to his senses, Freevill concocts a bizarre plot. The friends stage a quarrel, after which Freevill goes into hiding. Claiming Francischina's favors as his promised reward for killing Freevill, Malheureux is deceived when she betrays him to the law. Meanwhile, Freevill has vanished, and with him, the corroborating evidence of the hoax. Condemned to hang, Malheureux is saved only at the gallows by Freevill, who justifies his friend's anguish as the price that must be paid for moral enlightenment.

The Dutch Courtesan is a comic morality play whose end is psychological and social, rather than religious, salvation. It proceeds by establishing a dialectic between love and lust, defined at the outset by Freevill, who sees no moral inconsistency between his former lust for Francischina and his present love for Beatrice. Whoring, no less than marriage, is a valid expression of man's nature. This Malheureux denies, arguing for a rigid line of demarcation between virtue and vice and thereby against the reality of the human condition. A "snowy" man of cloistered virtue, Malheureux must be brought face-to-face with an exemplum of his folly in the alluring person of Francischina. Undeniably a good man, as evidenced by his refusal to betray Freevill at Francischina's behest, Malheureux must be brought to the foot of the scaffold to attain self-knowledge. Regarding himself as above passion, he becomes "passion's slave"; proffering himself as Freevill's moral tutor, he becomes his moral pupil. One of Marston's most effective characterizations, he mirrors the playwright's moral torment. Regarding lust as the deadliest sin, his imagination nevertheless dwells on the loose sexuality he abhors. Shocked by the moral degeneracy of the beautiful Francischina, he eddies between frantic desire and consuming guilt. In this drama of initiation, Malheureux, like his creator, must learn to recognize and control his natural desires, not to annihilate them.

These lessons are farcically reinforced in a brilliant subplot that features Cocledemoy's gulling of the affected pseudo-Puritans, the Mulligrubs. By causing Mulligrub's false arrest for thievery and effecting his victim's release only at the point of execution, Cocledemoy, like Freevill, exposes and cauterizes moral absolutism. This subplot, combined with Tysefew's bantering wooing of Beatrice's sister, Crispinella, also functions to preserve the play's light tone.

By introducing a purely comic subplot, by inflating Malheureux's rhetoric, by layering Francischina's diatribes with a thick Dutch accent, and by establishing Freevill's beneficent control of the action, Marston invokes a world of comic absurdity as he dissipates its potential tragedy. A perceptive study in sexual psychology, *The Dutch Courtesan* balances and expands its author's moral vision.

The Fawn, Marston's frothiest comedy, recapitulates that vision and its modes of achievement. Like *The Dutch Courtesan*, it treats the perverted natural instincts resulting from repressed or misdirected sexuality; it also employs a double plot no less sophisticated than its predecessor's. Like *The Malcontent*, it is set in an Italian court corroded by folly and flattery; its hero is a disguised duke bent on reform. *The Fawn*'s lighter tone stems primarily from its unthreatened duke and its more farcical than sinister court intrigues.

Hercules, Duke of Ferrara, appears at the court of Gonzago, Duke of Urbin, disguised as Faunus, the consummate flattering courtier and a member of his son Tiberio's retinue. Tiberio's ostensible mission is to negotiate the marriage of Gonzago's fifteen-year-old daughter, Dulcimel, to his sixty-four-year-old father. Actually, Duke Hercules hopes that Dulcimel's charms will arouse his unnaturally aloof son to woo the girl for himself; to ensure that end, he monitors the action as Faunus. Because Dulcimel immediately falls in love with Tiberio and sets out to awaken the young man's latent feelings, Faunus is freed to deal with the corruption and hypocrisy of the court; nearly half the play is devoted to providing him with appropriate occasions to practice the art of flattery on the unsuspecting courtiers. Lulled into freely confessing their follies, Faunus' victims indirectly satirize themselves. Since vanity rather than Machiavellian intrigue marks Urbin's court, Faunus contents himself with exposing grotesqueries rather than reviling corruption. The stuff of satire—Nymphadora's claim to be the world's great lover, Herod's assertion of superiority, Dosso's impotence and his wife Garbetza's adultery with his brother, Zuccone's jealousy of his estimable wife Zoya—takes the form of sexual foibles. That these sins are merely skin-deep allows Marston to turn his satiric commentator from savage railer to witty practitioner of the courtly games he plans to expose. Moreover, the sexual waywardness of the minor characters functions as an implicit comment upon the sexual backwardness of Tiberio. The double plot of *The Fawn* therefore proceeds along parallel tracks, Faunus dealing with sexual excess, Dulcimel with sexual indifference. Successful resolution depends upon the ability of Faunus and Dulcimel to awaken Gonzago to the folly around him—his own as well as his court's.

Gonzago, Duke of Urbin, is one of Marston's most inspired comic creations. Delighting in words and garrulous in conversation, he imagines himself the consummate rhetorician. His several long-winded speeches, studded with odd bits of classical lore, are designed to bolster his self-image of a learned man of ripe wisdom; instead, they reveal him as an unknowing self-flatterer and, therefore, as a potential gull. Dulcimel plays upon her father's vanity to promote the very affair he would frustrate, using him as a go-between to inform the slow Tiberio of her interest. Shamelessly flattered by his daughter, Gonzago becomes her unwitting instrument; "hee shall direct the Prince the meanes the very way to my bed." Through four acts, Dulcimel, like Faunus, wields the weapon of flattery. "Dulcimel is not conducting an experiment in moral reformation through her flattery, but in the fifth act the Fawne exploits her work and draws the duke into the web in which he has trapped the rest of his victims," notes Philip Finkelpearl in *John Marston of the Middle Temple* (1969).

The final act is played on a two-level stage: Tiberio climbs a "tree" to join Dulcimel above, while Hercules remains below. The marriage of the young lovers presumably coincides with the several judgments rendered by Cupid's Parliament. Symbolic of healthy and natural love, the union of Dulcimel and Tiberio implicitly condemns the courtiers, who have violated

Cupid's laws. Paraded before the court and arraigned upon Faunus' evidence, they are exposed and released. Finally, Gonzago is indicted for his pretensions to wisdom and, more serious, for his attempts to obstruct life's natural flow. "What a slumber have I been in," cries the duke, whose court promises to be healthier hereafter.

In its comic characterizations, in its tonal consistency, and in its technical assurance, *The Fawn* is a masterly achievement. Marston's fusion of satiric force and content, apparent in *The Malcontent* and *The Dutch Courtesan*, is no less perfect in *The Fawn*.

Sophonisba is Marston's attempt at high Roman tragedy. Full of high moral sentiment expressed in consistently lofty verse, it impressed T. S. Eliot as Marston's best play. Its purpose, implicit in its alternate title, *The Wonder of Women*, is to portray human perfection in the person of its heroine, Sophonisba. To evoke her ideal virtue, Marston employs his characteristic tactic of pitting individual honor and integrity against a corrupt world. It is in the altered relationship between character and context, however, that *Sophonisba* embodies Marston's tragic design. Earlier protagonists manipulated adversaries and events; Sophonisba is victimized by them. A Malevole or a Hercules recognized surrounding evil, satirically castigated it, and finally dispersed or reformed it. Sophonisba, no less perceptive, can only reaffirm her virtue in a world whose evil she cannot alter and can evade only by suicide. The wildly chaotic settings for court intrigues have yielded to a harder, more frightening world of realpolitik.

Before the end of the second act, the main characters and the political world they inhabit are sharply defined. A note of discord is struck early, when the news that Carthage has been invaded disrupts the nuptials of Sophonisba and the famed Carthaginian general Massinissa. When she selflessly postpones marital consummation in the face of her husband's martial duty, she elicits the first of his many expressions of awe at her character: "Wondrous creature, even fit for Gods, not men...a pattern/ Of what can be in woman." Much of the remainder of the play consists of tableaux that present repeated assaults upon Sophonisba's unassailable virtue, each designed to spotlight her moral grandeur. In similar fashion, political evil surfaces in the scene immediately following Massinissa's departure for battle. No sooner does he leave than the senators of Carthage plot to betray him and Sophonisba for an alliance with the powerful Syphax. Their treachery backfires when Syphax, driven by lust for Sophonisba, who had earlier rejected him, deserts his army in his frenzy to reach her. Syphax's forces defeated, Massinissa and Sophonisba are reunited. Their happiness is, however, as illusory as it is brief. Syphax, his lust frustrated by Sophonisba's virtue and his prestige tarnished by Massinissa's victory in single combat, conceives a final act of vengeance. Arguing, ironically, that Sophonisba's virtues of loyalty to Carthage and constancy to Massinissa will tempt the latter to break his oath of allegiance to Rome, Syphax convinces the Roman general Scipio to demand that she be delivered up to Roman captivity. Confounded by the excruciating choice of betraying his allies or his wife, Massinissa crumbles. No such dilemma exists for Sophonisba, whose immediate decision to commit suicide implicitly condemns her husband's failure to do so. A good and courageous man, albeit Sophonisba's moral inferior, Massinissa is reduced to mixing the poisoned wine for her supremely stoic gesture. Eulogizing her—"O glory ripe for heaven"—he measures her distance from ordinary mortals.

The meaning of Sophonisba's suicide transcends its dramatic function of saving Massinissa by eliminating his moral dilemma. For Marston's heroine, suicide is a welcome escape from "an abhord life" of Roman captivity; it has become virtue's only possible response to the world's depravity. For the playwright, her death creates a dramatic impasse. An obsessive moralist from the outset of his literary career, Marston found in satiric comedy the means of exposing, castigating, and reforming evil. Abandoning satire for pure tragedy, he traps Sophonisba in a world of omnipresent evil which she can recognize but not alter. Thus, the final outcome of the struggle of individual integrity against the corrupt world is martyrdom. After *Sophonisba*, Marston's eventual desertion of the stage for the pulpit may have been the only viable extension of that struggle.

Other major works

POETRY: *The Metamorphosis of Pigmalion's Image and Certaine Satyres*, 1598; *The Scourge of Villainie*, 1598.

Bibliography
Caputi, Anthony. *John Marston, Satirist*, 1961.
Ellis-Fermor, Una. *The Jacobean Drama*, 1936, 1958.
Finkelpearl, Philip J. *John Marston of the Middle Temple*, 1969.
Ingram, R. W. *John Marston*, 1978.
Kernan, Alvin. *The Cankered Muse: Satire of the English Renaissance*, 1959.
Kirsch, Arthur C. *Jacobean Dramatic Perspectives*, 1972.

Lawrence S. Friedman

EDWARD MARTYN

Born: Masonbrook, Ireland; January 31, 1859
Died: Dublin, Ireland; December 5, 1923

Principal drama

The Heather Field, wr. c. 1893, pr., pb. 1899; *Maeve*, pb. 1899, pr. 1900; *An Enchanted Sea*, pb. 1902, pr. 1904; *The Place-Hunters*, pb. 1902; *The Tale of a Town*, pb. 1902, pr. 1905; *Romulus and Remus*, pb. 1907; *Grangecolman*, pr., pb. 1912; *The Dream Physician*, pr., pb. 1914.

Other literary forms

Edward Martyn is known exclusively as a playwright, although he also published a novel, *Morgante the Lesser* (1890), under the pseudonym "Sirius." The novel's combination of wit and scatology makes Martyn a remote relation of Jonathan Swift and François Rabelais, and as a shaggy-dog story, it owes a debt to Laurence Sterne. In addition, the novel belongs to a rich Gaelic and Anglo-Irish tradition of satires on learning. Its interest is confined exclusively to literary history, however, thanks to its turgid style and flaccid pace. Perhaps its most surprising aspect is its authorship. Nothing in the rigorous Ibsenite realism of his major plays, or in the ascetic idealism of his private life, would lead one to suspect that Martyn ever perpetrated a work which might well be ascribed to Alfred Jarry.

Achievements

Martyn has a permanent, if minor, place in the history of the Irish Literary Revival. As this cultural phenomenon undertook no less than to change, or indeed to review, the mind of a nation, a minor contribution to it should not necessarily be considered negligible. William Butler Yeats, in one of his summaries of Martyn's achievements, dismissively mentions Martyn merely as one of Lady Augusta Gregory's neighbors who "paid for our first performances" (those, that is, of the Irish Literary Theatre, the company, which, in 1904, became the Abbey Theatre). In fact, Martyn was a founding member of the Irish Literary Theatre, and his play *The Heather Field* was the company's second production. Moreover, Martyn brought to the company a set of theatrical ideals, heavily influenced by the drama of Henrik Ibsen, which offered an alternative to Yeats's concept of "peasant drama." This alternative remained underdeveloped, and partly as a result, Martyn's playwriting career stagnated. In *The Heather Field*, however, Martyn demonstrated, intriguingly but embryonically, how his approach could have spoken in realistic terms about contemporary Irish idealism.

Far from being merely the nascent Irish theater's well-disposed financier, Martyn was as committed to the Revival as was any of its other initiators.

Despite more lasting contributions to other spheres of Irish culture and the fact that he was, by temperament, better equipped to be a critic than an artist, Martyn's position in the anterooms of fame is assured. He gave significant impetus to one of the twentieth century's most distinctive theatrical undertakings.

Biography

Edward Martyn was born to an illustrious family of Irish Catholic aristocrats at Masonbrook, near Loughrea, County Galway, on January 31, 1859. His father died the following year, and Edward and his brother were reared in the Martyn family home, Tulira Castle (which he subsequently inherited).

When Martyn was eight years old, the family moved to Dublin, where Martyn briefly attended Belvedere College. A further move, to London, led to his enrollment, in 1870, at Beaumont College, Windsor (like Belvedere, a prominent Jesuit school). Completing his secondary education in 1876, Martyn—in an unusual move for a Catholic—entered Christ Church College, Oxford, in 1877. There he had an undistinguished career and left, without taking his degree, in 1879, though not before falling under the influence of the aesthetic philosophy of Walter Pater.

The following year found Martyn in Paris, in the company of his cousin and subsequent nemesis, the Irish novelist George Moore. Paris gave him access to such contemporary artistic movements as Symbolism and Impressionism (Martyn had an important collection of Impressionist paintings, notably of works by Edgar Degas). Extensive travel in Europe put him in touch with other important cultural developments, such as Wagnerism and Hellenism. The latter proved an important enthusiasm on Martyn's return to Tulira Castle, and he divided his time between Tulira and London artistic circles, in which he cultivated the acquaintance of, among others, Arthur Symons and Aubrey Beardsley.

In 1885, however, Martyn underwent a spiritual crisis of some severity, resulting in the replacement of virtually all the modern tastes which he had formed with a more pious and ascetic regimen. The most important survivors of this reevaluation were the drama of Ibsen and the music of Giovanni Palestrina. It is tempting, with this crisis in mind, to view Martyn's contribution to the Irish Literary Theatre as, in part, rehabilitative. The crisis certainly contributed to the scathing attitude, and essentially inchoate argument, of his pseudonymous novel, *Morgante the Lesser*.

The Irish Literary Theatre was founded by Yeats, Martyn, and Lady Gregory in 1899, and in its early days, Martyn, as well as Yeats, was its principal playwright. By 1902, however, Martyn had resigned from the venture, partly because of artistic differences with Yeats, but partly also because of the arrival of George Moore. (Moore was later to subject Martyn to merciless satire in his three-volume memoir of those years, *Hail and Fare-well*, 1911-1914—treatment to which Martyn eventually responded in kind in *The Dream Physician*.)

The matter at issue between Moore and Martyn was the latter's play *The Tale of a Town*. In response to Yeats's criticism of it, Moore revised the piece, which was then staged under the title *The Bending of the Bough* (pr. 1900). After resigning from the Irish Literary Theatre, Martyn continued his playwriting career. He directed a large share of his energies to other areas of Irish culture, however, particularly to music.

In 1902, after protracted negotiations, the Palestrina Choir was established at the Pro-Cathedral, Dublin. The choir was exclusively Martyn's idea, and at the time of its inauguration he referred to it as "the chief interest of my life." This interest reflected an unorthodox approach to bringing art to the people. A unique expression of the Irish Literary Revival's ethos, the choir was financed almost exclusively by Martyn. As a result of this venture's success, Martyn devoted further time and money to beautifying provincial churches with tapestries, stained glass, and similar ornamentation.

After his break with Yeats and Moore, Martyn also developed a strong interest in, and commitment to, the Gaelic League, an organization devoted to the restoration of the Irish language. Martyn believed Irish to be second only to Greek among the languages of man; as a practical expression of his commitment, he set about rehabilitating traditional Irish music. He was instrumental in organizing an annual outlet for amateur performers called Feis Ce oil (music festival). At one of these, a tenor named James Joyce performed. Perhaps the most substantial expression of Martyn's involvement with the non-Yeatsian Revival was his presidency of Sinn Fein (the Revival's political manifestation) from 1904 to 1908.

In 1906, Martyn helped establish the Theatre of Ireland. Its principles were identical to those of the more successful Irish Theatre, which Martyn founded in 1914, assisted by Thomas MacDonagh and Joseph Plunkett, both of whom were executed for their parts in the Easter Rising of 1916. These principles echo Martyn's lifelong admiration of drama which was intellectual in theme and which availed itself of contemporary European dramaturgical models. Despite numerous vicissitudes, the Irish Theatre managed to remain open until 1920.

Martyn's activities on behalf of the Irish Theatre marked the end of his public life. He died in Dublin on December 5, 1923, a lonely and neglected figure. He was unmarried.

Analysis

Edward Martyn made his name as a dramatist with *The Heather Field*, and his subsequent works comprise a series of not very startling variations on that play. Without being autobiographical, *The Heather Field* draws on important features of Martyn's life. It is set in the wild country of the author's native western Ireland. The action takes place in the context of the Land War, as the struggle between peasants and landlords over conditions of tenure was called. The play is not absolutely contemporaneous with the events it relates; the Land War was at its height from the late 1870's to the mid 1880's, and had simmered down considerably by the turn of the century. Nevertheless, the play's references to events still fresh in the minds of an Irish audience emphasize Martyn's rejection of prehistoric material as the vehicle of his vision and have something in common with the belief of James Joyce (another Ibsenite) that art may be won from the life of one's own unpromising times. This belief is implicit in all of Martyn's plays. Regardless of whether one accepts that the handling of the belief conforms to the tenets of realism, the plays' intellectual bases are firmly grounded in realism.

In addition, the protagonist of *The Heather Field*, Carden Tyrrell, is a landlord, as Martyn himself was. He is given a surname whose Irish associations are as notable in their own right as is the name Martyn. Tyrrell is provided with one of Martyn's own formative experiences, that of hearing exalted song from the choir of Cologne Cathedral. Tyrrell is also an "improving" landlord—that is, one who takes an interest in his property (which a great number of Irish landlords did not). In fact, the play contains an unexamined paradox concerning Tyrrell's social commitments: He makes every effort to reclaim land and enlarge his holdings, yet he is notably unsympathetic to the causes of the Land War. This paradox is subsumed under the more divisive and irreconcilable aspects of Tyrrell's case. Martyn is less interested in his protagonist's social situation than in his psychological condition. It should be noted, however, that *The Heather Field* is an important step forward in the representation of typical Irish types not as figures of fun but as serious embodiments of predicaments experienced by the majority of conscious humanity. By remaining faithful to conditions with which he was intimately familiar, Martyn helped to enlarge the stock of Irish dramatic characters; by dignifying stereotypes, he offered the basis for a new dramatic perspective on Irish life.

The plot of *The Heather Field* is somewhat spare. Tyrrell conceives an overweening ambition to reclaim the wild, infertile areas of his demesne. To this end, he has risked his fortune draining the heather field of the title. This project is, ostensibly, a success: Productive grass has evidently supplanted pretty, barren heathland. As a result, Tyrrell is determined to go forward and put the whole of his property in financial jeopardy in order to expand his reclamation scheme. Barry Ussher, a friend and neighbor, attempts to dissuade Tyrrell from his rash ambition, but to no avail. Moreover, Tyrrell's wife, Grace (like most of Martyn's protagonists, Tyrrell is unsuitably married, a fate which the author himself assiduously avoided), is aggressively opposed to the scheme, so much so that she attempts to have her husband certified as insane. Only the timely intervention of Barry Ussher thwarts such a development, Tyrrell being so engrossed in his dream of fertility that he cannot perceive Grace's tactics or defend himself against the two doctors summoned to the house to carry out Grace's design. As events reveal, however, official certification of insanity becomes a formality. In the third act, spring has come round again and with it the triumph of heather over grass. The result is that Tyrrell, refusing to accept that nature has declined to answer his needs, loses his mind; he cannot tell past from present, or anything else about himself and the real world which has frustrated his dreams.

Establishing a theme that was to recur in Martyn's work, *The Heather Field* is a critique of idealism—or perhaps of idealism in a solipsistic formulation. Tyrrell does not recognize that his ambition is flawed on practical grounds. He cannot accept the fact that the world will not necessarily accommodate the needs he foists on it. His indifference to society, both in the polite sense of the word and in the historical sense, throws him back on his own psychic resources, which wilt under the pressure. Tyrrell's isolation is subjectively crucial and objectively crippling: The belief that the reclamation scheme is the signature of his integrity leads inevitably to his disintegration; as practical dramatic evidence of his situation, Tyrrell seems to exist in the play in order to contest what everyone else says to him rather than adjust to it. The only relaxation of this intransigent manner occurs in exchanges with his young son, Kit, who is being reared as a child of nature. These exchanges ironically portray the child as father to the man: The child's genuine, naïve wonder of the same state of mind—a pursuit of the natural which requires the face of nature to be redrawn.

One of the rewards of *The Heather Field*, therefore, is in identifying the protagonist's problems from an intellectual standpoint. In terms of its theatrical dynamics, however, the play is less satisfactory. The dialogue is written in prose of a rather leaden variety, and the scenes are conceived as set pieces in an argument rather than as occasions in a man's life. These drawbacks are nevertheless redeemed by the strength of Tyrrell's commitment to his ideal: It does, after all, cost him everything. The audience's involvement with his fate is sustained by the persuasiveness with which the ideal is conveyed: It is clear that for Tyrrell, the heather field and the dream of rehabilitation which it duplicitously facilitates offer the possibility of beauty, renewal, and completeness. It is an alternative to history, both personal (his marriage) and social (the Land War). Tyrrell claims to hear voices when he is out in the field, the voices of a German choir, the definitive experience of beauty which he received in his formative years, and it is these voices he welcomes when nature fails and madness overwhelms him.

The author's unsparing revelation of his protagonist's irreconcilable tensions gives the play its dramatic strength and also lends to it a cultural significance of which Martyn may have only been incidentally aware: The play is a fascinating and idiosyncratic example of a distinctively Irish genre, comprising works, in a variety of literary forms, which deal with the decline of the Big House, the generic term for the homes of the landed gentry.

As noted, Martyn's other plays repeat the themes of *The Heather Field*, but whereas *The Heather Field* contains a degree of tacit sympathy for Tyrrell (if only because all the other characters are narrower in spirit than he is), the critique of idealism in later plays is rather more bitter. In fact, what causes subsequent works to have destructive endings is not idealism of the characters as such, but its frustration.

Grangecolman is a case in point. The action is set in the Colman family home, a large old house outside Dublin, and the plot is concerned with the hauntings of an irrecoverable past. This theme is conveyed with a symbolic explicitness that borders on the obtuse and that, at the same time, leaves the intellectual burden of the play vague and generalized.

The household consists of old Michael Colman, the last of his line, his daughter Catherine, and her ne'er-do-well husband, Lucius Devlin. Michael is an antiquarian, a pursuit which in the Irish literature of the generation before Martyn's epitomized impotent reclusiveness. Catherine, who, with her husband, espouses the contemporary feminism, is a doctor, but her career has been blighted because of Lucius' irresponsible financial specula-tions. To assist him with his research, Michael hires young Clare Farquhar. Her grace and energy have a restorative effect on the old man's morale. This development, in turn, arouses Catherine's hostility.

Early in the play, the notion of the house's decline is introduced. Incur-sions, by thieves from the outside and ghosts from within, are feared; Miss Farquhar, handling a revolver, promises to deal with intruders of whatever kind. The audience soon learns, however, of the depth of Catherine's jeal-ousy of Clare, whose vitality and resolve are at odds with Catherine's self-abnegating temperament. Catherine's hostility erupts in her peremptory dismissal of Clare from her duties.

Ignorant of this development, Michael proposes marriage to Clare, a step which Catherine naturally opposes, using the occasion to voice the ideals of feminism and independence, which, for all of her enthusiasm for them, have evidently driven her into a dead end. Leaving the scene in an agitated state, she later returns, impersonating the family ghost. Clare takes the revolver and kills her.

Undoubtedly the plot's Gothic machinery gets in the way of the play's intellectual brooding. Nevertheless, there is no escaping the ideological im-passe to which Catherine's idealism has led. Once again, the world resists the pressure placed by the mind upon it, with catastrophic results for the mind's proprietor. The contrived nature of the scenario diminishes the play's surface plausibility, while at the same time drawing our attention to the situation's latent incoherence. In the dialogue, Martyn shows himself to be as tone-deaf as ever to the rhythms of human speech, but the consistency of the play's gloom and pessimism in a sense works to sanction its shortcomings. It seems remarkable that a committed Catholic such as Martyn continued to write plays which implicitly deny the possibility of faith. The depiction of conditions that are apparently beyond redemption—a prominent feature throughout Martyn's work—is given its most funereal presentation in *Grangecolman*, a play which, in the hands of a more adept man of the theater, would fully realize itself as a plainsong dirge for past, present, and future; for cultural recuperation, social commitment, and personal vanity.

In his last play, *The Dream Physician*, Martyn resorted to an uncharacteristic mode which perhaps he should have cultivated—namely, satire. (*The Tale of a Town* is the other major dramatic example of Martyn's satiric powers.) The basic framework of the plot is no more than a pretext for the author to have the last word about the role of Yeats and George Moore (particularly the latter) in the Irish Literary Revival. The surgery which exposes these luminaries' pretensions in act 4 is wholly out of keeping with the play's stilted pace, but the results are hilarious. Moore is presented as the fraudulent, malicious, self-seeking George Augustus Moon, while Yeats is caricatured as Beau Brummell, whose self-appointed destiny is to save the soul of his people with the aid of a banjo.

The plot concerns Shane Lester, who has betrayed his Anglo-Irish origins by becoming President of, and later Member of Parliament for, an Irish Nationalist group. His wife, Audrey, a social butterfly, cannot forgive Shane for this shift in allegiance, and she and her husband have a violent fight, during the course of which Audrey believes that she has killed him. Nothing will expunge this fantasy—the dream of the title. Audrey is confined to bed in a semicatatonic state, despite Shane's numerous entreating visits. A nurse, Sister Farnan, is engaged to care for Audrey, and it is she who suggests that the patient will snap out of her dream if confronted with a reality to which she cannot possibly assent. This reality is provided by the antics of Moon and company, and exposure to it has the desired therapeutic effect: The play ends with Audrey and Shane reconciled. Moon's posturing makes him the dream physician; the imbalance resulting from his pretensions make it impossible to take seriously what he represents. By virtue of experiencing that impossibility, Audrey is restored to a reality which she can take seriously, her husband's.

Clearly, however, *The Dream Physician* is itself imbalanced, formally and thematically. Martyn was unable to work out a unified relationship between the more general theme of Shane's idealism, embodied in his nationalist leanings, and the more local and personal bouts of character assassination, which have little or nothing to do directly with Shane. This failure places the play in danger of being a unique example of a hopelessly implausible genre, the revenge farce. After the sobriety of most of its predecessors, however, it is pleasant to encounter a spirited Edward Martyn. The caricatures of Moore and Yeats show all the signs of being an insider's work. Less successful are the cartoons of Lady Gregory (Sister Farnan) and James Joyce. Joyce was allegedly the model for Otho, Audrey's insufferable brother, who finally comes to life when he denounces Moon because his beloved, Moon's grandniece, "a woman of genius" who signs her poetic effusions "La Mayonaise" (Mayo was George Moore's native county), proves to be nonexistent.

The uncharacteristic note on which Martyn's playwriting career ended is perhaps symptomatic. Inspired by the most impressive contemporary models and fortified by the principles derived from them, Martyn had perhaps too clear an intellectual formula for his work, and an insufficiently coherent aesthetic approach. Adherence to his formula made the work repetitive, two-dimensional, and lacking in vitality. Like so many of his protagonists, Martyn failed to live up to the promise of his ideals. Yet those ideals, particularly in their eschewal of sentimentality, and the works which attempt to articulate them, provide an important perspective from which to view the theatrical accomplishments of his contemporaries.

Other major work
NOVEL: *Morgante the Lesser*, 1890 (as Sirius).

Bibliography
Courtney, Sister Marie-Thérèse. *Edward Martyn and the Irish Theatre*, 1956.
Gwynn, Denis. *Edward Martyn and the Irish Revival*, 1930.
Setterquist, Jan. *Ibsen and the Beginnings of Anglo-Irish Drama, Volume II: Edward Martyn*, 1960.

George O'Brien

JOHN MASEFIELD

Born: Ledbury, England; June 1, 1878
Died: Burcote Brook, England; May 12, 1967

Principal drama

The Campden Wonder, pr. 1907, pb. 1909 (one act); *The Tragedy of Nan*, pr. 1908, pb. 1909; *Mrs. Harrison*, pb. 1909 (one act); *The Tragedy of Pompey the Great*, pr., pb. 1910; *The Witch*, pr. 1911 (adaptation of a Norwegian play); *Philip the King*, pr. 1914 (one act); *The Faithful*, pr., pb. 1915; *The Sweeps of Ninety-Eight*, pr., pb. 1916; *Good Friday: A Dramatic Poem*, pb. 1916, pr. 1917; *The Locked Chest*, pb. 1916, pr. 1920 (one act); *Esther*, pr. 1921 (adaptation of Jean Racine's play); *Melloney Holtspur: Or, The Pangs of Love*, pb. 1922, pr. 1923; *A King's Daughter: A Tragedy in Verse*, pr. 1923; *Tristan and Isolt: A Play in Verse*, pr. 1923, pb. 1927; *The Trial of Jesus*, pb. 1925, pr. 1927; *The Coming of Christ*, pb. 1928; *Easter: A Play for Singers*, pr. 1929; *End and Beginnings*, pb. 1933; *A Play for St. George*, pb. 1948.

Other literary forms

John Masefield is noted for his lyric and narrative poetry, and because of poems such as "Sea Fever" and "Cargoes," he will continue to be read. For more than sixty years, however, he was prolific in many other genres as well. Between 1902 and 1966, Masefield wrote more than forty volumes of poetry or verse plays and more than twenty novels, in addition to short stories, essays, reviews, biographies, historical works, addresses, and prefaces, totaling about fifty books in all. Masefield's first book of verse was *Salt-Water Ballads* (1902); his narrative poem, *The Everlasting* (1911), caused a sensation with its realistic diction. Masefield wrote eight other book-length narrative poems, the most important being *The Window in the Bye Street* (1912), *The Daffodil Fields* (1913), *Reynard the Fox* (1919), *Right Royal* (1920), and *King Cole* (1921). As his sea poems and ballads are about the life of the common sailor, his narrative verse tells about the lot of the rural folk of the Malvern Hills in his native Herefordshire.

Masefield's fiction is varied and uneven; his most popular and successful novels were his books about the sea and strange lands, written in the vein of Joseph Conrad and Robert Louis Stevenson—tales such as *Captain Margaret* (1909), *The Bird of Dawning* (1933), and *Victorious Troy* (1935). While not a great critic, Masefield was a thoroughly professional man of letters who turned out well-focused articles and reviews by the hundreds, as well as book-length studies. In the field of history, Masefield gave accounts of World War I debacles in *Gallipoli* (1916) and *The Battle of the Somme* (1919); he told the story of the evacuation of Dunkirk in *The Nine*

Days Wonder (1941). In addition, Masefield wrote about maritime history in *Sea Life in Nelson's Time* (1905), *On the Spanish Main* (1906), and *The Conway from Her Foundation to the Present Day* (1933). Masefield's auto-biographical works include *In the Mill* (1941), *New Chum* (1944), *So Long to Learn* (1952), and *Grace Before Ploughing* (1966).

Achievements

Masefield's plays have lost much of their appeal for stage audiences, but some of his dramatic work, such as that written about the common people, has a vitality to recommend it, particularly his most successful play, *The Tragedy of Nan*, which reveals Masefield's ability to tell a vivid story in dramatic terms. It is not likely that any of his plays will become standard reading in drama courses, nor are any likely to be revived for production, yet Masefield should be commended for trying to infuse the English commercial theater in the early twentieth century with dramatic works of serious artistic intent. In the years after World War I, Masefield largely abandoned this ambition; the postwar plays were the products of an avocation rather than a true vocation. Though some of these plays were staged by local amateur dramatic clubs, Masefield wrote them primarily for his own edification and for the entertainment of his family and friends.

Although Masefield was writing plays after George Bernard Shaw, Henrik Ibsen, August Strindberg, and Anton Chekhov had established the dimensions of early modern drama, his dramatic values have the conventionalities of Victorian theater. Despite their conventional manner, his plays never appealed to a wide popular audience, nor, for the most part, did they satisfy the critics. Masefield's endeavors as a playwright did, however, enhance his reputation in Georgian literary circles, and his mastering of the dramatic conventions enabled him to write novels with well-constructed plots and carefully focused characterizations.

Whatever the merits of his drama, it is for his achievements as a poet that Masefield will be remembered: His tenure as England's poet laureate, from 1930 until his death in 1967, was one of the longer ones.

Biography

John Edward Masefield was born on June 1, 1878, in the small town of Ledbury in rural Herefordshire, England; he was the son of George Edward and Carol Parker Masefield. Masefield's father, a fairly successful solicitor, died at the age of forty-nine following a period of mental disorder that may have been caused by the death of Masefield's mother, who died from complications following childbirth in 1885. Thus left an orphan when he was only six years old, Masefield was taken in by his aunt and uncle, who reared him in pleasant circumstances in a Victorian country house called The Priory. There, young Masefield learned to love the waters, woods, and flowers of Herefordshire, and from his aunt's teaching he acquired a love for literature, particularly the narrative poems of Henry Wadsworth Longfellow. In 1888, Masefield was sent to the King's School in Warwick as a boarding student. Homesick and unhappy at Warwick, Masefield ran away from school, and though he was to return, it was obvious that this experience with formal education was not to produce the desired results. Masefield was allowed to join the merchant navy, leaving home at thirteen and enlisting as a midshipman; he was posted to the H. M. S. *Conway*, a famous training ship. During his days as apprentice seaman, he took long voyages to South America and around Cape Horn, but the ardors of a sailor's life were not to his liking, and he jumped ship in New York, giving up his berth as sixth officer on the White Star liner *Adriatie*. The young Masefield's disgraceful behavior caused his uncle to disinherit him, and Masefield was forced to take whatever work he could find. For some time, he lived a nearly vagrant life in Greenwich Village, where he started to write poetry seriously. Masefield remained in New York for two years before returning to London in 1897, where he took a post as a bank clerk, a position he held for three years, during which time he started to publish some of his own verse and to meet some of the London literati, becoming acquainted with William Butler Yeats, Lady Augusta Gregory, and John Millington Synge, along with others whom he came to know during regular gatherings in Bloomsbury. Masefield's first book of poems, *Salt-Water Ballads*, was published in 1902 and enjoyed immediate success, becoming popular with the public and critics alike.

Masefield met Constance Crommelin in 1903, and they were married the same year, when he was twenty-five years old and his bride was thirty-five. Despite the difference in their ages, the marriage seems to have been as happy as most. Masefield acquired a job as an editor and settled in Greenwich with his wife and baby daughter. In 1904, Masefield received an offer to write for the *Manchester Guardian*, but newspaper writing deflected him from his main interest at this period—writing plays. He managed to turn out a series of dramas, despite the demands of producing reviews and articles for the *Manchester Guardian* seven days a week. Although most of Masefield's early dramatic writings were left unfinished or destroyed, he completed and published his first play, *The Campden Wonder*, in 1907. In addition to writing another six plays in the years before World War I, he also produced novels, stories, sketches, his first long verse narratives, and more ballads and poems, although he considered himself to be primarily a playwright. In 1910, about the time of the birth of his son Lewis, he become involved with Elizabeth Robins, an American actress and leader of the suffragettes. Although she was nearly fifty and he was only thirty-one, he became totally enamored of her; for her part, she accepted Masefield's attentions with reservation, and their affair was conducted under the guise of an imaginary mother-son relationship, he calling her "mother" and she addressing him as her "little son." Most of Masefield's ardor went into his letters; he often wrote her as many as two a day. Their actual meetings were confined primarily to rendezvous at the British Museum, where "mother" and "son" would tour the galleries. Finally, Robins, having tired of Masefield's filial pose and the maternal role imposed on her, called off the relationship.

After a period of desolation caused by Robins' withdrawal, Masefield moved his family to an old manor house in the Berkshire hills. It was at this time that he wrote the long narrative poem *The Everlasting*, which established his fame as the premier poet of the Georgian period.

Masefield's life as a literary country squire was disrupted by the start of World War I. Although he tried to enlist in the army, Masefield was not able to join a combat branch because of his poor medical record, but he was accepted for service in the British Red Cross, going to France in 1914 with the British Expeditionary Force; later, in 1915, he was posted to the Dardanelles, where he participated in the debacle at Gallipoli. Because of his literary reputation, he was relieved of his duties as a field officer and sent by the Red Cross to promote the war effort with two lecture tours of the United States.

As the war ended, Masefield moved his residence again, settling at Boar's Hill, near Oxford. His neighbors there included Gilbert Murray, Sir Arthur Evans, and Robert Bridges, and Masefield became the landlord for a young war-poet, Robert Graves, to whom he leased a cottage on his property. Masefield also became a friend to Edmund Blunden, another war-scarred writer who was returning to Oxford to be a professor of poetry. The two young veterans saw Masefield as a mentor who, like them, was opposed to modernists such as Ezra Pound, T. S. Eliot, and Edith Sitwell, and stood, like them, rooted in the native English tradition.

The postwar years were good ones for Masefield. He was the originator of annual verse recitals called the Oxford Recitations and devoted himself to writing plays again as well as history books about the war. He founded a local amateur theatrical company in 1919 that put on the plays of Euripides, William Shakespeare, and John Galsworthy. The Hill Players, as they were called, performed in a theater called the Music Room from 1922 until 1932, staging several experimental plays by young, unknown playwrights as well as some of Yeats's later plays and Masefield's own *Tristan and Isolt* and *The Trial of Jesus*. In effect, Masefield had created his own private theater, where he could try out his plays without worrying about commercial success. He could give young dramatists a vehicle for their plays and could cast his friends and family in the parts.

At the end of the decade, Masefield was named poet laureate, and in 1930, he moved from Boar's Hill to Pinbury Park, near Cirencester in

Gloucestershire. There, Masefield lived in a grand house with great rows of oak trees, playing his part as a public figure with quiet dignity, but, as before, another world war disturbed his serene life.

Masefield once again offered his services to the nation and, during the dark days of the early war years, produced an inspiring story of the escape of the British Army from the beaches of Dunkirk. Personal grief came to him in this war: His son Lewis was killed in action in the African desert while serving with the Royal Ambulance Corps. The aging Masefield never fully recovered from the heartbreak caused by his son's death. In the years after the war, his life was given over to letter writing, by which he kept up a wide range of friendships, and to completing his sequence of autobiographical works. His official duties as poet laureate kept him occupied in cultural affairs, promoting the Royal Academy of Dramatic Art and serving as president of the National Book League. In the autumn of 1959, Mrs. Masefield became ill, and she died in 1960 at the age of ninety-three. Masefield's life became increasingly reclusive, but he continued to write; among the works required by his office were poems upon the deaths of T. S. Eliot and President John F. Kennedy. Indeed, Masefield's energy as a writer seemed inexhaustible, and he produced his last book, *In Glad Thanksgiving* (1966), when he was eighty-eight years old. The next year, on May 12, 1967, he died and was cremated; his ashes were placed in the Poets' Corner of Westminster Abbey, though he had requested that they should be scattered in the winds and waters of his native downs.

Analysis

Very early in his career as a writer, John Masefield developed an interest in playwriting. His deep study of Shakespeare and his personal association with Yeats, Lady Gregory, and Synge instilled in Masefield a desire to revive the English drama as his friends were attempting to rekindle the drama of Ireland by infusing it with the vitality of mythic and folk elements. Masefield saw what could be done with folk materials in plays such as Synge's *Riders to the Sea* (pb. 1903) and *In the Shadow of the Glen* (pr. 1903); his own first play, *The Campden Wonder*, is a one-act drama in the expressionistic-symbolic mode of Yeats, to whom it was dedicated. Using the colloquial idiom, it deals with a brutal story that Masefield had heard about a hanging in Chipping Campden of three innocent people. This first effort was followed by several more one-act plays: *Mrs. Harrison*, a sequel to *The Campden Wonder* and also an exercise in sustained naturalism; *The Sweeps of Ninety-Eight*, an amusing comedy with a historical background concerning the outwitting of the British Navy by an Irish rebel in 1798; and another short play, *The Locked Chest*, which is a suspenseful drama about a clever wife who tricks her confused husband.

Good Friday, also written during this period, is a morality play in rhymed

verse. Its subject is the Passion of Christ, and Masefield employs an austere style in imitation of the cycle plays of medieval drama, but his modern
idiomatic phrases are somewhat out of keeping with the spirit of the original. Nevertheless, the play contains a moving account of the Crucifixion,
simple and vivid in its effects:

> We were alone on the accursed hill
> And we were still, not even the dice clicked
> On to the stone . . .
> And now and then the hangers gave a groan,
> Up in the dark, three shapes with arms outspread.

Overall, in the period between 1907 and 1916, Masefield finished ten plays.
During this decade, he produced some of his most important dramatic
works, including longer, full-length plays such as *The Tragedy of Nan*, *The
Tragedy of Pompey the Great*, *Philip the King*, and *The Faithful*.

The first of these, *The Tragedy of Nan*, was produced at the New Royalty Theatre under the direction of Harley Granville-Barker; it had a long
and successful stage run in repertory theaters in England and abroad.
Based on a true "country tragedy" of the early nineteenth century, it is a
play with the capacity to move audiences. The poignant plot details the
plight of Nan Hardwick, an orphaned charity girl whose father is hanged
for stealing sheep. She is taken in by a stingy uncle whose family is unkind
to her, but her life is made bearable by the attention paid her by Dick
Gurvil, a local youth of uncertain moral fiber who has plans to marry Nan.
Her chances for happiness are destroyed when her mean-spirited aunt, who
wants him for a husband to one of her own daughters, reveals to Dick that
Nan is a murderer's daughter. Fearful that he cannot expect a dowry from
Nan and that he will be disinherited by his own father, he breaks off their
engagement and marries one of Nan's cousins. Nan realizes the defective
character of her lover, but her pain and humiliation at losing him are nevertheless acute. In an ironic turn of events, it is discovered that her father
was the victim of a miscarriage of justice: He was innocent of the charges,
and she is paid a large sum of money in compensation for his death. Her
former fiancé realizes that she is a richer prize than the cousin, so he turns
to her again with a proposal of marriage. In a fury at his duplicity and
temerity, Nan stabs him in the heart with a bread knife, saying that he
must be killed to keep him from preying on any more innocent women.
She then throws herself in the Severn River, closing the play on a note of
unrelieved tragedy.

Although a summary of the play makes it appear like a study in naturalism, it is, in fact, less so than Masefield's early plays; nevertheless, some
contemporary drama critics indicted the drama for its use of dialect, vicious
characters, and commonplace scenes to tell an ugly story. In general, *The*

Tragedy of Nan seems most to echo Thomas Hardy's novel *Tess of the D'Urbervilles* (1891): Both are rustic melodramas that feature pure, beautiful country girls who are the playthings of cruel fate. Like Hardy's Tess, Nan is truly a tragic protagonist, and her death induces the proper feeling of catharsis in the audience.

Masefield followed *The Tragedy of Nan* with *The Tragedy of Pompey the Great*, which was written during the winter of 1908-1909 and produced for the stage in 1910, opening at the Aldwych Theatre in London under the direction of Harcourt Williams. Masefield began this history play as a one-act drama in which he tried to dramatize the life of the ill-fated Roman general as it was depicted in Sir Thomas North's translation (1579) of Plutarch' *Parallel Lives* (105-115). The events of the story required a fuller treatment, however, and Masefield expanded his play into a complete three-act drama. The tragic career of Pompey, who goes down to defeat with brave dignity in his struggle with Caesar, embodies a theme often found in Masefield's work: the idea that the greatest victories are those of the spirit. Masefield draws Pompey's character in more complimentary terms than history does, making him into a magnanimous, peace-loving general.

As a play, *The Tragedy of Pompey the Great* has some arresting scenes, with battles on land and sea which provide an opportunity for striking stage effects, but as Aristotle reminds us in *The Poetics*, spectacle is the lowest artistic ingredient of the drama. The main weakness of this play, though, is its lack of dramatic tension. Masefield idealizes Pompey as a highly principled aristocratic leader who opposes Caesar's mob appeal and egalitarian policies. Masefield's Pompey, much like Shakespeare's Brutus, is motivated by a patriotic desire to preserve the ideals of republican Rome. Unfortunately, Caesar is not among the *dramatis personae* of Masefield's play; as a result, there is no dramatic tension between Pompey and a worthy antagonist. Instead, there is only an extended exposition of Pompey's character. Pompey's tentative idealism is no match for the single-minded Caesar's ambition; his efforts at compromise and his rational appeals to avert civil war are not successful, and strife breaks out with seeming inevitabilty. In this respect, some reviewers saw the play as an effort by Masefield to warn audiences of the threat to peace which international tensions posed in the period just before the outbreak of World War I.

One of Masefield's next plays, *The Faithful*, a total departure from any of his previous dramatic works, reflects the vogue for Oriental culture that swept England and France during the early years of the twentieth century. Using Japanese rather than Roman history as his subject, Masefield— inspired perhaps by Yeats's adaptations of Nō plays—tried a more experimental form of drama in *The Faithful*. The play opened at the Birmingham Repertory Theatre in 1915 and ran until 1918. After the end of the war, it had a run of more than forty performances on Broadway, where it enjoyed a critical rather than a commercial success. The play is about the forty-seven rōnin, whose tragic story Masefield at first planned to tell in a verse narrative because he could not envision a dramatic structure for the story. Inspired in part by Granville-Barker's productions of Shakespeare's *Twelfth Night* and *The Winter's Tale*, which, Masefield said, "showed me more clearly than any stage productions known to me the power and sweep of Shakespeare's constructions . . . ," he created a play of considerable lyric eloquence—a play that has all the blood and gore of a Jacobean tragedy, presented with a ritualistic air that mutes the violence and that invests the action with a timeless quality.

The action, set in medieval Japan, revolves around a revenge plot. The play's villain is an upstart tyrant named Kira, a newly rich daimyo, or feudal lord, who causes the death of a young rival, Asano. In the conflict that results, Asano's followers try to avenge their leader, but the rebels are routed and their families are scourged by the ruthless Kira. Finally, however, the tide turns, and Kira is executed by one of Asano's followers, the heroic Kurano. The curtain comes down with all the survivors preparing to commit hara-kiri. The pseudo-Japanese quality of the drama annoyed some of the play's critics, who questioned its historical and cultural credibility, but Masefield should be given credit for his attempted synthesis of Western and Oriental dramatic modes. All in all, *The Faithful* is an interesting example of the impact of Japanese theater on the dramatic arts in England.

Only a few of Masefield's post-World War I plays attracted any serious critical attention. One that did was a fantasy melodrama entitled *Melloney Holtspur*, a seriocomic ghost story about the way in which the peccadilloes of a past generation are passed on to the present. Written in the spirit of the supernaturalism of Sir James Barrie, the play was praised for its upbeat treatment of such solemn themes as ancestral sins and atonement. In addition, Masefield translated Jean Racine's play *Berenice*; he also adapted Racine's *Esther*. Masefield's last effort at playwriting was *A Play for St. George*; this drama in verse and prose, which was never staged, treats the famous legend of England's patron saint.

Masefield was always more the poet than the dramatist. His plays nevertheless retain historical interest, both as expressions of his many-sided talent and as reflections of diverse trends in British drama of the late nineteenth and the early twentieth century.

Other major works

NOVELS: *Captain Margaret*, 1909; *Multitude and Solitude*, 1909; *Lost Endeavour*, 1910; *The Taking of Helen*, 1923; *Sard Harker*, 1924; *Odtaa*, 1926; *The Hawbucks*, 1929; *The Bird of Dawning*, 1933; *Victorious Troy*, 1935; *Basilissa*, 1940.

SHORT FICTION: *A Mainsail Haul*, 1905; *A Tarpaulin Muster*, 1907.

POETRY: *Salt-Water Ballads*, 1902; *Ballads*, 1903; *The Everlasting*, 1911; *The Window in the Bye Street*, 1912; *The Story of a Round-house and Other Poems*, 1912; *Dauber: A Poem*, 1913; *The Daffodil Fields*, 1913; *Philip the King and Other Poems*, 1914; *The Cold Cotswolds*, 1917; *Rosas*, 1918; *A Poem and Two Plays*, 1919; *Reynard the Fox: Or, The Ghost Heath Run*, 1919; *Enslaved and Other Poems*, 1920; *Right Royal*, 1920; *King Cole*, 1921; *The Dream*, 1922; *Sonnets of Good Cheer to the Lena Ashwell Players*, 1926; *Madsummer Night and Other Tales in Verse*, 1936; *Ode to Harvard*, 1937; *Some Verses to Some Germans*, 1939; *Gautama the Enlightened and Other Verse*, 1941; *Natalie and Masie Pavilastukay: Two Tales in Verse*, 1942; *Wonderings (Between One and Six Years)*, 1943; *I Want! I Want!*, 1944; *On the Hill*, 1949; *Poems*, 1953; *The Bluebells and Other Verse*, 1961; *Old Raiger and Other Verse*, 1964; *In Glad Thanksgiving*, 1966.

NONFICTION: *Sea Life in Nelson's Time*, 1905; *On the Spanish Main*, 1906; *Shakespeare*, 1911; *Gallipoli*, 1916; *The Battle of the Somme*, 1919; *Chaucer*, 1931; *The Conway from Her Foundation to the Present Day*, 1933; *The Nine Days Wonder*, 1941; *In the Mill*, 1941; *New Chum*, 1944; *So Long to Learn*, 1952; *Grace Before Ploughing: Fragments of Autobiography*, 1966; *The Letters of John Masefield*, 1979.

TRANSLATION: *Berenice*, 1922 (of Jean Racine's play).

MISCELLANEOUS: *A Book of Sorts: Selections from the Verse and Prose*, 1947.

Bibliography

Fisher, Margery. *John Masefield*, 1963.

Handley-Taylor, Geoffrey. *John Masefield: A Bibliography*, 1960.

Montague, Charles Edward. "Mr. Masefield's Tragedies," in *Dramatic Values*, 1925.

Smith, Constance Babington. *John Masefield*, 1956.

Spark, Muriel. *John Masefield*, 1953.

Sternlicht, Sanford. *John Masefield*, 1977.

Stevenson, Lionel. "Masefield and the New Universe," in *The Sewanee Review*. XXXVIII (July, 1929), pp. 336-348.

Thomas, Gilbert. *John Masefield*, 1933.

Hallman B. Bryant

PHILIP MASSINGER

Born: Salisbury, England; November 24, 1583 (baptized)
Died: London, England; March 18, 1640

Principal drama

The Fatal Dowry, pr. 1616-1619, pb. 1632 (with Nathaniel Field); *Sir John van Olden Barnavelt*, pr. 1619, pb. 1883 (with John Fletcher); *The Custom of the Country*, pr. c. 1619-1620, pb. 1647 (with Fletcher); *The Little French Lawyer*, pr. 1619-1623, pb. 1647 (with Fletcher); *The Virgin Martyr*, pr. c. 1620, pb. 1622 (with Thomas Dekker); *The False One*, pr. c. 1620, pb. 1647 (with Fletcher); *The Double Marriage*, pr. c. 1621, pb. 1647 (with Fletcher); *The Maid of Honor*, pr. c. 1621, pb. 1632; *The Unnatural Combat*, pr. c. 1621, pb. 1639; *The Duke of Milan*, pr. c. 1621-1622, pb. 1623; *A New Way to Pay Old Debts*, pr. 1621-1622(?), pb. 1633; *The Beggar's Bush*, pr. before 1622, pb. 1647 (with Fletcher); *The Prophetess*, pr. 1622, pb. 1647 (with Fletcher); *The Bondman*, pr. 1623, pb. 1624; *The Renegado: Or, The Gentleman of Venice*, pr. 1624, pb. 1630; *The Parliament of Love*, pr. 1624, pb. 1805; *The Elder Brother*, pr. 1625(?), pb. 1637 (with Fletcher); *The Roman Actor*, pr. 1626, pb. 1629; *The Great Duke of France*, pr. 1627(?), pb. 1636; *The Picture*, pr. 1629, pb. 1630; *Believe as You List*, pr. 1631, pb. 1849; *The Emperor of the East*, pr. 1631, pb. 1632; *The City Madam*, pr. 1632(?), pb. 1658; *The Guardian*, pr. 1633, pb. 1655; *A Very Woman: Or, The Prince of Tarent*, pr. 1634, pb. 1655; *The Bashful Lover*, pr. 1636, pb. 1655; *The Dramatic Works of Thomas Dekker*, 1953-1961 (4 volumes, Fredson Bowers, editor; includes collaborations with Dekker); *The Dramatic Works in the Beaumont and Fletcher Canon*, 1966-1976 (4 volumes, Bowers, editor; includes collaborations with Fletcher); *Selected Plays of Philip Massinger*, 1978 (Colin Gibson, editor).

Other literary forms

Philip Massinger wrote a few commemorative poems, commendations of other playwrights, and dedicatory epistles in verse and prose. These have been collected by Donald Lawless in a 1968 monograph, *The Poems of Philip Massinger with Critical Notes*. Massinger's reputation, however, rests firmly on his plays.

Achievements

Massinger's missing plays are the stuff of legend: An eighteenth century book dealer, Joseph Warburton, bought and stacked away in a closet an undetermined number of Massinger manuscripts, which his cook mistook for scrap and used, sheet by sheet, to line pie plates and start fires. What outlived the cook is a body of competently, sometimes brilliantly, plotted plays which are variations on three or four themes and character types.

In the past, critics such as Arthur Symons and Ronald Bayne have complained that Massinger's works offer no new insights into the relationship between man and society, no existential questions about the right and wrong of a character's course. They found his thinking conventional and his heroines smug. Later critics, such as Mark Mugglio and A. P. Hogan attempted to rescue Massinger from such charges by arguing that he was subtly challenging the very assumptions his plays seem to support.

In fact, Massinger's plays do make conventional assumptions about art, society, and human motives. Art teaches pleasantly; society naturally forms a hierarchy in which those of good blood, well educated, rule over men of less exalted natures. Humans act from love, greed, ambition, or simple fellowship. Working from these assumptions, Massinger dramatizes the unsuccessful attempts of citizens who wish to rise above their natural stations. He twits the younger generation for its impatience; he upholds loyalty as an almost ultimate value, and he polishes with loving care his portraits of the loyal and the innocent, the gruff and the greedy.

Though he does not challenge his culture's values, Massinger can still fascinate and delight a modern audience for three reasons. First, he fills his scenes with accurate observations of daily details. He savors the dodges by which a shrewd merchant secures a mortgage, the puff pastries and sherry sauces which a good chef can concoct, the pearl necklaces and tavern reckonings upon which social status so often depends. Even in his most serious plays, one finds him lavishing stage time on the petty rituals and daily clutter which make men feel comfortably at home in the middle class. Through Massinger, one becomes intimate with the Renaissance Everyman, a hearty and surprisingly broad-minded figure.

Second, Massinger composes good, though not memorable, poetry and satisfying plots. His characters can dependably explain themselves and can use the common stock of images. Having apprenticed himself to such masters of double and triple plots as Thomas Dekker and John Fletcher, Massinger could weave most pleasing tapestries of contrasting threads. The saint's sweetness shows grandly against a background of sinners; the jealous man's frenzy, against the loyal anger of his wife.

Third, Massinger had an apparently lifelong fascination with the way that passion attacks reason. He continually examines the "something snapped" movement of a character's mind. In a Massinger character, passion's attack can numb the will as suddenly as the wasp's sting paralyzes the spider. Like Robert Burton in his *The Anatomy of Melancholy* (1621), Massinger concentrates sometimes on symptoms, sometimes on causes, sometimes on cures for the victims of jealousy or of "heroical love." His impassioned characters may be enrapt by Providence (as in *The Virgin Martyr*) or entrapped by their own possessive natures (as in *A New Way to Pay Old*

Debts) or by the lure of other characters (as in *The Maid of Honor*); whatever the causes, they act with a compulsiveness and are cured, if they are cured at all, by mechanisms that call into question the notion of free will perhaps more strongly than their creator intended.

Biography

Philip Massinger was baptized on November 24, 1583, at Salisbury, England, the son of Arthur and Anne Crompton Massinger. His father, "an honest gentleman and a loving man," served as trusted retainer to the powerful Henry Herbert, Earl of Pembroke. As Pembroke's retainer, Arthur Massinger held various minor political offices, sat three times in Parliament, and handled many of the earl's financial affairs. Massinger's mother came from a similarly professional family, but one whose political connections were smudged by more or less open Roman Catholicism. (Young Massinger may well have grown up Catholic; he treats Papists sympathetically, and their doctrines underlie at least three of his plays.) Early editors speculated that Massinger was reared as a page in a Pembroke household, where he could become familiar with the routines of gentry life. At the age of eighteen, he entered Oxford University, his father's alma mater. Though he may have stayed there until Arthur's death around 1606, he left without a degree.

Massinger's whereabouts after leaving Oxford are conjectural; probably he worked as an actor. By 1613 he was certainly scriptwriting in London, collaborating with other scriptwriters for hungry London audiences. Since playwriting paid very little, Massinger lived for some time on the fringes of poverty. In two letters, he seeks cash advances "without which we cannot be bailed" from prison for debt. Like a modern young screenwriter, he joined forces with one or another of the more established writers—Thomas Dekker, Nathaniel Field, Robert Dabourne—and worked for several of London's major production companies. Though Massinger wrote tragedies, tragicomedies, and comedies throughout his career, there was a general drift toward lighter plays as his career advanced.

By 1617, Massinger had begun what became his most fruitful writing partnership—with John Fletcher, who had succeeded William Shakespeare as chief writer for the King's Men, a highly acclaimed acting company. Massinger and Fletcher worked together on at least a dozen (and perhaps as many as nineteen) plays, mostly tragicomedies. In 1625, when Fletcher died in the great London plague, Massinger succeeded him as the company's chief writer; from then until his own sudden death in March, 1640, Massinger wrote almost exclusively for the King's Men.

Analysis

It is in Philip Massinger's studies of passion, whether the conclusion is tragic or comic, that one sees most clearly both his strengths and his limitations—both his famous seriousness as a dramatist and teacher, and the problems critics find with his use of conventions. Four plays particularly illustrate Massinger's "anatomy" of passion and will: *The Virgin Martyr, The Maid of Honor, The Picture,* and *A New Way to Pay Old Debts.*

In *The Virgin Martyr,* Massinger collaborated with Dekker to produce a hagiography with a decidedly Romish coloring. Massinger believed in ritual, ceremony, order, and in the power of prayer to change determinations. With a certainty bordering on superstition, he believed that those who adhere to a set body of moral codes will have an almost magical effect on their world.

Dorothea, the virgin martyr, has such an effect. She adheres to Christian dogma and practices the virtues of generosity, compassion, self-control, and rational argument. She gladly accepts martyrdom as payment for three benefits: heaven for herself; conversion of Antoninus, the young Roman who loves her; and a gift of fruit and flowers for Theophilus, her prosecutor. At her dying request, "A holy fire/ yields a comfortable heat" in Antoninus; soon thereafter, Theophilus, receiving his miraculous bouquet, sets about becoming Rome's next Christian martyr. Thus, prayer's power triumphs—perhaps over the free will of the converts.

Yet *The Virgin Martyr,* contrary to what the title leads us to expect, is not entirely Dorothea's story; her self-control in the face of physical torment is merely the simplest of several versions of self-control tested. Massinger gives as much attention to Antoninus, the governor's son, and Artemia, the emperor's daughter. Antoninus passionately loves Dorothea, yet when Artemia chooses him for her consort, he cannot safely refuse. He temporizes, then rushes off to pursue Dorothea again. The Christian virgin, completely occupied with prayer and good works, shows no interest in a pagan lover. She would rather feed the poor and instruct the ignorant.

Antoninus does not love Dorothea for her virtue—he simply loves her, irrationally. Of Artemia's proposal, he complains, "When I am scorched/ With fire, can flames in any other quench me?/ What is her love to me, greatness, or empire,/ That am slave to another?" That Dorothea's love brings him "assured destruction" bothers him not a whit, and when he attempts to color his passion with reason, the attempt largely fails.

Artemia, like Antoninus, covers passion with reasonable answers, yet ultimately, the pagan princess exercises a self-control that makes her admirable. Given her choice of husband, she bypasses kings and follows her affection for Antoninus; when she finds that he loves Dorothea, she impulsively wants him dead. She orders his execution but soon relents. Regaining control, she gives up her interest in him, "That all may know, when the cause wills, I can/ Command my own desires." At the play's end, she chooses a more appropriate husband, the Emperor Maximinus, grounding love and affection to him on a clearly rational basis.

The question of will is examined from two other perspectives as well—those of Theophilus' daughters and of Dorothea's servants. The daughters, at the play's start, have newly renounced their Christianity and returned to their father's pagan gods. Tortures and reasoning had not worked, but the knowledge that their father chose his cultural convictions over even paternal feelings brought the girls back to Jove's altar. Massinger casts their conversion from Christianity in convincing psychological terms; their father's will has overwhelmed them. (Later, Dorothea uses reason to bring them back to Christ.)

The other perspective is that of Dorothea's two reprobate servants, Hircius and Spungius, who provide a not very comic commentary on their mistress' intellectualism. Drunkard and whoremaster respectively, they squander, with mechanical predictability, money entrusted to them for the poor. They embrace Christianity or paganism, depending on which sect puts the readiest cash into their hands. They claim no will at all. As Spungius says, "The thread of my life is drawn through the needle of necessity, whose eye, looking upon my lousy breeches, cries out it cannot mend them." Derogatory comparisons and flat punch lines give these characters some cleverness but no will. Their conversations counterpoint Dorothea's rational control.

Several of the themes and characters of *The Virgin Martyr* turn up in later Massinger works. *The Unnatural Combat*, for example, is the study of a father's incestuous passion for his daughter. Malefort, the father, habitually does as he pleases; he has dispatched prisoners of war, disregarded friendship, done away with one wife to make room for a second. Massinger has his audience learn these things gradually as he builds a picture of an effective military leader, but one whose power comes from utterly undisciplined appetites. Malefort gradually loses the sympathy of the audience until, halfway through the play, he kills his own son in a duel. His saving grace has been his care for his daughter. Now he suddenly realizes that he wants the girl incestuously, and the habit of taking what he wants—of unbridled, undisciplined will—is so strong in him that his real and painful struggle to give her up is doomed to fail.

The Malefort character resembles that of Theophilus in *The Virgin Martyr* and has even stronger resemblance to the Duke of Milan in the play of that title. There, the possessive will of Duke Sforza demands that, should he die, his chaste and innocent wife be killed, lest she someday enjoy a second love. Sforza's possessive will, like Malefort's, derives from his habitual and public indulgence of his appetite for Marcelia, and, like Malefort's, it is fatal. Domitian and his wife in *The Roman Actor* share the same lack of disciplined will.

The willful will-lessness Massinger portrays in these characters is op-

posed in the likes of Dorothea and Artemia. Massinger is particularly interested in the influence of such characters on others. In *The Renegado*, for
example, the stalwart Christian hero converts the equally stalwart pagan
heroine by having a Jesuit sprinkle her with holy water as she passes by, a
rapid-transit baptism. In this case, the ritual itself effects the change in
will. (Such a belief in ritual's power to summon up prevenient grace served
as a kind of watershed in the early seventeenth century, separating Papists
from Anglicans. Thus, critics tend to think Massinger was a Catholic.) In a
humanized, toned-down form, Massinger's interest in the way wills fixate,
interact, and change informs three of his mature works, *A New Way to Pay
Old Debts*, *The Picture*, and *The Maid of Honor*. These three plays are
vintage Massinger; all three deserve close study.

In *A New Way to Pay Old Debts*, Massinger packs the *deus ex machina*
in mothballs and stores it backstage along with the thunderbolts and heavenly flowers. The play, often considered his masterpiece, depends on
human goodwill and gets most of its energy from one man's bad will. *A
New Way to Pay Old Debts* transfers the single-minded bad man of *The
Unnatural Combat* to the world of London city comedy, reshaping him into
a Sir Giles Overreach, a character based on the real-life monopolist Sir
Giles Mompesson. Sir Giles moves so firmly over Massinger's stage that,
despite a highly conventional comic plot, the play almost loses its status as
comedy.

A New Way to Pay Old Debts contains all the conventions of Jacobean
double-plot comedy. In one of its plots, Frank Wellborn, Overreach's
nephew, schemes to regain the land his uncle has deceitfully appropriated.
In the other plot, Wellborn's younger friend, Tom Allworth, schemes to
win Overreach's daughter Margaret. Each plotter uses a similar device.
Wellborn asks Widow Allworth, Tom's mother, to pretend that she is
infatuated with him; Overreach jumps to furnish Wellborn with riches as
bait to catch the wealthy lady. Allworth asks Lord Lovell, his employer, to
pretend that he is infatuated with Margaret Overreach. Her father jumps
to furnish Margaret with riches, a marriage contract, and all things necessary for eloping with a lord. Thus, Wellborn regains his wealth and Tom
Allworth gets Margaret. To complete the symmetry of the plots, Widow
Allworth and Lord Lovell become a loving couple.

The play is rich in imagery; a gang of butlers and chefs at the Allworth
house, with names like Furnace and Order, keep up a running account of
the way various schemers use food and fancy dress as weapons in their battle of wits. Among Overreach's retainers is a crooked, pathetically thin
judge whose perpetual hunger mirrors the insatiable appetites of his master. The vignettes of taverners and tailors clamoring for payment and the
scenes of banqueting and muted bits of courtship would make the play a
good one even without its gargantuan villain. Yet for most audiences, the

play belongs to Sir Giles—and he goes mad.

The role, like that of Shylock in Shakespeare's *The Merchant of Venice* (pr. c. 1596-1597), is a rich one. Sir Giles has more land, more money, more luxuries, and more dreams than any other two characters combined. A commoner by birth, he has parlayed small sums into huge fortunes. Early in the play, he gives detailed instructions for ruining a neighbor and appropriating his land—beginning with cutting his fences, firing his barns, and trampling his grain; moving on through protracted lawsuits and phony writs; and concluding with the forced sale of the land for a fraction of its worth. Bitter against those who claim aristocratic status from birth, Overreach relishes the knowledge that his servants are the widows of gentlemen he has ruined, that his daughter wears elaborately jeweled dresses, that his home far outshines those of the gentry.

Yet despite this bitterness, Sir Giles wants more than anything else to see his daughter married to a nobleman, to call her "right honorable" and bounce young lordlings on his knee. To achieve that aim, he virtually orders the girl to prostitute herself to Lord Lovell so that a marriage between them will be necessary. He oversees preparations for her courtship with a vigor and a compulsiveness that almost win the sympathy of modern democratic audiences, whatever their original effect may have been. When he finds that his plans have failed—that she has eloped not with a lord but with a dependent page—he goes mad.

Critics disagree on whether Massinger intended Sir Giles's ambition to gain the sympathy it does. Certainly, Massinger did not believe that usurers should cheat the poor or that citizens and lords should intermarry. He does, however, structure the play's last scene so that Sir Giles, at last sure of his goal, receives one irreversible blow after another. When Wellborn counsels the "true valor" of repentance after the penultimate revelation, Sir Giles replies, "Patience, the beggar's virtue/ Shall find no harbour here." Though he has competently manipulated people throughout his career and has adopted patience when it suited his purpose, the anger he has hidden earlier has cut a deep underground channel in him, and now it floods out in murderous fury. When others prevent his carrying out his threats, his mind snaps. In his frenzy, he cries out one last lucid line before drowning in hallucinations: "Why, is not the whole world/ Included in myself?" It is a question Massinger's tragic protagonists—Malefort or Sforza—might have asked, one that Sigmund Freud would have found revealing.

In *A New Way to Pay Old Debts*, Massinger examines human will in the context of greed and social ambition. In *The Picture*, the context is jealousy and trust. The play teaches that loyalty begets loyalty, while mistrust begets mistrust. When soldier Mathias goes to Hungary to seek fortune as a mercenary, he leaves behind his lovely wife, Sophia. He secretly takes with him, however, a magic picture of her, a likeness that will turn yellow if she is sexually tempted and black if she is unfaithful to him. Mathias soldiers so well that meek King Ladislaus and his gorgeous wife Honoria stand indebted to him. His boasts about his wife, however, arouse Honoria's envy. Like the spoiled and willful villains of Massinger's early tragedies, she decides to destroy what stands in her light, namely the constant love of Mathias and his wife. She sends goatish courtiers off to seduce Sophia and offers herself to Mathias. In a series of parallel scenes, Mathias, strengthened by the Picture, resists Honoria while his wife resists Ubaldo and Ricardo. The courtiers (and her husband's long delay in returning home) eventually convince Sophia that her husband is unfaithful; in jealous anger, she decides that she, too, will embrace wantonness. As the lines of the Picture turn yellow and begin to blacken, Mathias, in anger, gives in to the queen's kisses. Conscience, religion, and "love to goodness for itself," however, soon recall Sophia from her wayward schemes. As the Picture correspondingly regains its natural colors, Mathias finds it easy to lecture the queen on the value of married love.

The Picture trumpets Massinger's theme of will. Honoria has been badly spoiled. Her husband proclaims himself her slave, gives her charge of the treasury, and knocks timidly at her bedroom door at night, unsure of admission, while dependable observers voice authorial comments on such submissiveness. Willfulness reigns so supremely in Honoria that she sees Mathias and Sophia's loyalty as something else for her to overcome. "I thought one amorous glance of mine could bring all hearts to my subjection," she complains. "I cannot sit down so with mine honour." Accustomed to having her way, she no longer questions whether her way is just.

It takes the Picture, indirectly, to save her. A day's journey from the palace waits a good woman, one capable of doubt and anger but essentially honorable. While Honoria and Mathias circle each other like amateur wrestlers looking for a headlock, Sophia manages her household in Bohemia. As the match in Hungary gets tougher, she loses her sense of humor, punishing servants for pranks. When she succeeds in bringing her suspicions and fears under control and chooses "goodness for itself," the long-distance reformations begin: First Mathias chooses chastity, then Honoria learns humility, and Ladislaus gains in fortitude.

This growth in the characters' virtue comes through a magic totem, just as Theophilus' conversion had come from flowers and the pagan princess' Christianity had come through a sprinkle of water. The problem of *deus ex machina* has thus surfaced again, yet in *The Picture* Massinger backs away from superstition. Sophia is outraged to learn that her husband relies on a picture instead of doing, as she has, the very hard work of trusting one's spouse. Her sense of humor becomes astringent: She will teach the courtiers a lesson, so she pretends to make assignations, robs them of their clothes, dresses them in women's garb and sets them to work spinning wool. She will teach Mathias, too, so she disorders the house for his home-coming, ignores his royal guests, and pretends to have become promiscu-ous. In the play's final scene, it takes the entire cast's pleading to keep Sophia from entering a convent.

Sophia's lessons work. The lecherous courtiers renounce womanizing. Her pretense rouses an almost murderous wrath in her husband; when he is made aware how unjust and unstable his jealousy makes him, he learns to value trust. The royal Hungarians also find a better marital balance. Sophia's actions produce these effects directly, not through flowers or thun-derbolts. Her will is strong enough to affect the other characters' wills, in a purely human way.

The anatomy of will shapes *The Maid of Honor* as fully as it does *The Picture*, yet the test cases differ. Sophia and Mathias, Honoria and Ladislaus, have to learn to control but not ignore their jealousies. In *The Maid of Honor*, the test case is the oath. Almost every character in the play makes and wants to break an oath, yet for Massinger oath-breaking inevitably signals a disordered will. (Massinger rarely questions whether a conventionally condemned action is right or wrong but rather whether the character has will enough to choose the course assumed right. In his better plays, such as this one, even the very good characters are capable of moral failure.)

The title character, Camiola, is a lovely, charmingly honest young maid. She cherishes oaths; being naturally inclined to "deal in certainties," she likes having things spelled out, contracted. She believes in the social order that has produced her. When the king's brother, Bertaldo, sends eye beams toward her, she tells him she loves him but denies his passionate suit. "Reason, like a tyrant," forbids a match between his royal blood and even the richest and fairest of citizens, which she grants herself to be. Besides, she is convinced that "when what is vow'd to heaven is dispens'd with/ To serve out ends on earth, a curse must follow," and Bertaldo, as a Knight of Malta, has vowed lifelong celibacy. Thus, at the play's start, she sacrifices her love.

Such a sacrifice, however, is not easily made. Like any self-confident, honest, and infatuated young woman, Camiola sees in his "sweet presence/ Courtship and loving language" evidence that Bertaldo possesses "so clear a mind, . . . furnished with Harmonious faculties moulded from Heaven." She proclaims that her passion for Bertaldo rests on his solid virtues, on "the judgment of my soul." (In fact, her catalog of his virtues relies heavily on the superficial.) Because she is rich and charming, she has had little need for or practice in renunciations. When he leaves, she is sure her sun has set forever. Her passions fight so fiercely against reason that she first takes to her bed, then tries to recover by amusing herself with the vain suit of a fop, Signior Sylli, himself a prodigious breaker of oaths.

Bertaldo, frustrated, embarks on a time-honored cure for the constellation of feelings that Robert Burton called "heroical love." He goes to war: An ally of Sicily has invaded the kingdom of Duchess Aurelia and is in need of assistance. The war is patently unjust, as even the ally's ambassador admits, but Bertaldo needs a fight, and his brother, King Roberto, allows him to go. In fighting against the duchess, Bertaldo is breaking yet another of his knightly oaths, to protect the innocent. Back in Sicily, his brother the king sends an ambassador of his own to Duchess Aurelia. His mission: to swear falsely that Bertaldo is fighting without the king's consent. Most of the play's characters see promises as convenient ways to get what they want. They use oaths willfully. Fulgentio, the king's favorite, for example, uses them to turn the king against his brother, and, when Camiola scorns him, he swears to tell "every man in every place" that she is a strumpet.

Because Camiola is strong-willed rather than willful, she keeps her resolutions even when they are inconvenient. Yet once, temporarily, she falters. She has refused Bertaldo on two counts—the difference in their social classes and his vow. When, in the course of battle, he is captured and refused ransom by his brother, she gladly sends fifty thousand gold crowns to redeem him. Buying him from slavery, she believes, makes her his social equal and thus frees her to marry him. In her exuberance at finding a way around the problem of class, she apparently forgets his vow. She sends off a betrothal contract with the ransom money. She employs as messenger a man who, she knows, loves her loyally from a distance. Anticipating Bertaldo's gratitude, she lives a dance of glee, daydreaming their future together.

In a play about the importance of vows, Philip Massinger, moralist, will not let a heroine, no matter how charming, build a happy future on broken promises. Bertaldo does sign the betrothal agreement but almost immediately finds himself the object of another infatuation. The normally level-headed Duchess Aurelia, like Camiola, sees his courtly bearing as proof of a wise and noble nature. Forgetting past offenses, she offers him marriage, a dukedom, and a papal dispensation from his vow of celibacy. Bertaldo, like the spoiled Honoria, has few scruples. He accepts and returns home in triumph, doubly promised.

Massinger's conclusion owes much to Shakespeare's *All's Well That Ends Well* (pr. c. 1602-1603). Bertaldo, like Bertram, is publicly exposed. The duchess shakes off her infatuation and Camiola wins fair title to the now repentant man. Then, in a plot twist destined to perplex readers for centuries, Camiola abandons the court, abandons Bertaldo—whom she now pities as a weakling—and marries herself to the Church as a nun.

Massinger may have intended Camiola's decision as a comic resolution, but several things qualify the reaction audiences have to it. Though she has proved strong-willed and loyal, Camiola is very young. She has misjudged Bertaldo's character through her own inexperience. She has a flair for drama that needs careful control. She choreographs the entire last scene of the play, from exposing Bertaldo to taking the veil, deliberately arranging events to "deserve men's praise, and wonder too," and she does so immediately upon learning of his betrayal. Thus, the will, which has guided her throughout the play in delightfully good-hearted ways, shows itself even in the act of renouncing itself.

The shaping and testing of will is certainly not Massinger's only theme, but its development in several of his major plays amply illustrates both his talents and his limitations. Whether the will is tested by the demands of religion, the lure of lucre, the icy grip of jealousy, or the sweetness of an infatuation, Massinger manages to stir the theme deep into a play, to arrange characters and events to illustrate it. If he did not challenge the social or psychological conventions of his day as John Webster or John Ford did, he did make dramatically vivid and sometimes convincing cases for the wisdom of those conventional attitudes.

Other major works

POETRY: *The Poems of Philip Massinger with Critical Notes*, 1968 (Donald Lawless, editor).

MISCELLANEOUS: *The Plays and Poems of Philip Massinger*, 1976 (5 volumes; Philip Edwards and Colin Gibson, editors).

Bibliography

Ball, Robert. *Amazing Career of Sir Giles Overreach*, 1939.

Cruickshank, A. H. *Philip Massinger*, 1920.

Dunn, T. A. *Philip Massinger: The Man and the Playwright*, 1957.

Edwards, Philip. "Massinger the Censor," in *Essays in Honor of Hardin Craig*, 1962.

Evenhuis, Francis. *Massinger's Imagery*, 1973.

Fothergill, R. A. "The Dramatic Experience of Massinger's *The City Madam* and *A New Way to Pay Old Debts*," in *University of Toronto Quarterly*. XLIII (1973), pp. 68-86.

Gross, Alan G. "Social Change and Philip Massinger," in *Studies in English Literature, 1500-1900*. VII (1967), pp. 329-342.

Logan, Terence. "Philip Massinger," in *The Later Jacobean and Caroline Dramatists: A Survey*, 1978.

Makkink, H. J. *Philip Massinger and John Fletcher: A Comparison*, 1927.

Maxwell, B. *Studies in Beaumont, Fletcher and Massinger*, 1938.

Elizabeth Spalding Otten